Tort Law in South Africa

Tort Law in South Africa

Max Loubser

This book was originally published as a monograph in the International Encyclopaedia of Laws/Tort Law.

Founding Editor: Roger Blanpain
General Editor: Frank Hendrickx
Volume Editor: Britt Weyts

Wolters Kluwer

Published by:
Kluwer Law International B.V.
PO Box 316
2400 AH Alphen aan den Rijn
The Netherlands
E-mail: international-sales@wolterskluwer.com
Website: lrus.wolterskluwer.com

Sold and distributed by:
Wolters Kluwer Legal & Regulatory U.S.
7201 McKinney Circle
Frederick, MD 21704
United States of America
Email: customer.service@wolterskluwer.com

ISBN 978-94-035-2623-2

e-Book: ISBN 978-94-035-2624-9
web-PDF: ISBN 978-94-035-2625-6

This title is available on www.kluwerlawonline.com

The Author

Max Loubser was born on 8 December 1948 in Somerset West, South Africa. He studied at the University of Stellenbosch, South Africa where he obtained both BA (Law) and LLB degrees cum laude. He was awarded a South Africa-at-large Rhodes scholarship for study at the University of Oxford, UK where he obtained the degree DPhil in 1977.

He was Professor of Private Law at the University of Stellenbosch from 1977 to 2012 and is now Professor Emeritus and Research Associate. The law of delict is his special area of interest.

His publications include books on prescription, third-party compensation in motor vehicle accident cases, sport and the law and numerous articles in legal journals and chapters in books.

He is a partner and director of a firm of attorneys in Stellenbosch, Cluver Markotter Inc. The focus of his practice is general commercial law.

The Author

Table of Contents

List of Abbreviations

(A)	Appellate Division of the Supreme Court of South Africa (1947–1994)
ACJ	Acting Chief Justice
AD	Appellate Division (pre-1947 Reports)
AJ	Acting Judge
AJ	*Acta Juridica*
AJA	Acting Judge of Appeal
ANC	African National Congress
All SA	The All South African Law Reports
Art.	Article
Arts	Articles
BCLR	Butterworths Constitutional Law Reports
BGB	*Bürgerliches Gesetzbuch*
Bpk.	*Beperk* (Limited)
(C)	Cape Provincial Division
C	*Codex* in *Corpus Iuris Civilis*
CC	Close Corporation
(CC)	Constitutional Court
cf.	Compare
CJ	Chief Justice
(Ck)	Ciskei Supreme Court
COIDA	Compensation for Occupational Injuries and Diseases Act
Co	Company
CPD	Cape Provincial Division Reports (pre-1947 Reports)
D	*Digesta* in *Corpus Iuris Civilis*
(D)	Durban and Coast Local Division
DP	Deputy President (of Supreme Court of Appeal)
(E)	Eastern Cape Provincial Division
Ed	edition, editor
Eds	editors

List of Abbreviations

(HL)	House of Lords
I	*Institutiones* in *Corpus Iuris Civilis*
Inc	Incorporated
J	Judge
JA	Judge of Appeal
LAWSA	The Law of South Africa
Ltd	Limited
(N)	Natal Provincial Division
(NC)	Northern Cape Provincial Division
NCOP	National Council of Provinces
NLR	Natal Law Reports (pre-1947 Reports)
(O)	Orange Free State Provincial Division
OPD	Orange Free State Provincial Division (pre-1947 Reports)
PAC	Pan Africanist Congress
PH	Prentice Hall Reports
Plc	Public Limited Company
Pty.	Proprietary
Pvt	Private (Company)
(R)	Rhodesia High Court
(RA)	Rhodesia High Court Appellate Division
reg.	Regulation
SA	South Africa
(SA)	South African Law Reports
SALJ	*South African Law Journal*
SCA	Supreme Court of Appeal of South Africa (post-1994)
(SECL)	South Eastern Cape Local Division
Stell LR	*Stellenbosch Law Review*
SWA	South West Africa Provincial Division
(T)	Transvaal Provincial Division
THRHR	*Tydskrif vir Hedendaagse Romeins-Hollandse Reg*
(Tk)	Transkei
TPD	Transvaal Provincial Division (pre-1947 Reports)
TRC	Truth and Reconciliation Commission
TS	Transvaal Supreme Court (pre-1910 Reports)
Tvl	Transvaal
VAT	value-added tax
VOC	*Vereenigde Oost-Indische Compagnie* (Dutch East India Company)
(W)	Witwatersrand Local Division

WLD	Witwatersrand Local Division (pre-1947 Reports)
ZASCA	South African Supreme Court of Appeal judgments published by the Southern African Legal Information Institute (SAFLII), at http://www.saflii.org/. Judgments of other courts are published on the same website for free public access.

List of Abbreviations

General Introduction

§1. General Background of the Country

I. Geography

1. South Africa covers an area of some 1.2 million square kilometres, comprising almost the whole of the subcontinent of Africa. A plateau that covers the largest part of the country dominates the topography. It is separated from surrounding areas of generally lower elevation by the Great Escarpment that is highest in the east in the Lesotho region and lowest in the sandy Kalahari in the west. The central part of the plateau comprises the Highveld, and the Great Karoo region lies to the south of the Orange River. Between the escarpment and the sea, there is little genuine coastal plain, with exceptions in northern KwaZulu/Natal and in parts of Western Cape.

The coastline of some 2,700 kilometres is characterized by fairly steep slopes rising rapidly inland. Few flooded river valleys or natural harbours occur. Long stretches of beach are common. The greater part of the country is drained to the Atlantic Ocean by the Orange River, which rises in the Lesotho Highlands, and its tributaries. The plateau is drained to the Indian Ocean by the Limpopo system. All South African rivers are highly seasonal in flow, and few offer a suitable gradient and volume to allow navigation by even small crafts for more than a few kilometres from the river mouths.

II. History

2. The earliest inhabitants of the area now known as South Africa were the Khoikhoi and San (the 'Hottentots' and 'Bushmen' of early European terminology), and these groups were scattered across the subcontinent. The Khoikhoi were pastoralists, herding sheep and later cattle. The San were hunter-gatherers. African or Bantu-speaking peoples migrated to southern Africa hundreds of years ago, establishing themselves in the well-watered eastern coastal region, later spreading out across the interior plateau, with a culture centred around cattle-keeping. They did not extend their settlements into the arid western or the winter-rainfall southwestern regions. These regions remained the preserve of the Khoikhoi and San, until Europeans put down roots at the Cape of Good Hope.

3. In 1652, the Dutch East India Company (VOC) set up a station in Table Bay (Cape Town) to provision passing ships on voyages to and from the Dutch East

Indies. From 1657, European settlers were allotted farms by the VOC in the arable regions around Cape Town, where wine and wheat became the major products. In response to the colonists' demand for labour, the VOC imported slaves from East Africa, Madagascar and its possessions in the East Indies.

The VOC founded this settlement at the Cape as a private commercial venture. The VOC had a charter from the government of the Netherlands to exercise administrative authority at the Cape and according to its directive the law to be applied within the territories governed by the VOC was that of the Province of Holland, but neither the VOC nor the Province of Holland had authority to legislate for the Cape settlement.[1] The only body authorized to legislate for overseas Dutch territories was the central government of the Netherlands, the Estates-General. Legislation applicable in the Province of Holland and the common law of that province became part of the law of South Africa through their incorporation into the works of seventeenth- and eighteenth-century Dutch institutional writers, who were accepted as authoritative in South Africa.[2]

The founding legal language was Dutch, which formed the basis for the development of a new indigenous language – Afrikaans. Dutch and its derivative Afrikaans were the dominant languages of government and law, from 1652 until the end of the initial period of Dutch occupation in 1795.

4. Roman law, as received and partially reformulated in the Netherlands, and particularly in the Province of Holland, thus became the common law of South Africa, known as Roman-Dutch law. The authoritative sources of the Roman-Dutch law were the Dutch legal writers of the time, but the boundaries of the source materials were imprecisely defined in respect of both time and space.[3] Under Dutch rule, the quality of the administration of justice was uneven, and there was no separation of judicial and executive authority. Also, because the Cape was settled for commercial purposes and ruled by a trading company, there was never an extensive commitment to invest in legal or other administration.[4]

5. In 1795, governance of the Cape was first taken over by the British for a period of eight years. The British governed at the request of the Dutch until 1803, during the upheavals of the Napoleonic wars. From 1803 to early 1806, there was another spell of Dutch rule, which ended when the Dutch sided with the French in a renewed Anglo-French war, as a result of which the British fleet took over the Cape in January 1806. The British retained the Cape at the end of hostilities in Europe in 1815, and it remained a British colony until the four British colonies in South Africa united and became self-governing as the Union of South Africa in 1910.

1. Eduard Fagan in *Southern Cross: Civil Law and Common Law in South Africa*, 38–39 (Reinhard Zimmermann & Daniel Visser eds., Juta & Co. Ltd 1996).
2. Fagan, *supra*, n. 1, at 39–41.
3. Fagan, *supra*, n. 1, at 41.
4. Fagan, *supra*, n. 1, at 47.

Roman-Dutch law officially remained the common law of the Cape Colony, according to the rule of English law that the laws of a conquered country remain in place until altered by legislation.

The advent of British rule was accompanied by an increase in the number of immigrants from Britain, notably the settlement in 1820 of several thousand British in the Eastern Cape. The original colonists, known as the Boers, were at this time already extending white settlement beyond the borders of the Cape Colony. In the 1830s, several thousand Boers from the interior districts began a series of migrations northwards, and this movement became known as the Great Trek. The Boers (*Voortrekkers*, as they were called) later coalesced in two landlocked republics to the north, the South African Republic (Transvaal) and the Orange Free State.

6. The administration of justice in the Cape Colony was revamped under British rule, notably by introduction of the First Charter of Justice in 1827. The Charter instituted the Cape Supreme Court, manned by four (later three) legally qualified and full-time judges imported from Britain.[5] English civil and criminal procedure and rules of evidence were introduced, with important consequences also for substantive law.[6]

Notable legislative measures included the adoption of Ordinance 50 of 1828 that guaranteed equal civil rights for 'people of colour' within the Cape Colony and a proclamation for the emancipation of slaves that came into force in the Cape Colony in 1834. The slaves were subjected to a four-year period of 'apprenticeship' with their former owners and obtained full freedom on 1 December 1838.

Apart from the law of procedure and evidence, the Charter of Justice introduced in the Cape Colony did not alter the law generally, but instead required that the courts exercise jurisdiction according to the laws in force in the Colony.[7] The intention was to introduce English law gradually, and this happened in due course by wholesale importation by statute of English law, mainly in the field of commercial law, as in the law on companies, insurance, insolvency and negotiable instruments.[8]

The tendency to apply English law instead of Roman-Dutch law was strengthened by various factors: the inability of many nineteenth century South African judges to understand Dutch, the exclusive use of English in the courts, the requirement that barristers be trained in Britain, the continued importation of judges from Britain and the adoption of the Privy Council as the final Court of Appeal.[9] The trade and legal links with Britain and its empire increased and the links with the Netherlands decreased, compounded, as far as the legal links are concerned, by the codification of the common law of the Netherlands in the early nineteenth century.

7. Britain continued the expansion of its rule in southern Africa by annexing the territory of Natal, with its harbour Port Natal (Durban), in 1843. The Colony of Natal developed a system of political and legal dualism, whereby the British-ruled

5. Fagan, *supra*, n.1, at 51.
6. *See* H.J. Erasmus in *Southern Cross: Civil Law and Common Law in South Africa*, 141–161 (Reinhard Zimmermann & Daniel Visser eds., Juta & Co. Ltd 1996).
7. Fagan, *supra*, n.1, at 55–56.
8. Fagan, *supra*, n.1, at 56.
9. Fagan, *supra*, n.1, at 57.

Colony also recognized the rule of African chiefs in their territories and African customary law was codified. The development of sugar plantations in the subtropical coastal lowlands of Natal led to the importation of Indian indentured labourers from 1860, and many Indian traders and market gardeners followed. It was here that Mohandas Gandhi from the mid-1890s developed the strategy of passive resistance against racial discrimination. Although Indians gradually moved into the Transvaal and elsewhere, they remain concentrated mainly in Natal.

In 1853, the Cape Colony was granted representative government, followed in 1872 by self-government. The franchise was formally non-racial, but also based on income and property qualifications. The result was that Africans and 'coloured' people formed a minority of the electorate.

8. The discovery of valuable minerals in the interior of southern Africa in the late 1800s heralded the development of the mining industry. The discovery of large deposits of diamonds in the sparsely populated north western territory, where the city of Kimberley developed, drew tens of thousands of people to the first great industrial hub in Africa. In 1871, the British annexed the diamond fields as the Colony of Griqualand West, and it was incorporated into the Cape Colony in 1880. By 1888, the consolidation of diamond claims had led to the creation of the De Beers mining company under the control of Cecil John Rhodes. He later became Prime Minister of the Cape Colony (1890–1896) and, through his chartered British South Africa Company, he also acquired control of the northern territories now known as Zambia and Zimbabwe.

The mineral discoveries had a major impact on the subcontinent as a whole, and to this day mining is of major importance in the South African economy. A railway network linking the interior to the coastal ports revolutionized transportation and energized agriculture. Coastal cities such as Cape Town, Port Elizabeth, East London and Durban experienced an economic boom as port facilities were upgraded.

9. In a further step to expand British rule in southern Africa, the South African Republic (Transvaal) was annexed by Britain in 1877, on the basis, as claimed, that the majority of its inhabitants desired to become British subjects. Boer resistance led to British withdrawal in 1881.

The discovery of the Witwatersrand goldfields in 1886 led to an influx of English-speaking immigrants (the *Uitlanders*) into the South African Republic. Their demand for franchise rights was supported by Britain and the British mining magnates, including Cecil John Rhodes. This led to the plot by Rhodes and his friend Dr Leander Starr Jameson to launch a raid into the Transvaal in late December 1895 (the Jameson raid). The raid's failure saw the end of Rhodes' political career, but Sir Alfred Milner, British High Commissioner in South Africa from 1897, continued efforts to establish British rule throughout the subcontinent. This led to the Anglo-Boer War 1899–1902.

In the first phase of the Anglo-Boer War, the Boer forces achieved success and took the initiative, besieging the frontier towns of Mafeking and Kimberley in the northern Cape and Ladysmith in northern Natal. Some colonial Boers from the Cape and Natal rebelled and joined the forces of the Boer republics. After a large expeditionary force under Lords Roberts and Kitchener arrived, the British made rapid advances. President Kruger fled the Transvaal shortly before Pretoria fell in June 1900.

The formal conquest of the two Boer republics was followed by a prolonged guerrilla campaign. Small, mobile groups of Boers denied the imperial forces of their victory by disrupting rail links and supply lines. Commandos swept deep into colonial territory. The British were at a disadvantage in unfamiliar terrain, and the Boers had superior skills as horsemen and sharpshooters.

The British responded with a scorched earth policy. This included farm burnings and looting and the setting up of concentration camps for non-combatants, in which some 26,000 Boer women and children died from disease. There was also large-scale incarceration of black (including coloured) people in this phase of the war, in racially segregated camps. They too suffered from appalling conditions and some 14,000 are estimated to have died.

10. The Treaty of Vereeniging of 1902 eventually ended the war, and the British agreed to leave the issue of rights for Africans to be decided by a future self-governing (white) authority. During 1907 and 1908, the two former Boer Republics were granted self-government with a whites-only franchise. The National Convention drew up a Constitution and Britain's reconstruction regime resulted in a white-ruled dominion – a union of the former Boer republics with Natal and the Cape called the Union of South Africa that came into being on 31 May 1910. The nineteenth century model of formally non-racial franchise was retained in the Cape, but was not extended elsewhere, where rights of citizenship were confined to whites alone.

Planning for a segregation-oriented structuring of society was already evident in a 1905 report by the South African Native Affairs Commission, and continued to evolve into the system later known as apartheid. In 1913, the first Union Government enacted the Natives Land Act, which defined the remnants of African communal or tribal land, and declared illegal all land purchases or rent tenancy outside these reserves. The reserves ('homelands' as they were subsequently called) eventually comprised about 13% of South Africa's land surface. Administrative and legal dualism reinforced the division between white citizens and black non-citizens. In these and other ways, the foundations of segregation or 'apartheid' were laid.

From the outset, the integration of black Africans into the emerging urban and industrial society of South Africa followed the pattern of short-term, recurrent labour migrancy. Migrant African labourers were drawn from reserved communal or tribal areas and had no political rights in the urban areas, while their families and dependants remained in the reserves. This system formed the basis of the system of segregation later known as apartheid.

11. After World War II and particularly with the advent of the Nationalist government in 1948, a more rigorous and authoritarian system of segregation was adopted. In the mid-1950s, the government engineered the overriding of an entrenched clause in the 1910 Constitution of the Union to remove coloured voters from the common voters' roll. It enforced residential segregation and engaged in large-scale expropriation of land and enforced removal of black and coloured people from specific 'group areas'. Black resistance groups such as the African National Congress (ANC) were eventually banned, and an extensive State security apparatus was developed.

In 1961, the government under Dr HF Verwoerd declared South Africa a republic, after winning a whites-only referendum on the issue. A new currency, the Rand, and a new flag, anthem and coat of arms were introduced. South Africa also withdrew from the British Commonwealth.

The architects of apartheid, among whom the academic and later Prime Minister H.F. Verwoerd, propounded a theory of multinationalism. The policy, that was termed 'separate development', divided the African population into ethnic 'nations', each with its own 'homeland' and the prospect of 'independence'. Four of these 'homeland' structures (Transkei, Bophuthatswana, Venda and Ciskei) were declared 'independent', a status which the international community did not recognize.

12. In the long history of black resistance and struggle against apartheid generally and against specific discriminatory measures, the following groups and events feature prominently: The ANC; the Pan Africanist Congress (PAC); the Defiance Campaign of the early 1950s; the formation of the Congress Alliance; the Freedom Charter of 1955; the prosecution of more than 150 anti-apartheid leaders (including Nelson Mandela) for treason, in a trial that started in 1956 and ended in acquittals in 1961; the killing of sixty-nine PAC demonstrators at Sharpeville in March 1960; the arrest and trial of members of the armed resistance group *Umkhonto we Sizwe* (Spear of the Nation) in 1963 (the 'Rivonia trial') and the subsequent conviction for sabotage and imprisonment of Nelson Mandela and others; the youth uprisings in Soweto and elsewhere in 1976; the Black Consciousness Movement, led by Steve Biko, who died in detention in 1977; the United Democratic Front and the Mass Democratic Movement in the 1980s; worker resistance through the Congress of South African Trade Unions (COSATU) and the National Council of Trade Unions; and the Inkatha movement that stressed Zulu ethnicity and traditionalism, with its main support in the rural areas of KwaZulu.

13. In the 1980s, the South African government embarked on a series of piecemeal reforms, such as the recognition of black trade unions and the 1983 Constitution, that afforded coloured and Indian minorities limited participation in separate and subordinate Houses of Parliament. However, pressures on the apartheid government mounted, both internally and externally, in the form of international financial, trade, sport and cultural sanctions and boycotts. The collapse of global communism, the withdrawal of Soviet and Cuban support for the MPLA regime in neighbouring Angola, and the negotiated independence of Namibia (from 1919 administered by South Africa as South-West Africa, in terms of a League of Nations mandate), foreshadowed radical change in South Africa.

14. Change came when FW de Klerk became State President in 1989 and, at the opening of Parliament in February 1990, announced the unbanning of the ANC and other liberation movements and the release of political prisoners, notably Nelson Mandela. Constitutional negotiations followed, and in April 1994 South Africa held its first democratic election under an interim Constitution. The ANC emerged with a large majority and formed a new government, with Nelson Mandela as President. The Constitution was finally adopted in 1996.[10] The country is now divided into nine provinces, each with its own provincial government structure, with competencies in areas delineated in the Constitution.

15. South Africa has achieved a peaceful transition to democracy. A prominent step along the way of transition was the constitution of the Truth and Reconciliation Commission (TRC) in 1996, chaired by 1984 Nobel Peace Prize winner Archbishop Emeritus Desmond Tutu, to advance the reconciliation process. The TRC was empowered to investigate apartheid-era human rights abuses committed between 1960 and 10 May 1994, to grant amnesty to those who committed politically motivated crimes and to recommend compensation to victims of abuses. The TRC's mandate was part of the larger process of reconciling the often conflicting political, economic and cultural interests held by the many people that make up South Africa's diverse population. The TRC completed its work in 2001. South Africa is now a democracy, politically and economically prominent in Africa, with a progressive Constitution that has changed its legal system fundamentally.

III. Political System

16. South Africa is a constitutional democracy and the Constitution is the supreme law. The present Constitution of South Africa was certified by the Constitutional Court on 4 December 1996, was signed by then President Mandela on 10 December 1996, and came into effect on 3 February 1997. The Constitution provides for a federal system with significant powers reserved for the nine provincial governments.

17. Government is three-tiered, with representatives being elected at the national, provincial and local levels. The main institutions of the national government are a bicameral Parliament and an executive presidency. The Parliament consists of the National Assembly, with four hundred members, and the National Council of Provinces (NCOP), with ninety members. The members of the National Assembly are elected by a proportional representation system through party lists, with universal adult suffrage. The NCOP members consist of provincial officials chosen to reflect provincial parties' relative strengths. Elections for the bicameral Parliament occur every five years. The National Assembly passes legislation, amends the Constitution, and oversees activities of the provinces in accordance with the Constitution. The NCOP passes legislation that pertains specifically to the provinces.

18. The president is elected by the National Assembly for a five-year term, and an elected president is restricted to serving two terms. The president is responsible for appointing the deputy president and cabinet, as well as leading his party in the

10. Act 108 of 1996.

passage of legislation. The president oversees the day-to-day operation of the government and distributes power and functions among the deputy president, ministers and the deputy ministers. The president can call for new elections by dissolving Parliament if a majority of representatives seek its dissolution and at least three years have lapsed since the last election. The National Assembly, however, may pass a no-confidence resolution that excludes or includes the president. If the majority of the National Assembly votes 'no confidence' in the government, the president must reconstitute his cabinet. In the event that the National Assembly passes a no-confidence resolution that includes the president, both the president and his government must resign. The National Assembly must select a replacement from within its ranks.

19. Each province has an elected legislature and chief executive – the provincial premier. Although in forming a federal system, in practice the nature of the relationship between the central and provincial governments continues to be the subject of considerable debate, particularly among groups desiring a greater measure of autonomy from the central government. A key step in defining the relationship came in 1997 when provincial governments were given more than half of central government funding and permitted to develop and manage their own budgets.

20. The Bill of Rights contained in the Constitution provides extensive guarantees, including equality before the law; the prohibition of unfair discrimination; the right to life, human dignity, privacy, property, and freedom and security of the person; freedom of speech, religion, assembly and association. The Bill of Rights also deals with social and economic rights in respect of a safe environment, housing, education and healthcare.

21. The Constitution provides for a fully independent judiciary, including a nine-member Constitutional Court. It further provides for an independent corruption watchdog, the Public Protector and for independent commissions on human rights, gender equality and the restitution of land rights.

22. After winning an overwhelming victory in the first democratic election in 1994, the ANC has also won all the subsequent elections. The ANC is the ruling party at a national level, and in all but one province. The COSATU and the South African Communist Party (SACP) are in a formal alliance with the ruling ANC, and thus do not stand separately for election.

The main opposition parties are the Democratic Alliance (DA) and the Economic Freedom Fighters (EFF). Other political parties represented in Parliament include the Inkatha Freedom Party (IFP), the Congress of the People (COPE), and the African Christian Democratic Party (ACDP).

23. The current political agenda of government is broadly directed at the political and economic transformation of the South African society and economy, involving issues such as black economic empowerment (BEE); the correction of social imbalances; promoting growth and investment; job creation; programmes to improve the delivery of essential social services to the majority of the population;

and combating HIV/AIDS. Since the abolition of apartheid, levels of political violence in South Africa have dropped dramatically, but organized and violent crime, including a high level of violence against women and children, remain areas of grave concern.

IV. People

24. According to the 2011 census, the population was 51.77 million, of which 51.4% were female and 48.7% male. According to population groups, 79.2% were classified as Black African, 8.9% as white, 8.9% as coloured and 2.5% as Indian/ Asian.

Eleven languages (Afrikaans, English, Ndebele, North Sotho, South Sotho, Swazi, Tsonga, Tswana, Venda, Xhosa, and Zulu) have official status under the Constitution. The main 'black' languages are Zulu (IsiZulu), Xhosa (IsiXhosa), Sotho (Sesotho), Pedi (Sepedi), Tswana (Setswana), Venda (Tshivenda), Swazi (SiSwati), Ndebele (IsiNdebele) and Tsonga (Xitsonga).

The African population is heterogeneous, composed mainly of four linguistic groups. The largest is the Nguni, including various Ndebele, Swazi, Xhosa and Zulu peoples, who constitute more than half the African population of the country and form the majority in the eastern coastal regions. The second largest is Sotho-Tswana, which includes numerous Sotho, Pedi and Tswana peoples and forms a majority in some northern areas. The last two are the Tsonga, or Shangaan, concentrated in Northern and Mpumalanga provinces, and the Venda, concentrated in Northern province. The original Khoikhoi and San peoples of South Africa scarcely exist as distinct groups inside the country today.

The majority of South Africans of European extraction (i.e., British, Dutch, German, French, Portuguese) speak either English or Afrikaans as a home language, with Afrikaans in the majority.

The people formerly classified as 'Coloured' is composed of mixed-race descendants of Africans, Indians and other Asians and Europeans. Several distinct ethnic groups can be identified, such as the Malays, largely descended from Islamic slaves brought from Indonesia under Dutch rule, and the Griquas, who can trace their origins to Khoikhoi communities beyond the border of the Cape Colony in earlier centuries. Those formerly classified as Coloured are concentrated in the western half of the country, particularly in Western and Northern Cape and the westernmost parts of Eastern Cape province, where they form a majority in most districts. The home language of the majority of 'Coloured' people is Afrikaans.

The Indians in South Africa mostly speak English (as well as languages such as Gujarati, Hindi and Urdu). They are the descendants of immigrant traders and indentured workers that came to South Africa in the second half of the nineteenth century. Today, the large majority live in KwaZulu/Natal and to a lesser extent in Gauteng. Almost all Indian South Africans live in urban areas.

The majority of South Africans understand either English or Afrikaans, but possibly half of the adult population in fact speaks neither of these. According to the 2011 census, the home language percentages are the following: IsiZulu (22.7%); IsiXhosa (16%); Afrikaans (13.5%); English (9.6%); Sepedi (9.1%); Setswana

(8%); Sesotho (7.6%); Xitsonga (4.5%); SiSwati (2.6%); Tshivenda (2.4%); IsiNdebele (2.1%); and others (1.6%). There is no single language that can claim majority status for the entire population. English dominates to an increasing extent as *lingua franca* in official, educational and formal business spheres.

The largest category of religious affiliation is Christian, estimated to be more than 70% of the population (the *2011* census did not include any questions about religion), and the largest churches are the independent African Christian churches, varying in size from small groups to millions of members. The largest other Christian denominations, drawing members from all ethnic groups, are the Methodist, Roman Catholic, Anglican and Dutch Reformed churches. The other major religions are Hinduism, among the majority of Indians; Islam, among many Indians and Malays; and Judaism, among a minority of the white population.

V. Economy

25. In the years since World War II, South Africa has experienced highly variable growth rates, including some years when its growth rate was among the highest in the world. Its gross domestic product (GDP) is the largest in Africa. South Africa's economy long was dependent on agriculture and mining and on the export of commodities and import of manufactured goods. Since World War II, the country has built a well-developed manufacturing base, though it continues to import manufactured goods and remains dependent on the export of primary products.

The economy is essentially based on private enterprise, but the State participates in many ways. Public corporations for the production of oil from coal, steel and electricity were set up. Privatized but still State-controlled corporations own the railways, the national airline, harbour facilities, fuel pipelines and telecommunications.

Central government taxation consists primarily of income taxes on individuals and businesses and a value-added tax (VAT) on transactions. Provincial governments depend mainly on transfer payments from the central government, while property taxes and levies on businesses provide the main support for local governments. VAT is levied across the board, at a flat rate of 15%, with a limited range of goods and services which are subject to VAT at a zero rate or are exempt from VAT. The corporate tax rate is 28%, and a dividends tax of 20% is withheld by the entities paying the dividends to individuals. The highest (marginal) rate of personal income tax is 45%.

Diamonds, gold and coal are historically the most important minerals, but there are many others of importance, including iron ore, platinum, manganese, chromium, copper, uranium, silver, beryllium and titanium. No commercially exploitable deposits of oil have been found, but natural gas in moderate quantities exists off the southern coast. Known coal deposits are large, and oil is made from coal at two large plants. South Africa produces by far the most electricity in Africa, from mainly coal-burning power stations. The State-controlled electricity company Eskom supplies about 95% of South Africa's electricity and more than 50% of Africa's energy needs.

Hydroelectric potential is limited, though the government has developed projects on a number of rivers; and more significant are the projects to import electricity from stations on the Zambezi at Cahora Bassa, Mozambique and on rivers in the Lesotho Highlands.

Agriculture is of major importance, especially as a provider of employment. Arid conditions prevail generally, except in the well-watered, fertile soils of the Western Cape river valleys, the KwaZulu/Natal coast, and the Highveld of Mpumalanga and the Free State, where conditions are favourable for extensive cereal cultivation.

§2. Legal System

I. Primacy of Legislation and Codification

26. The private law of South Africa has never been codified, and the Roman-Dutch law heritage has remained as a living source of law. The Roman-Dutch law of delict was the product of an action-based Roman law (in particular the *actio legis Aquiliae* and the *actio iniuriarum*) that was generalized and shorn of its penal elements to provide general rules for compensation in respect of damage caused *dolo aut culpa*.[11] English cases have also been influential, but, in respect of South African private law generally and the law of delict in particular, Roman-Dutch law has been the dominant source of law.

The important difference between South African private law and that of most other modern civil law systems is that South African private law, for the most part, continues to exist in an uncodified form as *ius commune*, or common law. Legislation overrides and may change certain common law rules, and certain areas of the law of delict are governed by specific legislation,[12] but the *ius commune* and decided cases constitute the basic source of law. Cases decided by higher courts bind lower courts in terms of the stare decisis doctrine, and the development of the law is shaped by judges reasoning 'from case to case' in the tradition of common law judges.[13] The Constitution is the highest law and section 8(1) of the Constitution provides that the Bill of Rights applies to all law (whether that law be legislation, common law or customary law). Thus constitutional rights and values affect all areas of the law, including the law of delict, as set out in section IV below.

---

11. *See* generally on this development F.H. Lawson & B.S. Martkesinis, *Tortious Liability for Unintentional Harm in the Common Law and the Civil Law*, vol. 1, 39–41 (Cambridge U. Press, 1982).
12. The following are examples of legislation governing certain aspects of the law of delict: the Apportionment of Damages Act 34 of 1956, governing contributory negligence and the position of joint wrongdoers; the Assessment of Damages Act 9 of 1969, governing the effect of life insurance and certain other benefits on damages.
13. *See Southern Cross: Civil Law and Common Law in South Africa* 10 (Reinhard Zimmermann & Daniel Visser eds., Juta & Co. Ltd 1996).

II. Courts and the Judiciary

A. The Constitution

27. Section 165 of the Constitution of the Republic of South Africa (1996)[14] (hereinafter 'the Constitution') vests the courts with 'the judicial authority of the Republic'.[15] This section provides that the courts are 'subject only to the Constitution and the law',[16] and that 'no person or organ of state' may interfere with their functioning.[17] The judiciary must apply the Constitution and the law 'impartially and without fear, favour or prejudice'.[18]

The Constitution is the highest law. Some courts have jurisdiction to decide whether legislation or State action complies with the Constitution. They can then, in various ways, undo whatever is unconstitutional and their orders bind 'all persons ... and organs of state'.[19]

The integrity and independence of the courts are therefore entrenched in the Constitution. In addition, the Constitution enjoins organs of State to assist and protect the courts to ensure their independence, impartiality, dignity, accessibility and effectiveness.[20]

The Constitution provides for a Constitutional Court,[21] a Supreme Court of Appeal,[22] High Courts,[23] magistrates' courts[24] and special courts established in terms of an Act of Parliament with a status similar to that of either High Courts or magistrates' courts.[25]

The Constitutional Court, the Supreme Court of Appeal and the High Courts have the inherent power to protect and regulate their own process and to develop the common law, taking into account the interests of justice.[26]

14. Act 108 of 1996.
15. Section 165(1).
16. Section 165(2).
17. Section 165(3).
18. Section 165(2).
19. Section 165(5).
20. Section 165(4).
21. Section 166(a).
22. Section 166(b).
23. Section 166(c).
24. Section 166(d).
25. Section 166(e).
26. Section 173.

B. The Constitutional Court

28. In constitutional matters (issues involving the interpretation, protection or enforcement of the Constitution[27]) the Constitutional Court, with its seat in Johannesburg, is the highest court in the country.[28] It can adjudicate in constitutional matters only.[29] It is also the final Court of Appeal in constitutional cases. It is possible to bring a constitutional matter directly before the Constitutional Court, and this court can also hear an appeal directly from any other court.

The Supreme Court of Appeal and High Courts also have jurisdiction in constitutional matters. In some cases, the Constitutional Court has a final say and in others an exclusive say. For instance, the Constitutional Court finally decides the question whether a matter is a constitutional issue.[30] A High Court or the Supreme Court of Appeal can give judgment on the constitutionality of an Act of Parliament or a provincial legislature as well as conduct of the president. The Constitutional Court must finally confirm any nullification of such act or conduct.[31]

Matters in which the Constitutional Court has an exclusive say are the following:

- disputes between organs of state;[32]
- abstract review, that is the testing of the constitutionality of parliamentary and provincial bills;[33]
- the constitutionality of constitutional amendments;[34]
- compliance with constitutional obligations by Parliament or the president;[35] and
- the certification of provincial constitutions.[36]

The Constitutional Court consists of a president, a deputy president and nine other judges.[37] A matter before the court must be heard by at least eight judges.[38]

C. The Supreme Court of Appeal

29. The Supreme Court of Appeal (formerly the Appellate Division of the Supreme Court of South Africa) has its seat in Bloemfontein. The court consists of a chief justice, a deputy chief justice and the number of judges of appeal determined by legislation.[39]

---

27. Section 167(7).
28. Section 167(3)(a).
29. Section 167(3)(b).
30. Section 167(3)(c).
31. Section 167(5).
32. Section 167(4)(a).
33. Section 167(4)(b) and (c) read with secs. 80 and 122.
34. Section 167(4)(d).
35. Section 167(4)(e).
36. Section 167(4)(f).
37. Section 167(1).
38. Section 167(2).
39. Section 168(1).

The Supreme Court of Appeal is only a Court of Appeal and not a Court of First Instance. It is the final Court of Appeal in all non-constitutional matters.[40] It can also hear appeals in constitutional matters,[41] except those in which the Constitutional Court has an exclusive say. In constitutional matters, a further appeal lies from the Supreme Court of Appeal to the Constitutional Court. This holds for all constitutional matters and not only those in which the Constitutional Court has a final say.

D. The High Courts

30. The High Courts, each headed by a judge president, are the successors to the former provincial and local divisions of the Supreme Court of South Africa.

The geographical borders of the former provincial divisions of the Supreme Court coincided, by and large, with those of the four former provinces (Transvaal, the Cape Province, Natal and the Orange Free State). The seats of these courts were in provincial capitals (Pretoria, Cape Town, Pietermaritzburg and Bloemfontein). There were two additional provincial divisions in the geographically extensive Cape Province, namely in Grahamstown for the Eastern Cape and in Kimberley for the Northern Cape. The former independent States within South Africa had their own court structures with the seats of the High Courts in their respective capitals (Umtata, Mmabatho, Thohoyandou and Bisho).

The provincial divisions had comprehensive jurisdiction within a certain geographic area (mostly a whole province) and over specific persons. Provincial divisions could also hear appeals.

The three local divisions of the Supreme Court (in Johannesburg, Durban and Port Elizabeth) functioned within the territory of provincial divisions. With the exception of the Witwatersrand Local Division in Johannesburg, local divisions did not have jurisdiction in appeals. As Courts of First Instance, a local division and the provincial division in whose territory it was situated, had concurrent jurisdiction.

Under the Constitution the Supreme Court has been renamed as the High Court and the seats of the High Court have been rationalized.[42] Currently, the seats of the High Court are the following: Eastern Cape High Court, Bhisho; Eastern Cape High Court, Grahamstown (renamed Makhanda in 2018); Eastern Cape High Court, Mthatha; Eastern Cape High Court, Port Elizabeth; Free State High Court, Bloemfontein; KwaZulu-Natal High Court, Durban; KwaZulu-Natal High Court, Pietermaritzburg; Limpopo High Court, Thohoyandou; North Gauteng High Court, Pretoria; South Gauteng High Court, Johannesburg; North West High Court, Mafikeng; Northern Cape High Court, Kimberley; and Western Cape High Court, Cape Town.

---

40. Section 168(3)(a) and (b).
41. According to s. 168(3) the Supreme Court of Appeal may decide 'appeals in any matter'.
42. Schedule 6 item 16(6).

The High Courts can resolve any justiciable dispute except insofar as their jurisdiction has been limited by legislation. The Constitution provides that certain matters in which High Courts would normally have jurisdiction, can be assigned by an Act of Parliament to other courts of equal status.[43]

The Constitution also gives the High Courts jurisdiction in all constitutional matters except those in which the Constitutional Court has an exclusive say or those that have been assigned by an Act of Parliament to another court of equal status.[44] This means that a High Court can also, as a Court of First Instance, hear cases on constitutional issues in which the Constitutional Court has a final say.

Judges from a particular High Court sit from time to time in towns and cities away from the seat of that court. Mainly criminal cases are heard in this way. Such a court is known as a circuit court.

E. Magistrates' Courts

31. The Constitution includes magistrates' courts as part of the court system.[45] They may decide any matter determined by an Act of Parliament, but they may not rule on the constitutionality of any legislation or conduct of the president.[46]

Magistrates' courts consist of two main groups, namely district courts and regional courts.

A district court is a Court of First Instance within a limited area (called a magisterial district) and with limited civil as well as criminal jurisdiction. There are certain limitations on the civil jurisdiction of magistrates' courts in general:

- In terms of the Magistrates' Courts Act,[47] there are certain kinds of civil cases that magistrates' courts cannot hear, for example divorce cases, disputes in which the validity or interpretation of a will is at issue, and cases in which someone's mental status is to be determined.
- A case in which specific performance is claimed may be heard by a magistrate's court provided that damages are also claimed in the alternative.[48]
- The jurisdiction of magistrates' courts is also limited in respect of the amount involved in the dispute.[49]

In cases where the amount in dispute exceeds the maximum figures, it is still possible for a magistrate's court to hear civil cases in which such larger amounts are claimed, provided that all the parties concerned consent to the jurisdiction of the court in writing.[50]

43. Section 169(a)(ii) and (b).
44. Section 169(a).
45. Section 166(d).
46. Section 170.
47. Act 32 of 1944, s. 17.
48. Section 46(2)(c).
49. Section 29(a), (b), (d), (e), (f) and (g).
50. Section 45.

Litigants cannot consent to the jurisdiction of a magistrate's court, however, where the court has no jurisdiction because of *the nature of the cause of action.* Parties in a matrimonial dispute, for instance, cannot consent to the hearing of their divorce case in a magistrate's court.

The criminal jurisdiction of a magistrate's court is also limited. It may not hear criminal cases in which an accused is on trial on charges of crimes such as murder, rape and high treason.[51] In addition, there are limits to the maximum sentence which a magistrate's court can impose.[52]

Regional courts instituted for particular regional divisions (i.e., a number of magisterial districts together function in practice exclusively as criminal courts even though they also have civil jurisdiction. Their civil jurisdiction is the same as that of the district courts, but their criminal jurisdiction is considerably wider. They can hear more serious criminal cases in which heavier sentences can be imposed. For example, regional courts can also hear rape cases and even certain kinds of murder cases but not treason cases.[53] There are limits to the maximum jail sentence and the maximum fine they can impose.[54]

The Constitution[55] makes it clear that magistrates' courts cannot test legislation of any kind or the conduct of the president against the Constitution. They can, however, pass judgment on the constitutionality of administrative action. A magistrate can, for instance, decide whether an arrest or a detention of an accused person in a criminal case complies with the provisions of section 35 of the Constitution. If not, he can order the release of the accused.

F. Special Courts

32. Special courts deal with specialized litigation. There are special higher as well as lower courts. Special higher courts are presided over by judges. Examples of such courts are the Land Claims Court, water affairs courts and a special court for income tax appeals. Examples of special lower courts are children's and maintenance courts and Equality Courts. Equality Courts are courts designed to deal with matters covered by the Promotion of Equality and Prevention of Unfair Discrimination Act 4 of 2000, also known as the Equality Act. Equality courts are specialized courts designated to hear matters relating to unfair discrimination, hate speech and harassment. In areas where the local population still lives according to customary law, the courts of the chiefs and the headmen have limited civil and criminal jurisdiction.[56]

---

51. Section 89(1).
52. Section 92(1).
53. Section 89(2).
54. Section 92(1).
55. Section 170.
56. Sections 12 and 20 of the Black Administration Act 38 of 1927.

G. Small Claims Courts

33. The small claims courts, which have functioned in South Africa since 1985 and were instituted by the Small Claims Courts Act,[57] do not form part of the normal court structure. These courts hear civil disputes in which the amount in dispute does not exceed a periodically set maximum. They are able to deal with cases cheaply and quickly. The presiding officials (called commissioners) have legal qualifications (and are usually attorneys or law lecturers) and offer their services on a voluntary basis. The procedures in these courts are more informal than in the normal courts, and no legal representatives are permitted. The underlying idea is that parties should be on as equal a footing as possible. Legal persons or personae (such as companies) cannot sue anyone in a small claims court, but they themselves can be sued.

III. Distinction Between Public and Private Law

34. The terms 'public law' and 'private law' are used descriptively in South African law, to indicate, on the one hand, the area of law dealing with the organization of the State, the relationship between different organs of State and between the State and its citizens (public law); and on the other hand the area of law dealing with the relationship between persons (natural and legal), in respect of matters such as family, contract, delict and property (private law).

There is a considerable overlap between the areas of public and private law and the distinction is largely artificial, because the State increasingly intervenes in the area of private law, to regulate matters such as labour relations, employment equity and consumer contracts. Furthermore, the Constitution,[58] as the supreme law, affects all other areas of law, public and private. Section 8(1) of the Constitution provides that the Bill of Rights applies to all law (whether legislation, common law or customary law) and further provides that the Bill of Rights binds 'the legislature, the executive, the judiciary and all organs of State'. The State itself must respect, protect, promote and fulfil the rights contained in the Bill of Rights.[59] Thus constitutional rights and values affect all areas of the law, including public and private law.

The distinction between public and private law therefore does not entail the application of different rules, substantive or procedural. The distinction simply indicates a broadly different area of operation and function, and historically different sources, as indicated in the following section IV.

57. Act 61 of 1984.
58. Act 108 of 1996.
59. Section 7(2).

IV. Sources of Private Law

35. The South African legal system can be described generally as a mixed system comprising elements of civil law and common law.[60] South African law has developed from a civilian (Roman-Dutch) background and has had a substantial measure of English law grafted on to it.[61]

As indicated in section I above, Roman-Dutch law, mainly that of the province of Holland, was introduced after the first Dutch settlement in South Africa in 1652. During subsequent periods of British rule in South Africa, the English law of procedure was introduced and in other areas of the law English cases and statute law were influential. Key statutes in the field of commercial law, for example those dealing with companies and bills of exchange, were based on English models.

A renewed appreciation for and reassessment of the civilian basis of South African law appeared from the South African legal literature from the late 1930s onwards. This reflects what has been termed a *bellum juridicum* between proponents on the one side of the English and on the other side of the civilian or Roman-Dutch legal heritage.[62] The *bellum juridicum* has been well documented[63] and involved a serious legal debate, but there were also strong nationalistic and political

60. *See* generally *Southern Cross: Civil Law and Common Law in South Africa* 3 (Reinhard Zimmermann & Daniel Visser eds., Juta & Co. Ltd 1996).

61. *Supra*, n. 9.

62. A debate, at times acrimonious, about the nature and characterization of the sources of South African law. *See* Edwin Cameron, *Legal Chauvinism, Executive-Mindedness and Justice – LC Steyn's Impact on South African Law*, 99 S. African L. J. 38, 43–44 (1982): 'Two views are opposed. The one asserts that the Roman-Dutch common law introduced at the Cape in 1652 upon its colonization by Dutch settlers has remained in force unabridged as the subsidiary law which South African courts are obliged to apply. Except where this body of law has been explicitly or implicitly abolished by statute, or where it has fallen into desuetude in terms of the well-defined and narrow judicial doctrine recognizing such a process, it is the sole non-statutory source of rules, legal principles and writings wielding cogent force. Elements of English law have undeniably been introduced into contemporary Roman-Dutch law by legislation and in some instances by the courts. But English-born statutory provisions must always be interpreted subject to the principles of the Roman-Dutch common law. And it must be remembered that judicial importation of English doctrines frequently occurred as a result of inadvertence or misdirection; the growths so engrafted must not be nurtured, and where possible must be subjected to the purgative effects of reinterpretation in the context of "our own" legal doctrines. Naturally, however, no contemporary Roman-Dutch lawyer would seek to exclude the enriching influences of appropriate comparative investigations into related (particularly Continental) legal systems. On this basis, English law may be examined like any other to assess its possible persuasive effect. The second view urges that modern South African law is the product of a centuries-old process which initially involved the fusion in Renaissance Europe of Roman concepts with customary and local law. In addition to other systems, this produced the Roman-Dutch law that was transplanted to the Cape in the seventeenth century. However, the process of development by no means stopped there. The coming of the British in 1806 had profound effects on the nature and basis of the common law applicable in South Africa. Litigants, legal practitioners, judges and legislators triggered an immense infusion of English doctrines and concepts that added to the two components of the hybrid that already existed a third. The result is that South African law is a "mixed" system, containing and drawing upon both English and Romanist-European elements. English law has been a tributary giving power and direction to our legal current.'

63. Edwin Cameron, *supra*, n. 62, at 43–44; *Southern Cross: Civil Law and Common Law in South Africa* 22–24 (Reinhard Zimmermann & Daniel Visser eds., 1996); and Annél van Aswegen in the same volume at 563–564.

undercurrents, and language also played a part in the orientation of the jurists towards either the English or Roman-Dutch legal heritage.

New Afrikaans-language law faculties were established at Stellenbosch in 1920 and Pretoria in 1930, and others followed.[64] Many of the professors at the new law faculties had studied in Europe, particularly in the Netherlands and Germany, and their students later followed. They were exposed to the principled structure of the civilian codified systems, in contrast with the more casuistic nature of the English system of precedent. When the products of these faculties later became members of the judiciary they often showed a preference for the civilian legal heritage, in some cases despite the established precedents of English law.[65] The scholarship of English-speaking jurists, not surprisingly, was often firmly rooted in the English tradition.

The dust of this debate about the sources of South African law has now settled and the mixed nature of the South African legal system is generally accepted, particularly in the field of private law. The advent of the new Constitution of 1996, with its Bill of Rights, has changed fundamentally the nature of the South African legal system and also the nature of legal reasoning and debate. Constitutional rights and values influence all areas of the law, including private law generally and the law of delict in particular.

English has effectively become the language of the courts.

§3. Function of the Law of Delict

36. The law of delict forms part of the law of obligations and the wider field of private law. Private law generally recognizes and protects certain individual interests and harmonizes conflict between the interests of different individuals. The law of delict recognizes and protects certain individual interests against wrongful infringement and provides for compensation or damages in the event of such infringement. The person responsible for the wrongful infringement is liable to compensate for the damage caused by the infringement; and the person who suffered harm or damage has the corresponding right to claim compensation. Delictual liability therefore implies an obligation, with a right and a correlative liability or duty.

A delict occurs when the act of one person wrongfully and culpably causes damage to another. Accordingly, the elements of a delict and requirements for delictual liability in South African law are the following: an act, causation, damage, unlawfulness and fault. In general, delictual liability arises whenever the act of one person wrongfully and culpably causes damage to another, irrespective of the nature of the act or the kind of interest affected by the act. The law of delict is based on the general principles that developed around the elements of delictual liability, and this generalizing approach gives the system flexibility and enables the law of delict to

64. *See* generally Derek van der Merwe, *Die impak van toenemende eentaligheid in die regstelsel op Afrikaans as juridiese vaktaal*, 40(3) Tydskrif vir Geesteswetenskappe, 255, 256–258 (2000).

65. W.J. Hosten, *Kodifikasie in Suid-Afrika –'n Heroorweging*, Huldigingsbundel vir WA Joubert 59, 62–63 (1988).

deal with new situations and to afford protection to a whole spectrum of rights and interests. This is in contrast with some of the restrictions inherent in the Common lLaw system of individual torts and the codified European systems where a general clause specifies the interests protected by the law of delict, as for instance in section 823 of the German Civil Code, which refers to injury to life, body, health, freedom, property or 'other rights'.

However, the South African law of delict is not a wholly uniform system, and it distinguishes between delicts involving patrimonial damage (*damnum iniuria datum*) and those involving injury to personality rights (*iniuria*). This distinction derives from two important actions in Roman law, namely the *actio legis Aquiliae* that dealt (in its developed form) with negligent or intentional causing of patrimonial loss; and the *actio iniuriarum* that dealt with intentional injury to personality rights. The action for negligent causing of pain and suffering, arising from the infringement of physical or mental bodily integrity, has some of the characteristics of an Aquilian action and some of the *actio iniuriarum*. The South African law of delict also recognizes various forms of liability without fault, such as for damage caused by animals and vicarious liability of an employer for a delict by an employee in the course of employment.

§4. Relationship Between Delict and Criminal Law

37. The law of delict is essentially directed at protecting private interests and providing compensation for loss or harm, whereas the criminal law is directed at protecting the public interest and imposing penal sanctions on the wrongdoer. However, the wrongful causing of loss or harm to another will in many cases constitute both a delict and a crime, for example in cases of theft, fraud, assault and intentional damage to property. Many delicts are not crimes, for example negligent damage to property and negligent causing of bodily harm. Also, many crimes are not delicts, for example treason, interfering with the course of justice, trading in prohibited substances.

Compensation can be awarded in criminal proceedings to the victim of crime, in terms of section 300(1) of the Criminal Procedure Act 51 of 1977:

> Where a person is convicted by a superior court, a regional court or a magistrate's court of an offence which has caused damage to or loss of property (including money) belonging to some other person, the court in question may, upon the application of the injured person or of the prosecutor acting on the instructions of the injured person, forthwith award the injured person compensation for such damage or loss.

In the case of theft of property, an award of compensation can also be made in terms of section 301 of the Criminal Procedure Act 51 of 1977:

> Where a person is convicted of theft or of any other offence whereby he has wrongfully obtained any property, and it appears to the court on the evidence that such person sold such property or part thereof to another person who had

no knowledge that the property was stolen or wrongfully obtained, the court may, on the application of such purchaser and on restitution of such property to the owner thereof, order that, out of any money of such convicted person taken from him on his arrest, a sum not exceeding the amount paid by the purchaser be returned to him.

§5. Relationship Between Contractual and Delictual Liability

38. Delict and breach of contract in South African law both concern the wrongful causing of loss or harm and both involve recovery of compensation. However, there are some important differences. The purpose of remedies based on breach of contract is either to enforce the contract or to obtain compensation for the non-fulfilment of its terms. The purpose of a remedy based on delict is to obtain compensation for the infringement of a right or breach of a duty. In delict, there is a right of recovery for patrimonial or non-patrimonial harm (such as pain and suffering or injury to reputation), whereas in contract there is no right of recovery for non-patrimonial harm.[66] Fault is generally a requirement for delictual liability, whereas liability for breach of contract is generally not based on fault. The Apportionment of Damages Act 34 of 1956 applies where the action for damages is based on delict, but not where it is based on contract.[67] The time for computation of damages may differ. Claims in delict and contract may be subject to the jurisdiction of different courts. The extent of vicarious liability in delict is different from that in contract. Claims in delict and contract are subject to different rules of private international law. Contractual claims are actively transmissible, whereas some delictual claims are not. Where actions both in contract and in delict are available on the same facts, the onus of proving or disproving negligence may differ according to the choice of action, as in the case of damage done to goods deposited with another.

Although the distinction between contract and delict, fully accepted in the nineteenth century, is said to have become somewhat unfashionable,[68] there is arguably still an important difference between the values underlying contract and a delict.[69] Contract law is based, in large part, on the notion that people should be free to do

66. *Administrator Natal v. Edouard* 1990 (3) SA 581 (A) 595–596.
67. The issue of contributory negligence in a contractual setting was considered at length by the Supreme Court of Appeal in *Thoroughbred Breeders' Association v. Price Waterhouse* 2001 (4) SA 551 (SCA). The case concerned the contractual liability of auditors for negligently failing to discover that the financial manager of a company (their client) was involved in large-scale theft from the company. It appeared that the company itself was careless in failing to exercise proper supervision over the activities of the financial manager, despite its awareness that the manager had previously been convicted of theft. Both forms of negligence contributed to the company's loss, but the court held that the company's fault was comparatively negligible, and that the Apportionment of Damages Act 34 of 1956 does not apply to contractual claims for damages: the concepts of contributory negligence or preponderance of fault historically pertain to the law of delict, and the Apportionment of Damages Act was intended to remedy the all-or-nothing approach in delictual actions. The auditors were therefore liable in full.
68. Weir, Complex Liabilities in International Encyclopedia of Comparative Law XI Ch 12 at 12–14.
69. *See* generally Annél van Aswegen, Die Sameloop van Eise om Skadevergoeding uit Kontrakbreuk en Delik (unpublished LL D thesis, *University of South Africa*, 1991); Thomas C. Galligan Jr, *Contortions along the Boundary Between Contracts and Torts*, 69 Tul. L. Rev. 457, 459 (1994).

as they choose and to maximize their personal utilities, with the corollary that a contracting party also accepts the risks of the contract. The law of delict or tort, on the contrary, requires one person to make compensation to another if he or she acts in a way that the community determines to be unlawful or actionable. Intentional causing of harm to another is mostly clearly unlawful and exposes one to liability. Also, the failure to act as a reasonable person under the circumstances can, in many cases, result in liability for negligence. One may view the reasonable person standard as the symbolic point at which society arrests unfettered freedom of action.[70] The traditional distinction between contract and delict is therefore founded on the difference between obligations voluntarily assumed and obligations imposed by societal norm.

39. These two branches of law have historically existed side by side. In Roman law, a *concursus actionum* between contract and delict was recognized in several instances, although the consequences of such concurrence were not mapped out clearly.[71] Concurrence of contract and delict in modern South African law is particularly relevant in cases involving liability for negligent performance of professional services. Courts in different legal systems have accepted that the contractual relationship between a professional person and his client, in addition to an implied duty to act with reasonable care and skill, also gives rise to a delictual duty with similar content.

Breach of contract involving the negligent performance of service may give rise to a delictual action, either as an alternative remedy to an action for breach of contract, in cases where professional services are performed negligently; or as an exclusively delictual action, for example where the defendant in the pre-contractual phase negligently or intentionally misrepresented facts, inducing the plaintiff to enter into the contract.[72] The negligent performance of contractual duties that causes loss or harm to a person outside the contractual relationship may also give rise to a delictual action by such an outsider, as in cases of misrepresentation, negligent advice, defective workmanship or the 'disappointed beneficiary' cases.[73]

40. There is no general *non cumul* rule in South African law: the same conduct may constitute either a breach of contract or a delict and there may be a concurrence of actions in delict and contract, affording the plaintiff a choice of proceeding either in delict or in contract against the same defendant. Concurrence of contract and delict is particularly relevant in cases involving liability for negligent performance of professional services. The contractual relationship between a professional

70. Thomas C. Galligan Jr, *Contortions along the Boundary Between Contracts and Torts*, 69 Tul. L. Rev. 457, 460 (1994).
71. D19 2 25; D19 2 43; D10 2 16 5; D17 2 50; D9 2 18; D13 6 7 1; D44 7 34 2; D13 6 18 1; D92 27 11; D9 2 27 34; D9 2 42; and cf. generally Annél van Aswegen, Die Sameloop van Eise om Skadevergoeding uit Kontrakbreuk en Delik (unpublished LL D thesis, *University of South Africa*, 1991) 30; and *Lillicrap, Wassenaar and Partners v. Pilkington Brothers* 1985 (1) SA 475 (A) at 496.
72. *Bayer SA (Pty) Ltd v. Frost* 1991 (4) SA 559 (A) 570.
73. *See Pretorius en andere v. McCullum* 2002 (2) SA 423 (K); *BOE Bank Ltd v. Ries* 2002 (2) SA 39 (SCA).

person and his client generally implies that the professional person has a duty to act with reasonable care and skill, but the relationship may also give rise to a delictual duty with a similar content.

41. In South African law, concurrence of contract and delict has been recognized in respect of the relationship between doctor and patient in a case where the alleged harm was physical and not purely economic;[74] and also between attorney and client in respect of pure economic loss,[75] although in the leading case concerning an attorney's liability to his client the client's action was treated as a contractual action.[76] In the leading case of *Lillicrap, Wassenaar & Partners v. Pilkington Bros (SA) (Pty) Ltd*,[77] which dealt with an engineer and client relationship where professional negligence caused pure economic loss, the Supreme Court of Appeal has held that the client has a contractual remedy and no concurrent action in delict. A key consideration was that this case did not involve an infringement of rights of property or person, but only the infringement of a contractual duty to perform specific professional work with due diligence. There was no 'independent' duty for the purposes of delictual liability. In the view of most commentators, this judgment implied that only a contractual remedy is available where pure economic loss (as opposed to physical damage or personal injury) is caused by negligent performance of a contractual duty, notably in the relationship between a client and a professional practitioner.[78]

42. However, in later cases there appears to have been a more open approach. The yardstick to determine whether there is a legal duty for the purposes of delictual liability within a contractual relationship is the general criterion of reasonableness or *boni mores*, involving the 'policy-based aspect of the "duty of care" concept, by means of which the scope of delictual liability is judicially controlled'.[79] The criterion of reasonableness involves a value judgment, based on considerations of morality and policy and the court's perception of the legal convictions of the community. The following are examples of this more general approach.

43. The Supreme Court of Appeal has recognized delictual liability of a builder towards the owner who had contracted with the builder.[80] The Supreme Court of Appeal has also recognized delictual liability for a negligent misstatement by a bank

---

74. *Van Wyk v. Lewis* 1924 AD 428.
75. *Rampal (Pty) Ltd v. Brett Wills and Partners* 1981 (4) SA 360 (D).
76. *Mouton v. Die Mynwerkersunie* 1977 (1) SA 119 (A); and *see also Bouwer v. Harding* 1997 (4) SA 1023 (SE), where the liability of an attorney to a client was the subject of an action for breach of contract, and the attorney was found to be in breach of his contractual duties by negligently failing to advise the client correctly on the tax implications of structuring a sale of property in a particular manner.
77. *Lillicrap, Wassenaar and Partners v. Pilkington Brothers (SA) (Pty) Ltd* 1985 (1) SA 475 (A).
78. J.R. Midgley, *The Nature of the Inquiry into Concurrence of Actions*, 621 S. African L. J. 107 (1990); Annél van Aswegen, *Die Toets vir die Bestaan van 'n "Onafhanklike Delik" in die Geval van Kontrakbreuk*, 55 THRHR 271, 273–274 (1992).
79. *Shell and BP SA Petroleum Refineries (Pty) Ltd v. Osborne Panama SA* 1980 (3) SA 653 (D) 659.
80. *SM Goldstein & Co. (Pty) Ltd v. Cathkin Park Hotel (Pty) Ltd* 2000 (4) SA 1019 (SCA) para. 7 at 2.

manager that caused loss to a customer (account holder) of the bank, distinguishing the *Lillicrap* case on the basis that 'Lillicrap decided that no claim is maintainable in delict where the negligence relied on consists in the breach of a term in a contract'.[81] A financial services company can be liable to a client in delict for the grossly negligent advice of an employee, on the basis of vicarious liability, despite the existence of a contractual relationship between the company and the client.[82] An employer owes a common law duty to its employees to take reasonable care for their safety. This includes a duty to protect them from psychological harm caused by, for example, sexual harassment by co-employees. The legal convictions of the community require an employer to take reasonable steps to prevent sexual harassment of its employees in the workplace and to compensate the victim for harm caused thereby should it negligently fail to do so. The fact that there was a contractual relationship between the employee and the employer does not alter the position – there can be a concurrence of delictual and contractual actions arising from the same set of facts.[83] Where a negligent misrepresentation by one party to a contract induced the other party to enter into the contract and the negligent misrepresentation was not incorporated as a term of the contract, the party induced by the negligent misrepresentation to enter into the contract would, in many instances, have a claim in delict against the other for his pure economic loss flowing from his conclusion of the contract.[84]

44. In *Freddy Hirsch Group (Pty) Ltd v. Chickenland (Pty) Ltd*,[85] one company bought spices from another for use in its food business, and it turned out that the spices containing a banned colourant. The court held that the plaintiff had an alternative claim in delict for economic loss caused by delivery to it of the defective spices. The court accepted that the same facts may give rise to a claim for damages *ex contractu* and alternatively *ex delicto*, but also that the breach of a contractual duty is not per se wrongful for the purposes of Aquilian liability.[86] The negligent causing of pure economic loss is not prima facie wrongful, but in this case policy considerations such as knowledge of the potential harm, the fact that the loss was single and determinate, and the manufacturer's general duty to take reasonable steps to ensure that defective products do not reach the market indicated wrongfulness for the purposes of delictual liability.

45. The courts thus recognize an overlap of delict and breach of contract in cases of property damage or bodily harm. Courts may also recognize this overlap in some cases of pure economic loss, where the delictual action is based on a general duty to prevent loss, as opposed to a duty deriving from a specific term of a contract. However, in some cases, contract 'trumps' delict, so that the existence of a contract

81. *Holtzhausen v. ABSA Bank Ltd* [2004] JOL 12962 (SCA) para. 6.
82. *Pinshaw v. Nexus Securities (Pty) Ltd and Another* 2002 (2) SA 510 (C).
83. *MEDIA 24 Ltd and Another v. Grobler* 2005 (6) SA 328 (SCA) 350, para. 69.
84. *Thatcher and Another v. Katz and Another* 2006 (6) SA 407 (C) 412D-E, para. 16.
85. 2011 (4) SA 276 (SCA).
86. Paragraph 33.

between the parties is a defence to an action in delict.[87] The leading cases illustrating this approach are *Lillicrap*, discussed above, and *Trustees, Two Oceans Aquarium Trust v. Kantey & Templer (Pty) Ltd.*[88]

46. In the *Trustees, Two Oceans Aquarium Trust* case, the appellants were trustees of a trust that leased and operated an aquarium. They claimed damages in delict for pure economic loss that resulted from the negligent design by the respondent structural engineers of the exhibit tanks at the aquarium. They alleged that the respondent's negligence began before the contract between them was concluded, but that even at that stage, the respondent was under a legal duty to act without negligence when deciding on an appropriate design for the tanks. The court held that negligently causing pure economic loss was wrongful, and therefore actionable, only where the defendant had been under a legal duty not to act negligently. The court determined whether such a legal duty existed by considering relevant public or legal policy that was consistent with constitutional norms. The appellants were asking the court to accept that a legal duty existed that up until then was not recognized by our law. Therefore, they were asking the court to extend the limits of delictual liability. Whether the court would oblige depended upon whether there were any considerations of public or legal policy that required the extension. The approach of the South African courts is not to extend the scope of the Aquilian action to new situations unless there are positive policy considerations that favour the extension. However, in this case, there was no need for the extension sought because of the following:

- It was intended from the outset that if the project proceeded at all, it would be governed by a contractual relationship that would be created once the trust was formed.
- It was foreseen from the outset that the trust could not possibly suffer any damages through the negligent conduct of the respondent before the contract was concluded.
- The trust could have protected itself against this risk of harm by inserting, either in the agreement between the joint venture and the respondent, or in the contract of formal appointment of the respondent, appropriate contractual stipulations that covered conduct occurring before the trust was formed. There was no reason to extend the Aquilian action to rescue a plaintiff who could have avoided the risk of harm by contractual means, but who failed to do so.

47. In a contractual context, the same set of facts may give rise to cumulative liability, both in contract and in delict, as in the case where breach of contract causes patrimonial loss and also injury to dignity or reputation. Both a contact action for

---

87. *Nashua Mobile (Pty) Ltd v. GC Pale CC t/a Invasive Plant Solutions* 2012 (1) SA 615 (GSJ); *Nortje v. Fakie* 2013 (1) SA 577 (KZP).
88. 2006 (3) SA 138 (SCA).

recovery of patrimonial loss and a delict action (the *actio iniuriarum*) for recovery of compensation for the injury to personality rights may be available.[89]

A contractual relationship, such as that between an employer and employee, may give rise to a legal duty not to cause financial loss to the other contract party, even though no breach of contract is involved. The case of *Joubert v. Impala Platinum Ltd*[90] is an example of this type of situation. The case involved administrative duties of an employer in respect of a master insurance policy entered into between the employer and an insurance company, providing cover for the employer's employees. In terms of the policy, the employer had a contractual duty towards the insurer to give notice of an employee's claim as soon as possible after an accident and to transmit the claim to the insurer as soon as possible. The employer failed to transmit the claim and the employee forfeited compensation as a result. The court held that the employer was liable in delict towards the employee for negligent omission to fulfil a duty of care towards the employee.

48. Pre-contractual liability in delict can arise where a party to a prospective contract in the pre-contractual phase negligently misrepresents facts, inducing another party to enter into the contract. This is not 'true' concurrence of contract and delict, because the delictual liability for pure economic loss arises in the pre-contractual phase and is not an alternative to contractual liability, unless the representation is reinforced in the form of a contractual warranty.

The South African Appeal Court recognized in 1991 in *Bayer South Africa (Pty) Ltd v. Frost*[91] that negligent misstatement inducing a contract can give rise to a delictual claim for damages. The plaintiff purchased a new type of herbicide spray for use in his vineyards. An agent of the seller recommended that spraying be done by helicopter and undertook to supervise the spraying operations. During spraying the herbicide drifted to adjacent lands and caused extensive damage to crops. The seller was held liable in delict for negligent misstatement, a recognized delictual cause of action which, the court held, should have no different application in contractual context.

49. Interaction between delictual and contractual liability also occurs in the case of indemnity insurance. Loss or harm caused by a delict may be covered by insurance, in which case both a delictual action against the wrongdoer and a contractual claim against the insurer will be available. The insured (plaintiff) is then entitled to both the damages recovered from the wrongdoer and the proceeds of the insurance claim. However, in the case of indemnity insurance the insured who has recovered damages equal to or in excess of the insurance payment from the wrongdoer will be obliged in terms of the insurance contract to repay the insurance benefit, to prevent double compensation. Alternatively, where the insured has not claimed damages from the wrongdoer the insurer will be entitled to institute such a claim against the

89. *Jockie v. Meyer* 1945 AD 354 367–368; *Guggenheim v. Rosenbaum* (2) 1961 (4) SA 21 (W); *Ndamse v. University College of Fort Hare* 1966 (4) SA 137 (E); *Klopper v. Volkskas Bpk* 1964 (2) SA 421 (T) 425.
90. 1998 (1) SA 463 (B).
91. 1991 (4) SA 559 (A).

wrongdoer in the name of the insured, without cession of action, in terms of the principle of subrogation. In respect of liability insurance, this principle also entitles the insurer to defend a delictual claim in the name of its insured, so as to limit or exclude liability.

The operation of the principle of subrogation is described as follows in *Commercial Union Insurance Company of South Africa Ltd v. Lotter*:[92]

> It is trite law that an insurer under a contract of indemnity insurance who has satisfied the claim of the insured is entitled to be placed in the insured's position in respect of all rights and remedies against other parties which are vested in the insured in relation to the subject-matter of the insurance. This is by virtue of the doctrine of subrogation, which is part of our common law.

By operation of the principle of subrogation, many delictual actions ostensibly instituted by the person who suffered harm, or ostensibly defended by the wrongdoer, are in fact conducted by insurance companies. In many cases, no delictual action would have been instituted were it not for the existence of indemnity insurance.

§6. Protected Interests

50. The South African law of delict serves to protect a wide spectrum of subjective rights, such as personality rights, real rights, personal rights, immaterial property rights, personal immaterial property rights and also other legally recognized interests. There is no closed list of protected rights or interests, and liability is determined by application of general principles in respect of conduct, causation, damage, unlawfulness and fault. The application of these general principles is influenced by moral, economic and other considerations and liability depends essentially on whether the perpetrator unreasonably caused harm to another person, and not so much on the particular nature of the right or interest affected. As noted in section 2 above, this generalizing approach gives the system flexibility and enables the law of delict to deal with new situations and to afford protection to a whole spectrum of rights and interests. This is in contrast with codified European systems where a general clause specifies the interests protected by the law of delict, as for instance section 823 of the German Civil Code, that refers to injury to life, body, health, freedom, property or 'other rights'.

51. Consideration of the nature and extent of protected rights and interests in delict raises the question of a 'superior value factor': are some rights or interests rated more worthy of protection than others? The law of delict serves to protect rights and interests (to both tangibles and intangibles) that are of value to persons generally. Rights and interests obviously differ in value and also in the nature of

92. 1999 (2) SA 147 (SCA) 154. *See also Ackerman v. Loubser* 1918 OPD 31, *Teper v. E McGees Motors (Pty) Ltd* 1956 (1) SA 738 (C); and *Avex Air (Pty) Ltd v. Borough of Vryheid* 1973 (1) SA 617 (A) at 625H.

their value and cannot always be given efficient protection against all infringements. The existence and extent of protection might thus be dictated by moral, economic and other policy considerations. How highly the law of delict rates a right or interest might appear from the extent of protection the law gives to it relatively to other rights or interests.[93] The Road Accident Fund Act,[94] for example, provides for a statutory compensation scheme for bodily injury or death resulting from motor vehicle accidents, but not for property damage. The Aquilian liability for injury to a person or tangible property is older and more comprehensive than liability for causing pure economic loss. The spectre of 'opening the floodgates' and potentially unlimited liability to an unlimited class of persons, and the fact that the economic consequences of conduct might have a far wider impact than physical consequences, are policy considerations that inhibit the recognition of liability for pure economic loss. Likewise, for historical and policy reasons, the statutory protection afforded to patents, trademarks, designs and copyright varies in duration and extent.

52. A number of rights included in the Bill of Rights (Chapter 2 of the Constitution[95]) also enjoy protection in the common law of delict, including the rights to life, bodily and psychological integrity, human dignity, bodily freedom and privacy. In respect of constitutionally protected rights and interests (*see* further section 7 below) the constitutional court has indicated that the rights to life[96] and to human dignity[97] are fundamental:[98]

> The rights to life and dignity are the most important of all human rights, and the sources of all other personal rights in chapter 3 … [We] are required to value these two rights above all other.

However, the infringement of a constitutional right is not conclusive for delictual liability. As noted in section 7 below, many of the rights entrenched in the Bill of Rights are also protected and kept in balance with competing rights by the general principles of the law of delict. The assessment of unlawfulness for the purposes of liability often involves a conflict of rights, as in the case of defamation, where one person's right to freedom of expression[99] and another's right to human dignity (including reputation)[100] come into conflict.[101] There may also be a conflict between the constitutional right to property[102] and freedom of competition in terms of the Competition Act,[103] for instance where a trader who dominates a particular market

93. *See* F.H. Lawson & B.S. Markesinis, *Tortious Liability for Unintentional Harm in the Common Law and the Civil Law*, 49 (1982).
94. Act 56 of 1996.
95. Act 108 of 1996.
96. Section 11 of the Constitution Act 108 of 1996.
97. Section 10.
98. *S v. Makwanyane* 1995 (3) SA 391 (CC) 451.
99. Section 16 of the Constitution Act 108 of 1996.
100. Section 10.
101. *See*, for example, *Khumalo and Others v. Holomisa* 2002 (5) SA 401 (CC).
102. Section 25 of the Constitution Act 108 of 1996.
103. Act 89 of 1998.

may be ordered to share an 'essential facility' with a rival.[104] There have been attempts to call in aid the constitutional right to engage freely in economic activity,[105] or to choose a trade, occupation or profession freely,[106] particularly to have a contractual restraint of trade declared invalid,[107] but these have not yet met with success.

53. Factors such as the extent of interference with or disturbance of a right or interest, the extent of harm, the reasonable foreseeability and preventability of harm, the relationship between the parties, and moral, economic and other policy considerations determine whether or not and to what extent the law of delict affords protection to a particular right or interest; and there is no closed list or hierarchy of protected rights and interests.

§7. The Constitution and the Law of Delict

54. The relationship between the law of delict and the Constitution[108] concerns the application of the Constitution's Bill of Rights in a delict action between private parties. The terms 'horizontal', 'direct' or 'indirect' are often used to describe the application of the Constitution in this context. By 'horizontal' is meant the application of the Bill of Rights between private persons or entities, as opposed to the application between citizens and organs of State. By 'direct operation' is meant that the Bill of Rights could be the basis of a substantive right held by one person against another. By 'indirect operation' is meant that the Bill of Rights might only influence a court's interpretation and development of the law in deciding on rights and duties between private persons. The values encapsulated in fundamental rights provisions may be brought to bear indirectly in interpreting or filling out private law norms.

55. Section 8(1) of the Constitution provides that the Bill of Rights applies to all law (whether that law be legislation, common law or customary law) and further provides that the Bill of Rights binds four types of public agencies, namely 'the legislature, the executive, the judiciary and all organs of State'. The State (a term not defined in the Constitution – only an 'organ of State' is defined in section 239) must respect, protect, promote and fulfil the rights contained in the Bill of Rights.[109] The Constitution defines an 'organ of State' as any State department, any other institution which exercises a power or performs a function in terms of the Constitution or

---

104. Section 8(b); and *see SAD Holdings Ltd and Another v. South African Raisins (Pty) Ltd and Another*[2000] 2 All SA 326 329, where the Competition Tribunal ordered a company dominant in the raisin market to share specially designed containers, which it owned, with a rival.
105. Section 26(1) of the interim Constitution Act 200 of 1993.
106. Section 22 of the Constitution Act 108 of 1996.
107. *See Waltons Stationery Company (Pty) Ltd v. Fourie and Another* 1994 (1) BCLR 50 (O); *Kotze en Genis (Edms) Bpk v. Potgieter en Andere* 1995 (3) BCLR 349 (C).
108. Act 108 of 1996.
109. Section 7(2).

a provincial constitution, and any institution which exercises a public power or performs a public function in terms of any legislation (but excluding a court or a judicial officer).

56. Section 8(2) of the Constitution provides that certain constitutional rights apply directly to private persons or entities. According to this section, a provision of the Bill of Rights (i.e., a right) 'binds a natural or a juristic person', but only 'if and to the extent that it is applicable' to a natural or juristic person, 'taking into account the nature of the right and the nature of any duty imposed by the right'. In terms of section 8(2), the Bill of Rights undoubtedly has direct application to natural and juristic persons in some circumstances, but it is a restricted form of direct application, in that only certain constitutional rights will apply in such a manner and the application might only be to a certain extent. The courts will be required to decide in an ad hoc manner whether or not a particular constitutional right binds a private natural or juristic person.

57. The only guidance provided by section 8(2) is that regard should be had to the nature of the right and the nature of any correlative duty. The constitutional right under consideration might provide further guidance, inasmuch as it contains an 'internal application provision' which serves to make clear that the right does (or does not) apply against private agencies. For example, the formulation of the provisions dealing with the right to just administrative action[110] and the rights of arrested persons[111] indicate that these rights apply only against the State. In contrast, the formulation of the right to equality,[112] and of the right of access to information,[113] indicate that obligations might be imposed on private persons. In the absence of an internal indication of application, courts will be required to make a value judgment on whether or not it would be appropriate for the constitutional right under consideration to impose burdens on private persons. In terms of section 8(2), this will depend in large part on 'the nature of the right and the nature of any duty imposed by the right'.

58. Section 8(3) of the Constitution applies only where a court seeks to apply a provision of the Bill of Rights to a natural or juristic person in terms of section 8(2). Section 8(3) contains two directives to a court in such a case.

(1) To give effect to a constitutional right which binds a private person, a court is required to apply (or, if necessary, develop) the common law to the extent that legislation fails to give effect to that right. The application of constitutional rights to private persons is mandated in a particular manner – it must occur by means of the common law. This provision is reinforced by section 39(2) of the Constitution, which provides that when a Court develops the common law, it

110. Section 33.
111. Section 35.
112. Section 9.
113. Section 32.

must 'promote the spirit, purport and objects of the Bill of Rights'. The Constitution thus involves both a direct and indirect horizontal application, because even where a constitutional right applies directly to a private person in terms of section 8(2), it is the common law which is required to be applied or developed to give effect to the constitutional right.

(2) When a court applies a constitutional right to a private person in terms of section 8(2), it is empowered to develop rules of the common law so as to limit such a right provided that the limitation is in accordance with section 36(1) of the Constitution. The limitation is required to comply with the criteria contained in the general limitation clause. Section 8(3)(b) is of particular importance in a dispute between private persons who both rely on constitutional rights. In such a situation of competing constitutional rights, section 8(3)(b) of the Constitution requires that a court consider whether infringement of the one right by a common law rule which serves to protect the other right can be justified in terms of the general limitation clause.

59. In a delictual action between private persons, the application of the Constitution involves two stages, as illustrated by the judgment of the Constitutional Court in *Khumalo and Others v. Holomisa.*[114] This case deals with the question whether the plaintiff in a defamation action should be required to allege and prove that the defamatory statement is untrue. The defendants attacked the common law rule which requires of the plaintiff only to allege and prove the publication of a defamatory statement pertaining to him or her. In terms of this rule, it is then for the defendant to allege and prove that the statement was true, and that the publication was in the public interest. The rule was attacked on the basis of an alleged conflict with the right of freedom of expression guaranteed by section 16 of the Constitution. The plaintiff argued that the rule is justified on the basis of the protection of human dignity (including reputation and privacy) guaranteed by section 10 of the Constitution.

(1) The first issue was whether these constitutional rights bind private persons in terms of section 8(2) of the Constitution, and if so to what extent. The Constitutional Court had to consider this question with regard to the nature of the rights and the nature of any correlative duties. The court considered that the defendants were members of the media who are expressly identified as bearers of constitutional rights to freedom of expression. There can be no doubt that the law of defamation does affect the right to freedom of expression. Given the 'intensity' of the constitutional right in question, coupled with the potential invasion of that right which could be occasioned by persons other than the State or organs of State, the court held that the right to freedom of expression is of direct horizontal application in this case, as contemplated by section 8(2) of the Constitution.[115]

(2) If a constitutional right does apply to private persons, as in this case, then at the second stage of the inquiry the court is required to apply or develop the

114. 2002 (5) SA 401 (CC).
115. Paragraph 33 of the judgment.

common law to give effect to that right. The Constitutional Court here considered whether the common law rule which requires the defendant to allege and prove truth and public benefit in a defamation action unjustifiably limits the right to freedom of expression. If it did, it would be necessary to develop the common law in the manner contemplated by section 8(3) of the Constitution, including a possible limitation of a conflicting right in accordance with section 36(1) of the Constitution. The court held that the common law rule in question does not unjustifiably limit the constitutional right to freedom of expression, mainly because a defendant who cannot establish the truth, or finds it disproportionately expensive or difficult to do so, may show that in all the circumstances the publication was reasonable. In determining whether publication was reasonable, a court will have regard to the individual's interest in protecting his or her reputation and privacy in the context of the constitutional commitment to human dignity.

60. The application of the Bill of Rights as described above will not necessarily involve extensive new development of the law of delict. The general principles of delict have developed as criteria or guidelines to achieve an equitable balance between conflicting rights and an equitable allocation or distribution of risk and loss. Many of the rights entrenched in the Bill of Rights are in any event protected and kept in balance with competing rights by the general principles of the law of delict. However, the application of the Bill of Rights in the law of delict, as in other areas of private law, clearly has an impact on the style of judicial reasoning, inasmuch as the courts more often engage with normative issues rather than to rely on 'authority reasons' in a formalistic way. The general or open-ended principles of law of delict, in particular the element of unlawfulness, is informed by applicable constitutional values.

61. In *Dendy v. University of the Witwatersrand*[116] the Supreme Court of Appeal considered whether the law relating to infringements of dignity needed to be developed. The court accepted that it had an obligation to ensure that the common law is consistent with the Constitution, but also noted that any development must be done within the common law's paradigm. A court must first to enquire whether the existing common law should be developed. If the answer is no, then that would be the end of the inquiry. If the answer is yes, it should enquire what development should occur. In this case, the court concluded that the common law had not been found wanting and was not in need of reform. Dendy could have vindicated his rights 'by the remedies of review or a relatively simple application to compel production of the documentation and the reasons sought', but chose not to do so, seeking instead to bring a novel claim in delict.

62. In *Minister of Safety and Security v. Van Duivenboden*[117] the police had information showing that the person who had shot Van Duivenboden was unfit to possess a firearm, but they failed to investigate further. In holding the police liable

116. 2007 (5) SA 382 (SCA).
117. 2002 (6) SA 431 (SCA).

for Van Duivenboden's injuries, the court noted that public functionaries and public authorities were not on the same level as ordinary citizens. With reference to the norm of accountability the Supreme Court of Appeal said:[118]

> When determining whether the law should recognise the existence of a legal duty in any particular circumstance what is called for is not an intuitive reaction to a collection of arbitrary factors but rather a balancing against one another of identifiable norms. Where the conduct of the State, as represented by the persons who perform functions on its behalf, is in conflict with its constitutional duty to protect rights in the Bill of Rights, in my view, the norm of accountability must necessarily assume an important role in determining whether a legal duty ought to be recognised in any particular case. The norm of accountability, however, need not always translate constitutional duties into private law duties enforceable by an action for damages, for there will be cases in which other appropriate remedies are available for holding the State to account. Where the conduct in issue relates to questions of State policy, or where it affects a broad and indeterminate segment of society, constitutional accountability might at times be appropriately secured through the political process or through one of the variety of other remedies that the courts are capable of granting.

63. The Constitution serves both an oversight and a supportive role. Delictual rules that run contrary to constitutional rights and values must be amended, while those that are compatible with the values of the Constitution are supported and strengthened. The Constitution informs public policy, determining in the final instance whether, as a matter of public policy, it is reasonable to attach delictual liability to certain conduct. For example, in *DE v. RH*[119] the Constitutional Court held that the act of adultery was no longer wrongful and therefore should not give rise to a cause of action under the actio iniuriarum for contumelia and loss of consortium. The action for adultery brought by the innocent spouse had a deleterious impact on the constitutional rights to privacy, freedom and security of the person and freedom of association of both the adulterous spouse and the defendant third party. The key issue for the court was whether the act of adultery meets the element of wrongfulness for the purposes of delictual liability; and the pivotal question concerns wrongfulness. The common law, including the law of delict, had to be developed in accordance with public policy, infused with constitutional norms. Madlanga J, for the majority, said that the right of a non-adulterous spouse that is implicated by the act of adultery is the right to dignity. Undoubtedly, adultery has the potential to infringe the non-adulterous spouse's right to dignity, but this potential infringement of dignity must be weighed against the infringement of the fundamental rights of the adulterous spouse and the third party to privacy, freedom of association and freedom and security of the person. These rights demand protection from State intervention in the intimate choices of, and relationships between people. The majority of the court concluded that the act of adultery by a third party does not constitute

118. Paragraph 21.
119. 2015 (5) SA 83 (CC).

wrongfulness for purposes of a delictual claim of contumelia and loss of consortium; as a matter of public policy it is not reasonable to attach delictual liability to it.

§8. STRUCTURE OF THE LAW OF DELICT

64. As noted in section 2 above, the South African law of delict is the product of the action-based Roman law (in particular the *actio legis Aquiliae* and the *actio iniuriarum*), that was received in the Netherlands prior to codification, shorn of its penal elements, generalized to provide for compensation in respect of damage caused *dolo aut culpa*[120] and transplanted to South Africa in the seventeenth century, as Roman-Dutch law.

I. The *Aquilian* Action

65. The delict of *damnum iniuria datum* was created by the *lex Aquilia*, a plebiscite of 286 or 287 BC. The *actio legis Aquiliae* was originally a penal action which also served to compensate a victim for damage suffered by the wrongful killing (*occidere*) or wounding (*urere, frangere* and *rumpere*) of slaves and four-footed animals belonging to the class of *pecus*. The original limited scope of the *lex Aquilia* was gradually widened by means of juristic interpretation and praetorian extension of actions, to include not only positive conduct but also omissions, and to include cases where the conduct of the wrongdoer created conditions from which, with the concurrence of other circumstances, death resulted (*causam mortis praestare*) or patrimonial loss was caused. The foundations for the general principles governing the extended Aquilian action in Roman-Dutch law and later in South African law are set out in the following paragraphs.

66. The causing of harm must have been unlawful or wrongful (*iniuria*). A person caused harm unlawfully or wrongfully (*contra ius*) if he acted without a right (*nullo iure, non iure*). Conversely, harm caused where a person acted in pursuance of a right (*iure*) was justified, for example in cases of self-defence, necessity, consent, public authority and the exercise of a private right.

67. Fault (*culpa*) was required for liability in classical Roman law and was imputed where the wrongdoer acted either intentionally (*dolo*) or negligently (*culpa*). Generally *culpa* was the failure to observe the standard of care and diligence of a *bonus paterfamilias* in the circumstances. The defendant must have been capable of acting intentionally or negligently (*doli capax*, *culpae capax*) and an insane person or an infant was therefore exempt from delictual liability. Where the plaintiff contributed to the harm by his own negligent conduct, the negligent wrongdoer was absolved from liability by operation of the principle of set-off of fault

120. *See* generally on this development F.H. Lawson & B.S. Markesinis, *Tortious Liability for Unintentional Harm in the Common Law and the Civil Law,* vol. 1, 39–41 (Cambridge U. Press, 1982).

(*culpa compensatio*). There was no apportionment of blame – contributory negligence was an absolute defence. However, where the defendant acted intentionally the contributory negligence of the plaintiff was no defence.

68. A causal connection between the wrongful act of the defendant and the harm to the plaintiff was required. The requirement of causation was implied by texts dealing with multiple causative acts and the significance of an interruption in a chain of causation.

69. To succeed, the plaintiff had to prove that he had suffered patrimonial harm (*damnum*) – a concept that, by extensive interpretation, came to mean the real pecuniary loss (*id quod* interest) of the plaintiff.

70. Originally only the owner (*erus*) could claim damage, but in the course of time the Aquilian action was extended to the bona fide possessor, the injured free man, the father whose child had been killed or injured, the pledgee, the usufructuary, a rural tenant, the holder of a right of servitude and the beneficiary under a will.

II. The *Actio Iniuriarum* for *Iniuria* or *Contumelia*

71. The concept of *iniuria* in its general sense meant unlawfulness or wrongfulness and in its particular sense referred to the delict *iniuria* or *contumelia.* This delict had its origin in certain penal provisions contained in the Twelve Tables, in respect of various forms of aggression upon the person or reputation of another, for example an incantation intended to disgrace (*malum carmen*), or the public vituperation of another, or the severance, mutilation or permanent disablement of a limb (*membrum ruptum*). In the second century BC, the *praetorian edictum generale* introduced a comprehensive *actio iniuriarum aestimatoria*, allowing judges to assess penalties for the acts of physical aggression contemplated in the Twelve Tables. Subsequent praetorian edicts extended the *actio iniuriarum* to other forms of aggression against the person or reputation of another, for example public abuse (*convicium*), imputations on the chastity of a person (*adtemptata pudicitia*) and conduct directed to infringement of a person's reputation (*infamandi causa*). As a result of extensive interpretation of the *edictum generale*, the *delict iniuria* acquired a wider meaning, to include any form of wilful physical aggression upon the person of another or wilful infringement of the personality of another. The essence of the delict was the intentional impairment of the personality of a person. Conduct in pursuance of a right was not wrongful and did not constitute an *iniuria.*

The *actio iniuriarum* was a purely penal action for the imposition of a pecuniary penalty payable to the plaintiff as a *solatium* for the injury to his personality. Where the wrong was particularly reprehensible (*atrox*), the defendant was punished more severely. Like other penal actions the *actio iniuriarum* was neither actively nor passively transmissible, unless *litis contestatio* had taken place.

The *actio iniuriarum* in Roman law was the foundation for the further development of an action under that name in Roman-Dutch law and later in South African law.

III. The Action of Dependants

72. The action of dependants for loss of support resulting from the death of a breadwinner was unknown in Roman law, but was recognized in Roman-Dutch law, probably under the influence of customary Germanic law. Most Roman-Dutch writers did not attempt a systematic classification of the action, but apparently considered it to be an independent delictual action, available to any dependant who was legally entitled to and actually received support from the deceased. In many cases, the dependants would also be heirs in the estate of the deceased, but the action was available to dependants for loss of support, and not to heirs for the loss of a potentially greater inheritance that could have been accumulated in the estate through the earning capacity of the deceased. Costs incurred by the estate for the medical treatment of the deceased prior to death and for funeral expenses were recoverable.

The action of dependants as developed in Roman-Dutch law forms part of and has undergone further expansion in modern South African law.

IV. The Action for Pain and Suffering

73. In Roman law as represented in the Justinian codification, the Aquilian action for bodily injury was also available to a free man, but only for loss of income and medical expenses. In Roman-Dutch law, an action for the recovery of compensation for pain and bodily disfigurement resulting from wrongfully inflicted bodily injuries was recognized. The action probably developed under the influence of customary Germanic law. Although sometimes classed under the *actio legis Aquiliae*, the action for pain and suffering was a separate and distinct delictual remedy for the recovery of a *solatium* and was neither actively nor passively transmissible, unless *litis contestatio* had taken place.

The action for pain and suffering as developed in Roman-Dutch law has remained virtually unchanged as part of the modern South African law of delict.

V. Other Actions

74. In Roman-Dutch law, an action was afforded to the parents of a child wrongfully injured, to recover loss of income and medical expenses. This action is still part of modern South African law, as a form of the Aquilian action. The master of a domestic servant wrongfully injured was also afforded an action in Roman-Dutch law, to recover damages for the loss of the services of the servant. It is doubtful whether an action based on the injury of a domestic servant still forms part of modern South African law, and it is in any event clear that there is no such action relating to employees generally.[121]

Certain other Roman actions in delict were recognized in Roman-Dutch law and still form part of modern South African law, although their importance has greatly

121. *Union Government v. Ocean Accident and Guarantee Corporation Ltd* 1956 (1) SA 577 (A).

declined as a result of the ever-widening scope of the Aquilian action for patrimonial loss. These actions include the following: the *actio Pauliana*, for recovery of an object (or its value) alienated by a debtor in fraud of a creditor; the *actio ad exhibendum*, for recovery of an object (or its value) held or alienated mala fide; the *condictio furtiva*, for recovery of loss as a result of theft; and the *actio aquae pluviae arcendae* and the *interdictum quod vi aut clam*, for removal of a structure obstructing the natural flow of water and for recovery of limited damages.

Certain Roman actions involving strict liability still form part of South African law, as set out in Part I below.

Part I. Liability for One's Own Acts

Chapter 1. General Principles

75. In Roman-Dutch law, a generalization of the principles of delictual liability occurred, to the extent that every unlawful and blameworthy causing of harm was in principle regarded as a delict. Conduct that could give rise to delictual liability included acts of commission or omission and also spoken words. Although unlawfulness and fault were not clearly distinguished, both were by implication recognized as elements of delictual liability. A causal connection between conduct and harm was required. The generalization of the principles of liability is an important characteristic of the modern South African law of delict, distinguishing it from the English law of torts which, despite the unifying force and influence of the concept of negligence, is still a system of individual torts. The South African law of delict consists of a body of principles and concepts founded on historically developed broad bases of liability. In this respect, it resembles the European civilian systems of law. This generalized approach has been formulated as follows in *Perlman v. Zoutendyk*:[122]

> Roman Dutch Law approaches a new problem in the continental rather than the English way, because in general all damage caused unjustifiably (injuria) is actionable, whether caused intentionally (dolo) or by negligence (culpa).

In general, therefore, the South African law of delict recognizes that the causing of harm by unlawful and blameworthy (culpable) conduct gives rise to delictual liability.

76. In general, the elements of a delict and requirements for delictual liability in South African law are the following:

- human conduct (that must be voluntary);
- factual causation (often said to imply that the defendant's conduct is a *conditio sine qua non* for plaintiff's harm);
- legal causation (requiring a sufficiently close relationship between conduct and harm to make it just and reasonable to impose liability; often determined by foreseeability);

122. 1934 CPD 151.

- compensable damage or harm (determined with reference to the plaintiff's position had the delict not been committed); and
- fault (presupposing accountability and consisting in either intent, with regard to the factual result and the unlawfulness of causing it; or negligence, based on reasonable foreseeability and preventability of the harm and the unlawfulness of causing it); and
- unlawfulness (according to the general criterion of reasonableness – rooted in public policy, the legal convictions of the community or *boni mores*).

The general principles of the law of delict have developed around these elements or requirements. In general, all these elements or requirements must be present for delictual liability to arise, regardless of the type of right or interest infringed. Delicts involving infringement of diverse rights or interests – such as property, bodily integrity, reputation, privacy, goodwill of a business, trade secrets – are all governed by the same general principles, but the nature of the protected right or interest will determine the kind of conduct, infringement, fault and damage required for liability in each case.

77. The general principles of delictual liability are adaptable for application to novel situations. Notwithstanding the inherent elasticity of the general principles, the courts adopt a conservative approach to the extension of delictual liability, guided by considerations of public policy, practical convenience and above all by what is considered just and equitable. The tests for unlawfulness, negligence and legal causation, in particular, have a strong policy base. The determination of unlawfulness by application of the general criterion of reasonableness – rooted in public policy, the legal convictions of the community or *boni mores* – plays a dominant role in fixing and limiting liability, in many instances replacing the traditional focus on foreseeability of harm.

The following elements of and requirements for delictual liability are examined below: conduct, unlawfulness, fault, capacity for liability.

§1. Conduct

78. A delict involves human conduct in the form of a positive act or omission whereby one person (the actor or perpetrator) wrongfully and culpably causes damage or harm to another. The characteristics of an act or conduct that gives rise to delictual liability are that it is a human act, a voluntary act, and either a positive act or an omission. A delict might also involve harm caused by animals, for example where owners of domestic animals are held liable for the harm done by such animals. Human conduct might involve the use of animals or inanimate as instruments to cause harm.

79. A defendant's involuntary act does not give rise to delictual liability. Conduct is voluntary if it is subject to the control of the actor's will. This implies mental capacity to direct muscular activity or to refrain from such activity. An infant or an insane person usually has the mental capacity to act, but not to be held accountable for such an act. Whether the actor's conduct was voluntary depends on mental capacity at the time of the conduct. An act that is physically enforced (i.e., where there is absolute compulsion or *vis absoluta*), is involuntary. Conduct that involves a reflex action, or that is performed in a state of unconsciousness as during sleep, amnesia, epileptic fit, extreme intoxication, an extremely emotional state, a heart attack, or hysterical dissociation, will not be regarded as voluntary and gives rise to the defence of automatism. Impulsive or spontaneous acts are not genuinely reflexive and are therefore voluntary, as in the case where the driver loses control of a vehicle when reacting to a bee sting or a burning match falling into his lap.[123]

80. Defences based on involuntariness or automatism have to be scrutinized with great care.[124] The onus of proving a voluntary act on a balance of probabilities is on the plaintiff.[125]

If, for example, the defendant alleges that he had suffered a black out while driving a car, the plaintiff must prove 'that the defendant was negligent and this includes proof that the negligence relied upon consisted of a voluntary act'.[126] Where the defendant's vehicle had suddenly moved on to the incorrect side of a straight stretch of road in broad daylight and there was evidence that he had suffered a fall shortly before the collision and that the fall was of sufficient severity to warrant medical attention, the plaintiff must discharge the onus of proving that the defendant's conduct in driving to the incorrect side of the road was a voluntary act. To succeed with the claim, the plaintiff must therefore prove, on a balance of probabilities, that the defendant did not have a black out.

81. A person who voluntarily enters into a state of unconsciousness, for example self-induced intoxication, with the intention of causing harm to another in that state (a course of conduct known as *actio libera* in causa) will be liable in delict on the basis of the voluntary conduct preceding the state of unconsciousness.

82. Similarly, liability will ensue where a person negligently allows a state of unconsciousness to develop, for example by falling asleep while driving, or by failing to prevent a reasonably foreseeable health-related condition. In *Wessels v. Hall and Pickles (Coastal) (Pty) Ltd*,[127] the defendant, while driving a vehicle, suffered a hypoglycaemic attack resulting in a diabetic coma. He lost control of the vehicle and caused an accident. The defendant was aware of his diabetic condition and of the possibility of sudden attacks and knew what precautionary measures were necessary. He was held to have been negligent for failing to take reasonable precautions. In every case, the circumstances at the time of the preceding voluntary

123. *See S v. Smit* 1963 (4) SA 824 (GW); *S v. Crockart* 1971 (2) SA 496 (RAD); *S v. Erwin* 1974 (3) SA 438 (C).
124. *Molefe v. Mahaeng* 1999 (1) SA 562 (A) 567.
125. *Molefe v. Mahaeng* 1999 (1) SA 562 (A) 568.
126. *Ibid.*
127. 1985 (4) SA 153 (C).

conduct will be taken into account to determine whether the state of unconsciousness and the concomitant possibility of harm to others were reasonably foreseeable and preventable.

83. Delictual liability may be based on either a positive act (any form of physical activity or statement) or an omission. It is often difficult to distinguish between positive conduct and conduct by way of an omission. This is particularly true in cases involving a continuous course of conduct, where the failure to take precautionary measures along the way may be seen as an omission or as legally deficient positive conduct. For example, failing to stop at a stop sign and colliding with an oncoming vehicle constitutes positive conduct (driving), but also an omission (failing to stop). The failure to stop indicates deficient (negligent) positive conduct. In such a case, it is legally irrelevant whether the occurrence is described as an omission or as positive conduct. However, an action based on the failure to take precautionary action which would not have been an integral part or stage of the course of conduct in which the defendant was engaged, would essentially be based on an omission. For example, a delictual action against a jogger who sees a child drowning in a river but carries on without attempting a rescue, or against a policeman who fails to assist a person being assaulted by another,[128] would essentially be based on an omission.

84. The scope of liability based on omission is restricted, because of potentially indeterminate delictual liability which would be against the public interest. There is no general duty to prevent harm to others – one is generally in law not compelled to be your brother's keeper. The same restrictive approach is followed in the case of liability for harm attributable to statements, because the harmful effects of the spoken or written word may be widespread. Liability for the harmful effects of an omission or statement is therefore imposed only in special circumstances indicating a duty to prevent harm. The existence of such a duty is essentially a question of unlawfulness, as discussed in section 2 below.

§2. Unlawfulness

I. Unlawfulness in South African Law: Comparative Perspective

85. In most systems of delict or tort, there are traces of the concept of unlawfulness or wrongfulness, but there is no uniformity in the use of the expression.[129] In a wide sense, the expression indicates a combination of reprehensible conduct and the infringement of an interest that is deemed worthy of legal protection, but

128. *Minister van Polisie v. Ewels* 1975 (3) SA 590 (A).
129. *European Group on Tort Law Principles of European Tort Law Text and Commentary* 28 (Springer-Verlag/Wien 2005).

this description is so wide that it can be taken to refer to the concept of delictual liability generally.[130] Unlawfulness is closely linked to the central idea of tort law, as formulated by Prosser:

> So far as there is one central idea, it would seem that it is that liability must be based upon conduct which is socially unreasonable. The common thread woven into all torts is the idea of unreasonable interference with the interests of others.[131]

86. In English tort law, there is no catalogue of protected rights and interests and both the required standard of conduct and the scope of protection are integrated into the concept of a duty of care.[132] This was also the approach of South African courts in earlier cases, as will be shown below. It has been said that a broad idea of wrongfulness is reconcilable with the English law of tort, at the highest level of abstraction, if only because there are situations where the causing of damage is not actionable.[133] The mechanism to control the ambit of tort liability is normally the duty of care. However, the foreseeability-based duty of care (as famously formulated by Lord Atkin in *Donaghue v. Stevenson*[134]) is not a conclusive test of liability, because it does not take account of instances where liability based on foreseeability is sometimes excluded or restricted, including cases of pure economic loss; cases of justification on grounds such as defence or consent; and cases of omission (the law does not recognize a general duty to act positively to ward off foreseeable danger from another person).[135] In these instances, the courts employ – in addition to foreseeability – notions of 'proximity', 'neighbourhood', 'fairness', 'assumption of responsibility', 'reliance' and 'special relationship' to control the scope of liability for negligence.[136] These concepts have been described as 'little more than convenient labels to attach to the features of different specific situations which, on a detailed examination of all the circumstances, the law recognizes pragmatically as giving rise to a duty of care of a given scope'.[137] The courts have shown an increased willingness to bring policy questions into the open and, even if it is

---

130. *Ibid*; W.V. Horton Rogers, *Unification of Tort Law: Wrongfulness*, 39 (Helmut Koziol, ed., Kluwer Law International 1998). But from another point of view the concept is almost meaningless since 'wrong'/'wrongfulness' may be regarded as merely a shorthand description of the situations in which tort liability is imposed. The same can be said of the following comment, made in the context of a discussion of protected interests in European systems of tort law: 'It all boils down to the fact that negligent conduct must be legally wrong or that damage needs to be legally relevant'; *see* Cees van Dam, *European Tort Law* 141, para. 701-1 (Oxford U. Press, 2006).
131. Cited by W.V. Horton Rogers, *Unification of Tort Law: Wrongfulness*, 40 (Helmut Koziol ed., Kluwer Law International 1998).
132. Gerhard Wagner, *The Oxford Handbook of Comparative Law*, 1013–1014 (Matthias Reimann & Reinhard Zimmermann eds., Oxford U. Press, 2006).
133. W.V. Horton Rogers, *Unification of Tort Law: Wrongfulness* 40 (Helmut Koziol ed., Kluwer Law International 1998).
134. [1932] AC 562.
135. W.V. Horton Rogers, *Unification of Tort Law: Wrongfulness* 41–42 (Helmut Koziol ed., Kluwer Law International 1998); and *see* F.H. Lawson & B.S. Markesinis, *Tortious Liability for Unintentional Harm in the Common and the Civil Law*, I, (Cambridge Stud. Intl. & Comp. L 95 (1982)).
136. *See* Tony Weir, *Tort Law*, 34–54 (Oxford U. Press, 2002).
137. Lord Bridge in *Caparo Industries v. Dickman* [1990] 1 All ER 568 574.

found that injury was a foreseeable result of the defendant's negligence, the existence of a duty of care may be denied on the basis that policy concerns necessitate a restrictive approach in determining the ambit of 'neighbourhood' for purposes of the duty of care.[138]

87. In German law, the concept of unlawfulness (*Rechtswidrigkeit*) is somewhat contentious. Unlawfulness for the purposes of section 823 I of the BGB essentially turns on the infringement of the interests that are specifically protected by that section, such as life, physical integrity, health, property and other similar rights (not including pure economic loss). These are said to be 'absolutely protected interests' and the notion of unlawfulness to be 'outcome-related', an approach to unlawfulness known as *Erfolgsunrechtslehre.*[139] However, in cases of indirect infringement of rights and omission the notion of unlawfulness is said to involve an evaluation of conduct in terms of certain societal norms, an approach to unlawfulness known as *Verhaltensunrechtslehre.*[140] Where an act infringes one of the protected interests only indirectly, there is no unlawfulness in terms of this approach, unless it can be shown that the defendant has failed to satisfy the standard of care demanded by the society. This duty-oriented approach is even more necessary in the case of liability for omissions. One of the most fertile sources of this development in German law was the idea that a preceding dangerous or potentially dangerous activity or state of affairs gives rise to a duty of care. From this idea, the courts developed the *Verkehrssicherungspflichten* or societal duties.[141] The purpose of the duties is to delineate the range of relationships that will be protected against careless interference and the range of persons who could be held liable for a harmful result, and also the precise content of the duty, if it is found to exist. All this is decided as a matter of judicial policy, involving consideration of factors such as the gravity of the harm, probability of occurrence, the cost of prevention and the social utility of the activity in question, as developed by the courts in an extensive body of case law.[142] There is some uncertainty as to whether these duties relate to conduct, unlawfulness or negligence, but it appears not to make appreciable difference to the final practical result.[143]

The existence of the *Verkehrssicherungspflichten* indicates that the law of delict requires a value or policy judgment on the existence of a legal duty not to cause or to prevent harm, concerning the range of relationships and interests that will be protected against careless interference and the range of persons who could be held liable for a harmful result. Whether this value judgment is made in the context of

---

138. Mark Lunney & Ken Oliphant, *Tort Law Text and Materials* 119 (2nd ed. 2003).
139. Gert Brüggemeier, *Common Principles of Tort Law A Pre-statement of Law* 77 (Brit. Inst. Intl. Comp. L. 2004).
140. Helmut Koziol, *Unification of Tort Law: Wrongfulness* 131 (Helmut Koziol ed., Kluwer Law International 1998).
141. *See* generally Basil S. Markesinis & Hannes Unberath, *The German Law of Torts: A Comparative Treatise*, 85–86 (4th ed., Hart 2002).
142. *See also* Cees van Dam, *European Tort Law* 402–403 (Oxford U. Press, 2006); Helmut Koziol, *Unification of Tort Law: Wrongfulness*, 131 (Helmut Koziol ed., Kluwer Law International 1998).
143. Basil S. Markesinis & Hannes Unberath, *The German Law of Torts A Comparative Treatise*, 81 (4th ed., Hart 2002); Hein Kötz & Gerhard Wagner Deliksrecht 54–55 (10th ed., Luchterhand Fachb. 2001).

unlawfulness or negligence is a matter of structure. The specific content of the duty and whether there has been a breach of the duty would mostly be dealt with in the context of negligence.

88. The draftsmen of the *Principles of European Tort Law* could not find sufficient common ground among the legal systems of Europe to formulate a unitary concept of unlawfulness or wrongfulness, and it has been said that they have 'essentially dodged the thorny issue of "wrongfulness"'.[144] The proposed common principles provide that damage may be attributed to the person 'whose conduct constituting fault has caused it' and that the concept of damage denotes harm to a legally protected interest. The concept of 'protected interests' includes life, bodily integrity and mental integrity, as interests enjoying the most extensive protection, followed by property rights. For protection of pure economic interests or contractual relationship the extent of protection depends on factors such as proximity and awareness.[145]

89. In South African law, unlawfulness or wrongfulness (the terms are interchangeable) has been said to mean that harm was caused in a legally reprehensible or unreasonable manner, involving both the factual infringement of an interest and the violation of a legal norm.[146] This general definition is to a certain extent circular (the concepts 'legally reprehensible' and 'violation of a legal norm' in turn depend on the notion of unlawfulness) and is at the same time imprecise on whether the standard of reasonableness essentially concerns the nature and extent of protected interests, blameworthy conduct, or an overall value judgment. As shown below, unlawfulness can involve all these elements.

II. Function of Unlawfulness

90. To describe unlawfulness in the South African law of delict more precisely, it is first necessary to determine its function. It is a requirement for delictual liability that is supplementary to:

(a) conduct (that must be voluntary);
(b) factual causation (often said to imply that the defendant's conduct is a *conditio sine qua non* for plaintiff's harm);
(c) legal causation (requiring a sufficiently close relationship between conduct and harm to make it just and reasonable to impose liability; often determined by foreseeability);
(d) compensable damage or harm (determined with reference to the plaintiff's position had the delict not been committed); and

144. Gerhard Wagner, *The Oxford Handbook of Comparative Law*, 554 (Matthias Reimann & Reinhard Zimmermann eds., Oxford U. Press, 2006).
145. *See* Arts 2:101 and 2:102 of the Principles, in *European Group on Tort Law – Principles of European Tort Law Text and Commentary* (Springer-Verlag/Wien 2005).
146. Neethling, Potgieter & Visser, *Law of Delict* 31 (5th ed., Butterworths 2006).

(e) fault (presupposing accountability and consisting in either intent, with regard to the factual result and the wrongfulness of causing it; or negligence, based on reasonable foreseeability and preventability of the harm).

91. Unlawfulness supplements the inquiry into liability in respect of the following matters:

- The requirement of voluntary conduct says little about the circumstances where liability will be imposed for an omission. This question resolves itself into an inquiry into the existence of a duty not to cause harm negligently or intentionally. Is the harm that was caused within the actor's scope of responsibility, as in the case of liability for an omission?
- The requirement of damage deals with the *effects* of infringement of a right or interest, but does not explain *what interests* will be protected or to what extent interests will be protected (physical integrity and tangible property are generally recognized as fully protected interests and the infringement of such an interest by positive conduct can be said to be prima facie unlawful,[147] but in the case of pure financial loss, privacy, reputation, mental distress the extent of protection is often regarded as a question of unlawfulness).
- The requirements of conduct, causation, damage and fault do not adequately deal with the balancing of conflicting rights or interests (reputation versus free speech; enjoyment of property versus harm to a neighbour; freedom of competition versus harm to trading goodwill; freedom of action versus a duty to protect).
- The conclusion that the defendant's conduct culpably caused the plaintiff's damage is not sufficient for imposing liability. The causing of damage that would otherwise be unlawful can be justified, for instance on the basis of defence, necessity, consent or statutory authority.
- The requirement of fault generally deals with the blameworthiness of the actor's conduct, but not with the weight to be given to intent or a reprehensible motive on the part of the actor; and also not comprehensively with the effects of mistake on the part of the actor, for instance in cases of putative justification. Intent, awareness of the possibility of harm, a reprehensible motive, and conscious negligence (recklessness) can be indicators of unlawfulness. The reasonableness of the actor's conduct is mostly an issue that belongs in the domain of fault, but history and the vagaries of case-to-case legal development have on occasion made this an unlawfulness issue (for instance in the case of qualified privilege as a defence to a defamation claim, reasonable publication of a falsity for the purposes of a defamation claim and some cases of putative defence), as shown below.
- The requirements of conduct, causation, damage and fault do not explicitly leave scope for policy considerations relating, *inter alia*, to guarding against indeterminate liability; guarding against the hampering or disrupting of public administration; the availability of an alternative remedy; or the maintenance of free competition. Rights and duties in delict are legal constructs that reflect the scope

147. *See* P.Q.R. Boberg, *The Law of Delict Vol. 1 Aquilian Liability* 32 (1984): 'it is settled law that all harm to person or property caused by a positive act is prima facie wrongful'.

of protection that the law affords. For example, the law of delict offers protection in certain limited circumstances for economic loss resulting from personal injury or damage to property of third persons. The 'right' to such protection is correlative to the 'duty' of the actor to refrain from causing the loss, but the content of both reflect a value judgment on the appropriate extent of protection, as judicially determined.

- Under a fault-based system the requirement of either negligence or intent acts as an important filter in the evaluative process to decide whether liability should be imposed. Where liability is strict the elimination of the fault requirement does not mean that all risk of harm is indiscriminately transferred to the defendant who caused the harm. Strict liability does not mean absolute liability, and the requirement of unlawfulness, based on reasonableness and policy, remains in place.

III. Unlawfulness: Summary of Nature and Function

92. Unlawfulness supplements and overarches the other elements of delict, adding a further value- or policy-based dimension to the inquiry into liability and requiring the exercise of judicial discretion, with the aim to achieve an appropriate balance between the interests of the plaintiff, the defendant's interests and freedom of action and the interests of society.

93. The inquiry into unlawfulness involves the application of wide and evaluative criteria and the exercise of judicial discretion.[148] The criteria are reasonableness (sometimes referred to as 'general reasonableness'), 'the legal convictions prevailing in the community', and the *boni mores*; and the application of these criteria in the final instance involves public policy.[149] Judicial reasoning in the application of these wide and evaluative criteria is reducible to the following factors, which are often interrelated:

(a) policy considerations indicating whether the law of delict should intervene in respect of the type of harm-causing (*inter alia* the social or economic consequences of imposing liability – in particular potential indeterminate liability (opening the floodgates); the availability of alternative remedies; and the need for accountability of public bodies or officials);
(b) consideration of relevant constitutional or other statutory rights and duties (*inter alia* the right to freedom and security of the person, the right to privacy, the right to freedom of expression);
(c) a typology of factual circumstances that indicate a duty not to cause or to prevent harm in the particular situation (*inter alia* the proportionality of the risk of harm and the cost of prevention, control over a dangerous object or situation, awareness of danger, prior conduct creating danger, a relationship imposing responsibility, professional knowledge);

148. Anton Fagan, *Rethinking Wrongfulness in the Law of Delict* 122 S. African L. J. 90, 90–91 (2005).
149. *Mukheiber v. Raath* 1999 (3) SA 1065 (SCA) para. 25; and *see* generally Annél van Aswegen, *Policy Considerations in the Law of Delict*, 56 *THRHR* 171, 180 (1993) (add footnotes 26 and 27).

(d) the nature of the defendant's conduct (harm-causing by positive conduct is generally more readily considered to be unlawful than harm-causing by omission; and physical harm-causing is generally more readily considered to be unlawful than harm-causing by speech);
(e) the nature of the defendant's fault and state of mind (intentional harm-causing is generally more readily considered to be unlawful than negligent harm-causing; and a motive to harm is indicative of unlawfulness); and
(f) the nature of the interest sought to be protected (the causing of physical injury and damage to property is considered to be prima facie unlawful, while the causing of pure economic loss or emotional distress is not; and in the case of certain forms of harm such as nuisance and damage to reputation unlawfulness is often judged by balancing conflicting interests).

94. With all the other elements of liability (conduct, causation, harm and fault) proved or assumed to be present, unlawfulness involves a further value judgment on whether the affected interest of the plaintiff deserves protection from the defendant's action or lack of it, so that the burden of damage should be shifted from plaintiff to defendant. Unlawfulness is thus essentially concerned with the scope of protection afforded to various rights and interests, the scope of responsibility to act and overall policy considerations relating to the question whether the law of delict should intervene.

95. In *Le Roux and Others v. Dey* (Freedom of Expression Institute and Restorative Justice Centre as Amici Curiae)[150] Brand AJ described wrongfulness as follows:

> [122] In the more recent past our courts have come to recognise, however, that in the context of the law of delict: (a) the criterion of wrongfulness ultimately depends on a judicial determination of whether – assuming all the other elements of delictual liability to be present – it would be reasonable to impose liability on a defendant for the damages flowing from specific conduct; and (b) that the judicial determination of that reasonableness would in turn depend on considerations of public and legal policy in accordance with constitutional norms. Incidentally, to avoid confusion it should be borne in mind that, what is meant by reasonableness in the context of wrongfulness has nothing to do with the reasonableness of the defendant's conduct, but it concerns the reasonableness of imposing liability on the defendant for the harm resulting from that conduct.

96. Unlawfulness is mostly not contentious in cases involving positive conduct causing bodily injury or damage to property. It is settled law that all harm to person

150. 2011 (3) SA 274 (CC) para. 122.

or property caused by a positive act is prima facie unlawful.[151] Unlawfulness is mostly contentious in cases involving omission, pure economic loss and a conflict of rights.

Various aspects of unlawfulness will be dealt with in detail below.

IV. Unlawfulness: An Attribute of Conduct?

97. As said above, unlawfulness supplements and overarches all the other elements of delict. Unlawfulness is not an attribute of conduct alone, but characterizes the outcome of a causal sequence involving conduct and the causation of harm.[152] Walker, writing on the law of Scotland, expresses this as follows:

> The act or omission by itself is not wrongful or delictual unless it brings about as an immediate consequence some harm to a legally protected interest of another person. The law of delict is concerned with harms, with wrongs to, or infringements of, the interests of others, not with the bare conduct whereby those harms come about.[153]

In this respect, the law of delict differs from criminal law, where a particular act is sometimes prohibited and therefore characterized as unlawful (e.g., dangerous driving or possession of a prohibited substance). Where a crime is defined substantively in terms of a particular causal sequence (e.g., culpable homicide, involving the negligent causing of the death of a human being), unlawfulness characterizes the outcome of the causal sequence involving conduct and the causation of harm, as in the case of delict. Some commentators nevertheless appear to hold the view that unlawfulness turns on the reasonableness of conduct,[154] and unlawfulness is often linked to conduct in expressions such as 'unlawful conduct' or 'wrongful conduct'.[155] This usage may often simply reflect looseness or inaccuracy of expression, rather than a conscious attempt to convey that unlawfulness is an attribute of conduct alone. The blameworthiness of the actor's conduct can be relevant to unlawfulness, but it will not necessarily be decisive, as shown below.

---

151. *See Lillicrap, Wassenaar and Partners v. Pilkington Brothers (SA) (Pty) Ltd* 1985 (1) SA 448 (A) 497; P.Q.R. Boberg, *The Law of Delict Vol. 1 Aquilian Liability* 32 (1984).
152. *Mukheiber v. Raath* 1999 (3) SA 1065 (SCA) para. 25.
153. *See* David M. Walker, *The Law of Delict in Scotland*, 33 (2nd ed., W. Green 1981). *See also* at 36: '... the fact that conduct can be said to be legal or lawful in the sense of not being prohibited or punishable goes no distance at all in a delict case to exonerate a defender. A great deal of delictual conduct is undoubtedly lawful, and does not become unlawful for any purpose of the civil law merely because it causes harm.'
154. Anton Fagan, *Rethinking Wrongfulness in the Law of Delict* 122 S. African L. J. 90, 90–91 (2005) refers to this view as the 'standard academic view' (which he disputes) and cites textbooks on delict where this view is propounded.
155. *Olitzki Property Holdings v. State Tender Board and Another* 2001 (3) SA 1247 (SCA) para. 12; *Steenkamp NO v. The Provincial Tender Board of the Eastern Cape* [2006] JOL 18364 (CC) para. 37.

V. Unlawfulness Concerns Conduct and Consequences

98. Unlawfulness concerns both the actor's conduct and its consequences, which may be separated in time and space. The separation between an act and its consequences is a matter of degree. An act of assault may cause immediate injury, whereas the act of building a wall unsafely may not have harmful effects until much later, when the wall collapses.[156]

99. An illustrative case is *Pinchin v. Santam Insurance Co. Ltd*,[157] involving an act of negligent driving that caused an accident and injuries to a pregnant woman, who later gave birth to a child with brain damage. The unborn child (*nasciturus*) did not have legal personality at the time of the accident, and it was therefore argued on behalf of the negligent driver that he could not have unlawfully harmed the unborn child at the time of the accident. An answer to this argument could have been that the harmful effects of the defendant's act manifested itself later when the child was born; and at that time the completed causal sequence could be characterized as unlawful. The case was not decided on this basis, however. The Court held that the child could have an action on account of the *nasciturus* fiction, which entails that an unborn child should be regarded as already born if this is in the child's interest. Nevertheless the action did not succeed, because the causal relationship between the mother's injuries and the brain damage of the child could not be proved. In *RAF v. Mtati*,[158] a case dealing with similar facts, the Supreme Court of Appeal held that the damage occurred when the child was born with injuries; and at that time the completed causal sequence could be characterized as unlawful.

100. Another instance illustrating that unlawfulness can only be determined once the consequences of an act are known is that of a surgeon performing an operation which, even if performed competently, involves the risk of harmful side effects. If the surgeon goes ahead with the operation without beforehand fully informing the patient of the risks, the operation is performed without the patient's informed consent. If the harmful side effects then occur, the surgeon will have caused the harm unlawfully. If, however, the operation is completely successful and no harmful side effects occur, there is no unlawfulness, despite the fact that the operation was performed without the patient's informed consent.[159]

---

156. *See* the following cases on liability for subsidence: *John Newmark & Co. (Pty) Ltd v. Durban City Council* 1959 (1) SA 169 (D); *Desraj v. Durban City Council* 1964 (1) SA 427 (N); *Gijzen v. Verrinder* 1965 (1) SA 806 (D); *Tsimatakopoulos v. Hemingway, Isaacs & Coetzee CC* 1993 (4) SA 428 (C).
157. 1963 (2) SA 254 (W).
158. 2005 (6) SA 215 (SCA).
159. *See Broude v. McIntosh and Others* 1998 (3) SA 60 (SCA), where Marais JA referred to this situation and expressed the view that there is no principle of law by which the characterization as unlawful or lawful of an intentional act objectively involving the doing of bodily harm to another could be postponed until its consequences are known. It is suggested, however, that this view is open to criticism. In the event of a completely successful operation, there is no harm or damage for the purposes of the law of delict, despite the fact that the patient might have chosen not to undergo the operation had he known of the risks; and in the law of delict the characterization of an act as unlawful or lawful can often only be done once the consequences of the act are known.

VI. Unlawfulness: A Matter of Law

101. Unlawfulness is a matter of law.[160] The courts do not hear evidence on the issue of unlawfulness as such, but the onus is on the plaintiff to make factual allegations and eventually present evidence that justifies the inference of unlawfulness, which is a matter for judicial determination. If the matter of unlawfulness is raised by way of exception, the court must decide whether the factual allegations in the pleadings, if eventually proved, establish a legal duty not to cause damage in the manner alleged, in accordance with relevant policy considerations.[161] In exception proceedings relating to unlawfulness, the court must assume the other elements of the delict, such as causation and negligence.[162]

102. In *Axiam Holdings Ltd v. Deloitte & Touche*,[163] it was alleged that the auditors had owed a duty to third parties to warn them that certain financial statements and their audit opinion were incorrect, alternatively to warn them that it had not conducted the audit properly, and that they should not rely on the statements and the audit opinion; and that their failure in this regard was negligent and constituted a misrepresentation within the meaning of section 20(9)(b)(ii) of the Public Accountants' and Auditors' Act.[164] The auditors raised an exception, on the basis that the allegations in the pleadings did not justify the conclusion that the auditors owed a legal duty to the third parties. The majority of the court held that the unlawfulness of the harm-causing by omission to speak could not in this case be decided on exception. The matter had to go to trial; it was premature to decide on exception whether a legal duty could be said to exist.[165]

103. In some cases, the courts are prepared to decide on the facts as alleged in the pleadings whether unlawfulness can be established. In *Trustees, Two Oceans Aquarium Trust v. Kantey & Templer (Pty) Ltd*,[166] engineers negligently recommended an inadequate system of waterproofing for aquarium tanks. This meant that expensive additional work had to be done on the aquarium. The work was done in a pre-contractual phase, and the parties later entered into a detailed contract and could have provided in the contract for liability arising from the pre-contractual

---

160. *Carmichele v. Minister of Safety and Security and Another (Centre for Applied Legal Studies Intervening)* 2001 (4) SA 938 (CC) at para. 7; *Cape Town Municipality v. Bakkerud* 2000 (3) SA 1049 (SCA) paras. 14–17; *Cape Metropolitan Council v. Graham* 2001 (1) SA 1197 (SCA) para. 6; *Olitzki Property Holdings v. State Tender Board and Another* 2001 (3) SA 1247 (SCA) paras 11 and 31; *BOE Bank v. Ries* 2002 (2) SA 39 (SCA) para. 13 and *Minister of Safety and Security v. Van Duivenboden* 2002 (6) SA 431 (SCA) para. 16.
161. *Lillicrap, Wassenaar and Partners v. Pilkington Brothers (SA) (Pty) Ltd* 1985 (1) SA 448 (A); *Trustees, Two Oceans Aquarium Trust v. Kantey & Templer (Pty) Ltd* 2006 (3) SA 138 (SCA) para. 9.
162. *Trustees, Two Oceans Aquarium Trust v. Kantey & Templer (Pty) Ltd* 2006 (3) SA 138 (SCA) paras 5 and 10.
163. 2006 (1) SA 237 (SCA).
164. Act 80 of 1991.
165. *See* paras 22–25 of the judgment.
166. 2006 (3) SA 138 (SCA).

work. As the aquarium owners did not do this, the court decided, on policy grounds, that they could not sue in delict. The facts alleged did not establish the delictual element of unlawfulness.

104. If the defendant relies on a ground of justification for the causing of harm the onus is on him to allege and eventually present evidence of facts that may justify an inference of such a justification.[167] Justification is a part of the inquiry into unlawfulness and a matter of law.

VII. The General Criteria for Determining Unlawfulness

105. Every decision on unlawfulness is ad hoc and based on the facts of the particular case, but over time the courts have accepted a typology of factual indicators of a duty to prevent harm, certain guidelines for weighing up conflicting interests and certain policy considerations for limitation of liability. The general criteria or standards for determining unlawfulness are reasonableness (sometimes referred to as 'general reasonableness'), 'the legal convictions prevailing in the community' and the *boni mores*. The application of these criteria in the final instance involves public policy.[168]

The importance of policy considerations for the South African law of delict is obvious from the number of reported cases expressly acknowledging that the decision was determined or influenced by such considerations.[169] Policy considerations play a decisive role in determining unlawfulness, because of the application of the so-called open-ended standards of 'general reasonableness', 'the legal convictions prevailing in the community', and *boni mores*.[170]

106. The general criteria or standards for determining unlawfulness are of a legal rather than a social, moral, ethical or religious nature,[171] but the criteria do reflect societal values. In applying the concept of the legal convictions of the community, the court is not concerned with what the community regards as socially, morally, ethically or religiously right or wrong, but whether or not the community regards a particular act or form of conduct as unlawful for the purposes of delictual liability. The legal convictions of the community must be taken as the legal convictions of the legal policymakers of the community, such as the legislature and

167. *Malahe v. Minister of Safety and Security* 1999 (1) SA 528 (SCA) 534, 537; *Clarke v. Hurst* 1992 (4) SA 630 (D) 650.
168. *Mukheiber v. Raath* 1999 (3) SA 1065 (SCA) para. 25; and *see* generally Annél van Aswegen, *Policy Considerations in the Law of Delict*, 56 *THRHR* 171, 180 (1993) (add footnotes 26 and 27).
169. *See Argus Printing and Publishing Co. Ltd v. Inkatha Freedom Party* 1992 (3) SA 579 (A); *Indac Electronics (Pty) Ltd v. Volkskas Bank Ltd* 1992 (1) SA 783 (A); *Compass Motor Industries (Pty) Ltd v. Callguard (Pty) Ltd* 1990 (2) SA 520 (W); *International Shipping Co. (Pty) Ltd v. Bentley* 1990 (1) SA 680 (A); *Administrator, Natal v. Edouard* 1990 (3) SA 581 (A).
170. *See* generally M.M. Corbett, *Aspects of the Role of Policy in the Evolution of Our Common Law*, 52 S. African L. J. (1987); Annél van Aswegen, *Policy Considerations in the Law of Delict*, 56 *THRHR* 171 (1993).
171. *Minister of Safety and Security v. Hamilton* 2004 (2) SA 216 (SCA), para. 16.

judges.[172] In *Clarke v. Hurst*,[173] this interplay between the legal concept of unlawfulness and the fundamental values of society was described as follows:

> Wrongfulness is tested according to society's legal, as opposed to its moral, convictions, but at the same time morality plays a role in shaping society's legal convictions. If it is accepted, as I think it should, that law is but a translation of society's fundamental values into policies and prescripts for regulating its members' conduct, then the Court, when it determines the limits of such a basic concept as wrongfulness, has to have regard to the prevailing values of society.

107. The inquiry into unlawfulness can focus either on the infringement of a right or on the breach of a legal duty, but in the final analysis it involves an assessment of reasonableness and public policy. The court must weigh up the interests of the persons involved and also take into account the interests and convictions of the community at large. The personal views of the judge or the parties or a segment of the community are not the measure of what should be regarded as lawful or unlawful.[174]

108. The meaning of 'general reasonableness', *boni mores* and 'the legal convictions of the community' has been summarized in the following judgments:

> In *Du Plessis v. Road Accident Fund*,[175] the question before the court was whether the right to support of one partner in a same-sex relationship could form the basis of a claim for loss of support against the person who negligently caused the death of the other partner, or, put differently, whether the killing of the deceased had to be considered to have been a wrongful act as against the plaintiff. The court held that the question had to be answered in the light of the prevailing boni mores. The legal convictions of the community were informed by the norms and values of society as embodied in the Constitution of the Republic of South Africa, Act 108 of 1996, which norms and values in this case indicated a wrongful infringement of the plaintiff's right to support.[176]

---

172. *See Schultz v. Butt* 1986 (3) SA 667 (A), 679D-E; *Premier Hangers CC v. Polyoak (Pty) Ltd* 1997 (1) SA 416 (A), 422E-F; and *Minister of Safety and Security v. Van Duivenboden*, 2002 (6) SA 431 (SCA), para. 16.
173. 1992 (4) SA 630 (D) 652.
174. The court will take account of the views of a substantial group within the community where the reputation of the plaintiff within that group is in issue in a defamation action, albeit that views within that group differ from views in the community at large, *see Mohamed v. Jassiem* 1996 (1) SA 673 (A).
175. 2004 (1) SA 359 (SCA).
176. Paragraphs 17 and 18, at 368E–F and 369A/B–C.

In *Minister of Safety and Security v. Hamilton,*[177] the court referred to the formulation in *Van Eeden v. Minister of Safety and Security (Women's Legal Centre Trust, as Amicus Curiae)*[178] to assess the unlawfulness or otherwise of an omission or failure to act:

> [9] … An omission is wrongful if the defendant is under a legal duty to act positively to prevent the harm suffered by the plaintiff. The test is one of reasonableness. A defendant is under a legal duty to act positively to prevent harm to the plaintiff if it is reasonable to expect of the defendant to have taken positive measures to prevent the harm. The Court determines whether it is reasonable to have expected of the defendant to have done so by making a value judgment based, *inter alia*, upon its perception of the legal convictions of the community and on considerations of policy. The question whether a legal duty exists in a particular case is thus a conclusion of law depending on a consideration of all the circumstances of the case and on the interplay of the many factors which have to be considered.
>
> [10] In applying the concept of the legal convictions of the community the Court is not concerned with what the community regards as socially, morally, ethically or religiously right or wrong, but whether or not the community regards a particular act or form of conduct as delictually wrongful. The legal convictions of the community must further be seen as the legal convictions of the legal policy makers of the community, such as the Legislature and Judges.

109. The concepts of 'the legal convictions of the community' and *boni mores* purport to be objective, normative standards for determining unlawfulness, but conclusions reached on the basis of these standards alone would be impenetrable to analysis and unverifiable. Courts do not hear evidence on the content of the legal convictions of the community or the *boni mores*. These are general guidelines for the value judgment required of a court when assessing unlawfulness. It has been said that these general criteria provide the courts with 'a legal standard firm enough to afford guidance to the court, yet flexible enough to permit the influence of an inherent sense of fair play'; and this standard is based on 'the general sense of justice of the community, the *boni mores*, manifested in public opinion'.[179]

---

177. 2004 (2) SA 216 (SCA) at para. 16.
178. 2003 (1) SA 389 (SCA) per Kriegler J. Similar factors are noted in the discussion of wrongfulness in The Law of South Africa, Butterworths-LexisNexis (LAWSA), Vol. 8, part 1, first reissue, at para. 51, which concludes: 'It is now openly acknowledged that the inquiry into wrongfulness involves considerations of public and legal policy and that courts are required to render a value judgment as to what society's notion of justice demands, either to protect the plaintiff's interests or to give judicial sanction to the defendant's conduct.'
179. Per Van Dijkhorst J in *Atlas Organic Fertilizers (Pty) Ltd v. Pikkewyn Ghwano (Pty) Ltd* 1981 (2) SA 173 (T) 188.

110. Unlawfulness therefore requires a value judgment, but the court is not absolved from the need for an open and structured process of reasoning, with reference, *inter alia*, to the specific rights and interests involved; the relationship between the parties; relevant provisions of the Constitution and of other legislation; and relevant policy considerations.[180] The following are illustrative cases.

In *Telematrix (Pty) Ltd t/a Matrix Vehicle Tracking v. Advertising Standards Authority SA*,[181] the court held that the Advertising Standards Authority of South Africa (the ASA) did not owe a legal duty towards an advertiser who had suffered a loss because of an incorrect decision by one of the ASA organs. The relevant policy consideration is the protection of the independence of persons or bodies with an adjudicative function to serve the public interest, which imposes on them a duty to act impartially. These persons or bodies (including the judiciary, arbitrators and other administrative tribunals) should be able to adjudicate fearlessly. The threat of an action for damages could interfere with their prompt dealings of litigation and disputes. Although both the person harmed and the loss suffered due to an incorrect decision are foreseeable, negligently causing harm is not considered wrongful.

In *Freddy Hirsch Group (Pty) Ltd v. Chickenland (Pty) Ltd*,[182] the court held that the plaintiff had an alternative claim in delict for economic loss caused by delivery to it of spices containing a banned colourant. The delictual claim was based on the defendant's awareness that breach of contract by delivery of spices containing the banned colourant would or could reasonably cause losses to the plaintiff, including the costs associated with the recall and replacement of the affected products. The court accepted that the same facts may give rise to a claim for damages *ex contractu* and alternatively *ex delicto*, but also that the breach of a contractual duty is not per se unlawful for the purposes of Aquilian liability[183] The negligent causing of pure economic loss is not prima facie unlawful, but in this case policy considerations such as knowledge of the potential harm, the fact that the loss was single and determinate, and the manufacturer's general duty to take reasonable steps to ensure that defective products do not reach the market indicated wrongfulness for the purposes of delictual liability.

111. In summary, the reasoning of the courts on unlawfulness is reducible to the following specific (and often interrelated) factors:

(a) policy considerations indicating whether the law of delict should intervene in respect of the type of harm-causing (*inter alia* the social or economic consequences of imposing liability – in particular potential indeterminate liability (opening the floodgates), the availability of alternative remedies and the need for accountability of public bodies or officials);

---

180. *See*, for example, *Carmichele v. Minister of Safety and Security and Another* 2001 (1) SA 489 (SCA) at para. [7]; *Cape Town Municipality v. Bakkerud* 2000 (3) SA 1049 (SCA) paras [14]–[32]; *Cape Metropolitan Council v. Graham* 2001 (1) SA 1197 (SCA) para. [6]; *Olitzki Property Holdings v. State Tender Board and Another* 2001 (3) SA 1247 (SCA) paras [11] and [31]; *BOE Bank Ltd v. Ries* 2002 (2) SA 39 (SCA) para. [13].
181. 2006 (1) SA 461 (SCA) para. 12.
182. 2011 (4) SA 276 (SCA).
183. Paragraph 33.

(b) consideration of relevant constitutional or other statutory rights and duties (*inter alia* the right to freedom and security of the person, the right to privacy, the right to freedom of expression);
(c) a typology of factual circumstances that indicate a duty not to cause or to prevent harm in the particular situation (*inter alia* the proportionality of the risk of harm and the cost of prevention, control over a dangerous object or situation, awareness of danger, prior conduct creating danger, a relationship imposing responsibility, professional knowledge);
(d) the nature of the defendant's conduct (harm-causing by positive conduct is generally more readily considered to be unlawful than harm-causing by omission);
(e) the nature of the defendant's fault (intentional harm-causing is generally more readily considered to be unlawful than negligent harm-causing); and
(f) the nature of the interest sought to be protected (causing physical injury and damage to property is considered to be prima facie unlawful, whereas the unlawfulness of nuisance and damage to reputation, for example, is often judged in balance with a conflicting interest of the defendant).

VIII. The Constitution and Unlawfulness in the Law of Delict

112. The Constitution[184] has had an important effect in giving content to the criteria of 'general reasonableness', *boni mores*, and 'the legal convictions of the community'. One of the most important areas where the Constitution has an impact is in conflict-of-rights situations. For example, where there is a potential conflict between freedom of expression and the administration of justice, for example, the Supreme Court of Appeal in *Midi Television (Pty) Ltd v. Director of Public Prosecutions*[185] said the following:

> [19] In summary, a publication will be unlawful, and thus susceptible to being prohibited, only if the prejudice that the publication might cause to the administration of justice is demonstrable and substantial and there is a real risk that the prejudice will occur if publication takes place. Mere conjecture or speculation that prejudice might occur will not be enough. Even then publication will not be unlawful unless a court is satisfied that the disadvantage of curtailing the free flow of information outweighs its advantage. In making that evaluation it is not only the interests of those who are associated with the publication that need to be brought to account but, more important, the interests of every person in having access to information. Applying the ordinary principles that come into play when a final interdict is sought, if a risk of that kind is clearly established, and it cannot be prevented from occurring by other means, a ban on publication that is confined in scope and in content and in duration to what is necessary to avoid the risk might be considered.

184. Act 108 of 1996.
185. [2007] SCA 56 (RSA) para. 19.

113. Another important area affected by the Constitution is that of state liability for omissions. In a number of cases, victims of violent crime have instituted actions against the state for the failure, mostly by the police, to hold dangerous criminals in custody, or to provide effective protection against crime, or to exercise properly their duties in respect of firearm licensing.

114. In the case of *Carmichele v. Minister of Safety and Security and Another (Centre for Applied Legal Studies Intervening)*,[186] the plaintiff was the victim of a violent attack by a person with a prior conviction for violence who was released on his own recognizances while awaiting trial on a new charge, also involving violence against women. The plaintiff alleged that the state through the investigating police officers and the prosecutors had a legal duty to protect him, which it unlawfully failed to do by not opposing the release of the accused at the bail hearing. The Constitutional Court held that in applying the pre-constitutional common law test for unlawfulness for the purposes of delictual liability, the courts must have regard to sections 8(3) and 39(2) of the Constitution, which require that the common law must be developed if necessary, to give effect to constitutional rights and to reflect the spirit, purport and objects of the Bill of Rights.[187] The court said the following in this regard:

> Following this route it might be easier to cast the net of unlawfulness wider because constitutional obligations are now placed on the State to respect, protect, promote and fulfil the rights in the Bill of Rights and, in particular, the right of women to have their safety and security protected. However, it is by no means clear how these constitutional obligations on the State translate into private law duties towards individuals. (paragraph 57)

115. The court in *Carmichele* indicated that a consequence of such an approach might be:

(a) to accentuate the objective nature of unlawfulness as one of the elements of delictual liability, particularly in the context of a bail hearing where the roles and general duties of investigating officers and prosecutors are more clearly defined than would normally be the case;
(b) to define it more broadly; and
(c) to allow the elements of fault and remoteness of damage to play the greater role in limiting liability.[188]

The court took into account the record of the accused, the knowledge that the police had of his threatening conduct, and the right of women and other vulnerable groups in particular to have their safety and security protected in terms of section 12(1)(c) of the Constitution (a section providing that everyone has right to freedom from violence). The court in this case did not undertake the exercise of developing

186. 2001 (4) SA 938 (CC).
187. Paragraphs 32–37.
188. Paragraph 57.

the common law itself, but indicated different ways of developing the common law to give effect to the constitutional rights and values, in particular the element of unlawfulness.[189] The court held that the trial court should not have granted an order for absolution from the instance and remitted the case to the High Court for the trial to proceed.

116. In subsequent cases, the courts have reiterated that where a legal duty to act positively to prevent harm is in issue, the general test for determining unlawfulness applies.[190] The concept of the legal convictions of the community must now necessarily incorporate the norms, values and principles contained in the Constitution. The Constitution is the supreme law of the country, and no law, conduct, norms or values that are inconsistent with it can have legal validity, which has the effect of making the Constitution a system of objective, normative values for legal purposes.[191] However, the Constitution can neither be regarded as the exclusive embodiment of the delictual criterion of the legal convictions of the community, nor does it mean that this criterion will lose its status as an agent in shaping and improving the law of delict to deal with new challenges. The entrenchment of fundamental rights and values in the Bill of Rights, however, enhances their protection and affords them a higher status in that all law, State actions, court decisions and even the conduct of natural and juristic persons may be tested against them and all private law rules, principles or norms, including those regulating the law of delict, are subjected to, and thus given content in the light of the basic values in the Bill of Rights.

117. The fundamental values enshrined in the Constitution include human dignity, the achievement of equality and the advancement of human rights and freedoms, non-racialism and non-sexism (sections 1(a) and (b) of the Constitution). In terms of section 12(1)(c), everyone has the right to freedom and security of the person, which includes the right to be free from all forms of violence from either public or private sources. Section 12 should be read with section 7(2) of the Constitution which imposes a duty on the State to 'respect, protect, promote and fulfil the rights in the Bill of Rights'.

118. In *Minister of Safety and Security v. Van Duivenboden*,[192] the majority of the Supreme Court of Appeal concluded that while private citizens might be entitled to remain passive when the constitutional rights of other citizens are under threat,

---

189. At para. 57.
190. *See* the judgment of this Court in *Carmichele* at para. 7; and *Cape Town Municipality v. Bakkerud* 2000 (3) SA 1049 (SCA) paras 14–17; *Cape Metropolitan Council v. Graham* 2001 (1) SA 1197 (SCA) para. 6; *Olitzki Property Holdings v. State Tender Board and Another* 2001 (3) SA 1247 (SCA) paras 11 and 31; *BOE Bank v. Ries* 2002 (2) SA 39 (SCA) para. 13 and *Minister of Safety and Security v. Van Duivenboden*, 2002 (6) SA 431 (SCA) para. 16.
191. *Minister of Safety and Security v. Van Duivenboden* 2002 (6) SA 431 (SCA) para. 17.
192. 2002 (6) SA 431 (SCA).

and while there might be no similar constitutional imperatives in other jurisdictions, in South Africa the State has a positive constitutional duty to act in the protection of the rights in the Bill of Rights.[193] Furthermore, as held by the Constitutional Court in *Carmichele*,[194] the State is obliged under international law to protect women against violent crime and against the gender discrimination inherent in violence against women. This obligation is imposed on the State by section 39(1)(b) of the Constitution, read with the preamble to the *Universal Declaration of Human Rights*; Article 4(d) of the *Declaration on the Elimination of Violence against women* and Article 2 of the *Convention on the Elimination of All Forms of Discrimination against Women.*

119. In terms of section 205(3) of the Constitution, the police must 'prevent, combat and investigate crime, to maintain public order, to protect and secure the inhabitants of the Republic and their property and to uphold and enforce the law'; and under the South African Police Service Act 68 of 1995 the functions of the police include the maintenance of law and order and the prevention of crime. The police service is thus one of the primary agencies of the State responsible for the discharge of its constitutional duty to protect the public in general and women in particular against the invasion of their fundamental rights by perpetrators of violent crime.[195]

120. In *Van Duivenboden*, the majority of the court emphasized[196] that the very existence of the State's constitutional duty to act in protection of the rights in the Bill of Rights necessarily implies the norm of public accountability, and pointed out that section 41(1) of the Constitution expressly provides that all spheres of government and all organs of State within such sphere must provide government which is not only effective, transparent and coherent, but also government which is accountable. The court held[197] that this norm must necessarily assume an important role in determining whether a legal duty ought to be recognized in any particular case; and the court held that certain police officers who were in possession of information that reflected adversely upon the fitness of a person to possess firearms owed a legal duty to members of the public to take reasonable steps to act on that information in order to prevent harm.

121. An important consideration in favour of recognizing delictual liability for damages on the part of the State in cases of failure to provide protection against violent crime is that there is no other practical and effective remedy available to the victim of violent crime. Conventional remedies such as review and mandamus or interdict do not afford the victim of crime any relief at all. The only effective remedy is a private law delictual action for damages.[198] This is illustrated by the case

193. Paragraph 20.
194. 2001 (4) SA 938 (CC) para. 62.
195. *Minister of Law and Order v. Kadir* 1995 (1) SA 303 (A) at 321F; and the Constitutional Court's judgment in *Carmichele* para. 62.
196. Paragraph 20.
197. Paragraph 21.
198. *See Van Eeden v. Minister of Safety and Security* 2002 (4) SA 346 (SCA) para. 19.

of *Van Eeden v. Minister of Safety and Security*,[199] which concerned the control that the police were required to exercise over a known dangerous criminal in police custody. The court held that the manner in which the police performed their functions relating to the detection of crime and the apprehension of criminals were matters in which public policy may well require that police should have a wide discretion. However, the court held that the recognition of a legal duty of control in this case would neither disrupt the efficient functioning of the police, nor will it necessarily require additional resources or inhibit the proper performance by the police of their primary functions or lead to defensive policing. The court was satisfied that the imposition of liability on the State in this case would not open the floodgates of litigation and result in limitless liability on public authorities and functionaries, because the requirements for establishing negligence and causation provide sufficient practical scope for limiting liability.

IX. Unlawfulness and the Infringement of a Right

122. Unlawfulness can focus either on the infringement of a right, or on the breach of a duty.[200] In many cases, the courts accept unlawfulness without referring to the general criteria of reasonableness, *boni mores*, the legal convictions of the community, or concomitant policy considerations, because it is settled law that all harm to person or property caused by a positive act is prima facie unlawful.[201] It is simply accepted as unlawful to cause harm to another in the form of bodily injury or property damage, because such conduct involves the infringement of a recognized right to bodily integrity or to property. In the absence of some form of justification, like self-defence or necessity, the infringement of a recognized subjective right is unlawful. In such cases, the law is settled and it is unnecessary to apply the general criteria or standards of reasonableness, *boni mores* or the legal convictions of the community.[202]

123. Unlawfulness mostly occurs in the form of the infringement of a right that belongs within one of the settled categories of rights.[203] These settled categories are:

- real rights in respect of movable or immovable property;
- personal rights in respect of an act or performance required from another person, such as payment of a debt;

---

199. 2002 (4) SA 346 (SCA).
200. The approach to the inquiry into unlawfulness as formulated in the New Dutch Civil Code (Art. 162.2) reflects a similar approach, characterizing as unlawful the infringement of a right (*inbreuk op een recht*), or conduct infringing a statutory duty (*wettelijke plicht*) or with that which according to the unwritten law is proper in the community (*hetgeen volgens ongeschreven recht in het maatschappelijk verkeer betaamt*).
201. *See Lillicrap, Wassenaar and Partners v. Pilkington Brothers (SA) (Pty) Ltd* 1985 (1) SA 448 (A) 497; P.Q.R. Boberg, *The Law of Delict Vol. 1, Aquilian Liability 32* (1984).
202. *See Universiteit van Pretoria v. Tommie Meyer Films (Edms) Bpk* 1977 (4) SA 376 (T) 383; *Lillicrap, Wassenaar and Partners v. Pilkington Brothers (SA) (Pty) Ltd* 1985 (1) SA 448 (A) 497.
203. *See Universiteit van Pretoria v. Tommie Meyer Films (Edms) Bpk* 1977 (4) SA 376 (T) 387; *Clarke v. Hurst* 1992 (4) SA 630 (D) 651.

- personality rights in respect of aspects of human personality such as bodily integrity, dignity or reputation; and
- immaterial property rights in respect of intangible products of the human mind such as patents, trademarks or copyright.

The courts accept that unlawfulness in the law of delict mostly involves the infringement of a subjective right belonging within one of these settled categories.[204] There is no closed list of protected rights, however, and to these settled categories may also be added subcategories or new categories of rights, such as personal immaterial property rights in the form of the right to earning capacity or personal goodwill; the right to information; and rights to privacy, identity, goodwill and trade secrets.[205]

124. Generally, the law of delict recognizes a protectable right or interest in respect of something of value that is capable of independent existence, so that the person who has the right or interest may enjoy, use or dispose it.[206] Every such right therefore has an interest as its object. Typical examples of such interests are movable or immovable property that constitutes the object of a right of ownership or some other real right; an act of payment or delivery that constitutes the object of a personal right to enforce such payment or delivery; aspects of personality such as dignity, privacy or reputation; and intellectual property such as a patent or trademark. The law of delict characterizes as unlawful the causing of harm to another person by the unreasonable infringement of that person's right to enjoyment, use or disposal of such an interest.

125. Infringement of a right involves disturbing or curtailing the ability or opportunity of the holder of the right to enjoy, use or dispose of the interest that is the object of the right.[207] This occurs, for instance, by damaging or appropriating property belonging to another; or inducing breach of contract so that a debt owed to another person is not paid; or causing a breach of privacy or damage to reputation; or appropriating a patented process or a trademark. Factual disturbance or curtailment is not enough; the infringement must be unreasonable in terms of general criteria or standards based on *boni mores*, the legal convictions of the community and in the final instance public policy.[208]

---

204. *Universiteit van Pretoria v. Tommie Meyer Films (Edms) Bpk* 1977 (4) SA 376 (T) 382, 387; *Mukheiber v. Raath* 1999 (SCA) para. 25.
205. *See Hawker v. Life Offices Association of South Africa* 1987 (3) SA 777 (C), where the infringement of the right to earning capacity was in issue; and J. Neethling, *Die Reg op die Verdienvermoë en die Reg op Korrekte Inligting as Selfstandige Subjektiewe Regte*, THRHR 101 (1990).
206. On the doctrine of subjective rights generally *see Universiteit van Pretoria v. Tommie Meyer Films (Edms) Bpk* 1977 (4) SA 376 (T) 381-4; J. Neethling, *Delict*, 49–55; Van der Vyfer *Huldigingsbundel WA Joubert* 201 et seq.; Joubert *Grondslae van die Persoonlikheidsreg* (1953) 118–121.
207. *See* generally J. Neethling, *Delict* (Butterworths) 53–55.
208. *See Bester v. Calitz* 1982 (3) SA 864 (O) 879, where it is stated that the factual infringement of a subjective right to personal dignity, even though it causes a measure of harm, will not necessarily be regarded as unreasonable and will therefore not necessarily be unlawful.

126. In the process of determining unlawfulness where the infringement of a right is concerned, the courts will look at the following:

- whether a legally recognized right or interest is involved;
- whether there has been a factual disturbance or curtailment of such a right or interest that affects, for instance, the ability to enjoy, use or dispose of the right or interest; and
- whether the disturbance or curtailment is unreasonable according to the *boni mores* or legal convictions of the community. In some cases, unreasonableness is easily determined or readily assumed.

127. As noted above, it is settled law that all harm to person or property caused by a positive act is prima facie unlawful.[209] In other cases, the courts apply the general criteria or standards to assess the alleged infringement of a right, as illustrated by the following cases.

128. In *Universiteit van Pretoria v. Tommie Meyer Films (Edms) Bpk*,[210] the infringement of a university's right to its good name, privacy and goodwill was in issue. In a fictional film dealing with the unhappy experiences of a sportsman of colour against the background of life at university, the film-maker depicted fictional characters at the university in an unfavourable light. It was held that the university itself was not personified by these characters; that a university is an institution in the public domain; that there should be scope for creating fiction against the background of such an institution without having to obtain its consent; and that the university was not directly associated with certain characters that were portrayed as unpleasant in the story. A university does have a personality right to its good name as well as a right to goodwill as a patrimonial interest, but the extent of the infringement of these rights did not justify the conclusion that the film unlawfully caused harm to the university.

129. In *Gien v. Gien*,[211] there was a dispute between neighbouring landowners over the disturbance resulting from the owner's use of a noise apparatus to deter animals and birds from feeding on crops. The apparatus emitted loud bangs day and night and allegedly caused an excessive disturbance of peace in the whole neighbourhood. There was also a history of ill feeling between the neighbours. It was held that where rights of ownership come into conflict, reasonableness and fairness should determine the issue. The respective interests of the parties should be weighed up in an objective manner. Relevant factors were the extent of the disturbance as determined by the type and time of the noise, the degree of its persistence and the locality involved; the value of the crops allegedly protected by the noise; possible alternative and less disruptive measures; and a possible motive to cause harm or to

---

209. *See Lillicrap, Wassenaar and Partners v. Pilkington Brothers (SA) (Pty) Ltd* 1985 (1) SA 448 (A) 497; P.Q.R. Boberg, *The Law of Delict Vol. 1 Aquilian Liability* 32 (1984).
210. 1977(4) SA 376 (T); 1979 (1) SA 441 (A).
211. 1979 (2) SA 1113 (T).

irritate. In weighing up these factors, the court decided that the use of the noise apparatus caused an excessive disturbance and therefore unlawfully infringed the neighbour's rights of ownership.

130. In *Schultz v. Butt*,[212] the applicant Butt, the designer of a twin-hulled glass-fibre boat named 'Butt-Cat', sought to interdict a competitor Schultz from manufacturing and marketing a boat with an identical hull design. Years of experience, expertise and effort and substantial costs had gone into the 'Butt-Cat' hull design and the venture was a financial success. Schultz got hold of a 'Butt-Cat' hull and used it to construct a mould and then used the mould to manufacture replica hulls for a boat named 'Supercat', that was sold in competition with the 'Butt-Cat'. Schultz went further and registered the hull as a model with the Registrar of Designs. Butt applied for an interdict against Schultz and an order for cancellation of the registration of the design, on the basis, *inter alia*, of unlawful competition. The issue was essentially whether the infringement by Schultz of Butt's unregistered rights in respect of the design was unlawful.

The court in *Schultz v. Butt* held that competitive conduct may fall within 'a category of clearly recognized illegality',[213] as in the case of trading in contravention of an express statutory prohibition, fraudulent misrepresentation concerning one's own product, passing off one's product as that of a competitor and injurious falsehoods concerning a competitor's product. However, unlawfulness in competition is not limited to these categories and can also be determined by criteria such as fairness and honesty in competition.[214] In this case, the question was whether it can be unlawful to copy a design that is in the public domain and not protected by copyright, patent or design legislation. In the application of the criteria of fairness and honesty, the court considered on the one hand that the design was in the public domain and that imitation is the lifeblood of competition, but on the other hand that it may be intolerable to allow one manufacturer to appropriate the product of another's invention and development without licence or compensation. In this case, Schultz used one of Butt's hulls, that was developed over a long period, with considerable expenditure of time, labour and money, to make a mould with which to make boats in competition with Butt. Furthermore, he 'added impudence to dishonesty' by obtaining a design registration in his own name for the hull designed by Butt.[215] In the view of the court, this conduct constituted unlawful competition.

131. In *Stewart and Another v. Botha and Another*,[216] the Supreme Court of Appeal refused to recognize a 'wrongful life' claim by a child born disabled. The question of unlawfulness involved consideration of the content of the duty owed to the child by the medical practitioners (to advise the mother properly, so as to enable her to make an informed decision on whether or not to abort the foetus) and the corresponding right of the child. The court held that this question essentially involved

212. 1986 (3) SA 667 (A).
213. *Schultz v. Butt* 1986 (3) SA 667 (A) at 678.
214. *Schultz v. Butt* 1986 (3) SA 667 (A) at 678.
215. *Schultz v. Butt* 1986 (3) SA 667 (A) at 683.
216. 2008 (6) SA 310 (SCA); [2008] ZASCA 84.

a choice between life with disabilities on the one hand and non-existence on the other. Making that choice in favour of non-existence not only involves a disregard for the sanctity of life and the dignity of the child, but also involves an arbitrary, subjective preference for some policy considerations and the denial of others. Therefore, the essential question when adjudicating a claim of this kind is whether the particular child should have been born at all. That is a question that goes so deeply to the heart of what it is to be human that it should not even be asked of the law. For that reason, the court refused to recognize the action of the child. However, in *H v. Fetal Assessment Centre*,[217] the Constitutional Court took a different view, holding that H, a boy with Down's syndrome, who was represented by his mother, sued the Fetal Assessment Centre for his damages flowing from its alleged failure to warn his pregnant mother that there was a high risk of him being born with the syndrome. H alleged that had his mother been informed of the risk she would have terminated the pregnancy. The damages he claimed were for his past and future medical expenses, for disability and for loss of amenities of life. The Constitutional Court decided that the common law might be developed to recognize the child's claim. Under the Constitution children have the right to have their best interests given paramount importance in every matter concerning them. That includes a prenatal medical expert misdiagnosis that results in the child being born with a disability. The best interests of the child may require that the loss should not in those circumstances lie with the child. Translated into legal terms, that would mean that there may be a legal duty not to cause that loss. Failure to do so might breach that duty and infringe the child's right under section 28(2) of the Constitution.

132. The cases referred to above illustrate how the courts set about giving specific content to the concepts of reasonableness, *boni mores* and legal convictions of the community when assessing the alleged infringement of rights. The process of reasoning often involves one or more of the following legal, factual and policy questions:

- Can one or both of the parties rely on a constitutional or other right?[218] However, the existence of a right, even if it is a constitutional right, is not conclusive, because the assessment of unlawfulness often involves a conflict of rights.[219]

217. 2015 (2) SA 193 (CC).

218. *See* for instance *National Media Ltd v. Bogoshi*[1998] 4 All SA 347 (SCA), a case involving the constitutional right to personal dignity on the one hand and the right freedom of expression on the other, in the context of defamation, and in particular the question whether the media should be strictly liable for a defamatory publication. The court rejected the rule of strict liability for defamation as formerly applied to the media and held that the standard of reasonableness should apply. Although the constitutional position was referred to, the court essentially based its judgment on the common law. *See* further the section on the law of delict and the constitution.

219. *See* for instance *Gien v. Gien* 1979 (2) SA 1113 (T), involving conflicting rights of neighbouring landowners, i.e., the right to live in peace and quiet versus the right to protect crops by using a noise emitting apparatus.

- What is the extent of the disturbance or harm caused? Where one person furthers his own interests at the cost of harm to another, the extent of the harm will be a factor in the assessment of unlawfulness.[220]
- What is the social or economic value or purpose of the conduct causing the harm? It may be reasonable to cause a measure of harm to another if this is an inevitable result of protecting one's own substantially more valuable interests.[221] This is the policy consideration underlying the recognition of necessity as a ground of justification in the law of delict.[222]
- Did the person who caused the harm know or foresee that his conduct could cause the harm; or did he have the motive to cause harm? Prior knowledge or actual foresight of the possibility of harm makes the causing of that harm more unreasonable. The degree or extent of the risk of harm will also be a factor in determining the defendant had knowledge or foresight of the possibility of harm. However, the existence of knowledge, foresight or motive is not conclusive in determining unlawfulness and will be taken into account together with other factors.[223] Intent, motive and awareness of risk are relevant to both fault and unlawfulness, as discussed below in the section on unlawfulness, fault and reasonableness of conduct.[224]

---

220. *See* for instance *Gien v. Gien, supra*, where the extent of the nuisance caused to a neighbouring landowner was taken into account; and *Mpongwana v. Minister of Safety and Security* 1999 (2) SA 794 (CPD) 803-4, where the seriousness of the plaintiff's injury was taken into account as one of the factors in the overall assessment of unlawfulness.
221. *See* for instance *Gien v. Gien, supra*, where the purpose served by using a noise emitting apparatus, i.e., to protect crops from animals and birds, was weighed up against the nuisance caused by the apparatus to a neighbour.
222. *See* Part IV, Ch. 2, §3 below.
223. *See* for instance *Coronation Brick (Pty) Ltd v. Strachan Construction Co. (Pty) Ltd* 1982 (4) SA 371 (D) 386-7, where knowledge of the existence of an underground cable was taken into account in deciding whether economic loss was unlawfully caused by cutting the cable; *Shell and BPSA Petroleum Refineries (Pty) Ltd v. Osborne Panama SA* 1980 (3) SA 653 (D) 659, where damage to a mooring buoy in Durban harbour caused economic loss to the charterer of an oil tanker because of the consequent delay in offloading the cargo, but liability was not imposed because it had not been shown that the defendant did foresee or should have foreseen the possibility of loss (on account of delay and liability for demurrage) to the charterer specifically, this kind of loss being foreseeable only in relation to an unascertained class of potential victims, namely the owners or charterers of all vessels intending the discharge oil at that particular mooring buoy; and only insofar as the plaintiff-charterer was a member of that unascertained class was its loss reasonably foreseeable; *Arthur E Abrahams and Gross v. Cohen* 1991 (2) SA 301 (C) 311, where the professional administrators of a deceased estate were held to have unlawfully caused loss to the beneficiaries of an insurance policy that was an asset in the estate, by failing to collect the proceeds of the policy timeously, while knowing who the beneficiaries were and that they would suffer loss as a result of delay; *Indac Electronics (Pty) Ltd v. Volkskas Bank Ltd* 1992 (1) SA 783 (A) 799, where the liability of a collecting bank to the true owner of a cheque was in issue; and the court held that there is a need for protection of the true owner of a cheque that was incorrectly collected and credited; particularly because the true owner relies on the collecting banker to look at the named payee on the face of the cheque before collecting and crediting the proceeds to an account; and the collecting banker undertaking this responsibility in the course of his professional services is or should be aware that the failure to take reasonable care may result in loss to the true owner of the cheque..
224. The distinction between taking into account the defendant's state of mind as a factor relating to unlawfulness and taking it into account for the purpose of determining fault is not always clearly

- Was the conduct causing the harm fraudulent or dishonest? Where one person furthers his own interests at the cost of harm to another, the existence of fraud or dishonesty makes the causing of harm more unreasonable.[225]
- What practical measures could be taken to avert the harm? The courts have regard to the probable success, the relative ease and the expense of practical steps that the defendant could have taken to avert the harm.[226]
- Was the harm caused in the course of rendering professional services and was there a failure of professional competence or skill? Where the defendant renders professional services and professes to possess special skills, knowledge and competence the courts will more readily accept that it is unreasonable to cause harm to a person depending on the defendant's professional competence.[227]
- What are the legal, social and economic implications of imposing liability for the infringement? Are other public policy considerations relevant to the case? The courts shy away from imposing liability, for instance, where neither the harm nor the number of persons affected are finite and the recognition of liability raises the spectre of indeterminate liability to an indeterminate class of persons.[228]

X. Unlawfulness and Breach of Duty

133. The inquiry into unlawfulness often focuses on the existence of a duty, notably in cases where the actor's conduct takes the form of an omission (failure to prevent harm to another person); or the plaintiff suffers pure economic loss (manifesting itself, for instance, in the diminishing of the plaintiff's financial status quo, or the generating of expenses, or the frustration of an expectation of gain); or where breach of a statutory duty is involved. Breach of a legal duty to prevent harm to another also involves infringement of the right of the other person not to be harmed,

---

made by the courts, see for instance the reference to reasonable foreseeability in *Shell and BP SA Petroleum Refineries (Pty) Ltd v. Osborne Panama SA* 1980 (3) SA 653 (D) 659, as set out in the previous footnote.

225. *See Schultz v. Butt* 1986 (3) SA 667 (A), where the respondent's dishonesty in not only copying a design, but also registering it in his own name, was taken into account by the court in its finding that he had acted unlawfully towards the applicant.

226. *See* for instance *Coronation Brick (Pty) Ltd v. Strachan Construction Co. (Pty) Ltd* 1982 (4) SA 371 (D) 384, where the court took into account that a contractor who knew of the existence of an underground cable could have taken steps to prevent the cutting of the cable: and *Arthur E Abrahams and Gross v. Cohen* 1991 (2) SA 301 (C) 311, where the professional administrators of a deceased estate could easily have taken steps timeously to collect the proceeds of an insurance policy that was an asset in the estate, thereby preventing loss to the beneficiaries.

227. *See* for instance *Indac Electronics (Pty) Ltd v. Volkskas Bank Ltd* 1992 (1) SA 783 (A) 799, where it was held that a collecting banker undertakes a professional responsibility towards the true owner of a cheque to collect and credit the proceeds of the cheque for the benefit of the payee.

228. *See Shell and BP SA Petroleum Refineries (Pty) Ltd v. Osborne Panama SA* 1980 (3) SA 653 (D) 659–660; and *Mpongwana v. Minister of Safety and Security* 1999 (2) SA 794 (CPD) 802-3, where the plaintiff based her claim for damages on the failure of the police to protect her from injury resulting from an attack on a taxi in which she was travelling, at a time when a volatile and violent relationship between two rival taxi organizations existed. The court referred to policy considerations such as the implications of holding policemen liable for damages arising from instances of dereliction of duty; and the time, expense and diversion of police manpower involved in defending numerous claims for damages based on alleged police dereliction of duty.

because to every obligation there is a right and a duty side; and a legal duty is the converse of a right.[229] Approaching the assessment of unlawfulness from the duty side simply means a difference in the initial focus of the inquiry. The general criteria for determining unlawfulness remains the same – the question is whether the defendant unreasonably or contrary to the *boni mores* or the legal convictions of the community failed to prevent harm to the plaintiff.[230]

134. In the breach-of-legal-duty cases, the causing of harm cannot be said to be prima facie unlawful (there is no clear right to be protected from such harm or loss); and the focus is on the existence of a duty. This inquiry often turns on responsibility and relationship issues. Typical cases are claims by a resident against a local authority for failure to repair a public facility or warn of danger; by a member of the public against the police for failure to provide protection; by a customer against a bank for furnishing incorrect information or making an incorrect payment; by a client against a financial advisor for careless handling of investments; or by a client against a professional (engineer, accountant, doctor) for inadequate professional services. The concept of duty in these cases ties in with the general function of the inquiry into unlawfulness, namely to determine whether the affected interest of the plaintiff (judged either on its own or in balance with a conflicting interest of defendant) deserves protection from the defendant's action or lack of it, so that the burden of damage should be shifted from plaintiff to defendant. As noted above, unlawfulness is essentially concerned with the scope of protection afforded to various interests, the scope of responsibility to act and policy considerations relating to the question whether the law of delict should intervene.

The courts approach the assessment of unlawfulness from the duty side in cases of liability for pure economic loss, omissions and breach of a statutory duty, as indicated in the following sections. However, the approach of the courts to the 'duty' inquiry has not been a uniform one.

135. In some earlier cases, the courts dealt with questions relating to unlawfulness by following the 'duty of care' approach of English law, holding that harm is not actionable unless the defendant has a duty of care not to cause it; and that the duty of care is essentially based on foreseeability. This was a contentious approach, which, in one commentator's view, 'brought trouble and strife',[231] and which attracted criticism on the basis that the concept of a 'duty of care' is an unnecessary and misleading import from English law, which conflates negligence and unlawfulness. In answer to criticism of the 'duty of care' approach, Schreiner JA in *Union*

---

229. *See Mukheiber v. Raath* 1999 (3) SA 1065 (SCA) para. 27, where it was held that the assessment of unlawfulness in the context of misrepresentation required that one must ask the question: 'was there in the particular circumstances an invasion of the rights of the claimant as a consequence of the misrepresentation? Conversely, was there a legal duty upon the defendant before making the representation, to take reasonable steps to ensure that it was correct?'

230. *See Marais v. Richard* 1981 (1) SA 1157 (A) 1168; *Minister van Polisie v. Ewels* 1975 (3) SA 590 (A) 596-7; *Administrateur, Natal v. Trust Bank van Afrika Bpk* 1979 (3) SA 824 (A) 833-4; *Lillicrap, Wassenaar and Partners v. Pilkington Brothers (SA) (Pty) Ltd* 1985 (1) SA 448 (A) 498.

231. P.Q.R. Boberg, *The Law of Delict Vol. 1 Aquilian Liability* 30–31 (1984).

Government v. Ocean Accident & Guarantee Corporation Ltd,[232] refusing the claim of an employer for economic loss resulting from the negligent injury of its employee by the defendant, lauded the 'duty of care' concept for its convenience as a 'device of reasoning' to control the scope of liability:

> The expression 'duty of care' has sometimes been criticized as introducing an unnecessary complication into the law of negligence, but, apart from the fact that it is endorsed by considerable authority in this Court, it is so convenient a way of saying that it is the plaintiff himself and no other, whose right must have been invaded by the careless defendant, that the complication seems rather to be introduced by the effort to avoid its use. The duty of care is in our case law rested upon foreseeability and this gives rise to a measure of artificiality. But this is really unavoidable for, if there is to be control over the range of persons who may sue, the test must be that of the reasonable man; what he would have foreseen and what action he would have taken may not be calculable according to the actual weighing of probabilities, but the device of reasoning on these lines helps to avoid the impression of delivering an unreasoned moral judgment *ex cathedra* as to how the injurer should have behaved. The duty of care fits conveniently into the reasoning process and even if it is no more than a manner of speaking it is a very useful one.

136. The 'duty of care' approach as set out in the *Union Government* case is explicitly based on the test of the reasonable person and asks if harm was reasonably foreseeable and what action a reasonable person would have taken to prevent harm. This inquiry into 'duty' is indistinguishable from the test for negligence and largely utilizes the flexible concept of foreseeability, which, although it 'may not be calculable according to the actual weighing of probabilities,' nevertheless enables the court to avoid the appearance of 'an unreasoned moral judgment ex cathedra'. Evidently this approach conflates unlawfulness and negligence and utilizes the flexible concept of foreseeability to cover value judgments and policy considerations that often remain unexpressed.

137. In a series of subsequent cases, the courts have moved away from applying the concept of a 'duty of care' in the context of unlawfulness, focusing the inquiry instead on the existence of a 'legal duty'. This development was summarized by Brand JA in *Trustees, Two Oceans Aquarium Trust v. Kantey & Templer (Pty) Ltd*:[233]

> Likewise, the 'legal duty' referred to in this context must not be confused with the 'duty of care' in English law which straddles both elements of wrongfulness and negligence (*see* e.g., *Knop v. Johannesburg City Council* 1995 (2) SA 1 (A) at 27B-G; *Local Transitional Council of Delmas v. Boshoff* 2005 (5) SA 514 (SCA) in paragraph [20]). In fact, with hindsight, even the reference to 'a legal duty' in the context of wrongfulness was somewhat unfortunate. As was

---

232. 1956 (1) SA 577 (A) 585B-D.
233. 2006 (3) SA 138 (SCA) para. 11.

pointed out by Harms JA in *Telematrix (Pty) Ltd t/a Matrix Vehicle Tracking v. Advertising Standards Authority SA* 2006 (1) SA 461 (SCA) in paragraph [14], reference to a 'legal duty' as a criterion for wrongfulness can lead the unwary astray. To illustrate, he gives the following example:

'(T)here is obviously a duty – even a legal duty – on a judicial officer to adjudicate cases correctly and not negligently. That does not mean that the judicial officer who fails in the duty, because of negligence, acted wrongfully.' (See also *Knop v. Johannesburg City Council* (*supra*) at 33D-E.)

138. The courts now mostly refer to a 'legal duty' instead of a 'duty of care' when dealing with unlawfulness, but this fairly consistent current terminology[234] has not produced a uniform approach to unlawfulness. In some cases, the courts accept that the question of foreseeability of harm forms part of the inquiry into unlawfulness. This approach is challenging to analysis, because it utilizes the concept that is central to negligence, namely foreseeability, but nevertheless disavows the conflation of unlawfulness and negligence. The resurgent support for a foreseeability-based concept of legal duty in the context of unlawfulness appears to

234. References to 'duty of care' in the context of unlawfulness still occur. *See* the judgment of Moseneke DCJ in *Steenkamp NO v. The Provincial Tender Board of the Eastern Cape* 2007 (3) BCLR 300 (CC) paras 36–37.

owe much to the often-cited work of Millner on negligence.[235] The judgment of Lewis JA in *Premier, Western Cape v. Faircape Property Developers (Pty) Ltd*[236] is an example of this approach:

> [42] The foreseeability of harm to the plaintiff is also 'a relevant consideration in the determination of lawfulness' (per Hefer JA in *Government of the Republic of South Africa v. Basdeo*) ...
> Accordingly, even if it were to be found that the Minister's conduct had been negligent, this would not entail, necessarily, a finding that it was also wrongful. One must ask whether it was wrongful. ... In answering that question one must consider also, therefore, whether the Minister should have foreseen that his conduct might cause prejudice or loss to persons like Faircape, whose applications are granted.

---

235. *Negligence in Modern Law* (1967). The following passages at pages 25 and 26 have often been cited by the courts:

> The law lays down two tests for ascertaining the existence of a duty of care; firstly, that the injury was such as a reasonable man would have foreseen and guarded against; secondly, that the nature of the interest infringed was one which the law protects against negligent conduct. These two elements must occur to give rise to a duty of care. Now it is plain that the first test is in no way different from the test applied in order to decide the 'negligence issue', that is, in order to answer the question: was the defendant's conduct negligent? It reiterates the identical abstract standard of reasonableness. If a reasonable man, placed in the circumstances of the defendant, would have foreseen that his conduct might endanger or prejudice others in regard to their legally protected interests, then the defendant is deemed to have been under a legal duty towards such others to exercise appropriate care. [25]
>
> The duty concept, on the contrary, shows abounding vitality. The key to this paradox is the utility of this concept as a device of judicial control over the area of actionable negligence on grounds of policy. Here, the ascertainment of liability is linked to the second of the two elements of duty of care referred to above. This second element is not at all concerned with reasonable foresight; it is to do with the range of interests which the law sees fit to protect against negligent violation. It is only when this policy function of the duty of care concept is ignored and the matter examined exclusively in terms of reasonable foresight, that the conclusion that the duty concept is redundant, 'an unnecessary fifth wheel on the coach', is inescapable. Even so, the concept serves in practice as a mode of addressing that part of the negligence issue which is concerned with the risk to the particular plaintiff, and the reasoning of a judgment may be clothed in the language of 'duty', whatever the hidden springs of the decision may be.
>
> Divorced from its role as a monitor of policy, the duty of care concept becomes dispensable, and is in fact dispensed with in other systems of law. The Roman law, as Buckland pointed out, made no reference to a precedent duty of care in the Aquilian action, which is a remedy somewhat analogous to the negligence action of the common law. Culpa, unlike negligence, was not defined with reference to a particular person or class. Failure to take that care which a reasonable man, the *bonus paterfamilias* or *paterfamilias diligens*, would take, was culpa, and, if damage to property resulted, there was liability (subject only to a causal nexus). This was unlawful damage, *damnum injuria datum*, and the 'unforeseeable plaintiff' rode home with the rest. Modern civil law still maintains this approach. [26]

See the references to these passages by Rumpff CJ in *Administrateur, Natal v. Trust Bank van Afrika Bpk* 1979 (3) SA 824 (A) 833E-H; and by Hefer JA in *Government of the Republic of South Africa v. Basdeo* 1996 (1) SA 355 (A) 368–369.

236. 2003 (6) SA 13 (SCA).

> [46] One of the enquiries, then, for determining whether the Minister was under a legal duty to prevent harm to Faircape is whether the Minister should have foreseen that his conduct 'might endanger or prejudice others in regard to their legally protected interests'? A similar question is inevitably repeated when one is determining the issue of negligence. In the context of determining wrongfulness, the question relates only to whether there should be a legal duty imposed on the Minister not to infringe a legal interest of an applicant. And it is but one of several enquiries that must be pursued in order to determine whether, as a matter of legal policy, an official or member of government should be visited with liability for damages. Would a reasonable Minister have foreseen that an applicant for the removal of restrictions would be prejudiced or would suffer loss if the application were granted? Again, the answer must be no. [Footnotes omitted]

According to this passage, the question of foreseeability is 'inevitably repeated' in the course of the enquiries into unlawfulness and negligence. For the purposes of unlawfulness 'it is but one of several enquiries that must be pursued' to determine whether, as a matter of legal policy, liability for damages should be imposed. It is not explained why foreseeability must be determined twice; whether it is in effect the same question that is asked twice or a 'similar question'; and how unlawfulness can properly perform the function of indicating in which cases of negligently caused harm liability should be imposed, if it shares a central attribute with negligence.[237]

139. Another example of the foreseeability-based approach to unlawfulness is the following passage in the judgment of Scott JA in *Gouda Boerdery BK v. Transnet Ltd*:[238]

> [12] ... Where the element of wrongfulness gains importance is in relation to liability for omissions and pure economic loss. The inquiry as to wrongfulness will then involve a determination of the existence or otherwise of a legal duty owed by the defendant to the plaintiff to act without negligence: in other words to avoid negligently causing the plaintiff harm. This will be a matter for judicial judgment involving criteria of reasonableness, policy and, where appropriate, constitutional norms. If a legal duty is found to have existed, the next inquiry will be whether the defendant was negligent. ... The courts have in the past sometimes determined the issue of foreseeability as part of the inquiry into wrongfulness and, after finding that there was a legal duty to act reasonably, proceeded to determine the second leg of the negligence inquiry, the first (being foreseeability) having already been decided. If this approach is adopted, it is important not to overlook the distinction between negligence and wrongfulness. [Footnotes omitted.]

---

237. *See* R.W. Nugent, *Yes, It Is Always a Bad Thing for the Law: A Reply to Professor Neethling*, 123 S. African L. J. 557, 560 (2006).
238. 2005 (5) SA 490 (SCA).

According to this passage, the question of foreseeability is 'sometimes' determined as part of the inquiry into unlawfulness and, if a legal duty to act reasonably is found, the second leg of the negligence inquiry follows; the first leg (foreseeability) having already been decided. This seems to indicate a split inquiry into negligence – the first leg of the inquiry being merged with the inquiry into unlawfulness and the second leg standing on its own. It is not explained why this makes sense logically or what the practical benefits are.

140. It appears therefore that, although the unlawfulness terminology has changed from 'duty of care' to 'legal duty', the courts still on occasion regard reasonable foresight as a key requirement for existence of a legal duty, and thus for unlawfulness. Adherence to reasonable foresight for the purposes of the unlawfulness inquiry in effect leaves the 'duty of care' approach alive and well. Reasonable foreseeability, with its focus on the perspective of the actor, connotes blameworthiness of conduct, which is at the heart of the concept of fault. Unlawfulness is essentially concerned with the scope of protection afforded to various interests, the scope of responsibility to act and policy considerations relating to the question whether the law of delict should intervene. If reasonable foresight is a shared attribute of unlawfulness and negligence, these two elements are at least partly conflated. However, such conflation is disavowed in the judgments referred to above, where it is said that the elements of unlawfulness and negligence are distinct, although they are intertwined. The extent of the independence of these two elements is therefore left uncertain, which is bad for both the logic and the practice of the law.

141. In *Telematrix (Pty) Ltd t/a Matrix Vehicle Tracking v. Advertising Standards Authority SA*[239] Harms JA said the following in this regard:

> But the fact that an act is negligent does not make it wrongful, although foreseeability of damage may be a factor in establishing whether or not a particular act was wrongful. To elevate negligence to the determining factor confuses wrongfulness with negligence and leads to the absorption of the English law tort of negligence into our law, thereby distorting it.

142. Unlawfulness and negligence should be distinguishable if it is accepted that the negligent causing of (reasonably foreseeable) harm will in some cases not attract liability.[240] If it is argued that the causing of reasonably foreseeable harm in some cases does not attract liability because the foreseeability of harm is outweighed by policy factors, then it remains uncertain what mere foreseeability of harm adds to the unlawfulness inquiry. Foreseeability should be (and is in the great majority of cases) left to the domain of negligence, where it is a well-defined concept, extensively developed in case law.

239. 2006 (1) SA 461 (SCA) para. 12.
240. *See* R.W. Nugent, *Yes, It Is Always a Bad Thing for the Law: A Reply to Professor Neethling*, 123 S. African L. J. 557, 562 (2006).

143. What is it that should be done or not be done in terms of the legal duty? The formulation of the concept of legal duty in case law is not uniform, and the duty has been described variously as a duty not to cause harm, or to prevent harm, or to act reasonably. In some judgments and academic comment, it is said that the legal duty, breach whereof renders the negligent causing of harm unlawful, is a duty *to act without negligence*.[241] However, to say that 'the legal duty, breach whereof renders negligent conduct wrongful, is a duty *to act without negligence*',[242] is to conflate negligence and unlawfulness (wrongfulness). The statement is in any event challenging to analysis, because breach of a duty not to be negligent is nothing more or less than negligence; and the statement in effect says that negligence renders negligent conduct wrongful.

144. While it is true that liability based on negligence is dependent upon a duty not to be negligent, duty is an indicator of unlawfulness in its fullest sense and is not confined to negligence. If liability for negligence is in issue, the 'legal duty owed by the defendant to the plaintiff to act without negligence' in effect means a legal duty 'to avoid negligently causing the plaintiff harm'.[243] Unlawfulness presupposes that all the other requirements for liability either have been met, or will be met, and the legal duty required for unlawfulness in its full sense seems to be best described as *the legal duty not to cause damage negligently or intentionally by voluntary action or inaction.*[244]

145. The existence of a legal duty for purposes of unlawfulness is broadly explained in terms of 'the legal convictions of the community', 'general reasonableness' or *boni mores*.[245] As noted above, judicial reasoning in the application of these wide and evaluative criteria to determine the existence of a legal duty is reducible to the following (often interrelated) factors:

---

241. *See Gouda Boerdery BK v. Transnet* 2005 (5) SA 490 (SCA) para. 12; *Trustees, Two Oceans Aquarium Trust v. Kantey & Templer (Pty) Ltd* 2006 (3) SA 138 (SCA) para. 12; and Anton Fagan, *Rethinking Wrongfulness in the Law of Delict*, 122 S. African L. J. 90, 110 (2005).
242. Anton Fagan, *Rethinking Wrongfulness in the Law of Delict*, 122 S. African L. J. 90, 110 (2005).
243. *Gouda Boerdery BK v. Transnet* 2005 (5) SA 490 (SCA) para. 12.
244. Walker, writing on the law of Scotland, expresses this as follows: an obligation *ex delicto* arises where there was conduct 'in breach of a logically prior or antecedent obligation imposed by law not to cause or allow to happen the kind of harm which has happened'; *see* David M. Walker, *The Law of Delict in Scotland* 13 (2nd ed., W. Green 1981).
245. In *Sea Harvest Corporation (Pty) Ltd v. Duncan Dock Cold Storage (Pty) Ltd*, 2000 (1) SA 827 (SCA) at 838 Scott JA said the following:

> If the omission which causes the damage or harm is without fault, that is the end of the matter. If there is fault, whether in the form of *dolus* or culpa, the question that has to be answered is whether in all the circumstances the omission can be said to have been wrongful or, as it is sometimes stated, whether there existed a legal duty to act. (The expression 'duty of care' derived from English law can be ambiguous and is less appropriate in this context. *See Knop v. Johannesburg City Council* 1995 (2) SA 1 (A) at 27D-E). To find the answer the Court is obliged to make what in effect is a value judgment based, *inter alia*, on its perceptions of the legal convictions of the community and on considerations of policy. The nature of the inquiry has been formulated in various ways.

(1) Policy considerations indicating whether the law of delict should intervene in respect of the type of harm-causing include the social or economic consequences of imposing liability – in particular potential indeterminate liability (opening the floodgates); the availability of alternative remedies; the need for accountability of public bodies or officials; and potential hampering of persons or bodies in the exercise of functions in the public interest. The following are examples:

(i) In *Shell and BPSA Petroleum Refineries (Pty) Ltd v. Osborne Panama SA*,[246] the court refused to impose liability for the causing of economic loss to the charterer of an oil tanker, delayed outside the Durban harbour as a result of the negligent causing of damage to a mooring buoy in the harbour. The court was unwilling to recognize a legal duty towards the charterer as one of an indeterminate number of similarly placed potential claimants.

(ii) In *Lillicrap, Wassenaar and Partners v. Pilkington Brothers (SA) (Pty) Ltd*,[247] the Appellate Division held that a legal duty in delict did not fit comfortably into the setting of a detailed business contract for professional services, *inter alia* because recognition of an action in delict could entail the circumvention of contractual terms and could create 'a trap for the unwary' within the contractual relationship.[248]

(iii) In *Steenkamp NO v. The Provincial Tender Board of the Eastern Cape*,[249] the court refused to recognize a legal duty on the part of a tender board towards a successful tenderer, whose tender award was later set aside on account of negligence in the process of awarding the tender. The court took into account, *inter alia*, whether an imposition of liability for damages would be likely to have a 'chilling effect' on performance of administrative or statutory functions by members of the board.[250]

(iv) The result is likely to be different where there is fraud in the process of awarding a tender.[251]

---

246. 1980 (3) SA 653 (D).

247. 1985 (1) SA 448 (A).

248. *See*, however, *Pinshaw v. Nexus Securities (Pty) Ltd and Another* 2002 (2) SA 510 (C), where it was held that the existence of a contract between an asset management company and its client did not preclude the existence of a legal duty in delict on the part of the company's employee towards the client; and *Holtzhausen v. ABSA Bank Ltd* Case No. 280/03, judgment delivered on 17 Sep. 2004 (SCA), where it was held that an action is maintainable in delict for a negligent misstatement causing pure pecuniary loss even if a concurrent action is available in contract. The denial of an action in delict in *Lillicrap, Wassenaar and Partners v. Pilkington Brothers (SA) (Pty) Ltd* 1985 (1) SA 475 (A) was regarded as being limited to the case where the negligence alleged consists in the breach of a term of a contract. In *Trustees, Two Oceans Aquarium Trust v. Kantey & Templer (Pty) Ltd* 2006 (3) SA 138 (SCA) it was held that public policy does not require extension of the Aquilian action to rescue plaintiff who was in position to avoid risk of harm by contractual means but failed to do so.

249. [2006] JOL 18364 (CC) para. 42.

250. *See also*, for non-recognition of the claim of an unsuccessful tenderer, *Olitzki Property Holdings v. State Tender Board and Another* 2001 (3) SA 1247 (SCA).

251. *Minister of Finance and Others v. Gore NO* 2007 (1) SA 111 (SCA). The court held that negligent conduct causing pure economic loss was wrongful only if, as a matter of legal and public policy, there existed a legal duty (para. 82 at 138G–H); and that there were no considerations of public or

(v) In *Telematrix (Pty) Ltd t/a Matrix Vehicle Tracking v. Advertising Standards Authority SA*,[252] it was held that the Advertising Standards Authority of SA (the ASA) did not have a legal duty for purposes of delictual liability towards an advertiser who suffered a loss because of an incorrect decision by one of the ASA organs. The relevant policy consideration is the protection of the independence of persons or bodies entrusted with an adjudicative function that serves the public interest and that imposes on them a duty to act impartially. Such persons or bodies (including the judiciary, arbitrators and other administrative tribunals) should be enabled to adjudicate fearlessly. The threat of an action for damages could unduly hamper the expeditious consideration and disposal of litigation and disputes. Although both the person harmed and damage suffered as a result of an incorrect decision are foreseeable, the negligent causing of harm is not considered unlawful.

(2) Constitutional rights may, in the context of the law of delict, imply a legal duty not to cause harm or to prevent harm to another person. Rights that may imply such a duty include the sanctity of life, the right to freedom and security of the person, the right to privacy and the right to freedom of expression. In *Du Plessis v. Road Accident Fund*,[253] the question before the court was whether the right to support of one partner in a same-sex relationship could form the basis of a claim for loss of support against the person who negligently caused the death of the other partner, or, put differently, whether the killing of the deceased had to be considered to have been a wrongful act as against the plaintiff. The court held that the question had to be answered in the light of the prevailing *boni mores*. The legal convictions of the community are informed by the norms and values of society as embodied in the Constitution of the Republic of South Africa, Act 108 of 1996, which norms and values in this case indicated an unlawful infringement of the plaintiff's right to support.[254]

(3) The typology of factual circumstances that indicate a duty not to cause or to prevent harm in particular situations include the following: proportionality of the risk of harm and the cost of prevention, control over a dangerous object or situation, awareness of danger, prior conduct creating danger, a relationship imposing responsibility, professional knowledge. The case of *Administrateur, Transvaal v. Van der Merwe*[255] is illustrative of the process or reasoning involved. Liability for an omission was in issue, and the court determined the existence of a legal duty to prevent harm by means of an inquiry into the proportionality of the risk of harm and the cost of prevention. The question was whether provincial authorities had a duty in respect of a minor road to make firebreaks or to take other precautionary measures against fires breaking out and spreading to adjoining land. The court held that to determine whether a

---

legal policy which dictated that the State should not be liable for the provincial officials' fraudulent conduct in the course of a public tender process.

252. 2006 (1) SA 461 (SCA) para. 12.
253. 2004 (1) SA 359 (SCA).
254. Paragraphs 17 and 18, at 368E–F and 369A/B–C.
255. 1994 (4) SA 347 (A) 361H/I-362A/B; 363C.

positive act or an omission is such that it can be branded as unlawful, the different interests of the parties, their relationship with one another and the social consequences of imposing liability in the kind of case in question, *inter alia*, should be weighed. Factors which play an important role in that process are, *inter alia*, the probable or possible extent of the prejudice to others; the degree of risk of such prejudice eventuating; the interests which the defendant and the community or both have in the act or omission in issue; whether there were reasonably practicable measures available to the defendant to avoid the prejudice; what the chances were of the measures being successful; and whether the cost involved in taking such measures was reasonably proportional to the damage which the plaintiff could suffer. Affordability and proportionality between the potential damage and the potential cost of prevention should be brought into account in deciding the question of unlawfulness. On application of this proportionality test, the court found that the control and supervision of the Administrator over all public roads was only of a permissive nature, and that the applicable legislation did not impose any obligations on the Administrator to make firebreaks or take other precautionary measures against veld fires breaking out and spreading to adjoining land. Given the nature of the road in question, the fact that it was seldom used, and the cost of preventative measures the mere fact that the Administrator exercised control and supervision over all public roads did not in itself create a duty for purposes of delictual liability. In the absence of a positive danger-creating act, the mere control of property and the failure to exercise such control with resultant prejudice to another is not per se unlawful. The crucial issue is whether the precautionary measures which the controller should, according to the aggrieved party, have taken in order to prevent the prejudice can in the circumstances be reasonably and practicably required of him. The underlying philosophy is that a consequence is only unlawful if in the light of all the circumstances it can reasonably be expected of the defendant to act.

(4) The nature of the defendant's conduct is taken into account: harm-causing by positive conduct is generally more readily considered to be unlawful than harm-causing by omission; and the context in which the conduct occurred will be taken into account. In *BOE Bank Ltd v. Ries*,[256] for example, the Supreme Court of Appeal refused to recognize a legal duty on the part of an insurance broker towards an intended beneficiary under a life insurance policy, where the broker had failed to ensure that the policyholder signs the necessary form to nominate the beneficiary. The court took into account that the conduct of the broker did not amount to the assumption of any professional responsibility regarding the signing of the form: he became involved in the process in passing, by doing a favour for a colleague and in effect acting as a messenger, without undertaking any professional responsibility. Although it was foreseeable that the intended beneficiary would obtain no benefit from the policy if the holder failed to sign the necessary nomination form before his death, foreseeability of loss was not in itself enough to indicate a legal duty.

256. 2002 (2) SA 39 (SCA) paras 13–26.

(5) The nature of the defendant's fault and state of mind (motive) is taken into account: intentional harm-causing is more readily considered to be unlawful than negligent harm-causing; and a motive to cause harm will indicate unlawfulness. These matters are dealt with in the following section of unlawfulness, fault and reasonableness of conduct.
(6) The nature of the interest sought to be protected is taken into account: a duty not to cause or to prevent physical injury and damage to property is more readily recognized than a duty not to cause or to prevent pure economic loss, as indicated in the section below on pure economic loss.

XI. Unlawfulness, Fault, and Reasonableness of Conduct

146. The relationship between unlawfulness and fault is somewhat contentious, as noted in section X above. Issues in contention include whether the inquiry into unlawfulness involves a strictly ex post facto perspective and excludes an ex ante or actor-oriented perspective; and whether taking into account such factors would 'make wrongfulness depend, in part at least, on fault' and would 'reverse the ordering of wrongfulness and fault' that sees wrongfulness or unlawfulness as logically anterior to fault.[257]

147. The distinction between the ex ante perspective for determining fault and the ex post facto perspective for determining unlawfulness can be misleading. The determination of both unlawfulness and fault is necessarily done ex post facto. The events have already occurred and the requirements for both these elements of the delict are determined with the perspective of hindsight, but with a different focus. The focus of unlawfulness is wide and includes within its ambit all the other elements of liability (conduct, causation, affected interest, harm and fault), and essentially involves a value judgment on whether the affected interest of the plaintiff deserves protection from the defendant's action or lack of it. Fault is essentially concerned with the blameworthiness of the conduct of the actor: was the conduct at the time of acting directed to the causing of harm with knowledge of unlawfulness (intent); or was harm at that point, from the perspective of the actor, reasonably foreseeable and preventable (negligence)? Insofar as fault is relevant to the inquiry into unlawfulness, as set out below, the inquiry into unlawfulness includes an ex ante perspective; while the final value judgment on whether the affected interest of the plaintiff deserves protection from the defendant's action or lack of it is reached by the court with an overall ex post facto perspective.

148. The ordering of the inquiry does not mean that either unlawfulness or fault logically precedes the other. The courts on occasion deal with negligence first and a finding that the actor was not negligent then obviates the inquiry into unlawfulness.[258] inquiryFault can also be determined after proof of or on the assumption that

257. Anton Fagan, *Rethinking Wrongfulness in the Law of Delict*, 122 S. African L. J. 90, 96 (2005).
258. *Mostert v. Cape Town Municipality* 2001 (1) SA 105 (SCA) para. 43; *Local Transitional Council of Delmas and Another v. Boshoff* 2005 (5) SA 514 (SCA).

there is an unlawful causing of harm.[259] If this assumption proves to be unfounded, either because the actor did not in fact cause the harm or because it is not reasonable or in accordance with 'the legal convictions prevailing in the community' or the *boni mores* to impose liability, the 'fault' is simply irrelevant or 'legally neutral'.[260] Likewise unlawfulness can be determined on the assumption that there is fault, simply because the court finds it convenient to deal with the unlawfulness issue first. If fault is a requirement for liability and it turns out there is no fault, the assessment of unlawfulness then becomes irrelevant. In *Local Transitional Council of Delmas and Another v. Boshoff*,[261] the court said the following on the order and manner of inquiry into the elements of unlawfulness and fault:

> Depending on the circumstances it may be appropriate to enquire first into the question of wrongfulness, in which event it may be convenient to assume negligence for the purpose of the inquiry (see e.g., *Van Duivenboden* at 442A-B (SA)). On the other hand, it may be convenient to assume wrongfulness and then consider the question of negligence (see *Gouda Boerdery Bpk* in paragraph [12]).

149. The nature of the fault that is proved or assumed (in particular intent or conscious negligence) and fault-related factors (in particular awareness of the risk of harm or motive to cause harm) may be relevant to unlawfulness. Intentional causing of harm will mostly be devoid of social utility and therefore unlawful. The unlawfulness of harm-causing misrepresentation, for example, can depend on whether this occurred intentionally or negligently. In *Minister of Finance and Others v. Gore NO*,[262] the court said the following in this regard:

> [86] … We do not think that it can be stated as a general rule that, in the context of delictual liability, state of mind has nothing to do with wrongfulness. Clear instances of the contrary are those cases where intent, as opposed to mere negligence, is itself an essential element of wrongfulness. These include intentional interference with contractual rights (see e.g., *Dantex Investment Holdings (Pty) Ltd v. Brenner and Others NNO*) and unlawful competition (see e.g., *Geary & Son (Pty) Ltd v. Gove*). [Footnotes omitted][263]

---

259. *Gouda Boerdery BK v. Transnet* 2005 (5) SA 490 (SCA) para. 12.
260. *See* R.W. Nugent, *Yes, It Is Always a Bad Thing for the Law: A Reply to Professor Neethling*, 123 S. African L. J. 557, 559 (2006).
261. 2005 (5) SA 514 (SCA) para. 20.
262. 2007 (1) SA 111 (SCA) para. 86.
263. *See also* para. 87.
In the language of the more recent formulations of the criterion for wrongfulness:

> In cases of pure economic loss, the question will always be whether considerations of public or legal policy dictate that delictual liability should be extended to loss resulting from the conduct at issue. Thus understood, it is hard to think of any reason why the fact, that the loss was caused by dishonest (as opposed to bona fide negligent) conduct, should be ignored in deciding the question. We do not say that dishonest conduct will always be wrongful for the purposes of imposing liability, but it is difficult to think of an example where it will not be so.

150. Intentional causing of harm to others will not always be unlawful, for instance where justified criticism harms the reputation of another, or fair competition causes financial loss to a trade competitor. If all other things are equal, a court might accept that there is unlawfulness only if harm was caused intentionally, because intent is more blameworthy. However, everything will depend on the circumstances, and intent will not conclusively indicate unlawfulness. The passenger on the bus who knowingly offers bad investment advice to other passengers, who are complete strangers to him, probably will not be liable if his bad advice is followed, because in the area of investment advice he owes no duty towards his fellow-passengers.

151. A motive to cause harm to another in itself does not necessarily make the causing of harm unlawful, but motive may be taken into account by the court, together with other circumstances, in the assessment of unlawfulness. For instance, where a landowner exercises his rights of ownership in a manner calculated to cause extensive harm to a neighbour, with little benefit to himself, his motive to harm may influence the court to decide that the harm was caused unlawfully.[264] In the area of unlawful competition, a motive to harm rather than to compete will also be taken into account to determine unlawfulness.[265]

152. A court that is undecided on the question of unlawfulness after weighing up conflicting interests and taking into account policy considerations, may therefore consider the blameworthiness of the actor's conduct. Intent, motive to harm, or awareness of the possibility of harm indicates an enhanced degree of blameworthiness, bringing fault or fault-related factors into the unlawfulness inquiry, which may tip the scale to the side of unlawfulness and resultant liability.

153. Where the blameworthiness of the actor's conduct (reasonableness or lack of it) is taken into account in the context of unlawfulness this is (or should be) judged from the perspective of the actor (the ex ante point of view).[266] This happens, as shown above, mainly in cases where there is an enhanced degree of blameworthiness on the part of the actor. However, there are also some instances where the courts take into account the absence of blameworthiness on the part of the actor (reasonableness of conduct), as a form of justification, indicating that harm was not caused unlawfully. The following are examples of cases where either an enhanced degree of blameworthiness or the absence of blameworthiness (reasonableness of conduct) may be relevant to the unlawfulness inquiry:

– A driver in a fit of road rage deliberately crashes into the vehicle of another person and kills the driver, but thereby inadvertently saves a number of pedestrians who would otherwise have been injured by the other driver. If all aspects of the

264. *See Gien v. Gien* 179 (2) SA 1113 (T) 1121 (causing excessive noise to deter animals and birds from causing damage to crops); *Kirsh v. Pincus* 1927 TPD 199 (planting deciduous trees along a boundary so that falling leaves will cause harm to a neighbour.
265. *See Bress Designs (Pry) Ltd v. GY Lounge Suite Manufacturers (Pty) Ltd* 1991 (2) SA 455 (W).
266. Anton Fagan, *Rethinking Wrongfulness in the Law of Delict*, 122 S. African L. J. 90, 95–96 (2005).

situation are considered (applying the comprehensive perspective of the unlawfulness inquiry) the saving of the pedestrians could be considered an 'extenuating' factor, but the intentional causing of harm indicates an enhanced degree of blameworthiness, which may tip the scale to the side of unlawfulness and resultant liability.

- A man injures his friend when pulling the trigger of a gun which he mistakenly but reasonably believes to be a toy. The causing of injury is prima facie unlawful, because injury was caused to another person by a positive act. However, liability should not be imposed, because the reasonable mistake excludes fault in the form of negligence (a reasonable person would also not have foreseen the injury). In this case the lack of blameworthiness of the actor (the reasonableness of his conduct) should be considered relevant to fault. An enhanced degree of blameworthiness (of which there is none) would also have been relevant to unlawfulness.

–In cases of putative defence, the courts have on occasion taken into account the reasonableness of the actor's belief. For example, a woman shoots her neighbour because she mistakenly and reasonably believes him to be an intruder (a reasonable person in her position would also have believed that the victim posed a threat).[267] In this case, the lack of blameworthiness of the actor (the reasonableness of her belief that her conduct is justified) excludes fault, both in the form of negligence, because a reasonable person in her position would also have caused the injury, and in the form of intent, because she lacked knowledge of unlawfulness.[268] Arguably, only an enhanced degree of blameworthiness (of which there is none) should be relevant to unlawfulness. However, in some of these cases the courts in effect conflate unlawfulness and fault. The foundations of this reasonableness of conduct approach to unlawfulness were laid at a time when the concept of unlawfulness in the law of delict was poorly developed, if at all. The judgments on putative defence are by provincial divisions and there is a convincing dissent in the latest of them, the judgment in *Kgaleng v. Minister of Safety and Security*.[269] However, in *Mugwena and Another v. Minister of Safety and Security*, the Supreme Court of Appeal also applied the test of a reasonable person in the context of unlawfulness, to determine whether the causing of injury was justified by defence.[270] The two approaches will almost invariably produce the same result, but the *Kgaleng* approach seems preferable, because it takes account of the reasonableness of the belief in the threat with reference to the well-defined concepts of intent and negligence. The court said the following:

- The defendants may yet escape liability on the basis that the second defendant's bona fide (although erroneous) belief that his conduct was justified, excluded consciousness of wrongfulness – and thus fault in the form of *dolus* – on his part, and provided a reasonable man would not have reacted differently to the way in which the second defendant reacted under the circumstances – thereby excluding fault in the form of culpa.[271]

---

267. *Ibid.*, at 97–99.
268. *See Dantex Investment Holdings (Pty) Ltd v. Brenner* 1989 (1) SA 390 (A) 396-7.
269. 2001 (4) SA 854 (W).
270. 2006 (4) SA 150 (SCA) 158–159.
271. At 865–866, para. 16.

– In defamation cases, the reasonableness of conduct has been recognized as a defence. The Supreme Court of Appeal has recognized that the publication of a false and defamatory statement will be lawful if 'upon consideration of all the circumstances of the case, it is found to have been reasonable to publish the particular facts in the particular way and at the particular time' (the so-called *Bogoshi* defence).[272] The courts have also upheld the defence of qualified privilege if a reasonable person in the position of the person who made the statement would have believed that a duty or interest existed which entitled him to make the defamatory statement.[273] In these cases, the approach of the courts is to allow freedom of speech in circumstances where the person who made the statement did so reasonably. The reasonableness or lack of blameworthiness of conduct indicates that the defence is closely related to the basic concerns of fault. In effect it is indistinguishable from a defence excluding fault, based on absence of intent (because there is no consciousness of wrongfulness), or on absence of negligence (because the defendant's conduct is reasonable). The defence of qualified privilege has its origins in English law, where a distinction between fault and unlawfulness is not recognized. It should be dealt with in modern South African law as a defence excluding unlawfulness, but it is apparently regarded as a defence excluding fault. It illustrates an area of the law on defamation where unlawfulness and fault overlap. The *Bogoshi* case illustrates a similar phenomenon. Reasonableness of the publication, equated with absence of negligence, was held to exclude unlawfulness. The judgment is certainly not a model of structured analysis of the roles of unlawfulness and negligence in the law of defamation. It is arguable that the court intended to deal with two defences, both turning on the reasonableness of the defendant's conduct: the one negating unlawfulness and the other negating negligence.[274] This is how the Supreme Court of Appeal itself interpreted the *Bogoshi* judgment in the subsequent case of *Mthembi-Mahanyele v. Mail & Guardian Ltd*,[275] albeit, arguably, that the court failed to clarify the basis of the distinction between the two defences.[276] As in the case of qualified privilege, the consideration of reasonableness or blameworthiness of conduct that is at the heart of the *Bogoshi* defence indicates that this defence is closely related to the basic concerns of fault. It is barely distinguishable from a defence excluding negligence, based on the reasonableness of the defendant's conduct. Insofar as it is dealt with as a defence excluding unlawfulness, it overlaps with fault. The lack of clarity around the *Bogoshi* defence is at least partly the result of the radical change of course by the Supreme Court of Appeal on the fault requirement for defamation involving the media. The court jettisoned the earlier no-fault liability without making clear what is to replace it. On the basis of the judgment in the *Mthembi-Mahanyele* case, it is now clear that the Supreme Court of Appeal

---

272. Anton Fagan, *Rethinking Wrongfulness in the Law of Delict*, 122 S. African L. J. 90, 101–106 (2005), with reference to *National Media Ltd v. Bogoshi* 1998 (4) SA 1196 (SCA) at 1212G–H.
273. Anton Fagan, *Rethinking Wrongfulness in the Law of Delict*, 122 S.African L. J. 90, 99–101 (2005).
274. *Ibid.*, at 102 refers to, but does not agree with, such arguments.
275. 2004 (6) SA 329 (SCA) paras 45–47.
276. Anton Fagan, *Rethinking Wrongfulness in the Law of Delict*, 122 S. African L. J. 90, 105–106 (2005).

intends to recognize the reasonableness of a publication as a defence that could exclude either unlawfulness or negligence, confirming the possibility of overlap between these two elements of delict.

154. The discussion and examples above indicate that an enhanced degree of blameworthiness of conduct (absence of reasonableness) is relevant to unlawfulness; and that the courts have also on occasion taken into account the reasonableness of conduct (absence of blameworthiness), as judged from the perspective of the actor (ex ante), in the unlawfulness inquiry. Arguably, however, the reasonableness of the actor's conduct is more accurately dealt with in the domain of fault, where both intent and negligence take account of reasonableness in terms of established and well-defined principles.

155. Cases involving liability for negligent failure to prevent harm also illustrate that the issues of unlawfulness and negligence are often closely related. If the question is whether a local authority is liable for harm caused by or related to public property, such as a pedestrian's injury resulting from a hole in a pavement,[277] or a child's injury on a broken merry-go-round,[278] or a shop-owner's loss through flooding from a burst pipe,[279] or a landowner's losses resulting from the establishment of an informal settlement adjacent to his land,[280] the unlawfulness and the negligence issues both involve consideration of the extent of the risk and of the possible harm, the cost of repair or prevention, and the resources available to the local authority. If the pavement, merry-go-round, pipe or settlement was under the control of the local authority, with concomitant responsibility to maintain or administer it, the existence of a legal duty not to cause harm (unlawfulness) will generally not be contentious. However, liability will not be imposed if the local authority was unaware of the state of disrepair and could not reasonably have foreseen it, perhaps owing to the informational and organizational constraints under which it operates, or if preventative measures would be costly out of all proportion to the harm. In these circumstances, the failure to repair or to prevent harm will not be negligent. If the issue is essentially whether the public authority had the duty to exercise control, rather than the extent of the control or preventative measures required, it is more likely to be treated as an issue of unlawfulness than an issue of negligence.[281]

156. It appears therefore that there is an overlap and interrelationship between unlawfulness and fault. This does not indicate a logical grey area or a lack of clear

277. *Cape Town Municipality v. Bakkerud* 2000 (3) SA 1049 (SCA).
278. *Cape Town Municipality v. April* 1982 (1) SA 259 (C).
279. *Mostert v. Cape Town City Council* 2001 (1) SA 105 (SCA).
280. *Local Transitional Council of Delmas and Another v. Boshoff* 2005 (5) SA 514 (SCA).
281. *See Administrateur Transvaal v. Van der Merwe* 1994 (4) SA 347 (A) 349, where it was held that, in the absence of a positive danger-creating act, a provincial authority did not have a legal duty to control a fire that started alongside a minor road. In *Local Transitional Council of Delmas and Another v. Boshoff* 2005 (5) SA 514 (SCA) the court accepted that a local authority with control over an informal settlement adjacent to the plaintiff's land had a legal duty towards the owner of the adjacent land, and could not claim immunity from liability for his losses, but the nature and extent of the preventative steps required of the local authority was a question of negligence.

definition of the elements of delict. Liability must be determined rationally and consistently and a certain measure of overlap does not in itself detract from either rationality or consistency. A theory of delict comprising elements fitted into perfectly separated compartments is not an end in itself. Unlawfulness and fault have broadly different focus areas (blameworthiness of conduct in the case of fault, and overall balancing of interests and determination of the scope of responsibility in the case of unlawfulness), but there are also commonalities: both these elements of delict are essentially based on reasonableness and involve value judgments. To try and separate out factors pertaining to unlawfulness and fault into compartments presents a risk: 'scholars' theoretical attachments can blind them to practical common sense.[282]

XII. Pure Economic Loss, Including Liability for Negligent Misrepresentation

157. Liability for pure economic loss, where the plaintiff's loss is financial and there is no personal injury or damage to the plaintiff's property, often does not involve the infringement of a right that is from the outset clearly identifiable within the settled categories of rights (real, personal, personality, or intellectual property rights). In such cases, the courts tend to focus on the existence of a legal duty to prevent economic loss. The negligent causing of pure economic loss is not necessarily unlawful. In *Telematrix (Pty) Ltd t/a Matrix Vehicle Tracking v. Advertising Standards Authority SA*,[283] Harms JA said the following in this regard:

> [13] When dealing with the negligent causation of pure economic loss it is well to remember that the act or omission is not prima facie wrongful ('unlawful' is the synonym and is less of a euphemism) and that more is needed. Policy considerations must dictate that the plaintiff should be entitled to be recompensed by the defendant for the loss suffered (and not the converse as Goldstone J once implied unless it is a case of prima facie wrongfulness, such as where the loss was due to damage caused to the person or property of the plaintiff). In other words, conduct is wrongful if public policy considerations demand that in the circumstances the plaintiff has to be compensated for the loss caused by the negligent act or omission of the defendant. It is then that it can be said that the legal convictions of society regard the conduct as wrongful, something akin to and perhaps derived from the modern Dutch test 'in strijd ... met hetgeen volgens ongeschreven recht in het maatschappelijk verkeer betaamt' (contrary to what is acceptable in social relations according to unwritten law). [Footnotes omitted.]

282. Anton Fagan, *Rethinking Wrongfulness in the Law of Delict*, 122 S.African L.J. 90, 127 (2005).
283. 2006 (1) SA 461 (SCA) para. 13.

158. The recognition of liability for pure economic loss was summarized as follows by Grosskopf JA in *Lillicrap, Wassenaar & Partners v. Pilkington Bros (SA) (Pty) Ltd:*[284]

> It is clear that in our law Aquilian liability has long outgrown its earlier limitation to damages arising from physical damage or personal injury. Thus, for instance, in *Administrateur, Natal v. Trust Bank van Afrika Bpk* 1979 (3) SA 824 (A) this Court held that Aquilian liability could in principle arise from negligent misstatements which caused pure financial loss, i.e., loss which was caused without the interposition of a physical lesion or injury to a person or corporeal property.

159. In earlier cases, the courts sometimes referred to the concept of a 'duty of care' in the context of liability for pure economic loss. In later cases, the phrase 'legal duty' has been adopted as an appropriate indication of unlawfulness, because the concept of a 'duty of care', derived from English law, connotes an aspect of negligence. In *Knop v. Johannesburg City Council,*[285] Botha JA remarked as follows in this regard:

> In the phraseology of our law the 'policy-based or notional duty of care' is more appropriately expressed as a 'legal duty', in consonance with the requirement of wrongfulness as an element of delictual liability and the underlying concept of legal reprehensibility in respect of the causing of pure economic loss.

160. A typical instance requiring determination of a 'legal duty' is where incorrect information supplied by the defendant is acted upon by the plaintiff, resulting in financial loss. The question is then whether the plaintiff had a right to correct information and the defendant a duty to supply such information. If no contractual relationship between the parties existed a right to information cannot be assumed from the outset and the assessment of unlawfulness therefore proceeds from the duty side. The focus of the inquiry is on whether factual and policy considerations indicate the existence of a legal duty to provide correct information.

161. In the leading case of *Administrateur, Natal v. Trust Bank van Afrika Bpk,*[286] the court applied the general criterion of reasonableness to determine whether an act of misrepresentation is to be regarded as wrongful for the purposes of delictual liability. The court accepted that the criterion of reasonableness involves policy considerations and Rumpff CJ quoted the following passage from Fleming's *Law of Torts* as being correct also for South African law:

---

284. 1985 (1) SA 475 (A) at 498.
285. 1995 (2) SA 1 (A) 27. *See also Administrateur, Natal v. Trust Bank van Afrika Bpk* 1979 (3) SA 824 (A), at 832H–833A.
286. 1979 (3) SA 824 (A), at 833–834.

> In short, recognition of a duty of care is the outcome of a value judgment that the plaintiff's invaded interest is deemed worthy of legal protection against negligent interference by conduct of the kind alleged against the defendant. In the decision whether or not there is a duty, many factors interplay: the hand of history, our ideas of morals and justice, the convenience of administering the rule and our social ideas as to where the loss should fall. Hence, the incidence and extent of duties are liable to adjustment in the light of the constant shifts and changes in community attitudes.

In the *Administrateur, Natal* case, the defendant bank acted on behalf of a person who claimed compensation from the provincial authorities for expropriation of property. Compensation was eventually paid to him via the bank, but it turned out that he was not the owner of the property concerned. The provincial authorities then claimed the amount that they paid out as damages for alleged negligent misrepresentation by the bank. The action failed, because the provincial authorities themselves had initially identified the claimant as owner of the property, and the court held that the bank had no legal duty to verify the facts and that the plaintiff's own mistake therefore caused the loss.

162. Prior to the judgment in the *Administrateur, Natal* case, the law on delictual liability for economic loss caused by negligent misrepresentation was not clear. Under the influence of the English law, which only recognized liability for intentional misrepresentation,[287] the Appellate Division was reluctant to recognize a legal duty in respect of financial loss caused by negligent misrepresentation,[288] although such a duty was recognized in a few cases in judgments of provincial divisions of the Supreme Court.[289] Liability for negligent misrepresentation where a duty to provide correct information existed is now well established.

163. The Appellate Division also recognized in 1991 that a negligent misstatement inducing a contract can give rise to a delictual claim for damages.[290] The court

---

287. *Derry v. Peek* (1889) 14 AC 337.

288. *See Herschel v. Mrupe* 1954 (3) SA 464 (A), where the Appellate Division by a majority decided not to recognize liability on the part of a car owner who, through her attorney, had supplied incorrect information on the identity of the third-party insurer of her car, with the result that the victim of an accident involving the car instituted action against the wrong insurance company and incurred wasted costs.

289. *See Perlman v. Zoutendyk* 1934 CPD 151 328, where the court was prepared to recognize that a sworn appraiser of land could be liable to a bank that had lent money on mortgage to the owner of land on the strength of a sworn appraisement that had (it was later decided on the facts that the appraiser is not liable). *See also Suid-Afrikaanse Bantoetrust v. Ross en Jocobz* 1977 (3) SA 184 (T). In *EG Electric Co. (Pty) Ltd v. Franklin* 1979 (2) SA 702 (E) the court recognized that a registered electrician, who on instructions of the seller of a house had supplied a certificate that the electrical wiring of the house complied with municipal regulations, owed a legal duty to the purchaser of the house who had relied on the correctness of the certificate and later had to incur costs to rectify defective wiring.

290. *See Bayer South Africa (Pty) Ltd v. Frost* 1991 (4) SA 559 (A). In this case, the plaintiff had purchased a new type of herbicide spray for use in his vineyards. An agent of the seller recommended that spraying be done by helicopter and undertook to supervise the spraying operations. During the spraying operations, the herbicide drifted to adjacent lands and caused extensive damage to crops.

held that the relationship of parties engaged in pre-contractual negotiations gives rise to a legal duty not to make a misstatement, and the breach of such a duty can lead to delictual liability for economic loss caused by the misstatement.

164. In *Mukheiber v. Raath*,[291] the parents of a healthy and normal child (their fourth) instituted action in delict against a gynaecologist, alleging that he had negligently misrepresented to them that the wife had been sterilized after the birth of their third child. Relying on this representation they had failed to take contraceptive measures, with the result that the fourth child was conceived and born. The parents claimed damages from the doctor for pure economic loss, in the form of confinement costs and maintenance of the child until he becomes self-supporting. The Supreme Court of Appeal held that the doctor had a legal duty to desist from making any representation on the matter of sterilization until he had taken reasonable steps to ensure the accuracy of the representation. The factual and policy considerations indicating the existence of such a duty were the following: the special relationship between the doctor and the parents who consulted him; the material risk that the situation involved, that is, the risk of the conception and birth of an unwanted child; the fact that this risk should have been obvious to the mind of the doctor; the fact that it should also have been obvious to the doctor that the parents would rely on what he told them, and that the correctness of the representation was of vital importance to them, and that that they could suffer serious damage if the representation was incorrect; and the fact that the representation related to technical matters concerning a surgical procedure about which the parents would necessarily be ignorant and the doctor should be knowledgeable. As far as public policy considerations are concerned, the court held that the parents' reasons for wanting the sterilization were socio-economic and family reasons, that were socially acceptable and not *contra bonos mores*. The recognition of a legal duty in this case would not impose too heavy a burden on the doctor: professional people must not act negligently and should not make unsolicited misrepresentations. Through misrepresentation, the doctor therefore had unlawfully caused financial loss to the parents.

165. In *Shell and BPSA Petroleum Refineries (Pty) Ltd v. Osborne Panama SA*[292] the defendant's employee caused damage to a mooring buoy in Durban harbour and that in turn caused economic loss to the charterer of an oil tanker waiting outside the harbour, because of the consequent delay in discharging the cargo and additional liability for charter fees. The court held that the defendant did not owe a legal duty to the plaintiff to avert such economic loss, because it had not been shown that the defendant should have foreseen the possibility of such a loss to the charterer specifically. In the view of the court, this kind of loss was foreseeable only in relation to an unascertained class of potential victims, namely the owners or charterers of all vessels intending the discharge oil at that particular mooring buoy. Only

---

The seller was held liable in delict for negligent misstatement. The court held that negligent misstatement was a recognized cause of action in delict; and that the same principles applied where the misstatement was made in a pre-contractual context.

291. 1999 (3) SA 1065 (SCA).

292. 1980 (3) SA 653 (D).

insofar as the plaintiff-charterer was a member of that unascertained class was its loss reasonably foreseeable. The court was therefore unwilling to recognize a legal duty on the part of the defendant towards one of an unknown number of potential claimants.

166. In *Fourway Haulage v. SA National Roads Agency*,[293] the Supreme Court of Appeal considered a number of policy considerations in deciding on liability for economic loss. A big truck, carrying asbestos dust, was on its way to Durban harbour from a mine in Zimbabwe. The driver negligently caused a collision on a toll road. The truck overturned and spilled its cargo on and around the road. Because of the hazardous nature of asbestos powder, the spillage required extensive cleaning and decontamination operation. As a result, the toll road had to be closed for twenty-four hours, and the Roads Agency lost the revenue that would otherwise have been collected at two nearby toll plazas. The Roads Agency instituted an action in delict against the driver and his employer (Fourway Haulage), for damage suffered in the form of lost toll revenue for twenty-four hours.

The court accepted that liability will more readily be imposed for a single loss of a single identifiable plaintiff occurring but once and which is unlikely to bring in its train a multiplicity of actions, but held that in this case the loss claimed was suffered by a single plaintiff and was finite in its extent. But the absence of indeterminate liability itself will not automatically give rise to the imposition of liability where, despite the absence of indeterminate liability, the plaintiff was in a position to avoid the risk of the loss by contractual means. In this case, the Roads Agency could, in the court's view, be said to be 'vulnerable' to the risk of the loss that eventuated, because it could not readily protect itself against that risk by concluding a contract with every user of the toll road. Another policy factor taken into account was whether the extension of delictual liability would impose an additional burden on the defendant which would be unwarranted or which would constitute an unjustified limitation of the defendant's activities. The court decided that this was not so, because Fourway's driver was already under an obligation towards other users of the road to drive with reasonable care. Imposing liability on him – and his employer – for economic loss resulting from his negligent driving would thus not foist any additional burden upon him at all. Finally, Fourway Haulage argued that it should not be saddled with the Roads Agency's loss because it would be more appropriate to spread the burden by increasing toll fees in order to accommodate losses of this kind. The court did not agree with this argument and saw no reason why innocent users of the toll road should effectively be held responsible for the negligent conduct of Fourway's employee. Spreading the loss more widely might alleviate the burden imposed upon the individual innocent motorist, but it did not detract from the principle that it would cause prejudice to the innocent in favour of the negligent driver.

167. In *Franschhoekse Wynkelder (Ko-operatief) Bpk v. South African Railways and Harbours*[294] the plaintiff, a wine-making co-operative, instituted an action for

293. 2009 (2) SA 150 (SCA), at paras 23–27.
294. 1981 (3) SA 36 (C).

damages against the defendant, the South African Railways and Harbours, arising out of the spraying, by defendant, of the undergrowth alongside one of its railway lines with a weed killer. This had contaminated the soil in vineyards of farms adjoining the railway line. The owners of these farms were members of the co-operative, and in terms of its constitution the members were obliged to deliver grapes to plaintiff for the purpose of making wine. The plaintiff alleged that vines growing on the contaminated soil were destroyed or damaged, and that, as a result, the plaintiff would not receive grapes from such farms, causing plaintiff damage, which was alleged to have been foreseeable. Defendant excepted to the claim on the ground, *inter alia*, that it was not in law liable to plaintiff for any damage, because defendant's conduct was not unlawful vis-à-vis plaintiff. The court held that it had not been alleged by plaintiff that there was any special relationship between the parties; and no circumstances or facts alleged by plaintiff allowed the conclusion that defendant had a legal duty to prevent harm to the plaintiff. There were also no considerations of public policy that justified the recognition of such a legal duty and the exception was therefore upheld.

168. The reasoning of the courts when dealing with an alleged breach of a legal duty to prevent pure economic loss to another often involves one or more of the following legal, factual and policy questions:

- Did a special relationship between the parties give rise to a legal duty for the defendant to prevent economic loss to the plaintiff?[295] A relationship of trust or authority or a long-standing business relationship can give rise to such a duty.[296] A contractual relationship between the parties is also an example of a special relationship that can give rise to delictual liability for causing pure economic loss. For instance, a person engaged in pre-contractual negotiations with another has a legal duty not to make a misstatement; and the breach of such a duty can lead to delictual liability for the economic loss caused by a negligent misstatement.[297] As far as liability for damages is concerned, the effect of finding that a legal duty not to make a misstatement existed in delict is practically the same as finding that the statement was a contractual warranty, that is, that the person who made the statement was assuming contractual responsibility for its correctness. If there is no such contractual warranty, and therefore no remedies for breach of contract, the contractual relationship can nevertheless for the purposes of the law of delict entail a legal duty to furnish correct information concerning a matter arising from

295. *See Franschhoekse Wynkelder (Ko-operatief) Bpk v. South African Railways and Harbours* 1981 (3) SA 36 (C); *Mukheiber v. Raath* 1999 (SCA) para. 28.
296. *Bowley Steels (Pty) Ltd v. Dalian Engineering (Pty) Ltd* 1996 (2) SA 393 (T).
297. *Bayer South Africa (Pty) Ltd v. Frost* 1991 (4) SA 559 (A).

the contract or relating to its implementation.[298] The law of delict can thus intervene in a contractual relationship to provide compensation for the financial loss suffered as a result of misinformation.[299]

- Was a duty to prevent economic loss provided for or implied by a statutory provision? The existence of such a statutory duty will be determined according to the normal rules of statutory interpretation, with regard to the intention of the legislature as it appears from the wording of the statutory provision.[300] For instance, a statutory duty to provide correct information could indicate that the failure to provide information or the furnishing of incorrect information is unlawful.[301] The assessment of unlawfulness in the case of breach of a statutory duty is discussed in more detail below.
- What is the extent of the economic loss caused? Where one person furthers his own interests at the cost of harm to another, the extent of the harm will be a factor in the assessment of unlawfulness.[302]
- What is the social or economic value or purpose of the conduct causing the economic loss? It may be reasonable to cause a measure of loss to another if this is an inevitable result of protecting one's own substantially more valuable interests.[303] This is the policy consideration underlying the recognition of necessity as a ground of justification in the law of delict.[304]

---

298. Cf. *Herschel v. Mrupe* 1954 (3) SA 464 (A) 490; *Administrateur, Natal v. Bijo* 1978 (2) SA 256 (N) 261; *Western Alarm System (Pty) Ltd v. Coini and Co.* 1944 CPD 271 276; *Bayer South Africa (Pty) Ltd v. Frost* 1991 (4) SA 559 (A) 575; and *McCann v. Goodall Group Operations (Pty) Ltd* 1995 (2) SA 718 (C) 726.
299. *See* in this regard *Bayer South Africa (Pty) Ltd v. Frost* 1991 (4) SA 559 (A) 569C-D; and on the concurrence of contractual and delictual actions in respect of negligent misrepresentation, *see* M.M. Loubser, *Concurrence of Contract and Delict*, 2 Stell L. Rev. 146–147 (1997).
300. *See* for instance *Knop v. Johannesburg City Council* 1995 (2) SA 1 (A), where it was held that a local authority charged with the implementation of zoning provisions did not have a duty to prevent economic loss to a person who incurred wasted costs when his application for permission to subdivide property was granted, but it then later appeared that the permission was in contravention of an existing zoning plan. *See also Minister of Law and Order v. Kadir* 1995 (1) SA 303 (A) 319 where policemen investigated the scene of an accident caused by a package falling off a delivery vehicle, the driver of which had driven on without stopping. The policemen failed to obtain the names and addresses of possible witnesses before these people left the scene of the accident. The court held that the policemen did not have a legal duty towards the victim of the accident, who was later unable to institute a civil claim for damages against the possibly negligent and unknown driver of the vehicle. The police had a statutory duty in terms of s. 5 of the Police Act 7 of 1958 to deter crimes, track down criminals and protect the public against crimes. However, Hefer JA stared at 321: 'Viewing the matter objectively, society will take account of the fact that that the function of the police relate in terms of the Act to criminal matters and were not designed for the purpose of assisting civil litigants.' This decision is criticized by Burchell in 1995 S. African L. J. 214–216.
301. *See Herschel v. Mrupe* 1954 (3) SA 464 (A) 490; *International Shipping Co. (Pty) Ltd v. Bentley* 1990 (1) SA 680 (A) 694.
302. *See* for instance *Gien v. Gien, supra*, where the extent of the nuisance caused to a neighbouring landowner was taken into account; and *Mpongwana v. Minister of Safety and Security* 1999 (2) SA 794 (CPD) 803-4, where the seriousness of the plaintiff's injury was taken into account as one of the factors in the overall assessment of unlawfulness.
303. *See* for instance *Gien v. Gien, supra*, where the purpose served by using a noise emitting apparatus, i.e., to protect crops from animals and birds, was weighed up against the nuisance caused by the apparatus to a neighbour.
304. *See* Part IV, Ch. 2, §3 below.

- Did the defendant know or foresee that his conduct could cause the economic loss; or, even more unreasonable, did he have the motive to cause economic loss? Prior knowledge or foresight of the possibility of harm makes the causing of that harm more unreasonable. The degree or extent of the risk of harm will in turn be a factor in determining the defendant had knowledge or foresight of the possibility of harm. However, the existence of knowledge, foresight or motive is not conclusive in determining unlawfulness and will be taken into account together with other factors.[305] The question here is only knowledge or foresight, not whether the defendant had intention to cause the harm; nor whether the harm was reasonably foreseeable and preventable and therefore negligently caused: these questions are dealt with in the process of determining fault, in the form of either intention or negligence.[306]
- Was the conduct causing the economic loss fraudulent or dishonest? Where one person furthers his own interests at the cost of harm to another, the existence of fraud or dishonesty makes the causing of harm more unreasonable.[307]

---

305. *See* for instance *Coronation Brick (Pty) Ltd v. Strachan Construction Co. (Pty) Ltd* 1982 (4) SA 371 (D) 386–387, where knowledge of the existence of an underground cable was taken into account in deciding whether economic loss was unlawfully caused by cutting the cable; *Shell and BPSA Petroleum Refineries (Pty) Ltd v. Osborne Panama SA* 1980 (3) SA 653 (D) 659, where damage to a mooring buoy in Durban harbour caused economic loss to the charterer of an oil tanker because of the consequent delay in offloading the cargo, but liability was not imposed because it had not been shown that the defendant did foresee or should have foreseen the possibility of loss (on account of delay and liability for demurrage) to the charterer specifically, this kind of loss being foreseeable only in relation to an unascertained class of potential victims, namely the owners or charterers of all vessels intending the discharge oil at that particular mooring buoy; and only insofar as the plaintiff-charterer was a member of that unascertained class was its loss reasonably foreseeable; *Arthur E Abrahams and Gross v. Cohen* 1991 (2) SA 301 (C) 311, where the professional administrators of a deceased estate were held to have unlawfully caused loss to the beneficiaries of an insurance policy that was an asset in the estate, by failing to collect the proceeds of the policy timeously, while knowing who the beneficiaries were and that they would suffer loss as a result of delay; *Indac Electronics (Pty) Ltd v. Volkskas Bank Ltd* 1992 (1) SA 783 (A) 799, where the liability of a collecting bank to the true owner of a cheque was in issue; and the court held that there is a need for protection of the true owner of a cheque that was incorrectly collected and credited; particularly because the true owner relies on the collecting banker to look at the named payee on the face of the cheque before collecting and crediting the proceeds to an account; and the collecting banker undertaking this responsibility in the course of his professional services is or should be aware that the failure to take reasonable care may result in loss to the true owner of the cheque; and *Delphisure Group Insurance Brokers Cape (Pty) Ltd v. Kotzé and Others* [2011] 1 All SA 109 (SCA) paras [23]–[26], where incorrect crop insurance information was provided by an insurance broker to a specific group of farmers. In respect of the role of motive to cause harm, *see* para. 120 above. *See also Mukheiber v. Raath* 1999 (SCA) para. 28.
306. The distinction between taking into account the defendant's state of mind as a factor relating to unlawfulness and taking it into account for the purpose of determining fault is not always clearly made by the courts, see for instance the reference to reasonable foreseeability in *Shell and BP SA Petroleum Refineries (Pty) Ltd v. Osborne Panama SA* 1980 (3) SA 653 (D) 659, as paraphrased in the previous footnote. In *MTO Forestry (Pty) Ltd v. Swart NO* 2017 (5) SA 76 (SCA) the Supreme Court of Appeal held that foreseeability of harm should not be considered in determining wrongfulness, but should be confined to rubrics of negligence and causation.
307. *See Schultz v. Butt* 1986 (3) SA 667 (A), where the respondent's dishonesty in not only copying a design, but also registering it in his own name, was taken into account by the court in its finding that he had acted unlawfully towards the applicant.

- What practical measures could be taken to avert the economic loss? The courts have regard to the probable success, the relative ease and the expense of practical steps that the defendant could have taken to avert the loss.[308] The ability or lack of ability of the plaintiff to protect himself against the economic loss is also taken into account.[309]
- Was the economic loss caused in the course of rendering professional services and was there a failure of professional competence or skill? Where the defendant renders professional services and professes to possess special skills, special or exclusive knowledge or professional competence the courts will more readily accept that it is unreasonable to cause economic loss to a person depending on the defendant's professional competence or relying on the correctness of information furnished in a professional capacity.[310]
- Was the economic loss caused by a person holding a public office, such as that of notary, sworn appraiser or auditor. Such a person has 'a kind of patent of credibility and efficiency conferred upon him by public authority' and members of the public are 'invited and entitled to repose confidence and trust in the acts of such persons performed in their respective capacities'.[311]
- What are the legal, social and economic implications of imposing liability for the infringement? Are other public policy considerations relevant to the case? The

---

308. *See* for instance *Coronation Brick (Pty) Ltd v. Strachan Construction Co. (Pty) Ltd* 1982 (4) SA 371 (D) 384, where the court took into account that a contractor who knew of the existence of an underground cable could have taken steps to prevent the cutting of the cable; and *Arthur E Abrahams and Gross v. Cohen* 1991 (2) SA 301 (C) 311, where the professional administrators of a deceased estate could easily have taken steps timeously to collect the proceeds of an insurance policy that was an asset in the estate, thereby preventing loss to the beneficiaries.
309. *See Indac Electronics (Pty) Ltd v. Volkskas Bank Ltd* 1992 (1) SA 783 (A) 799, where the liability of a collecting bank towards the true owner of a cheque was in issue and where the court took note of the ability of the bank to protect itself against liability by obtaining insurance cover.
310. *See Indac Electronics (Pty) Ltd v. Volkskas Bank Ltd* 1992 (1) SA 783 (A) 799, where it was held that a collecting banker undertakes a professional responsibility towards the true owner of a cheque to collect and credit the proceeds of the cheque for the benefit of the payee; and *see* further. In *EG Electric Co. (Pty) Ltd v. Franklin* 1979 (2) SA 702 (E) where the court recognized that a registered electrician, who on instructions of the seller of a house had supplied a certificate that the electrical wiring of the house complied with municipal regulations, owed a legal duty to the purchaser of the house who had relied on the correctness of the certificate and later had to incur costs to rectify defective wiring. *See also Herschel v. Mrupe* 1954 (3) SA 464 (A) 472; *Currie Motors (Pretoria) (Pty) Ltd v. Motor Union Ins Co. Ltd* 1961 (3) SA 872 (T) 876-7; *Siman and Co. (Pty) Ltd v. Barclays National Bank Ltd* 1984 (2) SA 888 (A) 913; *Lillicrap, Wassenaar and Partners v. Pilkington Brothers (SA) (Pty) Ltd* 1985 (1) SA 448 (A) 509; *Bayer South Africa (Pty) Ltd v. Frost* 1991 (4) SA 559 (A) 575; *Standard Chartered Bank of Canada v. Nedperm Bank Ltd* 1994 (4) SA 747 (A) 770; *McCann v. Goodall Group Operations (Pty) Ltd* 1995 (2) SA 718 (C) 726 727; *Jowell v. Bramwell-Jones* 1998 (1) SA 836 (W) 882; *Mukheiber v. Raath.* 1999 (3) SA 1065 (SCA) para. 28; *Viv's Tippers (Edms) Bpk v. Pha Phama Staff Services (Edms) Bpk t/a Pha Phama Security [2011] 1 All SA 34 (SCA)* paras [8], [21].
311. *Herschel v. Mrupe* 1954 (3) SA 464 (A) 488; *Perlman v. Zoutendyk* 1934 CPD 151 328.

courts shy away from imposing liability, for instance, where neither the economic loss nor the number of persons affected are finite and the recognition of liability raises the spectre of indeterminate liability to an indeterminate class of persons.[312]

– In *Country Cloud Trading CC v. MEC, Department of Infrastructure Development*[313] the Department of Infrastructure Development entered into a building contract with iLima. When the project ran into difficulties iLima borrowed ZAR 12 million from Country Cloud. The loan agreement was subject to the condition that the Department would repay Country Cloud's ZAR 12 million out of the amount payable by the Department to iLima in terms of the building contract. The Department later cancelled the building contract, thereby committing breach of contract, and this resulted in iLima's liquidation and a loss to Country Cloud, who then sued the Department in delict. The central issue was whether the Department had wrongfully caused harm to Country Cloud. Country Cloud's claim was for pure economic harm and it could not show that the Department had wrongfully infringed its rights or had a legal duty not to cause it economic harm. Country Cloud relied on State accountability, but this consideration does not always give rise to a private law duty, particularly if, as in this case, the Department did not act dishonestly or corruptly. Also, Country Cloud could have attempted to take steps to protect itself against non-payment by iLima, by claiming repayment from iLima's liquidator under the loan agreement, or taking cession of iLima's claim for breach of contract against the Department, or by calling for payment from a surety.

Not all economic interests are protected by the law of delict. To determine whether an unlawful infringement of a protected interest occurred, the courts focus on the existence of a legal duty not to cause economic loss, and this involves a value judgment based on factual and policy considerations as set out above.

XIII. Liability for Omissions, Including Omissions by Public Bodies or Officials

169. Liability for an omission involves an inquiry into the existence of a legal duty to prevent the harm. There is no general right to be protected from harm by others and, conversely, no general legal duty to act positively to prevent harm to

312. *See Shell and BP SA Petroleum Refineries (Pty) Ltd v. Osborne Panama SA* 1980 (3) SA 653 (D) 659–660; *Franschhoekse Wynkelder (Ko-operatief) Bpk v. South African Railways and Harbours* 1981 (3) SA 36 (C); and *Mpongwana v. Minister of Safety and Security* 1999 (2) SA 794 (CPD) 802-3, where the plaintiff based her claim for damages on the failure of the police to protect her from injury resulting from an attack on a taxi in which she was travelling, at a time when a volatile and violent relationship between two rival taxi organizations existed. The court referred to policy considerations such as the implications of holding policemen liable for damages arising from instances of dereliction of duty; and the time, expense and diversion of police manpower involved in defending numerous claims for damages based on alleged police dereliction of duty. *See* further *Mukheiber v. Raath* 1999 (SCA) para. 28.

313. 2015 (1) SA 1 (CC).

others.[314] A duty to act positively to prevent harm is recognized for the purposes of delictual liability only where the failure to act was unreasonable, according to the *boni mores* or the legal convictions of the community.[315] The omission itself is not characterized as unlawful: the focus is on the whole of the causal sequence beginning with the failure to act and ending with the harmful consequences that could have been prevented by positive action.[316] The inquiry into unlawfulness involves an objective and ex post facto judgment based on the criteria of reasonableness, *boni mores* and the legal convictions of the community. The court must weigh up the interests of the persons involved and also take into account the interests and convictions of the community at large.

170. In a line of cases prior to the decision of the Appellate Division in *Minister van Polisie v. Ewels*,[317] the courts adhered to the view that liability for an omission can only be imposed where the prior conduct of the defendant had created a risk of harm or a new source of danger and the defendant then failed to prevent the harm from occurring. This view was first adopted by the Appellate Division in 1912 in *Halliwell v. Johannesburg Municipality.*[318] The *Halliwell* case and similar cases subsequently dealt with the liability of a local authority for injury to a person using a public road or other amenity (hence the reference to these cases as 'municipality cases'). The judgments in these cases often involved subtle distinctions between situations where the defendant simply failed to prevent harm and where such failure was preceded by the creation of a risk of harm or the introduction of a new source of danger. This 'prior conduct' approach to liability for an omission held sway for more than four decades, in spite of criticism in certain judgments.[319]

171. Eventually, the Appellate Division broke away from the 'prior conduct' approach in the leading case of *Minister van Polisie v. Ewels*,[320] where it was held that there can be liability in delict for a mere omission, not preceded by conduct that created a risk of harm or that introduced a new source of danger. In this case, the court imposed liability in a situation where the plaintiff was assaulted by an off-duty policeman in a police station in the presence of a more senior policeman, who failed to prevent the assault. The decision of the Appellate Division in the *Ewels*

---

314. *Minister van Polisie v. Ewels* 1975 (3) SA 590 (A) 596; *Nkumbi v. Minister of Law and Order* 1991 (3) SA 29 (E) 35; *Macadamia Finance Ltd v. De Wet* 1991 (4) SA 273 (T) 278.
315. *See Minister van Polisie v. Ewels* 1975 (3) SA 590 (A) 596-7; *Administrateur, Natal v. Trust Bank van Afrika Bpk* 1979 (3) SA 824 (A) 833-4; *Lillicrap, Wassenaar and Partners v. Pilkington Brothers (SA) (Pty) Ltd* 1985 (1) SA 448 (A) 498; *Nkumbi v. Minister of Law and Order* 1991 (3) SA 29 (E) 35; *Macadamia Finance Ltd v. De Wet* 1991 (4) SA 273 (T) 278; *Kadir v. Minister of Law and Order* 1992 (3) SA 737 (C) 740; *McCann v. Goodall Group Operations (Pty) Ltd* 1995 (2) SA 718 (C) 722-3; *Administrateur Transvaal v. Van der Merwe* 1994 ($) SA 347 (A) 358; *Mukheiber v. Raath* 1999 (3) SA 1065 (SCA) para. 26.
316. *Mukheiber v. Raath* 1999 (3) SA 1065 (SCA) para. 25.
317. 1975 (3) SA 590 (A).
318. 1912 AD 659.
319. *See Silva's Fishing Corporation (Pry) Ltd v. Maweza* 1957 (2) SA 256 (A) 264-5. *See also Regal v. African Superslate (Pty) Ltd* 1963 (1) SA 102 (A); and *Minister of Forestry v. Quathlamba (Pty) Ltd* 1973 (3) SA 69 (A) 82.
320. 1975 (3) SA 590 (A).

case has been of great significance, not only in respect of liability for omissions, but also in respect of the criteria for assessment of unlawfulness generally.[321]

172. Following the *Ewels* case, the courts regard the essential question to be whether a legal duty existed to prevent harm to others, on the basis of reasonableness and public policy. In terms of the wide and evaluative criteria used by the courts in this regard, a legal duty will be recognized where the failure to prevent harm not only evokes moral indignation, but is regarded as so unreasonable, according to the *boni mores* or legal convictions of the community, that it should be regarded as unlawful, so that liability should be imposed for the loss suffered.[322] In addition to these wide and general criteria, the courts take into account policy considerations indicating whether the law of delict should intervene (*inter alia* the social or economic consequences of imposing liability; the availability of alternative remedies; and the need for accountability of public bodies or officials) relevant constitutional or other statutory rights and duties; and a typology of factual circumstances that indicate a duty not to cause or to prevent harm in the particular situation.

173. The 'prior conduct' approach to liability of local authorities for omissions was finally discarded in *Cape Town Municipality v. Bakkerud*,[323] where the general criterion of reasonableness – involving the policy-based standard of *boni mores* or legal convictions of the community – was accepted. Specific content is given to this general criterion by taking into account a typology of factual considerations, such as the extent of the danger, the period of time for which it existed, the resources of the public authority and prior warning. The typology of factual considerations relevant to the wrongfulness inquiry will for the most part also be relevant to the negligence inquiry. The need to prove both the existence of a legal duty to prevent harm and negligence limits claims against public authorities.

174. Mostert v. Cape Town City Council, a case involving a damaging leak from the defendant's water main, illustrate the factors relevant in cases involving local authorities. Weighing the technical evidence as to the likelihood of collapse of the pipeline against the high cost of replacement, the court judged that it could not reasonably have been expected of the council to replace the pipe. The conduct of the city council was therefore found not to have been negligent. Noting that 'an unbending adherence to logic'[324] might dictate that wrongfulness is the prior inquiry, and the reasonableness of requiring the council to replace the pipeline might also have been dealt with under that heading, Schutz JA remarked that logic is one thing, utility sometimes another. In many if not most delicts involving property damage or

321. *See Van der Merwe Burger v. Munisipaliteit van Warrenton* 1987 (1) SA 899 (C), *Rabie v. Kimberley Munisipaliteit* 1991 (4) SA 243 (NC) 258; *Cape Town Municipality v. Butters* 1996 (1) SA 473 (C) 477 479–480; *Longueira v. Securitas of South Africa (Pty) Ltd* 1998 (4) SA 258 (W) 262-3.

322. *See Minister van Polisie v. Ewels* 1975 (3) SA 590 (A) at 597.

323. 2000 (3) SA 1049 (SCA).

324. Per Schutz JA at 120–121.

injury the issue of unlawfulness is uncontentious, as the action is founded upon conduct which, if held to be culpable, would be prima facie wrongful.[325] This was such a case. If the council was negligent in not preventing the burst of the pipe, the test for wrongfulness – the general, policy-based criterion of reasonableness, or the community's sense of what the law ought to be – would have been met, and liability would be imposed upon the council.

175. The reasoning of the courts in cases involving an alleged breach of a legal duty to act positively to prevent harm to others often involves one or more of the following factual and policy considerations:

- Did prior conduct of the defendant create a risk of harm and therefore also the duty to prevent such harm? Prior conduct creating a risk of harm or a new source of danger is no longer a requirement for liability based on an omission, as shown above, but such prior conduct is still an important factor indicating the existence of a duty to act positively to prevent harm to another.[326]
- Did the defendant have control over a dangerous or potentially dangerous object? Control may be actually exercised, or the right, obligation or ability to exercise control may flow from rights of ownership or possession or from an agreement or statutory provision. For instance, the fact that a provincial administration exercises control and supervision over all public roads in the province in terms of a statutory provision is an important factor in determining whether the administration had a legal duty to prevent the spreading of a fire that had started on the side of a minor public road.[327] The actual exercise of control, or the right, obligation or ability to exercise control is not in itself conclusive, but it is an important factor indicating the existence of a legal duty in respect of a particular occurrence of harm.[328] The degree and scope of the control that is required cannot be laid down generally, but should be determined on the basis of all the facts of the particular case and with reference to the harm that occurred. The essential question is whether precautionary measures could be reasonably and practicably required of the person or body in control in respect of the harm that occurred.[329] The owner, occupier or person in control of property generally has a duty to control fire on

325. P.Q.R. Boberg, *Law of Delict* at 32 says in this regard: 'it is settled law that all harm to person or property caused by a positive act is prima facie wrongful'.
326. *See Minister van Polisie v. Ewels* 1975 (3) SA 590 (A) 597. In *Administrateur Transvaal v. Van der Merwe* 1994 (4) SA 347 (A) 349 it is stated that, in the absence of a positive danger-creating act, the provincial authority with control over a minor road does not necessarily have a legal duty to prevent the spreading of a fire that started alongside the road. In *Local Transitional Council of Delmas and Another v. Boshoff* 2005 (5) SA 514 (SCA), the court accepted that a local authority who set up and administered an informal settlement adjacent to the plaintiff's land had a legal duty towards the owner of the adjacent land, and could not claim immunity from liability for his losses.
327. *Administrateur Transvaal v. Van der Merwe* 1994 (4) SA 347 (A).
328. *Administrateur Transvaal v. Van der Merwe* 1994 (4) SA 347 (A) 359 360; *Local Transitional Council of Delmas and Another v. Boshoff* 2005 (5) SA 514 (SCA).
329. *Administrateur Transvaal v. Van der Merwe* 1994 (4) SA 347 (A) 359–360; *Faiga v. Body Corporate of Dumbarton Oaks* 1997 (2) SA 651 (W) 665; *Kritzinger v. Steyn* 1997 (3) SA 686 (C).

the property[330] and to prevent injury to persons, even trespassers on the property;[331] and the same applies to the owner or person in control of a firearm[332] or an animal.[333] Teachers in charge of schoolchildren on an excursion have a duty to ensure that bunk beds in a bungalow with a cement floor are safe for young children to sleep in.[334] Did the defendant have an obligation in terms of a rule of common law or statute law to act positively to prevent harm to others? For instance, the owner of lower land is obliged to provide lateral support for the higher land of his neighbour;[335] and is generally required of an owner to prevent that harmful substances flow or otherwise escape from his property to neighbouring land.[336] The existence of a statutory duty will be determined according to the normal rules of statutory interpretation, with regard to the intention of the legislature as it appears from the wording of the statutory provision.[337] For instance, a statutory

330. *See Minister of Forestry v. Quathlamba (Pty) Ltd* 1973 (3) SA 69 (A); *Steenberg v. De Kaap Timber (Pty) Ltd* 192 (2) SA 169 (A); *Dews v. Simon's Town Municipality* 1991 (4) SA 479 (C) 485; *Gouda Boerdery BK v. Transnet* 2005 (5) SA 490 (SCA) para. 13; *Minister of Water Affairs and Forestry and Others v. Durr and Others* 2006 (6) SA 587 (SCA) paras 12–13, 17.
331. *See Kritzinger v. Steyn* 1997 (3) SA 686 (C), where it was held that an owner does not generally have a duty towards trespassers, whose presence are not reasonably foreseeable.
332. *See Maylett v. Du Toit* 1989 (1) SA 90 (T).
333. *See Kruger v. Coetzee* 1966 (2) SA 428 (A); *S v. Fernandez* 1966 (2) SA 259 (A); *R v. Eustace (2)* 1948 (3) SA 859 (T); *Bristow v. Lycett* 1971 (4) SA 223 (RA); *Zietsman v. Van Tonder* 1989 (2) SA 484 (T).
334. *Hawekwa Youth Camp and Another v. Byrne* [2010] 2 All SA 312 (SCA).
335. *See D and D Deliveries (Pty) Ltd v. Pinetown Borough* 1991 (3) SA 250 (D) 253; *John Newmark and Co. (Pty) Ltd v. Durban City Council* 1959 (1) SA 169 (D); *Gijzen v. Verrinder* 1965 (1) SA 806 (D).
336. *See Regal v. African Superslate (Pty) Ltd* 1963 (1) SA 102 (A) 109, where this general duty was acknowledged, but liability was not imposed, because the circumstances would have required the owner to erect costly weir in a river to prevent some harm to land downstream during flooding of the river.
337. In *Minister van Polisie v. Ewels* 1975 (3) SA 590 (A) 595-6 the Appellate Division held that the failure by a policemen in a specific instance to carry out his duties as set out in s. 5 of the Police Act 7 of 1958, namely to maintain law and order and to prevent and investigate crime, did not mean that such a breach of duty necessarily constituted unlawfulness for the purposes of delictual liability. *See also Nkumbi v. Minister of Law and Order* 1991 (3) SA 29 (E) 34-5. In *Administrateur Transvaal v. Van der Merwe* 1994 (4) SA 347 (A), a farmer claimed damages from the provincial administration for failure to prevent the spreading of a fire from the side of a road onto his land. Section 4 of the Roads Ordinance 22 of 1957 provides that '(a)ll public roads within the province shall be under the control and supervision of the Administrator'. The court held that the control and supervision of the Administrator over all public roads is only of a permissive nature. The ordinance confers certain powers on the Administrator, for example the making and maintenance of public roads, the installation of traffic signs etc. It does not impose any obligations on the Administrator in respect of the making of firebreaks or the taking of other precautionary measures against veld fires breaking out and spreading to the land of others (*see* at 359H–J). In *Knop v. Johannesburg City Council* 1995 (2) SA 1 (A), it was held that a local authority charged with the implementation of zoning provisions did not have a duty to prevent economic loss to a person who incurred wasted costs when his application for permission to subdivide property was granted, but it then later appeared that the permission was in contravention of an existing zoning plan. *See also Minister of Law and Order v. Kadir* 1995 (1) SA 303 (A) 319 where policemen investigated the scene of an accident caused by a package falling off a delivery vehicle, the driver of which had driven on without stopping. The policemen failed to obtain the name and address of the driver. The court held that the policemen did not have a legal duty towards the victim of the accident, who was later unable to institute a civil claim for damages against the possibly negligent and unknown driver of the

duty to provide correct information could indicate that the failure to provide information is unlawful for the purposes of the law of delict.[338]

- Did a special relationship between the parties give rise to a legal duty for the defendant to prevent harm to the plaintiff?[339] The mere fact of such a special relationship is not conclusive, but it will be an important factor indicating a legal duty to prevent harm and will be considered along with all the other circumstances of the case. A relationship of trust or authority or a long-standing business relationship can give rise to such a duty.[340] A contractual relationship can likewise give rise to duty to prevent harm to the other party or to the contract or a third party.[341] Other examples are the relationship between a policeman and a member of the public,[342] a prison officer and a prisoner[343] and an employer and his employee.[344]
- Did the defendant create the expectation that he would protect the interests of the plaintiff? For instance, a security firm that has undertaken to provide security services for an office building or parking garage, in terms of a contract with the owner, may have a legal duty toward third parties who rely on the security services for protection of their person or property.[345] The creation of such an expectation is not conclusive, and the court will take into account whether the plaintiff could reasonably have relied on the security services for protection and also all the other circumstances of the case.[346]

---

vehicle. The police had a statutory duty in terms of s. 5 of the Police Act 7 of 1958 to deter crimes, track down criminals and protect the public against crimes. However, Hefer JA stared at 321: 'Viewing the matter objectively, society will take account of the fact that that the function of the police relate in terms of the Act to criminal matters and were not designed for the purpose of assisting civil litigants.' This decision is criticized by Burchell in 1995 S. African L. J. 214–216.

338. *See Herschel v. Mrupe* 1954 (3) SA 464 (A) 490; *Da Silva v. Coutinho* 1971 (3) SA 123 (A) 140; *International Shipping Co. (Pty) Ltd v. Bentley* 1990 (1) SA 680 (A) 694.
339. *See Franschhoekse Wynkelder (Ko-operatief) Bpk v. South African Railways and Harbours* 1981 (3) SA 36 (C); *Mukheiber v. Raath* 1999 (SCA) para. 28.
340. *See Jowell v. Bramwell-Jones* 1998 (1) SA 836 (W), concerning the duty of trustees towards the beneficiaries of the trust; and *Arthur E Abrahams and Gross v. Cohen* 1991 (2) SA 301 (C) 311, where it was held that the professional administrators of a deceased estate had a duty to prevent financial loss to the beneficiaries in the estate; and *see Bowley Streels (Pty) Ltd v. Dalian Engineering (Pty) Ltd* 1996 (2) SA 393 (T), concerning a long-standing business relationship and the duty to disclose the sale of the business.
341. *See Greenfield Engineering Works (Pty) Ltd v. NKR Construction (Pty) Ltd* 1978 (4) SA 901 (N); *Bayer South Africa (Pty) Ltd v. Frost* 1991 (4) SA 575 (A); *Cathkin Park Hotel v. JD Makesch Architects* 1993 (2) SA 98 (W) 100; *McCann v. Goodall Group Operations (Pty) Ltd* 1995 (2) SA 718 (C) 726 727: *Joubert v. Impala Platinum* 1998 (1) SA 463 (BHC).
342. *Minister van Polisie v. Ewels* 1975 (3) SA 590 (A).
343. *Mtati v. Minister of Justice* 1958 (1) SA 221 (A).
344. *Joubert v. Impala Platinum* 1998 (1) SA 463 (BHC).
345. *See Compass Motors Industries (Pty) Ltd v. Callguard (Pty) Ltd* 1990 (2) SA 520 (W).
346. *See* the remarks in *Longueira v. Securitas of South Africa (Pty) Ltd* 1998 (4) SA 259 (W) 261–262; and *see Viv's Tippers (Edms) Bpk v. Pha Phama Staff Services (Edms) Bpk t/a Pha Phama Security* (2010) 4 SA 455 (HHA).

- Did the defendant know or foresee that his conduct could cause the harm; or, even more unreasonable, did he have the motive to cause harm? Prior knowledge or foresight of the possibility of harm makes the causing of that harm more unreasonable.[347]
- What practical measures could be taken to avert the harm? The courts have regard to the probable success and the relative ease and expense of practical steps that the defendant could have taken to avert the loss.[348] The ability or lack of ability of the plaintiff to protect himself against the harm is also taken into account.[349]
- Did the failure to prevent harm occur in the course of rendering professional services and was there a failure of professional competence or skill?[350]
- Did a person holding a public office, such as that of notary, sworn appraiser or auditor, fail to prevent harm in the course of his official duties?[351]
- What are the legal, social and economic implications of imposing liability for the infringement? Are other public policy considerations relevant to the case?[352]

---

347. *See Van der Merwe Burger v. Munisipaliteit van Warrenton* 1987 (1) SA 899 (C) 908, where the court stated that knowledge on the part of a municipality of a dangerous situation within its area of authority may burden it with a duty to prevent harm, even though the municipality did not create a risk of harm by prior conduct. In *Rabie v. Kimberley Munisipaliteit* 1991 (4) SA 243 (NC), the fact that the municipality had been aware that a traffic light was malfunctioning, but failed to investigate and repair it, resulted in liability. *See also Langley Fox Business Partnership (Pty) Ltd v. De Valence* 1991 (1) SA 1 (A), where the liability of a builder in respect of a dangerous condition on a building premises was in issue. The danger had been created by a subcontractor; and in his minority judgment Botha JA considered the essential question to be whether the builder was aware of the dangerous condition created by the subcontractor.
348. *See Regal v. African Superslate (Pty) Ltd* 1963 (1) SA 102 (A) 109, where the court recognized the general duty of a landowner to prevent harmful substances from his land from flowing onto neighbouring land, but liability was not imposed, because the circumstances would have required the owner to erect costly weir in a river to prevent some harm to land downstream during flooding of the river. *See also Coronation Brick (Pty) Ltd v. Strachan Construction Co. (Pty) Ltd* 1982 (4) SA 371 (D) 384, where the court took into account that a contractor who knew of the existence of an underground cable could have taken steps with relative ease to prevent the cutting of the cable: and *Arthur E Abrahams and Gross v. Cohen* 1991 (2) SA 301 (C) 311, where the professional administrators of a deceased estate could easily have taken timely steps to collect the proceeds of an insurance policy that was an asset in the estate, thereby preventing loss to the beneficiaries. *See also Local Transitional Council of Delmas and Another v. Boshoff* 2005 (5) SA 514 (SCA) para. 26.
349. *See Indac Electronics (Pty) Ltd v. Volkskas Bank Ltd* 1992 (1) SA 783 (A) 799, where the liability of a collecting bank towards the true owner of a cheque was in issue and where the court took note of the ability of the bank to protect itself against liability by obtaining insurance cover.
350. *See Arthur E. Abrahams and Gross v. Cohen* 1991 (2) SA 301 (C), concerning professional administrators of a deceased estate; and *Jowell v. Bramwell-Jones* 1998 (1) SA 836 (W), concerning the duty of trustees towards the beneficiaries of the trust.
351. *See* the *Arthur E Abrahams and Gross* and *Jowell* cases referred to in the previous footnote; and *see* further *The Cape of Good Hope Bank v. Fischer* (1886) 4 SC 368, where a Registrar of Deeds was held liable for failing to register a bond in favour of the plaintiff; and *Macadamia Finance Ltd v. De Wet* 1991 (4) SA 273 (T), concerning the failure by liquidators of a company to insure assets of a company under their control.
352. *See Shell and BP SA Petroleum Refineries (Pty) Ltd v. Osborne Panama SA* 1980 (3) SA 653 (D) 659–660; *Franschhoekse Wynkelder (Ko-operatief) Bpk v. South African Railways and Harbours* 1981 (3) SA 36 (C); and *Mpongwana v. Minister of Safety and Security* 1999 (2) SA 794 (CPD) 802–803, where the plaintiff based her claim for damages on the failure of the police to protect her from injury resulting from an attack on a taxi in which she was travelling, at a time when a volatile and violent relationship between two rival taxi organizations existed. The court referred to policy

The factual and policy considerations outlined above serve to give specific content to the general criteria for determining unlawfulness as set out in the *Ewels* case, providing both certainty and flexibility for further judicial development of the law on liability for omissions.[353]

XIV. Breach of a Statutory Duty

176. Where the breach of a statutory duty resulted in harm unlawfulness depends on the content and purpose of the statutory duty and the implications of breach of the duty. It must be determined, according to the rules of statutory interpretation and with regard to the intention of the legislature and the wording and purpose of the statutory provision, whether the breach of duty was unlawful for purposes of delictual liability.

177. According to the judgment in *Knop v. Johannesburg City Council*,[354] a case involving the erroneous granting of an application for subdivision of property by a local authority, the legislative intention is to be ascertained with reference to the nature of the powers conferred, the nature of the duties involved in their exercise, the procedures prescribed for their exercise and for persons aggrieved to obtain redress and the objects sought to be achieved by the legislature. The focus is on the content and purpose of the statutory duty and the implications of breach of the duty, rather than on the infringement of the plaintiff's right. The mere fact that the defendant acted in breach of a statutory duty is not conclusive in respect of unlawfulness for the purposes of delictual liability. Where it is alleged that the breach of a statutory duty caused harm to the plaintiff it must be determined, according to the rules of statutory interpretation and with regard to the intention of the legislature and the wording and purpose of the statutory provision, whether the breach of duty could give rise to a delictual remedy.[355]

---

considerations such as the implications of holding policemen liable for damages arising from instances of dereliction of duty; and the time, expense and diversion of police manpower involved in defending numerous claims for damages based on alleged police dereliction of duty. *See* further *Mukheiber v. Raath* 1999 (3) SA 1065 (SCA) para. 28.

353. *See* generally Dale Hutchison, *Southern Cross Civil Law and Common Law in South Africa*, 627–628 (Zimmerman & Visser eds., Juta & Co. Ltd 1996).

354. 1995 (2) SA 1 (A) 28.

355. In *Minister van Polisie v. Ewels* 1975 (3) SA 590 (A) 595–596, the Appellate Division held that the failure by a policemen in a specific instance to carry out his duties as set out in s. 5 of the Police Act 7 of 1958, namely to maintain law and order and to prevent and investigate crime, did not mean that such a breach of duty necessarily constituted unlawfulness for the purposes of delictual liability. *See also* in this regard *Nkumbi v. Minister of Law and Order* 1991 (3) SA 29 (E) 34–35. In *Administrateur Transvaal v. Van der Merwe* 1994 (4) SA 347 (A), a farmer claimed damages from the provincial administration for failure to prevent the spreading of a fire from the side of a road onto his land. Section 4 of the Roads Ordinance 22 of 1957 provides that '(a)ll public roads within the province shall be under the control and supervision of the Administrator'. The court held that the control and supervision of the Administrator over all public roads is only of a permissive nature. The ordinance confers certain powers on the Administrator, for example the making and maintenance of public roads, the installation of traffic signs, etc. It does not impose any obligations on the Administrator in respect of the making of firebreaks or the taking of other precautionary measures

178. In *Knop v. Johannesburg City Council*,[356] the process of interpretation to determine whether a delictual remedy arises from the breach of a statutory duty or negligent exercise of a statutory power is stated as follows:

> The essence of the plaintiff's claim is that the Council caused him loss by the negligent exercise of a statutory power. The source of the power being statutory, it is necessary to examine the legislation by which it was brought into being, for it is self-evident that the intention of the legislature is an important, and may possibly be a decisive, feature of the circumstances material to the determination of whether or not a legal duty existed. The legislative intention is to be ascertained with reference to the nature of the powers conferred, the nature of the duties involved in their exercise, the procedures prescribed for their exercise and for persons aggrieved by it to obtain redress, and the objects sought to be achieved by the legislature.

In this case, the local authority granted an application for subdivision of a property in error; and then later informed the applicant that the approval could not stand, because it was in conflict with an existing town planning scheme. The applicant claimed damages for losses incurred as a result of the delayed development of the property. The court took into account as a matter of policy that there was an administrative procedure for an aggrieved person to obtain redress in the event of refusal of his application; and that potential liability in delict could unduly hamper the local authority in carrying out its statutory duty to consider and dispose of such applications expeditiously. The application in this case was defective, because it did not comply with the existing town planning scheme; and it was for the applicant to ensure such compliance. In the circumstances, it would be contrary to the objective criterion of reasonableness to hold the local authority liable for damages; and would also offend the legal convictions of the community.[357]

---

against veld fires breaking out and spreading to the land of others. (*See* at 359H–J.) In *Knop v. Johannesburg City Council* 1995 (2) SA 1 (A), it was held that a local authority charged with considering applications for subdivision of property did not unlawfully cause economic loss to a person whose application for subdivision of a property was first granted in error. The local authority then informed the applicant that the approval could not stand, because it was in conflict with an existing town planning scheme. The applicant was unsuccessful with his claim for losses suffered as a result of the delayed development of the property. *See also Minister of Law and Order v. Kadir* 1995 (1) SA 303 (A) 319 where policemen investigated the scene of an accident caused by a package falling off a delivery vehicle, but failed to record the name of the driver and the particulars of the vehicle. This information would have enabled the plaintiff, who was injured in the accident, to claim damages from the driver. The court held that the policemen did not have a legal duty towards the plaintiff to record such information. The police had a statutory duty in terms of s. 5 of the Police Act 7 of 1958 to deter crimes, track down criminals and protect the public against crimes. However, as Hefer JA stared at 321: 'Viewing the matter objectively, society will take account of the fact that that the function of the police relate in terms of the Act to criminal matters and were not designed for the purpose of assisting civil litigants.' This decision is criticized by Burchell in 1995 S. African L. J. 214–216. *See also Lascon Properties (Pty) Ltd v. Wadeville Investment Co. (Pty) Ltd* 1997 (4) SA 578 (W).

356. 1995 (2) SA 1 (A) 28.

357. At 33.

179. In *Da Silva v. Coutinho*,[358] it was held that the owner of a motor vehicle was liable in delict for failing to comply with a statutory duty to provide the plaintiff with a declaration of insurance in respect of the motor vehicle. Compliance with this duty would have enabled the plaintiff, who was injured in an accident involving the motor vehicle, to claim damages from the insurance company concerned. In effect the defendant had therefore unlawfully caused the plaintiff's loss. A statutory duty to provide correct information could indicate that a failure to provide such information, resulting in harm to the plaintiff, is unlawful for the purposes of delictual liability.[359]

180. In the context of unlawful competition, the 'licence' cases deal with the situation where one trader alleges that he is incurring losses as a result of competition from another trader, who does not hold the necessary statutory licence or permit to trade, or who otherwise contravenes a statutory duty or prohibition. In *Patz v. Greene and Co.*,[360] for instance, a trader who conducted business in the vicinity of a mining compound applied for an interdict against a rival trader who traded on claim land, in contravention of a specific statutory prohibition. The court accepted in principle that it is unlawful to cause loss to a rival trader through conduct expressly prohibited by statute.[361]

181. The typical factual and policy considerations that will be taken into account by the courts in deciding whether the breach of a statutory duty will be regarded as unlawful for the purposes of delictual liability, include the following:

> Did the breach of statutory duty cause or materially contribute to the harm?[362] Was the imposition of the statutory duty intended to benefit the plaintiff as one of a specific class of persons?[363] Where the statute was enacted in the public interest and not to protect individual interests, the court may refuse to recognize an action for damages,[364] but may nevertheless grant an interdict.[365] Was

358. 1971 (3) SA 123 (A).
359. *See Herschel v. Mrupe* 1954 (3) SA 464 (A), where the Appellate Division by a majority decision did not impose liability; and *International Shipping Co. (Pty) Ltd v. Bentley* 1990 (1) SA 680 (A) 694.
360. 1907 TS 427.
361. The court nevertheless did not grant the interdict, because the application did not contain all the necessary allegations to found the cause of action.
362. *Da Silva v. Coutinho* 1971 (3) SA 123 (A) 140.
363. If the statutory provision is aimed at protecting the interests of a particular group, the courts have been prepared to accept that the plaintiff need not prove damages; it will be presumed; *see Bedfordview Town Council v. Mansyn Seven (Pty) Ltd* 1989 (4) SA 599 (W) 601–602; *Van den Berg; Schoeman v. Unie en Suidwes-Afrika Verseleringsmaatskappy Bpk* 1989 (4) SA 721 (C) 727–728. Where the statutory provision serves the public interest generally any member of the public will have a remedy (interdict or a claim for damages) if he can prove that he has actually suffered patrimonial loss as a result of the illegal trading; *see United Dairies Co-op Ltd v. Searle* 1974 (4) SA 117 (E) 126; *Bedfordview Town Council v. Mansyn Seven (Pty) Ltd* 1989 (4) SA 599 (W) 601–602; *Van den Berg; Schoeman v. Unie en Suidwes-Afrika Verseleringsmaatskappy Bpk* 1989 (4) SA 721 (C) 727–728. *See also Da Silva v. Coutinho* 1971 (3) SA 123 (A) 140.
364. *Ellis v. Vickerman* 1954 (3) SA 1001 (C).
365. *Herbst v. Ditmar* 1970 (1) SA 238 (T).

the harm suffered by the plaintiff of a kind that the statute intended to guard against?[366] Are alternative procedures or remedies provided for in the statute to aid persons aggrieved by the alleged breach of the statutory duty?[367] Are other sanctions, including criminal sanctions, provided for in the event of breach of the statutory duty? However, where a statute provides for a criminal sanction this does not necessarily exclude a civil remedy.[368] What are the practical implications of recognizing a delictual remedy for breach of the statutory duty; for instance would potential liability hamper a local authority in carrying out its statutory duties,[369] or the police in carrying out their normal duties?[370]

182. In *Lascon Properties (Pty) Ltd v. Wadeville Investment Co. (Pty) Ltd*, where a duty under regulation to prevent the escape of contaminated water was in issue, the court said the following:[371]

> In my view, the regulation was prima facie enacted for the benefit of the owners of land which might be polluted as a result of the actions of a mining company. (See Franklin and Kaplan The Mining and Mineral Laws of South Africa at 169.) This having been the purpose of the regulation, it seems to me that the Legislature would not have imposed an obligation to prevent the escape of noxious water without intending persons harmed thereby to be entitled to be compensated by the person permitting the water to escape. 'For, if it were not so, the statute would be but a pious aspiration' (per *Lord Simonds in Cutler v. Wandsworth Stadium Ltd* [1949] AC 398 (HL) at 407 ([1949] 1 All ER 544 at 548B).

183. In *Premier, Western Cape v. Faircape Property Developers (Pty) Ltd*,[372] the Supreme Court of Appeal confirmed that state officials, including employees of local authorities, and members of government at every level, are accountable for their decisions. They must perform their statutory duties without negligence. Where they do not exercise due care, in circumstances where they owe a duty to members of the public to act responsibly and without causing loss or harm, they should be held liable for the damage that they have caused. However, the specific duties required by the legislation in question should be determined. In this case, which involved the grant of an application to remove restrictive conditions of title from land, there was no duty cast by legislation on the minister to check that the applicant had complied with all the procedures laid down. The minister was required only to satisfy himself that it was desirable, in the interests of the area (*inter alia*), to remove the restrictive conditions of title.

366. *Ibid.*
367. *Knop v. Johannesburg City Council* 1995 (2) SA 1 (A) 33; *Von Moltke v. Costa Areosa (Pty) Ltd* 1975 (1) SA 255 (C).
368. *Da Silva v. Coutinho* 1971 (3) SA 123 (A) 135–138.
369. *Knop v. Johannesburg City Council* 1995 (2) SA 1 (A) 33.
370. *Minister of Law and Order v. Kadir* 1995 (1) SA 303 (A) 318.
371. 1997 (4) SA 578 (W) 583C-D.
372. 2003 (6) SA 13 (SCA).

184. In *Steenkamp NO v. The Provincial Tender Board of the Eastern Cape,*[373] factors relevant to the assessment of unlawfulness, in a case concerning a claim for damages by a successful tenderer whose tender award was later set aside on account of negligence on the part of the tender board, were set out as follows:

> Our courts –*Faircape, Knop, Du Plessis* and *Duivenboden* – and courts in other common law jurisdictions readily recognize that factors that go to wrongfulness would include whether the operative statute anticipates, directly or by inference, compensation of damages for the aggrieved party; whether there are alternative remedies such as an interdict, review or appeal; whether the object of the statutory scheme is mainly to protect individuals or advance public good; whether the statutory power conferred grants the public functionary a discretion in decision-making; whether an imposition of liability for damages is likely to have a 'chilling effect' on performance of administrative or statutory function; whether the party bearing the loss is the author of its misfortune; whether the harm that ensued was foreseeable. It should be kept in mind that in the determination of wrongfulness foreseeability of harm, although ordinarily a standard for negligence, is not irrelevant. The ultimate question is whether on a conspectus of all relevant facts and considerations, public policy and public interest favour holding the conduct unlawful and susceptible to a remedy in damages. [Footnotes omitted.]

185. The question whether the breach of a statutory duty that causes harm is unlawful for the purposes of delictual liability involves a process of statutory interpretation, according to the normal rules of interpretation, but additionally involves a value or policy judgment based on factual and policy considerations as set out above.

§3. Fault

I. General

186. Fault is generally required for delictual liability, in addition to unlawfulness, so that a defendant can be held liable for the wrongful causing of harm only if the harmful conduct was also legally blameworthy. Legal blameworthiness on the part of the defendant is indicated either by a reprehensible state of mind, subjectively determined (intent or *dolus*), or by a lack of proper care, objectively determined (negligence or culpa). Fault in either form can be attributed to a person only if the person is accountable (culpae capax).

187. In general, the principle of 'no liability without fault' applies in the South African law of delict. Despite the dominance of this principle, there are a number of recognized instances of strict liability, as set out below in more detail, in Part II, Chapter 1 (Vicarious Liability) and in Part III (Forms of Strict Liability).

373. [2006] JOL 18364 (CC) para. 42.

188. Certain Roman actions involving strict liability were recognized in Roman-Dutch law and still form part of modern South African law. These actions include the *actio de pauperie* for damage done by domestic animals acting *contra naturam sui generis*, the *actio de pastu* for damage done by grazing animals, and the *actio de effusis vel deiectis* and the *actio positi vel suspensi* for the recovery of damage from the occupier of a building from which something was thrown (*effusis vel deiectis*) or from which something fell down (*positi vel suspensi*).

189. Vicarious liability is a form of transferred liability and fault plays a part, because the employer takes on liability for the wrongdoing of an employee, but only to the extent that the employee was at fault. The general rule is that an employer is vicariously (strictly) liable for the delict of its employee committed in the course and scope of employment. The principles of vicarious liability are set out in detail below, in Part II, Chapter 1.

190. Other instances of strict liability are provided for in legislation, dealt with in Part III, Chapter 5 below, for example damage caused by aircraft,[374] fire caused by rail transport,[375] damage caused by nuclear energy[376] and damage to telecommunication lines.[377]

II. Intent

191. Intent (*dolus* or *animus iniuriandi*) involves the will to cause harm and awareness that the causing of harm is wrongful. In *Dantex Investment Holdings (Pty) Ltd v. Brenner and Others NNO*,[378] the Appellate Division held that 'it is now accepted that *dolus* encompasses not only the intention to achieve a particular result, but also the consciousness that such a result would be wrongful or unlawful'. Intent is determined subjectively and involves a legal conclusion about the state of mind of the defendant at the time of the relevant conduct, concerning the will to cause harm and awareness of the wrongfulness of such causing of harm. Intent is generally a requirement for liability in cases of *iniuria*, that is, delicts involving the infringement of personality rights.

192. In *Le Roux and Others v. Dey*,[379] Harms DP analysed the background and implications of the requirement of consciousness of wrongfulness (coloured intent) and decided that intention for the purposes of the *actio iniuriarum* does not require consciousness of wrongfulness. However, on appeal the Constitutional Court

374. Aviation Act 74 of 1962, s. 11.
375. Clause 2(1) of Schedule 1 of the Legal Succession to the South African Services Act 9 of 1989.
376. Nuclear Energy Act 92 of 1982, s. 41(1).
377. Post Office Act 44 of 1958, s. 108.
378. 1989 (1) SA 390 (A) 396.
379. [2010] ZASCA 41 para. 39.

decided that it was unnecessary for the Supreme Court of Appeal to have decided on this issue, and it was also unnecessary for the Constitutional Court to do so.[380]

193. Intent can take different forms. Direct intent of *dolus* directus is present when the actor directs his will to the attainment of a particular harmful result, with whatever motive, and with awareness that the causing of harm is wrongful. Indirect intent or *dolus* indirectus is present where the actor directs his will to the attainment of a particular harmful result, with whatever motive, while at the same time being aware that another result will inevitably also occur and that the causing of the other result is wrongful. Intent with knowledge of the possibility of a harmful result or *dolus* eventualis is present when the actor directs his will to the attainment of a particular result, harmless or harmful, with whatever motive, while at the same time being aware that another harmful result may possibly also occur and that the causing of the other result is or may possibly be wrongful.[381] The awareness for purposes of *dolus* indirectus and *dolus* eventualis is determined subjectively: the defendant must actually be aware that the other harmful result will inevitably (*dolus* indirectus) or may possibly occur (*dolus* eventualis) and that the causing of such other result is or may possibly be wrongful. In respect of *dolus* eventualis, it is sometimes said that subjective awareness of a possible harmful result in itself is not enough; the defendant must also have 'reconciled' himself or herself with the occurrence of such a result or must have acted with a reckless disregard of the foreseen possible consequences. This essentially means that the defendant acted with awareness that the harmful result might possibly occur, and that it cannot be written off as an unlikely possibility. Lack of such awareness in circumstances where a reasonable person would have been aware might constitute negligence.

In *Director of Public Prosecutions, Gauteng v. Pistorius*[382] Pistorius had shot and killed his girlfriend Reeva through a toilet cubicle door when he allegedly mistook her for a thief. The court a quo found Pistorius guilty of culpable homicide and held that he could not be convicted of murder, as dolus had not been proved. On appeal, the Supreme Court of Appeal considered especially whether dolus in the form of dolus eventualis had been present, for if it had been, Pistorius should have been found guilty of murder instead of culpable homicide. The court stated:[383]

> In contrast to dolus directus, in a case of murder where the object and purpose of the perpetrator is specifically to cause death, a person's intention in the form of dolus eventualis arises if the perpetrator foresees the risk of death occurring, but nevertheless continues to act appreciating that death might well occur, therefore 'gambling' as it were with the life of the person against whom the act

---

380. *Le Roux and Others v. Dey (Freedom of Expression Institute and Restorative Justice Centre as amici curiae)* 2011 (3) SA 274 (CC) para. 137.
381. In *Frankel Pollak Vinderine Inc v. Stanton* 2000 (1) SA 425 (W) 438. Wunsh J said: '*Dolus eventualis* is present if the defendant foresaw a consequence, i.e., in a case like the one under consideration that a third party had a right or claim to the property, as a "real or concrete possibility" (*S v. Ngubane* 1985 (3) SA 677 (A) at 680A) or as a "reasonable possibility" (*S v. Beukes en 'n Ander* 1988 (1) SA 511 (A) at 522C-J).'
382. 2016 (2) SA 317 (SCA).
383. Paragraph 26.

> is directed. It therefore consists of two parts: (1) foresight of the possibility of death occurring, and (2) reconciliation with that foreseen possibility. This second element has been expressed in various ways. For example, it has been said that the person must act 'reckless as to the consequences' (a phrase that has caused some confusion as some have interpreted it to mean with gross negligence) or must have been 'reconciled' with the foreseeable outcome. Terminology aside, it is necessary to stress that the wrongdoer does not have to foresee death as a probable consequence of his or her actions. It is sufficient that the possibility of death is foreseen which, coupled with a disregard of that consequence, is sufficient to constitute the necessary criminal intent.

Pistorius sought to deny the presence of dolus eventualis by insisting he did not have the necessary intention to kill Reeva, as he had believed a thief, not Reeva, had been concealed in the toilet. In this regard the court said:[384]

> although a perpetrator's intention to kill must relate to the person killed, this does not mean that a perpetrator must know or appreciate the identity of the victim. A person who causes a bomb to explode in a crowded place will probably be ignorant of the identity of his or her victims, but will nevertheless have the intention to kill those who might die in the resultant explosion.

The court said further:[385]

> What was in issue, therefore, was not whether the accused had foreseen that Reeva might be in the cubicle when he fired the fatal shots at the toilet door but whether there was a person behind the door who might possibly be killed by his actions.

194. Intent and motive must be distinguished. Motive indicates the actuating impulse or reason for intent. Intent or *animus iniuriandi* does not necessarily imply any ill will or spite towards the person harmed and the motive for intentionally causing harm might even be a laudable one. The fact that the motive for an assault might be laudable does not negative the fact that the intended assault might nevertheless be unlawful. An improper motive might be of evidentiary value to prove the existence of intent.

195. Given that intent is determined subjectively and awareness of wrongfulness is an element of intent, it follows that ignorance of unlawfulness or a mistaken belief in the lawfulness of a course of conduct excludes intent. Logically, the subjective nature of intent implies that any bona fide ignorance or mistake concerning the elements of intent, factual or legal, excludes intent. In *Maisel v. Van Naeren*[386] the owner of an apartment building wrote to a tenant alleging conduct constituting a nuisance to fellow tenants. The owner sent a copy of the letter to the Rent Board,

384. Paragraph 31.
385. Paragraph 32.
386. 1960 (4) SA 836 (C).

thereby publishing its defamatory content, in the honest but mistaken belief that the board had jurisdiction in the matter under the Rents Act and that the publication was therefore privileged. In the circumstances the publication was unlawful, but the owner was held not to be liable for defamation, because his mistake excluded awareness of unlawfulness as an element of intent or *animus iniuriandi*. However, causing harm in the unreasonable belief that it is justified to do so may entail liability for negligence.

196. The onus to prove intent is on the plaintiff.[387] In some cases, the plaintiff is assisted by a presumption of intent. In defamation cases, for example, the plaintiff must allege and prove only that the defendant published defamatory material referring to the plaintiff. This gives rise to two rebuttable presumptions, one being that the publication was unlawful and the other that the material was published with intent or *animo iniuriandi*.[388] The onus is then on the defendant to rebut the presumptions by proving a defence which negates the inference of unlawfulness and intent. Because intent is subjective and involves a state of mind and because the defendant's own assertions in respect of his or her state of mind are of little or no value, the existence or absence of intent must be determined by having regard to all external facts and circumstances from which inferences as to state of mind can be drawn.[389] It is sometimes said that a person can be taken to have intended the necessary, natural and probable consequences of his or her conduct, but this is not a rule of law or a legal presumption, and the existence or absence of intent must in each case be inferred from the nature of the act and from the surrounding circumstances.

III. Negligence

A. General

197. Negligence indicates failure to apply the degree of care that a reasonable person (diligens paterfamilias in Roman law) would have exercised in the same situation. The test for negligence was authoritatively formulated as follows in *Kruger v. Coetzee*:[390]

> For the purposes of liability culpa arises if –
>
> a. a *diligens paterfamilias* in the position of the defendant –

---

387. *Dantex Investment Holdings (Pty) Ltd v. Brenner* 1989 (1) SA 390 (A) 396; *Minister of Justice v. Hofmeyr* 1993 (3) SA 131 (A) 154; *Tödt v. Ipser* 1993 (3) SA 577 (A) 584; *Jansen van Vuuren v. Kruger* 1993 (4) SA 842 (A) 849.

388. *Suid-Afrikanse Uitsaaikorporasie v. O'Malley* 1977 (3) SA 394 (A) 402–403; *Sayed v. Editor, Cape Times, and Another* 2004 (1) SA 58 (C) 61D.

389. *Maisel v. Van Naeren* 1960 (4) SA 836 (C) 840.

390. 1966 (2) SA 428 (A) 430.

- would foresee the reasonable possibility of his conduct injuring another in his person or property and causing him patrimonial loss; and
- would take reasonable steps to guard against such occurrence; and

b. the defendant failed to take such steps.

198. The test focuses on three elements: reasonable foreseeability of harm; reasonable precautions to prevent the occurrence of such foreseeable harm; and the failure to take such reasonable precautions. In the above formulation, the test refers only to injury to person or property and patrimonial loss, but the same principles apply in respect of other forms of harm, as in claims for pure economic loss and for pain and suffering.

199. A reasonable person is expected to be aware of his or her physical inability or lack of skill and experience and to act or take precautions accordingly. Conversely, the existence of any higher-than-normal level of knowledge or experience will be taken into account. An expert or professionally qualified person is required to act in accordance with standards of knowledge, skill and care that are reasonable for the particular field of expertise. The test for negligence in effect becomes that of a reasonable person endowed with those particular qualities of knowledge and skill.

200. Any failure to adhere to the standard of a reasonably prudent person, however slight the deviation from the required standard, constitutes negligence. The degree of deviation from the standard of a reasonably prudent person becomes relevant in cases of contributory negligence, where the negligence of each of the persons involved is expressed as a percentage of deviation from the applicable standard, for the purpose of an apportionment of damages.

B. Duty of Care

201. In earlier cases, the courts sometimes referred to the concept of a 'duty of care' in the context of both negligence and unlawfulness. In later cases, the phrase 'legal duty' has been adopted as an appropriate indication of unlawfulness, because the concept of a 'duty of care', derived from English law, connotes an aspect of negligence. In *Administrateur, Natal v. Trust Bank van Afrika Bpk*[391] and *Knop v. Johannesburg City Council*,[392] and subsequent cases the Appellate Division has accepted that the expression 'legal duty' is to be preferred in the context of unlawfulness and that such a duty is based on general reasonableness, involving policy considerations and the value judgment that the plaintiff's invaded interest is deemed

391. 1979 (3) SA 824 (A), at 833–834.
392. 1995 (2) SA 1 (A) 27. *See also Administrateur, Natal v. Trust Bank van Afrika Bpk* 1979 (3) SA 824 (A), at 832H–833A.

worthy of legal protection against negligent interference by the defendant. The concept of 'legal duty' as applied in the context of unlawfulness, and the relationship between unlawfulness and fault, are dealt with in Part 1, Chapter 1, section 2 above.

202. The standard of care required in a particular case is sometimes formulated in terms of a 'duty', for example when it is asserted that the driver of a car has a duty to keep a proper lookout for pedestrians crossing the street. This 'duty' does not have the status of a specific legal principle or rule, and merely indicates the person and the circumstances that will be taken into account in the application of the legal standard of reasonable care. The concept of 'duty' and the 'duty of care' approach to negligence have now given way to a large extent to the recognition that a standard of reasonable care applies in all circumstances. This standard is given specific content with reference to the 'reasonable person', involving an inquiry into whether the harm in question was reasonably foreseeable and could reasonably be prevented by taking steps to guard against its occurrence. Where the courts formulate the inquiry into negligence in 'duty of care' terminology the approach is hardly different, inasmuch as a 'duty of care' is said to arise when a reasonable person in the position of the defendant would have foreseen harm and would have taken steps to guard against it.[393]

C. The Reasonable Person

203. The criterion of the reasonable person is the embodiment of an external and objective standard of care. The qualities, experience, idiosyncrasies and judgment of the particular defendant are in principle irrelevant. The hypothetical reasonable person has been characterized as follows:

> The concept of the bonus paterfamilias is not that of a timorous faintheart always in trepidation lest he or others suffer some injury; on the contrary, he ventures out into the world, engages in affairs and takes reasonable chances. He takes reasonable precautions to protect his person and property and expects others to do likewise.[394]

204. A reasonable person has the knowledge required for his work or enterprise. The reasonable person is reasonably attentive and has the reasonable degree of alertness and concentration necessary for using his senses to perceive the surroundings and recognize any danger involved. The standard of reasonable care implies that the defendant is endowed with the mental, intellectual and emotional capacities of an ordinary prudent person (diligens paterfamilias). In *Weber v. Santam Versekeringsmaatskappy Bpk*,[395] Joubert JA said that it serves no purpose to consider the anthropomorphic attributes of the diligens paterfamilias, because it represents an abstract

393. *See Cape Town Municipality v. Paine* 1923 AD 207 217; *Peri-Urban Areas Health Board v. Munarin* 1965 (3) SA 367 (A) 373; P.Q.R. Boberg, *The Law of Delict* 274.
394. *Herschel v. Mrupe* 1954 (3) SA 464 (A) 490.
395. 1983 (91) SA 381 (A), at 410–411.

and objective standard of what the court regards as reasonable in the circumstances, as explained by Lord Wright in *Fibrosa Spolka Akcyjna v. Fairbairn Lawson Combe Barbour Ltd*:[396]

> The Court is thus taken to assume the role of the reasonable man, and decides what the reasonable man would regard as just on the facts of the case. The hypothetical 'reasonable man' is personified by the Court itself. It is the Court which decides.

205. The law of negligence makes no allowance for a person's extraordinary lack of intelligence, education or emotional stability, or for any personal idiosyncrasies. For example, the tendency to be hyper-careful and to expect extraordinary harm will not be taken into account when determining whether the harm was reasonably foreseeable.[397] Physical handicaps and infirmities, such as blindness or deafness, and lack of physical strength are treated as part of the circumstances to be taken into account by the reasonable person. The conduct of a physically disabled person must be reasonable in the light of his or her knowledge of the disability. For example, a person with knowledge of a medical condition that could affect his ability to drive safely should take steps necessary to prevent the occurrence of the risk.[398]

206. The reasonable person has no special skills and lack of skill or knowledge is not per se negligence. However, the reasonable person will not voluntarily engage in any potentially dangerous activity without the required knowledge or skill, in accordance with the principle as expressed in the maxim of Roman law: where skill is required, lack of it will be regarded as negligence (imperitia culpae adnumeratur).[399] It is negligent to engage voluntarily in any potentially dangerous activity unless one has the skill and knowledge usually associated with the proper discharge of the duties connected with such an activity. The following was said in this regard in *Durr v. ABSA Bank Ltd*:[400] 'It is not negligent not to be a lawyer. But those who undertake to advise clients on matters including an important legal component do so at their peril if they have not informed themselves sufficiently on the law.'

D. Foreseeability of Harm

207. Foreseeability is central to the test for negligence. The question is not whether the reasonable person would have foreseen harm as a likelihood or probability, but whether a reasonable person would recognize the possibility of harm as real enough to warrant precautionary measures. The requirement of foreseeability

396. (1942) 2 All ER 122 (HL) at 140G.
397. *AA Mutual Insurance v. Manjani* 1982 (1) SA 790 (A).
398. *Wessels v. Hall & Pickles* 1985 (4) SA 153 (C).
399. *Durr v. ABSA Bank Ltd* 1997 (3) SA 448 (SCA) 460 (manager of broking division of bank); *Minister of Safety and Security v. Rudman* 2005 (2) SA 16 (SCA) (police should be aware of inadequate knowledge of first aid).
400. 1997 (3) SA 448 (SCA) 462.

can be understood in an abstract sense, indicating that *some harm* must be foreseeable to *someone*; or in a more specific sense (sometimes referred to as a concrete or relative sense), indicating that *the kind of harm in issue* must have been foreseeable to *a person in the position of the plaintiff*. The formulation of the test for negligence in *Kruger v. Coetzee*,[401] cited above, is an example of foreseeability in the abstract sense, whereas the following formulation of the test in *Mukheiber v. Raath and Another*[402] is an example of a more specific understanding of foreseeability:

> For the purposes of liability culpa arises if (a) a reasonable person in the position of the defendant (i) would have foreseen harm of the general kind that actually occurred; (ii) would have foreseen the general kind of causal sequence by which that harm occurred; (iii) would have taken steps to guard against it, and (b) the defendant failed to take those steps.

208. In *Sea Harvest Corporation (Pty) Ltd and Another v. Duncan Dock Cold Storage (Pty) Ltd and Another*,[403] Scott JA declined to opt for either of the two approaches to negligence, preferring the following general approach:

> [I]n the ultimate analysis the true criterion for determining negligence is whether in the particular circumstances the conduct complained of falls short of the standard of the reasonable person. Dividing the inquiry into various stages, however useful, is no more than an aid or guideline for resolving this issue.

The facts of the *Sea Harvest* case were that a cold storage facility in the Cape Town harbour area was set alight by a distress flare which had been fired from a boat in the harbour by an unknown person during celebrations on New Year's Eve. The roof sheets were non-combustible, but the fibreglass guttering, though requiring a 'fairly substantial heat source' to ignite, was combustible, as was the polystyrene core of the insulation panels used for the roof and the cold rooms. The high-intensity flame of the flare set the guttering alight and the entire facility burnt down. The question was whether persons with responsibility for the design of the building (the port engineer and project engineer) should have provided for a sprinkler system in the roof. The court held that, having regard to the circumstances of the case, the question of culpability had to be determined not simply by asking whether fire, any fire, had been foreseeable but whether a reasonable person in the position of the project engineer or the port engineer would have foreseen the danger of fire emanating from an external source on the roof of the building with sufficient intensity to ignite the gutter.[404] Given that the building was relatively isolated in relation to other buildings in the harbour area; that there was nothing about its locality rendering it more vulnerable to fire; and that the region was not prone to lightning of the kind which would set fire to buildings; save for a burning flare, it was difficult to

401. 1966 (2) SA 428 (A) 430.
402. 1999 (3) SA 1065 (SCA) 1077E-F.
403. 2000 (1) SA 827 (SCA) 839F.
404. Paragraph [24] at 841E–F/G.

conceive of any other source of fire which could have set the roof alight from above.[405] Furthermore, bearing in mind that distress flares had been designed to burn out at a height of not less than 150 feet and that, notwithstanding the long-standing practice of firing off flares to celebrate the New Year, a fire had never been caused in that fashion, the possibility of a flare landing while still burning and setting fire to the gutter of a building constructed with an otherwise non-combustible shell was so remote as not to have been reasonably foreseeable.[406]

209. The foreseeability of harm depends on a consideration of all the circumstances, but the courts typically focus on the following questions:

- How likely is it that a person in the position of the plaintiff would have suffered harm?[407] A reasonable person would also have regard to the class of persons likely to be harmed. If the general category or class of persons was reasonably foreseeable, it does not matter that the particular plaintiff ought not to have been part of that class. For example, if harm to passengers was reasonably foreseeable to the driver of a vehicle, all passengers are foreseeable plaintiffs, even those who had no right to be on board. In road accident cases, the courts have often emphasized that the driver of a vehicle must be on the lookout at all times where children are about, and to expect and be prepared to avoid the consequences of impulsive and irrational conduct by children of whose presence he is aware; and also where he should reasonably have expected the presence of children.[408]
- Was the *kind of harm* that occurred (as opposed to the specific harm) reasonably foreseeable?[409] When assessing the evidence the approach of the courts is mostly not general, but rather focused on the kind of harm in issue, such as bodily injury, property damage, pure economic loss, or emotional shock. The issue is not whether some harm, irrespective of its nature, was foreseeable, but whether the *kind of harm* which did occur was reasonably foreseeable. In nervous or emotional shock cases, for example, the plaintiff must prove that a reasonable person in the defendant's position would have foreseen the possibility of the plaintiff (as one of a group of persons with a close relationship or affinity to the injured person) would suffer nervous shock.[410] The particular harm, or the particular extent of the harm or manner of its occurrence, need not be reasonably foreseeable.[411]

---

405. Paragraph [25] at 841F/G–H.
406. Paragraph [27] at 842C–F.
407. *Workman's Compensation Commissioner v. De Villiers* 1949 (1) 474 (C); *Government of the RSA v. Basdeo* 1996 (1) SA 355(A); *Palsgraf v. Long Island Railroad Co.* (1928) 248 NY 339; *Bourhill v. Young* [1943] AC 92 (HL).
408. *Santam Insurance Co. Ltd v. Nkosi* 1978 (2) SA 784 (A) 789.
409. *Murray v. Union & SWA Insurance Co.* 1979 (2) SA 825 (D); *Minister van Polisie v. Van Aswegen* 1974 (2) SA 101 (A).
410. *Bester v. Commercial Union Versekeringsmaatskappy van SA Bpk* 1973 (1) SA 769 (A); *Masiba v. Constantia Insurance Co. Ltd* 1982 (4) SA 33 (C); *Majiet v. Santam Ltd* 1997 (4) All SA 555 (C); *Clinton-Parker v. Administrator, Transvaal* 1996 (2) 37 (W); *Barnard v. Santam Ltd* 1999 (1) SA 202 (SCA); *RAF v. Sauls* 2002 (1) SA 961 (SCA).
411. In *Mukheiber v. Raath and Another* 1999 (3) SA 1065 (SCA) 1077E-F, the test for negligence is formulated as follows: for the purposes of liability culpa arises if (a) a reasonable person in the position of the defendant (i) would have foreseen harm of the general kind that actually occurred;

Extraordinary vulnerability to bodily injury is generally not reasonably foreseeable, but as long as some injury was foreseeable, the specific nature and extent need not have been foreseeable, by application of the maxim: 'You take your victim as you find him.'[412]

- Was the general manner of occurrence of the harm (general kind of causal sequence, as opposed to the specific turn of events) reasonably foreseeable?[413]
- How likely was it that harm might occur? In the English case of *Bolton v. Stone*,[414] a cricket ball was hit out of the ground and struck and injured a person in a quiet public road adjacent to the ground. The chance that a ball would be hit out of the ground into the road was not a far-fetched improbability: it had happened six times in twenty-eight years. Nevertheless, in the circumstances the risk was so slight that a reasonable person would not have foreseen and guarded against it. However, even though the risk of harm is slight, the possible extent of harm may be so substantial that a reasonable person would have foreseen and guarded against it.
- If harm does occur, what is the likely extent of the damage? In *Lomagundi Sheetmetal and Engineering (Pvt.) Ltd v. Basson*,[415] sparks caused by welding on the roof of a silo ignited bales of fodder stacked against the silo far below. The risk of the fodder being ignited by the welding was slight, but in the event of fire extensive damage would result, and the cost and difficulty of guarding against fire were minimal. A reasonable person would therefore have foreseen and guarded against the possibility of harm. The chance or likelihood of harm and the extent of the possible harm are interrelated factors. A reasonable person would take precautions to prevent foreseeable harm if the risk of harm is high or almost a certainty, even though the extent of the harm that is likely to occur is slight; and likewise where the risk is slight, but the extent of the foreseeable harm is substantial.

E. Preventing Harm

210. A reasonable person will take reasonable measures to prevent the occurrence of foreseeable harm. The factors typically taken into account by the courts in this regard include the following:

(ii) would have foreseen the general kind of causal sequence by which that harm occurred; (iii) would have taken steps to guard against it, and (b) the defendant failed to take those steps.' In *Sea Harvest Corporation (Pty) Ltd and Another v. Duncan Dock Cold Storage (Pty) Ltd and Another* 2000 (1) SA 827 (SCA) 839F, the court warned against piecemeal reasoning: '[I]n the ultimate analysis the true criterion for determining negligence is whether in the particular circumstances the conduct complained of falls short of the standard of the reasonable person. Dividing the inquiry into various stages, however useful, is no more than an aid or guideline for resolving this issue'.

412. *Wilson v. Birt (Pty) Ltd* 1963 (2) 508 (D); *Masiba v. Constantia Insurance Co. Ltd* 1982 (4) SA 333 (C).
413. *Kruger v. Van der Merwe* 1966 (2) SA 266 (A); *Mafesa v. Parity Versekeringsmaatskappy Bpk* 1968 (2) SA 603 (O); *Sea Harvest Corporation (Pty) Ltd and Another v. Duncan Dock Cold Storage (Pty) Ltd and Another* 2000 (1) SA 827 (SCA).
414. 1951 AC 150.
415. 1973 (4) SA 523 (RA).

– Did the degree of the risk of the occurrence of harm and the likely extent or gravity of the possible consequences, if the risk of harm materializes, require more extensive protective measures? For example, how likely is it that a child might climb up a pylon supporting power cables above a railway line;[416] or that animals might wander on a road?[417] Where a landslide occurred in a mountain pass after heavy rains, the presence of signs warning against falling rocks was held not to be adequate: in view of the extent of the risk, the road should have been closed.[418]
– The magnitude of the risk must be weighed up against the social utility of the risk-creating conduct. The question here is whether 'the game is worth the candle'. A fire brigade or ambulance, for example, might proceed at speeds that would amount to negligent driving on the part of an ordinary driver of a car, while the necessary higher speed requires an appropriate level of skill and experience. Similarly, persons engaged in the burning of fire-belts create necessary risks, but at the same time they are required to take special precautions against the risk of the fire running out of control. The utility of keeping lawns and playing fields around schools tidy by using a lawnmower does not outweigh the risk of injury to children playing in the vicinity.[419] The importance of cattle ranching as a farming activity in South Africa might justify the risk of allowing cattle to roam freely on large tracts of land crossed by an unfenced public road.[420] However, generally the owner or person in control of cattle will be required to take steps to prevent the cattle straying onto a public road, which steps could include a padlock to secure a gate that keeps the cattle away from the public road, or installing a cattle grid at the access point to the public road, both being easy, inexpensive and effective measures to prevent the cattle from straying onto the public road.[421]
– Where a municipality undertakes construction work alongside a busy road concomitant risks should be reasonably guarded against, but all risks cannot be excluded.[422]
– The cost and burden of possible precautionary measures must be balanced against the risk. This might require an overall cost-benefit analysis: whether the extent of possible harm exceeds the cost of prevention; for example, the cost of installing devices in trains to prevent departure from a station before all the doors are closed;[423] or the cost of replacing an entire section of pipeline to prevent the occasional occurrence of a burst, even though such a burst might cause considerable damage.[424] Where the risk can be eliminated or minimized without substantial difficulty, disadvantage or expense, a reasonable person would take the necessary precautions.

---

416. *Stratton v. Spoornet* 1994 (1) SA 803 (T).
417. *Mkhwanazi v. Van der Walt* 1995 (4) SA 589 (A); *Jordaan v. Krone Broers* 1999 (3) All SA 57 (C).
418. *Cape Metropolitan Council v. Graham* 2001 (1) SA 1197 (SCA).
419. *Knouwds v. Administrateur, Kaap* 1981 (1) SA 544 (C).
420. *Botes v. Van Deventer* 1966 (3) SA 182 (A).
421. *Enslin v.* Nhlapo 2008 (5) SA 146 (SCA).
422. *Pretoria City Council v. De Jager* 1997 (2) SA 96 (A).
423. *Khupa v. SA Transport Services* 1990 (2) SA 627 (W).
424. *Mostert v. Cape Town City Council* 2001 (1) SA 105 (SCA).

- In *Maylett v. Du Toit*,[425] for example, Maylett was shot in the leg by Du Toit's three-year-old son, who had picked up Du Toit's revolver, unobserved, and removed it from its holster. Not only had Du Toit created the danger by leaving the revolver where it could be reached by the child, but he also could have taken effective precautions without any difficulty, either by unloading the weapon or by putting it out of reach.
- In *Shabalala v. Metrorail*,[426] the Supreme Court of Appeal considered the reasonable steps that the railway company Metrorail could take to protect commuters from armed robbery on their trains. The court noted that the grounds of negligence that Shabalala relied on were of a general nature and 'relate to a systemic failure on the part of the respondent'. In other words, the alleged failure did not relate to a failure on the part of an individual employee to act in a specific manner in relation to the incident in question, but to a general failure on Metrorail's part to put measures in place that would ensure the safety of commuters. It was evident that Metrorail had adopted measures to minimize or prevent crime on the trains by employing security guards on the trains and on the station platforms. Therefore, the question was whether Shabalala had discharged the burden of establishing that those measures were unreasonably inadequate in the circumstances, and that had better precautions been taken, the harm would not have occurred. The court emphasized that the precautionary steps which Metrorail did take were not necessarily unreasonably inadequate simply because foreseeable harm occurred. Metrorail could not be expected to provide an absolute guarantee against harm from criminal activity on its trains. Based on the facts, it appeared that avoiding the attack would have required at least one security guard in each train coach. The court found that such a requirement would be unreasonable, because of the cost, in view of the large number of coaches involved. It might have been reasonable to require security guards on every coach where lines have been identified as being particularly vulnerable to criminal activities, but no evidence to this effect had been tendered. The court therefore dismissed the plaintiff's appeal. What would have been the likely success of preventative steps? For example, in a case where policemen were charged with culpable homicide, for negligently causing the death of children by failing to undertake a more extensive search when the children went missing, they were found not guilty, because the search was likely to have been unsuccessful.[427]

F. Factors Relevant to the Standard of Care

211. The standard of care required is determined by objective evaluation, and considerable evidentiary weight attaches to whether or not the conduct complied

425. 1989 (1) SA 90 (T) 94.
426. 2008 (3) SA 142 (SCA).
427. *S v. Van As* 1967 (4) SA 594 (A).

with normal and generally accepted practice. Generally accepted practice is indicative of the nature and extent of care and precautions in particular situations.[428] However, the generally accepted practice is not necessarily conclusive. The overriding standard in every instance is that of a reasonable person in the particular situation.

212. For some situations, the appropriate standard of care is prescribed by statutory provision. A breach of a statutory duty is indicative of negligence, but not conclusive.[429] However, where a statute, regulations, or police standing orders prescribe certain conduct or precautions, a breach of duty or failure to take such precautions will be a strong indication of negligence.[430]

213. Reasonable care depends also on certain legitimate assumptions about the conduct of other persons. In general, a person is entitled to assume that the rules and conventions that normally govern the behaviour of persons in particular situations will be observed.[431] For example, the reasonable driver of a motor vehicle will foresee the possibility of negligent conduct on the part of other drivers.[432] It is reasonably foreseeable that other drivers sometimes approach intersections at too high speeds, or suddenly and without warning slow down or stop. The reasonable driver adjusts his own standard of care accordingly. However, in the absence of indications to the contrary, a driver is entitled to assume that others will obey traffic signs. Generally, a reasonable person would not anticipate gross negligence on the part of others. In road accident cases, the courts have often emphasized that the driver of a vehicle must be on the lookout at all times where children are about, and to expect and be prepared to avoid the consequences of impulsive and irrational conduct by children of whose presence he is aware; and also where he should reasonably have expected the presence of children.[433]

214. An error of judgment may be indicative of negligence, but some errors of judgment are reasonable, for instance in emergencies or in situations fraught with risk, such as a complicated medical procedure. However, an error of judgment occasioned by a lack of the required degree of knowledge, skill and diligence will constitute negligence.[434]

---

428. *Colman v. Dunbar* 1933 AD 141 157; *Van Heerden v. SA Pulp & Paper Industry* 1946 AD 382.
429. *Clairwood Motor Transport Co. (Pty) Ltd v. Akal & Sons* 1959 (1) SA 183 (N); *Bekker v. Du Toit* 1974 (3) SA 248 (O).
430. *Botha v. Minister van Veiligheid en Sekuriteit* 2003 (6) SA 568 (T) 581–582; *Minister of Safety and Security v. Carmichele* 2004 (3) SA 305 (SCA).
431. *Butters v. Cape Town Municipality* 1993 (3) SA 521 (C); *Masureik (t/a Lotus Corporation) v. Welkom Municipality* 1995 (4) SA 745 (O).
432. *Moore v. Minister of Posts and Telegraphs* 1949 (1) SA 815 (A) 826.
433. *Santam Insurance Co. Ltd v. Nkosi* 1978 (2) SA 784 (A) 789.
434. *Mouton v. Die Mynwerkersunie* 1977 (1) SA 119 (A) 143.

G. Sudden Emergency and Special Dangers

215. The test for negligence requires that the conduct of the defendant be assessed in the particular circumstances prevailing at the time. The pressure created by a sudden emergency or imminent danger, resulting from the careless conduct of another person or from some unforeseeable event, will be taken into account. In general, a person confronted by a situation of sudden emergency is not in a position to evaluate carefully the best course of action to follow, and an error of judgment is more likely to occur.[435] However, this allowance for the pressure of a sudden emergency will not be made where the defendant's own negligence created the situation of imminent danger;[436] or where the conduct was unreasonable even if allowance for the emergency is made.[437] In determining whether conduct in a situation of imminent danger was reasonable, the courts take into account that certain activities, for example the driving of a car, require the ability to cope with dangerous situations that are likely to arise.[438]

216. Particular care and vigilance is required in situations generally known to be dangerous.[439] Where a person deals with an inherently dangerous thing, or is in control of a dangerous situation, that person is required to act with greater care. Examples of dangerous things or situations include handling loaded firearms, transporting dangerous criminals[440] and slippery floors in supermarkets.[441] Where young children are present at the side of a road or where the presence of children is reasonably to be expected, the reasonable motorist would exercise greater care and take precautions against the possibility that a child could behave unpredictably.[442] In road accident cases, the courts have often emphasized that the driver of a vehicle must be on the lookout at all times where children are about, and to expect and be prepared to avoid the consequences of impulsive and irrational conduct by children of whose presence he is aware; and also where he should reasonably have expected the presence of children.[443]

H. Experts

217. A person who engages in a profession, trade, calling or any other activity that demands special knowledge and skill must not only exercise reasonable care,

---

435. *Samson v. Winn* 1977 (1) SA 761 (C).
436. *Brown v. Hunt* 1953 (2) SA 540 (A)
437. *Walpole v. Santam Insurance Co. Ltd* 1973 (1) SA 357 (T).
438. *S v. Crockart* 1971 (2) SA 496 (RA) (driver reacting to burning match); *S v. Erwin* 1974 (3) SA 438 (C) (driver reacting to bee sting).
439. *Brauns v. Shoprite Checkers (Pty) Ltd* 2004 (6) SA 211 (E) (wet shop floor).
440. *Van der Spuy v. Minister of Correctional Services* 2004 (2) SA 463 (SE).
441. *Brauns v. Shoprite Checkers (Pty) Ltd* 2004 (6) SA 211 (E); *Checkers Supermarket v. Lindsay* [2009] ZASCA 26.
442. *Keown v. Ned-Equity Versekeringsmaatskappy Bpk* 1984 (1) SA 656 (A) 661–662.
443. *Santam Insurance Co. Ltd v. Nkosi* 1978 (2) SA 784 (A) 789.

but also measure up to the standard of competence of a reasonable person professing such knowledge and skill. In assessing the attributes required, a court will have regard to the general level of knowledge and skill of members of the branch of the profession to which the practitioner belongs.[444] The liability of professionals is dealt with under specific cases of liability in Part I Chapter 2 below.

I. Inexperience and Lack of Skill

218. Where a beginner's lack of skill exposes the public to a risk of harm, no allowance will be made for lack of proficiency and experience. For example, an inexperienced doctor or driver on a public road cannot rely on lack of knowledge, experience or skill.

219. The relationship between a beginner and the person harmed might be such that a lower than the ordinary reasonable standard of care and skill will be required. In *African Flying Services (Pty) Ltd v. Gildenhuys*,[445] a flying instructor was injured as a result of the inexperience of his pupil in flying an aeroplane. The instructor allowed his pupil to fly his aeroplane, which the pupil crashed, and the instructor claimed damages from the pupil. The accident did not cause harm to anyone else. In assessing whether the pupil had been negligent, Tindall JA in a separate judgment[446] indicated that, because the instructor knowingly entrusted his interests to his inexperienced pupil, the standard against which the pupil's conduct had to be measured needed to be adjusted downwards to take into account the risks inherent in the lack of skill and experience of a pupil. In effect, he had consented to such a lower standard of competence by voluntarily exposing himself to the risks inherent in allowing a novice to fly.

J. Children

220. The negligence of a child could involve three questions, namely the question of accountability (dealt with in Part 1 Chapter 1 section 4 below), the question of negligence, and, where other persons were also at fault, the question of contributory negligence and apportionment of damages in terms of the Apportionment of Damages Act 34 of 1956 (dealt with in Part IV Chapter 3 below).

---

444. *Van Wyk v. Lewis* 1924 AD 438 444; *Esterhuizen v. Administrator, Transvaal* 1957 (3) SA 710 (T); *Pringlev. Administrator, Transvaal* 1990 (2) SA 379 (W); *Castell v. De Greeff* 1993 (3) SA 501 (C); *Deysel v. Truter* 2005 (5) SA 598 (C) (medical practitioners); *Mouton v. Die Mynwerkersunie* 1977 (1) SA 119 (A) 143 (attorney); *Standard Chartered Bank of Canada v. Nedperm Bank Ltd* 1994 (4) SA 747 (A) 762; *Durr v. ABSA Bank Ltd* 1997 (3) SA 448 (SCA) (bank); *Minister of Safety and Security v. Carmichele* 2004 (3) SA 305 (SCA) 325–327; *Minister of Safety and Security v. Hamilton* 2004 (2) SA 216 (SCA) 238 (police officers); *Randaree v. Dixon* 1983 (2) SA 1 (A) (civil engineer); *SM Goldstein & Co. (Pty) Ltd v. Cathkin Park Hotel (Pty) Ltd* 2000 (4) SA 1019 (SCA) (builder).

445. 1941 AD 230.

446. *African Flying Services (Pty) Ltd v. Gildenhuys* 1941 AD 230 at 245.

221. The accountability of children is determined on a subjective basis, taking into account the mental ability of the child, but the ordinary objective test is applied to determine negligence on the part of a child, so that the conduct of the child is tested against the standard of the reasonable person in the particular situation.[447] If both accountability and negligence have been established, and another person was also at fault, the contributory negligence of the child is determined by establishing the degree to which its conduct deviated from the standard of the reasonable person. However, for purposes of contributory negligence of the child, the courts have made some allowance for the child's lack of maturity, on the basis that contributory negligence for the purposes of apportionment of damages should be determined according to the standard of what is just and equitable.

K. Proof of Negligence

222. The onus of proving negligence on a balance of probabilities is on the plaintiff. The maxim res ipsa loquitur is invoked when the occurrence indicates the likelihood of negligence, for instance when a vehicle was being driven on the wrong side of the road at the time of an accident. Where the maxim res ipsa loquitur is applicable the onus of proof does not shift to the defendant, but an evidential burden then rests on the defendant to produce some evidence to explain the apparently negligent conduct, thereby to rebut the inference of negligence.[448] Where a statutory presumption of negligence is applicable the onus is on the defendant to rebut the presumption of negligence.[449]

§4. Capacity, Accountability, Imputability

223. For the imposition of liability, the law of delict requires that the defendant must at least have had the mental and intellectual capacity to comprehend and avoid the causing of harm in a particular situation. The defendant can be held accountable for his or her state of mind (intent) or lack of reasonable care only if at the time of acting one had this capacity. Accountability or imputability on the part of the defendant is therefore a prerequisite for the existence of fault: the law of delict requires a certain minimum mental capacity to be held responsible for one's actions.

224. A person has capacity for fault or is accountable (*culpae capax*) if he or she has the mental ability to comprehend both the facts of a potentially harmful situation and the unlawfulness of causing harm. This means the defendant must have had

447. *Jones v. Santam Bpk* 1965 (2) SA 542 (A) 551; *Eskom Holdings Ltd v. Hendricks* 2005 (5) SA 503 (SCA) 511–512.

448. *Arthur v. Bezuidenhout and Mieny* 1962 (2) SA 566 (A); *Sardi v. Standard & General Insurance Co. Ltd* 1977 (3) SA 776 (A) 780.

449. *See*, for example, s. 34 of the National Veld and Forest Fire Act 101 of 1998, considered in *Gouda Boerdery BK v. Transnet* 2005 (5) SA 490 (SCA); and s. 26 of the Electricity Act 41 of 1987, considered in *Malherbe v. Eskom* 2002 (4) SA 497 (O) 504; and *Eskom Holdings Ltd v. Hendricks* 2005 (5) SA 503 (SCA).

the mental ability to appreciate the danger involved in a particular situation and to take precautionary measures to avoid it, the ability to control impulsive conduct and the ability to distinguish between what is lawful and wrongful and to act in accordance with this distinction.[450] Accountability is determined subjectively, and a person may lack the required mental ability to be accountable on account of factors such as youth, mental illness or a drug-induced condition.

225. The issue of accountability in the law of delict arises mostly where children are involved. The accountability of children is determined on a subjective basis, taking into account the mental ability of the child.[451] In *Weber v. Santam Versekeringsmaatskappy Bpk*,[452] the Appellate Division confirmed the distinction previously drawn in *Jones NO v. Santam Bpk*[453] between the issue of capacity on the part of a child to commit a wrong on the one hand, and the issue of fault on the other. In doing so, it declined to follow the view that there was a need to introduce a subjective element into the concept of negligence in the case of children, by requiring no more than a degree of care expected of a child of the age and maturity of the one in question. Instead, the court in *Weber* held that the inquiry into capacity is subjective, while the inquiry into fault is objective. This means that once a child is found to have the necessary capacity, negligence is to be determined in accordance with the standard of the ordinary (adult) reasonable person.

226. In *Weber*, both Jansen JA and Joubert JA undertook an exhaustive analysis of the Roman and Roman-Dutch authorities and confirmed the rule that an *infant* (a child under 7 years of age) is culpae incapax, while children between the ages of 7 and puberty (12 in the case of girls and 14 in the case of boys) are presumed to lack capacity until the contrary is proved by the party alleging negligence. In *Eskom Holdings Ltd v. Hendricks*,[454] Scott JA expressed the opinion that this gender-based distinction between girls and boys may well be unjustifiable, and that the more appropriate cut-off point would be 14 years for children of both sexes, as would appear to be the case in the criminal law.[455] A youth between the ages of 14 and 21 is presumed to be accountable.

227. Factors to be considered in assessing the child's ability include age, intelligence, knowledge, education and maturity. In the case of a road accident involving a child under the age of puberty, for instance, the question will be whether the child at the time of the accident was old enough to have and had the intelligence to appreciate the particular danger to be avoided, had knowledge of how to avoid it or of the precautions to be taken against it, and was sufficiently mature to be able to

450. *Weber v. Santam Versekeringsmaatskappy Bpk* 1983 (1) SA 381 (A) 403, 410.
451. *Jones v. Santam Bpk* 1965 (2) SA 542 (A) 551; *Eskom Holdings Ltd v. Hendricks* 2005 (5) SA 503 (SCA) 511–512.
452. 1983 (1) SA 381 (A).
453. 1965 (2) SA 542 (A).
454. 2005 (5) SA 503 (SCA) para. 16.
455. *See R v. K* 1956 (3) SA 353 (A); *Attorney-General, Transvaal v. Additional Magistrate for Johannesburg* 1924 AD 421 at 434.

control irrational or impulsive acts. The courts are careful not to overemphasize factors such as intelligence and education. The inherent weaknesses associated with youth, especially the tendency of young children to act irrationally and impulsively, are taken into account.[456]

228. In *Jones NO v. Santam Bpk*,[457] the court stated the position as follows:

> If it be decided in any particular case that a child under puberty is old enough to have and does have the intelligence to appreciate a particular danger to be avoided, that he has a knowledge of how to avoid it or of the precautions to be taken against it, and further that he is sufficiently matured or developed so as to be able to control irrational or impulsive acts, then it would be proper to hold that a failure to control himself or to take the ordinary precautions against the danger in question is negligent conduct on his part; in other words that child, in relation to the particular acts or omissions complained of in the particular circumstances, was culpae capax.

229. In *Weber v. Santam Versekeringsmaatskappy Bpk*,[458] it was held that where the issue is whether or not a child is culpae capax, care should be taken not to place 'an old head on young shoulders'. It should not be too readily accepted, purely on the ground of a child's training, that it has attained a sufficient degree of development and maturity to control irrational or impulsive acts. If the child's acts and omissions are to be measured against the standard of the adult, it must be asked whether it is sufficiently mature in regard to the situation at issue to comply with that standard.

230. In *Eskom Holdings Ltd v. Hendricks*,[459] Hendricks' son, Jacques (who was 11 years and 8 months old), sustained serious injuries when he went too close to a high voltage power line that was suspended from one of the power company Eskom's pylons. To reach the point where the accident occurred, Jacques had to climb to a height of 14 metres above the ground after first going through an anti-climbing device. Apparently, Jacques, his younger brother, and a younger friend were taking their dog for a walk when they challenged each other to see who could climb the highest. As Jacques was climbing, he stopped to take rest and the glass insulators, which he described as greenish glass saucers, caught his eye. Out of curiosity, he climbed further out onto the cross-arm of the pylon to feel their texture. According to an expert's evidence, Jacques' head came too close to the power line that was suspended from the cross-arm immediately above him. The strong voltage caused the current to jump across the space between the power line and Jacques' head. The shock, from 66,000 Volts, flung the boy from his perch. Hendricks claimed damages and Eskom denied liability and also claimed contributory negligence on Jacques' part. In assessing whether Jacques was indeed *culpae capax* at

456. *Weber v. Santam Versekeringsmaatskappy Bpk* 1983 (1) SA 381 (A) 400–401.
457. 1965 (2) SA 542 (A) at 554.
458. 1983 (1) SA 381 (A) 410.
459. 2005 (5) SA 503 (SCA).

the time of the incident, the court referred to *Weber v. Santam Versekerings-maatskappy Bpk*, and reiterated that it needed to recognize the inherent weakness in children to act irrationally and impulsively due to their tender age. Therefore, although children can distinguish between right and wrong, they will often not be able to act in accordance with that appreciation, because they can become so engrossed in their play that they become oblivious to other considerations. The court had no doubt that Jacques had appreciated that if he climbed past the anti-climbing device he ran the risk of falling and hurting himself. However, while he was climbing, the glass insulators, which had nothing to do with why Jacques climbed up the pylon, attracted his attention. His fascination by these glass saucers prompted him to climb towards them so that he could touch them. The court said that Jacques' emotional and intellectual maturity had to be assessed according this particular conduct. On the evidence, the court concluded that Jacques' conduct was typical of the impulsive behaviour in which children sometimes engage, and that this was an instance where the warning against 'placing an old head on young shoulders' should be heeded. The court held that the conduct in question (i.e., touching the insulators out of curiosity) was indicative of Jacques' inability to act in accordance with any appreciation he may have had of the danger involved. Accordingly, the court held that Eskom had failed to rebut the presumption that Jacques was *culpae incapax* at the time of the accident, and so he had not been contributorily negligent.

231. While the accountability of children is determined on a subjective basis, the ordinary objective test is applied to determine negligence on the part of a child, so that the conduct of the child is tested against the standard of the reasonable person in the particular situation.[460] If both accountability and negligence have been established, and another person was also at fault, the contributory negligence of the child is determined by establishing the degree to which its conduct deviated from the standard of the reasonable person. However, for purposes of contributory negligence of the child the courts have made some allowance for the child's lack of maturity, on the basis that contributory negligence for the purposes of apportionment of damages should be determined according to the standard of what is just and equitable.

232. The accountability of a person whose mental ability was impaired as a result of some form of mental illness, severe provocation, or the influence of alcohol or some other drug, is determined according to the principles as set out above, by enquiring whether, at the time when harm was caused, he or she had the necessary mental ability to comprehend the facts of the potentially harmful situation, to distinguish between what is lawful and unlawful, and to act in accordance with this distinction.

233. The influence of alcohol or some other drug might bring about incapacity, but the voluntary consumption of alcohol or drugs by a person who is at that time accountable might in itself be negligent, where it was reasonably foreseeable that the resultant impairment of mental ability could have harmful consequences. For

---

460. *See* in respect of the negligence of children Ch. 1 §3 above.

instance, a person who drives a motor vehicle after consuming alcohol, and then causes an accident in a state of intoxication, will be liable for setting in motion a course of events leading to the harmful consequences, even though he or she might no longer have been accountable at the time of the accident.[461]

---

461. *See*, in criminal law, *S v. Chretien* 1981 (1) SA 1097 (A); *S v. Stellmacher* 1983 (2) SA 181 (SWA); *S v. Arnold* 1985 (3) SA 256 (C).

Chapter 2. Specific Forms of Liability

§1. Liability of Professionals

I. General

234. A person who engages in a profession, trade, calling or any other activity that demands special knowledge and skill must not only exercise reasonable care, but also measure up to the standard of competence that is reasonable to expect of a person professing such knowledge and skill. The general test for negligence is therefore adapted to accommodate situations where special knowledge or skill is required. In assessing liability of a professional or expert, the court will have regard to the general level of knowledge and skill of members of the relevant branch of the profession or area of expertise. The reasonable expert criterion does not require the highest skill and expertise, but courts use it to assess the 'general level of skill and diligence possessed and exercised at the time by members of the branch of the profession to which the practitioner belongs'.[462] Therefore, one can take into account the specific branch of an area of expertise when determining negligence. For example, a medical practitioner who is a specialist will be required to exercise a greater degree of skill than a medical practitioner who is a general practitioner, due to the difference in their levels of specialization and skill.

235. The relationship between a professional and his or her client is primarily a contractual one, giving rise to potential liability for breach of contract. However, some concurrence of contractual and delictual liability can occur within this relationship: it is accepted that the contractual relationship between a professional person and his or her client, in addition to a duty to act with reasonable care and skill as an implied term of the contract, under certain circumstances also gives rise to a delictual duty with a similar content, as discussed above in the General Introduction, section 5. Where the performance of professional services constitutes either a breach of contract or a delict, the plaintiff has a choice of proceeding either in delict or in contract against the same defendant.

236. The relationship between a professional and a client can also give rise to an exclusively delictual action, for example where one party in the pre-contractual phase negligently or intentionally misrepresented facts to the other, inducing entry into the contract.[463] In addition, a professional person or expert may also under certain circumstances incur delictual liability towards third parties, in cases where misrepresentation, negligent advice, or defective workmanship affects third parties, for example in the 'disappointed beneficiary' cases, where a beneficiary does not benefit from a will, because a professional advisor was negligent in drafting or executing the will.[464]

---

462. *Van Wyk v. Lewis* 1924 AD 438 at 444.
463. *Bayer SA (Pty) Ltd v. Frost* 1991 (4) SA 559 (A) 570.
464. *See Pretorius en andere v. McCullum* 2002 (2) SA 423 (K); *BOE Bank Ltd v. Ries* 2002 (2) SA 39 (SCA).

237. In South African law, concurrence of contract and delict has been recognized in respect of the relationship between doctor and patient in a case where the alleged harm was physical and not purely economic;[465] and also between attorney and client in respect of pure economic loss,[466] although in the leading case concerning an attorney's liability to his client the client's action was treated as a contractual action.[467] In the leading case of *Lillicrap, Wassenaar & Partners v. Pilkington Bros (SA) (Pty) Ltd*,[468] which dealt with an engineer and client relationship where professional negligence caused pure economic loss, the Supreme Court of Appeal has held that the client has a contractual remedy and no concurrent action in delict. A key consideration was that this case did not involve an infringement of rights of property or person, but only the infringement of a contractual duty to perform specific professional work with due diligence. There was no independent duty for the purposes of delictual liability. In the view of most commentators, this judgment implied that only a contractual remedy is available where pure economic loss (as opposed to physical damage or personal injury) is caused by negligent performance of a contractual duty, notably in the relationship between a client and a professional person.[469] However, in *Pinshaw v. Nexus Securities (Pty) Ltd and Another*,[470] it was held that the existence of a contract between an asset management company and its client did not preclude the existence of a legal duty in delict on the part of the company's employee towards the client; and in *Holtzhausen v. ABSA Bank Ltd*,[471] it was held that an action in delict for a negligent misstatement causing pure pecuniary loss is maintainable against a bank, even if a concurrent action is available in contract. The denial of an action in delict in the *Lillicrap, Wassenaar* case was in the *Holtzhausen* case regarded as being limited to the case where the negligence alleged consists in the breach of a term of a contract. In *Trustees, Two Oceans Aquarium Trust v. Kantey & Templer (Pty) Ltd*,[472] it was held that public policy does not require extension of the Aquilian action to rescue plaintiff who was in position to avoid risk of harm by contractual means but failed to do so.

238. Both in contract and in delict, the liability of professionals is based on the expectation of a reasonable degree of specialized knowledge, competence and skill.

---

465. *Van Wyk v. Lewis* 1924 AD 428.
466. *Rampal (Pty) Ltd v. Brett Wills and Partners* 1981 (4) SA 360 (D).
467. *Mouton v. Die Mynwerkersunie* 1977 (1) SA 119 (A); and *see also Bouwer v. Harding* 1997 (4) SA 1023 (SE), where the liability of an attorney to a client was the subject of an action for breach of contract, and the attorney was found to be in breach of his contractual duties by negligently failing to advise the client correctly on the tax implications of structuring a sale of property in a particular manner.
468. *Lillicrap, Wassenaar and Partners v. Pilkington Brothers (SA) (Pty) Ltd* 1985 (1) SA 475 (A).
469. J.R. Midgley, *The Nature of the Inquiry into Concurrence of Actions*, 107 S. African L. J. 621 (1990); *Annél van Aswegen Die Toets vir die Bestaan van 'n 'Onafhanklike Delik' in die Geval van Kontrakbreuk*, 55 THRHR 271, 273–274 (1992).
470. 2002 (2) SA 510 (C).
471. Case No. 280/03, judgment delivered 17 Sep. 2004 (SCA).
472. 2006 (3) SA 138 (SCA).

This standard is applied not only to members of the established and organized professions, such as medical doctors,[473] legal practitioners,[474] and accountants and auditors,[475] but also to other specialized occupations, such as bankers,[476] investment advisors[477] and sworn appraisers of land.[478] The said standard is also applied to technicians, such as electricians;[479] and to others with a special competence for performing certain tasks or handling certain equipment, such as petrol station attendants;[480] farmers using special equipment;[481] persons engaged in burning firebelts;[482] and drivers of motor vehicles.[483]

It is negligent to engage voluntarily in any potentially dangerous activity unless one has the skill and knowledge usually associated with the proper discharge of the duties connected with such an activity. The following was said in this regard in *Durr v. ABSA Bank Ltd*:[484] 'It is not negligent not to be a lawyer. But those who undertake to advise clients on matters including an important legal component do so at their peril if they have not informed themselves sufficiently on the law.'

239. The test for negligence where professional knowledge or expertise is concerned has two components: the possession of the necessary knowledge or skill, and the exercise of necessary care and diligence. The ordinary reasonable person or diligens paterfamilias is replaced by the reasonable expert and, in assessing the

473. *See Wyk v. Lewis* 1924 AD 438, *Buls & Another v. Tsatsarolakis* 1976 (2) SA 891 (T); *Richter v. Estate Hamman* 1976 (3) SA 226 (C); *Blyth v. Van den Heever* 1980 (1) SA 191 (A) 221; *Pringle v. Administrator, Tvl* 1990 (2) SA 379 (W) 384–385; *Castell v. De Greef* 1993 (3) SA 501 (C) 509; *Broude v. McIntosh and Others* 1998 (3) SA 60 (SCA); *Mukheiber v. Raath* 1999 (3) SA 1065 (SCA).
474. *Bruce v. Berman* 1963 (3) SA 21 (T); *Honey and Blanckenberg v. Law* 1966 (2) SA 43 (R); *Broderick Properties (Pty) Ltd v. Rood* 1964 (2) SA 310 (T); *Reinecke v. Incorporated General Insurances Ltd* 1974 (2) SA 84 (A); *Mouton v. Die Mynwerkersunie* 1977 (1) SA 119 (A); *Mazibuko v. Singer* 1979 (3) SA 258 (W); *Rampal (Pty) Ltd v. Brett Wills & Partners* 1981 (4) SA 360 (D); *Slomowitz v. Kok* 1983 (1) SA 130 (A). As to the duty of a lawyer towards an opponent in litigation, *see Barlow Rand Ltd t/a Barlow Noordelike Masjinerie Mpy v. Lebos* 1985 (4) SA 335 (T); *Pretorius v. McCullum* 2002 (2) 423 (C), and *see* generally J.R. Midgley, *Lawyers Professional Liability*, 120–132.
475. *International Shipping Co. (Pty) Ltd v. Bentley* 1990 (1) SA 680 (A); *Thoroughbred Breeders' Association v. Price Waterhouse* 2001 (4) SA 551 (SCA); *NPC Electronics Ltd v. Taitz Kaplan & Co.* [1998] 1 All SA 390 (W); *Axiam Holdings Ltd v. Deloitte & Touche* 2006 (1) SA 237 (SCA).
476. *Siman & Co. (Pty) Ltd v. Barclays National Bank Ltd* 1984 (2) SA 888 (A); *BOE Bank Ltd v. Ries* 2002 (2) SA 39 (SCA); *Holtzhausen v. ABSA Bank Ltd* Case no 280/03, judgment delivered 17 Sep. 2004 (SCA).
477. *Durr v. ABSA Bank Ltd* 1997 (3) SA 448 (SCA); *Pinshaw v. Nexus Securities (Pty) Ltd and Another* 2002 (2) SA 510 (C).
478. *Perlman v. Zoutendyk* 1934 CPD 151 328.
479. *EG Electric Co. (Pty) Ltd v. Franklin* 1979 (2) SA 702 (E).
480. *Brown v. Hunt* 1953 (2) SA 540 (A).
481. *Wessels v. Bouwer* 1971 1 PH J9 (NC) (involving the use of a tractor-driven hammer-mill to crush maize cobs).
482. *Van Wyk v. Hermanus Municipality* 1963 (4) SA 285 (C); *Simon's Town Municipality v. Dews* 1993 (1) SA 191 (A).
483. *R v. Du Toit* 1947 (3) SA 141 (A); *S v. Claasen* 1962 (3) SA 308 (O); *Palm v. Elsley* 1974 (2) SA 381 (C); *Beswick v. Crews* 1965 (2) SA 690 (A) 705; *Griffiths v. Netherlands Insurance Co. of SA Ltd* 1976 (4) SA 691 (A) 695; *Butt v. Van der Camp* 1982 (3) SA 819 (A) 826.
484. 1997 (3) SA 448 (SCA) 462.

attributes required, a court 'will have regard to the general level of skill and diligence possessed and exercised at the time by members of the branch of the profession to which the practitioner belongs'.[485] The courts also take into consideration the branch of the profession to which the practitioner belongs. In respect of the medical profession, for example the level of knowledge and skill required will be determined not only by the kind of practice (general practitioner or specialist), but also by the nature of the duties the practitioner is carrying out at the time (specialist duties or general duties, for example, as the casualty officer on duty at a hospital). An error of judgment may be indicative of negligence, but some errors of judgment are reasonable, for instance in emergencies or in situations fraught with risk, such as a complicated medical procedure. However, an error of judgment occasioned by a lack of the required degree of knowledge, skill and diligence will constitute negligence.[486]

240. The test for negligence requires that the conduct of the defendant be assessed in the particular circumstances prevailing at the time. In that sense, locality considerations will also be relevant to the inquiry into professional negligence. However, as far as the level of knowledge and skill expected of a professional is concerned, it is not likely that a lower level of competence will be required of a professional practising in a particular locality, for instance a rural area. In *Van Wyk v. Lewis*,[487] Innes CJ applied a general standard when assessing the competence of a surgeon, without considering the circumstances or practices in the particular locality. Wessels JA in the same case indicated that the level of skill and care to be expected could differ according to locality.[488] The courts are bound to take into account the surrounding circumstances (such as lack of facilities) when assessing care and diligence, but are unlikely to adapt the level of competence expected of a professional according to locality.

241. As indicated in the section on fault (Chapter 1 section 3 above), the standard of care required is determined by objective evaluation, and considerable evidentiary weight attaches to whether or not the conduct complied with normal and generally accepted practice. The generally accepted practice in a particular profession or area of expertise will be indicative of the nature and extent of care and precautions in particular situations.[489] However, the generally accepted practice is not necessarily conclusive. The overriding standard in every instance is that of a reasonable person in the particular situation.

---

485. *Van Wyk v. Lewis* 1924 AD 438 444. *See also Blyth v. Van den Heever* 1980 (1) SA 191 (A) 221; *Randaree v. W H Dixon & Associates* 1983 (2) SA 1 (A) 4; *Pringle v. Administrator, Tvl* 1990 (2) SA 379 (W) 384–385; *Castell v. De Greef* 1993 (3) SA 501 (C) 509.
486. *Mouton v. Die Mynwerkersunie* 1977 (1) SA 119 (A) 143.
487. 1924 AD 438 444.
488. 1924 AD 438 457.
489. *Colman v. Dunbar* 1933 AD 141 157; *Van Heerden v. SA Pulp & Paper Industry* 1946 AD 382.

II. Medical Practitioners

242. A medical practitioner engages in a profession that demands special knowledge, skill and care, and should measure up to the standard of competence that is reasonable to expect of a person of that profession.[490] The relationship between medical practitioner and patient is mostly contractual, but not necessarily, for example where medical services are rendered to an unconscious person. The relationship entails the duty to act with reasonable care and skill, as an implied term of the contract, or as a duty imposed by the law of delict. Concurrence of contract and delict has been recognized in respect of the relationship between doctor and patient in a case where the harm was physical and not purely economic.[491]

243. In *Van Wyk v. Lewis*,[492] Wessels JA said the following on the standard of competence and care expected of a medical practitioner (a surgeon):

> [T]he surgeon [must perform] the operation with such technical skill as the average medical practitioner in South Africa possesses and [must] apply that skill with reasonable care and judgment … [he] is not expected to bring to bear on a case entrusted to him the highest possible professional skill but is bound to employ reasonable skill and care and is liable for the consequences if he does not.

The courts also take into consideration the branch of the medical profession to which the practitioner belongs. The level of knowledge and skill required will be determined by the kind of practice (general practitioner or specialist), but also by the nature of the duties the practitioner is carrying out at the time. A general practitioner may be required to carry out specialist duties, for example in radiology, when acting as the casualty officer on duty at a hospital. Competence will then be assessed at the level of a general practitioner, but this should include the knowledge and judgment as to when it is necessary to call upon the services of a specialist.

244. In this regard, Bekker J said the following in *Esterhuizen v. Administrator, Transvaal*:[493]

> [A] general practitioner is not expected to have the same degree of knowledge and skill and experience as a specialist has. … The question is what is the common knowledge in the branch of the profession to which the accused belongs.

490. *See Mitchell v. Dixon* 1914 AD 519 525. *Van Wyk v. Lewis* 1924 AD 438, *Buls & Another v. Tsatsarolakis* 1976 (2) SA 891 (T); *Richter v. Estate Hamman* 1976 (3) SA 226 (C); *Blyth v. Van den Heever* 1980 (1) SA 191 (A) 221; *Pringle v. Administrator, Tvl* 1990 (2) SA 379 (W) 384–385; *Castell v. De Greef* 1993 (3) SA 501 (C) 509; *Broude v. McIntosh and Others* 1998 (3) SA 60 (SCA); *Mukheiber v. Raath* 1999 (3) SA 1065 (SCA).

491. *Van Wyk v. Lewis* 1924 AD 428.

492. 1924 AD 438 456.

493. 1957 (3) SA 710 (T) 723.

245. In *Buls & Another v. Tsatsarolakis*,[494] the standard applied was that of an average general practitioner, carrying on his duties as a casualty officer in a public hospital, and not that of a specialist orthopaedic surgeon.

246. Liability for medical practitioners may arise not only from clinical work, such as prescribing medicine or the performance of a procedure, but also from the failure to inform patients properly about risks presented by medicine or medical procedures. Patients must be informed of the material aspects of the risk of harm.[495] In *Castell v. De Greef*,[496] the court reviewed the South African law in this regard comprehensively and held that, for a patient's consent to constitute a defence, the doctor is obliged to warn a patient of a material risk inherent in the proposed treatment; and that a risk is material if, in the circumstances of the particular case:

– a reasonable person in the patient's position, if warned of the risk, would be likely to attach significance to it; or
– the medical practitioner is or should reasonably be aware that the particular patient, if warned of the risk, would be likely to attach significance to it.[497]

247. If a medical procedure involves the risk of harmful side effects even if performed competently, the patient must be informed of the material aspects of the risk of harm. Questions of unlawfulness, causation and negligence arise in this regard. If, for example, a surgeon operates without beforehand fully informing the patient of the risks, the operation is performed without the patient's informed consent. If harmful side effects occur, and the patient would not have undergone the operation if informed of the risk, the surgeon will have caused the harm unlawfully. If the failure to inform the patient was also negligent in terms of the standard of a reasonable practitioner in the relevant branch of the medical profession, the practitioner will be liable. If, however, the operation is completely successful and no harmful side effects occur, there is no unlawful causing of harm, despite the fact that the operation was performed without the patient's informed consent.[498]

248. In cases of children born disabled, a medical practitioner can be liable towards the parents for failing to advise them properly as to the risks of disability, so as to enable them to make an informed decision on abortion, but in *Stewart and*

494. 1976 (2) SA 891 (T) 894.

495. *See* generally *Esterhuizen v. Administrator, Transvaal* 1957 (3) SA 710 (T) 719; *Santam Insurance Co. Ltd v. Vorster* 1973 (4) SA 764 (A) 781; *Castell v. De Greeff* 1994 (4) SA 408 (C) 425.

496. 1994 (4) SA 408 (C).

497. *Castell v. De Greeff* 1994 (4) SA 408 (C) at 426.

498. *See Broude v. McIntosh and Others* 1998 (3) SA 60 (SCA), where Marais JA referred to this situation and expressed the view that there is no principle of law by which the characterization as unlawful or lawful of an intentional act objectively involving the doing of bodily harm to another could be postponed until its consequences are known. It is suggested, however, that this view is open to criticism. In the event of a completely successful operation there is no harm or damage for the purposes of the law of delict, despite the fact that the patient might have chosen not to undergo the operation had he known of the risks; and in the law of delict the characterization of an act as unlawful or lawful can often only be done once the consequences of the act are known.

Another v. Botha and Another,[499] the Supreme Court of Appeal refused to recognize a 'wrongful life' claim by a child born disabled. The question of unlawfulness involved consideration of the content of the duty owed to the child by the medical practitioners and the corresponding right of the child. The court held that this question essentially involved a choice between life with disabilities on the one hand and non-existence on the other. Making that choice in favour of non-existence not only involves a disregard for the sanctity of life and the dignity of the child, but also involves an arbitrary, subjective preference for some policy considerations and the denial of others. Therefore, the essential question when adjudicating a claim of this kind is whether the particular child should have been born at all. That is a question that goes so deeply to the heart of what it is to be human that it should not even be asked of the law. For that reason, the court refused to recognize the action of the child.

However, in H v. Fetal Assessment Centre,[500] the Constitutional Court decided differently. The plaintiff instituted a claim on behalf of her minor child who suffered from Down's syndrome. She alleged that the defendant had acted negligently by failing to inform her that there was a high risk of her child being born with Down's syndrome. She alleged that, if she had known of this risk, she would have had an abortion. The High Court disallowed the claim, holding that, while South African law recognizes a claim by a mother for damages for harm caused by a prenatal misdiagnosis, it does not recognize such a claim brought by the child. The Constitutional Court unanimously decided that the existing position, which deprives a child of the right to claim damages for a prenatal misdiagnosis, may not be in the child's best interests and found that, in theory, such a claim may exist. The court referred the matter back to the High Court, since a decision on the validity of the child's claim might involve complex factual and legal considerations which the High Court was best placed to assess. The High Court would have to decide whether the elements of a delict had been satisfied, or whether a new remedy should be developed to allow a child to recover compensation for any harm he or she may have suffered.

249. Medical practitioners can also be held liable for economic loss in cases of unwanted pregnancy resulting in the birth of a normal child. In *Mukheiber v. Raath*,[501] the parents of a healthy and normal child (their fourth) instituted action in delict against a gynaecologist, alleging that he had negligently misrepresented to them that the wife had been sterilized after the birth of their third child. Relying on this representation, they had failed to take contraceptive measures, with the result that the fourth child was conceived and born. The parents claimed damages from the doctor for pure economic loss, in the form of confinement costs and maintenance of the child until he becomes self-supporting. The Supreme Court of Appeal held that the doctor had a legal duty to desist from making any representation on the matter of sterilization until he had taken reasonable steps to ensure the accuracy of the representation. The factual and policy considerations indicating the existence

499. 2008 (6) SA 310 (SCA); [2008] ZASCA 84 .
500. 2015 (2) SA 193 (CC).
501. 1999 (3) SA 1065 (SCA). *See also* the contractual claim in *Edouard v. Administrator, Natal* 1989 (2) SA (D).

of such a duty were the following: the special relationship between the doctor and the parents who consulted him; the material risk that the situation involved, that is, the risk of the conception and birth of an unwanted child; the fact that this risk should have been obvious to the mind of the doctor; the fact that it should also have been obvious to the doctor that the parents would rely on what he told them and that the correctness of the representation was of vital importance to them, and that that they could suffer serious damage if the representation was incorrect; and the fact that the representation related to technical matters concerning a surgical procedure about which the parents would necessarily be ignorant, and the doctor should be knowledgeable. As far as public policy considerations are concerned, the court held that the parents' reasons for wanting the sterilization were socio-economic and family reasons, that were socially acceptable and not *contra bonos mores*. The recognition of a legal duty in this case would not impose too heavy a burden on the doctor: professionals must act with due care and should not make unsolicited misrepresentations. Through misrepresentation, the doctor therefore had unlawfully caused financial loss to the parents and was held liable.

250. In *Premier, Kwazulu-Natal v. Sonny and Another*,[502] a doctor failed to inform a pregnant patient of the meaning of an ultrasound scan which indicated possible Down's syndrome, or of the importance of the patient returning for a second scan. This, coupled with a nurse's subsequent misdirection, resulted in the patient not returning for the scan, and not having further tests to diagnose the syndrome within the time allowed to terminate the pregnancy. The child was eventually born with Down's syndrome, and the patient and her husband sued successfully for the costs of maintaining their daughter.

251. In deciding on the liability of medical practitioners, the court will take into account all the circumstances, including the nature of the work and the nature of the alleged failing (error of judgment, lack of required knowledge or care). In *Oppelt v. Department of Health, Western Cape*[503] the plaintiff suffered a serious spinal cord injury in a rugby match. He was taken to a government hospital for treatment. The medical professionals failed to provide him with timeous appropriate medical treatment (a 'closed reduction') and the delay meant that he became paralysed from the neck down. The plaintiff sued the provincial government for damages in delict. The trial court allowed his claim, but this decision was overturned by the Supreme Court of Appeal. In a further appeal, the Constitutional Court found that the medical professionals had been negligent and that the plaintiff's harm had been caused wrongfully. Regarding wrongfulness, the court held that there was a legal duty in the circumstances for the medical professionals to provide the plaintiff with timeous medical treatment, in part because section 27(3) of the Constitution requires that emergency medical treatment be provided to those who require it. The defendant could not justify the delay through citing a need for it to adhere to hospital protocols regarding the transfer of patients to other healthcare facilities.

502. 2011 (3) SA 424 (SCA).
503. 2016 (1) SA 325 (CC).

III. Legal Practitioners

252. The legal profession in South Africa is divided into two branches, involving practice either as an attorney or as an advocate. Broadly stated, attorneys deal directly with clients, whereas advocates take instructions from attorneys, who act in this regard in terms of a mandate received from a client. Advocates have the right to appear in the higher courts. The division between the two branches of the profession has been bridged by the Right of Appearance in Courts Act,[504] in terms of which attorneys under certain conditions also have the right to appear in the higher courts in the Republic (including the Supreme Court of Appeal and Constitutional Court). Generally, members of both branches of the profession are required to have specialized knowledge, skill and care; and a practitioner must measure up to the standard of competence of a reasonable man professing such attributes.[505]

A. Attorneys

253. The relationship of attorney and client is a contractual one. This relationship imposes the duty, by way of an implied term, to perform professional services with the knowledge, competence, skill and care that can reasonably be expected of a member of the profession. Failure to exercise this standard of care is a breach of this implied term of the contract.[506] An attorney will not be guilty of negligence merely because he committed an error of judgment, whether on matters of discretion or law.[507] However, an error of judgment may be indicative of negligence, in particular where the practitioner should have realized that the work required a degree of expertise which he or she did not possess. Also, an error of judgment occasioned by a lack of the required degree of knowledge, skill and diligence will constitute negligence.[508] Where an attorney does not exercise the required skill and care and the client suffers loss, the damages will be those that normally flow from the breach or may reasonably be supposed to have been in the contemplation of the parties as likely to result from it.[509]

254. Apart from liability for damages which arises in contract, an attorney may also be held liable in delict. As noted in section I above, concurrence of contract and delict has been recognized in respect of the relationship between attorney and

504. Act 62 of 1995.
505. *See* generally J.R. Midgley, *Lawyers' Professional Liability,* 120–132 (Juta & Co. Ltd 1992).
506. *Honey & Blanckenberg v. Law* 1966 (2) SA 43 (R); *Bruce v. Berman* 1963 (3) SA 21 (T) 23; *Mouton v. Die Mynwerkersunie* 1977 (1) SA 119 (A); *Groom v. Crocker* 1938 (2) All ER 394 (CA) 401–402.
507. *Honey & Blanckenberg v. Law* 1966 (2) SA 43 (R).
508. *Mouton v. Die Mynwerkersunie* 1977 (1) SA 119 (A) 143.
509. *Lavery & Co. Ltd v. Jungheinrich* 1931 AD 156 169; *Whitfield v. Phillips* 1957 (3) SA 318 (A) 325; *Saif Ali v. Sydney Mitchell & Co. & P* 1978 (3) All ER 1033 (HL).

client in respect of pure economic loss,[510] although in the leading case concerning an attorney's liability to his client, the client's action was treated as a contractual action.[511]

255. In *Roestoff v. Cliffe Dekker Hofmeyr Inc*[512] fraudsters managed to access the plaintiff's bank account by Internet 'phishing' and stole ZAR 350,000 from it. They then transferred ZAR 200,000 of this amount into the defendant attorneys' trust account. The defendant firm was not aware that the money had been stolen and subsequently transferred the money to a third party. The plaintiff sued the firm for loss of the money, claiming that it, as a firm of attorneys, had a legal duty to ascertain the source of the money before allowing the money to be paid out to a third party. The court held that, although the plaintiff had been unknown to the firm, there was a duty on it not to be negligent in respect of deposits made into its trust account. This means that attorneys are generally obliged to verify the source of unidentified trust account deposits before dealing with them. However, in this instance the firm had not been negligent, as there had been nothing to alert it to the fact that the deposit had been obtained fraudulently. In addition, the fraudsters had misled the firm as to the source of the deposit, and the plaintiff himself had been negligent in failing to heed the bank's warnings on its Internet banking website about the prevalence of Internet fraud.

256. In *Steyn NO v. Ronald Bobroff & Partners*[513] the claim was against a firm of attorneys alleged by the appellant to be specialists in the field of personal injury claims. The appellant contracted the firm to lodge a claim with the Road Accident Fund in respect of personal injuries suffered by her minor son in a motor vehicle accident. The appellant alleged that it was a tacit term in the contract of professional services between them that the respondent would execute the mandate with reasonable diligence, care and skill; and further, that the firm had been negligent in executing the mandate, in that it had failed to prosecute the claim timeously, which resulted in the Road Accident Fund paying out the appellant's claim some fourteen-and-a-half months later than it otherwise would have done. The appellant's claim was for damages in the form of the interest that would have been earned on the capital sum over the fourteen-month period, had it been invested. The court found that the appellant had failed to adduce clear evidence proving that the respondent had acted negligently and, in particular, evidence of how a reasonable attorney would have prosecuted the claim in the circumstances. Accordingly, her claim for damages failed.

---

510. *Rampal (Pty) Ltd v. Brett Wills and Partners* 1981 (4) SA 360 (D).

511. *Mouton v. Die Mynwerkersunie* 1977 (1) SA 119 (A); and *see also Bouwer v. Harding* 1997 (4) SA 1023 (SE), where the liability of an attorney to a client was the subject of an action for breach of contract, and the attorney was found to be in breach of his contractual duties by negligently failing to advise the client correctly on the tax implications of structuring a sale of property in a particular manner.

512. 2013 (1) SA 12 (GNP).

513. 2013 (2) SA 311 (SCA).

257. Liability in delict towards a third party outside the contractual relationship can also arise, for instance in a 'disappointed beneficiary' case, where a benefit conferred in a will does not flow to the intended beneficiary, because the attorney was negligent in the drafting or execution of the will.[514] An attorney conducting litigation on behalf of a client has a duty to act with integrity and care not only towards his or her client, but also towards the court and the opponent; but this duty is likely to be considered a matter of professional ethics rather than a basis for delictual liability.[515]

B. Advocates

258. There is authority in South African common law for the view that advocates are not liable for an error, lack of expertise or mistake of fact or law, particularly where this concerns the handling of a case in court.[516] This immunity from liability is rooted in the policy consideration that it is not in the interests of the administration of justice that a court should have to conduct what effectively amounts to a retrial of a case heard in another court, to determine whether the alleged error or lack of expertise was negligent and the cause of harm to the client. This was also the approach to liability of barristers in English law, but the position has changed.[517] There is no authoritative South African case dealing generally with the liability of advocates for negligence, but the courts are likely to impose the same standard of knowledge, competence, skill and care that is expected of other legal professionals, rather than maintaining an historical immunity based on a questionable distinction between the handling of a case in court and other professional work.

259. In deciding on the liability of legal practitioners, the court will take into account all the circumstances, including the nature of the work (advisory, or the conduct of litigation) and the nature of the alleged failing (error of judgment, lack of required knowledge or care).

IV. Engineers, Builders, Architects

260. Professionals involved in the construction industry, such as engineers, builders and architects, must, like other professionals, exercise reasonable care in their work, and must measure up to the standard of competence that is reasonable to expect of a person professing such knowledge and skill.

---

514. *See Pretorius en andere v. McCullum* 2002 (2) SA 423 (K).
515. *Barlow Rand Ltd t/a Barlow Noordelike Masjinerie Mpy v. Lebos* 1985 (4) SA 341 (D).
516. J.R. Midgley, *Lawyers' Professional Liability* 1 ff.
517. *See Rondel v. Worsley* 1966 (3) All ER 657 (CA) and *Rondel v. Worsley* 1967 (3) All ER 993 (HL); *Saif Ali v. Sydney Mitchell & Co. & P* 1978 (3) All ER 1033 (HL).

261. The case of *Lillicrap, Wassenaar & Partners v. Pilkington Bros (SA) (Pty) Ltd*[518] dealt with an engineer and client relationship where professional negligence caused economic loss. The testing of the ground structure prior to the building of a glass factory was inadequate, with the result that the levels inside the factory were defective, and extensive repair work had to be done. The engineering firm was initially in a direct contractual relationship with the client, and later in the position of a subcontractor. The Supreme Court of Appeal held that the client has a contractual remedy and no concurrent action in delict. A key consideration was that this case did not involve an infringement of rights of property or person, but only the infringement of a contractual duty to perform specific professional work with due diligence. There was no independent duty for the purposes of delictual liability. In the view of most commentators, this judgment implied that only a contractual remedy is available where pure economic loss (as opposed to physical damage or personal injury) is caused by negligent performance of a contractual duty, notably in the relationship between a client and a professional person.[519]

262. In *Tsimatakopoulos v. Hemingway, Isaacs & Coetzee CC*,[520] it was held that a firm of engineers was liable in delict for negligently designing a defective wall. The engineers had contracted with their client to design a retaining wall on the client's property and had negligently designed the wall with inadequate strength, so that it leaned over. The client had sold the property to the plaintiff, who had to incur the cost of restoring the stability of the wall.[521] The principle on which the judgment was based was the same as those accepted in cases involving pure economic loss, namely that a party to a contract can have a legal duty and be liable in delict to a person who is not a party to the contract: and the recognition of such a legal duty is:

> the outcome of a value judgment that the plaintiff's interest is deemed worthy of legal protection against negligent interference by conduct of the kind alleged against the defendant.[522]

There was no contractual nexus between the plaintiff and the engineers. In respect of the question whether the plaintiff had an independent claim in delict against the engineers, it was irrelevant that the original client might have had a claim in contract against the engineers, and that the plaintiff might have been able to take cession of such a claim. The real issue was how far the engineers' legal duty should be extended in any given situation. A professional engineer should have foreseen that wall would not remain stable, and that the property on which it was built could be sold to another person, and that his negligence was likely to cause harm to the subsequent owner.

---

518. *Lillicrap, Wassenaar and Partners v. Pilkington Brothers (SA) (Pty) Ltd* 1985 (1) SA 475 (A).
519. J.R. Midgley, *The Nature of the Inquiry into Concurrence of Actions*, 107 S. African L. J. 621 (1990); Annél van Aswegen, *Die Toets vir die Bestaan van 'n 'Onafhanklike Delik' in die Geval van Kontrakbreuk* 55 THRHR 271, 273–274 (1992).
520. 1993 (4) SA 428 (C).
521. 1993 (4) SA 428 (C).
522. At 431H–I.

263. The case of *SM Goldstein & Co. (Pty) Ltd v. Cathkin Park Hotel (Pty) Ltd*[523] involved a delictual action for damages by the owner of a hotel against the building contractor responsible for building the hotel in accordance with an architect's design. A fireplace for an open fire in the lobby of the hotel was built as designed by the architect, but the design created a fire hazard and did not comply with the installation instructions of the manufacturer of the Jetmaster firebox built into the fireplace. In due course, a fire broke out as a result of the faulty design of the fireplace and the hotel was extensively damaged. Although the building contractor had built it in accordance with the architect's design as the building contract required, it had failed to comply with the installation instructions of the manufacturer as the building contract also required. It was common cause that it would have been manifest to any builder that the construction of the fireplace in accordance with the architect's design was unsafe. The court held that a builder generally had a legal duty to both the owner and third parties to refrain from building something which was manifestly unsafe. The foreseeability of the harm was also a relevant consideration in deciding on the existence of a legal duty and wrongfulness. The building contractor had therefore acted both wrongfully and negligently and was liable in delict for the owner's loss.

Although the *SM Goldstein* case, like the *Tsimatakopoulos* case, did not deal with pure economic loss, the approach to determining the existence of a legal duty and wrongfulness corresponds to that adopted by the courts in cases involving pure economic loss. The court in this case did not even refer to the question of concurrence of delictual and contractual actions, accepting that in cases involving foreseeable harm a builder has a legal duty towards the owner and third parties to build safely, with the apparent implication that this duty arises independently from his contract with the owner. This case also confirms that recognition of delictual liability for pure economic loss within a contractual relationship is subject to the qualification that the contract party who elects to sue in delict should not be able to circumvent contractual immunities, waivers, or other limitations of liability to which he agreed. Such clauses can be invoked against a delictual claim by way of a defence, as happened in this case. However, on the facts of this case and on the wording of the building contract, the court decided that the builder could not rely on the liability exemption clause contained in the contract.

264. In *Pienaar and Others v. Brown and Others*,[524] the Supreme Court of Appeal held that the test for liability of a building contractor as employer of an independent subcontractor, for damage negligently caused by the subcontractor, consists of three broad questions: (1) Would a reasonable man have foreseen the risk of danger in consequence of the work he employed the contractor to perform? If so, (2) would a reasonable man have taken steps to guard against the danger? If so, (3) were such steps duly taken in the case in question? The liability in these cases is personal, not vicarious, and it is not a question of the liability of the employer being passed to the independent contractor, and thence to any subcontractor, but a question of the respective individual liability of each of them. Only where the answer to

523. 2000 (4) SA 1019 (SCA).
524. 2010 (6) SA 365 (SCA).

the first two questions is in the affirmative does a 'legal duty arise, the failure to comply with which can form the basis of liability'.[525]

On a proper reading of the National Building Regulations and Building Standards Act 103 of 1977, there is nothing to suggest that a failure to comply with its requirement to submit plans for a building in terms of section 4(1), read with section 7, would necessarily lead to liability for damage caused by collapse of part of the building work. There must be a causal link between the failure to submit the plans and the collapse of the building work.[526]

265. In deciding on the liability of professionals involved in the construction industry, the court will take into account all the circumstances, including the nature of the work and the nature of the alleged failing (error of judgment, lack of required knowledge or care).

V. Accountants and Auditors

266. The liability of accountants and auditors to their clients is primarily contractual and is governed by the same principles that apply to attorneys, engineers and other professionals. The duties of an auditor towards his client was extensively considered by the Supreme Court of Appeal in *Thoroughbred Breeders' Association v. Price Waterhouse*,[527] where it was held that contributory negligence in terms of the Apportionment of Damages Act[528] does not apply in the contractual relationship between auditor and client.

267. The delictual liability of accountants and auditors to third parties (non-clients), who rely on a negligently formulated opinion, certificate, report or statement, is governed by legislation. The legislation essentially recognizes a duty on the part of an auditor or accountant towards a third party if the auditor knew or could reasonably be expected to know the third party would act on the information furnished to him or her.[529]

268. A potential investor or lender to a company should be entitled to rely on the company's audited financial statements; that is, the statements give a correct and clear picture of the company's financial position. In the event of incorrect or misleading statements, an investor or lender may claim delictual damages from the auditor. Section 46(2) and (3) of the Auditing Profession Act 26 of 2005 describes when an auditor will be liable for an opinion, report or statement:

(1) In respect of any opinion expressed or report or statement made by a registered auditor in the ordinary course of duties the registered auditor does not

525. Paragraph [11] at 368H–369B.
526. Paragraph [16] at 370D E, read with para. [7] at 367H–I.
527. 2001 (4) SA 551 (SCA).
528. Act 34 of 1956.
529. Section 20(9)(b) of the Public Accountants' and Auditors' Act 80 of 1991.

incur any liability to a client or any third party, unless it is proved that the opinion was expressed, or the report or statement made, maliciously, fraudulently or pursuant to a negligent performance of the registered auditor's duties.

(2) Despite subsection (2), a registered auditor incurs liability to third parties who have relied on an opinion, report or statement of that registered auditor for financial loss suffered as a result of having relies thereon, only if it is proved that the opinion was expressed, or the report or statement was made, pursuant to a negligent performance of the registered auditor's duties and the registered auditor:

(a) knew, or could in the particular circumstances reasonably have been expected to know, at the time when the negligence occurred in the performance of the duties pursuant to which the opinion was expressed or the report or statement was made:
  - that the opinion, report or statement would be used by a client to induce the third party to act or refrain from acting in some way or to enter into the specific transaction into which the third party entered, or any other transaction of a similar nature, with the client or any other person; or
  - that the third party would rely on the opinion, report or statement for the purpose of acting or refraining from acting in some way or of entering into the specific transaction into which the third party entered, or any other transaction of a similar nature, with the client or any other person; or

(b) in any way represented, at any time after the opinion was expressed or the report or statement was made, to the third party that the opinion, report or statement was correct, while at the time the registered auditor knew or could in the particular circumstances reasonably have been expected to know that the third party would rely on that representation for the purpose of acting or refraining from acting in some way or of entering into the specific transaction into which the third party entered, or any other transaction of a similar nature, with the client or any other person.

269. In terms of these provisions, an auditor will not incur liability to a client or any third party in respect of a report or opinion expressed by him unless it was given maliciously, fraudulently or pursuant to negligent performance of the auditor's duties. Section 46(3) provides that if the report was made negligently, the auditor will be liable to a third party who relied on it. However, this is only if the third party can prove that the auditor knew or could, in the particular circumstances, reasonably have been expected to know that the client would use the opinion or report to induce the third party to act or refrain from acting, or that the third party would rely on the opinion or report.

270. Arguably, every auditor knows or ought reasonably to foresee that the annual financial statements of a company are widely used by investors and lenders for investment and business decisions. Also, one would reasonably expect an auditor to know that the client or the third party would act as contemplated in section

46(3)(a)(ii). However, for the purposes of this section, the requisite knowledge or foreseeability depends on the circumstances of each case.

271. There are different frameworks for auditing in South Africa. In terms of the Companies Act,[530] the auditors have a duty to ensure that the presentation of a company's financial position in the financial statements complies with the financial reporting standards applicable to the type of company. If an auditor does not ensure compliance with such practice, this constitutes a breach of the auditor's statutory duties and is likely to amount to negligence. The South African Institute of Chartered Accountants (SAICA), in conjunction with the Accounting Practices Board, also produces frameworks for auditing. A company must disclose which auditing framework it has adopted. An auditor's failure to ensure that the financial statements conform to the applicable standards is a breach of his statutory duty in terms of the Companies Act and is likely to amount to negligence.

272. In *International Shipping Co. (Pty) Ltd v. Bentley,*[531] a financing company in 1977 made facilities available to a group of companies. Thereafter, Bentley was appointed auditor to the group. From 1979, he issued unqualified financial statements that were to some extent false or misleading. The company alleged that it had relied on the statements in reviewing its facilities to the group and in deciding to increase the facilities. The group was liquidated in 1981, and the financing company suffered loss. The court found that Bentley's conduct was wrongful and blameworthy, and a *conditio sine qua non* of the company's loss, but a number of other factors had intervened and the ultimate loss was regarded as being too remote for Bentley to be held liable.

273. In *NPC Electronics Ltd v. Taitz Kaplan & Co,*[532] the plaintiff had relied on unqualified reports by the defendant firm of accountants and auditors on the financial statements of certain companies, prior to selling and delivering goods to these companies and making additional credit facilities available to them. The companies were subsequently liquidated. There was no contractual or other relationship between the parties. The court held that the auditor in this case did not conduct a proper auditing procedure and failed to carry out its duties in terms of the Companies Act. However, the defendant did not know and could not reasonably be expected to foresee that the plaintiff would rely on the reports for this purpose. In the circumstances, the defendant did not have a legal duty to prevent the loss of the plaintiff, and there was consequently no wrongfulness. Even if there were such a duty and wrongfulness, the plaintiff did not prove that the defendant had factually or legally caused its loss. The loss suffered by a third party reading financial statements and using them in a manner unknown to the auditors should not be the responsibility of the auditors. Imposing liability in this case would place an unreasonably onerous burden on the auditors.

530. Act 71 of 2008, s. 84(4)(b).
531. 1990 (1) SA 680 (A) 700.
532. [1998] 1 All SA 390 (W).

274. In *Axiam Holdings Ltd v. Deloitte & Touche*,[533] it was alleged that the auditors had owed a duty to third parties to warn them that certain financial statements and their audit opinion were incorrect, alternatively to warn them that it had not conducted the audit properly, and that they should not rely on the statements and the audit opinion; and that their failure in this regard was negligent and constituted a misrepresentation within the meaning of section 20(9)(b)(ii) of the Public Accountants' and Auditors' Act (which then applied).[534] The auditors raised an exception, on the basis that the allegations in the pleadings did not justify the conclusion that the auditors owed a legal duty to the third parties. Navsa JA said the following on liability of auditors for negligent misstatement:

> It is true that decisions by courts on whether to grant or withhold a remedy for negligent misstatement causing economic loss, are made conscious of the importance of keeping liability within reasonable bounds. It is universally accepted in common law countries that auditors ought not to bear liability simply because it might be foreseen in general terms that audit reports and financial statements are frequently used in commercial transactions involving the party for whom the audit was conducted (and audit reports completed) and third parties. In general, auditors have no duty to third parties with whom there is no relationship or where the factors set out in the *Standard Chartered Bank* case are absent.[535]

The majority of the court held that the unlawfulness of the harm-causing by omission to speak could not in this case be decided on exception. The matter had to go to trial; it was premature to decide on exception whether a legal duty could be said to exist.

275. In deciding on the liability of accountants and auditors, the court will take into account all the circumstances, including the nature of the work (advisory or auditing) and the nature of the alleged failing (error of judgment, lack of required knowledge or care).

VI. Banks

276. Banking is an occupation that demands special knowledge and skill, and bankers must exercise reasonable care and measure up to the standard of competence that is reasonable to expect of a person professing knowledge and skill in banking. The relationship between bank and client is contractual, with express or implied terms, or both, in respect of the banking service contracted for. In addition, there may be a legal duty on the bank to provide the client with information, and potential liability for misinformation. Banking encompasses a wide variety of activities, which includes assisting clients in commercial transactions, dealing with

533. 2006 (1) SA 237 (SCA).
534. Act 80 of 1991.
535. Paragraph 18.

the collection of cheques, conducting foreign currency transactions, reporting on the creditworthiness of clients, reporting on the state of accounts, dealing with insurance matters and offering investment advice. The cases referred to below illustrate the potential liability of banks in these areas.

277. In *Administrateur, Natal v. Trust Bank van Afrika Bpk,*[536] the court applied the general criterion of reasonableness to determine whether an alleged act of misrepresentation on the part of a bank should be regarded as unlawful for the purposes of delictual liability. The court accepted that the criterion of reasonableness involves policy considerations. In this case, the defendant bank acted on behalf of a person who claimed compensation from the provincial authorities for expropriation of property. Compensation was eventually paid to him via the bank, but it turned out that he was not the owner of the property concerned. The provincial authorities then claimed the amount that they paid out as damages for alleged negligent misrepresentation by the bank. The action failed, because the provincial authorities themselves had initially identified the claimant as owner of the property, and the court held that the bank had no legal duty to verify the facts, and that the plaintiff's own mistake therefore caused the loss.

278. In *Indac Electronics (Pty) Ltd v. Volkskas Bank Ltd,*[537] it was held that a collecting banker can be liable under the extended *lex Aquilia* for negligence to the true owner of a cheque, where the owner was specified as the payee and the cheque was crossed and marked 'not negotiable', but the cheque was nevertheless collected for and the proceeds credited to another person. A delictual action for damages would be available to a true owner of a cheque who can establish:

(1) that the collecting banker received payment of the cheque on behalf of someone who was not entitled thereto;
(2) that in receiving such payment the collecting banker acted:
    (a) negligently; and
    (b) unlawfully.
(3) that the conduct of the collecting banker caused the true owner to sustain loss; and
(4) that the damages claimed represent proper compensation for such loss.

279. In deciding on principle in the *Indac* case that a collecting bank can be liable to the true owner of a cheque for damages suffered in the event of payment of the cheque to someone who was not entitled thereto, the court made a value judgment and referred to a number of policy considerations relevant to the existence of a legal duty on the part of the bank towards its client. The objection of limitless or indeterminate liability does not arise in this case, because the extent of the potential loss is finite (the face value of the cheque), and the potential claimants are easily predictable and are limited to the drawer or the payee (or someone holding title under him). Furthermore, each potential claim will arise separately from any other

536. 1979 (3) SA 824 (A), at 833–834.
537. 1992 (1) SA 783 (A) 797–801.

and will be related to a specific act on the part of the collecting banker. The collecting banker undertakes to provide a professional service to collect other persons' cheques payable to his client, and should be aware that failure to take reasonable care may result in loss to the true owner of the cheque. The collecting banker, by virtue of his or her calling, possesses or professes to possess special skill and competence in his field and can, or ought to, appreciate the significance of instructions on a cheque. The bank is thus able to reduce, if not avoid, loss to the true owner by exercising reasonable care in the collection of cheques. If there was no legal duty to take reasonable care, it would mean that the collecting banker need not examine or even look at the cheque to ascertain to whom it is payable. The crossing of a cheque would be of little consequence if no legal duty existed on the part of the collecting banker. The collecting banker is the only person who is in a position to know whether or not a cheque is being collected on behalf of a person who is entitled to receive payment, and the drawee bank has to rely on the collecting banker to ascertain this fact. The collecting banker is fully aware of this position, and it is therefore his duty to ensure that he only presents a cheque for payment on behalf of a client who is entitled to receive payment of the cheque. Whereas the drawer or true owner of a cheque is unable to take steps for protection against loss if the collecting banker negligently collects payment on behalf of the wrong person, the collecting banker does have a right of recovery. The bank would have a claim for reimbursement against a customer who was wrongly credited with the proceeds of the cheque. If that customer is unable to pay, it would be more appropriate to allocate the loss to the banker who chose to accept the customer's business, than to the innocent true owner of the cheque. Furthermore, a collecting banker could relatively inexpensively protect itself against such loss by obtaining insurance cover.

280. In *Siman & Co. (Pty) Ltd v. Barclays National Bank Ltd*,[538] the plaintiff had approached the defendant bank on a Friday afternoon to procure immediate forward cover for its foreign currency commitments incurred for overseas purchases, as it had heard that the Rand unit of currency would probably be devalued over that weekend. The defendant bank informed the plaintiff that it was then too late for the cover to be procured that afternoon, and that it could only be procured on the following Monday. The Rand was, in fact, devalued during that weekend and the plaintiff, when subsequently paying for its foreign commitments, had to pay much more in Rand than it would have cost it if it had procured the immediate forward cover on the Friday afternoon. The statement by the bank official on the Friday, that it was too late to obtain forward cover that day, was in fact incorrect. Consequently, the plaintiff instituted action against the bank for damages in the amount which it had to pay in excess of what it would have had to pay if it had obtained the forward cover on the Friday. The plaintiff alleged that it had been misled by the defendant's statement that it was too late to procure the required cover on the Friday afternoon, that such statement was false because the cover was still procurable, that the statement had been made negligently and had caused the plaintiff loss. The action was

538. 1984 (2) SA 888 (A).

dismissed by the trial court. On appeal, the majority of the Appellate Division confirmed that the action must fail, deciding that the bank official's conduct involved two relevant acts:

(1) a firm decision or refusal, taken and persisted in, not to procure any forward cover for the plaintiff that afternoon; or
(2) the defendant's intimation to the plaintiff of the reason for the refusal, that is, that it was too late to do anything that afternoon, which was the misstatement.

It was necessary to distinguish between the above two acts, as the plaintiff had for the purposes of its action selected and relied only on act (2), the defendant's misstatement, and had founded its cause of action thereon. The plaintiff had never relied on act (1), the refusal to obtain the forward cover, at any stage of the proceedings. On the facts, the plaintiff's loss had ensued in consequence of the defendant's refusal to procure the cover that afternoon, when there was still time to do so. The defendant's intimation to the plaintiff of its reasons for refusing, wrong though they were, were then of no consequence. (In a dissenting minority judgment, Corbett JA found that the bank official, acting in the course and scope of his employment, made a misstatement to the client; and in doing so the official acted negligently and unlawfully; and that the misstatement had caused the client's loss.)

281. In *Durr v. ABSA Bank Ltd*,[539] the appellant-plaintiff sought to recover from the respondent-defendant (the bank) damages for the loss of money which she and other members of her family had invested in certain companies that went insolvent shortly afterwards (the companies), on recommendation of the regional manager of the bank's broking division. The manager had described the investments as 'safe', 'very solid', 'very secure' and 'very sound', and had strongly recommended them. The plaintiff alleged that she had suffered loss as a result of the manager's negligent failure to exercise the degree of care and skill which she was entitled to expect of someone in his position, and for which failure the bank should be held vicariously liable. Her evidence was that she would never have thought of investing in the companies were it not for the advice of the manager; and that she believed the bank had financial experts who would examine prospective investments. The companies were represented in publicity material as having a sound financial base and brokers were offered commission at a rate substantially higher than that for comparable investments. Brokers were invited to marketing conferences and given glossy brochures and dossiers containing laudatory press cuttings. No prospectuses or financial statements were provided. The companies concerned did not have the audited financial statements or prospectuses required by law; and no financial statements were made available to brokers. The manager had obtained his information about the investments from the directors of the companies themselves and from attending their marketing conferences. Although the manager's real skills were confined to advising clients on planning their affairs having regard to income tax, estate duty and investments such as endowments, retirement annuities, unit trusts, fixed deposits, life

539. 1997 (3) SA 448 (SCA).

assurance and the like, he at no stage sought information or advice about the investment in the companies from people who were better placed to evaluate them.

The court held that two issues arose, namely:

(1) in general, what was the level of skill and knowledge required; and
(2) whether the standard against which that skill and knowledge should be judged was that of an ordinary or average broker or that of a regional manager of the broking division of a bank professing investment skill and offering expert investment advice.

The court held, as to (1), that ‘in deciding what is reasonable the court will have regard to the general level of skill and diligence possessed and exercised at the time by the members of the branch of the profession to which the practitioner belongs’, but that ‘the decision of what is reasonable under the circumstances is for the court; it will pay high regard to the views of the profession, but it is not bound to adopt them’. As to (2), the court held that, as a matter of law set in the factual context of the case, the relevant standard in this instance was not that of the average or typical broker of modest accomplishments, because acceptance of such standard would allow a definition chosen by a witness for his own purposes to dictate the result, making the inquiry of what was required of a particular kind of broker pointless. The appropriate standard was that of the regional manager of the broking division of a financial institution professing investment skills and offering expert investment advice. As to the manager’s negligence, the basic rule was as follows: ‘[L]ack of skill or knowledge is not per se negligent. It is, however, negligent to engage voluntarily in any potentially dangerous activity unless one has the skill and knowledge usually associated with the proper discharge of the duties connected with such an activity.’ In bringing the investments to the plaintiff’s attention and assuring her that he had investigated it and strongly recommended it, he had advised the plaintiff to embark upon what was, in effect, the potentially dangerous activity of money lending. The manager was under a duty to make enquiries about the companies and the bank, given that he had held himself out as expert investment advisor, without qualification, could not argue that he had not been under a duty to investigate the creditworthiness of the companies. The plaintiff had been entitled to see the manager as a man skilled to advise her on such matters and as one backed by a major financial institution, not as someone devoid of skills in assessing creditworthiness and unready to seek help. The manager had the duty to investigate the creditworthiness of the companies and should either have forewarned the appellant and her family where his skills ended, so as to enable them to appreciate the dangers of accepting his advice without further ado, or he should not have recommended the investment. The manager had therefore not performed his duties adequately and had negligently caused the plaintiff’s loss; and the bank was vicariously liable. On the basis of liability Schutz JA held:[540] ‘The claim pleaded relied upon contract, alternatively delict, but as the case was presented as one in delict, and as nothing turns upon the precise cause of action, I shall treat it as such.’

540. *Durr v. ABSA Bank Ltd* 1997 (3) SA 448 (SCA) at 453.

282. In *BOE Bank Ltd v. Ries*,[541] the Supreme Court of Appeal refused to recognize a legal duty on the part of an insurance broker in the employ of a bank towards an intended beneficiary under a life insurance policy, where the broker had failed to ensure that the policyholder signs the necessary form to nominate the beneficiary. The court took into account that the conduct of the broker did not amount to the assumption of any professional responsibility regarding the signing of the form: he became involved in the process in passing, by doing a favour for a colleague and in effect acting as a messenger, without undertaking any professional responsibility. Although it was foreseeable that the intended beneficiary would obtain no benefit from the policy if the holder failed to sign the necessary nomination form before his death, foreseeability of loss was not in itself enough to indicate a legal duty.

283. In *Holtzhausen v. ABSA Bank Ltd*,[542] it was held that an action is maintainable in delict against a bank for a negligent misstatement causing pure pecuniary loss, even if a concurrent action is available in contract. The denial of an action in delict in *Lillicrap, Wassenaar and Partners v. Pilkington Brothers (SA) (Pty) Ltd*[543] was regarded as being limited to situations where the negligence alleged consists in the breach of a term of a contract. The *Holtzhausen* case did not concern a term of the contract between bank and client. The client requested information from the bank, concerning the deposit by cheque of an amount into his account, for the purposes of a sale of diamonds. The client was wrongly informed that the amount had been deposited and parted with the diamonds. Hence, he suffered loss equal to the value of the diamonds, for which the bank was be held liable.

284. In deciding on the liability of banks, the court will take into account all the circumstances, including the nature of the services rendered to the client and the nature of the alleged failing (error of judgment, lack of required knowledge or care).

§2. Liability of Public Authorities

I. Widening Liability

285. The liability in delict of the State or government and of public authorities generally has been extended in South Africa during the last part of the twentieth century and into the twenty-first century; a development that can be attributed to both external and internal factors.

286. Across the world, the relationship between State administrations and their citizens changed during the twentieth century. The range of public services has widened considerably and the culture has also changed, in that members of the public are seen much more as active 'clients' or 'customers' whose needs have to be

541. 2002 (2) SA 39 (SCA) paras 13–26.
542. Case No. 280/03, judgment delivered 17 Sep. 2004 (SCA).
543. 1985 (1) SA 475 (A).

met.[544] The disappointed 'customer' of a public service feels justified in complaining if the service that is provided or procured by the State on his or her behalf is deficient, and readily claims compensation for injury or loss. The liability of the State or a public authority requires that a balance has to be struck between protecting the interests of the citizen and preserving the ability of the administration to function in the public interest; and generally the trend has been towards what Basil Markesinis has called a 'consumerist vision of public liability' under which 'compensating the damages suffered by citizens because of administrative activities can never be a wrong use of public money'.[545]

287. In South Africa, this trend towards expanded liability of public authorities has been supported by the adoption of a new Constitution,[546] with an extensive Bill of Rights, which has opened the way towards an expanded interpretation of unlawfulness in the law of delict. Criminality and the absence of a victim compensation scheme have led to a number of cases where the victims of crime have successfully claimed damages from the State, based on the unlawful failure of the police to provide protection.[547]

288. The Constitutional guarantee of just administrative action,[548] given detailed content in legislation,[549] has widened the scope for liability of public bodies based on negligent failure of administrative justice. The Constitutional Court has affirmed that '(i)n our constitutional dispensation, every failure of administrative justice amounts to a breach of a constitutional duty'. Such a breach might, but will not necessarily, give rise to delictual liability.[550] This has manifested itself in a number of cases dealing with irregular tender procedures. In *Steenkamp NO v. The Provincial Tender Board of the Eastern Cape*,[551] the Constitutional Court refused to recognize a legal duty on the part of a tender board towards a successful tenderer, whose tender award was later set aside on account of negligence in the process of awarding the tender. The court took into account, *inter alia*, whether an imposition of liability for damages would be likely to have a 'chilling effect' on performance of administrative or statutory functions by members of the board.[552] The result is likely to be different where there is fraud in the process of awarding a tender.[553]

---

544. *Tort Liability of Public Authorities in Comparative Perspective* xvii (Duncan Fairgriew, Mads Andenas, John Bell eds., Brit. Inst. Intl. & Comp. L. 2002).
545. *Ibid.*
546. Act 108 of 1996.
547. *Carmichele v. Minister of Safety and Security and Another (Centre for Applied Legal Studies Intervening)* 2001 (4) SA 938 (CC); *Van Eeden v. Minister of Safety and Security* 2002 (4) SA 346 (SCA); *Minister of Safety and Security v. Van Duivenboden* 2002 (6) SA 431 (SCA).
548. Act 108 of 1996, s. 33.
549. Promotion of Administrative Justice Act 2 of 2000.
550. *Steenkamp NO v. The Provincial Tender Board of the Eastern Cape*, Case No. CCT 71/05, judgment delivered by the Constitutional Court on 28 Sep. 2006, per Moseneke DCJ, para. 37.
551. [2006] JOL 18364 (CC) para. 42.
552. *See also*, for non-recognition of the claim of an unsuccessful tenderer, *Olitzki Property Holdings v. State Tender Board and Another* 2001 (3) SA 1247 (SCA).
553. *Minister of Finance and Others v. Gore NO* 2007 (1) SA 111 (SCA). The court held that negligent conduct causing pure economic loss was wrongful only if, as a matter of legal and public policy,

289. The potential liability of local authorities for omissions has widened, once the courts discarded the view that liability for an omission can only be imposed where the prior conduct of the defendant had positively created a risk of harm or a new source of danger. This development is set out in section V. Local Authorities below under liability of local authorities.

II. State Liability Act 20 of 1957

290. The State Liability Act 20 of 1957 restates the earlier abolition of immunity of the State against being sued for the acts of its employees performed under statutory authority; with the result that, within the limits imposed by the Act, the liability of the State is coextensive with that of the individual citizen.[554]

291. The concept of 'State' is not defined in the Act. In section 239 of the Constitution,[555] there is a definition of 'organ of State':

> Definitions
> In the Constitution, unless the context indicates otherwise –
> 'organ of state'means –
>
> a. any department of state or administration in the national, provincial or local sphere of government; or
> b. any other functionary or institution –
>   – exercising a power or performing a function in terms of the Constitution or a provincial constitution; or
>   – exercising a public power or performing a public function in terms of any legislation, but does not include a court or a judicial officer.

292. In terms of section 1(b) of the Institution of Legal Proceedings against Certain Organs of State Act of 2002,[556] an 'organ of state' includes defined as follows:

> 'organ of state' means –
>
> a. any national or provincial department;
> b. a municipality contemplated in section 151 of the Constitution;
> c. any functionary or institution exercising a power or performing a function in terms of the Constitution, or a provincial constitution referred to in section 142 of the Constitution;

---

there existed a legal duty (para. 82 at 138G–H); and that there were no considerations of public or legal policy which dictated that the State should not be liable for the provincial officials' fraudulent conduct in the course of a public tender process.

554. *East London Western Districts Farmers' Association and Others v. Minister of Education and Development and Others* 1989 (2) SA 63 (A) 69–70.
555. Act 109 of 1996.
556. Act 40 of 2002.

d. the South African Maritime Safety Authority established by section 2 of the South African Maritime Safety Authority Act, 1998 (Act 5 of 1998);
e. The South African National Roads Agency Limited contemplated in section 3 of The South African National Roads Agency Limited and National Roads Act, 1998 (Act 7 of 1998);
f. National Ports Authority Limited, contemplated in section 4 of the National Ports Act, 2005, and any entity deemed to be the National Ports Authority in terms of section 3 of that Act; [paragraph *(f)* substituted by section 88 of Act 12 of 2005.]

293. Section 1 of the State Liability Act confirms that actions can be brought against the state in any competent court, providing as follows:

> 1. Claims against the State cognizable in any competent court – Any claim against the State which would, if that claim had arisen against a person, be the ground of an action in any competent court, shall be cognizable by such court, whether the claim arises out of any contract lawfully entered into on behalf of the State or out of any wrong committed by any servant of the State acting in his capacity and within the scope of his authority as such servant.

In terms of this section, the State is liable for a delict of an employee or 'servant' acting 'in his capacity and within the scope of his authority as such servant', that is, in the course and within the scope of his or her employment.[557] State liability is to an extent qualified by express mention of 'contract' and 'wrong', but it is settled law that these are not intended to be the sole grounds of liability.[558] The courts will not decline to redress a violation of individual rights resulting from an administrative act simply because the latter is performed 'in the course of implementing a general policy'.[559] In effect, the State is vicariously liable for the acts of its employees on the same basis as an ordinary employer.[560] Liability is imposed on the State not only for acts committed by its employees, but also in cases of strict liability for damage done by animals (pauperies).[561]

---

557. State Liability Act 20 of 1957, s. 1; *Naidoo v. Minister van Polisie* 1976 (4) SA 954 (T) 956; *Mhlongo v. Minister of Police* 1978 (2) SA 551 (A) 566 et seq.; *Minister of Police v. Rabie* 1986 (1) SA 117 (A) 132; *Tshabalala v. Lekoa City Council* 1992 (3) SA 21 (A) 31 ff.; *Minister of Law and Order v. Kadir* 1995 (1) SA 303 (A).
558. *East London Western Districts Farmers' Association and Others v. Minister of Education and Development and Others* 1989 (2) SA 63 (A) 69–70.
559. *East London Western Districts Farmers' Association and Others v. Minister of Education and Development and Others* 1989 (2) SA 63 (A) 69–70.
560. Cf. *Minister of Finance v. Barberton Municipal Council* 1914 AD 335 345 350; *Union Government (Minister of Justice) v. Thorne* 1930 AD 47 51; *Dolf v. Heath* 1959 (1) SA 714 (E) 717; *Ingram v. Minister of Justice* 1962 (3) SA 225 (W) 231; *Mhlongo v. Minister of Police* 1978 (2) SA 551 (A) 567; *Minister van Polisie v. Gamble* 1979 (4) SA 759 (A) 765; *Minister of Police v. Rabie* 1986 (1) SA 117 (A) 132.
561. *SAR & H v. Edwards* 1930 AD 3 9.

294. In some earlier cases, it was held that the State is not liable where the statutory duty imposed on the employee allows the latter to exercise his personal discretion independent of the State;[562] with the onus of proving that the employee was exercising his personal discretion being on the State;[563] but such instances, if they do still occur at all, would be exceptional.[564]

295. In *Mhlongo v. Minister of Police*,[565] the position in terms of the State Liability Act 20 of 1957 in respect of liability for the conduct of the police was summarized as follows: the liability of the State for a wrong is founded on the provisions of section 1 of the Act. The remedial legislation, of which Act 20 of 1957 is the modern offspring, was intended as the sole foundation of State liability. The particular provisions of section 1 of the Act relevant to the liability of the State for the delict of a policeman are those to be found in the words 'any wrong committed by any servant of the State acting in his capacity and within the scope of his authority as such servant'. The view that all members of the police force are prima facie servants of the State is well entrenched in decisions of the Appellate Division. Although section 1 of Act 20 of 1957 speaks only of a State servant acting 'within the scope of his authority', the courts appear to have treated this as embracing the concept 'within the scope of his employment'. It has never been suggested that the State escapes liability for a wrongful act committed by a servant in his capacity as such simply because the act fell outside the 'scope of his authority', when it was clearly within the 'scope of his employment'. All members of the police force are prima facie servants of the State and consequently, when a wrongful act is committed by a member of the force in the course or scope of his employment, the State is prima facie liable. It is then for the State to show that in committing the wrongful act the policeman was engaged upon a duty or function of such a nature as to take him out of the category of servant pro hac vice. For the duty or function to take him out of the category of servant, it must be one which is personal to the policeman, in the sense that from its very nature it is divorced from the State. Finally, the mere fact that the duty or function is a statutory one, or that it confers discretion upon the policeman.

296. The issue whether the notion of an employee acting 'in his capacity and within the scope of his authority', in terms of section 1 of the State Liability Act 20

---

562. *Sibiya v. Swart* 1950 (4) SA 515 (A) 520 ff.; *Mazeka v. Minister of Justice* 1956 (1) SA 312 (A) 317; *Reddy v. Town Council for the Borough of Kloof* 1964 (3) SA 280 (D) 281 ff.; *Thompson t/a Maharaj & Sons v. Chief Constable Durban* 1965 (2) SA 296 (D) 302; *Dladla v. Minister of Police* 1973 (2) SA 714 (W) 720; *Sizani v. Minister of Police* 1980 (3) SA 1205 (SECL) 1210. It has been held, however, that a policeman who arrests another is carrying out a statutory duty and not a 'personal duty': *Naidoo v. Minister van Polisie* 1976 (4) SA 954 (T) 957; *Mhlongo v. Minister of Police* 1978 (2) SA 551 (A) 567.

563. *Union Government (Minister of Justice) v. Thorne* 1930 AD 47 51; *Sibiya v. Swart* 1950 (4) SA 515 (A); *Mazeka v. Minister of Justice* 1956 (1) SA 312 (A) 317; *Dames v. De Kok* 1958 (1) SA 773 (W) 774; *Dladla v. Minister of Police* 1973 (2) SA 714 (W) 719 ff.; *Mhlongo v. Minister of Police* 1978 (2) SA 551 (A) 567; *Minister of Police v. Mbilini* 1983 (3) SA 705 (A) 711.

564. *Minister of Police v. Rabie* 1986 (1) SA 117 (A) 132; *Mtetwa v. Minister of Health* 1989 (3) SA 600 (D) 606.

565. 1978 (2) SA 551 (A) 567.

of 1957, coincides with the notion of acting 'in pursuance of' duties under a particular statute, was decided in *Masuku and Another v. Mdlalose and Others*.[566] The question was whether a policeman acting 'in the course and scope of his employment' was invariably also acting 'in pursuance of' the Police Act (so that certain procedural restrictions in terms of that Act would apply). The wording of the pleadings in this case, that a policeman acted 'in his capacity and within the course and scope of his authority', in essence followed that of section 1 of the State Liability Act 20 of 1957. The wording of the allegation was therefore appropriate to an action founded on the principles of vicarious liability. It has to be read as an allegation that at the relevant time the policeman had acted in the course and scope of his employment as a servant of the State. The court held that the concepts 'in the course and scope of his employment' (or any of its equivalents) and 'in pursuance of' the Act were notionally distinct from each other. They derived from different sources and dealt with different incidents of liability. The former was primarily concerned with the common law principles of vicarious liability; the latter was of statutory origin and its meaning and ambit stemmed from the provisions of the Act. Furthermore, different policy considerations were at stake when dealing with the two concepts. The former favoured a plaintiff by making a master liable for the wrongs of his servant, thereby extending and establishing liability where it otherwise would not exist. It was thus expansive in both its purpose and effect. The latter was restrictive and benefitted a defendant. These inherent differences justified the conclusion that the two concepts legally did not entirely correspond. The issue could not be interpreted in vacuo. It was impossible to lay down precise rules governing the meaning of each of the concepts. They differed notionally. Their application had inevitably to depend on the facts and the circumstances of each particular case. Only when the relevant facts had been established would it be possible to determine, applying recognized principles, whether the acts complained of amounted to conduct 'within the course and scope of employment' or 'in pursuance of the Act' or both, or neither. While the concepts clearly overlapped, one could not predict with certainty that they would necessarily always be coextensive.

297. In terms of the general rule of vicarious liability, as applicable also in cases of State liability, there is no vicarious liability where the employee is engaged in his personal affairs, divorced from his employment.[567] However, the State (like other employers) can in certain circumstances be liable for intentional misconduct of its employees, for example in the case of policemen, where there is some connection between their misconduct and the carrying out of police duties.[568]

566. 1998 (1) SA 1 (SCA).

567. *Sizani v. Minister of Police* 1980 (3) SA 1205 (SECL) 1210; *Witham v. Minister of Home Affairs* 1989 (1) SA 116 (ZH) 125; *Minister van Wet en Orde v. Wilson* 1992 (3) SA 920 (A) 927 ff.; *Minister of Law and Order v. Ngobo* 1992 (4) SA 822 (A) 828.

568. *Minister of Police v. Rabie* 1986 (1) SA 117 (A); *Minister van Veiligheid en Sekuriteit v. Japmoco BK* 2002 (5) SA 649 (SCA); *Minister van Veiligheid en Sekuriteit v. Phoebus Apollo Aviation BK* 2002 (5) SA 475 (SCA) *Masuku and Another v. Mdlalose and Others* 1998 (1) SA 1 (SCA); *Smit v. Minister van Polisie* 1997 (4) SA 893 (T); *K v. Minister of Safety and Security* 2005 (6) SA 419 (CC).

298. The Constitutional Court has considered whether the common law principles on vicarious liability conforms with the spirit, purport and objects of the Bill of Rights, as intended in section 39(2) of the Constitution.[569] The court held that both the principles of vicarious liability and their application must conform to the normative framework of Constitution. On the issue of whether the State should be liable for rape committed by police officers while on duty, the court found the principles of vicarious liability to be consistent with constitutional norms. On application of the principles the court found that, subjectively viewed, the policemen acted in pursuit of own objectives, but, objectively, their conduct was sufficiently linked to their employment as policemen, and the State was held liable.

299. Section 2 of the State Liability Act 20 of 1957 is a procedural measure, providing that the political head of a State or provincial department should be cited in proceedings:

> 2. Proceedings to be taken against Minister of department concerned.
>
> 1. In any action or other proceedings instituted by virtue of the provisions of section *one*, the Minister of the department concerned may be cited as nominal defendant or respondent.
> 2. For the purposes of subsection (1), 'Minister' shall, where appropriate, be interpreted as referring to a member of the Executive Council of a province.

300. Section 3 of the Act prohibits execution, attachment or like process for the enforcement of judgments against the State:

> - Satisfaction of judgment. – No execution, attachment or like process shall be issued against the defendant or respondent in any such action or proceedings or against any property of the State, but the amount, if any, which may be required to satisfy any judgment or order given or made against the nominal defendant or respondent in any such action or proceedings may be paid out of the National Revenue Fund or a Provincial Revenue Fund, as the case may be.

Prior to the judgment that this section is unconstitutional (see the following paragraph), it was held that section 3 is no bar to obtaining an *Anton Piller* order against the State.[570] The Appellate Division took account of the principle that a statutory provision which clogs or hampers the ordinary rights of an aggrieved person to seek the assistance of the courts had to be restrictively construed and not be extended beyond its express limits. Section 3 refers to 'execution, attachment or like process' and did not assist the State in its opposition to an *Anton Piller* order, even assuming that authorizing the Deputy Sheriff to retain objects found on State premises amounted to an 'attachment or like process'. An insuperable difficulty confronting

569. *K v. Minister of Safety and Security* 2005 (6) SA 419 (CC).
570. *Shoba v. Officer Commanding, Temporary Police Camp, Wagendrift Dam, and Another; Maphanga v. Officer Commanding, South African Police Murder and Robbery Unit, Pietermaritzburg, and Others* 1995 (4) SA 1 (A) 20C-E.

the State, in a case where the order was aimed at the search of a police facility to look for torture apparatus allegedly kept there, was the fact that the section applied only to the attachment of 'property of the State'. There was no evidence to suggest that the alleged torture apparatus (if it existed) belonged to the State: on the contrary, it could be accepted that, if discovered, such apparatus would probably be disowned by the State.

301. In *Nyathi v. Member of the Executive Council for the Department of Health, Gauteng*,[571] the Constitutional Court held that section 3 of the State Liability Act is unconstitutional, because it makes an unjustifiable differentiation between a judgment creditor who obtains judgment against the State and a judgment creditor who obtains a judgment against a private litigant. The court held that section 3 effectively places the State above the law. The section thereby unjustifiably limits the rights to equality enshrined in section 9 of the Constitution and could also unjustifiably impair a litigant's right to dignity enshrined in section 10 of the Constitution. This decision was followed by the passing of the State Liability Amendment Act,[572] which allows the issue of a writ of execution or a warrant of execution against movable property owned by the State and used by the department concerned, but only after various notification procedures have been followed.

302. Prior to the judgment that this section is unconstitutional, it was held in *Jayiya v. Member of the Executive Council for Welfare, Eastern Cape, and Another*[573] that section 3 did not preclude contempt proceedings, and the introduction of civil imprisonment for officials not carrying out obligations resting upon the State. Also prior to the judgment that this section is unconstitutional, it was held in *Minister of Health & Another v. Brückner*[574] by the Labour Appeal Court that in actions against the State, where a minister is cited as the nominal defendant, section 3 is no bar to bringing an action against a public official or functionary (including a minister), for an order to compel that official or functionary to fulfil an obligation imposed upon him or her by law. Such an action is an action against the public official or functionary concerned and not an action against the State. The Act also does not prevent the institution of proceedings for contempt of court against a public official or functionary, who has been ordered by the court to carry out an obligation imposed upon him or her by law and who has failed or refused to carry out that obligation.

303. In the *Brückner* case, the respondent had been employed by the appellants until she was removed from her position and appointed to a lower-ranking position. She referred a dispute to arbitration, where it was found that she had been unfairly demoted, and the appellants were ordered to reinstate her to her original position. On application by the respondent, the award was made an order of court. Instead of reinstating the respondent to her previous position, the appellants offered her a

571. [2008] ZACC 8.
572. No. 14 of 2011.
573. 2004 (2) SA 611 (SCA) paras 15 and 16 at 619E–H.
574. [2007] JOL18898 (LAC).

newly created position in which, according to her, the duties were largely administrative. The respondent accordingly applied to have the appellants declared in contempt of court. The court a quo found that the appellants were in contempt of court and committed them to a fifteen-day prison sentence. The sentence was suspended for sixty days to enable the appellants to comply with the court order. It was held on appeal that the contempt order made was not precluded by section 3 of the State Liability Act, but that it was not competent for the trial court to have made an order of imprisonment against the appellants.

304. *Section 4* of the Act provides that limitations of liability, prescribed periods and conditions for claims against the State contained in other legislation are not affected by this Act:

> 4. Savings. – Nothing in this Act contained shall affect any provision of any law which –
>   a. limits the liability of the State or the national government or a provincial government or any department thereof in respect of any act or omission of its servants; or
>   b. prescribes specified periods within which a claim is to be made in respect of any such liability; or
>   c. imposes conditions on the institution of any action.

305. The application of special notice and limitation periods was an important feature of actions against the State and certain State organs prior to the introduction of a new constitution in South Africa in the last decade of the twentieth century. Once the interim Constitution[575] and the finalized Constitution[576] had come into operation, the constitutionality of these short and onerous notice and limitation periods was challenged, in terms of the constitutional guarantees of equality and access to the courts. In *Mohlomi v. Minister of Defence*,[577] the Constitutional Court declared the notice and limitation provisions contained in section 113(1) of the Defence Act[578] invalid, on the basis of inconsistency with the constitutionally guaranteed right of access to the courts. In *Hans v. Minister van Wet en Orde*,[579] the court reached the same conclusion in respect of the validity of provisions similar to section 32(1) of the Police Act.[580] The law on notice and limitation periods for actions against the State and organs of State was subsequently reformed by the Institution of Legal Proceedings against Certain Organs of State Act of 2002.[581] In terms of this Act, prescription periods for actions against 'organs of State' as defined in section 1 of the Act were brought in line with the provisions of the Prescription Act,[582] and a uniform notice period was introduced.

575. Act 200 of 1993.
576. Act 108 of 1996.
577. 1996 (12) BCLR 1559 (CC); 1997 (1) SA 124 (CC).
578. Act 44 of 1957.
579. 1995 (12) BCLR 1693 (C).
580. Act 7 of 1958.
581. Act 40 of 2002.
582. Act 68 of 1969.

III. Section 35 of the General Law Amendment Act 62 of 1955

306. Section 35 of the General Law Amendment Act 62 of 1955 is a procedural provision, setting an obligatory notice period for obtaining a rule nisioperating as an interim interdict against the State. The concept of 'State' is not defined in the Act, and regard should be had to the definition of 'organ of State' in section 239 of the Constitution,[583] cited above. Section 35 provides as follows:

> 35. Interim interdicts against the State – Notwithstanding anything to the contrary contained in any law, no court shall issue any rule nisi operating as an interim interdict against the Government of the Union including the South African Railways and Harbours Administration or the Administration of any Province, or any Minister, Premier or other officer of the said Government or Administration in his capacity as such, unless notice of the intention to apply for such a rule, accompanied by copies of the petition and of the affidavits which are intended to be used in support of the application, was served upon the said Government, Administration, Minister, Premier or officer at least seventy-two hours, or such lesser period as the court may in all the circumstances of the case consider reasonable, before the time mentioned in the notice for the hearing of the application. [section 35 amended by section 4 of Act 18 of 1996.]

This provision sets procedural conditions for interdicts against the state, but not for an *Anton Piller* order against the state.[584] The interpretation of this section is governed by the principle that a statutory provision which clogs or hampers the ordinary rights of an aggrieved person to seek the assistance of the courts had to be restrictively construed and not be extended beyond its express limits. An *Anton Piller* order could not be regarded as 'a rule nisioperating as an interim interdict': while a rule nisicontemplated that the relief sought would be granted at some future date, the *Anton Piller* order granted immediate relief and required the respondent forthwith – and without any opportunity to voice opposition – to submit to the search of his premises and to the other demands of the order; a rule nisiusually related to substantive relief while an *Anton Piller* order related merely to procedural relief, namely the preservation of evidence; and furthermore, the interim interdict attached to a rule nisiusually sought to maintain the *status quo ante*, whereas an *Anton Piller* order gave instant relief, subject to the possibility of later variation or discharge of the order.

583. Act 109 of 1996.

584. *Shoba v. Officer Commanding, Temporary Police Camp, Wagendrift Dam, and Another; Maphanga v. Officer Commanding, South African Police Murder and Robbery Unit, Pietermaritzburg, and Others* 1995 (4) SA 1 (A) 20C-E.

IV. State Liability for Public Schools

307. The State is liable for damage or loss for which a public school would otherwise be liable, in terms of the provisions of section 60(1) of the South African Schools Act.[585] Under the heading 'Liability of State', this section provides as follows:

> The State is liable for any damage or loss caused as a result of any act or omission in connection with any educational activity conducted by a *public school* and for which such *public school* would have been liable but for the provisions of this section.

308. In *MEC for Education, Western Cape Province v. Strauss*,[586] the plaintiff, a public school teacher, had been struck on the head by a discus while coaching discus-throwing at the school athletics field. She suffered extensive injuries and was permanently disabled. She sought to hold the defendant liable under section 60(1) of the South African Schools Act,[587] for the school's failure to enclose the discus circle with safety nets. The plaintiff had been employed by the governing body of the school, in terms of section 20(4) of the Act.

The defendant raised the special plea that section 60(1) of the Act was not applicable, because liability of an employer is generally excluded by section 35(1) of the Compensation for Occupational Injuries and Diseases Act (COIDA).[588] The plea succeeded: the Supreme Court of Appeal held that section 60(1) renders the State liable only in circumstances where the school would have been liable –'and for which such public school would have been liable'. If a school as employer would not have been liable to an employee by virtue of the provisions of section 35 of COIDA, the State would likewise not be liable in terms of section 60. COIDA provides for compensation for employees and section 35(1) expressly excludes liability on the part of the employer for damages in respect of any occupational injury or disease resulting in disablement or death. Since the school is not liable to the plaintiff, liability cannot be attributed to the State in terms of section 60(1).[589]

309. Section 60(1) of the Act has been described as an 'umbrella provision', establishing general State liability for damage or loss arising from any educational activity undertaken by a public school, on the basis that education is primarily a responsibility of the State.[590] In the case of *Technofin Leasing & Finance (Pty) Ltd*

585. Act 84 of 1996.
586. [2007] SCA 155 (RSA).
587. Act 84 of 1996.
588. Act 130 of 1993.
589. *See also Technofin Leasing & Finance (Pty) Ltd v. Framesby High School and Another* 2005 (6) SA 87 (SE) 92I-93C and 95D-E; *LUR vir Onderwys en Kultuur, Vrystaat v. Louw en 'n Ander* 2006 (1) SA 192 (SCA) paras 12–13, 196E-197B. *See also* the discussion of the latter case by P.J. Visser in 2006, (69) *THRHR* 523–528.
590. *Louw en 'n Ander v. LUR vir Onderwys en* D *Kultuur, Vrystaat, en 'n Ander* 2005 (6) SA 78 (O), [2006] 4 All SA 282 para. 13.

v. Framesby High School and Another,[591] Pickering J said that section 60(1) 'is couched in the broadest of terms and the State's liability is expressed in the most general language'. There is nothing in the section to indicate that it is restricted to delictual liability.

V. Local Authorities

310. Local authorities are for some purposes regarded as organs of State. In terms of section 239 of the Constitution,[592] an 'organ of state' includes '(a) any department of State or administration in the national, provincial or local sphere of government'. Also, in terms of section 1(b) of the Institution of Legal Proceedings against Certain Organs of State Act of 2002[593] an 'organ of state' includes 'a municipality contemplated in section 151 of the Constitution'. However, it has been held that a municipality is not included in the word 'State' for the purposes of section 3 of the State Liability Act.[594]

311. In *Mateis v. Ngwathe Plaaslike Munisipaliteit en Andere*,[595] a judgment had been obtained by a municipal pension fund against a municipality. The indebtedness arose from the failure of the municipality to pay deducted pension contributions from their employees' monthly salaries to the pension fund. A warrant of attachment and execution was issued and a sale in execution of all the municipality's movable assets was pending, when the applicant, an inhabitant of a town situated within the jurisdiction of the municipality, brought an application for the setting aside of the sale in execution. His argument was that the sale could not take place in the light of the provisions of section 3 of the State Liability Act. The court held that the concept 'State' was an amorphous juristic-political concept. It had no fixed, general meaning in legislation. The meaning of the word 'State' thus depended on every specific piece of legislation in which it occurred. What was clear from sections 2 and 3 of the State Liability Act was that it was concerned with the liability of the central or provincial government. The liability of a municipality, which is also a form of government, is not mentioned, neither with regard to cause of action, nor as possible defendant, nor as possible paying party; and a municipality is therefore excluded by implication. The Act also does not provide for a source from which the liability of a municipality could be satisfied, in contrast to the position with regard to central or provincial government – another clear indication that the legislature did not intend to deal with judgments against municipalities.

591. 2005 (6) SA 87 (SE) 92I-93C.
592. Act 109 of 1996.
593. Act 40 of 2002.
594. Act 20 of 1957.
595. 2003 (4) SA 361 (SCA).

312. The delictual liability of a local authority is for the most part coextensive with that of an individual. However, in respect of liability for omissions, individuals on the one hand and public bodies or officials on the other are often treated differently. In the determination of unlawfulness in cases based on omission by a local authority, the courts are guided by policy considerations concerning, for example, the need for accountability of public bodies or officials, the proportionality of the risk of harm and the cost of prevention, control over a dangerous object or situation, awareness of danger, prior conduct creating danger and a relationship imposing responsibility. The threshold for considering the failure by a local authority to prevent harm as unlawful was lowered, and the liability of local authorities for omissions correspondingly widened, when the courts discarded the view that liability of public authorities for an omission can only be imposed where the prior conduct of the defendant had positively created a risk of harm or a new source of danger.

313. In a line of cases often referred to as the 'municipality cases', the courts adhered to the view that liability for an omission can only be imposed where the prior conduct of the defendant had created a risk of harm or a new source of danger and the defendant then failed to prevent the harm from occurring. This view was first adopted by the Appellate Division in 1912 in *Halliwell v. Johannesburg Municipality*.[596] The *Halliwell* case and similar cases subsequently dealt with the liability of a local authority for injury to a person using a public road or other amenity (hence the reference to these cases as 'municipality cases'). The judgments in these cases often involved subtle distinctions between situations where the defendant simply failed to prevent harm, and where such failure was preceded by the creation of a risk of harm or the introduction of a new source of danger.

314. This 'prior conduct' approach to liability for an omission held sway for more than four decades, in spite of criticism in certain judgments.[597] Eventually, the Appellate Division broke away from this approach in the leading case of *Minister van Polisie v. Ewels*,[598] where it was held that there can be liability in delict for a mere omission, not preceded by conduct that created a risk of harm or that introduced a new source of danger. In this case, the court imposed liability in a situation where the plaintiff was assaulted by an off-duty policeman in a police station in the presence of a more senior policeman, who failed to prevent the assault. The decision of the Appellate Division in the *Ewels* case has been of great significance, not only in respect of liability for omissions, but also in respect of the criteria for assessment of unlawfulness generally.[599]

596. 1912 AD 659.

597. *See Silva's Fishing Corporation (Pry) Ltd v. Maweza* 1957 (2) SA 256 (A) 264-5. *See also Regal v. African Superslate (Pty) Ltd* 1963 (1) SA 102 (A); and *Minister of Forestry v. Quahlamba (Pty) Ltd* 1973 (3) SA 69 (A) 82.

598. 1975 (3) SA 590 (A).

599. *See Van der Merwe Burger v. Munisipaliteit van Warrenton* 1987 (1) SA 899 (C), *Rabie v. Kimberley Munisipaliteit* 1991 (4) SA 243 (NC) 258; *Cape Town Municipality v. Butters* 1996 (1) SA 473 (C) 477 479–480; *Longueira v. Securitas of South Africa (Pty) Ltd* 1998 (4) SA 258 (W) 262-3.

315. After the *Ewels* case, the courts regard the essential question to be whether a legal duty existed to prevent harm to others, on the basis of reasonableness and public policy. In terms of the wide and evaluative criteria used by the courts in this regard, a legal duty will be recognized where the failure to prevent harm not only evokes moral indignation, but is regarded as so unreasonable, according to the *boni mores* or legal convictions of the community, that it should be regarded as unlawful, so that liability should be imposed for the loss suffered.[600] In addition to these wide and general criteria, the courts take into account policy considerations indicating whether the law of delict should intervene (*inter alia*, the social or economic consequences of imposing liability; the availability of alternative remedies; and the need for accountability of public bodies or officials); relevant constitutional or other statutory rights and duties; and a typology of factual circumstances that indicate a duty not to cause or to prevent harm in the particular situation.

316. The 'prior conduct' approach to liability of local authorities for omissions was finally discarded in *Cape Town Municipality v. Bakkerud*,[601] where the general criterion of reasonableness – involving the policy-based standard of *boni mores* or legal convictions of the community – was applied to determine the liability of the Cape Town Municipality for the injuries of a woman who had stepped into a pothole in a pavement. The court took into account the area where the injury occurred, the period of time for which the dangerous situation had existed, and the resources needed to maintain the pavement in a safe condition. These factors were relevant to both the inquiry into unlawfulness and negligence, and the conclusion on the facts was that there was a legal duty on the part of the municipality to prevent the harm (failure to prevent the harm was unlawful); and negligence on the part of the municipality; and contributory negligence on the part of the plaintiff, for failing to be reasonably observant when walking on the pavement.

317. Factors such as the extent of the risk, the opportunity and efforts to become aware of risks and the cost of prevention, were taken into account in *Mostert v. Cape Town City Council*, a case involving a damaging leak from the city council's water main. Weighing the technical evidence as to the likelihood of collapse against the high cost of replacement, the court judged that it could not reasonably have been expected of the council to replace the pipe, and the city council was therefore not negligent. Schutz JA noted that reasonableness of requiring the council to replace the pipeline might also have been dealt with as a question of unlawfulness.[602] In most cases involving property damage or personal injury, the issue of unlawfulness is not contentious, as the action is founded upon conduct which, if held to be culpable, would be prima facie wrongful.[603] This was such a case. If the council had

600. *See Minister van Polisie v. Ewels* 1975 (3) SA 590 (A) at 597.
601. 2000 (3) SA 1049 (SCA).
602. Per Schutz JA at 120–121.
603. P.Q.R. Boberg, *Law of Delict* at 32 says in this regard: 'it is settled law that all harm to person or property caused by a positive act is prima facie wrongful'.

been negligent in not preventing the burst of the pipe, the threshold for unlawfulness – the general, policy-based criterion of reasonableness, or the community's sense of what the law ought to be – would have been crossed, and liability would have been imposed on the council.

318. In determining negligence and unlawfulness where local authorities and public facilities are involved the courts generally take account of a typology of factual considerations, of which the most common are the extent of the danger, the period of time for which it existed, the opportunity and efforts to become aware of the danger, the resources of the public authority and prior warning.

§3. Abuse of Rights

I. Introduction

319. The concept of abuse of rights in South African law does not refer to a distinct doctrine or distinct set of rules but rather ties in with the general principles of unlawfulness. Abuse of rights occurs in two forms, which overlap and have common features:

(1) Abuse of rights occurs where there is a conflict of rights. It is a concept that reflects the recognition that rights are not absolute, but often limited by other rights. Where there is a conflict of rights, involving, for example, reputation versus free speech, enjoyment of property versus harm to a neighbour, or freedom of competition versus harm to trading goodwill, the principles relating to unlawfulness are applied to determine whether there has been an abuse of rights, in the sense that the exercise of one right infringes upon another to an extent that is unreasonable, contrary to the legal convictions of the community, or *contra bonos mores*.
(2) Abuse of rights also occurs where statutory powers or processes are used unlawfully, for example, in cases of unlawful arrest and malicious prosecution.

II. Conflict of Rights

320. Abuse of rights in its conflict of rights form is typically at issue in neighbour disputes. For instance, where a landowner exercises his rights of ownership in a manner calculated to cause extensive harm to a neighbour, with little benefit to himself, this could amount to an abuse of rights. As set out in the section on unlawfulness, Chapter 1 section 2 above, motive can be a relevant factor in this regard.[604]

604. *See Gien v. Gien* 1979 (2) SA 1113 (T) 1121, which deals with the causing of excessive noise to deter animals and birds from causing damage to crops); and *Kirsh v. Pincus* 1927 TPD 199, which deals with the planting of deciduous trees along a boundary so that falling leaves will cause harm to a neighbour.

In the area of unlawful competition, a motive to harm rather than to compete will also be taken into account to determine unlawfulness.[605] The purpose served by the harmful conduct and the extent of the harm will be taken into account.[606] Other factors include prior knowledge or actual foresight of the possibility of harm, which is not conclusive in determining abuse of rights (unlawfulness), but will be taken into account together with other factors.[607] Fraud or dishonesty in the purported exercise of rights will also be indicative of abuse of rights (unlawfulness).[608]

321. The case of *Gien v. Gien*[609] is illustrative of an abuse of rights. The case involved a dispute between neighbouring landowners over the disturbance resulting from the one owner's use of a noise apparatus to deter animals and birds from feeding on his crops. The apparatus emitted loud bangs day and night and allegedly caused an excessive disturbance of the peace in the whole neighbourhood. There was also a history of ill feeling between the neighbours. It was held that where rights of ownership come into conflict, reasonableness and fairness should determine the issue. The respective interests of the parties should be weighed in an objective manner. Relevant factors were the extent of the disturbance as determined by the type and time of the noise, the degree of its persistence and the locality involved; the value of the crops allegedly protected by the noise; possible alternative and less disruptive measures; and a possible motive to cause harm or to irritate. In weighing

605. *See Bress Designs (Pry) Ltd v. GY Lounge Suite Manufacturers (Pty) Ltd* 1991 (2) SA 455 (W).
606. *Bloemfontein Town Council v. Richter* 1938 AD 195.
607. *See* for instance *Coronation Brick (Pty) Ltd v. Strachan Construction Co. (Pty) Ltd* 1982 (4) SA 371 (D) 386-7, where knowledge of the existence of an underground cable was taken into account in deciding whether economic loss was unlawfully caused by cutting the cable; *Shell and BPSA Petroleum Refineries (Pty) Ltd v. Osborne Panama SA* 1980 (3) SA 653 (D) 659, where damage to a mooring buoy in Durban harbour caused economic loss to the charterer of an oil tanker because of the consequent delay in offloading the cargo, but liability was not imposed because it had not been shown that the defendant did foresee or should have foreseen the possibility of loss (on account of delay and liability for demurrage) to the charterer specifically, this kind of loss being foreseeable only in relation to an unascertained class of potential victims, namely the owners or charterers of all vessels intending the discharge oil at that particular mooring buoy; and only insofar as the plaintiff-charterer was a member of that unascertained class was its loss reasonably foreseeable; *Arthur E Abrahams and Gross v. Cohen* 1991 (2) SA 301 (C) 311, where the professional administrators of a deceased estate were held to have unlawfully caused loss to the beneficiaries of an insurance policy that was an asset in the estate, by failing to collect the proceeds of the policy timeously, while knowing who the beneficiaries were and that they would suffer loss as a result of delay; *Indac Electronics (Pty) Ltd v. Volkskas Bank Ltd* 1992 (1) SA 783 (A) 799, where the liability of a collecting bank to the true owner of a cheque was in issue; and the court held that there is a need for protection of the true owner of a cheque that was incorrectly collected and credited; particularly because the true owner relies on the collecting banker to look at the named payee on the face of the cheque before collecting and crediting the proceeds to an account; and the collecting banker undertaking this responsibility in the course of his professional services is or should be aware that the failure to take reasonable care may result in loss to the true owner of the cheque. In respect of the role of motive to cause harm.
608. *See Schultz v. Butt* 1986 (3) SA 667 (A), where the respondent's dishonesty in not only copying a design, but also registering it in his own name, was taken into account by the court in its finding that he had acted unlawfully towards the applicant.
609. 1979 (2) SA 1113 (T).

these factors, the court decided that the use of the noise apparatus caused an excessive disturbance and therefore unlawfully infringed the neighbour's rights of ownership.

III. Abuse of Statutory Powers or Processes Generally

322. Liability for abuse of rights occurs when statutory powers or processes are used unlawfully, as in the case of unlawful arrest or imprisonment, the use of force in carrying out an arrest, unlawful seizure of goods in execution of judgment and malicious prosecution.

IV. Unlawful Arrest or Imprisonment

323. Unlawful arrest or imprisonment involves the deprivation of physical freedom without justification. A valid warrant, for instance, may justify the arrest. The lawfulness of arrest or imprisonment, or the lawfulness of the use of force in carrying out an arrest, depends on the interpretation of the relevant statutory powers of arrest or imprisonment.[610]

324. Unlawful arrest and unlawful imprisonment are forms of liability for *iniuria*, that is, infringement of personality rights (personal freedom and dignity), requiring intent (*animus iniuriandi*), but in an attenuated form, in the sense that it is not necessary for the plaintiff to establish that the wrongdoer was conscious of the wrongful nature of his act.[611] The courts have acknowledged that liability for unlawful arrest on the basis of an attenuated form of intent may not be strictly in accordance with the Roman-Dutch principles of liability for *iniuria*, but that it has practical consequences that are both sensible and just. The policy underlying this approach is that more comprehensive protection should be afforded against wrongful arrest as a serious encroachment upon the freedom of the individual. This approach is underscored by the constitutional protection of the right to freedom and security of the person.[612] The plaintiff must prove the arrest and that it involved unlawful deprivation of freedom, and it is then for the defendant to show that the arrest was justified.

325. The manner of detention of a prisoner may render the imprisonment unlawful, for example where the prisoner is detained in conditions amounting to effective

610. *Minister of Justice v. Hofmeyr* 1993 (3) SA 131 (A); *Shoba v. Minister van Justisie* 1982 (2) SA 554 (A); *Minister van Polisie v. Goldschagg* 1981 (1) 37 (A); *Macu v. Du Toit en 'n Ander* 1982 (1) SA 272 (C); *Minister van Wet en Orde v. Van den Heever* 1982 (4) SA 16(K); *Botha v. Lues* 1983 (4) SA 496 (A); *George v. Minister van Wet en Orde* 1987 (4) SA 222 (EC); *Prince v. Minister van Wet en Orde* 1987 (4) SA 231 (EC); *Govender v. Minister of Safety and Security* 2001 (4) SA 273 (SCA); *Ex Parte Minister of Safety & Security: In re S v. Walters* 2002 (4) SA 613 (CC).
611. *Minister of Justice v. Hofmeyr* 1993 (3) SA 131 (A) 157.
612. Section 12 of the Constitution of the Republic of South Africa, Act 108 of 1996.

solitary confinement, which constitutes an infringement of his basic rights to bodily integrity and to mental and intellectual well-being.[613]

V. Malicious Arrest, Imprisonment, Instigation of Prosecution or Other Legal Proceedings

326. Wrongful arrest or imprisonment on the one hand must be distinguished from malicious arrest, imprisonment or instigation of prosecution or other legal proceedings on the other. In *Relyant Trading (Pty) Ltd v. Shongwe*[614] the court explained the distinction between a wrongful arrest and a malicious deprivation of liberty. A wrongful arrest is one where the defendant is the person who unjustifiably interfered with the plaintiff's personal liberty. In contrast, a malicious arrest is one where the defendant is the person who set a lawful process in motion in terms of which the plaintiff was arrested and prosecuted. A claim for malicious prosecution requires that an arrest or prosecution be instigated with animus iniuriandi and in circumstances where there is no reasonable or probable cause for it.

327. The allegation of intention to injure (*animus injuriandi*, *dolus*) is necessary in an action for malicious arrest or the malicious instigating or launching of other legal proceedings, whereas an action for wrongful arrest does not require proof of *animus injuriandi* in the full sense of the term, including the consciousness on the part of the defendant that he is acting unlawfully.[615] Malicious arrest or the malicious instigating or launching of other legal proceedings involves improper use of the judicial machinery to deprive a person of his liberty or otherwise to cause him harm, under the guise of a valid judicial process. Malicious criminal proceedings may take the form of malicious prosecution,[616] malicious procurement of a search warrant,[617] or malicious arrest or imprisonment.[618] Malicious civil proceedings may consist of malicious arrest of a person under civil process,[619] malicious execution,[620] or malicious insolvency or liquidation proceedings.[621]

613. *Whittaker v. Roos and Bateman; Morant v. Roos and Bateman* 1912 AD 92 122–123; *Minister of Justice v. Hofmeyr* 1993 (3) SA 131 (A).
614. [2007] 1 All SA 375 (SCA).
615. *Tödt v. Ipser* 1993 (3) SA 557 (A) at 586F; *Morkel v. Kruger-Liptrot* 200 (4) All SA 623 (C) 627.
616. *Beckenstrater v. Rottcher & Theunissen* 1955 (1) SA 129 (A) 134; *Van der Merwe v. Strydom* 1967 (3) SA 460 (A) 467; *Prinsloo v. Newman* 1975 (1) SA 481 (A) 491.
617. *Henry Woolman v. James McQuade* (1890) 11 NLR 271.
618. *Thompson v. Minister of Police* 1971 (1) SA 371 (E) 374 ff.; *Prinsloo v. Newman* 1975 (1) SA 481 (A); *Makhanya v. Minister of Justice* 1965 (2) SA 488 (N).
619. *Spiegel v. Miller* (1881) 1 SC 264; *Van der Vyver v. Deary* (1896) 13 SC 435.
620. *Lee v. Van Riebeeck Ladies' Hairdressers (Pty) Ltd* 1962 (4) SA 181 (T) 183; *RL Weir & Co. v. De Lange* 1970 (4) SA 25 (E) 28.
621. *Estate Logie v. Priest* 1926 AD 312 315; *Beckenstrater v. Rottcher & Theunissen* 1955 (1) SA 129 (A) 135.

328. Malicious prosecution is an abuse of the process of the court by intentionally and wrongfully setting the law in motion on a criminal charge.[622] In a malicious prosecution action, the onus is upon the appellant to establish:

(a) that the defendant set the law in motion (instigated or instituted the proceedings);
(b) that the defendant acted without reasonable and probable cause;
(c) that the defendant was actuated by an indirect or improper motive (malice); and
(d) that the prosecution was unsuccessful.[623]

329. The action for malicious prosecution or for the malicious instigation or launching of other forms of legal proceedings is an *actio iniuriarum*, and fault in the form of intent or *animus iniuriandi* is therefore required.[624] Intent or *animus iniuriandi* involves not only the intention to injure but also consciousness of unlawfulness.[625] The courts have distinguished between intent or *animus iniuriandi* on the one hand and improper motive or malice on the other.[626] Malice has been characterized as the actuating impulse preceding intent,[627] or an improper or indirect motive,[628] or an absence of an honest belief in the guilt of the accused.[629] Malice is in some cases associated with *animus iniuriandi*,[630] or regarded as evidence of *animus iniuriandi*,[631] particularly indicating the 'consciousness of wrongfulness' aspect

622. *Lederman v. Moharal Investments (Pty) Ltd* 1969 (1) SA 190 (A) 196.
623. *See* generally *Beckenstrater v. Rottcher & Theunissen* 1955 (1) SA 129 (A) 133 ff.; *Van der Merwe v. Strydom* 1967 (3) SA 460 (A) 467; *Lederman v. Moharal Investments (Pty) Ltd* 1969 (1) SA 190 (A) 196; *Prinsloo v. Newman* 1975 (1) SA 481 (A) 491 ff. *Landman v. Minister of Police* 1975 (2) SA 155; *Heyns v. Venter* 2004 (3) SA 200 (T).
624. In *Prinsloo v. Newman* 1975 (1) SA 481 (A) 492 the court said in this regard: 'In actions of this nature the plaintiff's remedy is provided under the actio injuriarum, from which it follows that what has to be alleged and established is animus injuriandi.' *See also Lederman v. Moharal Investments (Pty) Ltd* 1969 (1) SA 190 (A) 196; *Ramakulukusha v. Commander, Venda National Force* 1989 (2) SA 813 (V) 837; *Ochse v. King William's Town Municipality* 1990 (2) SA 855 (E) 857. In *Heyns v. Venter* 2004 (3) SA 200 (T) 209 the view was expressed that liability for malicious prosecution should also be accepted in cases of gross negligence.
625. *Maisel v. Van Naeren* 1960 (4) SA 836 (C) 840 850 ff.; *Smit v. Meyerton Outfitters* 1971 (1) SA 137 (T) 139; *SA Uitsaaikorporasie v. O'Malley* 1977 (3) SA 394 (A) 403; *Ramsay v. Minister van Polisie* 1981 (4) SA 802 (A) 818–819; *Dantex Investment Holdings (Pty) Ltd v. Brenner* 1989 (1) SA 390 (A) 396; *Minister of Justice v. Hofmeyr* 1993 (3) SA 131 (A) 154.
626. *Basner v. Trigger* 1946 AD 83 95; *Moaki v. Reckitt & Colman (Africa) Ltd* 1968 (3) SA 98 (A) 104; *SA Uitsaaikorporasie v. O'Malley* 1977 (3) SA 394 (A) 405.
627. *Gluckman v. Schneider* 1936 AD 151 159.
628. *May v. Union Government* 1954 (3) SA 120 (N) 129; *Beckenstrater v. Rottcher & Theunissen* 1955 (1) SA 129 (A) 134; *Van der Merwe v. Strydom* 1967 (3) SA 460 (A) 467; *Lederman v. Moharal Investments (Pty) Ltd* 1969 (1) SA 190 (A) 196; *Prinsloo v. Newman* 1975 (1) SA 481 (A) 491. Such motive may, but need not, be spite or ill will: *Landman v. Minister of Police* 1975 (2) SA 155 (E) 156.
629. *Fyne v. The African Realty Trust Ltd* 1906 EDC 248 257.
630. *Beckenstrater v. Rottcher & Theunissen* 1955 (1) SA 129 (A) 140: *Heyns v. Venter* 2004 (3) SA 200 (T) 208.
631. *Moaki v. Reckitt & Colman (Africa) Ltd* 1968 (3) SA 98 (A) 104: *Heyns v. Venter* 2004 (3) SA 200 (T) 208.

of *animus iniuriandi*.[632] Proof that the defendant was actuated by malice has also been regarded as an indication of unlawfulness.[633]

330. The action for malicious prosecution requires that the defendant should have instigated the process. Inherent in the concept 'set the law in motion', 'instigate or institute the proceedings', is the causing of a certain result, that is, a prosecution, which involves the question of causality. This is especially a problem where, as in most instances, the necessary formal steps to set the law in motion have been taken by the police, and it is sought to hold the defendant responsible for the prosecution. In this regard, it has been accepted that where a person merely gives a fair statement of the facts to the police, and leaves it to the latter to take such steps as they deem fit, and does nothing more to identify himself with the prosecution, he is not responsible, in an action for malicious prosecution, to a person whom the police may charge. But if he goes further, and actively assists and identifies himself with the prosecution, he may be held liable. When an informer makes a statement to the police which is wilfully false in a material respect, and no prosecution would have been undertaken but for the false information, such an informer instigates a prosecution.[634]

331. The action for malicious prosecution or for the malicious instigation or launching of other forms of legal proceedings requires proof that the defendant had no reasonable and probable cause for instigating the proceedings. Reasonable and probable cause requires an honest belief based on reasonable grounds that the institution of the proceedings complained of was justified.[635] There must be sufficient facts known to the defendant from which a reasonable man could have concluded that the plaintiff had committed the offence in question, and a mere honest belief that the facts amount to an offence irrespective of the legal requirements is insufficient.[636]

332. The plaintiff in an action for malicious prosecution or for the malicious instigation or launching of other forms of legal proceedings may claim damages for infringement of personality rights, including bodily integrity, reputation, dignity and liberty.[637] The plaintiff may also recover damages for pecuniary loss suffered, according to Aquilian principles.[638] Such damages may include loss of earnings[639] and the costs incurred by the plaintiff in defending the charge.[640]

---

632. *Moaki v. Reckitt & Colman (Africa) Ltd* 1968 (3) SA 98 (A) 104.
633. *Heyns v. Venter* 2004 (3) SA 200 (T) 208.
634. *Lederman v. Moharal Investments (Pty) Ltd* 1969 (1) SA 190 (A) 196.
635. *May v. Union Government* 1954 (3) SA 120 (N) 129; *Beckenstrater v. Rottcher & Theunissen* 1955 (1) SA 129 (A) 135; *Van der Merwe v. Strydom* 1967 (3) SA 460 (A) 467; *Prinsloo v. Newman* 1975 (1) SA 481 (A) 495 ff.; *Landman v. Minister of Police* 1975 (2) SA 155 (E) 156; *Minister of Police and Another v. Mthalane* 1978 (3) SA 542 (N); *Ochse v. King William's Town Municipality* 1990 (2) SA 855 (E) 857; *Mthimkhulu v. Minister of Law & Order* 1993 (3) SA 432 (E) 439.
636. *Ochse v. King William's Town Municipality* 1990 (2) SA 855 (E) 858 ff.
637. *Ramakulukusha v. Commander, Venda National Force* 1989 (2) SA 813 (V) 851; *Ochse v. King William's Town Municipality* 1990 (2) SA 855 (E) 860; *Mthimkhulu v. Minister of Law & Order* 1993 (3) SA 432 (E) 441.
638. *Heyns v. Venter* 2004 (3) SA 200 (T) 208.

§4. INJURY TO PERSONALITY RIGHTS: REPUTATION, PRIVACY

I. Defamation

A. Nature of Defamation

333. Defamation consists in the wrongful and intentional publication of defamatory matter referring to another person and infringing that person's personality rights to reputation, good name and the esteem in which he or she is held by others. The plaintiff establishes the infringement of these personality rights by proving publication of defamatory material referring to the plaintiff. Defamation is a form of *iniuria* and the action for defamation is a form of the *actio inuriarum*, which generally offers protection for intentional injury to personality rights.[641] In the Bill of Rights contained in the Constitution,[642] reputation or good name is protected under the aegis of human dignity.[643] The law of defamation reflects a tension between two constitutionally protected rights: the right to reputation or good name as an aspect of human dignity on the one hand, and the right to freedom of expression, including freedom of the press and other media, on the other.[644]

B. Publication

334. It is an essential element of defamation that the defamatory statement be published, or made known, to some person or persons other than the person defamed, thus causing harm to the plaintiff in respect of reputation or the esteem of others. Publication is the act of making known a defamatory statement, or the act of conveying an imputation by conduct, to a person or persons other than the person defamed. The plaintiff must prove that the defamatory statement alleged was communicated to those to whom publication is alleged, and there is no publication when the person to whom publication is alleged does not understand the statement as defamatory of the plaintiff.[645] However, once the person addressed learns of the defamatory nature of the statement, there is publication, regardless of the length of time between communication and understanding.[646] The plaintiff must also prove that the publication can be attributed to the defendant.[647]

---

639. *Law and Others v. Kin and Another* 1966 (3) SA 480 (W) 482; *Heyns v. Venter* 2004 (3) SA 200 (T) 208.
640. *Mthimkhulu v. Minister of Law & Order* 1993 (3) SA 432 (E) 441.
641. *Argus Printing & Publishing Co. Ltd v. Esselen's Estate* 1994 (2) SA 1 (A) 23D-I.
642. Act 108 of 1996.
643. *Holomisa v. Argus Newspapers Ltd* 1996 (1) All SA 478 (W); 1996 (6) BCLR 836 (W); 1996 (2) SA 588 (W) 606E-F; *National Media Ltd v. Bogoshi* 1998 (4) All SA 347 (SCA); 1999 (1) BCLR 1 (SCA); 1998 (4) SA 1196 (SCA) 1216J-1217B; *Khumalo v. Holomisa* 2002 (8) BCLR 771 (CC); 2002 (5) SA 401 (CC) 418F-419D.
644. *Khumalo v. Holomisa* 2002 (5) SA 401 (CC) 418F-419D.
645. *Sutter v. Brown* 1926 AD 155 164; *Vermaak v. Van der Merwe* 1981 (3) SA 78 (N) 79–80.
646. *Vermaak v. Van der Merwe* 1981 (3) SA 78 (N) 83.
647. *Pretorius v. Niehaus* 1960 (3) SA 109 (O) 112–113.

335. The editor, proprietor, printer and publisher of a newspaper, journal or other document circulated generally may be liable for defamatory statements appearing in the publication.[648] Publication of the defamatory statement is presumed if it is proved that a book, newspaper, journal or other such document containing the statement has been sold or distributed to the public; that defamatory words have been spoken within the hearing of third persons; or that the defamatory statement was contained in a postcard or telegram which has been sent.[649] A person who repeats, confirms, or allows publication of a defamatory statement will be held to have published the statement.[650] Not only the writer of a defamatory report or letter published in a newspaper, but also the editor, printer, publisher and owner of the newspaper will be held liable.[651]

C. What Is Defamatory

336. A statement is defamatory if it has the effect of injuring a plaintiff's reputation by tending to lower the plaintiff in the estimation of right-thinking members of society.[652] It is sufficient if the estimation concerns the views held by a substantial and respectable section of the community.[653] The defamatory nature of the publication is determined by the test of whether a reasonable person of ordinary intelligence might reasonably understand the words or imputation in context to convey a meaning that is derogatory of the plaintiff's moral character or professional or business standing, or a meaning that elicits enmity, ridicule or contempt towards the plaintiff. Vulgar abuse or uncouth comments are not necessarily defamatory, either because the statement does not convey a particular meaning or because it would not lower the person to whom they refer in the estimation of right-thinking members of society.[654]

337. The question whether a statement is defamatory, either in its ordinary meaning or per se, involves a two-stage inquiry. The first is to establish the natural or ordinary meaning of the statement. The second is whether that meaning is defamatory.[655] The meaning of a statement under consideration does not necessarily correspond with its dictionary meaning.[656] The test to be applied is an objective one.[657]

---

648. *Suid-Afrikaanse Uitsaaikorporasie v. O'Malley* 1977 (3) SA 394 (A) 407; *Pakendorf v. De Flamingh* 1982 (3) SA 146 (A); *National Media Ltd v. Bogoshi* 1998 (4) SA 1196 (SCA).
649. *Pretorius v. Niehaus* 1960 (3) SA 109 (O) 112–113; *Simpson v. Williams* 1975 (4) SA 312 (N).
650. *Hassen v. Post Newspapers (Pty) Ltd* 1965 (3) SA 562 (W) 564–565.
651. *Robinson v. Kingswell*; *Argus Printing & Publishing Co. Ltd v. Kingswill* 1913 AD 513. For publication on an Internet website, *see Tsichlas v. Touch Line Media (Pty) Ltd* 2004 (2) SA 112 (W).
652. *Conroy v. Stewart Printing Co. Ltd* 1946 AD 1015 1018; *Botha v. Marais* 1974 (1) SA 44 (A).
653. *Mohamed v. Jassiem* 1996 (1) SA 673 (A) 709.
654. *Wood v. Branson* 1952 (3) SA 369 (T). Vulgar abuse, although not defamatory, can constitute an infringement of dignity; *Brenner v. Botha* 1956 (3) SA 257 (T) 262; *Bester v. Calitz* 1982 (3) SA 864 (O) 874.
655. *SA Associated Newspapers Ltd v. Samuels* 1980 (1) SA 24 (A) 30F-G; *Sindani v. Van der Merwe* 2002 (1) All SA 311 (SCA); 2002 (2) SA 32 (SCA) 36B-C.
656. *Sindani v. Van der Merwe* 2002 (1) All SA 311 (SCA); 2002 (2) SA 32 (SCA) 36C.
657. *Crawford v. Albu* 1917 AD 102 119; *Botha v. Marais* 1974 (1) SA 44 (A) 48.

The focus is not on the meaning that the maker of the statement intended to convey,[658] but on how a reasonable or right-thinking person of ordinary intelligence would understand the statement in its context.[659] A statement may have a primary and secondary meaning (innuendo). The primary meaning is the ordinary meaning in its context as understood by a reasonable person of ordinary intelligence. A statement may derive a secondary or unusual meaning (innuendo) from special circumstances, understood by a person having knowledge of special circumstances.[660]

338. The determination of what is considered defamatory is evaluative, and the evaluation is done by the courts according to the standard of the notional reasonable or right-thinking person of ordinary intelligence. In the final analysis, the understanding and the norms attributed to the notional reasonable or right-thinking person are those of the court itself, as interpreter of the norms it considers reasonable for society at a particular time. These norms, as interpreted by the courts, may change over time and are shaped by the Constitution:[661] the courts are bound to assume that reasonable or right-thinking members of society will subscribe to the norms and values of the Constitution. For example, in *Sindani v. Van der Merwe*[662] it was held, with reference to the constitutional imperative against racial discrimination, that the use of racially derogatory language, such as calling a white person 'white trash', is defamatory. However, in view of the constitutional imperative against discrimination on the basis of sexual orientation, calling someone homosexual, gay or a lesbian[663] may no longer be considered defamatory.

339. In *Le Roux & Others v. Dey; Freedom of Expression Institute and Another Amici Curiae*,[664] the defamatory material complained of was an image. Three school boys created a computer-generated image of their school principal's and deputy principal's heads superimposed on the bodies of two gay men, photographed naked sitting side by side, and in a sexually compromising position. The private parts /genitalia of the two naked men in the picture were covered by the school crest.[665] The manipulation of the photograph reflecting this image was amateurish and did not look like a real depiction of the principal and the deputy principal, Dr Dey. The image was published and circulated within the school and was seen by many learners.[666] The image was also placed on the school notice board for approximately

658. *Sutter v. Brown* 1926 AD 155 163.

659. *Johnson v. Rand Daily Mails* 1928 AD 190 204; *Demmers v. Wyllie* 1980 (1) SA 835 (A) 847–848; *Mthembi-Mahanyele v. Mail & Guardian Ltd* 2004 (3) All SA 511 (SCA); 2004 (11) BCLR 1182 (SCA); 2004 (6) SA 329 (SCA) 342F-343C.

660. *National Union of Distributive Workers v. Cleghorn & Harris Ltd* 1946 AD 984 992 997; *Argus Printing & Publishing Co. Ltd v. Esselen's Estate* 1994 (2) SA 1 (A) 21; *Mangope v. Asmal* 1997 (4) SA 277 (T) 284.

661. *Sokhulu v. New Africa Publications Ltd t/a 'The Sowetan Sunday World'* 2002 (1) All SA 255 (W); 2001 (4) SA 1357 (W).

662. 2002 (1) All SA 311 (SCA); 2002 (2) SA 32 (SCA).

663. *Vermaak v. Van der Merwe* 1981 (3) SA 78 (N).

664. 2011 (6) BCLR 577 (CC).

665. At para. 1.

666. At para. 15.

thirty minutes and was then removed.[667] Once the school boys were identified as the persons behind the act, they were disciplined by their school in an internal disciplinary hearing.[668] The boys apologized to the principal who accepted their apology and took no further action.[669] The deputy principal, Dr Dey did not accept their apology.[670] Instead, he sued the schoolboys for defamation on the basis of two claims: one based on defamation and the other on dignity.[671]

The High Court upheld both claims.[672] On appeal, the Supreme Court of Appeal upheld the defamation claim and found that the additional claim based on an affront to his dignity was ill-founded and required no further consideration.[673] The schoolboys then appealed to the Constitutional Court. The boys argued that the image was not defamatory. It was not representative of reality, and a reasonable viewer would not have understood it as conveying any actual facts about the plaintiff.[674] Furthermore, even if Dr Dey felt subjectively that his dignity had been impaired by the picture, this was not objectively justified.

Brand AJ held that the reasonable observer would infer some association between the two teachers, on the one hand, and the indecent situation described in the picture, on the other.[675]

In short, the vision created is one of two promiscuous men who allowed themselves to be photographed in what can only be described as a situation of sexual immorality, which would be embarrassing and disgraceful to the ordinary members of society. The manipulation in this way is obvious and crude. No reasonable person could ever think that the bodies on which the faces are pasted were actually those of the principal and Dr Dey.[676]

This raised the question – as the second leg of the two-stage inquiry – whether the picture, thus understood, could be regarded as defamatory of Dr Dey. That in turn depended on whether the message conveyed by the picture would probably undermine the esteem in which Dr Dey was held by others: that is, whether the reasonable observer would regard the picture as likely to undermine the respect and good name enjoyed by Dr Dey. The court considered the context of the publication, in this regard, and concluded that the picture was distributed among the teachers and learners of the school.[677] In his capacity as deputy principal, Dr Dey 'was a symbol of authority and discipline at the school'.[678] In this context, the reasonable observer would understand the image to associate the two teachers with the bodies and their behaviour, and, consequently:

---

667. At para. 17.
668. At para. 18.
669. At para. 20.
670. *Ibid.*
671. At para. 22.
672. At para. 24.
673. At para. 25.
674. At para. 102.
675. At para. 103.
676. At para. 98.
677. At para. 99.
678. *Ibid.*

> The whole purpose and effect of the association created by the picture is to tarnish the image of the two figures representing authority, to reduce that authority by belittling them and by rendering them the objects of contempt and disrespect, and to subject these two figures of authority to ridicule in the eyes of the observers who would predominantly be learners at the school.[679]

It followed that the average person would regard the picture as defamatory of Dr Dey:

> The aim might have been to destroy Dr Dey's image as a figure of authority but the net effect was to belittle and humiliate him as a person, to represent him as unworthy – or at least less worthy – of respect by the learners of the school, which is a classic example of defamation.[680]

There were two dissenting judgments, the first is the joint judgment by Froneman J and Cameron J, who found that Dr Dey was not defamed, but that his dignity was actionably injured. The second dissenting judgment is that of Yacoob J with whom Skweyiya J concurred (for different reasons), but both of whom based their reasoning on child law principles.

In *Cele v. Avusa Media Limited*[681] the plaintiff, a high-ranking politician who had made certain statements calling on the police to 'shoot to kill' when dealing with criminals, claimed that the Sowetan newspaper had insulted him by publishing a digitally altered image of him which depicted him as a sheriff in the 'Wild West'. The court held that the image would have been understood by reasonable readers of the Sowetan to mean that the plaintiff was taking a tough stance on crime and that, like a sheriff in the Wild West, he wanted criminals to be harshly dealt with by the police and brought to justice, either dead or alive. The court found that this image was satirical (a caricature or parody) and was protected by the right to freedom of expression. In addition, the court held that the image was not realistic and would not have been regarded by a reasonable person as a genuine depiction of the plaintiff. The court held that a reasonable person in the position of the plaintiff (in other words, a reasonable seasoned politician) would not have felt insulted and humiliated by the image. Accordingly, the interference with the plaintiff's right to dignity was not wrongful, and the action for insult failed.

340. Once the plaintiff establishes that the defendant has published a defamatory statement referring to plaintiff, it is presumed that the publication was both unlawful and intentional. The defendant must then raise a defence which rebuts either unlawfulness or intention.[682]

---

679. At para. 107.
680. At para. 109.
681. [2013] 2 All SA 412 (GSJ).
682. *Borgin v. De Villiers* 1980 (3) SA 556 (A) 571F; *Marais v. Richard* 1981 (1) SA 1157 (A) 1166F-1167A; *Neethling v. Du Preez, Neethling v. The Weekly Mail* 1994 (1) SA 708 (A) 770I-G; *National Media Ltd v. Bogoshi* 1998 (4) SA 1196 (SCA) 1215 ff.

D. Referring to the Plaintiff

341. The defamatory material must refer to the plaintiff, either expressly or by implication. In the latter instance, the test is whether the statement would lead an ordinary reasonable person to believe that it refers to the plaintiff.[683] Where the statement does not refer directly to the plaintiff by name, or in such a way that the plaintiff is readily identifiable, the plaintiff must allege and prove, as in the case of an innuendo, that there are special circumstances which make the statement applicable to him or her.[684]

342. Where an individual member of a class or group institutes a defamation action based on a defamatory statement that refers to a class or group, the plaintiff must allege and prove that the statement concerned him or her personally. The mere fact that the person belongs to the class referred to is not enough.[685] Whether the statement refers to the individual members will depend on such factors as the size of the class or group, the generality of the charge and the extravagance of the allegation; none of which factors is conclusive.[686]

343. Where a defamatory statement refers to a family member, the plaintiff will only succeed by establishing that the defamation also affects him or her. The Roman law doctrine of *iniuria per consequentias*, allowing an action on the basis of defamation of a family member, is no longer applied, and cases of so-called *iniuria per consequentias* are dealt with in accordance with general principles.[687]

E. Persons Who Can Sue for Defamation

344. Every natural person who suffers an infringement of reputation can sue for defamation, including a minor,[688] a judge,[689] or a public official.[690]

683. *Goodall v. Hoogendoorn Ltd* 1926 AD 11 15; *SA Associated Newspapers Ltd v. Estate Pelser* 1975 (4) SA 797 (A) 810; *A Neumann CC v. Beauty Without Cruelty International* 1986 (4) SA 675 (C) 679–680; *Williams v. Van der Merwe* 1994 (2) SA 60 (E) 63.
684. *Pienaar v. Argus Printing & Publishing Co. Ltd* 1956 (4) SA 310 (W). Evidence may be given by persons who understood the defamatory matter to refer to the plaintiff, but the court is not bound to accept such an expression of opinion by a witness: *Nasionale Pers Bpk v. Long* 1930 AD 87 98; *Sachs v. Werkerspers Uitgewersmpy (Edms) Bpk* 1952 (2) SA 261 (W) 265; *Geyser v. Pont* 1968 (4) SA 67 (W) 71.
685. *SA Associated Newspapers Ltd v. Estate Pelser* 1975 (4) SA 797 (A) 810.
686. *Bane v. Colvin* 1959 (1) SA 863 (C) 867; *A Neumann CC v. Beauty Without Cruelty International* 1986 (4) SA 675 (C) 680–686; *Sauls v. Hendrickse* 1992 (3) SA 912 (A) 918; *Williams v. Van der Merwe* 1994 (2) SA 60 (E) 64.
687. *SA Associated Newspapers Ltd v. Schoeman* 1962 (2) SA 613 (A) 618; *Meyer v. Van Niekerk* 1976 (1) SA 252 (T) 255.
688. *Welken v. Nasionale Koerante Bpk* 1964 (3) SA 87 (O).
689. *Argus Printing & Publishing Co. Ltd v. Esselen's Estate* 1994 (2) SA 1 (A) 23 33.
690. *Mthembi-Mahanyele v. Mail & Guardian Ltd* 2004 (3) All SA 511 (SCA); 2004 (11) BCLR 1182 (SCA); 2004 (6) SA 329 (SCA) 345D-349A 364D-365I.

345. Corporate entities also have a legally protected reputation and can sue for defamation. A trading corporation can sue if the defamation can reasonably be expected to cause it financial loss.[691] Proof of the extent of actual loss is not required,[692] but if the extent of such loss is proved, this can be claimed in the form of special damages, apparently also with the *actio iniuriarum*, although patrimonial loss is normally claimed under the *lex Aquilia*.[693] A non-trading corporation can also sue if the defamatory statement was calculated to cause it financial prejudice. This includes a political party[694] or university.[695] An unincorporated association has no action for defamation, but those responsible for the management of the association may sue if the defamatory material refers to them.

346. The State (including the central government and all corporate entities which are part of the government of the country) has no action for defamation.[696] An individual minister, however, may have an action if the statement is defamatory of the minister in respect of his or her conduct in the management of State affairs.[697] The State can be vicariously liable for a defamatory statement by a cabinet minister.[698]

F. Defences Generally and Onus of Proof

347. Where the plaintiff in defamation proceedings proves the publication of a relevant defamatory statement, two presumptions arise, namely that the publication was unlawful and that the defendant acted with *animus iniuriandi*. The onus is then upon the defendant to establish a defence that constitutes either a justification (e.g., truth and public benefit, qualified privilege or fair comment) or the absence of *animus iniuriandi* (e.g., a bona fide mistake as to an element of the defamation).[699] However, it will not be enough for the defendant to establish a defence in the form

691. *G.A. Fichardt Ltd v. The Friend Newspapers Ltd* 1916 AD 1; *Die Spoorbond v. SA Railways, Van Heerden v. SA Railways* 1946 AD 999 1007 1010–1011; *A Neumann CC v. Beauty Without Cruelty International* 1986 (4) SA 675 (C); *Dhlomo v. Natal Newspapers (Pty) Ltd* 1989 (1) SA 945 (A); *Caxton Ltd v. Reeva Forman (Pty) Ltd* 1990 (3) SA 547 (A).
692. *Dhlomo v. Natal Newspapers (Pty) Ltd* 1989 (1) SA 945 (A); *Caxton Ltd v. Reeva Forman (Pty) Ltd* 1990 (3) SA 547 (A).
693. *GA Fichardt Ltd v. The Friend Newspapers Ltd* 1916 AD 1 7; *Die Spoorbond v. SA Railways, Van Heerden v. SA Railways* 1946 AD 999 1011; *Caxton Ltd v. Reeva Forman (Pty) Ltd* 1990 (3) SA 547 (A) 560–561.
694. *Argus Printing & Publishing Co. Ltd v. Inkatha Freedom Party* 1992 (3) SA 579 (A).
695. *Universiteit van Pretoria v. Tommie Meyer Films (Edms) Bpk* 1979 (1) SA 441 (A), although the university was not successful in this case.
696. *Die Spoorbond v. SA Railways, Van Heerden v. SA Railways* 1946 AD 999; *Posts & Telecommunications Corporation v. Modus Publications (Pvt) Ltd* 1998 (3) SA 1114 (ZS).
697. *SA Associated Newspapers Ltd v. Estate Pelser* 1975 (4) SA 810 (A); *Williams v. Van der Merwe* 1994 (2) SA 60 (E); *Mthembi-Mahanyele v. Mail & Guardian Ltd Mthembi-Mahanyele v. Mail & Guardian Ltd* 2004 (3) All SA 511 (SCA); 2004 (11) BCLR 1182 (SCA); 2004 (6) SA 329 (SCA) 345D-349A 364D-365I.
698. *Mangope v. Asmal* 1997 (4) SA 277 (T).
699. *Borgin v. De Villiers* 1980 (3) SA 556 (A) 571F; *May v. Udwin* 1981 (1) SA 1 (A) 10; *Neethling v. Du Preez, Neethling v. The Weekly Mail* 1994 (1) SA 708 (A); *National Media Ltd v. Bogoshi*

of qualified privilege or fair comment if the plaintiff can prove that the defendant acted with malice or an improper motive, in which case the protection afforded by the defence will be forfeited.[700]

348. The rules on onus of proof in respect of defences in defamation cases are not uniform. In *Suid-Afrikaanse Uitsaaikorporasie v. O'Malley*,[701] it was decided that the presumption of *animus iniuriandi* placed only a duty to adduce evidence on a defendant, that is, some evidence indicating the absence of *animus iniuriandi*, as opposed to a full onus which would require the defendant to prove the absence of *animus iniuriandi* on a balance of probabilities. In some subsequent decisions, the Appellate Division apparently accepted that this applied also to defences excluding unlawfulness.[702] However, in *Neethling v. Du Preez, Neethling v. The Weekly Mail*,[703] it was decided specifically that the presumption of unlawfulness placed a full onus of proof on the defendant, so that the defendant who raises the defence of truth and public benefit, for example, must prove the truth of the defamatory statement on a balance of probabilities.

G. Truth and Public Benefit

349. Publication of defamatory material that is true and for the public benefit is justified and therefore lawful. The defamatory material need not be true in every respect: provided the gist of the defamation (the 'sting of the charge', or the 'gist of the defamation') is true, some exaggeration is accepted.[704] It is not an element of defamation that the defamatory statement is false. The plaintiff therefore need not allege or prove that the statement is untrue; it is for the defendant who wishes to rely on this defence to allege and prove, on a balance of probabilities, the truth and public benefit of the statement. This rule has been attacked on constitutional grounds as an undue restriction on the freedom of expression, but the Constitutional Court has held that the rule complies with the constitutional right of freedom of expression.[705] The Constitutional Court held that the rule did not unjustifiably limit the constitutional right to freedom of expression of the defendant in this case, mainly because a defendant who cannot establish the truth, or finds it disproportionately expensive or difficult to do so, may show that in all the circumstances the

---

1998 (4) All SA 437 (SCA); 1999 (1) BCLR 1 (SCA); 1998 (4) SA 1196 (SCA) 1215 ff.; *Khumalo v. Holomisa* 2002 (8) BCLR 771 (CC); 2002 (5) SA 401 (CC) 421 ff.

700. *Basner v. Trigger* 1946 AD 83 95 96 and *May v. Udwin* 1981 (1) SA 1 (A) 1.9.
701. 1977 (3) SA 394 (A) 401–403.
702. *Borgin v. De Villiers* 1980 (3) SA 556 (A) 571; *May v. Udwin* 1981 (1) SA 1 (A) 1 10; *Marais v. Richard* 1981 (1) SA 1157 (A) 1166; *Argus Printing & Publishing Co. Ltd v. Inkatha Freedom Party* 1992 (3) SA 579 (A) 591.
703. 1994 (1) SA 708 (A) 767–769.
704. *Johnson v. Rand Daily Mails* 1928 AD 190 205–207; *Smit v. OVS Afrikaanse Pers (Bpk)* 1956 (1) SA 768 (O) 772–774; *Kemp v. Republican Press (Pty) Ltd* 1994 (4) SA 261 (E) 264; *Independent Newspapers Holdings Ltd v. Suliman* 2004 (3) All SA 137 (SCA) 154e–155e.
705. *Khumalo and Others v. Holomisa* 2002 (5) SA 401 (CC).

publication was reasonable.[706] In determining whether publication was reasonable, a court will have regard to the individual's interest in protecting his or her reputation and privacy in the context of the constitutional protection of both freedom of expression and human dignity.

350. Truth alone is not a defence, the publication of the defamatory material must also be for the public benefit. Generally speaking, publication of the truth will be for the public benefit. However, the courts have held that there is justification for retaining public benefit as a separate requirement, provided that the interpretation given to the element of public benefit is not unduly restrictive.[707] Generally, it is for the public benefit that the truth about the character or conduct of a person should be known, but the fact that the plaintiff had in the past transgressed does not necessarily make such transgressions relevant to his or her present character.[708]

H. Privilege

351. Publication of defamatory material in privileged circumstances is justified and therefore lawful. In certain cases, the law regards the free flow of information as so important that it should not be hampered by the fear of liability for defamation.

352. Absolute privilege is conferred in terms of legislation dealing with the institutions of government. The most important absolute privilege is created by section 58(1) of the Constitution[709] in terms of which cabinet members and members of the National Assembly are completely protected against liability, both civil and criminal, for anything they have 'said in, produced before or submitted to' the National Assembly or any of its committees.[710] Similar protection is afforded by the

706. In terms of the earlier decision of the Supreme Court of Appeal in *National Media Ltd v. Bogoshi* 1998 (4) All SA 437 (SCA); 1999 (1) BCLR 1 (SCA); 1998 (4) SA 1196 (SCA) 1215 ff.; *Khumalo v. Holomisa* 2002 (8) BCLR 771 (CC); 2002 (5) SA 401 (CC).

707. *Graham v. Ker* (1892) 9 SC 185 187; *Coetzee v. Central News Agency* 1953 (1) SA 449 (W) 452; *Mahomed v. Kassim* 1973 (2) SA 1 (RA) 1G; *Deedat v. Muslim Digest* 1980 (2) SA 922 (D) 928; *Lyman v. Natal Witness Printing & Publishing Co. (Pty) Ltd* 1991 (4) SA 677 (N) 684–686; *Kemp v. Republican Press (Pty) Ltd* 1994 (4) SA 261 (E) 265–266; *Yazbek v. Seymour* 2000 (2) All SA 569 (E); 2001 (3) SA 695 (E) 701; *Allie v. Foodworld Stores Distribution Centre (Pty) Ltd* 2004 (1) All SA 369 (SCA), 2004 (2) SA 433 (SCA) 445A-D.

708. In *Graham v. Ker* (1892) 9 SC 185 at 187 De Villiers CJ said:

> the worst characters sometimes reform, and some of the inducements to reformation would be removed if stories as to past transgressions could with impunity be raked up after a long lapse of time. Public interest … would suffer rather than benefit from any unnecessary reviving of forgotten scandals. But the commission of recent offences against the law or against society stands on a different footing.

709. Act 108 of 1996.

710. *See Speaker of the National Assembly v. De Lille MP* 1999 (4) All SA 241 (SCA); 1999 (11) BCLR 1339 (SCA); 1999 (4) SA 863 (SCA).

Constitution with reference to proceedings in the NCOP[711] as well as in the provincial legislatures.[712] Absolute privilege confers immunity from liability even if the defendant made the defamatory statement out of malice or with an improper motive.

353. Qualified privilege is recognized where material is published while exercising a right, in discharging a duty, or in furthering a legitimate interest, to someone who has a similar duty or interest to receive it.[713] The duty or right may be legal, moral or social. The person to whom the material is published must have a similar right, duty or interest to receive the communication. The existence of a right or duty for the purposes of qualified privilege is determined by the reasonableness standard. The question is whether the circumstances, according to the standard of a reasonable person, created a duty or right which entitled the defendant to speak.[714]

Examples of qualified privilege in the cases concern, for example, statements about the creditors of a company in a report on its claim for insurance;[715] statements made by public officials to one another in the course of official duties;[716] statements by members of public bodies to other members at meetings of these bodies;[717] statements by a former employer to inform a prospective employer about the character of an employee;[718] inquiries as to creditworthiness;[719] statements by a member of a church about the morality of a minister of the church, to the elders of the church;[720] complaints by members of the public to disciplinary bodies about professional misconduct;[721] and defamatory disclosures to a priest.[722]

Newspapers cannot rely on qualified privilege on the basis of a duty to report to their readers and a correlative interest in the subject matter of newspaper reports on the part of their readers. The press generally has a duty to report,[723] but readers of the newspaper generally do not have a sufficient interest in the subject matter of

711. Section 71(1).
712. Section 117(1).
713. *Ehmke v. Grunewald* 1921 AD 575; *De Waal v. Ziervogel* 1938 AD 112; *Borgin v. De Villiers* 1980 (3) SA 556 (A) 577.
714. *De Waal v. Ziervogel* 1938 AD 112 123; *Benson v. Robinson & Co. (Pty) Ltd* 1967 (1) SA 420 (A) 426; *Borgin v. De Villiers* 1980 (3) SA 556 (A) 577; *Vincent v. Long* 1988 (3) SA 45 (C) 47–48; *Jansen van Vuuren v. Kruger* 1993 (4) SA 842 (A) 855; *Yazbek v. Seymour* 2000 (2) All SA 569 (E); 2001 (3) SA 695 (E) 701G.
715. *Maskowitz v. Pienaar* 1957 (4) SA 195 (A); *Faydene Shirt & Clothing Manufacturers (Pty) Ltd v. Levy* 1966 (1) SA 26 (D).
716. *McLean v. Murray* 1923 AD 406; *Young v. Kemsley* 1940 AD 258.
717. *Young v. Kemsley* 1940 AD 258 (municipal council); *Lotter v. De Villiers* 1946 TPD 569 (school committee); *Naude v. Whittle* 1958 (1) SA 594 (A) (farmers' association); *Allardice v. Dowdle* 1965 (1) SA 433 (D) (meeting of creditors).
718. *Borgin v. De Villiers* 1980 (3) SA 556 (A).
719. *Informa Confidential Reports (Pty) Ltd v. Abro* 1975 (2) SA 760 (T).
720. *De Waal v. Ziervogel* 1938 AD 112.
721. *Vincent v. Long* 1988 (3) SA 45 (C); *Yazbek v. Seymour* 2000 (2) All SA 569 (E); 2001 (3) SA 695 (E); *Strydom v. Bence* 2002 (4) All SA 539 (SE); *Botha v. Mthiyane* 2002 (4) BCLR 389 (W); 2002 (1) SA 289 (W).
722. *O v. O* 1995 (4) SA 482 (W).
723. *Zillie v. Johnson* 1984 (2) SA 186 (W) 196.

reports.[724] However, newspapers can rely on a defence of reasonableness of the publication, even in respect of statements that turn out to be false.[725]

Malice or an improper motive on the part of the defendant will nullify the defence of qualified privilege.[726]

354. Qualified privilege also exists in respect of oral or written statements made by legal representatives, parties to litigation and witnesses in the course of judicial or quasi-judicial proceedings, or statements by judicial officers in the exercise of their public office. The provisos for recognition of qualified privilege in the context of legal proceedings are that the statement should be relevant to the matters in issue and should have some foundation in the evidence or circumstances surrounding the proceedings.[727] The privilege recognized in such cases is provisional, and the publication will be unlawful if the defendant acted out of malice or with an improper motive, or where the defendant had no reasonable grounds for believing the truth of the material.[728] The onus is on the defendant to establish on a balance of probabilities that the statement was relevant and had some foundation in the evidence or circumstances surrounding the proceedings;[729] except in the case of a presiding officer, who will only be liable if the plaintiff can prove malice on his or her part.[730] Considerable latitude is allowed to legal practitioners in presenting the cases of clients, but a practitioner has no general licence to defame others in the course of legal proceedings.[731] Public policy requires that the approach to relevance should not be so strict that witnesses and deponents would be unduly fettered in their testimony or affidavits.[732]

355. Qualified privilege attaches to the publication of reports on proceedings of courts, Parliament and public bodies, on the basis that it is in the public interest to know what transpires in bodies entrusted with public duties. A substantially accurate and fair report on the proceedings of such bodies will be protected.[733] The qualified privilege is provisional, and the publication will be unlawful if the defendant acted with an improper motive.[734]

---

724. *Neethling v. Du Preez, Neethling v. The Weekly Mail* 1994 (1) SA 708 (A).
725. *National Media Ltd v. Bogoshi* 1998 (4) All SA 347 (SCA); 1999 (1) BCLR 1 (SCA); 1998 (4) SA 1196 (SCA).
726. *Poovalingam v. Rajbansi* 1992 (1) SA 283 (A); *Yazbek v. Seymour* 2000 (2) All SA 569 (E); 2001 (3) SA 695 (E).
727. *Gluckman v. Schneider* 1936 AD 151; *Pogrund v. Yutar* 1967 (2) SA 564 (A); *May v. Udwin* 1981 (1) SA 1 (A); *Joubert v. Venter* 1985 (1) SA 654 (A); *Majolica Pottery (Venda) (Pty) Ltd v. Barrow & Coetzee* 1999 (1) SA 1166 (C) 1180; *Van der Berg v. Coopers & Lybrand Trust (Pty) Ltd* 2001 (1) All SA 425 (SCA); 2001 (2) SA 242 (SCA).
728. *Pogrund v. Yutar* 1967 (2) SA 564 (A) 574; *Joubert v. Venter* 1985 (1) SA 654 (A) 702 704.
729. *Mohamed v. Jassiem* 1996 (1) SA 673 (A) 709; *Van der Berg v. Coopers & Lybrand Trust (Pty) Ltd* 2001 (2) SA 242 (SCA) 252.
730. *May v. Udwin* 1981 (1) SA 1 (A) 19–20.
731. *Pogrund v. Yutar* 1967 (2) SA 564 (A) 570.
732. *Van der Berg v. Coopers & Lybrand Trust (Pty) Ltd* 1998 (4) All SA 18 (C); 1998 (4) SA 890 (C) 905.
733. *Welken v. Nasionale Koerante Bpk* 1964 (3) SA 87 (O) 90; *De Flamingh v. Pakendorf, De Flamingh v. Lake* 1979 (3) SA 676 (T) 682. In *La Grange v. Schoeman* 1980 (1) SA 885 (E) the court made

I. Fair Comment

356. Publication of defamatory statements that constitute fair comment on true facts and that are shown to be in the public interest is lawful. The requirements that the courts have set for reliance on this defence are:

(a) that the defamatory statement must amount to *comment* or *opinion* as opposed to a statement of fact;
(b) that the comment must be fair (a genuine expression of opinion, relevant, free from malice and a reasonable inference from the facts);
(c) that the facts on which the comment is based must be substantially true and must be expressly stated or clearly indicated in the document or speech containing the defamatory statement;[735] and
(d) that the comment must relate to a matter of public interest.[736] Malice or improper motive will nullify the defence of fair comment.[737]

357. In *The Citizen 1978 (Pty) Ltd v. McBride (Johnstone and Others as Amici Curiae)*[738] McBride sued *The Citizen* newspaper, its editor and journalists for defamation. *The Citizen* had published a series of articles and editorials questioning McBride's suitability for the post of Ekurhuleni Metro Police Chief. It expressed the view that McBride was unsuitable for the post because (i) he was a 'criminal' and a 'murderer'; (ii) he was not contrite for the deaths he caused; and (iii) he had dubious dealings with alleged gun dealers in Mozambique in 1998. The articles referred to McBride's conviction in the apartheid-era for the planting of a bomb that had killed a number of people in a bar. McBride alleged that these articles neglected to add a crucial fact: McBride had been granted amnesty in terms of the Promotion of National Unity and Reconciliation Act 34 of 1995, and that in terms of section 20(10) of the Act his conviction was therefore deemed 'for all purposes' not to have taken place. He contended that the labels 'criminal' and 'murderer' therefore did not apply to him. The Supreme Court of Appeal upheld McBride's claim and found that the false statements could not sustain the defence of fair comment.

On appeal, a majority in the Constitutional Court found that the Reconciliation Act did not render the fact that McBride committed murder untrue. *The Citizen's* comments were based on an adequate exposition of the relevant facts and constituted comment on McBride's suitability for an important and prominent public post.

---

a distinction between the lawful publication of reports of judicial proceedings and the publication of the photograph of a person connected with the proceedings.

734. *Benson v. Robinson & Co. (Pty) Ltd* 1967 (1) SA 420 (A) 427E 432H.

735. *Crawford v. Albu* 1917 AD 102 131 (Innes CJ said in this case that 'there can be no fair comment upon facts which are not true'); *Yazbek v. Seymour* 2000 (2) All SA 569 (E); 2001 (3) SA 695 (E) 701.

736. *Marais v. Richard* 1981 (1) SA 1157 (A) 1167; *Johnson v. Beckett* 1992 (1) SA 762 (A) 779; *Moyse v. Mujuru* 1999 (3) SA 39 (ZS) 47; *Delta Motor Corporation (Pty) Ltd v. Van der Merwe* 2004 (4) All SA 365 (SCA); 2004 (6) SA 185 (SCA) 193H–194B.

737. *Minister of Justice v. SA Associated Newspapers Ltd* 1979 (3) SA 466 (C); *Johnson v. Beckett* 1992 (1) SA 762 (A).

738. 2011(8) BCLR 816 (CC).

The majority emphasized that protected comment need not be 'fair or just at all', in the sense in which these terms are commonly understood. Criticism is protected even if extreme, unjust, unbalanced, exaggerated and prejudiced, so long as it expresses an honestly held opinion, without malice, on a matter of public interest on facts that are true. *The Citizen* was thus entitled to express views on McBride's suitability for the post and even though the court considered *The Citizen's* coverage to be vengeful and distasteful it was nonetheless entitled to legal protection.

The judgments in this case raise fundamental issues concerning the defence of fair comment. Cameron J, who wrote the majority judgment, stated the following:

> So to dub the defence 'fair comment' is misleading. If, to be protected, comment has to be 'fair', the law would require expressions of opinion on matters of fact to be just, equitable, reasonable, level-headed and balanced. That is not so. An important rationale for the defence of protected or 'fair' comment is to ensure that divergent views are aired in public and subjected to scrutiny and debate. Through open contest, these views may be challenged in argument. By contrast, if views we consider wrong-headed and unacceptable are repressed, they may never be exposed as unpersuasive. Untrammelled debate enhances truth-finding and enables us to scrutinize political argument and deliberate social value.[739]
>
> Perhaps it would be clearer, and helpful in the understanding of the law, if the defence were known rather as 'protected comment'. A new name would not change the requirements. At common law, it was rightly held that 'fairness' in fair comment must draw on the general legal criterion of reasonableness. In our constitutional state, comment on matters of public interest receives protection under the guarantee of freedom of expression. Hence the values and norms of the Constitution determine the boundaries of what is protected. To call the defence 'protected comment' may illuminate the constitutional source and extent of the protection.[740]

Ngcobo CJ appears to accept a more exacting standard for the defence of fair comment, on the basis of the need to maintain a delicate balance between the protection of the right of everyone, including the press, to freedom of expression, and the need to respect human dignity:

> The requirement that a comment must be fair is consistent with the values that underlie our constitutional democracy. It underscores the need to balance freedom of expression, on the one hand, and the need to protect human dignity, on the other. By insisting that a comment must be fair, the common law demands that comment be fair having regard to the right to human dignity. The comment must be relevant to the matter commented upon, and it must not be actuated by malice. It underscores the proposition that freedom of expression does not enjoy a superior status to other rights enshrined in the Constitution. Indeed,

739. At para. 82.
740. At para. 84.

it gives effect to the constitutional commitment this Court articulated in Mamabolo[741] to 'three conjoined, reciprocal and covalent values' that are foundational to our Republic, namely, human dignity, equality and freedom.[742]

In my view, the requirement of fair comment is consistent with the need to respect and protect dignity. It maintains a delicate balance between the need to protect the right of everyone, including the press, to freedom of expression and the need to respect human dignity. This is the balance that the Constitution requires to be struck. I do not, therefore, share the view expressed by Cameron J that the word 'fair' is misleading. It must now be understood in the light of our Constitution, in particular the foundational values of human dignity and freedom upon which our constitutional democracy rests and the need to strike a balance between ensuring that freedom of expression is not stifled and insisting on the need to respect and protect human dignity.[743]

J. Reasonable Publication in the Public Interest

358. In *National Media Ltd v. Bogoshi*,[744] the Supreme Court of Appeal held that earlier cases establishing strict liability of the media for defamation were wrong, being in conflict with the right of free expression of the media. The court recognized that, even if none of the other defences excluding unlawfulness (such as truth for public benefit, fair comment or qualified privilege) could be relied upon, the publication of a false and defamatory statement will be lawful 'if upon consideration of all the circumstances of the case, it is found to have been reasonable to publish the particular facts in the particular way and at the particular time'.[745] Reasonableness will depend on factors such as the extent of research or enquiries preceding the publication, the opportunity for the plaintiff to respond, the seriousness of the defamation, the extent of publication and the public interest involved.[746]

The defence recognized in this case illustrates an area of the law on defamation where unlawfulness and fault overlap. Reasonableness of the publication, equated with absence of negligence, was held to exclude unlawfulness. The judgment is not a model of structured analysis of the roles of unlawfulness and negligence in the law of defamation, but it appears that the court intended to deal with two defences, both turning on the reasonableness of the defendant's conduct: the one negating unlawfulness and the other negating negligence. This is how the Supreme Court of Appeal itself interpreted the *Bogoshi* judgment in the subsequent case of *Mthembi-Mahanyele v. Mail & Guardian Ltd*,[747] although the court did not clarify the basis

741. *S v. Mamabolo (ETV and Others, intervening)* 2001 (3) SA 409 (CC).
742. At para. 157.
743. At para. 158.
744. 1998 (4) All SA 347 (SCA); 1999 (1) BCLR 1 (SCA); 1998 (4) SA 1196 (SCA).
745. *National Media Ltd v. Bogoshi* 1998 (4) SA 1196 (SCA) at 1212G–H.
746. *National Media Ltd v. Bogoshi* 1998 (4) SA 1196 (SCA) 1212–1213.
747. 2004 (6) SA 329 (SCA) paras 45–47.

of the distinction between the two defences.[748] The judgment in the *Mthembi-Mahanyele* case makes it clear that the Supreme Court of Appeal recognizes the reasonableness of a publication as a defence that could exclude either unlawfulness or negligence.

K. *Intent (Animus Iniuriandi)*

359. Defamation generally requires fault in the form of the intent to harm the reputation of the plaintiff by publication of defamatory material, concomitant with knowledge that the causing of harm is unlawful.

Where the plaintiff in defamation proceedings proves the publication of a defamatory statement referring to it, the presumption arises that the defendant acted with *animus iniuriandi*. This presumption may be rebutted by proof that the statement was published in the course of a quarrel or fight (*rixa*),[749] or in jest, so that the person or persons to whom it was published understood the statement merely as a jest and not in a defamatory sense.[750] The jurisprudential basis for excluding liability on account of *rixa* or jest has not been made clear, but conceivably knowledge of unlawfulness is absent in such cases.

360. The presumption of intent may also be rebutted by proof of a mistake on the part of the defendant, where the mistake is incompatible with the will to cause harm to the plaintiff's reputation and concomitant knowledge of unlawfulness. If, for example, the defendant can prove that publication of the defamatory statement occurred as a result of a genuine mistake, or if the defendant was under the bona fide but wrong impression that the occasion was privileged, the defendant will escape liability for lack of *animus iniuriandi*.[751]

361. The term 'malice' has sometimes been associated with intent or *animus iniuriandi*, but the prevailing view is that 'malice' is the actuating impulse preceding intent,[752] or an improper or indirect motive,[753] and is relevant when determining whether the defendant has exceeded the limits of the defences referred to above.

362. In *National Media Ltd v. Bogoshi*,[754] the Supreme Court of Appeal held that the press can also rely on absence of *animus iniuriandi* through a genuine mistake,

---

748. Anton Fagan, *Rethinking Wrongfulness in the Law of Delict*, 122 S. African L. J. 90, 105–106 (2005).

749. *Wood v. Branson* 1952 (3) SA 369 (T) 372; *Peck v. Katz* 1957 (2) SA 567 (T) 570–571.

750. *Masch v. Leask* 1916 TPD 114 116; *Glass v. Perl* 1928 TPD 264.

751. *Maisel v. Van Naeren* 1960 (4) SA 836 (C); *Suttonmere (Pty) Ltd v. Hills* 1982 (2) SA 74 (N); *Minister van Veiligheid en Sekuriteit v. Kyriacou* 2000 (4) SA 337 (O).

752. *Gluckman v. Schneider* 1936 AD 151 159.

753. *May v. Union Government* 1954 (3) SA 120 (N) 129; *Beckenstrater v. Rottcher & Theunissen* 1955 (1) SA 129 (A) 134; *Van der Merwe v. Strydom* 1967 (3) SA 460 (A) 467; *Lederman v. Moharal Investments (Pty) Ltd* 1969 (1) SA 190 (A) 196; *Prinsloo v. Newman* 1975 (1) SA 481 (A) 491. Such motive may, but need not, be spite or ill will: *Landman v. Minister of Police* 1975 (2) SA 155 (E) 156.

754. 1998 (4) All SA 347 (SCA); 1999 (1) BCLR 1 (SCA); 1998 (4) SA 1196 (SCA).

as long as the mistake was not due to the negligence of those for whom the defendant can be held responsible. It has been suggested that the negligence-based liability for defamation in media cases should be extended to defendants in other cases.[755]

L. *Damages*

363. The successful plaintiff in a defamation action is entitled to an award of general damages as compensation for injured feelings and for the hurt to his or her dignity and reputation. In addition, the plaintiff may recover as special damages patrimonial loss suffered as a result of the publication of the statement.[756] The court has a wide discretion in determining the award of general damages, having regard to all the circumstances of the case and the prevailing attitudes of the community.[757] Factors taken into account include the nature of the defamatory statement; the nature and extent of the publication; the reputation, character and conduct of the plaintiff; and the motives and conduct of the defendant.

II. Infringement of Privacy

364. The right to privacy is an aspect of the common law concept of dignity (dignitas); is specifically guaranteed by the Constitution;[758] and is protected by the law of delict as a personality right.[759] In *Jansen van Vuuren v. Kruger*,[760] Harms JA

755. *Marais v. Groenewald* 2002 (2) All SA 578 (T); 2001 (1) SA 634 (T).

756. *Die Spoorbond v. SA Railways*, *Van Heerden v. SA Railways* 1946 AD 999 1005. Although patrimonial loss is normally recovered under the *lex Aquilia*, the two kinds of damages are usually claimed in the same action; *see Caxton Ltd v. Reeva Forman (Pty) Ltd* 1990 (3) SA 547 (A) 560–561.

757. *Black v. Joseph* 1931 AD 132 146; *Gelb v. Hawkins* 1960 (3) SA 687 (A) 693; *Geyser v. Pont* 1968 (4) SA 67 (W) 79; *Kritzinger v. Perskorporasie van SA (Edms)Bpk* 1981 (2) SA 373 (O) 389; *Smith v. Die Republikein (Edms)Bpk* 1989 (3) SA 872 (SWA) 875; *Van der Berg v. Coopers & Lybrand Trust (Pty) Ltd* 2001 (1) All SA 425 (SCA); 2001 (2) SA 242 (SCA) 260. In nominal damages can also be awarded, as in *Zillie v. Johnson* 1984 (2) SA 186 (W) 197.

758. Section 14 of the Constitution (Act 108 of 1996) provides as follows: "Everyone has the right to privacy, which includes the right not to have – (a) their person or home searched; (b) their property searched; (c) their possessions seized; or (d) the privacy of their communications infringed." On the right to privacy in terms of Constitution, *see Rudolph v. Commissioner for Inland Revenue* 1994 (3) SA 771 (W) 773–775; *Park-Ross v. Director: Office for Serious Economic Offences* 1995 (2) SA 148 (C) 158 ff. 166–167; *Bernstein v. Bester* 1996 (2) SA 751 (CC) 783–799; *Case v. Minister of Safety & Security* 1996 (3) SA 617 (CC) 656 ff.

759. *See* generally *O'Keeffe v. Argus Printing & Publishing Co. Ltd* 1954 (3) SA 244 (C) 249 ('The unauthorized publication of a person's photograph and name for advertising purposes is in my view capable of constituting an aggression upon that person's *dignitas*'); *Kidson v. SA Associated Newspapers Ltd* 1957 (3) SA 461 (W) 467–468; *Mhlongo v. Bailey* 1958 (1) SA 370 (W) 371–372; *Universiteit van Pretoria v. Tommie Meyer Films (Edms) Bpk* 1977 (4) SA 376 (T) 384; *Jansen van Vuuren v. Kruger* 1993 (4) SA 842 (A) 849; *Jooste v. National Media Ltd* 1994 (2) SA 634 (C) 645; *National Media Ltd v. Jooste* 1996 (3) SA 262 (A) 271; *Bernstein v. Bester* 1996 (2) SA 751 (CC) 789.

760. 1993 (4) SA 842 (A) 849.

stated that the '*actio iniuriarum* protects a person's dignitas and dignitas embraces privacy. Although the right to privacy has on occasion been referred to as a real right or ius in rem ... it is better described as a right of personality'. The protection of privacy is afforded to natural persons[761] as well as juristic persons.[762]

365. The right to privacy can be infringed, for instance, by the unlawful intrusion upon the personal privacy of another or the unlawful publication or disclosure of private facts about another.[763] Examples include entry into a private residence,[764] secretly watching a person in a private place,[765] reading private documents,[766] listening to private conversations,[767] taking unauthorized blood tests,[768] unauthorized publication of photographs,[769] disclosing details of a private relationship,[770] disclosing that a person is HIV positive.[771] Clearly not all such intrusions or publications are unlawful; and 'in demarcating the boundary between lawfulness and unlawfulness in this field, the court must have regard to the particular facts of the case and judge them in the light of contemporary *boni mores* and the general sense of justice of the community as perceived by the court'.[772]

366. The unlawfulness of the invasion of privacy can be rebutted by proof of a ground of justification such as a privileged occasion[773] or truth and public interest. The question of public interest in private matters requires a balancing of conflicting rights and interests, with regard to factors such that the plaintiff is a public figure or was involved in a newsworthy event;[774] the extent of the invasion of the plaintiff's privacy;[775] the fact that the plaintiff exposed his or her privacy to the risk of

761. *See* cases cited in previous footnote.
762. *Financial Mail (Pty) Ltd v. Sage Holdings Ltd* 1993 (2) SA 451 (A) 462–463; *Janit v. Motor Industry Fund Administrators (Pty) Ltd* 1995 (4) SA 293 (A).
763. *Financial Mail (Pty) Ltd v. Sage Holdings Ltd* 1993 (2) SA 451 (A) 462.
764. *R v. Schonken* 1929 AD 36.
765. *R v. R* 1954 (2) SA 134 (N).
766. *Reid-Daly v. Hickman* 1981 (2) SA 315 (ZA) 323.
767. *Financial Mail (Pty) Ltd v. Sage Holdings Ltd* 1993 (2) SA 451 (A).
768. *Goldberg v. Union & South West Africa Insurance Co. Ltd* 1980 (1) SA 160 (E) 164; *Seetal v. Pravitha* 1983 (3) SA 827 (D) 861–862; *C v. Minister of Correctional Services* 1996 (4) SA 292 (T).
769. *O'Keeffe v. Argus Printing & Publishing Co. Ltd* 1954 (3) SA 244 (C); *Mhlongo v. Bailey* 1958 (1) SA 370 (W); *La Grange v. Schoeman* 1980 (1) SA 885 (E).
770. *Mhlongo v. Bailey* 1958 (1) SA 370 (W); *National Media Ltd v. Jooste* 1996 (3) SA 262 (A).
771. *Jansen van Vuuren v. Kruger* 1993 (4) SA 842 (A); *NM and Others v. Smith and Others (Freedom of Expression Institute as Amicus Curiae)* 2007 (5) SA 250 (CC), where the Constitutional Court held that an individual's HIV status, particularly within the South African context, deserved protection against indiscriminate disclosure due to the nature and negative social context of the disease, as well as the potential intolerance and discrimination that resulted from such disclosure.
772. *Financial Mail (Pty) Ltd v. Sage Holdings Ltd* 1993 (2) SA 451 (A) 462E-G.
773. *La Grange v. Schoeman* 1980 (1) SA 885 (E) 893–894; *Jansen van Vuuren v. Kruger* 1993 (4) SA 842 (A) 851ff.
774. *La Grange v. Schoeman* 1980 (1) SA 885 (E) 892–894; *Jooste v. National Media Ltd* 1994 (2) SA 634 (C) 645–646.
775. *Jooste v. National Media Ltd* 1994 (2) SA 634 (C) 646.

infringement;[776] the motive, disposition or purpose with which the defendant acted;[777] and the fact that the private facts were obtained through a wrongful act of intrusion.[778]

367. Intent (*animus iniuriandi*) is a requirement for *iniuria* in the form of infringement of privacy, involving consciousness of both the factual aspect of infringement and of the unlawfulness of infringement.[779] Intent could be excluded by mistake (entering the wrong room under the bona fide impression that it is the right one), or absence of consciousness of the unlawfulness.[780]*Animus iniuriandi* is presumed once the wrongfulness of the infringement of privacy has been proved.[781]

368. Damages in the form of satisfaction (solatium) can be recovered for infringement of privacy, and the extent is determined *ex aequo et bono.*[782] Factors that may play a part in the assessment of damages include extenuating factors such as an apology by the defendant;[783] that the information concerning the event was already known;[784] that the information would inevitably have become known at a later stage or that the publication was limited;[785] while aggravating factors include the wide circulation of the publication;[786] the risk of further dissemination of the private facts;[787] the intimate nature of such facts and the identification of the plaintiff by means of a photograph;[788] the abuse of a confidential relationship notwithstanding an express undertaking to the contrary;[789] and mental stress as a result of

776. *O'Keeffe v. Argus Printing & Publishing Co. Ltd* 1954 (3) SA 244 (C) 249; *Mhlongo v. Bailey* 1958 (1) SA 370 (W) 371–372; *Prinsloo v. SA Associated Newspapers Ltd* 1959 (2) SA 693 (W) 695.
777. *La Grange v. Schoeman* 1980 (1) SA 885 (E) 893–894; cf. *Jooste v. National Media Ltd* 1994 (2) SA 634 (C) 646.
778. *Financial Mail (Pty) Ltd v. Sage Holdings Ltd* 1993 (2) SA 451 (A) 463; *Motor Industry Fund Administrators (Pty) Ltd v. Janit* 1994 (3) SA 56 (W) 61; *Janit v. Motor Industry Fund Administrators (Pty) Ltd* 1995 (4) SA 293 (A). The publication or disclosure of unlawfully obtained facts may nevertheless be justified in exceptional circumstances by overriding considerations of public interest: *Financial Mail (Pty) Ltd v. Sage Holdings Ltd* 1993 (2) SA 451 (A) 463 465.
779. *S v. A* 1971 (2) SA 293 (T) 297; *Kidson v. SA Associated Newspapers Ltd* 1957 (3) SA 461 (W) 468; *Jansen van Vuuren v. Kruger* 1993 (4) SA 842 (A) 849 856–857.
780. *S v. I* 1976 (1) SA 781 (RA) 787; *Jansen van Vuuren v. Kruger* 1993 (4) SA 842 (A) 856–857. In *C v. Minister of Correctional Services* 1996 (4) SA 292 (T) 304–306 it was held that in respect of the infringement of the privacy of prisoners through blood tests for AIDS only an attenuated form of intent applies, and consciousness of unlawfulness is not required; the position being similar to unlawful arrest (*Whittaker v. Roos & Bateman, Morant v. Roos & Bateman* 1912 AD 92; *Minister of Justice v. Hofmeyr* 1993 (3) SA 131 (A)).
781. *Kidson v. SA Associated Newspapers Ltd* 1957 (3) SA 461 (W) 468.
782. *Jansen van Vuuren v. Kruger* 1993 (4) SA 842 (A) 857–858.
783. *Kidson v. SA Associated Newspapers Ltd* 1957 (3) SA 461 (W) 468–469.
784. *Jooste v. National Media Ltd* 1994 (2) SA 634 (C) 647.
785. *Jansen van Vuuren v. Kruger* 1993 (4) SA 842 (A) 858.
786. *Jooste v. National Media Ltd* 1994 (2) SA 634 (C) 647.
787. *Jansen van Vuuren v. Kruger* 1993 (4) SA 842 (A) 858.
788. *Jooste v. National Media Ltd* 1994 (2) SA 634 (C) 647.
789. *Jansen van Vuuren v. Kruger* 1993 (4) SA 842 (A) 857–858.

the disclosure or intrusion.[790] Patrimonial loss as a result of the infringement of privacy can be recovered with the Aquilian action. The remedy for threatening or continuous infringement of privacy is an interdict.[791]

§5. Interference by a Third Person with Contractual Relations

I. Negligent Interference with Contractual Relations

369. There is no general claim in South African law for economic loss suffered as a result of *negligent* interference with contractual relations, or what is sometimes referred to as 'contractual relational economic loss'.[792]

370. The only form of liability for *negligent* interference with a personal claim that is recognized in South African law is the Aquilian liability for negligently causing the death of a breadwinner and thereby depriving dependants of the support to which they were entitled from the deceased. This form of liability is founded in family law and the claim for loss of support was historically restricted to cases where a duty of support derives from a valid marriage, mainly concerning spouses and children. However, the group of claimants has been extended in modern law, to include those whose right to support derives from a relationship akin to marriage, but not constituting a legally valid marriage, for instance 'a solemn marriage in accordance with recognized and accepted faith',[793] and a same-sex permanent life relationship similar in other respects to marriage;[794] and the right to support of a divorced person under a court order dealing with maintenance after dissolution of the marriage;[795] and also to the right to support deriving from de facto adoption.[796]

371. Liability for *negligent* interference with a personal claim has not been extended to those whose loss as a result of the death or injury of another person derives solely from a contractual relationship. In Roman-Dutch law, claims by masters for loss of services caused by injuries to their domestic servants were recognized, but this liability was not extended to employees generally.[797] The leading case in this regard, *Union Government v. Ocean Accident & Guarantee Corporation Ltd*,[798] involved a claim brought by the government for loss suffered as a result

790. *Jansen van Vuuren v. Kruger* 1993 (4) SA 842 (A) 858; *C v. Minister of Correctional Services* 1996 (4) SA 292 (T) 306–307.
791. *Rhodesian Printing & Publishing Co. Ltd v. Duggan* 1975 (1) SA 590 (RA).
792. *See* generally Dale Hutchison, 'Relational Economic Loss (or Interference with Contractual Relations): The Last Hurdle,' in *Developing Delict: Essays in Honour of Robert Feenstra* (2000) 133 ff.; first published as *Acta Juridica 2000*, Juta, Cape Town.
793. *Amod v. MVA Fund* 1999 (4) SA 1319 (SCA).
794. *Du Plessis v. RAF Fund* 19 Sep. 2003 (SCA).
795. *Santam v. Henery* 1999 (3) SA 421 (SCA).
796. *Road Accident Fund v. Mohohlo* 2018 (2) SA 65 (SCA).
797. Dale Hutchison, 'Relational Economic Loss (or Interference with Contractual Relations): The Last Hurdle', in *Developing Delict: Essays in Honour of Robert Feenstra* 138 (Juta 2000), first published as *Acta Juridica 2000*, Juta, Cape Town.
798. 1956 (1) SA 577 (A) 585B-D.

of negligently caused injuries to a government employee (a magistrate). The court declined to expand Aquilian liability beyond the historical scope of the action of dependants. Schreiner JA pointed out the dangers inherent in expanding this action:[799]

> Once one goes beyond physical proximity and considers the possibilities that may arise out of the relationships, contractual or other, between the physically injured person and other persons who may suffer indirectly, though materially, through his incapacitation, one is immediately met with the prospects of an unmanageable situation. It is easy to imagine the absurdities that would arise if all persons contractually linked to the injured person could sue the careless injurer for the loss suffered by them. The case was put to us of the injured building contractor who in consequence of his injury has to discontinue his contract, so that his employees and the building owner and the architect and his subcontractors and their employees are all put to some loss. Insurance companies would also be a wide class of plaintiffs who could bring actions when persons insured by them were negligently injured or, presumably, killed, if the extension of liability contended for were recognized. In fact it would be a rare accident that did not give occasion for a crop of actions at the suit of persons who had made contracts with the injured party. The question whether in any particular case there is a liability under the *Lex Aquilia* towards a particular person cannot be satisfactorily answered by any such wide proposition as that contended for on behalf of the Government.

372. There has been a substantial expansion of liability for negligently caused economic loss in areas such as negligent misrepresentation,[800] but this expansion has stopped short of including liability for negligent interference with contractual relations, whether through death, injury or otherwise. In respect of damage to property, the courts have extended the right to recover damages to certain holders of contractual rights; but only where, concomitant with the contractual right and economic interest in the property, the holder of the right is also physically in possession of the property and bears the risk of damage, as in the case of the instalment-purchaser of a motor vehicle,[801] the instalment-purchaser of land,[802] or the borrower of a motor vehicle.[803]

373. The decision in the *Union Government* case has effectively blocked the expansion of liability for economic loss resulting from negligent interference with

799. *Union Government v. Ocean Accident & Guarantee Corporation Ltd* 1956 (1) SA 577 (A) at 585–586.
800. *See* the section on unlawfulness in respect of pure economic loss: Part 1, Ch. 1, §2, and the section on damages for pure economic loss: Part V, Ch. 2, §4.
801. *Lean v. Van der Mescht* 1972 (2) SA 100 (O).
802. *Smit v. Saipem* 1974 (4) 918 (A).
803. *Spolander v. Ward* 1940 CPD 24.

contractual relations generally.[804] The position is different where there is *intentional* interference with a contractual relationship.

II. Intentional Interference with Contractual Relations

374. Intentional interference with contractual relationship of others by a third party, for instance by inducing a breach of a contract, can give rise to delictual liability for the third party towards the contract party who suffered loss. In *Dun and Bradstreet (Pty) Ltd v. SA Merchants Combined Credit Bureau (Cape) (Pty) Ltd*,[805] this liability was described as follows:

> Moreover, incorporeal property, such as a personal right flowing from contract, also enjoys a measure of protection in that a delictual remedy is available to a party to a contract who complains that a third party has intentionally and without lawful justification invaded his enjoyment of such property by inducing the other party to the contract to commit a breach thereof. ...

375. In *Dantex Investment Holdings (Pty) Ltd v. Brenner and Others NNO*,[806] the Appellate Division accepted that intentional interference with contractual relations, with the intent also to cause harm, is an actionable delict. Both parties in this case accepted that intent (*dolus*) is a requirement for liability. The court assumed for the purposes of the case that the attitude of the parties was correct in respect of the requirement of intent (*dolus*), but Grosskopf JA also noted that:

> the question whether culpa might not constitute a sufficient element of fault to ground liability for damages for an unlawful interference with contractual relations was not raised or debated in argument. Since there was in any event no allegation of culpa in the pleadings I need say no more about this possibility.

In dealing with the requirement of intent (*dolus*), the court also accepted that it encompassed not only the intention to achieve a particular result, but also the consciousness that such a result would be unlawful.

The claim in the *Dantex* case was for delictual damages, based on the defendant's allegedly unlawful occupation of premises. The plaintiff alleged that it was entitled to occupy the premises from a certain date, in terms of a valid lease with a third party, and that since then the defendant had been in wrongful occupation of the premises, and despite demand had refused to vacate the premises, and that, arising out of the wrongful occupation, the plaintiff had suffered damages and would continue to suffer damages until the defendant vacated the premises. The plaintiff did not contend that it had a sufficient interest in the property to entitle it to institute

---

804. *See* generally Dale Hutchison, 'Relational Economic Loss (or Interference with Contractual Relations): The Last Hurdle', in *Developing Delict: Essays in Honour of Robert Feenstra* 133 ff (Juta 2000), first published as *Acta Juridica 2000*, Juta, Cape Town.

805. 1968 (1) SA 209 (C) 215G-H.

806. 1989 (1) SA 390 (A).

an Aquilian action for damage to its limited interest in the property. Instead, the plaintiff relied on the alleged deliberate interference by defendants with its contractual rights under the lease.

The defendant raised an exception on the basis that the pleadings of the plaintiff did not disclose a cause of action, arguing that the plaintiff had not alleged the requisite intent on the part of defendant. The plaintiff argued that it had sufficiently alleged all the elements of intent (*dolus*) as this concept was understood in the law of delict, namely that that the defendants had no right to occupy the premises, and that the defendants knew that the premises had been leased to the plaintiff. The court held that the allegations made by the plaintiff did not embrace all that was meant by intent (*dolus*). A plaintiff who based his claim for patrimonial loss on an intentional wrongful act on the part of the defendant had to allege and prove, *inter alia*, that the defendant intended to cause the plaintiff loss, whereas in this case all the plaintiff had alleged was that the defendants had acted with knowledge of the plaintiff's rights, and that the plaintiff in fact suffered loss. The pleadings were therefore not inconsistent with a belief on the part of the defendants that the plaintiff would not suffer damage by being kept out of the leased premises, and a state of facts in which such a belief could arise could easily be imagined.

The court held further that it was now accepted that intent (*dolus*) encompassed not only the intention to achieve a particular result, but also the consciousness that such a result would be wrongful or unlawful. Although there might be policy considerations in cases falling under the extended *lex Aquilia* why a plaintiff who relied on fault in the form of intent (*dolus*) should not be required to prove consciousness of unlawfulness, such considerations did not apply in this case. The plaintiffs should, therefore, have alleged consciousness of unlawfulness on the part of the defendants, but failed to do so. The pleadings were consistent with the existence of an honest dispute about the defendant's right to occupy the premises, and therefore failed to disclose a cause of action.

376. In *Lanco Engineering CC v. Aris Box Manufacturers (Pty) Ltd*,[807] the court confirmed that a party to a contract who seeks to recover delictual damages from a third party for interference with his contractual relationship has to prove an unlawful and culpable interference. Unlawfulness is determined according to the general criterion of reasonableness or the *boni mores* as perceived by the public. As far as culpability is concerned, it is clear that the action can be founded on intent (*dolus*), but whether culpa will also suffice has not yet been settled. As to the interference itself, it is neither necessary that the interference should result in a breach of contract by the party with whom the plaintiff had contracted, nor that the interference should consist of an inducement by the defendant upon such party to commit the breach. Nonetheless, inducement and breach are significant factors which should be weighed by the court in determining whether, according to public policy or the *boni mores* or the criterion of reasonableness, the particular interference in a contractual relationship should be regarded as unlawful.

The plaintiff in the *Lanco Engineering* case claimed damages for being prevented by the defendant from carrying on business at certain premises. The plaintiff

807. 1993 (4) SA 378 (D).

had concluded a lease of the premises with the owner, in terms of which it would take occupation on a certain date, but the defendant failed to vacate the premises on that date, although its own lease had expired. The plaintiff was able to take occupation of the premises only some two months later, as a result of which it suffered losses. The evidence indicated that the defendant was aware that the plaintiff was negotiating a lease for the premises with the owner. The defendant had asserted the conclusion of an oral lease agreement with the owner for the period in dispute and had sent a 'rental' cheque to the owner, purportedly in terms of this oral agreement. The court found the assertion of an oral lease to be untruthful, and that the attempt to send a 'rental' cheque for the period in dispute had been a dishonest and mischievous attempt to support the untruthful assertion. The court found that the defendant had been well aware that, should it fail to vacate the premises, the plaintiff would suffer losses. The court decided:

(a) that the defendant's failure to vacate the premises (holding over) had interfered with the plaintiff's contractual relationship;
(b) that the defendant had the necessary intent (*dolus*); and
(c) that, judged in terms of the general criterion of reasonableness and the *boni mores* as perceived by the public, the defendant's conduct, even though it did not constitute inducement of a breach of contract, had unlawfully caused the plaintiff losses.

In *Country Cloud Trading CC v. MEC, Department of Infrastructure Development*[808] the MEC, for the Department, had contracted with a third party, iLima, for the latter to build a hospital. To comply with its obligations under the contract iLima had borrowed ZAR 12 million from the appellant, Country Cloud. This loan agreement was subject to the condition that Tau Pride, the MEC's managing agent for the building contract, would repay Country Cloud the ZAR 12 million out of the amount payable by the MEC to iLima. Further, one Lupepe, the chief executive officer of iLima, was listed as a party to the loan agreement and stood as surety and co-principal debtor for the loan. The MEC subsequently cancelled its contract with iLima on the basis that iLima had made certain misrepresentations. This resulted in the eventual liquidation of iLima, because it was relying on the money from the construction contract. Due to iLima's precarious financial position, it failed to repay Country Cloud the money it had borrowed. Country Cloud then instituted a delictual claim against the MEC for the pure economic loss it had suffered, on the basis that the MEC had unjustifiably cancelled the contract with iLima in circumstances where it had foreseen that Country Cloud would suffer harm as a result. The Supreme Court of Appeal dismissed the plaintiff's claim. It held that the case did not fall under the established categories of intentional interference with contractual relations. It also held that there were insufficient policy-based considerations justifying a finding of wrongfulness for the purposes of expanding delictual liability in this context. On appeal, the Constitutional Court followed the line of reasoning adopted by the Supreme Court of Appeal, holding that Country Cloud's claim was

808. 2015 (1) SA 1 (CC).

not on par with the cases previously considered to amount to intentional interference with contractual relationships. It further refused to extend delictual liability to what was recognized as a novel situation, because the MEC's causing of pure economic loss to Country Cloud was not considered wrongful. The main policy-based reasons for the court's stance was that, although the MEC had foreseen Country Cloud's loss and could be regarded as having caused it intentionally, and although imposing liability for a foreseen and intended loss would not open the floodgates to limitless liability, Country Cloud was not vulnerable to the risk of harm. Country Cloud could have claimed repayment from iLima in terms of the loan agreement, could have taken cession of iLima's claim against the MEC, or could have called up Mr Lupepe's suretyship obligation.

In *Masstores (Pty) Ltd v. Pick 'n Pay Retailers (Pty) Ltd*[809] Masstores had concluded a lease agreement with the owner of a mall, Hyprop, in terms of which it was agreed that Masstores was not allowed to trade as a general food supermarket. The mall owner also entered into a separate lease agreement with Pick 'n Pay, which secured for Pick 'n Pay a right of exclusivity by providing that the lessor would not permit any other supermarket to be operated in the mall. When Masstores decided to launch its Foodco concept at its store, Pick 'n Pay argued that it was operating a general food supermarket and launched an interdict application against Masstores to restrain it from interfering with the lease agreement between Pick 'n Pay and the owner of the mall. The Supreme Court of Appeal found in favour of Pick 'n Pay, but the Constitutional Court disagreed, holding that there was no wrongfulness. It emphasized the need for free competition as a policy consideration and held that, generally, there is no legal duty on third parties not to infringe contractually based exclusive rights to trade. The court also followed its reasoning in Country Cloud and noted Pick 'n Pay's alternative contractual remedies that were available against the mall owner. It held that the law should hesitate before superimposing delictual liability on the contractual relationship between parties. The fact that Pick 'n Pay could have taken alternative steps to protect itself from avoiding loss was a further important consideration against a finding of wrongfulness.

377. The position as set out in the cases referred to above can be summarized as follows: There can be delictual liability for the unlawful and culpable interference with the contractual relations of others, where such interference causes loss to one or both the parties to the contract. Interference can take the form of inducing a breach of contract, but such inducement, or the occurrence of a breach of contract, is not a requirement for this form of liability. The unlawfulness of the causing of loss by interference is determined according to the general criterion of reasonableness or the *boni mores* as perceived by the public. As far as culpability is concerned, it is clear that the action can be founded on intent (*dolus*), which encompasses not only deliberate interference and causing of harm, but also the consciousness that causing harm in this manner is unlawful. Whether negligence (culpa) will also suffice to found liability has not yet been decided.

809. 2017 (1) SA 613 (CC).

§6. UNLAWFUL COMPETITION

I. Aquilian Liability for Unlawful Competition

378. It is generally recognized that remedies for patrimonial loss as a result of unlawful competition or unlawful trading are based on the *actio legis Aquiliae*. The accepted position is that there is a modern general Aquilian action for unlawful competition or unlawful trading in South African law.[810]

379. The Appellate Division recognized as early as 1922 that the *actio legis Aquiliae* may be invoked where patrimonial loss is caused through unlawful competition. In *Matthews v. Young*[811] the court stated:

> In the absence of special legal restriction a person is without doubt entitled to the free exercise of his trade, procession or calling … But he cannot claim an absolute right to do so without interference from another. Competition brings about interference in one way or another about which rivals cannot legitimately complain. But the competition … must itself remain within lawful bounds. All a person can, therefore, claim is the right to exercise his calling without unlawful interference from others. Such an interference would constitute an injuria for which an action under the lex Aquilia lies if it has directly resulted in loss.

380. The decision of Steyn CJ in *Geary and Son (Pty) Ltd v. Gove*[812] was a further step on the way towards the general recognition of the *actio legis Aquiliae* as the basis for protection against unlawful competition in South African law.[813] In *Atlas Organic Fertilizers (Pty) Ltd v. Pikkewyn Gwhano (Pty) Ltd*,[814] Van Dijkhorst J stated 'that the law of South Africa recognizes and grants a general action in the case of unlawful competition, based on the principles of the lex Aquilia'.[815] The

---

810. *See* generally Max Loubser, 'Principles and Policy in Unlawful Competition: An Aquilian Mask?' in *Developing Delict: Essays in Honour of Robert Feenstra* 168 ff. (Juta 2000); first published as *Acta Juridica 2000*, Juta, Cape Town, on which this section is substantially based.

811. 1922 AD 492 507.

812. 1964 (1) SA 434 (A).

813. Steyn CJ stated as follows (440–441):

> The plaintiff's action is Aquilian. It sues in delict. What it apparently seeks to allege is the wrongful interference by a competitor with its rights as a trader. Although there is no clear statement to that effect in the declaration as amplified, the right upon which the plaintiff may be presumed to rely is its right to attract custom … I do not propose to attempt a definition of the limits set to competition in trade by Aquilian liability, but whatever those limits are, it seems clear that interference of the nature indicated is recognized as an infringement of a trader's right sand therefore as a delict in our law.

814. 1981 (2) SA 173 (T) 186.

815. *See also Schultz v. Butt* 1986 (3) SA 667 (A) 678; *Dun and Bradstreet (Pty) Ltd v. SA Merchants Combined Credit Bureau (Cape) (Pty) Ltd* 1968 (1) SA 209 (C) 218; *Sea Harvest Corporation (Pty) Ltd v. Irvin & Johnson Ltd* 1985 (2) SA 355 (C) 359–360; *Union Wine Ltd v. E Snell and Co. Ltd* 1990 (2) SA 189 (C) 200–202; *Times Media Ltd v. SABC* 1990 (4) SA 604 (W) 606; *Aetiology*

courts have applied the general principles of Aquilian liability to many of the forms of unlawful competition that are recognized in South African law, such as passing off,[816] misrepresentation as to a rival's own performance,[817] acquisition and use of a competitor's trade secrets,[818] copying and adoption of a rival's performance,[819] competition in conflict with statutory provisions[820] and boycott.[821]

381. An important implication of the recognition of Aquilian liability in the context of unlawful competition is that new forms of protection against unlawful competition may be developed by the courts within the ambit of the principles of the *actio legis Aquiliae*, even in the absence of a direct precedent in case law. It is not necessary for an aggrieved competitor to bring his action within the framework of one of the recognized forms of unlawful competition or another particular form of delict.[822] This approach was confirmed by the Appellate Division in *Schultz v. Butt*:[823]

Today CC t/a Somerset Schools v. Van Aswegen 1992 (1) SA 807 (W) 816–820; *William Grant and Sons Ltd v. Cape Wine and Distillers Ltd* 1990 (3) SA 897 (C) 915.

816. *Atlas Fertilizers (Pty) Ltd v. Pikkewyn Ghwano (Pty) Ltd* 1981 (2) SA 173 (T) 201–202; *Lorimar productions Inc v. Sterling Clothing Manufacturers (Pty) Ltd, Lorimar Productions Inc v. OK Hyperama Ltd, Lorimar Productions Inc v. Dallas Restaurant* 1981 (3) SA 1129 (T) 1138 1152 ff.; *Salusa (Pty) Ltd v. Eagle International Traders* 1979 (4) SA 697 (C) 704; *Link Estates (Pty) Ltd v. Rink Estates (Pty) Ltd* 1979 (2) SA 276 (E) 281; *Moroka Swallows Football Club Ltd v. The Birds Football Club* 1987 (2) SA 511 (W) 519 520; *Pepsico Inc v. United Tobacco Co. Ltd* 1988 (2) SA 334 (W) 348; *Tie Rack plc v. Tie Rack Stores (Pty) Ltd* 1989 (4) SA 427 (T) 445.

817. *See Geary and Son (Pty) Ltd v. Gove* 1964 (1) SA 434 (A) 440–441; *Victor Products (SA (Pty) Ltd v. Lateulere Manufacturing (Pty) Ltd* 1975 (1) SA 961 (W); *Stellenbosch Wine Trust Ltd v. Oude Meester Group Ltd* 1977 (2) SA 221 (C); *Elida Gibbs (Pty) Ltd v. Colgate-Palmolive (Pty) Ltd (1)* 1988 (2) SA 350 (W) 357; *William Grant & Sons Ltd v. Cape Wine & Distillers Ltd* 1990 (3) SA 897 (C) 915; *Long John International Ltd v. Stellenbosch Wine Trust (Pty) Ltd* 1990 (4) SA 136 (D) 141.

818. *See Dun and Bradstreet (Pty) Ltd v. SA Merchants Combined Credit Bureau (Cape) (Pty) Ltd* 1968 (1) SA 209 (C); *Stellenbosch Wine Trust Ltd v. Oude Meester Group Ltd, Oude Meester Group Ltd v. Stellenbosch Wine Trust* 1972 (3) SA 152 (C); *Prok Africa (Pty) Ltd v. NTH (Pty) Ltd* 1980 (3) SA 687 (W) 696–697; *Atlas Organic Fertilizers (Pty) Ltd v. Pikkewyn Ghwano (Pty) Ltd* 1981 (2) SA 173 (T) 189–196; *Sibex Construction (SA) (Pty) Ltd v. Injectseal CC* 1988 (2) SA 54 (T) 63; *Meter Systems Holdings Ltd v. Venter* 1993 (1) SA 409 (W) 427.

819. *See Schultz v. Butt* 1986 (3) SA 667 (A) 678; *Bress Designs (Pty) Ltd v. GY Lounge Suite Manufacturers (Pty) Ltd* 1991 (2) SA 455 (W) 471–475; *The Concept Factory v. Heyl* 1994 (2) SA 105 (T) 115–117; *Payen Components SA Ltd v. Bovic Gaskets CC* 1994 (2) SA 464 (W) 473 ff.

820. *See Silver Crystal Trading (Pty) Ltd v. Namibia Diamond Corporation (Pty) Ltd* 1983 (4) SA 884 (D) 887.

821. *See Hawker v. Life Offices Association of South Africa* 1987 (3) SA 777 (C) 780–781.

822. *See Dun and Brandstreet (Pty) Ltd v. SA Merchants Combined Credit Bureau (Cape) (Pty) Ltd* 1968 (2) SA 209 (C) 218; *Stellenbosch Wine Trust Ltd v. Oude Meester Group (Pty) Ltd, Oude Meester Group Ltd v. Stellenbosch Wine Trust Ltd* 1972 (3) SA 152 (C) 161; *Victor Products (SA) (Pty) Ltd v. Lateurele Manufacturing (Pty) Ltd* 1975 (1) SA 961 (W) 965; *Sea Harvest Corporation (Pty) Ltd v. Irvin & Johnson Ltd* 1985 (2) SA 355 (C) 359–360.

823. 1986 (3) AS 667 (A) 678. *See also Payen Components SA Ltd v. Bovic Gaskets CC* 1994 (2) SA 464 (W) 473–474; *The Concept Factory v. Heyl* 1994 (2) SA 105 (T) 115; *Van Castricum v. Theunissen* 1993 (2) SA 726 (T) 732; *Aetiology Today CC t/a Somerset Schools v. Van Aswegen* 1992 (1) SA 807 (W) 817–818; *Bress Designs (Pty) Ltd v. GY Lounge Suite Manufacturers (Pty) Ltd* 1991 (2) SA 455 (W) 473; *Pepsico Inc v. United Tobacco Co. Ltd* 1998 (2) SA 334 (W) 348; *Tie*

In order to succeed in an action based on unfair competition, the plaintiff must establish all the requisites of Aquilian liability, including proof that the defendant has committed a wrongful act. In such a case, the wrongfulness which is a requisite of Aquilian liability may fall into a category of clearly recognized illegality as the illustrations given by Corbett J in *Dun and Bradstreet (Pty) Ltd v. SA Merchants Combined Credit Bureau (Cape) (Pty) Ltd* 1968 (1) SA 209 (C) at 216F-H, namely trading in contravention of an express statutory prohibition; the making of fraudulent misrepresentations by the rival trader as to his own business; the passing off by a rival trader of his goods or business as being that of his competitor; the publication by the rival trader of injurious falsehoods concerning his competitor's business; and the employment of physical assaults and intimidation designed to prevent a competitor from pursuing his trade. But it is not limited to unlawfulness of that kind.

382. In terms of this approach the influence of English law, in particular with regard to the development of passing off[824] and the protection of trade secrets and confidential information,[825] should therefore be reconciled with Aquilian principles.[826]

Rack plc v. Tie Rack Stores (Pty) Ltd 1989 (4) SA 427 (T) 445; *Moroka Swallows Football Club Ltd v. The Birds Football Club* 1987 (2) SA 511 (W) 520–521.

824. In *Boswell-Wilkie Circus (Pty) Ltd v. Brian Boswell Circus (Pty) Ltd* 1984 (1) SA 734 (N) 742 the court said in regard to a particular question concerning passing off:

> South African case law on the question is thin … Plenty can be found, on the other hand, in England. The persuasive authority of English decisions on passing off has long been accepted in this country.

825. In *Meter Systems Holdings Ltd v. Venter* 1993 (1) SA 409 (W) 427–428 Stegmann J stated:

> It is of course important to recognize the difference in the historical sources from which English law and South African law derive their modern remedies, and to avoid anything like a blind acceptance that an English decision in this field necessarily holds good for our own law. At the same time, it is also important not to overlook the fact that in both systems of law the rules governing what we call the delict of unlawful competition, and in particular the protection of confidential information, are in a process of development. English law is developing according to the principles of its rules of equity and modern Roman-Dutch law on … 'the broad and ample basis of the *lex Aquilia*' … No doubt there is room for development in different directions. Nevertheless, no inherent conflict of principle or legal policy has yet emerged in this field on the lines of their rules of equity, it can be of considerable assistance, in analysing and solving a similar problem on Aquilian principles, to have regard to their work. There can be no question of an uncritical or slavish adoption of English precedents in that a solution similar to that found by an English court is the appropriate solution according to the principles of our own law in this field … I consider that the passages from the English case law which I am about to refer to do not conflict with the principles of our own law and indeed provide a useful guide to appropriate solutions based on the principles of our own law.

826. *See* in this regard Stegmann J's approach in *Weber-Stephen Products Co. v. Alrite Engineering (Pty) Ltd* 1990 (2) SA 718 (T) 734–735:

383. The courts have therefore repeatedly and clearly endorsed the general application of Aquilian principles to cases of unreasonable competitive or trading conduct, but the tendency has been, nevertheless, to fit the cases into one of the established categories of unlawful competition. In *Payen Components SA Ltd v. Bovic CC and Others*,[827] Schutz JA said the following in this regard:

> Unlawful competition should not be added as a ragbag and often forlorn final alternative to every trade mark, copyright, design or passing off action. In most cases it is one of the established categories or nothing.

384. Within the established categories of unlawful competition, the general principles of Aquilian liability have been developed into certain sub-rules. This is illustrated by the decision of the Supreme Court of Appeal in *Caterham Car Sales & Coachworks Ltd v. Birkin Cars (Pty) Ltd*,[828] where the sub-rules concerning passing off were set out in detail. The essence of passing off is the misrepresentation that a particular business or product is the same as or connected to a business or product with an established reputation, belonging to the complainant. This misrepresentation concerning the trade source or connection of a product or service has the potential of causing a diversion of custom from the complainant's established product or service to the offender's rival product or service. In the *Caterham Car Sales* case the question was, essentially, whether a British manufacturer of replica Lotus cars was unlawfully made to suffer economic loss or potential economic loss by a South African manufacturer's misrepresentation that its similar replica Lotus cars were the same or connected with the British replicas. The court held that the essence of passing off is to protect a business against a misrepresentation of a particular kind, namely deception as to a trade source or business connection.[829] The component of the goodwill of a business that is harmed by means of a passing off is its reputation, and for this reason the first requirement for a successful passing off action is proof of the relevant reputation.

385. The detailed set of sub-rules as set out in the *Caterham Car Sales* case indicates that there may be some tension between the approach, on the one hand, that

---

> In passing off matters, our Courts have frequently looked to the analysis of the problem in English cases. Our law on the subject derives, of course, from the *actio legis Aquiliae* which is unknown in English law. Nevertheless, the analysis of the problem to be found in English cases is often illuminating and can be of assistance to solving the problem of how to apply the principles of our own law to the facts of a particular case.

See also Meter Systems Holdings Ltd v. Venter 1993 (1) SA 409 (W) 427–428; *Hoechst Pharmaceuticals (Pty) Ltd v. The Beauty Box (Pty) Ltd* 1987 (2) SA 600 (A) 613.

827. 1995 (4) SA 441 (A) 453G.

828. 1998 (3) SA 938 (SCA).

829. *Caterham Car Sales & Coachworks Ltd v. Birkin Cars (Pty) Ltd* 1998 (3) SA 938 (SCA) 947E-F.

the law of unlawful competition in South Africa is governed by the general principles of Aquilian liability (what may be called the generalized approach),[830] and the approach, on the other hand, that the general principles have hardened into sub-rules governing different categories of unlawful competition (what may be called the categorized approach).

386. In terms of the generalized approach unlawful competition concerns conduct in the course of trade that unlawfully causes economic loss or the potential of such loss – mostly by misrepresentation or misappropriation of a rival's product. An example of this approach is the statement of Didcott J, in *Union Wine v. E Snell & Co. Ltd*,[831] who said of the elements of passing off (reputation and the secondary meaning of an established product name):

> The need for some reputation or secondary meaning to be shown, term it what you will, is not a principle or rule of law. Proof of such is simply part and parcel of the factual cloth which must necessarily be weaved in order that a passing off may be demonstrated in a case of the present kind.

This approach displays scepticism about the idea of passing off as an independent delict with its own set of rules, but it was summarily rejected as 'incorrect' by the Supreme Court of Appeal in the *Caterham Car Sales* case, in a judgment which clearly represents an example of the categorized approach.[832]

387. The categorized approach to the law of unlawful competition and unlawful trading have induced the courts to shy away from recognizing forms of unlawful competition outside the established categories. It is an approach that tends to restrict the flexibility of the Aquilian action and tends to facilitate the introduction into South African law of many of the subtle categorizations that characterize the passing off action in English law. It encourages the construction of arguments on, for example, the precise nature of the reputation damaged by passing off; and on whether the misrepresentation constitutes a deception as to a trade source or to a business connection.[833]

---

830. *See Atlas Fertilizers (Pty) Ltd v. Pikkewyn Ghwano (Pty) Ltd* 1981 (2) SA 173 (T) 201–202; *Lorimar productions Inc v. Sterling Clothing Manufacturers (Pty) Ltd, Lorimar Productions Inc v. OK Hyperama Ltd, Lorimar Productions Inc v. Dallas Restaurant* 1981 (3) SA 1129 (T) 1138 1152 ff; *Salusa (Pty) Ltd v. Eagle International Traders* 1979 (4) SA 697 (C) 704; *Link Estates (Pty) Ltd v. Rink Estates (Pty) Ltd* 1979 (2) SA 276 (E) 281; *Moroka Swallows Football Club Ltd v. The Birds Football Club* 1987 (2) SA 511 (W) 519 520; *Pepsico Inc v. United Tobacco Co. Ltd* 1988 (2) SA 334 (W) 348; *Tie Rack plc v. Tie Rack Stores (Pty) Ltd* 1989 (4) SA 427 (T) 445.
831. 1990 (2) SA 180 (D) 183I-J.
832. *Caterham Car Sales & Coachworks Ltd v. Birkin Cars (Pty) Ltd* 1998 (3) SA 938 (SCA) 948B.
833. *Caterham Car Sales & Coachworks Ltd v. Birkin Cars (Pty) Ltd* 1998 (3) SA 938 (SCA) 947F-I.

II. Forms of Unlawful Competition

388. The most common forms of unlawful competition or unlawful trading are passing off (representing to others that one's business or product is the same as, or connected to, that of another);[834] misappropriation of confidential information or trade secrets (the use or disclosure of information that has commercial value and is imparted or received in confidence, often in a fiduciary or employment relationship);[835] other forms of misappropriation, concerning, for example, a name or label,[836] advertising image,[837] fictional character,[838] or the personal image of a celebrity;[839] harmful trading conduct outside the sphere of competition, for example in cases of misappropriation of another's advertising image or name;[840] or disparagement of the good name of a business or entrepreneur;[841] and boycotts (instigating others to exclude someone from a certain commercial activity).[842] There is no closed list, however.

389. The following cases illustrate the variety of forms of unlawful competition and the difficulties of categorization.

390. In *Stellenbosch Wine Trust Ltd and Another v. Oude Meester Group Ltd*,[843] Diemont J accepted that the misappropriation of a secret or confidential label design that had been developed by skill and industry of a competitor, and the use of the label to the detriment of the competitor constituted unlawful interference with the trade of another. In this regard, he said the following:[844]

---

834. *Caterham Car Sales & Coachworks Ltd v. Birkin Cars (Pty) Ltd* 1998 (3) SA 938 (SCA) 947I-J; *Blue Lion Manufacturing (Pty) Ltd v. National Brands Ltd* 2001 (3) SA 884 (SCA); *New Media Publishing (Pty) Ltd v. Eating Out Web Services CC* 2005 (5) SA 388 (C); *Media 24 Bpk v. Ramsay, Son & Parker (Edms) Bpk* 2006 (5) SA 204 (C); *Premier Trading Co. (Pty) Ltd and Another v. Sporttopia (Pty) Ltd* 2000 (3) SA 259 (SCA); *Klimax Manufacturing Ltd and Another v. Van Rensburg and Another* 2005 (4) SA 445 (O).

835. *Coolair Ventilator Co. (SA) (Pty) Ltd Liebenberg* 1967 (1) SA 686 (W); *Atlas Organic Fertilizers (Pty) Ltd v. Pikkewyn Ghwano (Pty) Ltd* 1981 (2) SA 173 (T); *Knox D'Arcy Ltd and Others v. Jamieson and Others* 1992 (3) SA 520 (W); *Meter Systems Holdings Ltd v. Venter* 1993 (1) SA 409 (W); *Gordon Lloyd Page & Associates v. Rivera and Another* 2001 (1) SA 88 (SCA); *Waste Products Utilization (Pty) Ltd v. Wilkes and Another* 2003 (2) SA 515 (W).

836. *Stellenbosch Wine Trust Ltd and Another v. Oude Meester Group Ltd* 1972 (3) SA 152 (C).

837. F.W. Mostert, *The Right to the Advertising Image*, S. African L. J. 413 (1982).

838. *Lorimar Productions Inc v. OK Hyperama Ltd, Lorimar Productions Inc v. Dallas Restaurant* 1981 (3) SA 1129 (T).

839. *See* H.J.O. van Heerden & J. Neethling, *Unlawful Competition* (1995) 201 n. 4 and 202 n. 5; J. Neethling, *Persoonlike Immaterieelgoedereregte: 'n Nuwe Kategorie Subjektiewe Regte?*, THRHR 316 (1987).

840. *See Capital Estate and General Agencies (Pty) Ltd v. Holiday Inns Inc* 1977 (2) SA 916 (A).

841. *See Caxton Ltd v. Reeva Forman (Pty) Ltd* 1990 (3) SA 547 (A) 560–561; *Woodlands Dairy (Pty) Ltd v. Parmalat SA (Pty) Ltd* 2002 (2) SA 268 (E).

842. *Murdoch v. Bullough* 1923 TPD 495; *Times Media Ltd v. South African Broadcasting Corporation* 1990 (4) SA 604 (W); *Deneys Reitz v. South African Commercial, Catering and Allied Workers Union* 1999 20 ILJ 1008 (W).

843. 1972 (3) SA 152 (C).

844. *Stellenbosch Wine Trust Ltd and Another v. Oude Meester Group Ltd* 1972 (3) SA 152 (C) 162B.

> His conduct amounts to deliberate misappropriation of a business asset which was acquired by another's skill and industry. It is difficult to appreciate how this conduct differs in principle from the conduct of a man who steals goods from the shelves of a rival's shop.

The court here recognized the appropriation of the label design as unlawful misappropriation or unlawful interference with the trade of another, 'within the principles of the *Lex Aquilia*'. In other cases too, the courts have held competitive or trading conduct to be unlawful if it essentially amounts to 'stealing from the shelves of another', that is, misappropriation in the form of copying or otherwise exploiting the product of another's creative abilities.

391. In *Dun and Bradstreet (Pty) Ltd v. SA Merchants Combined Credit Bureau (Cape) (Pty) Ltd*,[845] Corbett J held a company liable in damages for knowingly furthering its business with credit information compiled by its competitor by the exercise of skill and labour, information which was distributed by the competitor on a confidential basis to clients. Corbett J quoted with approval from the judgment of the United States Supreme Court in *International News Service v. Associated Press*[846] where the copying and commercial use of news material was held to constitute unfair competition and where it was held that:

> [D]efendant's conduct differs from the ordinary case of unfair competition in trade principally in this that, instead of selling its own goods as those of complainant, it substitutes misappropriation in the place of misrepresentation, and sells complainant's goods as its own.

The offending conduct in the *Dun and Bradstreet* case was misappropriation of the credit information, by unlawfully 'obtaining' and 'using' it.

392. In *Capital Estate and General Agencies (Pty) Ltd v. Holiday Inns Inc.*,[847] a well-known hotel group sought to restrain a property developer from using its trade name for a shopping centre and a complex of duplex flats. The parties were engaged in dissimilar trading activities, but the court held that the use of the *Holiday Inn* name constituted passing off, because there was the likelihood that members of the public would be deceived or confused by the misrepresentation that the undertakings of the parties were associated. Because there was no common field of activity and therefore no potential diversion of custom between the parties, this was not passing off in its established form. The offending conduct in essence involved the misappropriation of the *Holiday Inn* trade name, entailing damage or potential damage in the form of dilution of the commercial value and impact of its trade name and potential harm to its reputation.

---

845. 1968 (1) SA 209 (C).
846. 248 US 215 (1918).
847. 1977 (2) SA 916 (A).

393. In *Atlas Organic Fertilizers (Pty) Ltd v. Pikkewyn Ghwano (Pty) Ltd*,[848] Van Dijkhorst J, with reference to a number of earlier cases, accepted that it is a wrongful act knowingly to appropriate confidential information of a rival who has by the exercise of his skill and labour compiled it; and also that the law will not permit a person who has obtained knowledge of a production method evolved by the intellectual effort of another to bypass intellectual effort of his own and to use the method as a springboard to obtain an unfair advantage for himself.

394. In *Schultz v. Butt*,[849] the applicant Butt, the designer of a twin-hulled fibre-glass boat named 'Butt-Cat', sought to interdict a competitor Schultz from manufacturing and marketing a boat with an identical hull design. Years of experience, expertise and effort and substantial costs had gone into the 'Butt-Cat' hull design, and the venture was a financial success. Schultz got hold of a 'Butt-Cat' hull and used it to construct a mould and then used the mould to manufacture replica hulls for a boat named 'Supercat', that was sold in competition with the 'Butt-Cat'. Schultz went further and registered the hull as a model with the Registrar of Designs. Butt applied for an interdict against Schultz and an order for cancellation of the registration of the design, on the basis, *inter alia*, of unlawful competition. The issue was essentially whether the infringement by Schultz of Butt's unregistered rights in respect of the design was unlawful.

The court held that competitive conduct may fall within 'a category of clearly recognized illegality',[850] as in the case of trading in contravention of an express statutory prohibition, fraudulent misrepresentation concerning one's own product, passing off one's product as that of a competitor and injurious falsehoods concerning a competitor's product. However, unlawfulness in competition is not limited to these categories and can also be determined by criteria such as fairness and honesty in competition.[851] In this case, the question was whether it can be unlawful to copy a design that is in the public domain and not protected by copyright, patent or design legislation. In the application of the criteria of fairness and honesty, the court considered on the one hand that the design was in the public domain and that imitation is the lifeblood of competition, but on the other hand that it may be intolerable to allow one manufacturer to appropriate the product of another's invention and development without licence or compensation. In this case, Schultz used one of Butt's hulls, with a shape that was developed over a long period, with considerable expenditure of time, labour and money. Schultz used the hull to make a mould with which to make boats in competition with Butt. Furthermore, he 'added impudence to dishonesty' by obtaining a design registration in his own name for the hull designed by Butt.[852] In the view of the court, this conduct constituted unlawful competition.

The offending conduct in the *Schultz* case was essentially the misappropriation of the hull design, by 'obtaining', 'copying' and 'using' it unlawfully.

---

848. 1981 (2) SA 173 (T) 188.
849. 1986 (3) SA 667 (A).
850. *Schultz v. Butt* 1986 (3) SA 667 (A) 678.
851. *Schultz v. Butt* 1986 (3) SA 667 (A) 678.
852. *Schultz v. Butt* 1986 (3) SA 667 (A) 683.

395. In *Lorimar Productions Inc and Others v. Sterling Clothing Manufacturers (Pty) Ltd*,[853] the court refused the application of the producers of the *Dallas* television series to restrain the respondents from using characters, names and logos from the series to market a restaurant, items of clothing and other products. It was held that the appropriation by the respondents of such characters, names and logos from the series did not constitute passing off, because the parties were not in competition in respect of the restaurant business or clothing sales, and the applicant therefore suffered no loss as a result of a diversion of custom. The alternative basis for the applicant's case was unlawful competition, in that the respondents had foreclosed on the applicant's opportunities to merchandize the characters, names and logos themselves. The court held that the important factors in assessing unlawfulness were that the parties were not in competition with one another[854] and that the applicant could have obtained protection in terms of trademark legislation, but failed to do so.[855] The conduct of the respondents was not considered to be unlawful.

This case essentially involved the unauthorized appropriation by the respondents of the merchandising value of characters created by the applicant. If the applicant had proved that it had incurred damage as a result of such appropriation, in the form of foreclosed merchandising opportunities or harm to reputation, through the public's association of products of inferior quality with the applicant, the requirements of Aquilian liability were present. The commercial phenomenon of 'character merchandising'– held not to have been proved in this case, but later accepted in *Federation Internationale de Football and Others v. Bartlett and Others*[856] – should not be regarded as a sub-rule of a particular kind of passing off; it is simply an evidence of a particular kind of economic loss where a trader has appropriated for his own commercial use the fictional characters created by another.

396. In the *Union Wine Ltd v. Edward Snell & Co. Ltd* cases,[857] it was accepted in respect of the wine *Bellingham Johannisberger* that the *Johannisberger* component of the name had become distinctive of the wine over a period of more than thirty years, and that this component of the name had attracted goodwill.[858] It was further accepted that the producers of this wine would suffer loss of custom as a result of the marketing by a competitor of a wine called *Edward Snell Johannisberger*.[859] Yet, because passing off could not be proved (the bottles and labels were substantially different), protection against the appropriation of the *Johannisberger* component of the name was not afforded. The courts took into account that this component of the name could have been registered as a trademark, as the *Bellingham* name was, but it appears that they were unduly hesitant to recognize a form of

853. 1981 (3) SA 1129 (T).
854. At 1154H.
855. At 1156H.
856. 1994 (4) SA 722 (T).
857. 1990 (2) SA 180 (D); 1990 (2) SA 189 (C).
858. *Union Wine Ltd v. Edward Snell & Co. Ltd* 1990 (2) SA 189 (C) 198C.
859. *Union Wine Ltd v. Edward Snell & Co. Ltd* 1990 (2) SA 189 (C) 198E.

unlawful competition outside the category of passing off, in the absence of dishonest conduct.[860] However, deliberate copying casts doubt on the bona fides of a competitor,[861] and it is suggested that, on the facts as proved and in terms of the general principles of Aquilian liability, a good case was made for recognition that the producers of *Edward Snell Johannisberger* unlawfully misappropriated the *Johannisberger* name.

This argument can also be made in respect of a similar situation in *Reckitt & Colman SA (Pty) Ltd v. S C Johnson & Son (SA) (Pty) Ltd*,[862] where the name component *Neutra*, used in the product name *Haze Neutra Air*, was appropriated by a competitor as part of the name *Glade Neutra Air.*

397. The cases referred to above illustrate the recognition of Aquilian liability for unlawful misappropriation in the course of trade,[863] where the misappropriation involves an asset of appreciable commercial value, such as a name or label,[864] advertising image,[865] fictional character,[866] or the personal image of a celebrity.[867] It therefore seems unduly complicated to argue for the protection of a new kind of subjective right to interests such as 'character merchandising'[868] or 'advertising image'[869] or a 'right to publicity'.[870] Reference to a subjective right or 'property' in respect of these interests in effect means that the person making such a claim has

860. *See* the statement at 1981:

> 'In the absence of passing off there is no proof of any false representation or that respondent's wine misrepresents itself'; and the circle argument at 1991-J: 'I have not been referred to any South African decision in which a plaintiff was afforded protection against the use of his unregistered trade mark in the absence of dishonest or *wrongful* (italics added) conduct on the part of the defendant.'

861. *See Stellenbosch Wine Trust Ltd and Another v. Oude Meester Group Ltd* 1972 (3) SA 152 (C) 164F.
862. 1995 (1) SA 725 (T).
863. *See* in respect of the development of 'misappropriation' torts in American law, Wendy J. Gordon, *On Owning Information: Intellectual Property and the Restitutionary Impulse*, 78 Virginia L. Rev. 149, 152 (1992).
864. *Stellenbosch Wine Trust Ltd and Another v. Oude Meester Group Ltd* 1972 (3) SA 152 (C).
865. F.W. Mostert, *The Right to the Advertising Image*, S. African L. J. 413 (1982).
866. *Lorimar Productions Inc v. OK Hyperama Ltd, Lorimar Productions Inc. v. Dallas Restaurant* 1981 (3) SA 1129 (T).
867. *See* H.J.O. van Heerden & J. Neethling, *Unlawful Competition* (1995) 201 n. 4 and 202 n. 5; J. Neethling, *Persoonlike Immaterieelgoedereregte: 'n Nuwe Kategorie Subjektiewe Regte?*, THRHR 316 (1987).
868. *See Federation Internationale de Football and Others v. Bartlett and Others* 1994 (4) SA 722 (T).
869. *See* F.W. Mostert, *The Right to the Advertising Image*, S. African L. J. 413 (1982); J. Neethling, *Passing off and Misappropriation of the Advertising Value of Trade Names, Trade Marks and Service Marks*, SA Merc L.J. 306 (1993).
870. *See* J. Neethling, *Persoonlike Immaterieelgoedereregte: 'n Nuwe Kategorie Subjektiewe Regte?*, THRHR 316 (1987).

acquired commercial value – goodwill – in the form of a reputation in respect of a name or mark, and that potential economic loss justifies protection against passing off or misappropriation generally.[871]

It follows that domain name filching, the misappropriation of an established trade name of another, by registering it as an Internet domain name – usually with the intention of obtaining payment from the real 'owner' of the name – should constitute an unlawful misappropriation in terms of the general principles of Aquilian liability.[872] A remedy under section 5 of the Business Names Act[873] should also be available against locally resident offenders. In the absence of a general action for unlawful competition or trading in English law the practice of Internet domain name filching has been forced into the category of passing off – even in the cases where the registered domain name had never been used and where there was no trading, misrepresentation or diversion of custom.[874]

398. The concept of misappropriation features prominently in cases of unlawful competition that are sometimes categorized under the rubrics 'leaning on' (*aanleuning*),[875] or 'misappropriation of performance' (*prestasie-aanklamping*).[876] It seems that these categories simply reflect the application of general principles to specific situations, and categorization may complicate the law unnecessarily and reduce flexibility in the application of general principles of Aquilian liability for future development of the law.

399. It also seems unnecessary to categorize cases involving elements of both misrepresentation and misappropriation within the category of passing off, even if there is no common field of activity between the parties, as the court did in the *Capital Estate* case. Unlawful misappropriation can occur outside the sphere of competition, as in both the *Capital Estate* and *Lorimar* cases. The *Dun and Bradstreet* and *Schultz* cases and the trade secret cases[877] expressly recognize Aquilian liability for unlawful misappropriation of confidential information or a creative product.

871. *See Moroka Swallows Football Club Ltd v. The Birds Football Club and Others* 1987 (2) SA 511 (W) 526H-I; 530H-I.
872. *See* G.C. Webster & N.S. Page, *South African Law of Trade Marks, Unlawful Competition, Company Names and Trading Styles,* para. 15.26.17 (1999).
873. Act 27 of 1960.
874. *See Pitman Training Ltd v. Nominet UK* [1997] FSR 797 (ChD) 807; *Marks & Spencer plc v. One in a Million Ltd* [1998] FSR 265; *British Telecommunications plc v. One in a Million* [1999] FSR 1 (CA); and Rembert Meyer-Rochow, *The Application of Passing off as a Remedy Against Domain Name Piracy*, EIPR 405 (1998).
875. *See* H.J.O. van Heerden & J. Neethling, *Unlawful Competition* (1995) 201 ff.; F.W. Mostert, *Aanleuning: Skending van 'n Handelsmerk en die Reg op Werfkrag Buite Mededingingsverband,* THRHR 173 (1986).
876. *See* H.J.O. van Heerden & J. Neethling, *Unlawful Competition* (1995) 242 ff.; J. Neethling, *Misappropriation or Copying of a Rival's Performance as a Form on Unlawful Competition (Prestasieaanklamping),* S. African L. J. 711 (1993).
877. *See* generally H.J.O. van Heerden & J. Neethling, *Unlawful Competition* (Butterworths) 223–239.

III. Conduct and Causation

400. The delict of unlawful competition or unlawful trading, as do delicts generally, involves human conduct in the form of an act or omission, whereby one person unlawfully and culpably causes damage in the form of economic loss to another, by infringement of a right to goodwill. In the law of delict it is not the act or conduct by itself that is characterized as unlawful, but the causal sequence of an act and its harmful result.[878]

401. The infringement of the right to goodwill may occur in a direct manner, for example by disparagement of a competitor's business or product; or an indirect manner, for example by making a false representation about the nature or quality of one's own product. The infringement of the right to goodwill may involve only one substratum or component of goodwill, for example the reputation of a business or product,[879] or a trade secret.[880] The infringement may involve a wide and almost unlimited spectrum of conduct,[881] such as conduct producing deception or misrepresentation, as in the case of passing off or leaning on; appropriation of a competitor's trade secret, design, name, or entire performance; interference with a competitor's relationships; disparagement of a competitor's business or product; instigation of a boycott against a competitor; or pressure on his customers or employees. The major part of delictual competition law involves either a misrepresentation – in respect of the offender's own product, or his competitor's product, or an association or connection between his own product and that of his competitor; or a misappropriation – of another's name, mark, design, advertising image, trade secret or information.

402. Although there can be no unlawful competition where the parties involved are not in competition with each other,[882] trading conduct may entail delictual liability outside the sphere of competition, for example in cases of misappropriation of another's advertising image or name;[883] or disparagement of the good name of a business or entrepreneur.[884]

403. The main focus in actions for unlawful competition is invariably on the harmful result, that is, damage in the form of economic loss or potential loss, resulting from the infringement of the right to goodwill, and not so much on the nature of the conduct that produces the result. In this respect, the action for unlawful competition is no different from the general Aquilian action for patrimonial loss.

---

878. *Mukheiber v. Raath* 1999 (3) SA 1065 (SCA) 1075 para. 25.
879. *See Caterham Car Sales & Coachworks Ltd v. Birkin Cars (Pty) Ltd* 1998 (3) SA 938 (SCA) 947I-J.
880. *See* H.J.O. van Heerden & J. Neethling, *Unlawful Competition* (1995) 118.
881. *See* H.J.O. van Heerden & J. Neethling, *Unlawful Competition* (1995) 4.
882. *See Tie Rack plc v. Tie Rack Stores (Pty) Ltd* 1989 (4) SA 427 (T) 445–446.
883. *See Capital Estate and General Agencies (Pty) Ltd v. Holiday Inns Inc* 1977 (2) SA 916 (A).
884. *See Caxton Ltd v. Reeva Forman (Pty) Ltd* 1990 (3) SA 547 (A) 560–561.

IV. Fault

404. Unlawful competition generally involves intentional conduct.[885] Competitors will often sail as close to the wind as possible to gain an advantage in the market. In a case of passing off, for example, it will often be difficult to distinguish between an intention to compete and an intention to deceive.[886] Boberg, in an article on the role of fault in unlawful competition, wrote that all the cases in which unfair competition were held also to be unlawful competition involved deliberate dishonesty; and that the delict of 'unfair competition' was 'born and nourished in a climate of calculated depravity'.[887] This may be so, but as a matter of general principle, intention is not required; the delict of unlawful competition may involve negligent infringement of goodwill.[888] In this respect, also the action for unlawful competition is no different from the general Aquilian action for patrimonial loss.

V. Interests Protected

405. The Aquilian action for unlawful competition or unlawful trading essentially protects a trader from unlawfully being made to suffer economic loss by the trading conduct of another. The interest protected by the delictual action for unlawful competition is essentially the right to goodwill, that is, the right to attract custom or the totality of attributes that lure or entice clients or potential clients to support a particular business.[889] The infringement of the right to goodwill may affect only one substratum or component of goodwill, for example the reputation of a business, the name of a product, the get-up of a product, a trademark, or a trade secret.[890] In the case of passing off, for instance, the substratum or component of goodwill that is primarily affected is reputation.[891]

406. Is there a 'superior value factor' in unlawful competition; that is, are some of these substrata of goodwill rated more worthy of protection than others? The Aquilian liability for injury to a person or tangible property is older and more comprehensive than liability for causing pure economic loss, and for historical and

---

885. *See* generally D.P. Visser, 'Die Rol van Opset en die *Boni Mores* by Onregmatige Mededinging' 1989 *THRHR* 115.
886. *See*, for example, *Reckitt & Colman SA (Pty) Ltd v. SC Johnson & Son (Pty) Ltd* 1993 (2) SA 307 (A).
887. P.Q.R. Boberg, *The Role of Fault in Determining the Lawfulness of Competition*, 54 THRHR, 43–55 (1991).
888. *See Elida Gibbs (Pty) Ltd v. Colgate-Palmolive (Pty) Ltd* 1988 (2) SA 350 (W) 354G-H 357F-G; *Link Estates (Pty) Ltd v. Rink Estates (Pty) Ltd* 1979 (2) SA 276 (E) 281; and *see* generally J. Neethling & J.M. Potgieter, *Die rol van opset by onregmatige mededinging*, S. African L. J. 33 (1991).
889. *See Atlas Organic Fertilizers (Pty) Ltd v. Pikkewyn Ghwano (Pty) Ltd* 1981 (2) SA 173 (T) 182; *A Becker and Co. (Pty) Ltd v. Becker and Others* 1981 (3) SA 406 (A) 417A; *Caterham Car Sales & Coachworks Ltd v. Birkin Cars (Pty) Ltd* 1998 (3) SA 938 (SCA) G-H; and *see* generally H.J.O. van Heerden & J. Neethling, *Unlawful Competition* (1995) 94–96.
890. *See* H.J.O. van Heerden & J. Neethling, *Unlawful Competition* (1995) 118.
891. *See Caterham Car Sales & Coachworks Ltd v. Birkin Cars (Pty) Ltd* 1998 (3) SA 938 (SCA) 947I-J.

policy reasons the statutory protection afforded to patents, trademarks, designs and copyright varies in duration and extent. However, the moral, economic and other considerations that determine the unlawfulness of competitive conduct have much more to do with the reasonableness of the conduct causing the economic loss than with the particular substratum of goodwill affected by the competitive conduct. In short, the cases dealing with the Aquilian action in the context of competition do not indicate that some of the substrata of goodwill are rated more worthy of protection than others: it is the end result – actual or potential economic loss resulting from the infringement of goodwill – that matters the most. In the case of passing off, for instance, the essential question is whether the alleged misrepresentation causes economic loss or potential loss to the business of the complainant.[892]

407. Although one can often identify the substratum or component of goodwill that is primarily affected by a particular form of unlawful competition or trade, such as reputation,[893] or the advertising value of trademarks or trade names,[894] for the purposes of liability the proof of actual or potential loss to the complainant is the essential requirement.

VI. Unlawfulness

408. An act or conduct must *unlawfully* cause damage or harm to another for delictual liability to arise. The general nature of unlawfulness is dealt with in detail Chapter 1 section 2 above. Essentially, unlawfulness involves the question whether the causing of damage or harm to another offends against the legal criterion of reasonableness or *boni mores*, a criterion that involves an assessment of the legal convictions prevailing in the community with reference to a number of considerations, leading in the final instance to a decision based on public policy.[895] Application of the criterion of reasonableness or *boni mores* thus requires the weighing up and balancing of the interests of the parties concerned in the light of the interests of the community.

409. In *Atlas Organic Fertilizers (Pty) Ltd v. Pikkewyn Ghwano (Pty) Ltd.*,[896] Van Dijkhorst J described the nature of the inquiry into unlawfulness of competitive trading conduct as follows:

892. *See Caterham Car Sales & Coachworks Ltd v. Birkin Cars (Pty) Ltd* 1998 (3) SA 938 (SCA) 950B-D.
893. *See Caterham Car Sales & Coachworks Ltd v. Birkin Cars (Pty) Ltd* 1998 (3) SA 938 (SCA) 947I-J.
894. *See* B.L. Rutherford, *Onregmatige Mededinging Unlawful Competition* (J. Neethling ed., 1990), 55.
895. *Mukheiber v. Raath* 1999 (3) SA 1065 (SCA) para. 25; and *see* generally Annél van Aswegen, *Policy Considerations in the Law of Delict*, 56 THRHR 171, 180 (1993).
896. 1981 (2) SA 173 (T) 188.

> I have come to the conclusion that the norm to be applied is the objective one of public policy. This is the general sense of justice in the community, the *boni mores*, manifested in public opinion.
>
> In determining and applying this norm in a particular case, the interests of the competing parties have to be weighted, bearing in mind also the interests of society, the public weal. As this norm cannot exist *in vacuo*, the morals of the market place, the business ethics of that section of the community where the norm is to be applied, are of major importance in its determination.

410. Public policy as a general criterion for determining unlawfulness in competition and trading constitutes 'a legal standard firm enough to afford guidance to the court, yet flexible enough to permit the influence of an inherent sense of fair play'.[897]

411. Unlawfulness involves an objective assessment of a causal sequence. A motive to cause harm to another in itself does not make the causing of harm unlawful, although a reprehensible or improper motive may be taken into account by the court, together with other circumstances, in the assessment of unlawfulness. In the field of unlawful competition, a motive to harm rather than to compete will also be taken into account to determine unlawfulness.[898]

412. Within the established categories of unlawful competition, the courts may often determine unlawfulness without necessarily referring to the criteria of reasonableness, *boni mores*, the legal convictions of the community or concomitant policy considerations. It is settled law, for instance, that a representation by one person that his business or merchandise is that of another, creating a reasonable likelihood of confusion among customers or clients, constitutes unlawful competition in the form of passing off.[899] The application of these general criteria or standards becomes necessary where the conduct complained of caused harm to the goodwill of another, but it does not fall within one of the established categories of unlawful competition. In such cases, the general criteria or standards create judicial discretion and allow the courts to take account of policy considerations in developing the law.

413. There are two general approaches to assessment of unlawfulness in the law of delict. The first approach is to determine whether infringement of a subjective right has occurred; and the second is to determine whether breach of a duty has occurred. Unlawful competition will hardly ever turn on a breach of duty between competitors. Instead, it generally involves the infringement of the subjective right to goodwill, that is the right to attract custom (*werfkrag*), or the infringement of a specific component of goodwill, such as copyright, a patent, a trademark, a design,

---

897. Per Van Dijkhorst J in *Atlas Organic Fertilizers (Pty) Ltd v. Pikkewyn Ghwano (Pty) Ltd* 1981 (2) SA 173 (T) 188.

898. *See Bress Designs (Pry) Ltd v. GY Lounge Suite Manufacturers (Pty) Ltd* 1991 (2) SA 455 (W).

899. *Capital Estate and General Agencies (Pty) Ltd and Others v. Holiday Inns Inc. and Others* 1977 (2) SA 916 (A) 929C; *Caterham Car Sales & Coachworks Ltd v. Birkin Cars (Pty) Ltd* 1998 (3) SA 938 (SCA) 947E-F.

business or product name and reputation, a trade secret, or a personal immaterial property right in the form of the right to earning capacity or personal goodwill.[900]

414. What constitutes a subjective right in the context of unlawful competition? Generally, the law recognizes a subjective right in respect of an interest that has value and is capable of independent existence, so that the person who has the interest may enjoy, use or dispose of it.[901] Every subjective right therefore has an interest as its object. The interests protected by means of the Aquilian action for unlawful competition or trading, as examined in the preceding section, generally constitute goodwill or a substratum of goodwill. However, there is no closed list of subjective rights, and conduct harmful to an interest of appreciable commercial value, such as a name or label,[902] advertising image,[903] fictional character,[904] or the personal image of a celebrity,[905] may be characterized as unlawful without the need to identify a new category of subjective right. In non-competition cases involving pure economic loss, the courts recognize unlawfulness without defining the subjective right that is infringed, focusing instead on the infringement of a legal duty. The inquiry into unlawfulness, as set out in the passage from the *Atlas Organic Fertilizers* case cited above, essentially involves a weighing of the interests of the competing parties, bearing in mind also the interests of society, the morals of the market place and the business ethics of the commercial sector concerned.

415. What constitutes infringement? The law of delict characterizes as unlawful the causing of harm to another person by disturbing or curtailing the ability or opportunity of the holder of a subjective right to enjoy, use or dispose of the interest that is the object of the right. This occurs, for instance, by misappropriation or diminishing the business value or of a substratum or component of goodwill, such as a patented process, trademark, name or trade secret. Factual disturbance or curtailment is not enough; the disturbance or curtailment must be unreasonable in terms of general criteria or standards based on *boni mores*, the legal convictions of the community and in the final instance public policy.

---

900. *See* generally *Atlas Fertilizers (Pty) Ltd v. Pikkewyn Ghwano (Pty) Ltd* 1981 (2) SA 173 (T) 182; H.J.O. van Heerden & J. Neethling, *Unlawful Competition* (1995) 94–96; and *see also Hawker v. Life Offices Association of South Africa* 1987 (3) SA 777 (C), where the infringement of the right to earning capacity was in issue; and J. Neethling, *Die Reg op die Verdienvermoë en die Reg op Korrekte Inligting as Selfstandige Subjektiewe Regte*, THRHR 101 (1990).
901. On the doctrine of subjective rights generally *see Universiteit van Pretoria v. Tommie Meyer Films (Edms) Bpk* 1977 (4) SA 376 (T) 381–384; Joubert, *Grondslae van die Persoonlikheidsreg* (1953) 118–121.
902. *Stellenbosch Wine Trust Ltd and Another v. Oude Meester Group Ltd* 1972 (3) SA 152 (C).
903. F.W. Mostert, *Onregmatige Mededinging/Unlawful Competition* (J. Neethling ed., 1990), 55.
904. *Lorimar Productions Inc v. OK Hyperama Ltd, Lorimar Productions Inc v. Dallas Restaurant* 1981 (3) SA 1129 (T).
905. *See* H.J.O. van Heerden & J. Neethling, *Unlawful Competition* (1995) 201 n. 4 and 202 n. 5; J. Neethling, *Persoonlike Immaterieelgoedereregte: n Nuwe Kategorie Subjektiewe Regte?*, THRHR 316 (1987).

416. The factors generally determining the reasonableness or otherwise of competitive conduct broadly involve an assessment of the respective rights and obligations of the parties; the nature and extent of the harm that was caused; and the nature of the competitive conduct. It will be relevant whether the person who caused the harm knew that his conduct would cause the harm or had the motive to cause harm. However, the existence of knowledge, foresight or motive is not conclusive in determining unlawfulness and will be taken into account together with other factors.[906] The existence of fraud or dishonesty will be an important factor indicating unlawfulness.[907]

417. The unlawfulness of the misappropriation of a commercially valuable name, idea, design or other creative product is determined by application of general principles; and factors that will be taken into consideration include the freedom to imitate ideas or designs in the public domain,[908] the freedom to exploit an established market for a particular type of product established by a competitor,[909] the manner of copying,[910] the distinctiveness of the name or product copied,[911] the extent of the imitation and of the alleged offender's own contribution to the product,[912] the possibility of obtaining statutory protection for the product,[913] fraud or dishonesty[914] and a motive to harm rather than to compete.[915] In the absence of statutory protection, the misappropriation of a foreign trade name that does not form the substratum of any goodwill in South Africa will not be considered unlawful, because no damage is suffered.[916]

---

906. *See* for example *Bress Designs (Pty) Ltd v. GY Lounge Suite Manufacturers (Pty) Ltd* 1991 (2) SA 455 (W) 474J–476A; and *see* further generally *Coronation Brick (Pty) Ltd v. Strachan Construction Co. (Pty) Ltd* 1982 (4) SA 371 (D) 386–387; *Shell and BPSA Petroleum Refineries (Pty) Ltd v. Osborne Panama SA* 1980 (3) SA 653 (D) 659; *Arthur E Abrahams and Gross v. Cohen* 1991 (2) SA 301 (C) 311; *Indac Electronics (Pty) Ltd v. Volkskas Bank Ltd* 1992 (1) SA 783 (A) 799.
907. *See Schultz v. Butt* 1986 (3) SA 667 (A) 683H-I, where the respondent's dishonesty in not only copying a design, but also registering it in his own name, was taken into account by the court in its finding that he had acted unlawfully towards the applicant.
908. *See Premier Hangers CC v. Polyoak (Pty) Ltd* 1997 (1) SA 416 (A) 423H–424C; *Schultz v. Butt* 1986 (3) SA 667 (A) 681A-E; *Bress Designs (Pty) Ltd v. GY Lounge Suite Manufacturers (Pty) Ltd* 1991 (2) SA 455 (W) 474E-G.
909. *See Taylor & Horne (Pty) Ltd v. Dentall (Pty) Ltd* 1991 (1) SA 412 (A) 421I–422A.
910. *Schultz v. Butt* 1986 (3) SA 667 (A) 683H-I; *Bress Designs (Pty) Ltd v. GY Lounge Suite Manufacturers (Pty) Ltd* 1991 (2) SA 455 (W) 474E.
911. *See* for example *Reckitt & Colman SA (Pty) Ltd v. SC Johnson & Son (SA) (Pty) Ltd* 1995 (1) SA 725 (T) 733B-G.
912. *Bress Designs (Pty) Ltd v. GY Lounge Suite Manufacturers (Pty) Ltd* 1991 (2) SA 455 (W) 472I–473A; and *see* generally H.J.O. Van Heerden, *Onregmatige Mededinging/Unlawful Competition* (J. Neethling ed., 1990) 6 (Van Heerden in Neethling (ed.)) (also in *THRHR* 151).
913. *Lorimar Productions Inc v. Sterling Clothing Manufacturers (Pty) Ltd, Lorimar Productions Inc v. OK Hyperama Ltd, Lorimar Productions Inc v. Dallas Restaurant* 1981 (3) SA 1129 (T) 1156H; *Reckitt & Colman SA (Pty) Ltd v. SC Johnson & Son (SA) (Pty) Ltd* 1995 (1) SA 725 (T) 732F-G; *Premier Hangers CC v. Polyoak (Pty) Ltd* 1997 (1) SA 416 (A) 424I–476A.
914. *Schultz v. Butt* 1986 (3) SA 667 (A) 683H-I.
915. *Bress Designs (Pty) Ltd v. GY Lounge Suite Manufacturers (Pty) Ltd* 1991 (2) SA 455 (W) 474J–476A.
916. *Tie Rack plc v. Tie Rack Stores (Pty) Ltd and Another* 1989 (4) SA 427 (T).

VII. The Constitution and Unlawful Competition

418. The assessment of unlawfulness may involve the application of a constitutional right such as the right to freedom of trade, occupation and profession,[917] the right to property,[918] the right to equality[919] and the right to freedom of expression.[920] The existence of a constitutional right is not conclusive, however, and the assessment of unlawfulness often involves a conflict of rights.[921] There may also be a conflict between the constitutional right to property and an obligation in terms of the Competition Act,[922] for instance where a trader who dominates a particular market may be ordered to share an 'essential facility' with a rival.[923]

419. Reliance on constitutional rights has not been of much assistance to litigants in the field of competition law in recent years. Litigants have attempted to rely on the constitutional right to engage freely in economic activity[924] or to choose a trade, occupation or profession freely,[925] particularly in legal action to have a contractual restraint of trade declared invalid,[926] but these have not yet met with success.

420. The Constitution may be invoked to protect freedom of expression,[927] and this includes freedom of commercial expression. Advertising and the Code of the Advertising Standards Authority (ASA) are subject to the constitutional right to freedom of expression.[928] A professional or trade association's rules against certain forms of advertising may offend against the constitutional freedom of expression. However, such rules may also be regarded as an unlawful limitation on the right to compete in terms of Aquilian principles, without invoking the Constitution. A provision in the Pharmacy Board's Advertising Code, prohibiting the advertising of discounts on prescription medicines, has been held to be in conflict with society's *boni mores* and therefore unlawful in terms of Aquilian principles.[929]

---

917. Section 22 of the Constitution Act 108 of 1996.
918. Section 25 of the Constitution Act 108 of 1996.
919. Section 9 of the Constitution Act 108 of 1996.
920. Section 16 of the Constitution Act 108 of 1996.
921. *See* generally H.J.O. van Heerden & J. Neethling, *Unlawful Competition* (1995) 13–16.
922. Act 89 of 1998.
923. Section 8(b); and *see SAD Holdings Ltd and Another v. South African Raisins (Pty) Ltd and Another*[2000] 2 All SA 326 329, where the Competition Tribunal ordered a company dominant in the raisin market to share specially designed containers, which it owned, with a rival.
924. Section 26(1) of the interim Constitution Act 200 of 1993.
925. Section 22 of the Constitution Act 108 of 1996.
926. *See Waltons Stationery Company (Pty) Ltd v. Fourie and Another* 1994 (1) BCLR 50 (O); *Kotze en Genis (Edms) Bpk v. Potgieter en Andere* 1995 (3) BCLR 349 (C).
927. Section 16 of the Constitution Act 108 of 1996.
928. *See* generally Tanya Woker *Advertising Law in South Africa* (1999) 190–199.
929. *See Van der Westhuizen v. Scholtz en Andere* 1992 (4) SA 866 (O) 873–874.

Invoking the Constitution in a competition-related Aquilian action will oblige the courts to assess the common law principles of unlawful competition, and in particular the element of unlawfulness, in the light of the 'values that underlie an open and democratic society based on human dignity, equality and freedom'.[930]

VIII. Policy Considerations Generally

421. Policy considerations for the purposes of Aquilian liability for unlawful competition or trading relate in particular to the element of unlawfulness, and derive from the Constitution, as indicated in the preceding section, but also from various other sources.

422. The provisions of legislation in the field of competition law, such as the Trade Marks Act,[931] the Copyright Act,[932] the Harmful Business Practices Act,[933] the Business Names Act[934] and the Trade Practices Act[935] may be taken into account to determine unlawfulness in an Aquilian action. The courts have accepted that the clearest cases of unlawful competitive conduct are those where the conduct is prohibited by legislation.[936]

423. The relationship between the policy considerations underlying the Competition Act[937] on the one hand and the considerations that determine unlawfulness in a delictual action for unlawful competition on the other, has not been the subject of thorough analysis by the courts. The courts have often acknowledged the need for protection of free competition as an important policy consideration when assessing the unlawfulness of competitive conduct by confirming the need for free and active competition,[938] or by taking into account that by prohibiting competition an unlimited monopoly will be bestowed upon the complainant.[939] However, these general acknowledgements are usually not followed by any detailed analysis of the particular market conditions, to determine possible efficiency or technological gains if the complainant is protected against competition; or, alternatively, the pro-competitive

930. Section 39(1)(a).
931. Act 194 of 1993.
932. Act 98 of 1978.
933. Act 71 of 1988.
934. Act 27 of 1960.
935. Act 76 of 1976.
936. *See Dun and Brandstreet (Pty) Ltd v. SA Merchants Combined Credit Bureau (Cape) (Pty) Ltd* 1968 (2) SA 209 (C) 216E-G; *Silver Crystal Trading (Pty) Ltd v. Namibia Diamond Corporation (Pty) Ltd* 1983 (4) SA 884 (D & CLD) 888C. *See also* generally on competition in conflict with statutory provisions H.J.O. van Heerden & J. Neethling, *Unlawful Competition* (1995) 266 ff.
937. Act 89 of 1998.
938. *See* for example *Payen Components SA Ltd v. Bovic CC and Others* 1995 (4) SA 441 (A) 453B-C; *Union Wine Ltd v. Edward Snell & Co. Ltd* 1990 (2) SA 189 (C) 203D-E; *Bress Designs (Pty) Ltd v. GY Lounge Suite Manufacturers (Pty) Ltd* 1991 (2) SA 455 (W) 473H; *Schultz v. Butt* 1986 (3) SA 667 (A) 679E; *Lorimar Productions Inc v. Sterling Clothing Manufacturers (Pty) Ltd, Lorimar Productions Inc v. OK Hyperama Ltd, Lorimar Productions Inc. v. Dallas Restaurant* 1981 (3) SA 1129 (T) 1154G 1155A-B.
939. *Premier Hangers CC v. Polyoak (Pty) Ltd* 1997 (1) SA 416 (A) 426H.

effects of allowing the competition. If there is blatant imitation without significant pro-competitive gains, but some doubt as to potential diversion of custom or other damage, should the court favour the complainant and prohibit the imitation?[940]

Such questions have generally not been considered in delictual competition cases, where the courts focus on the particular dispute and seek to do justice between the parties, rather than seeking to deal with the broader canvas of competition policy by determining the pro-competitive or anticompetitive effects in the particular market. In commenting on policy considerations arising in delictual competition cases, the former Chief Justice Corbett stated as follows:[941]

> So here again, where unlawful competition is alleged and the case does not fall within one of the recognized categories of unlawfulness, the court is required to take a policy decision: a decision orientated by considerations of fairness and honesty, but at the same time guided by *boni mores* and the general sense of justice of the community.

424. The Aquilian action for unlawful competition or trading has therefore traditionally fulfilled the function of corrective justice rather than of distributive justice. The Aquilian action has shown its capacity to change over time, and out of occasional uncertainty ideas are born and choices are eventually made,[942] but it is not a vehicle for radical review or overhaul. The courts are conservative in extending Aquilian liability into new areas.[943]

425. The relationship between the delict of unlawful competition and legislation on anticompetitive trade practices, that is, between the private and the public competition law, has been the subject of much debate.[944] In Europe, and particularly in Germany, there is a school of thought that a distinction should be drawn between competition law in the sphere of delict on the one hand and public competition law and policy on the other. The argument is that if the general interest of consumers and competition policy were to override, the judges in delict cases would need to become economic policymakers.[945] The private law of unlawful competition – so the argument goes – has the goal of ensuring that competitors compete fairly and

---

940. *See* for example *Reckitt & Colman SA (Pty) Ltd v. SC Johnson & Son (SA) (Pty) Ltd* 1995 (1) SA 725 (T) 733–734, where the name component *Neutra*, used in the product name *Haze Neutra Air*, was appropriated by a competitor as part of the name *Glade Neutra Air*, and the court considered the total market for air fresheners and the applicant's share of it, and also the wasted costs of research, labelling, packaging and promotion should the interdict against use of the product name *Glade Neutra Air* be granted.
941. M.M. Corbett, *Aspects of the Role of Policy in the Evolution of our Common Law*, S. African L. J. 52, 62 (1987).
942. *See* generally on the relationship between economic torts and legislation on restrictive trade practices J.D. Heydon, *Law and Social Control* 133, 145 (Eugene Kamenka & Alice Erh-Soon Tay eds., 1980).
943. *See Lillicrap, Wassenaar and Partners v. Pilkington Brothers (SA) (Pty) Ltd* 1985 (1) SA 475 (A) 500C-E.
944. *See* generally Peter Joachim Kaufmann, *Passing Off and Misappropriation* (1986) IIC Studies in Industrial and Copyright Law, Volume 9, 7–30.
945. *Ibid.*, at 9.

ethically and not to make general competition policy.[946] Since the seventies, however, this dichotomy between private and public competition law has come under attack in Europe, and there is increasing recognition that private and public competition law are branches of the same tree. The implication is that the unlawfulness of individual competitive conduct should not only be determined in terms of fairness between the parties, but in terms of consequences to the economic order, by determining whether the competitive conduct hinders or stifles the competitive process of differentiation and imitation and whether an improvement of market choice and efficiency will result.[947]

Arguably, the provisions of the Competition Act[948] provide a policy framework, not only for public competition law, but also for delictual competition actions.[949] Courts may be required to take into account whether the conduct complained of constitutes a prohibited practice in terms of the Act, and also consider possible 'technological, efficiency or other pro-competitive gains'.[950] Generally, cases on unlawful competition reflect an inadequate analysis of competition economics and policy. It is significant that in assessing the validity of contractual restraints of trade, the courts take a wide view of public policy considerations.[951]

426. The practice of comparative advertising involves important policy issues.[952] There is scant case law on comparative advertising in the context of unlawful competition.[953] It is an area largely regulated by rulings in terms of the Code of the Advertising Standards Authority (ASA), to which advertisers voluntarily submit.[954] Comparative advertising gives rise to vexed questions in trademark law[955] There is an obvious potential for misrepresentation and the absolute truth or falseness of a comparison is seldom determinable – and it may be unfair to place the burden of proving falseness on the trader who suffers in the comparison.[956]

946. *Ibid.*, at 11.
947. *Ibid.*, at 11–15, 23.
948. Act 89 of 1998.
949. Section 65(2) of the Act envisages that in any action in a civil court a party may raise 'an issue concerning conduct that is prohibited in terms of this Act'.
950. *See* ss 4(1)(a) and 5(1).
951. *Magna Alloys and Research (SA) (Pty) v. Ellis* 1984 (4) SA 874 (A); and *see* generally H.J.O. van Heerden & J. Neethling, *Unlawful Competition* (Butterworths 1995) 26–29.
952. *See* generally Nancy S. Greiwe, *Antidilution Statutes: A New Attack on Comparative Advertising*, 72 Trademark Reptr. 178 (1981); Peter Joachim Kaufmann, *Passing Off and Misappropriation* (1986) 9 IIC Studies in Industrial and Copyright Law ch. II: *Is Better Worse Than Best? An Unfettered View of Comparative Advertising* 31–72.
953. *See Post Newspapers (Pty) Ltd v. World Printing and Publishing Co. Ltd* 1970 (1) SA 454 (W), where the alleged misrepresentation as to the comparative exposure value to advertisers of two publications was held to be mere puffery.
954. *See* generally Tanya Woker, *Advertising Law in South Africa* (Juta & Co. Ltd 1999) 190–199.
955. *See* O.H. Dean, *Onregmatige Mededinging/Unlawful Competition* 114 (J. Neethling ed., 1990); O.H. Dean, *Intellectual Property and Comparative Advertising*, 1 Stell L. Rev. 25 (1996); Ron Wheeldon, *Brand-Comparative Advertising Is It Unlawful, Really?* De Rebus 585 (September 1996); Ron Wheeldon, *Is Our Trade Mark Law Out of Step with the EC?* De Rebus 21 (September 2000); *Abbott Laboratories and Others v. UAP Crop Care (Pty) Ltd and Others* 1999 (3) SA 624 (C).
956. H.J.O. van Heerden & J. Neethling, *Unlawful Competition* (1995) 304–305.

However, the right of free commercial speech in terms of section 16 of the Constitution[957] overrides these considerations, and the courts will deal with such cases on the merits, taking into account such factors as the potential dilution of the selling power of the name or mark involved; whether the comparison is merely informative or also persuasive; whether it involves only technical information; whether the information is verifiable; whether the advertisement was in response to another trader's misleading advertisement; whether the comparison is selective; and generally the public interest in the dissemination of truthful commercial information.[958]

427. The conduct of a trader who is dominant in a particular market is governed by section 8 of the Competition Act.[959] This section prohibits certain instances of abuse of dominance in a relevant market, for example where a dominant firm charges an excessive price or engages in an exclusionary act such as inducing a supplier or customer not to deal with a competitor, refusing to supply scarce goods, or imposing discriminatory sale conditions. The policy considerations underlying this section are relevant where a delictual remedy for a refusal to do business is in issue. In *Times Media Ltd v. SABC*,[960] the SABC, the dominant national television broadcaster, refused to broadcast a television advertisement of the applicant's newspaper, the *Sunday Times*, because it contained a reference to M-Net, a rival of the SABC. The applicant claimed that this refusal amounted to a boycott and unlawful competition. This claim was dismissed, on the basis that there was no competition between the applicant and the SABC; and also on the basis that the SABC's conduct did not constitute a boycott of M-Net; and even if it did, the conduct was not unlawful, because the SABC could decide with whom and on what basis it will do business. It is submitted that the policy orientation of this judgment was too narrow, and that the court should have considered whether the conduct amounted to a restrictive practice in terms of the Maintenance and Promotion of Competition Act[961] that applied at the time.[962] It is submitted that in assessing the lawfulness of a refusal to do business the courts should now also take into account a possible abuse of a dominant position in a market, as provided for in the Competition Act.[963]

428. On parallel imports, the courts have held that an exclusive contractual right to distribute goods in South Africa is not a sufficient basis for an Aquilian remedy against a rival trader who engages in parallel importation of the same goods, with the same name, mark and get-up.[964] However, where the importer or distributor adds

---

957. Act 108 of 1996. See on commercial freedom of speech *City of Cape Town v. Ad Output Ltd* 2000 (2) SA 733 (C).
958. *See* Nancy S. Greiwe, *Antidilution Statutes: A New Attack on Comparative Advertising*, 72 Trademark Reptr. 178, 188–196 (1981).
959. Act 89 of 1998.
960. 1990 (4) SA 604 (W) 607.
961. Act 96 of 1979.
962. *See* H.J.O. van Heerden & J. Neethling, *Unlawful Competition* (1995) 308 n. 9.
963. *See* generally Mary Ellen Schill, *Refusals to Deal by Single-Firm Monopolists – Should We rob Peter to Save Paul?* 63 Notre Dame L. Rev. 214 (1988).
964. *Rusmarc (SA) (Pty) Ltd v. Hemdon Enterprises (Pty) Ltd* 1975 (4) SA 626 (W); *Taylor & Horne (Pty) Ltd v. Dentall (Pty) Ltd* 1991 (1) SA 412 (A).

his own get-up or distinctive mark to the product, thereby establishing his own reputation for the product, a parallel importer who imitates the get-up or mark may be liable on the basis of passing off.[965] Parallel importation has also given rise to vexed questions in trademark law[966] and copyright law.[967] The phenomenon also involves important policy issues. In the case of *Taylor & Horne (Pty) Ltd v. Dentall (Pty) Ltd*,[968] the court refused to afford a monopoly to an exclusive agent on the basis of his exclusive contractual rights. However, there are also other relevant considerations such as:

- the cost of establishing a local market which is then exploited by another (the 'free rider' argument);
- damage to the reputation of the sole agent by parallel importation of inferior quality goods with the same name, mark and get-up;
- damage to the reputation of the sole agent if inferior after-sales service is provided by the parallel importer; and
- the protection of local business initiatives against a global competitor, who may be willing to flood the local market.[969]

The kind of product that is involved and the availability for import of similar products in the world market will also be relevant. Furthermore, the relevant policy considerations for a developing country and a developed country may differ.[970]

429. Generally, unlawful competition cases in South Africa do not reflect a comprehensive analysis of policy considerations or the effects of the competitive conduct concerned on the market and economic order.

---

965. *Frank & Hirsch (Pty) Ltd v. Roopenand Brothers* 1987 (3) SA165 (D) 189; *Salusa (Pty) Ltd v. Eagle International Traders* 1979 (4) SA 697 (K) 704–705.
966. *Hampo Systems (Pty) Ltd v. Audiolens (Cape) (Pty) Ltd 1985* (4) SA 257 (K); *Frank & Hirsch (Pty) Ltd v. Roopenand Brothers* 1987 (3) SA165 (D) 173H; and *see* generally J. Moorcroft, *Handelsmerke en parallelle invoere*, 55 THRHR 103 (1992); Carin-Gretna Grobbelaar, *'n Regsvergelykende studie na die regmatigheid van parallelle invoere, getoets aan die beginsels van handelsmerkereg, outeursreg en mededingingsreg* Unpublished LLM Thesis University of Stellenbosch (1998); Andrew Clark, *Parallel Imports: A New Job for Customs?* European Intell. Prop. Rev. 1 (1999); Abraham van Melle, *Parallel Importing in New Zealand: Historical Origins, Recent Developments, and Future Directions*, European Intell. Prop. Rev. 63 (1999).
967. Abraham van Melle, *Parallel Importing in New Zealand: Historical Origins, Recent Developments, and Future Directions*, European Intell. Prop. Rev. 63 (1999).
968. 1991 (1) SA 412 (A) 422.
969. *See* Carin-Gretna Grobbelaar, *'n Regsvergelykende studie na die regmatigheid van parallelle invoere, getoets aan die beginsels van handelsmerkereg, outeursreg en mededingingsreg* Unpublished LLM Thesis University of Stellenbosch (1998) 182–186; Abraham van Melle, *Parallel Importing in New Zealand: Historical Origins, Recent Developments, and Future Directions*, European Intell. Prop. Rev. 63, 69–72 (1999).
970. Parallel importation has recently been permitted by changes to copyright law in New Zealand, whereas a trademark owner in the European Community can prevent parallel importation if the product has not yet entered the Community; *see* respectively Abraham van Melle, *Parallel Importing in New Zealand: Historical Origins, Recent Developments, and Future Directions*, European Intell. Prop. Rev. 63 (1999) and Andrew Clark, *Parallel Imports: A New Job for Customs?* European Intell. Prop. Rev. 1 (1999).

IX. Damages

430. The Aquilian action for unlawful competition or unlawful trading essentially protects a trader from unlawfully being made to suffer economic loss by the trading conduct of another. The interest protected by the delictual action for unlawful competition is generally the right to goodwill, that is, the right to attract custom or the totality of attributes that lure or entice clients or potential clients to support a particular business.[971] Damages are awarded according to the general principles applicable to patrimonial loss. Damage is normally attributable to a loss of custom to competitors.[972] In most cases, it is possible to show that some loss has been suffered,[973] but the extent of the loss is often difficult to prove with precision.[974] Consequently, the courts will tend not to require mathematically precise proof of loss and will, on the probabilities indicated by the evidence, make an assessment of the loss *ex bono et aequo*.[975] Often, the most effective remedy will be an interdict ordering the wrongdoer to cease the unlawful competition or trading.

§7. Product Liability

431. In South African common law delictual product liability is fault-based, within the common law framework of Aquilian liability. This form of liability currently therefore does not belong in the area of strict liability. However, strict liability has been introduced by legislation,[976] and this legislation brings South African law into line with the position in many other jurisdictions.

432. In the area of product liability, the law of delict supplements the limited scope of protection afforded by the law of contract. In the context of a contract of sale, a dealer in goods is liable for latent defects where he publicly professes to have attributes of skill and expert knowledge in respect of the goods sold. This was accepted by the Appellate Division in *Kroonstad Westelike Boere Ko-op Vereniging*

---

971. *See Atlas Organic Fertilizers (Pty) Ltd v. Pikkewyn Ghwano (Pty) Ltd* 1981 (2) SA 173 (T) 182; *A Becker and Co. (Pty) Ltd v. Becker and Others* 1981 (3) SA 406 (A) 417A; *Caterham Car Sales & Coachworks Ltd v. Birkin Cars (Pty) Ltd* 1998 (3) SA 938 (SCA) G-H; and *see* generally H.J.O. van Heerden & J. Neethling *Unlawful Competition* (1995) 94–96.
972. *See* generally *Dun & Bradstreet (Pty) Ltd v. SA Merchants Combined Credit Bureau (Cape)Pty Ltd* 1968 (1) SA 209 (C) 221; and *Harchris Heat Treatment (Pty) Ltd v. Iscor* 1983 (1) SA 548 (T).
973. *Van Heerden v. Paetzold* 1917 CPD 221 224 (concerning damages for the effect of malicious statements); *Atlas Organic Fertilizers (Pty) Ltd v. Pikkewyn Ghwano (Pty) Ltd* 1981 (2) SA 173 (T) 204–206 (concerning the assessment of loss of profit); *Link Estates (Pty) Ltd v. Rink Estates (Pty) Ltd* 1979 (2) SA 276 (E) 286–287.
974. *See Lorimar Productions Inc v. Sterling Clothing Manufacturers (Pty) Ltd* 1981 (3) SA 1129 (T) 1138; *Hushon SA (Pty) Ltd v. Pictech (Pty) Ltd* 1997 (2) All SA 672 (SCA); 1997 (4) SA 399 (SCA).
975. *International Tobacco Co. (SA) Ltd v. United Tobacco Co. (South) Ltd (1)* 1955 (2) SA 1 (W) 17; *Caxton Ltd v. Reeva Forman (Pty) Ltd* 1990 (3) SA 547 (A) 573; *Hushon SA (Pty) Ltd v. Pictech (Pty) Ltd* 1997 (4) SA 399 (SCA) 412–413.
976. Section 61 of the Consumer Protection Act 68 of 2008.

Bpk v. Botha;[977] and in *Langeberg Voedsel Bpk v. Sarculum Boerdery* Bpk Schutz JA obiter commented as follows on the *Kroonstad* decision:[978]

> But the passage of time may have weakened rather than strengthened the authority of the decision. If it ever be challenged in the future, that will be the time to decide whether it may and should be altered.
>
> It remains to add that it is not only in this small, if important, branch of the law of purchase and sale, but in the much wider field of product liability generally that our law may be perceived to have lagged behind.

433. In *Ciba-Geigy (Pty) Ltd v. Lushof Farms (Pty) Ltd en 'n Ander*,[979] the Appellate Division commented as follows on the scope of delictual liability for defective products:

> If a manufacturer produces and markets a product without conclusive prior tests, when the utilization thereof in the recommended manner is potentially hazardous to the consumer, such negligence on the part of the manufacturer may expose him to delictual liability to the consumer. Where the consumer does not acquire the product directly from the manufacturer, and the manufacturer is thus a third party, such liability amounts to what is sometimes termed 'product liability'. A contractual nexus between the manufacturer and the consumer is not required. Although the historical origin of the manufacturer's liability is an agreement between the manufacturer and the distributor, the liability, which arises from the manufacture and distribution of the product, extends via the other contracting party to any third party who utilizes the product in the prescribed manner and suffers damage as a result thereof. It follows as a matter of course that a manufacturer who distributes a product commercially, which, in the course of its intended use, and as the result of a defect, causes damage to the consumer thereof, acts wrongly and thus unlawfully according to the legal convictions of the community.

434. For the purposes of delictual liability, it is thus accepted that the manufacturer owes a legal duty to the persons acquiring and using the products not to expose them to harm. Van den Heever JA in *Herschel v. Mrupe*,[980] under reference to the Scottish House of Lords case of *Donoghue v. Stevenson*,[981] analysed the duty as follows:

> By putting into circulation potentially harmful things … the manufacturer is not merely exercising a legal right but encroaching upon the rights of others

977. 1964 (3) SA 561 (A).
978. 1996 (2) SA 565 (A) at 572F–H.
979. 2002 (2) SA 447 (SCA) para. 64 at 470B–C/D and para. 66 at D/E-G.
980. 1954 (3) SA 457 (A) at 487; and *see Combrinck Chiropraktiese Kliniek (Edms) Bpk v. Datsun Motor Vehicle Distributors (Pty) Ltd* 1972 (4) SA 185 (T).
981. [1932] AC 562, 1932 SC (HL) 31.

> not to be exposed, when going about their lawful occasions and when accepting the implied general invitation to acquire and use such commodities, to danger without warning and without their having a reasonable opportunity to become aware of such danger before use. In other words, it is an encroachment upon the rights of others to set hidden snares for them in the exercise of their own rights. To refrain from doing so is a duty owing to the world at large.[982]

435. Commenting on American developments in the field of product liability in 1975, Coetzee J in *A Gibb and Son v. Taylor and Mitchell Timber Supply Co.* commented that:[983]

> Possibly due to our own positivist backgrounds, the pace of this transition, particularly the Californian, must seem unbelievably brisk to South African lawyers. It is important to appreciate this general tendency and its strength when one examines, for comparative purposes, their solutions of problems similar to that in casu. American Judges and writers will confidently find duties to care to exist where we may still tread very warily and hesitantly. By reason of this very tempo of their expansion of liability they may serve a useful purpose by demonstrating a high water mark to South African eyes as the latter are presently focussed.

436. This 'high-water mark' has not even been approached. The South African plaintiff who claims in delict on account of harm caused by a defective product must prove the twin elements of wrongfulness and negligence. In the first instance, the plaintiff must show that the defendant has wrongfully caused damage by producing or distributing a *defective* product, in breach of its duty to the consumer. Thus the presence of a defect is a necessary element of wrongful conduct. In South African law, there is no absolute standard to assess the defectiveness of a product. The assessment of defectiveness forms part of the general inquiry into wrongfulness, involving consideration of 'the legal convictions of the community', *boni mores* or general reasonableness. The position in this regard has been summarized as follows:

> A manufacturer has a general duty to take reasonable steps to ensure that defective products do not reach the market or, if they do, to withdraw them from the market, or to take other steps to ensure that no harm ensues from the present of the product on the market. The criterion of reasonableness coupled with the community's concept of what behaviour is reasonable in given circumstances is flexible enough to take into account such factors as the type of product, the nature of the manufacturer's business enterprise, the customs and practices prevailing in a particular trade or industry, the amount of knowledge and expertise of potential purchasers and users of the product, abnormal use, and the specific stage in the production process during which a defect originated. The

982. 1954 (3) SA 464 (AD) at 486F; in *A v. National Blood Authority* (2001) 3 All ER 289.
983. 1975 (2) SA 457 (W).

last-mentioned factor may influence the duties of a manufacturer in different ways. At the stage of planning or design the manufacturer must take into account the most recent knowledge available in his field.[984]

437. To date the South African law of delict has not developed detailed rules for different forms of product defects (manufacturing, design or warning defects) and the courts apply general principles in this regard. This general approach has been interpreted to mean that a product will be considered defective if it is *unreasonably dangerous*. Van der Merwe and De Jager have said the following on the application of this test:

> The test is flexible enough to take into account such factors as the type of product, the nature of the manufacturer's business enterprise, the customs and practices prevailing in a particular trade or industry, the amount of knowledge and expertise of potential purchasers and users of the product, abnormal use, and the specific stage in the production process during which a defect originated. The last mentioned factor may influence the duties of a manufacturer in different ways. At the stage of planning or design the manufacturer must take into account the most recent knowledge available in his field.[985]

438. In addition to wrongfulness, the plaintiff must prove negligence on the part of the manufacturer or distributor. Negligence is determined by assessing the producer's actions against the standard of care expected of the diligens paterfamilias,[986] involving the questions whether a reasonable person would have foreseen the harm and would have taken steps to prevent it, and whether the defendant failed to take such steps.

439. The fault requirement for product liability in South Africa was tested in the leading case of *Wagener and Cuttings v. Pharmacare Ltd and Others*,[987] where the plaintiffs alleged that the manufacturer of a local anaesthetic was strictly liable for breach of its duty to ensure that the product was safe. The manufacturer raised an exception to this part of the particulars of claim on the basis that it disclosed no cause of action, for want of the allegation that there was *dolus* or culpa in the manufacture, sale or distribution of the product. The plaintiffs, referring to the development of forms of strict product liability in Europe and America, argued that the law in South Africa had reached the stage where such liability should be imposed; and that there was a constitutional imperative to develop the common law in this regard, to give proper effect to the constitutional right to bodily integrity. The court in the *Wagener* case said the following on the distinct elements of wrongfulness and negligence:

---

984. S. van der Merwe & F. de Jager, *Products Liability: A Recent Unreported Case*, S. African L. J. 83, 88 (1980).
985. S. van der Merwe & F. de Jager, *Products Liability: A Recent Unreported Case*, S. African L. J. 83, 88 (1980).
986. *A Gibb & Son (Pty) Ltd v. Taylor & Mitchell Timber Supply Co. (Pty) Ltd* 1975 (2) SA 457 (W).
987. 2003 (4) SA 285 (SCA).

> [7] In deciding the issues raised by the appeal it must be accepted, as regards the facts, that the Regibloc in question was manufactured by the respondent, that it was defective when it left the respondent's control, that it was administered in accordance with the respondent's accompanying instructions, that it was its defective condition which caused the alleged harm and that such harm was reasonably foreseeable. It must also be accepted, as far as the law is concerned, indeed it was not disputed, firstly, that the respondent, as manufacturer, although under no contractual obligation to the appellant, was under a legal duty in delictual law to avoid reasonably foreseeable harm resulting from defectively manufactured Regibloc being administered to the first appellant and, secondly, that that duty was breached. In the situation pleaded there would therefore clearly have been unlawful conduct on the part of the respondent: *Ciba-Geigy (Pty) Ltd v. Lushof Farms (Pty) Ltd.*[988] The essential inquiry is whether liability attaches even if the breach occurred without fault on the respondent's part.

The court acknowledged that it had a role to develop the common law, but declined to do so in this case, on the basis that such development should be done with circumspection and that the duty of making law is primarily that of the legislature. It was accepted that the manufacturer had wrongfully caused the harm by selling products not conforming to its own specifications (a manufacturing defect). However, liability would not be imposed without proof of fault on the part of the manufacturer. The case illustrates the difficulty of proving fault in respect of a defect in a certain batch of a pharmaceutical product, and raises the policy question whether the risk of such a defect should not be borne by the manufacturer.

440. Not only the manufacturer, but also the seller of the product may be at fault. In the case of the seller, the negligence issue will entail the question whether in the circumstances he had a duty to inspect the product before the sale.[989] In *Freddy Hirsch Group (Pty) Ltd v. Chickenland (Pty) Ltd*,[990] the Supreme Court of Appeal held that the plaintiff, Chickenland, had an alternative claim in delict for economic loss caused by delivery to it of spices containing a banned colourant. The delictual claim was based on the defendant's awareness that breach of contract by delivery of spices containing the banned colourant would or could reasonably cause losses to the plaintiff, including the costs associated with the recall and replacement of the affected products. The court accepted that while the same facts may give rise to a claim for damages *ex contractu* and alternatively *ex delicto*, the breach of a contractual duty is not necessarily wrongful for the purposes of Aquilian liability.[991] The negligent causing of pure economic loss is not prima facie wrongful, but in this case policy considerations such as knowledge of the potential harm, the fact that the

988. 2002 (2) SA 447 (SCA).
989. *A Gibb &Son v. Taylor & Mitchell Timber Supply Co.* 1975 (2) SA 457 (W).
990. 2011 (4) SA 276 (SCA).
991. Paragraph 33.

loss was single and determinate and the manufacturer's general duty to take reasonable steps to ensure that defective products do not reach the market indicated wrongfulness for the purposes of delictual liability.

441. The problem of proving defectiveness and negligence was one of the main catalysts for reform of the law on product liability in Europe in the 1980s. These problems still exist under the South African common law rules governing product liability, despite the potential application of the res ipsa loquitur doctrine, which in certain cases allows the inference that the product did not meet the appropriate standard or that the manufacturer was negligent.[992]

442. Another obstacle for the plaintiff in a product liability case is the onus to prove the causal link between the defect and the harm suffered. This may present an even more complex task than proving the existence of a defect, for it requires the plaintiff to draw together technical data about the product and the accident with evidence of the conduct of the individuals concerned as well as environmental factors. The problems of proof relating to the elements of defectiveness, negligence and causation facing the claimant under the rules of the common law form part of the policy background to the introduction of strict liability by legislation.[993] Strict liability for defective products under the Consumer Protection Act 68 of 2008 is discussed in Part III, Chapter 6 below.

992. *See Bayer South Africa (Pty) Ltd v. Viljoen* 1990 (2) SA 647 at 662.
993. Section 61 of the Consumer Protection Act 68 of 2008.

Part II. Liability for Acts of Others

Chapter 1. Vicarious Liability

§1. Employee/Employer

443. The doctrine of vicarious liability as it is applied in South Africa is predominantly English in derivation.[994] In the context of South African law, it has been described as 'perhaps the most comprehensive and far-reaching innovation we have taken from English law'.[995] South African and English courts approach the two cardinal features of the doctrine – the concept of an employee and that of acting in the course and scope of employment – in similar fashion, although there are differences in detail.

I. General Rule

444. The general rule as applied by South African courts is that an employer is vicariously liable, regardless of the absence of fault on its part, for the delicts of its employees when these are committed in the course and the scope of their employment.[996] The rule is 'founded upon public policy and convenience; for in no other way could there be any safety to third persons in their dealings either directly or indirectly with him through the instrumentality of agents'.[997] It has been accepted that in the context of the employment relationship the employer creates a risk for his own ends,[998] and that the employer's liability is therefore 'coextensive and identical in every respect with the liability of the servant';[999] or that the employer is considered to be the actor himself where he acts through an employee –*qui facit per*

994. For the historical development of vicarious liability in South Africa, and the influence of English law, *see* B. Jordaan, 'Employment Relations', in Zimmermann & Visser, *Southern Cross*, 389, 397 ff. *See* further Max Loubser & Elspeth Reid, *Mixed Legal Systems in Comparative Perspective–Property and Obligations in Scotland and South Africa* (Reinhard Zimmermann, Daniel Visser & Kenneth Reid eds., Juta 2004), on which this section is substantially based.
995. P.Q.R. Boberg, *Oak Tree or Acorn*, 83 S. African L. J. 150, 169 (1966).
996. *Crown Chickens (Pty) Ltd t/a Rocklands Poultry v. Rieck* 2007 (2) SA 118 (SCA); and *see* generally D.J. McQuoid-Mason, *Vicarious and Strict Liability*, 30 LAWSA, §255 (2002).
997. *Gifford v. Table Bay Dock and Breakwater Management Commission* (1874) 4 Buch 96.
998. D.J. McQuoid-Mason, *Vicarious and Strict Liability*, 30 LAWSA, §257 (2002).
999. *Botesv. Van Deventer* 1966 (3) SA 182 (A) 205.

alium facit per se.[1000] A further policy consideration is that employers are the best 'risk-absorbers' because they can distribute the risk of accidents cost-effectively by insurance and take precautionary measures by resource allocation or incentive devices tailored to their type of enterprise.[1001] Consequently, an employer who is liable as a result of a delict committed by an employee is bound *in solidum* with the employee to compensate the person who suffers damage as a result of the employee's delict.[1002]

II. Who Qualifies as an Employee?

445. The employment relationship or contract of service (*locatio conduction operarum*) and the contract of mandate or services (*locatio conductio operis*) are often regarded as distinguishable for purposes of vicarious liability in that the employee is subject to the control of the employer in respect of the nature of the work and the manner in which it is to be done, whereas the mandatory or independent contractor is not subject to the control of the person paying for the services.[1003] The current approach is to regard the right to exercise control and direction over the employee as merely one of the indicia of an employment relationship.[1004] A multifaceted test is applied,[1005] taking into account all the circumstances, such as the nature of the work, the manner of payment, dismissal, the manner of performing the work;, state of social and economic interdependence, authority to give instructions, membership of medical or pension fund, paid vacation, working hours, use of employer's premises and equipment, whether the work and the person performing it form an integral part of the business organization.[1006] Employees are subordinate to the control or directives of their employers, and service is terminated by death or on expiration of the agreed period. The mandatory or independent contractor, however, contracts to perform certain specified work and is ordinarily not subject to the directives of the employer. The employer is thus liable for the acts of independent contractor only in respect of operations where the duty of care towards third parties is regarded as non-delegable, such as when they involve an abnormal level of danger.[1007]

1000. D.J. McQuoid-Mason, *Vicarious and Strict Liability*, 30 LAWSA, §253 (2002).
1001. *See* Zweigert & Kötz, *Comparative Law*, 643–645.
1002. D.J. McQuoid-Mason, *Vicarious and Strict Liability*, 30 LAWSA, § 257 (2002).
1003. *Smit v. Workmen's Compensation Commissioner* 1979 (1) SA 51 (A) 61.
1004. *Smit v. Workmen's Compensation Commissioner* 1979 (1) SA 51 (A) 62.
1005. *Midway Two Engineering & Construction Services v. Transnet Bpk* 1998 (3) SA 17 (SCA) 23; *Stein v. Rising Tide Productions CC* 2002 (5) SA 199 (C).
1006. *Smit v. Workmen's Compensation Commissioner* 1979 (1) SA 51 (A) 62; *Gibbins v. Williams, Muller, Wright & Mostert Ingelyf* 1987 (2) SA 82 (T) 90.
1007. *Langley Fox Building Partnership (Pty) Ltd v. De Valence* 1991 (1) SA (A) 11.

III. Employment and Akin-to-Employment Relationships

446. Vicarious liability arises from all kinds of employment relationships, including those involving skilled or professional employees who act with a large measure of independence, such as medical doctors.[1008] Spouses and parents are generally not vicariously liable for delicts of the other spouse[1009] or a child,[1010] unless the spouse or the child was acting as employee or agent.[1011]

447. Individual members of a partnership are jointly and severally liable to a person other than a partner for any delict committed by a partner acting in the course of the partnership business or with the authority of his co-partners.[1012] For the purposes of vicarious liability, therefore, it is not his capacity as a partner but the capacity in which he acts for the partnership which is important.[1013]

448. As a general rule, a principal is not liable for the unauthorized acts of his agent even though the act was ancillary to the carrying out of his mandate,[1014] unless the agent was acting in his capacity as agent and within the scope of his actual or ostensible authority;[1015] or the agent was also an employee and acting within the course and scope of his employment.[1016]

449. It is recognized in South African law that the owner of a motor vehicle who allows another person to drive may be vicariously liable for the latter's negligent driving if the vehicle is being driven in his interest;[1017] and the relationship between the owner and the driver is such that the owner retains the right to control the manner in which the vehicle is driven. In the leading case, *Messina Associated Carriers v. Kleinhaus*,[1018] it was held that the true inquiry is whether the relationship between

1008. *See*, for example, *Esterhuizen v. Administrator Tvl* 1957 (3) SA 710 (T).
1009. *Oberholzer v. Oberholzer* 1947 (3) SA 294 (O) 297; *Van Schalkwyk v. Fölscher* 1974 (4) SA 967 (NC) 968; *Grove v. Ellis* 1977 (3) SA 388 (C) 390; *Erikson Motors (Welkom) Ltd v. Scholtz* 1960 (4) SA 791 (O) 795; *Opperman v. Opperman* 1962 (3) SA 40 (N) 45; *Hamman v. South West African People's Organization* 1991 (1) SA 127 (SWA) 139.
1010. *De Beer v. Sergeant* 1976 (1) SA 246 (T) 251; cf. *R v. Magundeane* 1940 SR 169 170; *Hamman v. South West African People's Organization*1991 (1) SA 127 (SWA).
1011. *Mkize v. Martins* 1914 AD 382.
1012. *Holland v. Simenhoff* 1923 AD 676 679; *Rodrigues v. Alves* 1978 (4) SA 834 (A) 842 ff.; *Lindsay v. Stofberg* 1988 (2) SA 462 (C) 467.
1013. *Rodrigues v. Alves* 1978 (4) SA 834 (A) 839.
1014. *Eksteen v. Van Schalkwyk* 1991 (2) SA 39 (T) 45 ff.
1015. *Colonial Mutual Life Assurance Society Ltd v. Macdonald* 1931 AD 412 442.
1016. *Eksteen v. Van Schalkwyk* 1991 (2) SA 39 (T) 45.
1017. In *Roman v. Pietersen* 1990 (3) SA 350 (C) it was held that the owner-interest requirement is satisfied even if a limited interest of a social nature is involved.
1018. 2001 (3) SA 868 (SCA).

the owner and the driver and the interest of the owner in the driving of the vehicle is sufficiently analogous to the situation of an employee driving in the course of and within the scope of employment.[1019]

IV. Employee of Two Employers

450. A person who is in the general employment of one employer may temporarily become the employee of another for the purposes of vicarious liability, typically where an employee is lent or hired by one employer to another. In the leading South African case of *Midway Two Engineering & Construction Services v. Transnet*,[1020] a lorry driver was engaged through a labour broker as a temporary employee to a temporary employer. Since the temporary employer was regarded as most closely associated with the risk-creating event, it was found to be vicariously liable. The fact that the agreement between the two employers labelled the driver as the employee of the labour broker was therefore not decisive.

451. The onus is on the general employer to show that, in the circumstances, it has deprived itself of control over its employee. The principle is that the general employer retains responsibility unless it can establish that the effect of the transfer was to constitute its employee pro hac vice as the employee of another.[1021]

V. Course and Scope of Employment

452. Generally, an employer is liable for any wrongful act done by employees while acting in the course and within the scope of their employment.[1022] Broadly speaking, employees act in the course of their employment when they are carrying out acts authorized by the employer or tasks authorized by the employer but by means of an unauthorized method.[1023] There is no liability when the employee has been carrying out tasks wholly unauthorized by the employer.[1024]

1019. The manager of a business which is the owner of a vehicle, or the agent of the owner of a vehicle, is not vicariously liable for a elict of a person to whom that manager or agent gives instructions on behalf of the employer of that person or the owner of the vehicle; *see H. Mohammed & Associates v. Buyeye* 2005 (3) SA 122 (C).

1020. 1998 (3) SA 17 (SCA). At 23 the court refers to the English case of *Mersey Docks and Harbour Board v.Coggins & Griffith (Liverpool) Ltd* [1947] AC 1 as authority in this regard.

1021. *Midway Two Engineering & Construction Services v. Transnet* 1998 (3) SA 17 (SCA) 23.

1022. *Crown Chickens (Pty) Ltd t/a Rocklands Poultry v. Rieck* 2007 (2) SA 118 (SCA).

1023. *See*, for example, *Costa da Oura Restaurant (Pty) Ltd t/a Umdloti Bush Tavern v. Reddy* 2003 (4) SA 34 (SCA). Vicarious liability was not imposed where an employee assaulted a restaurant customer outside the establishment, after the employee had abandoned his duties. It was regarded as a personal act of aggression, not done in furtherance of the employer's interests or under his express or implied authority; and the assault was not incidental to or in consequence of anything the employee was employed to do.

1024. In *Bezuidenhout NO v. Eskom* 2003 (3) SA 83 (SCA), it was held that an employee's conduct in transporting a passenger in contravention of an express prohibition was not performed in the course and within the scope of his employment. The employer had expressly forbidden the employee from carrying unauthorized passengers and had thus placed a limitation on the scope of

453. The 'standard test' for application of the general principle was set out in *Minister of Police v. Rabie*,[1025] where it was stated that an employer may be liable even if the employee acted solely for his or her own interests and purposes in a situation occasioned by his or her employment. The test is both subjective, in that the employee's intention is taken into account, and objective, in that the existence of a sufficiently close link between the employee's act for his or her own purposes and the business of his or her employer may render the employer vicariously liable. An employer is liable for acts which it did not authorize, provided such acts are so connected with acts that it did authorize that they may rightly be regarded as modes – although improper modes – of doing authorized acts. If the employee's act falls outside the work or particular class of work that he or she is employed to do, the employer is not liable.

454. The difficulty in the case law has often been to distinguish between:

(a) an unauthorized mode of carrying out authorized work (where the employer is liable);
(b) unauthorized conduct falling outside the employee's work (where the employer is not liable); and
(c) conduct involving the employer's time or equipment but aimed solely at furthering the employee's interests (a frolic of the employee's own, not rendering the employer liable; there is no vicarious liability where the employee is engaged in his personal affairs, divorced from his employment).[1026]

If an employee for his own purposes deviates from his employer's business, it is a question of degree whether the digression is so great in terms of space or time that it cannot reasonably be held that he is still acting within the course and scope of his employment. Thus an employer has been held liable where his employee caused damage while smoking on duty, notably in *Viljoen v. Smith.*[1027] Similarly, in *Feldman (Pty) Ltd v. Mall,*[1028] where a delivery vehicle was used to deliver parcels and the driver deviated to go for drinks and then negligently caused an accident while returning to work, the employer was held liable. But in *Carter & Co. (Pty) Ltd v. McDonald,*[1029] where the employee collided with a pedestrian while cycling to the

---

employment. It was not merely an instruction as to manner of performing the employer's business. Having regard to all relevant circumstances, it was unfair to hold the employer liable to a passenger who had in effect assumed the risk of association with the forbidden conduct of an employee. Also, in terms of both the subjective state of mind of employee and the objective test of a sufficiently close link between the employee's acts for his own purposes and the business of the employer, vicarious liability should not be imposed.

1025. 1986 (1) SA 117 (A), 134.

1026. *Sizani v. Minister of Police* 1980 (3) SA 1205 (SECL) 1210; *Witham v. Minister of Home Affairs* 1989 (1) SA 116 (ZH) 125; *Minister van Wet en Orde v. Wilson* 1992 (3) SA 920 (A) 927 ff.; *Minister of Law and Order v. Ngobo* 1992 (4) SA 822 (A) 828; *Costa da Oura Restaurant (Pty) Ltd t/a Umdloti Bush Tavern v. Reddy* 2003 (4) SA 34 (SCA).

1027. 1997 (1) SA 309 (A). An employee climbed through a fence on to neighbouring property to relieve himself during working hours, and negligently started a fire when smoking there.

1028. 1945 AD 733.

1029. 1955 (1) SA 202 (A).

market for his own purposes during working hours, it was held that the employee acted in his own interests, and the employer was therefore not liable. The employer does not necessarily escape liability because the harmful conduct of the employee was expressly prohibited, but this will depend on all the circumstances.[1030]

VI. Intentional Wrongdoing

455. It is a vexing question when an intentional wrong can be said to have been undertaken in the course of employment. In Salmond's often-cited formulation, vicarious liability arises when the employee has done 'fraudulently that which he was authorized to do honestly', but not when the employee's conduct was insufficiently 'connected with the authorized act as to be a mode of doing it'.[1031] This distinction hinges upon a close scrutiny of the employee's authorized functions, resolving often into a question of 'degree'.[1032] Particular problems arise where employees perform professional services, work independently and exercise discretion. In such cases, it is not always possible to delineate their duties exactly. Nevertheless, the notion of fraudulent or improper performance of authorized duties has often been applied by the courts.

456. In *Ess Kay Electronics (Pty) Ltd v. First National Bank of Southern Africa Ltd*,[1033] for example, a bank was found not to be liable when one of its employees misappropriated blank bank drafts. The employee's work had in fact included the control and administration of the bank's foreign exchange department, but the court ruled that there was no liability because the employee had been promoting his own interests to the exclusion of the bank's, and in acting wrongfully he had effectively disengaged himself from his appointed functions. The court in that case rejected the plaintiff's argument that there was a sufficiently close link between the unauthorized and wrongful acts of the employee and the work he was authorized to do. Although the employee exploited opportunities offered by his employment, his self-interested purpose in doing so removed his conduct from the category of authorized actions.

457. A similar situation occurred in *Absa Bank v. Bond Equipment Pretoria) (Pty) Ltd*,[1034] where cheques payable to the employer were paid into a bank account operated by the employee. Despite the fact that it was the employee's duty to collect and deposit cheques for his employer, the court ruled that in stealing the cheques for himself he could not be said to be performing his duties at all: he was on a frolic of his own.

1030. *See Bezuidenhout NO v. Eskom* 2003 (3) SA 83 (SCA), where it was held that an employee's conduct in transporting a passenger in contravention of an express prohibition was not performed in the course and within the scope of his employment.
1031. *Salmond and Heuston on the Law of Torts* 443 (21st ed., R.F.V. Heuston & R.A. Buckley eds., Sweet & Maxwell Ltd 1996).
1032. *Feldman (Pty) Ltd v. Mall* 1945 AD 733, 756 per Tindall JA.
1033. 2001 (1) SA 1214 (SCA).
1034. 2001 (1) SA 372 (SCA).

458. Clearly intentional wrongdoing does not always remove the employee from the scope of his or her employment, as illustrated by cases on State liability for police transgressions.[1035] The State (like other employers) can in certain circumstances be liable for intentional misconduct of its employees. In the case of policemen, the approach of the courts has been to establish whether there is some connection between their misconduct and the carrying out of police duties.[1036]

459. The Constitutional Court has considered whether the common law principles on vicarious liability conform to the spirit, purport and objects of the Bill of Rights, as intended in section 39(2) of the Constitution.[1037] The court held that both the principles of vicarious liability and their application must conform to the normative framework of the Constitution. On the issue whether the State should be liable for rape committed by police officers while on duty, the court found the principles of vicarious liability to be consistent with the constitutional norms. On application of the principles the court found that, subjectively viewed, the policemen acted in pursuit of their own objectives, but, objectively, their conduct was sufficiently linked to their employment as policemen, and the State was held liable.

460. In *Minister of Safety and Security v. Luiters*,[1038] both the Supreme Court of Appeal and the Constitutional Court decided that vicarious liability should be imposed on the State where an off-duty policeman pursued persons who had attempted to rob him and shot an innocent third party. A two-stage test was applied, namely:

(1) whether employee's acts were committed solely for the employee's purposes; and if so,
(2) whether there was sufficiently close link between employee's acts and employer's purposes and business.

It was held that in pursuing would-be robbers the policeman had acted in both his own interests and those of the police service. He intended to perform police duties. The fact that the policeman died not adhering to the rules of criminal procedure or police standing orders was no bar to liability.

1035. *Minister van Veiligheid en Sekuriteit v. Japmoco Bk* 2002 (5) SA 649 (SCA); *Minister van Veiligheid en Sekuriteit v. Phoebus Apollo Aviation Bk* 2002 (5) SA 475 (SCA).

1036. *Minister of Police v. Rabie* 1986 (1) SA 117 (A); *Minister van Veiligheid en Sekuriteit v. Japmoco BK* 2002 (5) SA 649 (SCA); *Minister van Veiligheid en Sekuriteit v. Phoebus Apollo Aviation BK* 2002 (5) SA 475 (SCA) *Masuku and Another v. Mdlalose and Others* 1998 (1) SA 1 (SCA); *Smit v. Minister van Polisie* 1997 (4) SA 893 (T); *K v. Minister of Safety and Security* 2005 (6) SA 419 (CC). In *Munengami v. Minister of Defence* 2007 (2) SA 320 (ZH) vicarious liability was not imposed where soldiers assaulted a civilian in pursuit of their own interests. The assault itself was not authorized and it did not constitute an unlawful execution of an authorized act.

1037. *K v. Minister of Safety and Security* 2005 (6) SA 419 (CC).

1038. 2006 (4) SA 160 (SCA); 2007 (2) SA 106 (CC).

461. In *Minister of Finance and Others v. Gore NO*,[1039] vicarious liability was imposed on the State for the conduct of public officials who fraudulently awarded a government tender. It was held that the conduct of the officials closely resembling duties performed in the course and within the scope of their employment. There was a sufficiently close link between their conduct and their employment, and policy considerations supported the imposition of vicarious liability for fraud.

462. In the Constitutional Court case of *K v. Minister of Safety and Security*,[1040] O'Regan J referred in her judgment[1041] to the English case of *Lister v. Hesley Hall Ltd*,[1042] where the House of Lords extensively reviewed the law on vicarious liability for intentional wrongdoing. The defendants in that case ran a school boarding house for children with emotional and behavioural difficulties. Following the conviction of the house warden on charges of having sexually abused some of the children, a group of former residents brought a claim against the company which ran the boarding house as vicariously liable for his wrongful conduct. The House of Lords held the company liable. It viewed the Salmond formulation simply as a 'broad test', not a 'precise proposition', and focused on a later passage by Salmond in which the employer is said to be liable when the employee's actions 'are so connected with acts which he has authorized that they may rightly be regarded as modes – although improper modes – of doing them'.[1043] Noting that absurdities could result from 'a preoccupation with conceptualistic reasoning',[1044] it adopted a broad approach in which 'it becomes inappropriate to concentrate too closely upon the particular act complained of', or indeed 'the purpose and the nature of the act'.[1045] The central factor was 'whether the warden's torts were so closely connected with his employment that it would be fair and just to hold the employers vicariously liable'.[1046] Applying this test, the court was satisfied that his sexual abuse of the children was closely and directly connected with the warden's performance of his duties at the school boarding house.

463. In *Minister of Safety and Security v. F*,[1047] the plaintiff, F, found herself stranded late at night, and an off-duty policeman offered to drive her home, using a police vehicle. Instead, he drove to a remote spot where he raped her. The important distinction between this case and the *K* case is that on this occasion the policeman was off-duty and for this reason the Supreme Court of Appeal held that this case fails the test for vicarious liability that was articulated in *K*. On appeal, the

1039. 2007 (1) SA 111 (SCA).
1040. 2005 (6) SA 419 (CC).
1041. *K v. Minister of Safety and Security* 2005 (6) SA 419 (CC) at 438.
1042. [2002] 1 AC 215.
1043. *Salmond and Heuston on the Law of Torts* (21st ed., R.F.V. Heuston & R.A. Buckley eds., Sweet & Maxwell Ltd 1996) 443.
1044. [2002] 1 AC 215, para. 16 per Lord Steyn.
1045. *Ibid.*, at para. 43 per Lord Clyde.
1046. *Ibid.*, at para. 28 per Lord Steyn.
1047. [2011] ZASCA 3.

Constitutional Court overturned the decision.[1048] Mogoeng J, who wrote the majority judgment, found that there was a sufficiently close link between the policeman's employment and F's assault and rape: the police vehicle facilitated the commission of the rape; F placed her trust in the policeman because he was a police official; and the State has a constitutional obligation to protect the public against crime. Consequently, the minister was held vicariously liable for the harm that F had suffered.

Froneman J, in a separate concurring judgment, agreed with the outcome, but found that the minister's liability was direct rather than vicarious, because the actions of the State officials are in effect the State's own actions, and the normative considerations for determining liability may be appropriately assessed as part of the wrongfulness inquiry.

In their minority judgment, Yacoob and Jafta JJ applied the same test as the majority but concluded that there was not a sufficient link between the delict and the employment of the policeman concerned: the policeman's criminal conduct was too far removed in space and time from his employment to render the use of the police vehicle and the presence of police dockets in vehicle sufficient to establish vicarious liability, even if due regard was had to the victim's vulnerability and age.

In *Minister of Safety and Security v. Booysen*[1049] a policeman, while on duty and in uniform, was dropped by a police vehicle at the home of his girlfriend and dined with her and her family. Later she and he sat outside together. There he drew his service pistol and shot her in the face, before turning the gun on himself, fatally. His girlfriend later sued the Minister of Safety and Security, asserting that the minister should be vicariously liable for the harm caused to her. The majority of the Supreme Court of Appeal decided that that there was an insufficiently close link between the policeman's act and his employment for vicarious liability to be imposed. On appeal the Constitutional Court decided that the case was purely about the application of the accepted test for vicarious liability, in particular about the weight to be attached to the different factors in the test. The case was not about the development of the test, which was a constitutional matter; and accordingly the Constitutional Court had no jurisdiction.[1050]

464. The measure of a 'close and direct connection' depends on a diverse range of subsidiary criteria, including the nature of the relationship between the employer and an injured third party. An employer who has assumed responsibility with regard to the plaintiff's person or possessions owes to the plaintiff duties which are more extensive than those owed by the public at large. The fact of a pre-existing relationship between the employer and the injured third party has been an important factor in some cases. Where employees have misappropriated goods entrusted to their care by their employers, the employers are generally held accountable for such wrongdoing, and in this regard the courts often take into account the employer's pre-existing duty to the owner of the goods.[1051]

1048. [2011] ZACC 37.
1049. [2016] ZASCA 201.
1050. *Booysen v. Minister of Safety and Security* 2018 (6) SA 1 (CC).
1051. *See* for example the Scottish case of *Central Motors (Glasgow) Ltd v. Cessnock Garage and Motor Co.* 1925 SLT 563 in which the court held that the employer had a personal duty to look

The same considerations apply with regard to employers entrusted with investments, and can explain the distinction between *Ess Kay Electronics (Pty) Ltd v. First National Bank of Southern Africa Ltd*[1052] and similar cases where the employer escaped liability, and *Greater Johannesburg Transitional Metropolitan Council v. Absa Bank*,[1053] where it did not. In both cases, the employee had caused loss to a third party by intentional doing which was patently for the employee's own ends. But in the former case, the employee bank had no prior connection with the third parties, and there was no duty to the world at large to prevent the loss of the bank's draft forms. In the latter, however, the employee bank was held liable when one of its employees appropriated unendorsed cheques (payable to the plaintiff and deposited with the bank for collection) and transferred the proceeds to her own account. In this case, it is arguable that the bank's role as collecting bank placed it under a specific obligation to the plaintiff to ensure that unendorsed cheques were credited to the correct account. It may be that the employer's liability in such circumstances is implicitly based on a primary, non-delegable duty to the injured person. However, the courts in South Africa have not expressly adopted this line of reasoning.

465. The South African courts follow a multifaceted approach based on the policy considerations underlying vicarious liability. Among these policy considerations is the question whether the employer in the circumstances is best able to and should equitably be the 'risk-absorber'. Many of the subsidiary factors determining the closeness of the connection between the harmful conduct and the employment are not in themselves decisive, such as the time and place of the act; the use of the employer's property or equipment by the employee; the extent to which the employer had authorized or prohibited the employee's conduct; and the extent to which the respective interests of employer and employee were served by the harmful act. However, the relationship between the employer and a third party may be of crucial importance: did a pre-existing relationship between the employer and the injured party create reliance on safety or security, and did the employee's wrongdoing constitute the realization of a risk created by the employer by entrusting the work to the employee?

§2. Independent Contractors

466. Generally in South African law, the employer of an independent contractor is not vicariously responsible for the wrongful acts of such a contractor,[1054] because

---

after a car left in its garage for safekeeping. Parallels are drawn in that case with the law of agency. The English cases of *Lloyd v. Grace, Smith & Co.*[1912] AC 716; *Morris v. CW Martin & Sons Ltd* [1966] 1 QB 716) were referred to in the South African case *Absa Bank v. Bond Equipment (Pretoria) (Pty) Ltd* 2001 (1) SA 372 (SCA).

1052. 2001 (1) SA 1214 (SCA).

1053. 1997 (2) SA 591 (W).

1054. *See* generally *Colonial Mutual Life Assurance Society Ltd v. Macdonald*; *Auto Protection Insurance Co. Ltd v. Macdonald (Pty) Ltd* 1962 (1) SA 793 (A) 799; *Smit v. Workmen's Compensation Commissioner* 1979 (1) SA 51 (A) 61; *Langley Fox Building Partnership (Pty) Ltd v. De Valence* 1991 (1) SA 1 (A).

the independent contractor undertakes to carry out a specific piece of work (*locatio conductio operis*)[1055] and is not normally subject to the control[1056] or directions of his employer in the performance of the work.[1057] Vicarious liability cannot be avoided by stating in a contract that a person is appointed as an independent contractor, if the relationship is in fact that of ordinary employment.[1058] The liability of an employer for harm done by an independent contractor is determined by the ordinary rule that a person must exercise the degree of care demanded by the circumstances.[1059] This will, for instance, require consideration of the nature and extent of the danger; the degree of expertise available to the employer and the independent contractor respectively; and the reasonably practicable means available to the employer to avert the danger.[1060] With regard to the liability of the owner of a building for damage caused when a building contractor left a temporary beam extending over a pavement, Goldstone AJA said the following in *Langley Fox Building Partnership (Pty) Ltd v. De Valence*:[1061]

> In my opinion, it follows from the aforegoing that in a case such as the present, there are three broad questions which must be asked, viz:
>
> 1. would a reasonable man have foreseen the risk of danger in consequence of the work he employed the contractor to perform? If so,
> 2. would a reasonable man have taken steps to guard against the danger? If so,
> 3. were such steps duly taken in the case in question?
>
> Only where the answer to the first two questions is in the affirmative does a legal duty arise, the failure to comply with which can form the basis of liability.

467. In *Chartaprops 16 (Pty) Ltd v. Silberman*,[1062] the plaintiff, Mrs Silberman, slipped and fell in one of the passageways of a shopping mall, where there was a pool of a slippery substance that had been spilt on the floor. The shopping mall was owned by, and under the control of Chartaprops, which had engaged a contractor, Advanced Cleaning, to keep the floors of the mall clean. Advanced Cleaning had a

1055. *Colonial Mutual Life Assurance Society Ltd v. Macdonald*; *Auto Protection Insurance Co. Ltd v. Macdonald (Pty) Ltd* 1962 (1) SA 793 (A) 799; *Smit v. Workmen's Compensation Commissioner* 1979 (1) SA 51 (A) 61; *Stein v. Rising Tide Productions CC* 2002 (5) SA 199 (C).
1056. The issue of control is not decisive, as pointed out in *Mtetwa v. Minister of Health* 1989 (3) SA 600 (D) 605; 'The deciding factor is the intention of the parties to the contract, which is to be gathered from a variety of facts and factors. Control is merely one of the indicia to determine whether or not a person is a servant or an independent contractor.'
1057. *Colonial Mutual Life Assurance Society Ltd v. Macdonald* 1931 AD 412 433; *Dukes v. Marthinusen* 1937 AD 12 17 23; *Munarin v. Peri-Urban Areas Health Board* 1965 (1) SA 545 (A) 549; *Smit v. Workmen's Compensation Commissioner* 1979 (1) SA 51 (A) 61; *Stein v. Rising Tide Productions CC* 2002 (5) SA 199 (C).
1058. *Goldberg v. Durban City Council* 1970 (3) SA 325 (N) 331.
1059. *Langley Fox Building Partnership (Pty) Ltd v. De Valence* 1991 (1) SA 1 (A) 11.
1060. *Langley Fox Building Partnership (Pty) Ltd v. De Valence* 1991 (1) SA 1 (A) 13.
1061. 1991 (1) SA 1 (A) 12H-J.
1062. 2009 (1) 265 (SCA).

system in place for cleaning the floors, so that every part of the floor should ordinarily have been passed over by one or other of their cleaners at intervals of no more than five minutes. Chartaprops itself regularly checked the contractor's performance. Each morning, its centre manager met the cleaning supervisor and personally inspected the floors of the mall to ensure that they had been properly cleaned. If he encountered litter or spillage, he would arrange for its immediate removal. The trial court found that the substance had been on the floor for thirty minutes or more when the incident occurred.

Mrs Silberman sued both Chartaprops and Advanced Cleaning for damages. The questions were:

- Was the owner Chartaprops negligent?
- Was the independent contractor, Advanced Cleaning, negligent?
- If Advanced Cleaning was negligent, was Chartaprops vicariously liable as the employer of Advanced Cleaning, even if Chartaprops itself was not negligent?

The majority of the court held that the correct approach to determine the liability of a principal, such as Chartaprops, for the negligence of an independent contractor, such as Advanced Cleaning, is to apply the fundamental rule that obliges a person to exercise the degree of care that the circumstances demand. In this case, the court should not apply the general policy of the law that the economic cost of the wrong should be borne by the legal entity immediately responsible for it. It should not shift the economic cost of negligence from Advanced Cleaning, the independent contractor with primary responsibility, to Chartaprops, because of the legal fiction of a non-delegable duty of the owner-employer to ensure safety in the shopping mall. Most operations entrusted to an independent contractor by an owner-employer are capable of being sources of danger to others. If courts were to hold the owner-employer vicariously liable in all such cases, the distinction between 'employee' and 'independent contractor' will all but disappear.

This was plainly not a case where the court could say that Chartaprops negligently selected an independent contractor, that it interfered with the work, or that it authorized or ratified the wrong. The harm was caused solely by the act or omission of the independent contractor, Advanced Cleaning, or its employees. Chartaprops did not merely content itself with contracting Advanced Cleaning to perform the cleaning services. It did more. Its centre manager met the cleaning supervisor every morning and personally inspected the floors of the mall on a regular basis to ensure that they had been properly cleaned. Chartaprops did all that a reasonable person could do to make sure that the floors of the mall were safe. The duty to make sure that the premises were safe could not have been discharged better than by employing a competent contractor, as Chartaprops had done. Advanced Cleaning had a legal duty in delict to third parties, to ensure that the floors were clean and safe, and negligently failed to discharge that duty. Therefore, only Advanced Cleaning was held liable to Mrs Silberman.

468. The liability of the employer of independent contractor is therefore governed by the ordinary principles of negligence, and the question is whether the harm was reasonably foreseeable and preventable by the employer of the independent contractor. The employer is required to undertake reasonable monitoring of the work done by the contractor but is not held liable as if it performed the work itself.

§3. Liability of Legal Entities for Acts of Their Organs

469. A corporation is liable for delicts committed by its employees in the course and within the scope of their employment, according to the general principles governing vicarious liability.[1063] Therefore, where fraud is alleged on the part of a company employee or agent acting in the course and within the scope of employment, the state of mind and knowledge of the employee or agent is in issue, and not the state of mind or knowledge of the company itself or its senior management.[1064] Where fraud on the part of the company itself is alleged, the state of mind or knowledge of the company itself or its senior management will be in issue.[1065]

470. A hospital authority is vicariously liable for the delicts of its employees (doctors, nurses and other employees) acting in the course and within the scope of their employment.[1066] A hospital can be liable even though the particular conduct of its employee was prohibited or the employee acted intentionally.[1067]

1063. *British SA Co. v. Crickmore* 1921 AD 107 111 118; *Rhodes Motors (Pvt) Ltd v. Pringle-Wood* 1965 (4) SA 40 (SRA) 46; *Rhostar (Pvt) Ltd v. Netherlands Bank of Rhodesia Ltd* 1972 (2) SA 703 (R) 708; *Ensor v. Syfret's Trust and Executor Co. (Natal) Ltd* 1976 (3) SA 762 (D) 763; *Stainer v. Palmer-Pilgrim* 1982 (4) SA 205 (O) 211; *Hamman v. South West Africa People's Organization* 1991 (1) SA 127 (SWA) 139.

1064. *Ensor v. Syfret's Trust and Executor Co. (Natal) Ltd* 1976 (3) SA 762 (D) 766.

1065. *Anderson v. Dickson (Intermenua (Pty) Ltd intervening)* 1985 (1) SA 93 (N) 110; *Ex parte Minister van Justisie: in re S v. SA Uitsaaikorporasie* 1992 (4) SA 804 (A) 807 ff.

1066. *Esterhuizen v. Administrator Tvl* 1957 (3) SA 710 (T); *Dube v. Administrator Tvl* 1963 (4) SA 260 (W); *Mtetwa v. Minister of Health* 1989 (3) SA 600 (D).

1067. *Zungu v. Administrator Natal* 1971 (1) SA 284 (D).

Chapter 2. Liability for Other Persons, Things and Animals

471. Outside the scope of vicarious liability, dealt with in Part II Chapter 1 above, and strict liability for harm done by animals, dealt with in Part III below, liability for harm caused by other persons, things or animals is governed by general principles. The elements of conduct, causation, damage, unlawfulness and fault must be present for liability to be imposed. All these elements are dealt with separately elsewhere and do not require additional comment here. This chapter is intended to present material that is illustrative of the liability arising from a relationship of control over other persons, things or animals. A relationship of control over other persons, things or animals is particularly relevant to the determination of unlawfulness and negligence in cases where harm is done by such a person, thing or animal.

§1. Persons

472. Relationships of control that can give rise to delictual liability for the acts of other persons include the parent-child relationship; other relationships involving authority over persons; and the care or supervision of persons who constitute a danger to society.

473. The general principles concerning the responsibility of parents for the conduct of children were set out in *De Beer v. Sargeant.*[1068] There is no absolute or strict liability for a parent on account of the delict of a minor child. Liability can flow:

- from a relationship of employment when the damage is committed within the scope of the child's employment or where the child is an agent of the parent;[1069]
- where the child acts as the vicarious doer on behalf of the parent; and
- from negligence, where the parent was in a position to interfere and for inadequate reasons failed to do so.

It is not necessary that the parent should necessarily be present, because negligence can also lie in failure to prevent the child from foreseeably causing damage. Parents, guardians or teachers are therefore not vicariously liable for delicts of children, but parents, guardians or teachers entrusted with the care of children are in a relationship of control, and failure to exercise a reasonable measure of control in a situation where the child causes harm to another person will indicate unlawful and negligent causing of harm on the part of the parent, guardian or teacher. The cases referred to below illustrate potential liability in this regard.

1068. 1976 (1) SA 246 (T) 251. The case involved the allegedly negligent failure of a parent to foresee and prevent damage done by a child to a toy belonging to another person.
1069. *Mkize v. Martins* 1914 AD 382.

474. The duty of teachers and supervisors to exercise reasonable care implies that conditions on school premises or sports field should be safe, and children should be protected as far as reasonably possible from injuring each other. In *Knouwds v. Administrateur, Kaap*,[1070] an 8-year-old girl was injured on the school grounds when she fell onto a lawn mower. She and another girl were racing over a lawn where a caretaker was operating a lawn mower. The other girl pushed her to prevent her from passing, and she was injured when she stumbled and put her hand on the lawn mower to maintain her balance. The court found the caretaking and teaching staff negligent: they should have foreseen and guarded against the possibility that young children might collide with the lawn mower as used at that particular time and place.

475. Reasonable care should be exercised where young children participate in any sport involving the risk of injury to the child himself or to his fellow players. In *Broom and Another v. The Administrator, Natal*,[1071] a teacher allowed the boys to play a game of baseball or 'rounders' for physical exercise. A cricket stump, without a metal tip to it, was used by the batsmen. The boys awaiting their turn to bat stood in a queue, in an informal line to the rear of the batsman. The plaintiff was fourth in such queue and stood some nineteen to twenty feet away from the batsman. When the batsman hit the ball the stump left his hand, travelled through the air and struck the plaintiff's head just behind his right ear. The plaintiff, assisted by his father and natural guardian, sued for damages alleged to have been sustained through the negligence of the teacher. The court found that there was no negligence because injuries in 'rounders' occur very seldom and are normally not serious, and the use of a cricket stump without a metal tip to it did not in itself constitute negligence.

476. The supervisor or coach of children playing sport must take into account factors such as the danger of the activity, the size, age and maturity of the players and whether they are beginners, intermediate, or advanced players. The coach must have the ability to recognize and respond to danger.[1072] The degree of prudence and care required of a parent, guardian or teacher in supervising or controlling children engaged in sport or play is that of a reasonably prudent person.[1073] This standard involves no more than the reasonable standard of care required in other walks of life. Yet a child's tendency to act impulsively and disregard danger, or to become so engrossed in a particular activity as to be oblivious of danger, will be taken into account by the reasonably prudent person, who will therefore exercise a higher

1070. 1981 (1) SA 544 (C) 553.
1071. 1966 (3) SA 505 (D).
1072. *See* generally Kelly, *Prospective Liabilities of Sport Supervisors*, Australian L.J. 669, 671–672.
1073. *Broom & Another v. Administrator, Natal* 1966 (3) SA 505 (D) 518.

degree of foresight and care in respect of children.[1074] However, it is only reasonable supervision and care that is required, and it is not reasonable to require continuous supervision of children on a school playground. An injury may result from children running races against each other, pushing or shoving, because that is what playgrounds are for.[1075]

477. A parent who is the owner and in control of a firearm has a legal duty to take reasonable steps to prevent a child from getting hold of the firearm and causing harm to others.[1076] In *Wessels v. Pretorius*,[1077] it was held that the father of a 16-year-old boy was liable for in effect giving permission to his son to drive his motor vehicle, in circumstances where it was held to have been reasonably foreseeable that the son could drive irresponsibly and could cause injury to others.

478. In road accident cases, the courts have often emphasized that the driver of a vehicle must be on the lookout at all times where children are about, and to expect and be prepared to avoid the consequences of impulsive and irrational conduct by children of whose presence he is aware; and also where he should reasonably have expected the presence of children.[1078]

479. Other relationships involving authority or control can give rise to liability, if there is negligence on the part of the person in control. In *Saayman v. Visser*,[1079] a homeowner was held not to be liable for the shooting of a 16-year-old boy by a security guard stationed at the owner's premises, on the basis that the owner was not negligent in relying on the expertise of the security company for hiring and training personnel. In other cases, the conduct and responsibilities of the police feature prominently. The leading case in this regard is *Minister van Polisie v. Ewels*,[1080] where the State was held liable for the failure of a station commander to intervene and prevent an assault on the plaintiff by a junior police officer, which occurred in the police station. The court jettisoned the principle that liability for an omission can only be imposed where prior conduct of the defendant had created a risk of harm or a new source of danger, and the defendant then failed to prevent the harm from occurring. The position of authority and control of the station commander indicated a legal duty to take reasonable steps to prevent harm, and liability was imposed for the negligent failure to do so.

480. Other cases of State liability for harm done by offenders, based on the failure of the police to prevent such harm, have arisen from the control of the police over the issue or withdrawal of firearm licences. In *Minister of Safety and Security v. Van Duivenboden*,[1081] the police negligently failed to act on reports that the

1074. *Knouwds v. Administrateur, Kaap* 1981 (1) SA 544 (C) 553.
1075. *See* the English case of *Ward v. Hertfordshire County Council* [1969] 1 WLR 790.
1076. *See Maylett v. Du Toit* 1989 (1) SA 90 (T).
1077. [2008] 1 All SA 131 (SCA).
1078. *Santam Insurance Co. Ltd v. Nkosi* 1978 (2) SA 784 (A) 789.
1079. Case (411/07) [2008] ZASCA 71 (30 May 2008).
1080. 1975 (3) SA 590 (A).
1081. 2002 (6) SA 431 (SCA).

offender had repeatedly threatened others with a firearm in a state of drunkenness. The court held that the police had negligently failed in their legal duty to implement the procedure for withdrawal of the offender's firearm licence. In *Minister of Safety and Security v. Hamilton*,[1082] the court held that the police had negligently failed in their legal duty to conduct an inquiry into the fitness of a person to be issued with a firearm licence. The offender in this case had a history of mental instability. The leading case of *Carmichele v. Minister of Safety and Security and Another (Centre for Applied Legal Studies Intervening)*[1083] concerned the negligent failure by the police and prosecuting authorities to exercise their legal duties concerning the process of granting of bail and the release of a suspect. The plaintiff was the victim of a violent attack by a person with a prior conviction for violence, who was released on his own recognizance while awaiting trial on a new charge, also involving violence against women.

481. The control of the police and prison authorities over dangerous offenders in detention can give rise to liability for harm done by such an offender, following an escape. *Van Eeden v. Minister of Safety and Security (Women's Legal Centre Trust, as Amicus Curiae)*[1084] concerned the control that the police were required to exercise over a known dangerous criminal in police custody. The court held that the recognition of a legal duty in this case would neither disrupt the efficient functioning of the police, nor will it necessarily require additional resources or inhibit the proper performance by the police of their primary functions or lead to defensive policing. The court was satisfied that the imposition of liability on the State in this case would not open the floodgates of litigation and result in limitless liability on public authorities and functionaries, because the requirements for establishing negligence and causation provide sufficient practical scope for limiting liability.

482. The cases referred to above are illustrative of the liability arising from a relationship of control over other persons, according to general principles of delictual liability, where the relationship of control is particularly relevant to the determination of unlawfulness and negligence.

§2. THINGS

483. The control over things that are dangerous by themselves, or dangerous in particular circumstances, can give rise to liability. Liability is not strict, but is governed by the general principles of delictual liability. These cases mostly concern the legal duty to prevent harm by guarding against consequences that are reasonably foreseeable and preventable. The cases referred to below are illustrative.

1082. 2004 (2) SA 216 (SCA).
1083. 2001 (4) SA 938 (CC).
1084. 2002 (4) SA 346 (SCA).

484. The owner, occupier or person in control of property generally has a duty to control fire on the property[1085] and to prevent injury to persons, even trespassers on the property;[1086] and the same applies to the owner or person in control of a fire-arm.[1087]

485. If the question is whether a local authority is liable for harm caused by or related to public property, such as a pedestrian's injury resulting from a hole in a pavement,[1088] or a child's injury on a broken merry-go-round,[1089] or a shop-owner's loss through flooding from a burst pipe,[1090] or a landowner's losses resulting from the establishment of an informal settlement adjacent to his land,[1091] the unlawfulness and the negligence issues both involve consideration of the extent of the risk and of the possible harm, the cost of repair or prevention and the resources available to the local authority. If the pavement, merry-go-round, pipe or settlement was under the control of the local authority, with concomitant responsibility to maintain or administer it, the existence of a legal duty not to cause harm (unlawfulness) will generally not be contentious. The fact that a provincial administration exercises control and supervision over all public roads in the province in terms of a statutory provision is an important factor in determining whether the administration had a legal duty to prevent the spreading of a fire that had started on the side of a minor public road.[1092] However, liability will not be imposed if the local authority was unaware of the state of disrepair and could not reasonably have foreseen it, perhaps owing to the informational and organizational constraints under which it operates, or if preventative measures would be costly out of all proportion to the harm. In these circumstances the court may find, either that there is no legal duty to prevent the particular kind of harm, or that the failure to repair or to prevent harm will not be negligent.

486. If the issue is essentially whether the public authority had the duty to exercise control, rather than the extent of the control or preventative measures required, it is more likely to be treated as an issue of unlawfulness than an issue of negligence.[1093] The degree and scope of the control that is required cannot be laid down generally, but should be determined on the basis of all the facts of the particular case

1085. *Minister of Forestry v. Quathlamba (Pty) Ltd* 1973 (3) SA 69 (A); *Dews v. Simon's Town Municipality* 1991 (4) SA 479 (C) 485; *Steenberg v. De Kaap Timber (Pty) Ltd* 1992 (2) SA 169 (A); *Gouda Boerdery BK v. Transnet* 2005 (5) SA 490 (SCA); *Minister of Water Affairs and Forestry and Others v. Durr and Others* 2006 (6) SA 587 (SCA).

1086. *See Kritzinger v. Steyn* 1997 (3) SA 686 (C), where it was held that an owner does not generally have a duty towards trespassers, whose presence are not reasonably foreseeable.

1087. *Maylett v. Du Toit* 1989 (1) SA 90 (T).

1088. *Cape Town Municipality v. Bakkerud* 2000 (3) SA 1049 (SCA).

1089. *Cape Town Municipality v. April* 1982 (1) SA 259 (C).

1090. *Mostert v. Cape Town City Council* 2001 (1) SA 105 (SCA).

1091. *Local Transitional Council of Delmas and Another v. Boshoff* 2005 (5) SA 514 (SCA).

1092. *Administrateur Transvaal v. Van der Merwe* 1994 (4) SA 347 (A).

1093. *See Administrateur Transvaal v. Van der Merwe* 1994 (4) SA 347 (A) 349, where it was held that, in the absence of a positive danger-creating act, a provincial authority did not have a legal duty to control a fire that started alongside a minor road. In *Local Transitional Council of Delmas and Another v. Boshoff* 2005 (5) SA 514 (SCA), the court accepted that a local authority with control over an informal settlement adjacent to the plaintiff's land had a legal duty towards the owner of

and with reference to the harm that occurred. The essential question is whether precautionary measures could be reasonably and practicably required of the person or body in control in respect of the harm that occurred.[1094]

§3. Animals

487. The control over animals that are dangerous by themselves, or dangerous in particular circumstances, can give rise to liability, according to the general principles of delictual liability. Liability for harm done by animals can also be strict (without fault), under certain conditions, as set out in Part III below.

488. Fault-based liability for harm done by animals mostly concern negligence on the part of the owner, in failing to guard against harmful consequences that are reasonably foreseeable and preventable. The cases referred to below are illustrative.

489. A number of cases deal with the presence of animals on roads,[1095] where the issues were typical of fault-based liability of owners for harm done by animals.[1096]

490. In *Kruger v. Coetzee*,[1097] Holmes JA said the following on the responsibility of an owner, in respect of horses which had wandered onto a road, causing an accident:

> As to the existence of a duty to take reasonable steps to guard against such an occurrence, these were the defendant's horses and it was he who was grazing them in the camp; and, although the gate was being left open by persons over whom he had no control, he was aware of this fact and continued to graze his horses there, conscious of the potential danger to motorists. In these circumstances, a diligens paterfamilias in the position of the defendant would not have shrugged his shoulders in unconcern; if there were reasonable precautionary steps which could have been taken, he would have taken them.

491. In *Botes v. Van Deventer*,[1098] a public road ran through a paddock of the plaintiff's farm. The paddock was fenced but the public road was not fenced off. In the fence of the paddock, there was an opening for a gate but there was no gate.

---

the adjacent land and could not claim immunity from liability for his losses, but the nature and extent of the preventative steps required of the local authority was a question of negligence.

1094. *Administrateur Transvaal v. Van der Merwe* 1994 (4) SA 347 (A) 359–360; *Faiga v. Body Corporate of Dumbarton Oaks* 1997 (2) SA 651 (W) 665; *Kritzinger v. Steyn* 1997 (3) SA 686 (C).

1095. *See*, for example, *Kruger v. Coetzee* 1966 (2) SA 428 (A); *Botes v. Van Deventer* 1966 (3) SA 182 (A); *Mkhwanazi v. Van der Walt* 1995 (4) SA 589 (A); *Jordaan v. Krone Broers* 1999 (3) All SA 57 (C).

1096. *See also* generally in respect of the control of animals *Bristow v. Lycett* 1971 (4) SA 223 (RA); *Zietsman v. Van Tonder* 1989 (2) SA 484 (T).

1097. 1966 (2) SA 428 (A) 431D.

1098. 1966 (3) SA 182 (A).

The plaintiff had allowed his stud race horses to run in this paddock, and early one morning, while it was still dark, near the opening for the gate, a heavy lorry belonging to the defendant and driven by his employee collided with the horses, causing severe injuries to three of them, with the result that they had to be destroyed. The collision occurred although the road was straight and open. The court found that the driver had been negligent, but that the plaintiff had also been negligent in that he had allowed valuable stud horses to be let loose in the paddock at night.

492. The case of *Mkhwanazi v. Van der Walt*[1099] concerned a claim for damages arising from a collision between a minibus and horses on a national road. The horses had strayed through farm gates, left open by visitors to farm, onto the national road. The question was whether the farmer's precaution of chaining the gates between the grazing camp and the road was sufficient. The leaving open of the farm gates by persons passing through was an everyday occurrence, and therefore reasonably foreseeable. A reasonable person would in the circumstances have taken additional precautions, such as padlocking the gates or erecting a grid at the gates. Taking into account the respective interests of the farmer and motorists, such precautions were so simple and inexpensive that any reasonable person would have taken one of them. The farmer's failure to take additional precautions was therefore negligent.

493. A number of cases deal with kept wild animals.[1100] In *Zietsman v. Van Tonder*,[1101] for example, the plaintiff claimed damages for injuries sustained when a wildebeest attacked him on the defendant's game farm. After entering the farm at the main entrance the plaintiff drove to the office, which was in an area protected by game-proof fencing and a gateway with a grid of pipes spanning it. Inside the area, the plaintiff got out of the motor car to use the toilets situated in a fenced area. On his way back to the vehicle, he was attacked and injured by a wildebeest. The court held that the defendant was negligent in failing to take measures to prevent dangerous animals from entering the fenced area. The defendant should reasonably have foreseen the possibility that a person in the fenced area could be injured by animals, in particular because the owner had knowledge that animals had previously been found inside the fenced area.

494. The cases referred to above are illustrative of fault-based liability arising from ownership of and control over animals, according to general principles of delictual liability, with negligence mostly the primary issue.

1099. 1995 (4) SA 589 (A).
1100. *See*, for example, *Bristow v. Lycett* 1971 (4) SA 223 (RA); *Zietsman v. Van Tonder* 1989 (2) SA 484 (T).
1101. 1989 (2) SA 484 (T).

Part III. Forms of Strict Liability

Chapter 1. Road and Traffic Accidents

495. Liability for damage caused in road and traffic accidents is generally fault-based, and the determination of negligence in road and traffic situations has given rise to an extensive body of case law.[1102]

§1. Strict Liability of Owner

496. The only form of strict liability that is recognized in the context of road and traffic accidents is that of the owner of a motor vehicle who allows another person to drive the vehicle. The owner is then vicariously liable for the latter's negligent driving if the vehicle is being driven in his interest;[1103] and the relationship between the owner and the driver is such that the owner retains the right to control the manner in which the vehicle is driven. In the leading case, *Messina Associated Carriers v. Kleinhaus*,[1104] it was held that the true inquiry is whether the relationship between the owner and the driver and the interest of the owner in the driving of the vehicle is sufficiently analogous to the situation of an employee driving in the course of and within the scope of employment.[1105] In most cases, where this form of strict liability was recognized the owner was a passenger in the vehicle and allowed another person to drive, while retaining at least the right to control the manner in which the vehicle is driven. In the *Messina Associated Carriers* case, it was recognized that the strict liability of the owner is not confined to cases where the owner is present, and that a situation akin to employment is the central feature of this form of strict liability.[1106]

1102. *See* generally P.Q.R. Boberg, *The Law of Delict* 368–375 (Juta & Company Ltd. 1984).
1103. In *Roman v. Pietersen* 1990 (3) SA 350 (C), it was held that the owner-interest requirement is satisfied even if a limited interest of a social nature is involved.
1104. 2001 (3) SA 868 (SCA).
1105. There is no basis for vicarious liability on the part of the manager of the business of the owner of a vehicle, or agent of the owner, for a delict of a person to whom he gives instructions on behalf of the employer of that person or the owner of the vehicle; *see H Mohammed & Associates v. Buyeye* 2005 (3) SA 122 (C).
1106. *Messina Associated Carriers v. Kleinhaus* 2001 (3) SA 868 (SCA) 875.

§2. Road Accident Fund Act

497. An important feature of the application of the law of delict to road and traffic accidents is the statutory provision for the transfer of liability from the negligent driver or the owner of a motor vehicle to the Road Accident Fund, in cases of loss or damage as a result of bodily injury or death. (Legislation is in preparation to replace this compensation system with a Road Accident Benefit Scheme (RABS), which will not be based on fault. The framework for the new scheme was published in 2011 in the document 'Policy for the Road Accident Benefit Scheme (RABS)'.[1107]

The key provision of the current compensation scheme is section 17 of the Road Accident Fund Act,[1108] which provides as follows:

> 17 Liability of Fund and agents
>
> (1) The Fund or an agent shall: … be obliged to compensate any person (the third party) for any loss or damage which the third party has suffered as a result of any bodily injury to himself or herself or the death of or any bodily injury to any other person, caused by or arising from the driving of a motor vehicle by any person at any place within the Republic, if the injury or death is due to the negligence or other wrongful act of the driver or of the owner of the motor vehicle or of his or her employee in the performance of the employee's duties as employee. Provided that the obligation of the Fund to compensate a third party for non-pecuniary loss shall be limited to compensation for a serious injury as contemplated in subsection (1A) and shall be paid by way of a lump sum.

Section 17 refers to the liability of the Fund or its agents, but the Fund no longer appoints insurance companies as claim-handling agents, as it did formerly. All claims are handled by the Fund itself. The Fund derives its income from a levy on the sale of fuel.[1109] The liability of the Fund replaces the liability of the driver or owner that would have otherwise existed in common law, except where the Fund is unable to pay compensation, conceivably for reasons of insolvency.[1110] The Fund is also not liable for 'compensation in respect of loss or damage resulting from emotional shock sustained by a person, other than a third party, when that person witnessed or observed or was informed of the bodily injury or the death of another person as a result of the driving of a

1107. Notice 815 of 2011, in Government Gazette No. 34765 of 21 Nov. 2011.
1108. Act 56 of 1996.
1109. Section 5.
1110. Section 21 provides as follows:

> When a third party is entitled under sec. 17 to claim from the Fund or an agent any compensation in respect of any loss or damage resulting from any bodily injury to or death of any person caused by or arising from the driving of a motor vehicle by the owner thereof or by any other person with the consent of the owner, that third party may not claim compensation in respect of that loss or damage from the owner or from the person who so drove the vehicle, or if that person drove the vehicle as an employee in the performance of his or her duties, from his or her employer, unless the Fund or such agent is unable to pay the compensation.

motor vehicle.' The claimant must therefore institute a common law action against the negligent driver or owner for loss or harm that results from emotional shock.[1111]

498. The transferred liability of the Fund applies only in respect of damage resulting from bodily injury or death, not in respect of property damage. The Road Accident Fund Act refers to the claimant as 'the third party', a concept not defined in the Act, but given content by implication: the liability transferred to the Fund in terms of section 17 is common law liability for negligently caused injury or death,[1112] and a 'third party' is any person who would have had a common law claim for damages arising from bodily injury or death. This includes claims for personal injury, as well as claims for loss or damage caused by the injury of others (parents or spouses incurring medical costs based on the duty to maintain a child or spouse, for example) and claims for loss of support caused by the death of a breadwinner.

499. Causation of loss or damage can be direct or indirect (caused by or arising from the driving of a motor vehicle). Indirectly caused injury or death that has been recognized as falling under section 17 includes, for example, injury from a fire following a negligently caused accident,[1113] and injury from an attack on a bus that was allowed to be driven in a dangerous area.[1114]

500. The liability of the Fund can arise from accidents 'at any place within the Republic', not just on public or other roads. The accident must involve the 'driving' of a 'motor vehicle'. The concept of 'driving' is partially defined in section 20, with deeming provisions, namely that a vehicle is 'deemed to be driven by the person in control of the vehicle'; and that 'a person who has placed or left a motor vehicle at any place shall be deemed to be driving that motor vehicle while it moves from that place as a result of gravity, or while it is stationary at that place or at a place to which it moved from the first-mentioned place as a result of gravity'; and that '(W)henever any motor vehicle has been placed or left at any place, it shall, for the purposes of this Act, be presumed, until the contrary is proved, that such vehicle

---

1111. Section 21 provides as follows: ' …

(1) No claim for compensation in respect of loss or damage resulting from bodily injury to or the death of any person caused by or arising from the driving of a motor vehicle shall lie:
   a. against the owner or driver of a motor vehicle; or
   b. against the employer of the driver.
(2) Subsection (1) does not apply:
   a. if the Fund or an agent is unable to pay any compensation; or
   b. to an action for compensation in respect of loss or damage resulting from emotional shock sustained by a person, other than a third party, when that person witnessed or observed or was informed of the bodily injury or the death of another person as a result of the driving of a motor vehicle.'

1112. The reference in s. 17 refers to injury or death 'due to the negligence or other wrongful act' is a reference to common law fault-based liability. Furthermore, s. 19(a) of the Act in effect excludes liability of the Fund where no common law liability exists.

1113. *Groenewald v. Protea Assurance Co. Ltd* 1979 (1) SA 354 (C).

1114. *General Accident Insurance Co. of SA Ltd v. Xheggo and Others* 1992 (1) SA 580 (A).

was placed or left at such place by the owner of such vehicle.' The definition of a 'motor vehicle' is contained in section 1 of the Act, which provides that it means 'any vehicle designed or adapted for propulsion or haulage on a road by means of fuel, gas or electricity, including a trailer, a caravan, an agricultural or any other implement designed or adapted to be drawn by such motor vehicle'.

501. The liability of the Fund is fault-based, and this requires proof of 'negligence or other wrongful act of the driver or of the owner of the motor vehicle or of his or her employee in the performance of the employee's duties as employee'. The negligence or other wrongful act can be (and mostly is) that of the driver, but it can also be related to the maintenance or use of the vehicle by the owner or an employee of the owner in the performance of duties.

502. Road accidents not involving 'driving' of a 'motor vehicle' or fault on the part of the driver, owner or employee of the owner as required by section 17, can only give rise to common law liability. Even if the requirements of section 17 are met, there are certain limitations on the liability of the Fund towards passengers in vehicles, as set out in section 18; and certain exclusions as set out in section 19. Claims under the Act are subject to prescription provisions contained in section 23, and must be instituted according to the procedural requirements as set out in section 24.

503. Where the Fund is liable to the third party in terms of the Act the negligent driver, the owner, or the employee of the owner normally incurs no liability,[1115] but in certain circumstances the fund has a right of recourse against the driver or the owner of the vehicle, as set out in section 25, including cases of driving without a licence and driving under the influence of alcohol or other drug.

1115. Section 21.

Chapter 2. Liability for Animals

§1. Background

504. Strict liability for harm done by animals is based on the consideration that animals create a source of danger in the human environment – they kick, butt, gore, stray on busy streets, attack, jump, chase and bite.[1116] Many other things also create danger, but the special risk of animals is their instinctive, unpredictable behaviour and their mobility.

505. The law of liability for damage done by animals developed in South Africa on the basis of the strict liability regime of the Roman *actio de pauperie* and edictal remedies.[1117] After early doubt on whether the *actio de pauperie* applied in South African law,[1118] the Appellate Division held in *O'Callaghan v. Chaplin*[1119] that it forms part of South African law, on the basis of a presumption of fault.[1120] It has subsequently been generally accepted as an action based on strict liability.

§2. Type of Animal

506. The *actio de pauperie* in Roman law applied to livestock and domestic animals and was gradually extended to all kinds of domesticated animals. In South African law, pauperian liability is now recognized for all kinds of domestic animals and livestock, and also for domesticated wild animals or other wild creatures employed for domestic use, such as bees.[1121]

507. The special risk of animals in a human environment is not only their aggression, but also their instinctive, unpredictable behaviour and mobility. The policy underlying the recognition of strict liability for harm done by animals therefore favours that liability should not be restricted to vicious or aggressive behaviour of animals. However, the tendency has been in South African cases to restrict liability to such behaviour, excluding liability for behaviour that would be described in human terms as over-friendly. There is no requirement that the animal must have shown previous signs of viciousness or unpredictable behaviour. This aspect is referred to below in the context of the type of behaviour giving rise to liability.

1116. *See* Reinhard Zimmermann, *The Law of Obligations: Roman Foundations of the Civilian Tradition* (1990; paperback edition, 1996) 1095; and *see* the remarks of Kumbleben JA in *Lever v. Purdy* 1993 (3) SA 17 (A) at 29C-G, accepting the creation of a risk or source of danger by the owner as the policy underlying the recognition of strict liability, but pointing out also that this underlying policy is not in itself the determinant of the content or ambit of liability.
1117. *See* generally C.G. van der Merwe, *Skuldlose Aanspreeklikheid vir Skade Veroorsaak deur Diere* (1970).
1118. *Parker v. Reed* (1904) 21 SC 496.
1119. 1927 AD 310.
1120. *O'Callaghan v. Chaplin* 378. *See also Bristow v. Lycett* 1971 (4) SA 223 (RA).
1121. *See* generally McQuoid-Mason, *LAWSA* vol. 1, para. 332.

§3. Person Liable

508. In South African law, the person liable is the owner of the animal at the time when the injury or damage was caused, ownership being determined in accordance with the accepted principles of property law. Control of the animal is not sufficient to found liability in respect of the *actio de pauperie*, but the person in control may be liable for negligence under the Aquilian action.[1122]

509. The special risk of animals in a human environment is their instinctive, unpredictable behaviour and mobility. The keeper of an animal is a party to creating or maintaining this risk and is in a position to contain the risk by controlling or restraining the animal and may benefit from keeping the animal. Therefore the policy considerations underlying the recognition of strict liability for harm done by animals favour that liability should include keepers and not be restricted to owners. In South Africa, the owner of an animal is liable even if he was not in possession of the animal at the time when it caused harm, but the owner can rely on the negligence of the keeper of the animal at the time as a defence.[1123]

§4. Type of Behaviour: The Contra Naturam Test

510. For liability under the *actio de pauperie* in South Africa, the animal must have acted contra naturam sui generis. In Roman law, the implication of this requirement was that the animal must have acted spontaneously and not as a result of an external factor, such as provocation; but the owner was liable if the animal reacted to stroking or patting. The contra naturam rule has been described as a conveniently flexible concept to determine where the risk of damage or injury should lie, and that it was neither meant to focus on the disposition of the individual animal (i.e., whether it was a generally placid or unruly horse), nor on the disposition of the species concerned (i.e., whether a horse or dog was by nature aggressive), but to indicate behaviour uncharacteristic of a domesticated animal in a human environment.[1124]

511. South African courts interpret the contra naturam rule inconsistently. Some cases refer to the innate wildness, viciousness or perverseness of the particular animal (a subjective approach), while others refer to what could be expected of a well-behaved animal of its kind (an objective or 'reasonable animal' approach).[1125] Typical of the latter approach is the much-discussed and even ridiculed judgment in *Da Silva v. Otto.*[1126] The appellant had been walking his dog on a leash in a public road in a residential area, when the respondent's dog ran out of an open side gate on

1122. *See* generally Part II, Ch. 2 above, on Aquilian liability for harm done by other persons, things or animals.
1123. *Lever v. Purdy* 1993 (3) SA 17 (A).
1124. *See* Reinhard Zimmermann, *The Law of Obligations: Roman Foundations of the Civilian Tradition* 1103 (1990; paperback edition, 1996).
1125. *See* generally McQuoid-Mason, *LAWSA* vol. 1, para. 334.
1126. 1986 (3) SA 538 (T).

the respondent's premises and attacked the dog on the leash. The Appellant, who carried a whip, hit the respondent's dog, which then bit him. The court found that the respondent had not acted negligently: the dog had never before bitten a person, and he had taken sufficient precautions against the possibility of the dog escaping from his premises. The court held furthermore that the appellant had also not acted negligently – he had not 'provoked' the dog by hitting it and was entitled to protect his dog against an attack. Nestadt J (with O'Donovan AJ) held that in such circumstances, where the injured person had acted lawfully and reasonably, the dog was presumed to have acted contra naturam sui generis. An objective test of the reasonable dog applies, and it was expected of the dog to distinguish between a lawful attack and an unlawful attack on itself.

In most decisions, the courts do not expressly apply this reasonable animal test, adopting rather a combination of a subjective and objective approach.[1127]

512. In *Fourie v. Naranjo and Another*,[1128] Fourie's dog had attacked and savaged his domestic worker. Naranjo hastened to the worker's assistance and was in turn attacked and bitten by the dog and also by another dog (not owned by Fourie) that was on the premises for the purposes of mating with Fourie's dog. Naranjo's wife witnessed the incident. Naranjo sued in respect of the injuries he sustained, and his wife sued for emotional shock and related medical expenses.

The court found that Fourie's dog had acted *contra naturam sui generis* according to the objective test of the reasonable dog; that Naranjo did not consent to the risk of injury when he entered the property (the defence of *volenti non fit iniuria* requires knowledge of, appreciation of, and consent to harm or the risk of harm); and that Naranjo had not been negligent in acting as he had done (this would have been a complete defence against the *actio de pauperie*).[1129]

A notable feature of this case is the award of damages for emotional shock in the context of the pauperien action. Fourie had contended that the wife's claim for emotional shock was not competent, as she had not been attacked by the dog. However, the court noted that is trite that an action in delict may lie for patrimonial or sentimental damages arising out of the infliction of emotional shock.[1130] It pointed out that a person bitten by a dog is entitled to damages not only for the direct injury sustained, but also for subsequent physical disorders caused by the nervous shock; that there is support for the view that damages may be claimed by a dependant for loss of support if an animal has caused the death of a breadwinner; and that the extent of Fourie's liability should be limited only in accordance with the flexible criterion of legal causation. There was thus no objection in principle to the *actio de pauperie* being extended to recover damages for emotional shock.[1131]

1127. McQuoid-Mason, *LAWSA* vol. 1, para. 334.
1128. 2008 (1) SA 192 (C).
1129. *See* paras 15–19.
1130. Paragraph 23.
1131. Paragraph 24.

513. Historically, strict liability for harm done by animals has been largely confined to violent conduct. However, the special risk of animals in a human environment is not necessarily their aggression, but their instinctive, unpredictable behaviour and mobility. The policy underlying the recognition of strict liability for harm done by animals suggests that liability for injury should not be restricted to vicious or aggressive behaviour of animals.

§5. Damage Caused by Foraging

514. South African law, following the Roman actio de pastu, recognizes strict liability for the owner of an animal that caused damage by eating plants, including any collateral damage caused by trampling while grazing, provided the animal had acted of its own volition.[1132] In this context also, the policy underlying the recognition of strict liability for damage caused by animals indicates that liability for such damage should not be restricted to certain acts such as 'foraging' or to certain species of animals.

§6. Defences

515. In South African law *vis maior*, for example, a sudden thunder clap that frightened an animal, provides a defence for the owner, but the extent of outside influence considered sufficient to exclude spontaneous conduct on the part of the animal is not always clear.[1133] Other defences are recognized where the plaintiff can be said to have brought the harm on himself by culpable conduct.[1134] The South African standard of own fault applied in this regard is restrictive from the point of view of plaintiffs – culpable conduct or at most 'substantial negligence or imprudence' will defeat the claim.[1135] Contributory negligence will not result in the apportionment of damages in terms of the Apportionment of Damages Act:[1136] South African courts have to date adopted an all-or-nothing approach, although not specifically excluding the possibility of apportionment.[1137] Other defences are voluntary assumption of the risk of harm,[1138] or unlawful presence at the place where the injury or damage occurred.[1139]

516. The owner of an animal is liable even if he was not in possession of the animal at the time when it caused harm, but the owner can rely on the negligence

1132. McQuoid-Mason *LAWSA* vol. 1, paras 337–339.
1133. McQuoid-Mason, *LAWSA* vol. 1, para. 335.
1134. *O'Callaghan v. Chaplin* 1927 AD 310 329.
1135. McQuoid-Mason, *LAWSA* vol 1, para. 335; *O'Callaghan v. Chaplin* 1927 AD 310 329.
1136. Act 34 of 1956.
1137. *See Svamvur v. Portwood* 1970 (1) SA 144 (R) 145; *Swart v. Honeyborne* 1981 (1) SA 974 (C) 976B.
1138. McQuoid-Mason, *LAWSA* vol. 1, para. 335.
1139. *Ibid.*

of the keeper of the animal at the time as a defence.[1140] In *Lever v. Purdy*,[1141] the plaintiff (respondent) had been bitten by a dog belonging to the owner (appellant). The incident occurred while the owner was overseas, leaving a custodian in charge of his house and dog. The custodian had summoned the plaintiff, a repairman, to the house and had advised him that there was a vicious dog on the premises. The plaintiff had requested the custodian to lock the dog away before his arrival at an agreed time. When the plaintiff arrived at the house and entered the premises the dog, not been locked away, bit him. It was common cause that the plaintiff had established the essentials of the *actio de pauperie* against the owner, but the question was whether the owner was exonerated by the negligence of the custodian.

Both Joubert ACJ[1142] and Kumbleben JA[1143] enumerated categories of culpable third-party conduct constituting a defence to pauperien liability. The first category involves inciting or provoking an animal to behave contra naturam sui generi, by striking, wounding, scaring or annoying the animal. The *causa causans* of the harm suffered is the inciting behaviour and not the animal's vicious propensities, and this is generally treated as an 'established exception' to pauperien liability. The second category involves culpable conduct which contributes to the injury, but falls short of being the causa causans of it, for example where a visitor facilitates injury by leaving open the owner's gate, so that a vicious dog can get out. The third category involves culpable lack of control of a vicious animal by the person to whom control of the animal has been entrusted, as in the *Lever* case. The majority of the Appellate Division held that the negligence by the custodian afforded the absent owner a defence to pauperien liability.

This decision is consistent with the risk principle – arguably the injury was caused by negligence of the custodian rather than by the materialization of a typical risk of owning a dog.[1144] However, the issues of strict liability of a custodian and joint and several liability of the owner and the custodian remain unresolved in South African law.

1140. *Lever v. Purdy* 1993 (3) SA 17 (A).
1141. 1993 (3) SA 17 (A).
1142. 21C-22A.
1143. 26E-H.
1144. *See* C.G. van der Merwe, *The Defence of Conduct of a Third Party in View of the Rationale for Strict Liability in Terms of the Pauperian Action Revisited*, 47 S.African L. J., 52–53 (1994).

Chapter 3. Liability for Buildings and Structures

517. South African law has retained remnants of the Roman law actio de deiectis vel effusis, available against the occupier of a building for damage caused by throwing or pouring an object or substance out of a building, and the actio de positis vel suspensis, applying a criminal fine against the occupier when an object fell from a building to the street below. However, there has been no significant development of strict liability by application of these actions in modern law, albeit that there has also been no unequivocal rejection of strict liability.[1145] The few claims brought in recent years have not had success.

518. In *Colman v. Dunbar*,[1146] a claim based on the actio de effusis et deiectis failed. This was not because the court refused to recognize the applicability of the Praetor's Edict, but rather because the action had been brought against a builder working on the premises (against whom there was no evidence of negligence) and only an occupier could be held liable.

519. A claim based on the *actio de effusis vel deiectis* was similarly unsuccessful in *Bowden v. Rudman*,[1147] but again because the facts of the case did not meet the terms of the Edict. Here the plaintiff claimed damages for an injury suffered due to a gate swinging open across a pavement, admittedly without negligence on the part of the occupier. The court ruled that the action was not available since it applied only to objects falling after being placed on, or suspended from, a building.

1145. *See* Reinhard Zimmermann, *The Law of Obligations: Roman Foundations of the Civilian Tradition* 1125 (1990; paperback edition, 1996), noting: 'In modern civil law systems none of these actions can be said to have prospered.'

1146. 1933 AD 141.

1147. 1964 (4) SA 686 (N).

Chapter 4. Unlawful Arrest

520. Unlawful arrest or imprisonment entails a form of strict liability for *iniuria* in South African law–*dolus* remains an ingredient of the cause of action, but in attenuated form, in the sense that the plaintiff need not establish that the wrongdoers (usually the State or its employees) were conscious of the wrongful nature of the act. The courts have noted that this form of strict liability may not be in accordance with the Roman-Dutch principles of liability for *iniuria*, but that it has practical consequences that are both sensible and just.[1148]

521. The policy underlying this approach is that more comprehensive protection should be afforded against unlawful arrest as a serious encroachment upon the freedom of the individual.[1149] This approach is underscored by the constitutional protection of the right to freedom and security of the person.[1150] The plaintiff must prove the fact of imprisonment or arrest and that it was unlawful, and it is then for the defendant to show that the imprisonment or arrest was justified.[1151] Consciousness of the unlawfulness of the arrest is not a requirement for liability. This approach is also followed in respect of detention or imprisonment, where the manner of detention of a prisoner may render it unlawful, for example where the prisoner is detained in conditions amounting to effective solitary confinement, which constitutes an infringement of his basic rights to bodily integrity and to mental and intellectual well-being.[1152]

522. The courts approach unlawful attachment of goods similarly. It is no defence for a sheriff who had unlawfully attached property that he believed, even reasonably, the attachment to be lawful, because consciousness of the unlawfulness of the attachment is not a requirement for liability.[1153]

523. Unlawful arrest or imprisonment involving a form of strict liability in South African law must be distinguished from malicious deprivation of liberty, which does require *animus iniuriandi*. Where improper use is made of the judicial machinery to deprive a person of his liberty under the guise of a valid judicial process, the plaintiff needs to prove that the defendant instigated the deprivation of liberty without reasonable and probable cause and also that the defendant acted *animo iniuriandi*, that is, with both factual intent and consciousness of the wrongful nature of his act.[1154]

1148. *Smit v. Meyerton Outfitters* 1971 (1) SA 137 (T) 139C-D; *Minister of Justice v. Hofmeyr* 1993 (3) SA 131 (A) 157.
1149. *Shoba v. Minister van Justisie* 1982 (2) SA 554 (C) 559B-D.
1150. Section 12 of the Constitution of the Republic of South Africa Act 108 of 1996.
1151. *Whittaker v. Roos and Bateman; Morant v. Roos and Bateman* 1912 AD 92 122–123; *Groenewald v. Minister van Justisie* 1972 (3) SA 596 (O) 599; *Donono v. Minister of Prisons* 1973 (4) SA 259 (C) 262; *Minister of Justice v. Hofmeyr* 1993 (3) SA 131 (A).
1152. *Whittaker v. Roos and Bateman; Morant v. Roos and Bateman* 1912 AD 92 122-3; *Minister of Justice v. Hofmeyr* 1993 (3) SA 131 (A).
1153. *Sheriff, Pretoria East v. Meevis* 2001 (3) 454 (SCA).
1154. *See* generally above Part I, Chapter 2, §3, on abuse of rights.

524. It is noteworthy that the strict liability for unlawful arrest or detention in South African law was affirmed in a few leading cases where the arrest or imprisonment was politically charged and where the need for protection of the freedom and security of the individual against the abuse of State power was particularly strong.[1155] The stricter-than-normal approach in South African law may partly at least be explained as a reaction of the courts against abuse of political power.

1155. *See Whittaker v. Roos and Bateman; Morant v. Roos and Bateman* 1912 AD 92 122–123 (alleged attempted sabotage in the context of a strike); *Smith and Lardner-Burke v. Wonesayi* 1972 (3) SA 289 (RA) 302 (arrest in the context of forced removal of persons); and *Minister of Justice v. Hofmeyr* 1993 (3) SA 131 (A) 157 (detention of opposition politician).

Chapter 5. Various Statutory Forms of Strict Liability

§1. Aviation

525. The Aviation Act[1156] imposes strict liability on the owner[1157] of an aircraft where material damage or loss is caused by the aircraft in flight, on taking off or landing, by any person in such aircraft, by any article falling from such aircraft, or to any person or property on land or water.[1158] The owner is not liable, however, if the damage or loss is caused or contributed to by the negligent or wilful act of the claimant.[1159] The intention appears to be to create a complete defence and to exclude the provisions of the Apportionment of Damages Act.[1160]

§2. Damage to Telecommunication Lines and Call Boxes

526. The Post Office Act[1161] imposes strict liability on any person who directly or indirectly injures or destroys any telecommunications lines or call boxes.[1162] However, where the telecommunications company is of the opinion that it is justified it may bear the whole or part of the expenses necessary to make good such injury or destruction.[1163] If the injury or destruction was caused through negligence on the part of any person, such person will also be guilty of an offence for which a fine may be imposed.[1164]

§3. Genetically Modified Organisms

527. The Genetically Modified Organisms Act[1165] provides that liability for damage caused by the use or release of a genetically modified organism should be borne by the user concerned, and the section refers neither to the need to prove fault nor to a presumption of fault.[1166] However, when such organism was in the possession of an inspector appointed under the Act,[1167] the user concerned at the time of such use or release may not be held liable for any damage unless such user foresaw

---

1156. Act 74 of 1962.
1157. In terms of s. 11(6), if the owner bona fide leases or rents out the aircraft to another person for a period exceeding fourteen days and no operative members of the crew are in the owner's employ, then the person to whom the aircraft was leased or rented out is responsible on the same basis as the owner would have been in terms of s. 11(2).
1158. Section 11(2).
1159. Section 11(3).
1160. Act 34 of 1956.
1161. Act 44 of 1958.
1162. Section 108; and *see Esterhuizen v. Minister van Pos & Telekommunikasiewese* 1978 (2) SA 227 (T) 229; *Telkom (SA) Ltd v. Duncan* 1995 (3) SA 941 (W) 943–945.
1163. Section 108.
1164. Section 108.
1165. Act 15 of 1997.
1166. Section 17(2).
1167. In terms of s. 15(1); and *see also* s. 15(4).

or should have foreseen such damage and could have or should have prevented the damage, but failed to take reasonable action to prevent such damage.[1168] Users are required to ensure that appropriate measures are taken to avoid an adverse impact on the environment which may arise from the use of genetically modified organisms.[1169]

1168. Section 17(2).
1169. Section 17(1).

Chapter 6. Product Liability

528. In South Africa, delictual liability for defective products under common law is fault-based, within the framework of Aquilian liability. This form of fault-based common law liability has been dealt with in Part I, Chapter 2, section 7. However, strict liability for defective products has been introduced by the Consumer Protection Act of 2008,[1170] which came into effect on 1 April 2011. This legislation brings the South African law on product liability into line with the position in many other jurisdictions.

529. Section 61 of the Consumer Protection Act provides:

> (1) Except to the extent contemplated in subsection (4), the producer or importer, distributor or retailer of any goods is liable for any harm, as described in subsection (5), caused wholly or partly as a consequence of:
> (a) supplying any unsafe goods;
> (b) a product failure, defect or hazard in any goods; or
> (c) inadequate instructions or warnings provided to the consumer pertaining to any hazard arising from or associated with the use of any goods irrespective of whether the harm resulted from any negligence on the part of the producer, importer, distributor or retailer, as the case may be.

530. The consumer will have an action against the producer, importer, distributor or retailer, without having to prove negligence. The consumer can be the purchaser or merely the user of the product,[1171] and the action is not limited by the ambit of whatever warranty was given for the product.

531. The Act defines 'goods' as follows:

(a) anything marketed for human consumption;
(b) any tangible object not otherwise contemplated in paragraph (a) including any medium on which anything is or may be written or encoded;
(c) any literature, music photograph, motion picture, game, information, data, software, code or other intangible product written or encoded on any medium, or a licence to use any such intangible product;
(d) a legal interest in land or any other immovable property, other than an interest that falls within the definition of 'service' in this section; and
(e) gas, water and electricity.

532. The wide and general definition of 'goods' includes all kinds of substances produced and tradable as commodities. In combination, paragraphs (a), (b) and (c) include any tangible object whether marketed for human consumption or otherwise, as well as a wide range of intangible products involving information. In addition to

1170. Section 61 of the Consumer Protection Act 68 of 2008.
1171. *See* definition of 'consumer' in s. 1.

goods produced by industrial process – from machinery to pharmaceuticals – it includes raw and processed foodstuffs. A 'tangible object' also includes natural substances such as body parts, blood products, minerals and water. Water is in any event mentioned specifically, together with gas and electricity.

533. Immovable property: the Act also covers land transactions. It includes in the definition of goods 'a legal interest in land or any other immovable property, other than an interest that falls within the definition of "service" in this section'. This involves liability for structural or design defects in buildings and hazards that occur on land. Damage to the product itself – the land or buildings – is apparently also recoverable.

534. Information products: the definition of 'goods' includes 'any literature, music, photograph, motion picture, game, information, data, software, code'. In this respect, the Act goes much further than its counterparts in Europe. The Act creates strict liability not only for mass-produced informational products like software packages, but also for the producer of defective software for products such as aeroplanes, cars or heart-lung machines. There appears to be no distinction between defective information accompanying the product, which renders it dangerous, and defective information obtained from the product (e.g., a recipe contained in a cookery book that encourages the use of potentially poisonous mushrooms).

535. Contaminated blood: contaminated blood and blood products also qualify as 'goods' (tangible object), and this means that the South African National Blood Service (SANBS) will potentially be liable for contaminated blood and blood products.

536. Defectiveness of goods: the remedies provided by section 61(1) are available for the causing of harm in consequence of (a) the supply of 'unsafe' goods; (b) a product 'failure', 'defect' or 'hazard' in goods; or (c) 'inadequate instructions or warnings' provided with goods. The definitions of these key terms, 'unsafe', 'failure', 'defect' or 'hazard' are contained in section 53. Therefore, strict liability can arise as a result of several alternative modes of conduct by the produce, importer, distributor or retailer of any goods. The scope of liability is determined by the definitions contained in sections 1 and 53.

537. Unsafe: according to section 53(1)(d), 'unsafe means that, due to a characteristic, failure, defect, or hazard, particular goods present an extreme risk of personal injury or property damage to the consumer or to other persons'. In turn, the subsections gives 'failure', 'defect' and 'hazard' their own statutory definitions, although it does not define 'extreme risk'. Liability arises if goods are 'unsafe' and present an 'extreme risk' 'due to a characteristic, failure, defect or hazard'. An accident occurs typically because of a failure in the manufacturing process of goods that has caused a safety problem, or a design defect in the goods that has rendered the goods unsafe to use.

538. Failure: 'Failure' means (according to section 53(1)(b)) that the product 'did not perform in the intended manner or to the intended effect'. This indicates a typical manufacturing defect, for example, where a machine tool malfunctions and causes injury, or the brakes of a car fail and causes an accident.

539. Defect: in the definition of 'defect', the Act broadly adopts a 'consumer expectations' standard. In terms of section 53(1)(a) a 'defect' means:

- any material imperfection in the manufacture of the goods or components, or in performance of the services, that renders the goods or results of the service less acceptable than persons generally would be reasonably entitled to expect in the circumstances; or
- any characteristic of the goods or components that renders the goods or components less useful, practicable or safe than persons generally would be reasonably entitled to expect in the circumstances.

This definition of 'defect' is complex, and is based on consumer expectations of performance, coupled with vague and overlapping notions of 'acceptable', 'useful', 'practicable' and 'safe'.

540. Hazard: a 'hazard', in terms of section 53(1)(c)(ii), means a characteristic that 'presents a significant risk of personal injury to any person, or damage to property, when the goods are utilized'. The liability referred to in section 61(1)(a) – the supply of 'unsafe' goods – therefore, *inter alia*, relates to supplying goods that present an 'extreme risk' of personal injury or property damage, due to a 'hazard', which is a characteristic that presents a 'significant risk' of personal injury to any person, or damage to property. This is a puzzling interplay of definitions. Even if it did make sense to link extreme risk and significant risk in this convoluted way, the different levels of risk are not defined and are difficult to distinguish. It is also difficult to see why a claimant would rely on an 'extreme risk' situation if it is also possible to rely on a 'significant risk' situation.

541. The Act refers to 'failure', 'defect' and 'hazard' alternately, so in effect, section 61(1)(b) refers to various alternative subcategories of liability. However, given that the same terms are all within the definition of 'unsafe' in 61(1)(a), these categories are in effect tautologous. If the criteria in sections 61(1)(a) and 61(1)(b) are alternatives, there appears to be no reason why a claimant should not simply rely on the lowest and most general of these standards in section 61(1)(b), which is that of a 'defect' that relates to whether the goods are 'acceptable', whatever judicial meaning can be ascribed to this.

542. Inadequate instructions or warnings provided to the consumer pertaining to any hazard: section 61(1)(c) refers to a situation where the consumer received inadequate instructions or warnings 'pertaining to any hazard arising from or associated with the use of any goods'. This refers to a situation, for example, where the goods are inherently dangerous, but could have been made safe by instructions for proper use or a warning making clear the risks of using the goods. An obvious example is toxic cleaning substances. In European and American law, there is a similar category of 'information' defect. However, in South Africa section 61(1) employs the vague concept of 'adequate' in this regard. Moreover, the focus is only on instructions or warnings 'pertaining to any hazard', bringing into this category also the uncertainties of the concepts of 'hazard' and 'significant risk', as discussed above. In short, section 61(1) in its present form, read with the definitions in sections 1 and 53(1), presents a convoluted array of different standards.

543. Who is a consumer? Section 1 of the Act defines a consumer in respect of any particular goods or services as follows:

(a) a person to whom those particular goods or services are marketed in the ordinary course of the supplier's business;
(b) a person who has entered into a transaction with a supplier in the ordinary course of the supplier's business, unless the transaction is exempt from the application of this Act by section 5(2) or in terms of section 5(3);
(c) if the context so requires or permits, a user of those particular goods or a recipient or beneficiary of those particular services, irrespective of whether that user, recipient or beneficiary was a party to a transaction concerning the supply of those particular goods or services;
(d) a franchisee in terms of a franchise agreement, to the extent applicable in terms of section 5(6)(b)–(e).

It is clear from this definition that a consumer includes the person to whom the goods or services are sold or supplied. The consumer is also the user of the goods or services, who was not a party to the transaction for the supply of the goods or services.

In *Eskom Holdings Ltd v. Halstead-Cleak*,[1172] the plaintiff, a cyclist who came into contact with a low-hanging live power line over a footpath and suffered severe burns, claimed damages under section 61 from Eskom as producer and distributor of the electricity. The plaintiff succeeded in the High Court, but lost on appeal, on the basis that he did not qualify as a 'consumer' vis-à-vis Eskom, because he (a) did not enter into any transaction with Eskom as a supplier or producer of electricity in the ordinary course of Eskom's business; and (b) was not at the time of his injury either a user, recipient or beneficiary of the electricity. For the meaning of 'user' the court referred to the Concise Oxford Dictionary,[1173] which defines 'utilize' as 'make practical and effective use of'.[1174] The injured plaintiff could hardly be regarded as a 'beneficiary' of the electricity. The court did not comment on the meaning of 'recipient', which arguably could have a wide meaning including a person who accidentally comes into contact with electricity, thereby inadvertently and unwillingly 'receiving' the electricity.

1172. 2017 (1) SA 333 (SCA).
1173. (2011) 2 ed.
1174. Paragraph 24.

544. Who is liable? The Act creates liability for 'the producer or importer, distributor or supplier'.[1175]'Supplier' and 'supply' have a particularly wide meaning, including 'sell, rent, exchange and hire in the ordinary course of business for consideration', and in respect of services, 'to sell the services, or to perform or cause them to be performed or provided, or to grant access to any premises, event, activity or facility in the ordinary course of business for consideration'. This covers leasing and seemingly also the common triangular arrangement in which a finance company buys goods from a retailer to supply to a customer on lease or hire purchase. The Act therefore appears to create strict liability for finance companies engaged in selling or leasing goods.

545. For what type of harm will liability be imposed? Section 61(6) imposes liability for the following types of harm:

(a) the death of, or injury to, any natural person;
(b) an illness of any natural person;
(c) any loss of, or physical damage to any property, irrespective whether it is movable or immovable; and
(d) any economic loss that results from harm contemplated in paragraph (a), (b) or (c).

Harm includes loss or damage of 'any property'. This apparently includes damage to the defective product itself. Loss may derive from the product itself in various ways, for example, the costs of replacement, repair, or remedying a safety hazard. The Act therefore allows significant additional compensation, over and above whatever contractual remedies may be available. The Act also expressly allows compensation for economic loss, thereby opening up a potentially vast area of liability, for example for loss of profit.

Defences

546. Section 61(4)(a) provides a defence where the characteristic that rendered the product unsafe was 'wholly attributable to compliance with any public regulation'. Compliance with legislation aiming to promote safety should not render the producer or supplier liable under section 61(4)(a). Compliance with codes of practice or voluntary standards would also not of itself provide a defence under section 61(4)(a). In the European experience, this defence is rarely invoked since 'as the purpose of most regulations is to make products safe, it will rarely be the case that compliance will force the producer to make an unsafe product'.[1176]

547. Section 61(4)(b)(i) provides a defence if the product defect 'did not exist in the goods at the time it was supplied by [the defendant] to another person alleged to be liable' (section 61(4)(b)(i)). The purpose of this provision would appear to be to allow the defendant to escape liability if the defect has arisen after the goods left

1175. All these terms are defined in s. 1.
1176. G Howells, *The Law of Product Liability* para. 4.211 (Howells ed., 2000).

his control. If goods have become defective due to mishandling or inappropriate modification, the producer and those who have supplied goods in their original, safe, condition should not be held liable.

Component parts (for instance nuts, bolts and industrial fasteners) also qualify as 'goods' as defined in section 1 of the Act. Section 61(4)(b)(i) allows the producer or supplier of a component part to escape liability if it can show that that component was sound at the point when it was delivered to the producer of the complex product.

548. Section 61(4)(b)(ii): Compliance with instructions. Section 61(4)(b)(ii) deals with the situation where a supplier (A) has passed on goods to another in the retail chain (B), and in doing so A has provided B with instructions, for example regarding their use or safekeeping. Where harm occurs as a result of compliance with these instructions, this subsection provides a defence for B, and also provides that A cannot use the defence in section 61(4)(b)(i) above to exonerate itself.

549. Section 61(4)(c): Defects not reasonably discoverable by the distributor or retailer. In terms of section 61(4)(c) there is no liability if, it is 'unreasonable to expect the distributor or retailer to have discovered' the product defect, 'having regard to that person's role in marketing the goods to consumers'. This exemption from liability is broadly drafted. There are many defects that one could not reasonably expect even a highly responsible distributor or retailer to discover, for instance the so-called development risks, which only become apparent in a new product once it has been used. Also, in many cases retailers sell packaged goods as delivered by a manufacturer or distributor, and cannot reasonably be expected to open the goods for inspection. To permit all 'reasonable' distributors and retailers to evade liability for latent defects significantly narrows the ambit of strict liability.

550. Section 61(4)(d): Time limit for claims. The introductory part of section 61(4) and its subsection 61(4)(d), read together, state that liability in terms of section 61 does not arise if the claim for damages is brought more than three years after the occurrence of certain events or the acquisition of certain knowledge. The Prescription Act 68 of 1969 generally deals with the effect of the passage of time on a 'debt'.[1177] Prescription begins to run as soon as the 'debt' is 'due'.[1178] Instead of using the established terminology of the Prescription Act, section 61(4)(d) refers to a 'liability' which 'does not arise' if the 'claim' is not 'brought' within three years. Section 61(4)(d) is probably intended to coexist with the operation of prescription under the Prescription Act, but it creates a number of interpretation problems in respect of matters such as the beginning of the period of prescription, knowledge on the part of the claimant of the facts from which the claim arises, delay of the running of prescription in the event of some disability on the part of the claimant and interruption of prescription. It is likely that the courts will interpret the prescription defence under section 61(4)(d) in accordance with the principles of prescription embodied in the Prescription Act 68 of 1969, discussed in Chapter 1 of Part IV below.

1177. *See* generally Max Loubser *Extinctive Prescription* (2nd ed, 2019) 1–8.
1178. Section 12(1) of the Prescription Act 68 of 1969.

Part IV. Defences and Exception Clauses

Chapter 1. Prescription

§1. Nature and Effect of Prescription

551. The Prescription Act 68 of 1969 provides for prescription periods in respect of different kinds of 'debt'. The concept of a 'debt' is not defined in the Act, but the courts have made it clear that the concept must be understood in a wide and general sense, to include any duty side of an obligation.[1179] The word 'debt' includes any liability arising from a delict, contract or any other source of obligation. The concept of a 'debt' in the context of the law of delict refers to the obligation to pay damages caused by the delict.

552. The Supreme Court of Appeal has emphasized the difference between a 'debt' and a 'cause of action' in a number of cases.[1180] A 'cause of action' is the factual basis or set of material facts that 'begets' the plaintiff's right of action and its correlative, the defendant's debt.[1181]

553. In terms of section 10 of the Prescription Act, the expiration of the applicable prescription period has the effect of extinguishing a debt. However, two principles embodied in the Act appear to be at odds with the notion that prescription extinguishes a debt: payment can discharge a debt after prescription has taken effect; and the courts do not take note of prescription unless the debtor raises it as a

1179. *See* generally Max Loubser *Extinctive Prescription* (2nd ed, 2019) 29–37; *CGU Insurance v. Rumdel Construction (Pty) Ltd* 2004 (2) SA 622 (SCA) para. 6 In; *Oertel v. Direkteur van Plaaslike Bestuur* 1983 (1) SA 354 (A) 369C-D, it was held that there is no indication in the 1969 Act that the expression 'debt' should be used in a narrow sense, and that it does not include statutory debts, i.e., public law debts. Hence the Act is applicable to public law debts, and therefore extinctive prescription runs against the State. For the purposes of extinctive prescription, there is no distinction to be made between so-called private and public law debts and the State. *See also City Treasurer & Rates Collector, Newcastle Town Council v. Shaikjee* 1983 (1) SA 506 (N); *Alberts v. Roodepoort-Maraisburg Municipality* 1921 TPD 133 136A-D.

1180. *CGU Insurance v. Rumdel Construction (Pty) Ltd* 2004 (2) SA 622 (SCA) para. 6, and the cases cited there.

1181. *CGU Insurance v. Rumdel Construction (Pty) Ltd* 2004 (2) SA 622 (SCA) para. 6.

defence.[1182] Arguably, therefore, the expiration of the prescription period does not extinguish the debt, but rather affords the debtor a complete defence against the creditor's claim.[1183]

§2. Prescription Periods

554. Different prescription periods apply to different kinds of debt, as set out in section 11 of the Act. A prescription period of three years applies in respect of any debt for which a specific other period is not provided for by section 11 or by any other Act of Parliament. Debts arising from delict fall within this general three-year category, unless another period is provided for by an Act of Parliament.

Section 11 provides that a thirty-year prescription period applies in respect of any debt secured by a mortgage bond;[1184] any judgment debt;[1185] any debt in respect of any taxation imposed or levied by or under law;[1186] and any debt owed to the State in respect of any share of the profits, royalties or any similar consideration payable in respect of the right to mine minerals or other substances.[1187] A fifteen-year prescription period applies in respect of any debt owed to the State and arising out of an advance or loan of money or a sale or lease of land by the State to the debtor, unless a longer period applies in respect of the debt in question.[1188] A six-year prescription period applies in respect of a debt arising from a bill of exchange or other negotiable instrument, or from a notarial contract, unless a longer period applies in respect of the debt in question.[1189]

1182. Section 17 of the Act.

1183. *See* Max Loubser *Extinctive Prescription* (2nd ed, 2019) ch. 1..

1184. Section 11(a)(i). *See Kilroe-Daley v. Barclays National Bank Ltd* 1984 (4) SA 609 (A) 622H-628C. Here the questions of whether s. 11(a)(i) was applicable to a surety's liability vis-à-vis a mortgage bond, and whether the wording of s. 408 of the Companies Act 61 of 1973 ('shall have the effect of a final judgment') means that confirmation of a liquidation account is tantamount to a judgment debt were considered. *See also Bankorp Ltd v. Leipsig* 1993 (1) SA 247 (W); *Jordan & Co. Ltd v. Bulsara* 1992 (4) SA 457 (E) 461D-H.

1185. Section 11(a)(ii). *See Wertheim v. Wertheim* 1976 (4) SA 633 (W) 633E-F. In *Blaas v. Athanassiou* 1991 (1) SA 723 (W) 725H-I, it was held that since, inter partes, an arbitrator's award, according to the applicable contract, has the status of a court order, it was akin to a judgment, and therefore subject to a prescriptive period of thirty years in terms of s. 11(a)(ii). *See also Kilroe-Daley v. Barclays National Bank Ltd* 1984 (4) SA 609 (A) 624H-628C; *Jordan & Co. Ltd v. Bulsara* 1992 (4) SA 457 (E) 461F-G.

1186. Section 11(a)(iii). In *Oertel v. Direkteur van Plaaslike Bestuur* 1983 (1) SA 354 (A) 369C-D, it was held that the expression 'debt' is applicable to public law debts, and there is no distinction to be made between so-called private and public law debts owed to the State. *See also Durban City Council v. Glenore Supermarket & Café* 1981 (1) SA 470 (D) 479G-481B; *Oertel v. Director of Local Government* 1981 (2) SA 77 (T) 84F-90H; *Electricity Supply Commission v. Stewarts & Lloyds of SA (Pty) Ltd* 1981 (3) SA 340 (A); *Kuhne & Nagel AG Zurich v. APA Distributors (Pty) Ltd* 1981 (3) SA 536 (W); *Rand Bank Ltd v. De Jager* 1982 (3) SA 418 (C); *EA Gani (Pty) Ltd v. Francis* 1984 (1) SA 462 (T); *Apex Mines Ltd v. Administrator, Tvl* 1986 (4) SA 581 (T) 599A-604A.

1187. Section 11(a)(iv).

1188. Section 11(b).

1189. Section 11(c).

§3. Beginning of Prescription

555. Prescription in respect of a debt begins to run as soon as the debt is due.[1190] A debt arising from delict is due as soon as it comes into being, when all the elements of the delict are present, or when it is 'owing and immediately payable', or 'immediately claimable', 'immediately exigible at the will of the creditor', or 'enforceable'.[1191] In *The Master v. IL Back & Co. Ltd*,[1192] it was held that the words 'debt is due' in section 12(1) mean there must be a liquidated monetary obligation presently claimable by the creditor, for which an action can be brought against the debtor. Damage is one of the elements of a delict and only after damage has occurred the cause of action becomes complete and the prescription period begins to run.[1193] This means that the injured party is in a position to claim payment immediately, and that the perpetrator of the delict does not have a defence to the claim for immediate payment. In *Truter & Another v. Deysel* 2006 (4) 168 (SCA), it was held that that for purposes of prescription 'cause of action' meant every *fact* which it was necessary for the plaintiff to prove in order to succeed in his claim. It did *not* comprise every piece of *evidence* which was necessary to prove those facts.[1194]

556. In terms of the once-and-for-all rule, all damages arising from a delict that constitutes a single cause of action must be claimed at the same time, including future or prospective damage. Prescription in respect of the debt arising from such a delict therefore begins to run as soon as some damage is caused. However, in the case of a continuing wrong causing continuing harm, the courts recognize that the cause of action in effect subsists continually (and the debt to pay damages remains due) over the period of time during which the harm occurs, so that the claimant can recover damages for the harm that occurred within the applicable prescription or limitation period.[1195]

1190. Section 12(1) of the Act.

1191. *See* generally Max Loubser *Extinctive Prescription* (2nd ed, 2019) 117–125. *See* further *Deloitte Haskins & Sells Consultants (Pty) Ltd v. Bowthorpe Hellerman Deutsch (Pty) Ltd* 1991 (1) SA 525 (A) 532 H. *See also Kotzé v. Ongeskiktheidsfonds van die Universiteit van Stellenbosch* 1996 (1) SA 645 (C); 1996 (3) SA 252 (C), indicating that extinctive prescription begins to run from the date when a 'debt' is claimable and not from when it is claimed (258H) and also that a creditor cannot by his unilateral arbitrary conduct postpone the commencement of prescription (259D-262C).

1192. 1983 (1) SA 986 (A).

1193. *Evins v. Shield Insurance Co. Ltd* 1980 (2) SA 814 (A) 839C-G. In *Oslo Land Corporation v. Union Government* 1938 AD 584, the spraying of excessively strong locust poison by a government agency caused death of cattle over next three years, but it was held that prescription began to run when the first damage occurred. In *John Newmark & Co. v. Durban City Council* 1959 (1) SA 169 (D), a case concerning damage that occurred when excavations alongside a wall caused it to collapse later. It was held that prescription began to run when the first subsidence occurred.

1194. Paragraph [19], at 174H–175A.

1195. On the concept of a continuing act causing continuing harm, *see* generally Loubser, *Extinctive Prescription,* 92–96 (1996). In *Slomowitz v. Vereeniging Town Council* 1966 (3) SA 317 (A), the plaintiff claimed damages for business losses suffered as a result of the unlawful closing of a road, from Feb. 1960 until 17 Dec. 1963. Summons had been served on 24 Mar. 1964. A limitation period applicable in this case required the action to be brought within six months of the time when the cause of action arose. The Appellate Division held that, on account of damage caused by the

557. The courts have refused consistently to allow a creditor to postpone the commencement of prescription by his unilateral and arbitrary conduct, for instance by not demanding payment and thereby delaying the date when the debt becomes due.[1196]

558. The Act provides in section 12(2) that if the debtor wilfully prevents the creditor from coming to know of the existence of the debt, prescription will not commence to run until the creditor becomes aware of the existence of the debt. It has been held that the word 'wilfully' in this subsection means 'deliberately' or 'intentionally'; it does not mean 'fraudulently'.[1197]

559. In terms of section 12(3) of the Act, a debt is not deemed to be due until the creditor has or ought to have had knowledge of the identity of the debtor, and of the facts from which the debt arises. This provision applies to debts arising from delict or any other source of obligation. The provisions of section 12(3) do not require a creditor to do more than what could reasonably be expected in the circumstances of a reasonable man.[1198]

560. A creditor will be deemed to have knowledge of the identity of the debtor, and the facts from which the debt arose, if he could have acquired it by exercising reasonable care. The debtor-defendant must allege and prove that the creditor had or ought to have had, the requisite knowledge on a particular date. On the question of the identity of a debtor can be said to be established, Diemont JA in *Gericke v. Sack*[1199] held as follows:

> In common parlance I apprehend that the identity of an individual can be said to be determined when one or more of his characteristics is established so that he is definitively recognisable or known … It may be that in some cases the debtor is so distinguished, or notorious, that no address is necessary, or in other cases that his name is so commonplace that a detailed address is called for. Regard will have to be had to the particular circumstances of each case, but for

---

continuance of the unlawful closing of the road, the claimant had a cause of action against the defendant throughout the period that the road remained closed. However, in view of the six-month limitation period, the plaintiff was only entitled to such damages as he could prove he sustained during the period six months prior to the serving of the summons on the defendant – for the period 25 Sep. to 17 Dec. 1963.

1196. *Kotze v. Ongeskiksheidsfonds van die Univesiteit van Stellenbosch* 1996 (3) SA 252 (C) 258H and 259D-262C.

1197. *Jacobs v. Adonis* 1996 (4) SA 246 (C) 250J-251B.

1198. *See Gericke v. Sack* 1978 (1) SA 821 (A) 832. For cases indicating when a creditor may be said to have knowledge of the identity of the debtor and the facts from which the debt arises, *see Gericke v. Sack* 825E-H. *See also Brand v. Williams* 1988 (3) SA 908 (C), where it was held that the knowledge of the guardian of an injured minor as to the identity of the defendant will not be imputed to the minor plaintiff. *See* further *Dube v. Banana* 1999 (1) BCLR 44 (ZH) in respect of prescription of a claim for damages following sexual abuse committed more than three years before the date of institution of the action.

1199. *Gericke v. Sack* 1978 (1) SA 821 (A) 829G-830A.

practical purposes it seems to me there should be sufficient information for the process-server to be able to identify the debtor by name and address.

561. The case of *Van Zijl v. Hoogenhout*[1200] concerned a claim by the adult survivor of child abuse. The abuse occurred between 1958 and 1967 and the plaintiff attained majority in 1973. The court found that the abuse affected the plaintiff's ability to attribute blame to the abuser. The plaintiff did not acquire 'meaningful' knowledge of the wrongs against her for the purposes of prescription before what the court described as a 'progressive course of self-discovery finally removed the blindfold she had worn since the malign influences … took over her psyche'. The defendant failed to establish on a balance of probability that knowledge of the facts from which the claim arose was acquired by the plaintiff, and the prescription commenced to run, before 1997.

562. In *Truter & Another v. Deysel*,[1201] the plaintiff had undergone eye surgery in 1993, but it was only in 2000 that he managed to secure medical opinion to the effect that the procedure was performed negligently. For that reason, the claim was instituted only in April 2000. The question was when the plaintiff had acquired knowledge of the facts from which the debt arose. The court held that in a delictual claim the requirements of fault and unlawfulness were not factual ingredients of the cause of action, but were legal conclusions to be drawn from the facts.[1202] For purposes of prescription 'cause of action' meant every *fact* which it was necessary for the plaintiff to prove in order to succeed in his claim. It did *not* comprise every piece of *evidence* which was necessary to prove those facts.[1203] The expert opinion indicating negligence in the performance of the medical procedure was not itself a *fact*, but, rather, *evidence*.[1204] The presence or absence of negligence is not a fact; it is a conclusion of law to be drawn by the court in all the circumstances of the specific case. Section 12(3) of the Prescription Act requires knowledge only of the material facts from which the debt arises for the prescriptive period to begin running – it does not require knowledge of the relevant legal conclusions, that is, that the known facts constitute negligence, or of the existence of an expert opinion which supports such conclusions.[1205]

§4. Delay of Prescription

563. In terms of section 13(1) of the Act, the completion of extinctive prescription will be delayed in certain circumstances. Where such circumstances or 'impediments' exist and the applicable period of prescription would, but for the provisions

1200. 2005 (2) SA 93 (SCA).
1201. 2006 (4) 168 (SCA).
1202. Paragraph [17], at 174E.
1203. Paragraph [19], at 174H–175A.
1204. Paragraph [20], at 175B.
1205. The court referred in this regard to M.M. Loubser, *Extinctive Prescription* (1996) 80 and the authorities cited there, in particular *Evins v. Shield Insurance Co. Ltd* 1980 (2) SA 814 (A) 838H-839A.

of section 13(1), be completed before or on, or within one year after the day on which the relevant impediment has ceased to exist, the period of prescription will not be completed before a year has elapsed after the day referred to in paragraph (i) of section 13(1), that is, a year after the date on which the relevant impediment has ceased to exist.[1206]

564. Completion of prescription will be delayed if:

(a) the creditor is a minor, or is insane, or is a person under curatorship, or is prevented by superior force, including any law or any order of court, from interrupting the running of prescription as contemplated in section 15(1);[1207]
(b) the debtor is outside the Republic;[1208]
(c) the creditor and the debtor are married to each other;[1209]
(d) the creditor and the debtor are partners and the debt is a debt which arose out of the partnership relationship;[1210]
(e) the creditor is a juristic person and the debtor is a member of the governing body of such juristic person;[1211]
(f) the debt is the object of a dispute subjected to arbitration;[1212]
(g) the debt is the object of a claim filed against the estate of a debtor who is deceased, or against the insolvent estate of a debtor, or against the company in liquidation; or
(h) the creditor or the debtor is deceased and an executor of the estate in question has not yet been appointed.[1213]

565. The implications of section 13 were considered by the Supreme Court of Appeal in *ABP 4x4 Motor Dealers (Pty) Ltd v. IGI Insurance Co. Ltd.*[1214] The court indicated that if a period of extinctive prescription of three years has commenced

---

1206. *See* generally *ABP 4x4 Motor Dealers (Pty) Ltd v. IGI Insurance Co. Ltd* 1999 (3) SA 924 (SCA) 930B.
1207. *See* on the interpretation of this subsection *Roux v. Santam Versekeringsmpy Bpk* 1977 (3) SA 261 (T); *Mattioda Construction (SA) (Pty) Ltd v. Everite Ltd* 1980 (3) SA 157 (W); *Magubane v. Minister of Police* 1982 (3) SA 542 (N); *Hartman v. Minister van Polisie* 1983 (2) SA 489 (A).
1208. In *Dithaba Platinum (Pty) Ltd v. Erconovaal Ltd* 1985 (4) SA 615 (T), it was held that an external company registered in SA was not a debtor outside the Republic as envisaged by s. 13(1)(b) and the running of prescription against such a company was not delayed.
1209. Section 13(1)(c).
1210. On s. 13(1)(d) *see Laconian Maritime Enterprises Ltd v. Agromar Lineas Ltd* 1986 (3) SA 509 (D) 513A-F; and *Van Staden v. Venter* 1992 (1) SA 552 (A).
1211. Section 13(1)(e).
1212. Section 13(1)(f). In *Murray & Roberts Construction (Cape) (Pty) Ltd v. Upington Munisipaliteit* 1984 (1) SA 571 (A) 582E-G, it was held that a dispute referred to an engineer in terms of a written agreement between the parties was 'a dispute subject to arbitration' as envisaged in s. 13(1)(f). *See also Members of the Sugar Industry Central Board v. Maritz* 1984 (4) SA 101 (T); *SA Breweries Ltd v. Grinaker Construction (Natal) (Pty) Ltd* 1986 (1) SA 191 (D); *Bankorp Ltd v. Hendler* 1992 (4) SA 375 (W); *Bank of Lisbon International Ltd v. Neves* 1992 (3) SA 349 (W) 353E-I; *Kilroe-Daley v. Barclays National Bank Ltd* 1984 (4) SA 609 (A); *Bankorp Ltd v. Leipsig* 1993 (1) SA 247 (W).
1213. Section 13(1)(h).
1214. 1999 (3) SA 924 (SCA) 930B.

running against a creditor and one of the 'impediments' listed in section 13 comes into being after two and a half years have run, but ceases to exist after the three years have run, the creditor will have one more year (calculated from the date when the impediment ceased to exist) within which to sue. If the impediment ceases to exist on the day when three years have run, the same applies. If the impediment ceases to exist when two and three-quarter years have run, the result is the same. In all three instances, the creditor will have another year (calculated from the date when the impediment ceased to exist) within which to sue. However, if the impediment comes into being after six months of the period of prescription have run, and ceases to exist six months later when two years of the original period of prescription still remain, the creditor is afforded no additional time to sue.

566. In *Jonker v. Rondalia Assurance Corporation of SA Ltd,*[1215] for example, it was held in respect of a minor that prescription commences running during minority, but where the relevant period of prescription is completed before the minor attains majority, prescription will not take effect before a year has elapsed after the attaining of majority. Should prescription be completed more than a year after the attaining of majority, prescription takes effect immediately.

§5. Interruption of Prescription by Service of Process

567. The 1969 Prescription Act provides for two kinds of interruption of prescription, namely judicial interruption by service of process on the debtor and interruption by acknowledgment of liability.

568. Section 15(1) of the 1969 Prescription Act provides for judicial interruption of extinctive prescription 'by the service on the debtor of any process whereby the creditor claims payment of the debt'. The requirements for effective judicial interruption are set out in subsections 15(2)–(6) of the Act.

The service of process on the debtor must be legally effective for interruption of prescription to occur. Mere issue of such process out of court is not sufficient. The service of process on the debtor must furthermore commence proceedings against the debtor in a legally effective manner. Where service of the process is premature in terms of a statutory provision, for example, legal proceedings are not effectively commenced and prescription will therefore not be interrupted.[1216] Service of process in an action instituted by or on behalf of a person without locus standi, for example by a minor without the assistance of his guardian, or by a company in liquidation prior to the appointment of a liquidator, or by or on behalf of a person who is not compos mentis, does not commence proceedings against the debtor in a

1215. 1976 (2) SA 334 (E) 336B-E.
1216. *Abrahamse & Sons v. SAR&H* 1933 CPD 626 637.

legally effective manner and will therefore not interrupt prescription in terms of section 15(1), unless such an action is ratified by the court. A summons served timeously may interrupt the running of prescription even if it discloses no cause of action or is otherwise excipiable.[1217]

569. Where two separate causes of action exist between a creditor and a debtor there is a separate debt corresponding to each cause of action. Service of summons on the debtor will interrupt prescription in respect of both debts only if the summons is substantively and procedurally effective as a means of commencing legal proceedings in respect of both debts.[1218] In *SANLAM v. Rainbow Diamonds (Edms) Bpk*,[1219] it was held that judicial interruption of prescription in respect of the capital did not ipso facto extend to the claim for mora interest. If any person is joined as a defendant on his own application, the process whereby the creditor claims payment of the debt will be deemed to have been served on such person on the date of such joinder.[1220]

570. In a situation where a plaintiff wishes to amend his claim for damages, the defendant could rely on prescription if the new claim is based upon a new cause of action and the relevant prescriptive period has run, but not if the new claim is part and parcel of the original cause of action, and merely represents a fresh quantification of the original claim by the addition of a further item of damages.[1221]

571. For the purposes of interruption 'any process whereby the creditor claims payment of the debt' includes a petition, a notice of motion, a rule nisi, a pleading in reconvention, a third-party notice referred to in any rule of court and any document by which legal proceedings are commenced.[1222] In *Cape Town Municipality v. Allianz Insurance Co. Ltd*,[1223] it was held that the service of process whereby the creditor claims a declaration that a debtor is liable to indemnify the creditor interrupts prescription in terms of section 15(1). An application for a winding-up order is not a legal process whereby the applicant claims payment of that debt, and the

---

1217. *Trans-African Insurance Co. Ltd v. Maluleka* 1956 (2) SA 273 (A); *Van Vuuren v. Boshoff* 1964 (1) SA 395 (T) 402F-H 403G; *Rooskrans v. Minister van Polisie* 1973 (1) SA 273 (T) 274G-H; *Sentrachem Ltd v. Prinsloo* 1997 (2) SA 1 (A) 15H-16B.

1218. *Evins v. Shield Insurance Co. Ltd* 1980 (2) SA 814 (A) 842F-G; *Park Finance Corporation (Pty) Ltd v. Van Niekerk* 1956 (1) SA 669 (T) 673A-C; *Erasmus v. Grunow* 1978 (4) SA 233 (O) 245E.

1219. 1982 (4) SA 633 (C) 643C-D.

1220. Section 15(5).

1221. *Evins v. Shield Insurance Co. Ltd* 1980 (2) SA 814 (A) 836C-E; *Wighman v. British Traders Insurance Co. Ltd* 1963 (3) SA 151 (W); *Schnellen v. Rondalia Assurance Corporation of SA Ltd* 1969 (1) SA 517 (W); *Lampert-Zakiewicz v. Marine & Trade Insurance Co. Ltd* 1975 (4) SA 597 (C) 601 602; *Mazibuko v. Singer* 1979 (3) SA 258 (W); *Mokoena v. SA Eagle Insurance Co. Ltd* 1982 (1) SA 780 (O) 784 786; *Standard General Insurance Co. Ltd v. Eli Lilly (SA) (Pty) Ltd (FBC Holdings (Pty) Ltd, Third Party)* 1996 (1) SA 382 (W) 385G-H; *Wavecrest Sea Enterprises (Pty) Ltd v. Elliot* 1995 (4) SA 596 (SECL) 600H-601D; *Willie's Plumbing Suppliers CC v. Ace Pools (East Rand) (Edms) Bpk* 1996 (1) SA 518 (W) 523E-524J; *Greater Johannesburg Transitional Metropolitan Council v. ABSA Bank Ltd t/a Volkskas Bank* 1997 (2) SA 591 (W) 601H-J 604I-J; *Stroud v. Steel Engineering Co. Ltd* 1996 (4) SA 1139 (W).

1222. Section 15(6).

1223. 1990 (1) SA 311 (C). *See also Desai v. Desai* 1996 (1) SA 141 (A) 147H-I.

service of such an application does not therefore have the effect of interrupting the running of prescription of a debt.[1224] Similarly, the service of a sequestration application will not interrupt the running of prescription.

572. The rules on interruption of prescription as set out above are subject to the provision in section 15(2) of the Act, that the interruption of prescription will lapse and the running of prescription will be deemed not to have been interrupted if the creditor does not successfully prosecute his claim to final judgment 'under the process in question',[1225] or abandons the judgment, or where the judgment is set aside.[1226] Should a plaintiff, for example, have absolution granted against him at the end of his case, he cannot be said to have successfully prosecuted his claim to final judgment; or, if an exception is taken to his claim and he cannot amend, but has to issue a fresh process, the process by which he commenced the proceedings is deemed not to have interrupted prescription.[1227]

If the running of prescription is interrupted by service of a process and the creditor successfully prosecutes his claim to final judgment and does not abandon the judgment or if the judgment is not set aside, prescription commences to run afresh on the day on which the judgment of the court becomes executable.[1228]

If the running of prescription is interrupted as contemplated in section 15(1) and the debtor acknowledges liability, and the creditor does not prosecute his claim to final judgment, prescription commences to run afresh from the day on which the debtor acknowledges liability or, if at the time when the debtor acknowledges liability, or any time thereafter, the parties postpone the due date of the debt, from the date upon which the debt again becomes due.[1229]

If the running of prescription is interrupted, and the creditor successfully prosecutes his claim under the process to final judgment, and the interruption does not lapse in terms of section 15(2), prescription commences to run afresh on the day on which the judgment of the court becomes executable.[1230]

§6. Interruption of Prescription by Acknowledgment of Liability

573. Extinctive prescription is interrupted by an express or tacit acknowledgment of liability by the debtor. 'Acknowledgment of liability' is not defined in the section 14(1) of the Prescription Act, and in deciding whether there has been an acknowledgement of liability interrupting prescription, the inquiry will be factual

---

1224. *Misnun's Heilbron Roller Mills Holdings (Pty) Ltd v. Nobel Street Central Investments (Pty) Ltd* 1979 (2) SA 1127 (W) 1129C; *Collett v. Priest* 1931 AD 290 299.
1225. In *Chauke v. President Insurance Co. Ltd* 1978 (2) SA 947 (W), it was held that the words 'under the process in question' in s. 15(2) meant 'in terms of the Rules of Court' governing the question (950 E-G). *See also Kuhn v. Kerble*1957 (3) SA 525 (A) 534A; *Sieberhagen v. Grunow* 1957 (3) SA 485 (C) 488–489.
1226. Section 15(2). *See Van der Merwe v. Protea Insurance Co. Ltd* 1982 (1) SA 770 (E) 773C-E.
1227. *Titus v. Union & SWA Insurance Co. Ltd* 1980 (2) SA 701 (Tk) 704C-E; *Union & SWA Insurance Co. Ltd v. Hoosein* 1982 (2) SA 481 (W) 484A-E.
1228. Section 15(4).
1229. Section 15(3).
1230. Section 15(4).

with regard to the intention of the debtor.[1231] It must be clear that the debtor had intended not merely to acknowledge that he had incurred the obligation, but also that the debt was in existence and that he was liable for it.[1232] The acknowledgement of liability need not amount to a fresh undertaking to discharge the debt. All that is required is an acknowledgement by the debtor of his liability under the debt.[1233] Such an acknowledgement can take the form of part payment, payment of interest, the giving of security, or the admission of liability in any other manner.[1234]

The acknowledgment of liability must be made by the debtor himself or his authorized agent; and must be made to the creditor himself or his agent.[1235]

574. If the running of prescription has been interrupted as contemplated in section 14(1), prescription will commence to run afresh from the day on which the interruption takes place or, if at the time of the interruption or at any time thereafter, the parties postpone the due date of the debt, on the date upon which the debt again becomes due.[1236]

§7. Waiver of Prescription

575. The question as to whether and how a debtor can renounce the right to rely on prescription, wholly or partially, involves questions of public policy. The courts will be reluctant to give effect to a term contained in a standard form contract

1231. *Agnew v. Union & South West African Insurance Co. Ltd* 1977 (1) SA 617 (A) 623A-C.

1232. *Estate Allie v. Cape Town Municipality* 1980 (1) SA 265 (C) 268D. In *Eerste Nasionale Bank van Suidelike Afrika Bpk v. Vermeulen* 1997 (1) SA 498 (O) 583G-I, it was held that payment, by the holder of an overdrawn account at a bank, of monies into that account constitutes an acknowledgement of the whole of the debt evidenced by the overdrawn account. Such a payment therefore interrupts the running of prescription in respect of the whole of the overdrawn account. *See also Road Accident Fund v. Mothupi* 2000 (4) SA 38 (SCA) paras [36]–[39], where Nienaber JA set out the key elements of acknowledgement of liability.

1233. *Benson v. Walters* 1984 (1) SA 73 (A) 87; and *see also Road Accident Fund v. Mothupi* 2000 (4) SA 38 (SCA) paras [36]–[39], where Nienaber JA set out the key elements of acknowledgement of liability.

1234. *Consolidated Textile Mills Ltd v. Weiniger* 1961 (3) SA 335 (O) 339H; *Petzer v. Radford (Pty) Ltd* 1953 (4) SA 314 (N) 318C. In the *Consolidated Textile Mills* case (314D-E), it was held that payment of an interim dividend cannot be regarded as an interruption of prescription running against the creditor of a company in liquidation.

1235. In *Pentz v. Government of the RSA* 1983 (3) SA 584 (A), a statement made to the South African Police Services, regarding a sum of money retained from a stolen cheque cashed by the second defendant, was held not to constitute an acknowledgement interrupting prescription, because it was not made to the creditor (defendant) or his agent, the police officer taking the statement not being an agent for the purposes of receiving such an acknowledgement. *See also Markham v. SA Finance & Industrial Co. Ltd* 1962 (3) SA 669 (A) 676F.

1236. Section 15(3).

whereby a debtor renounces the right to rely on prescription in advance.[1237] However, if the parties specifically negotiate such a renunciation, on the basis of particular circumstances or commercial considerations, the renunciation could be valid.[1238]

§8. The Prescription Act and Other Legislation on Prescription or Limitation

576. The provisions of Chapter III of the Prescription Act[1239] apply to any debt arising after its commencement.[1240] However, in terms of section 16(1) of the Act the provisions relating to extinctive prescription are only applicable insofar as they are not inconsistent with the provisions of other legislation which prescribes a specified period within which a claim is to be made or an action is to be instituted in respect of a debt, or which imposes conditions on the institution of an action for the recovery of a debt.[1241]

577. The provisions of section 16(1) are subject to a further proviso that the provisions of any law which, if the Act had not come into operation, would have applied to the prescription of a debt which arose or arises out of an advance or loan of money by an insurer to any person in respect of an insurance policy issued by such insurer before 1 January 1974, will continue to apply to the prescription of the debt in question in all respects as if the Act had not come into operation.[1242] Similarly, the provisions of any law which, immediately before the commencement of the Act, applied to the prescription of a debt which arose before such commencement, will continue to apply to the prescription of the debt in question in all respects as if the Act had not come into operation.[1243]

578. The provisions of the Act bind the State.[1244] This applies equally in respect of acquisitive and extinctive prescription insofar as a right of ownership or a limited real right can indeed be acquired.[1245]

1237. *Ryland v. Edros* 1997 (2) SA 690 (C) 713H-I. The court disagreed with the decision in *Nedfin Bank Bpk v. Meisenheimer* 1989 (4) SA 701 (T). *See also Friederich Kling GmbH v. Continental Jewellery Manufacturers, Speidel GmbH v. Continental Jewellery Manufacturers* 1995 (4) SA 966 (C); *ABSA Bank Bpk h/a Bankfin v. Louw* 1997 (3) SA 1085 (C) 1090A-D.
1238. *See* generally Max Loubser *Extinctive Prescription* (2nd ed. 2019) ch. 8.
1239. Act 68 of 1969.
1240. Section 16(1).
1241. *See Meintjies v. Administrasieraad van Sentraal-Tvl* 1980 (1) SA 283 (T) 289B-D; *Hartman v. Minister van Polisie* 1981 (2) SA 149 (O) 152A-E.
1242. Section 16(2)(b).
1243. Section 16(2)(a).
1244. Section 19.
1245. *Oertel v. Direkteur van Plaaslike Bestuur* 1983 (1) SA 354 (A) 369C-E.

§9. Procedure

579. A court may not of its own accord take notice of prescription.[1246]

580. A party to litigation who invokes prescription must do so in a document filed of record in the proceedings; and in an action the issue of prescription is raised by way of a special plea.[1247] The word 'proceedings' has a wide meaning, as has the reference to a party to litigation, so that prescription may be relied on in any proceedings, not only in an action.[1248]

§10. Onus

581. The onus is on the party invoking prescription to plead and prove the facts indicating that prescription has taken effect,[1249] including the date of the inception of the period of prescription,[1250] or deemed knowledge of the facts from which the debt arises on the part of the debtor, for determination of the date of the inception of the period of prescription.[1251]

The onus is on the creditor to allege and prove that the completion of prescription was delayed under the circumstances set out in section 13 of the Prescription Act,[1252] or the interruption of prescription through either an express or tacit acknowledgement of liability by the debtor,[1253] or by service of a legal process.[1254]

§11. Prescription and the Constitution

582. The application of special notice and limitation periods was an important feature of actions against the State and certain State organs prior to the introduction

---

1246. Section 17(1).
1247. Section 17(2). *See Grindrod (Pty) Ltd v. Seaman* 1998 (2) SA 347 (C) 350I-J.
1248. *Lipschitz v. Dechamps Textiles GmbH* 1978 (4) SA 427 (C) 413B-E; *Rand Staple-Machine Leasing (Pty) Ltd v. ICI (SA) Ltd* 1977 (3) SA 199 (W) 210H.
1249. *Gericke v. Sack* 1978 (1) SA 821 (A) 827 828C; *Groenewald v. Minister van Justisie* 1972 (3) SA 596 (O) 600B-D; *Mulungu v. Bowring Barclays & Associates (Pty) Ltd* 1990 (3) SA 694 (SWA) 697B; *De Szabo v. Swart* 1951 (3) SA 378 (T) 381G; *Avex Air (Pty) Ltd v. Borough of Vryheid* (2) 1972 (4) SA 676 (N) 678; *Dreyer v. Tuckers Land & Development Corporation (Pty) Ltd* 1981 (1) SA 1219 (T) 1129C.
1250. *Gericke v. Sack* 1978 (1) SA 821 (A) 827H-828A; *Santam Ltd v. Ethwar* 1999 (1) All SA 252 (SCA); 1999 (2) SA 244 (SCA) 256G-H.
1251. *Mulungu v. Bowring Barclays & Associates (Pty) Ltd* 1990 (3) SA 694 (SWA) 697B; *Administrator, Cape v. Olpin* 1996 (1) SA 569 (C) 573A-B; *Brand v. Williams* 1988 (3) SA 908 (C) 910A-C; *Van Staden v. Fourie* 1989 (3) SA 200 (A) 216A-B; *Hatem v. Oos-Randse Administrasieraad* 1984 (2) SA 276 (T) 281H-282A; *Salandia (Pty) Ltd v. Vredenburg-Saldanha Municipality* 1985 (3) SA 265 (C) 275A-B; *Johnson v. Blaikie & Co. (Pty) Ltd t/a FT Building Supplies* 1998 (2) All SA 38 (N) 47d-e.
1252. *Regering van die RSA v. SA Eagle Versekeringsmpy Bpk* 1985 (2) SA 42 (O) 47F-G.
1253. Section 14. *See Pentz v. Government of the RSA* 1983 (3) SA 584 (A); *Benson v. Walters* 1984 (1) SA 73 (A).
1254. *Du Bruyn v. Joubert* 1982 (4) SA 691 (W) 695–696A.

of a new Constitution in South Africa in the last decade of the twentieth century. Once the interim Constitution[1255] and the finalized Constitution[1256] had come into operation, the constitutionality of these short and onerous notice and limitation periods was challenged, in terms of the constitutional guarantees of equality and access to the courts. The Constitutional safeguards relating to prescription concern the adequacy of the prescription period and a concomitant notice period (where applicable).[1257]

583. In *Mohlomi v. Minister of Defence*,[1258] the Constitutional Court declared the notice and limitation provisions contained in section 113(1) of the Defence Act[1259] invalid, on the basis of inconsistency with the constitutionally guaranteed right of access to the courts. In *Hans v. Minister van Wet en Orde*,[1260] the court reached the same conclusion in respect of the validity of provisions similar to section 32(1) of the Police Act.[1261]

584. The law on notice and limitation periods for actions against the State and organs of State was subsequently reformed by the Institution of Legal Proceedings against Certain Organs of State Act of 2002.[1262]

§12. Institution of Legal Proceedings Against Certain Organs of State: Act 40 of 2002

585. This Act was introduced to regulate and to harmonize the periods of prescription of debts for which certain organs of State are liable, notably by the repeal or amendment of a large number of statutes, as listed in the Schedule to the Act. In terms of this Act prescription periods for actions for recovery of 'debts' from 'organs of State' as defined in section 1 have been brought in line with the provisions of the Prescription Act.[1263]

The Act also makes provision for certain transitional rules regarding prescription of debts that had not become prescribed at the date of its commencement.[1264]

The Act also provides for a uniform notice period and procedure for the purposes of intended legal proceedings against organs of State for the recovery of debts.[1265]

1255. Act 200 of 1993.
1256. Act 108 of 1996.
1257. *See* Iain Currie & Johan de Waal, *The Bill of Right Handbook,* 715–717 (5th ed., Juta & Co. Ltd 2005).
1258. 1996 (12) BCLR 1559 (CC); 1997 (1) SA 124 (CC).
1259. Act 44 of 1957.
1260. 1995 (12) BCLR 1693 (C).
1261. Act 7 of 1958.
1262. Act 40 of 2002.
1263. Act 68 of 1969.
1264. Section 1(2)–(4).
1265. Part 2 (ss 3–6).

§13. THE ROAD ACCIDENT FUND ACT 56 OF 1996

586. The Road Accident Fund Act 56 of 1996 provides for the transfer to the Road Accident Fund of certain forms of liability that would otherwise arise for the negligent driver or owner of a motor vehicle in terms of common law. The Road Accident Fund is liable in cases of loss or damage resulting from bodily injury or death, according to certain requirements as set out in section 17 of the Act. Claims against the fund are subject to prescription provisions contained in section 23 of the Act, which provides as follows:

> 23 Prescription of claim
>
> 1. Notwithstanding anything to the contrary in any law contained, but subject to subsections (2) and (3), the right to claim compensation under section 17 from the Fund or an agent in respect of loss or damage arising from the driving of a motor vehicle in the case where the identity of either the driver or the owner thereof has been established, shall become prescribed upon the expiry of a period of three years from the date upon which the cause of action arose.
> 2. Prescription of a claim for compensation referred to in subsection (1) shall not run against –
>   a. a minor;
>   b. any person detained as a patient in terms of any mental health legislation; or
>   c. a person under curatorship.
> 3. Notwithstanding subsection (1), no claim which has been lodged in terms of section 24 shall prescribe before the expiry of a period of five years from the date on which the cause of action arose.

587. Section 23 provides for a two-tier prescription system. A three-year prescription period, calculated from the date upon which the cause of action arose, applies for the lodging of a claim against the fund in terms of section 24 of the Act. In the event of failure to a lodge a claim within this three-year period, prescription takes effect and the claim is lost.[1266] If the claim is properly lodged within the three-year period, the second tier of the prescription system comes into operation; and to enforce the claim the claimant must institute action by having a summons served on the fund before the expiration of five years from the date on which the cause of action arose, in terms of section 23(3).

In terms of section 23(2), prescription does not run against a minor, or person detained under mental health legislation, or a person under curatorship. The subsection is silent on other grounds for suspension of the running of prescription on the basis of incapacity, such as unconsciousness, but such grounds will be recognized under common law.

The prescription of claims under the Road Accident Fund Act that arise from the driving of a motor vehicle where the identity of neither the driver nor the owner of

1266. *See Krischke v. Road Accident Fund* 2004 (4) SA 358 (W).

the vehicle is known (so-called hit-and-run claims) is governed by Regulations 2(3) and 2(4).[1267] These regulations provide for a shorter prescription period than normal (two years) and excludes suspension of the running of prescription on the basis of incapacity, but these provisions of the regulations have been held to be invalid for not being authorized under the Act.[1268]

§14. Apportionment of Damages Act 34 of 1956

588. In terms of the Apportionment of Damages Act,[1269] the period of extinctive prescription in respect of a claim for a contribution against and between joint and several wrongdoers is twelve months, calculated from the date of the judgment in respect of which a contribution is claimed or, where an appeal is made against such judgment, the date of the final judgment on appeal. Where the period of extinctive prescription governing any action which may be instituted against a joint wrongdoer by the plaintiff is governed by a law which prescribes a period of less than twelve months as the period within which legal proceedings must be instituted, or within which notice must be given that proceedings will be instituted, the provisions of such law will apply *mutatis mutandis* to any action for a contribution by a joint wrongdoer, the period or periods concerned being calculated from the date of judgment in the matter, instead of from the date of the original cause of action.[1270]

589. Notice of any action may, any time before the close of pleadings in such an action, be given by the plaintiff or by any joint wrongdoer who is not sued in that action, and such joint wrongdoer may thereupon intervene as a defendant in that action.[1271] A plaintiff who fails to give such notice may not proceed against the joint wrongdoer, except if the court is satisfied that there are good reasons save with the leave of the court on good cause shown why such notice was not given.[1272]

§15. Compensation for Occupational Injuries and Diseases Act (COIDA)

590. A claim for compensation in terms of the COIDA[1273] must be lodged by or on behalf of the claimant, in the prescribed manner, with the commissioner or the

1267. Regulations in terms of s. 26 of the Road Accident Fund Act 56 of 1996 were published in Government Gazette 17939 of 25 Apr. 1997. The regulations came into effect, with the Act, on 1 May 1997.
1268. *Moloi and Others v. Road Accident Fund* 2001 (3) SA 546 (SCA).
1269. Act 34 of 1956.
1270. Proviso to s. 2(6)(b).
1271. Section 2(2)(a) and (b). *See Commercial Union Assurance Co. Ltd v. Pearl Assurance Co. Ltd* 1962 (3) SA 856 (E).
1272. Section 2(4)(a).
1273. Act 30 of 1993.

employer or the mutual association concerned, within twelve months after the date of the accident or, in the case of death, within twelve months after the case of death.[1274]

If a claim for compensation is not lodged timeously, the claim may not be considered in terms of the Act, except where the accident concerned has been reported in terms of section 39.[1275] However, a claim for compensation by any seaman or airman may be lodged with the person in command of the ship or aircraft concerned, except if such seaman or airman is himself the person in command.[1276] If any seaman or airman meets with an accident outside the Republic, resulting in death, a claim for compensation may be instituted within twelve months after news of the death has been received by any dependant claiming compensation.[1277] The provisions of section 38 of the Act apply *mutatis mutandis* in respect of any failure to institute a claim, or in respect of any error or inaccuracy in a claim instituted in terms of section 43.[1278] A right to benefit in terms of the Act lapses if the accident in question is not brought to the attention of the commissioner or the employer or mutual association concerned, within twelve months after the date of such accident.[1279]

591. Section 23(4) of the Road Accident Fund Act[1280] provides that where a right of an 'employee' in terms of section 36 of the COIDA,[1281] to recover an amount from the person who caused the damage or loss, can be exercised against the Road Accident Fund, such a right shall for the purposes of the Road Accident Fund Act[1282] be deemed to be a right to claim compensation under section 17 of the Road Accident Fund Act,[1283] arising on the same date as the cause of action of the claimant under section 17.

1274. Section 43(1)(a).
1275. Section 43(1)(b).
1276. Section 43(2).
1277. Section 43(3).
1278. Section 43(4).
1279. Section 44.
1280. Act 56 of 1996.
1281. Act 30 of 1993.
1282. Act 56 of 1996.
1283. *Ibid.*

Chapter 2. Grounds of Justification

§1. Introduction

592. Grounds of justification are special circumstances that make the infringement of a right or breach of a duty reasonable and therefore lawful, whereas such infringement or breach would be unlawful in the absence of the special circumstances. Grounds of justification are simply applications of the general criterion of reasonableness, as applied to certain typical situations. For instance, where a person defends himself against an unlawful attack on his person or property and in the process injures the attacker, the injury may be justified on the ground of private defence. In *Clarke v. Hurst*,[1284] grounds of justification were described as follows:

> The stereotyped grounds of justification are specific grounds of justification of otherwise wrongful conduct which with the passage of time have become chrystallised, with their own rules limiting the scope of their application.

593. Grounds of justification deal with certain stereotyped situations where the application of the general criterion of reasonableness have become standardized to the extent that certain sub-rules, or a framework for the application of the general criterion, have developed. There is no closed list of grounds of justification, because such grounds merely represent applications of the general criterion of reasonableness, justifying an infringement of a right or breach of duty that would otherwise be unlawful.

594. The onus of proving that the infringement or breach is not unlawful is on the defendant, who has caused harm by what appears to be an infringement of a right or breach of a duty and therefore needs to justify the causing of such harm.[1285]

595. The most common grounds of justification are discussed below, namely private defence, necessity, provocation, consent, statutory authority, public authority, official command and disciplinary authority.

§2. Consent

596. Where a person capable of expressing his will indicates to another person his willingness to suffer some harm or to run the risk of suffering some harm, for a lawful purpose, the causing of such harm by the other person is justified. Consent is a ground of justification on the basis that it involves a waiver of rights in respect of the harm concerned; or on the basis that the causing of harm is reasonable in terms of the *boni* mores or the legal convictions of the community where the person affected has consented thereto for a lawful purpose. One could also say that consent

---

1284. 1992 (4) SA 630 (D) 650.

1285. *Mabaso v. Felix* 1981 (3) SA 865 (A); P.Q.R. Boberg, *The Law of Delict, Vol. 1 Aquilian Liability*, 644–652, 789–790, 792, 799 823–824.

is a ground of justification because a legal duty not to cause harm does not arise where consent to the harm has been given.[1286]

597. In Roman and Roman-Dutch law, the principle that consent can justify the causing of harm was expressed in the maxim *volenti non fit iniuria.*[1287] In South African law, this maxim and the principle that it embodies is applied not only in respect of the intentional causing of specific harm for a lawful purpose, as in the case of a medical operation, but also in respect of acceptance of a risk of harm that may be negligently caused in the course of a dangerous activity, as in the case of participation in a sport that involves the risk of injury.[1288] Consent in the latter form is sometimes also referred to as voluntary assumption of risk. Voluntary exposure to the risks of a dangerous activity will not necessarily constitute consent to suffer harm as a result of the negligence of others that also participate in the dangerous activity, but it may then nevertheless constitute contributory negligence in respect of the resultant harm. Whereas consent on the part of a plaintiff is a ground of justification and therefore a complete defence, excluding liability on the part of the defendant who caused the harm, contributory negligence on the part of the plaintiff has the effect of diminishing the damages to which he is entitled as a result of the harm caused by both his own and the defendant's negligent conduct.[1289]

598. Consent to of the intentional causing of harm for a lawful purpose, as in the case of a medical operation, involves a willingness to suffer specific harm, for example the removal of part of an organ as a result of cancer, with the inevitable pain and inconvenience accompanying such an operation. Consent to the risk of harm is less specific: it involves a willingness to run the risk of suffering some harm in the course of a dangerous activity such as a sport that involves the risk of injury.[1290] A particular situation may give rise to both forms of consent, as in the case of a medical operation involving not only some pain and inconvenience, but also the risk of complications or even death.[1291] A patient who is adequately informed of the risks and nevertheless decides to undergo the operation consents to

1286. *See* Von Bar, *Gemeineuropäisches Deliksrecht*, Band II, 534. In English law, it has been accepted that there is no duty of care in respect of harm that has been consented to; *see Dann v. Hamilton*[1939] 1 KB 509.

1287. D 47 10 1 5; De Groot 3 35 8; Voet 47 10 4.

1288. *See Santam Insurance Co. Ltd v. Vorster* 1973 (4) SA 764 (A) 775:

> In its simplest forms – of which express consent to a surgical operation or the tacit consent of participants in a contact sport such as rugby football afford clear illustrations – the defence gives rise to little or no difficulty. In practice, it is the application of this volens defence in what are conveniently known as 'risk' cases which presents problems. In such cases, the defence is variously designated as the 'voluntary assumption', 'voluntary acceptance', or 'voluntary encountering' of risk, or risk of injury.

1289. *See Santam Insurance Co. Ltd v. Vorster* 1973 (4) SA 764 (A) 778.

1290. *See Clarke v. Welsh* 1976 (3) SA 484 (A) (golf); *Boshoff v. Boshoff* 1987 (2) SA 694 (O) (squash).

1291. *See Esterhuizen v. Administrator, Transvaal* 1957 (3) SA 710 (T); *Castell v. De Greeff* 1994 (4) SA 408 (C); *Broude v. McIntosh* 1998 (3) SA 60 (A).

the pain and inconvenience that will inevitably occur, but also to the possibility of complications or death which may occur, but which is hoped will not occur.

599. The characteristics of and requirements for valid consent are set out in the following paragraphs.

600. Consent involves unilateral conduct on the part of the plaintiff whereby he indicates that he is willing to suffer harm or run the risk of some harm. No agreement or contract between plaintiff and defendant is required: the defendant who caused harm to the plaintiff when the latter was manifestly willing to suffer such harm can rely on consent as a defence without having to prove that there was consensus between the parties on the existence of consent.[1292] Where there was an agreement between the parties that the one will not hold the other liable for harm that may ensue (*pactum de non petendo*) the practical effect is the same as consent. Because consent involves unilateral conduct on the part of the plaintiff, he can revoke the consent at any stage prior to the causing of harm by the defendant. For example, a person who has consented to the publication of an article on her private life can revoke such consent prior to publication, and the publication would then be an unlawful invasion of privacy.[1293]

601. The consenting party must have indicated his consent in an externally apparent or manifest manner. In the absence of some external manifestation of consent, for instance where the plaintiff remained quiet and passive when the harm occurred, the plaintiff could of course simply deny that he had consented, and the defendant would not be able to prove the contrary.

602. Consent can be given verbally, either expressly or by implication, or tacitly, by conduct.[1294] Encouragement or invitation to cause harm will indicate consent,[1295] but mere acquiescence[1296] or knowledge that harm will ensue[1297] is not enough to constitute consent.

603. Consent must be given before the harm occurs. Because consent is a ground of justification that involves a waiver of rights in respect of the harm concerned, the causing of harm prior to the giving of consent will be unlawful; but the person who

1292. *Santam Insurance Co. Ltd v. Vorster* 1973 (4) SA 764 (A) 780–781.
1293. *Jooste v. National Media Ltd* 1996 (3) SA 262 (A).
1294. *Waring and Gillow Ltd v. Sherborne* 1904 TS 340 344–345; *Union Government (Minister of Railways) v. Matthee* 1917 AD 688 703; *Stoffberg v. Elliott* 1923 CPD 148.
1295. Cf. *Jordaan v. Delarey* 1958 (1) SA 638 (T). In this case, the plaintiff asked the defendant to repeat defamatory words in the presence of two policemen, which the defendant did. The court held that this request amounted to consent, but in such circumstances the request can also be interpreted as a challenge to the defendant, for the plaintiff to obtain evidence in order to vindicate his rights in court.
1296. Cf. *R v. Taylor* 1927 CPD 16 20. In the case of alleged rape, all the circumstances must be taken into account to determine whether passivity on the part of the woman implied consent or was the result of fear or realization that resistance would be useless; cf. *R v. M* 1953 (4) SA 393 (A).
1297. *Santam Insurance Co. Ltd v. Vorster* 1973 (4) SA 764 (A) 779.

suffers the harm may of course afterwards also waive the right to claim damages, either unilaterally or by way of an agreement not to claim (*pactum de non petendo*).

604. Consent must be given by a person capable of expressing his or her will, who must be the person who will suffer the harm. This does not mean that majority or full legal capacity is required for consent, but the person who consents must have the mental ability to appreciate the implications of his actions, to distinguish between right and wrong, and to act accordingly.[1298] All the circumstances of the case will be taken into account to determine whether the necessary capacity existed, including the nature and value of the interest affected and the age, intelligence, knowledge and experience of the person who is alleged to have consented. Because consent by a minor in respect of a patrimonial interest in effect amounts to the alienation of such an interest, the courts will be inclined to require full legal capacity for such consent, whereas a less strict approach may be followed in respect of a minor's consent to conduct affecting personality interests such as privacy or bodily integrity.[1299] In the case of someone not capable of expressing his or her will, such as a young child, consent may be given by someone who can lawfully express a will on behalf of the person lacking capacity, such as a parent or guardian. Where parents refuse to consent to an operation that is considered necessary in the opinion of a physician, or where the parents are deceased or incapacitated, the Minister of Health and Welfare can give the necessary consent.[1300] In an emergency, the medical superintendent of a hospital may consent to the medical treatment of a child.[1301] Consent to medical treatment of mentally ill persons are regulated by the Mental Health Act.[1302] The consent of a parent on behalf of a child must be reasonable and in the interests of the child: consent that the child may participate in a patently dangerous activity that is of no value or benefit to the child will be unreasonable and invalid.[1303]

605. Consent must be freely and voluntarily given. It will not readily be accepted that a person who was under moral, social or economic pressure has consented to suffer harm or to run the risk of harm; for instance in a situation where an employee undertakes dangerous work in the course of his employment,[1304] or submits to physical punishment.[1305]

606. Full prior knowledge of the nature and extent of the harm or the risk of harm is required. To be valid, consent must be informed consent, and the consenting party must have had information on the material aspects of the harm or the risk

1298. Cf. *S v. Marx* 1962 (1) SA 848 (N) 854; and also *R v. Taylor* 1927 CPD 16; *R v. Sagaye* 1932 NPD 236.
1299. Cf. Von Bar, *Gemeineuropäisches Deliksrecht*, Band II, 536.
1300. Section 39(1) of the Child Care Act 74 of 1983.
1301. Section 39(2) of the Child Care Act 74 of 1983.
1302. Act 18 of 1973.
1303. *See* P.Q.R. Boberg, *The Law of Delict Vol. 1 Aquilian Liability*, 732.
1304. *Waring and Gillow Ltd v. Sherborne* 1904 TS 340.
1305. *R v. McCoy* 1953 (2) SA 4 (SR); *S v. Collett* 1978 (3) SA 206 (RA).

of harm that is involved.[1306] This is of particular importance in the case of medical treatment. In *Castell v. De Greeff*,[1307] the court reviewed the South African law in this regard comprehensively and held that the requirements for informed consent in the context of medical treatment are as follows: For consent to operate as a defence:

(a) the consenting party must have had knowledge and been aware of the nature and extent of the harm or risk;
(b) the consenting party must have appreciated and understood the nature and extent of the harm or risk;
(c) the consenting party must have consented to the harm or assumed risk;
(d) the consent must be comprehensive, that is extend to the entire transaction, inclusive of its consequences.[1308]

Accordingly, for a patient's consent to constitute a justification that excludes unlawfulness in the context of medical treatment and its consequences, the doctor is obliged to warn a patient of a material risk inherent in the proposed treatment; a risk being material if, in the circumstances of the particular case:

(a) a reasonable person in the patient's position, if warned of the risk, would be likely to attach significance to it; or
(b) the medical practitioner is or should reasonably be aware that the particular patient, if warned of the risk, would be likely to attach significance to it.[1309]

607. The doctor's obligation to warn may be subject to the so-called therapeutic privilege, which permits medical practitioners to withhold disclosures which in their opinion would be detrimental to the patient in question, whatever the ambit of this 'privilege' may be in the light of the inroads that it might make on patient autonomy.[1310] Although expert medical evidence would be relevant to determine what the inherent risks of treatment (surgical or otherwise) are; and might also have a bearing on their materiality, this is not a question that ought to be answered on the basis of expert medical evidence alone: the ultimate question is whether the defendant's conduct conforms to the standard of reasonable care demanded by the law. That is a question for the court to decide and the duty of deciding it cannot be delegated to any profession or group in the community.[1311]

608. The consenting party must have been subjectively willing to suffer the harm, both where the harm is certain to occur through intentional conduct, as in the case of a medical operation, and where there is a risk of harm resulting from a dangerous activity. This requirement has been stated as follows:

1306. *See* generally *Esterhuizen v. Administrator, Transvaal* 1957 (3) SA 710 (T) 719; *Santam Insurance Co. Ltd v. Vorster* 1973 (4) SA 764 (A) 781; *Castell v. De Greeff* 1994 (4) SA 408 (C) 425.
1307. 1994 (4) SA 408 (C).
1308. *Castell v. De Greeff* 1994 (4) SA 408 (C) 425.
1309. *Castell v. De Greeff* 1994 (4) SA 408 (C) 426.
1310. *Ibid.*
1311. *Ibid.*

> Knowledge, appreciation, consent – these are the essential elements; but knowledge does not invariably imply appreciation, and both together are not necessarily equivalent to consent.[1312]

609. Where there is express consent, it is a matter of construction to determine what precisely is embraced by such consent. Where consent in the form of assumption of a risk is concerned the requirement of subjective willingness to suffer harm presents some difficulty. Mere knowledge of the possibility of harm is not enough to constitute consent; the maxim is *volenti non fit iniuria*, and not *scienti non fit iniuria.*[1313] Where the contention is that there was an assumption of the risk of harm, the question is whether the harm that eventually occurred was foreseen and accepted as falling within the ambit of the risk. The inquiry is subjective and foresight of the possible harm is a cardinal feature.[1314]

610. In *Lampert v. Hefer NO*,[1315] the plaintiff was a passenger in the sidecar of a motor cycle and was injured in an accident caused by the driver's negligence and the driver was killed in the accident. The plaintiff claimed damages from the driver's executor and the trial court upheld the defence of *volenti non fit injuria* on the ground that when the plaintiff entered the sidecar to commence the journey the driver was, to plaintiff's knowledge, in a highly intoxicated state. Plaintiff's application for leave to appeal in forma pauperis against the judgment of the trial court was refused by the Appellate Division. In delivering the main judgment, Fagan JA held that the defences of consent and contributory negligence may often overlap. In respect of consent by assumption of risk, he stated that 'serious intoxication in the driver of a motor vehicle must always involve a risk of accident'[1316] and concluded that the plaintiff, who had previously also travelled with the driver while he was intoxicated, must have or should have appreciated the risk of an accident and injury, even though she had been fortunate before. Her assumption of the risk on this occasion could therefore be relied upon as a complete defence by the defendant.

611. The *Lampert* case was decided before the Apportionment of Damages Act[1317] was in force; and the all-or-nothing rule of the common law still applied in respect of contributory negligence. It was therefore not vital for the purposes of the decision in the *Lampert* case to categorize the defence of assumption of risk specifically as either consent or contributory negligence; because either was a complete defence. In terms of the Apportionment of Damages Act,[1318] contributory negligence on the part of a plaintiff is not a complete defence, but leads to a reduction of the damages that the plaintiff is entitled to.[1319]

1312. *Waring and Gillow Ltd v. Sherborne* 1904 TS 340 344.
1313. *Santam Insurance Co. Ltd v. Vorster* 1973 (4) SA 764 (A) 779.
1314. *Ibid.*
1315. 1955 (2) SA 507 (A).
1316. *Lampert v. Hefer NO* 1955 (2) SA 507 (A) 514.
1317. Act 34 of 1956.
1318. *Ibid.*
1319. Section 1(1)(a).

612. Since contributory negligence has ceased to be a complete defence and it has become possible to produce a fair result by apportionment of damages, the courts have been reluctant to recognize consent in assumption of risk cases where there was negligence on the part of the defendant. In almost every case where the defence of consent in the form of assumption of risk has been raised, it has failed. The courts recognize such a defence in principle, but find on the facts that the plaintiff did not consent to the defendant's negligence and that the voluntary exposure to risk amounts to contributory negligence. Only in exceptional circumstances someone consents to run the risk of another person's negligence.[1320]

613. The leading case on consent in the form of assumption of risk is *Santam Insurance Co. Ltd v. Vorster*,[1321] where the plaintiff was a passenger in one of two cars that were being driven in a race on a country road. The drivers and passengers had placed bets on the outcome of the race. There was a collision when one driver attempted to overtake the other at a bend in the road. The plaintiff was severely injured and claimed damages on account of the negligence of both drivers. The defences of consent and contributory negligence were raised, on the basis that the plaintiff had known the risks of the race and had voluntarily exposed himself to those risks. It was held that, in addition to knowledge and appreciation of danger, the plaintiff must have foreseen the particular risk which culminated in the harm. The court held that it is inherently difficult to determine such foresight because of its subjective nature. Consent in the form of assumption of risk must therefore be determined by way of inference from the proved facts. The evidence of the plaintiff himself will carry little weight. The court must make an objective assessment of the relevant facts to determine what the inherent risks of the particular hazardous activity were and whether the risk which culminated in the harm fell within the ambit of these inherent risks. The essential question is therefore whether the plaintiff, despite his probable protestations to the contrary, must have foreseen the particular risk which culminated in the harm as part of the inherent risks of the hazardous activity, and should therefore be held to have consented thereto.[1322]

In the *Vorster* case, the court held that the inherent risks of the hazardous activity included that some mechanical defect could occur during the race, for instance the bursting of a tyre. The inherent risks did not include the acts of negligence on part of the drivers that caused the collision at a bend in the road. The defence of consent was therefore not upheld, but the court found contributory negligence on the part of the plaintiff for participating as a passenger in the hazardous activity. For the purposes of apportionment of damages, it was held that the plaintiff was equally at fault with the two drivers, and his damages were accordingly reduced by one-third.

614. Consent in the form of assumption of risk is also important in respect of sport-related injuries. Participation in sport often entails certain inherent risks of injury as a result of the conduct of other participants. A participant normally consents to the risk of injuries that occur reasonably within the normal course of a game

1320. *Santam Insurance Co. Ltd v. Vorster* 1973 (4) SA 764 (A) 778.
1321. 1973 (4) SA 764 (A).
1322. *Santam Insurance Co. Ltd v. Vorster* 1973 (4) SA 764 (A) 779–781.

or event. The fact that the injury-causing conduct of one player contravened the rules of the sport will not necessarily mean that the injury falls outside the ambit of another player's consent. A late tackle or running into an opponent in a dangerous manner may contravene the rules of a sport such as football or rugby, but it is nevertheless foreseeable in the normal course of a game.[1323] The position will be different where the injury is caused by gross contravention of the rules or deliberately dangerous conduct.[1324] To determine whether the injury occurred reasonably within the normal course of the game and therefore within the ambit of a participant's consent, all the circumstances will be taken into account. The following approach has been accepted in this regard:[1325]

> If the conduct is deliberately intended to injure someone whose presence is known, or is reckless and in disregard of all safety of others so that it is a departure from the standards which might reasonably be expected in anyone pursuing the competition or game, then the performer might well be held liable for any injury his act caused. There would, I think, be a difference, for instance, in assessing blame which is actionable between an injury caused by a tennis ball hit or a racket accidentally thrown in the course of play into the spectators at Wimbledon and a ball hit or a racket thrown into the stands in temper or annoyance when play was not in progress.

615. In *Boshoff v. Boshoff*,[1326] the plaintiff instituted action for damages as a result of injuries sustained when he was hit by his opponent's racket during a game of squash. The defence of consent was raised. The court held that injuries of this nature are reasonably to be expected in a social game of squash between amateurs. Although the plaintiff had not expressly admitted that he had accepted the risk of injury the court found that, had the plaintiff (an advocate) been asked before the match whether he consented to this risk of injury, he would have answered in the affirmative. It was therefore the 'will' of the plaintiff to run the risk of injury. Every intelligent person is, to a certain extent at least, master of his own fate and it is not *contra bonos mores* for a person capable of forming a will to consent to sustaining an injury or to run the risk of such injury in the course of lawful sport or physical recreation. A bona fide sportsman who causes injury to a fellow player in a reasonable manner as may be expected in the normal course of a game can rely on the defence of consent, on the basis that players know and accept the risk of injury in the normal course of the game. In this regard, the concept of volition does not require a positive desire to be injured, but a legal 'will' or acceptance of injury or the risk of injury. The defence of consent therefore succeeded.

1323. Cf. Von Bar, *Gemeineuropäisches Deliksrecht*, Band II, 542, 544–545.
1324. Cf. Von Bar, *Gemeineuropäisches Deliksrecht*, Band II, 544–545, referring to cases in European jurisdictions.
1325. *See Boshoff v. Boshoff* 1987 (2) SA 694 (O) 702, where this extract from the judgment in *Wooldridge v. Sumner and Another* [1962] 2 All ER 978 (CA) 983 is quoted with approval.
1326. 1987 (2) SA 694 (O).

616. In *Alex Roux v. Ryand Karel Hattingh,*[1327] a case involving a rugby injury, the court held that the conduct in question (deliberately causing the collapsing of a scrum) amounted to a serious violation of the rules of rugby and was not normally associated with the game, and was extremely dangerous, so that it would 'not have constituted conduct which rugby players would accept as part and parcel of the normal risks inherent to their participation in a game of rugby'. In the result, the causing of injury was wrongful and the justification of consent could not avail the defendant.

617. In sports injury cases, it will usually also be possible to rely on other defences, in addition to that of consent in the form of assumption of risk, namely absence of fault, that is, that the injury was not caused intentionally or negligently,[1328] or that the injury was caused lawfully because it was reasonable to cause such injury in the normal course of the game. In the *Boshoff* case, the court held that, even if the plaintiff had not consented, the causing of injury in the normal course of a game of sport would not be regarded as unlawful in terms of the general standard of reasonableness; and also alluded to the possible absence of fault.[1329]

618. The consent must be lawful, that is, be permitted in terms of the general standard of reasonableness, in accordance with the *boni mores* or the legal convictions of the community. Even if all the requirements for consent as set out above have been met, the consent will not be valid if the causing of harm as consented to offends against the *boni mores* or the legal convictions of the community or contravenes a statute; for example where a person consents to disfigurement or some other form of assault,[1330] or where a minor younger than the statutory age of consent agrees to sexual intercourse, or a woman agrees to sexual intercourse in circumstances amounting to seduction. It is also arguable that consent to the risk of injury in the course of a hazardous activity without any redeeming social value, for example a dangerous car race on a country road,[1331] or a ride with a drunken driver,[1332] should be regarded as *contra bonos mores* and therefore invalid; and that the injured person's voluntary exposure to such a risk should be regarded as contributory negligence,[1333] rather than as consent.

619. The existence of consent is a question of fact and the onus of proving facts that indicate the existence of consent is on the defendant.[1334] The courts do not

1327. [2012] ZASCA 132.
1328. *See Clarke v. Welsh* 1976 (3) SA 484 (A), where it was held that a person who hit a wayward golf shot from a tee and struck a fellow player who was standing slightly in front of the tee was not negligent in the circumstances of the case.
1329. *Boshoff v. Boshoff* 1987 (2) SA 694 (O) 702.
1330. *See R v. McCoy* 1953 (2) SA 4 (SR); *S v. Collett* 1978 (3) SA 206 (RA).
1331. *Santam Insurance Co. Ltd v. Vorster* 1973 (4) SA 764 (A).
1332. *Lampert v. Hefer NO* 1955 (2) 507 (A).
1333. *Santam Insurance Co. Ltd v. Vorster* 1973 (4) SA 764 (A) 778.
1334. *Santam Insurance Co. Ltd v. Vorster* 1973 (4) SA 764 (A) 779.

readily accept that there was consent to harm and approaches the defence of consent with circumspection.[1335] Where the defendant mistakenly thought that consent had been given, the causing of the harm will nevertheless be unlawful, but the defendant may escape liability because of absence of fault, that is, absence of the knowledge of unlawfulness as an element of intention.

620. Consent to the risk of death by a breadwinner, for example when taking part in a hazardous activity that may result in injury or even death, will not be a defence against a claim by dependants for loss of support where the death of the breadwinner has been caused by the negligence of another person. A claim for loss of support by dependants is based on the infringement of their right to support, and there is no basis in law for accepting that the breadwinner can by consent waive this right on their behalf and to their detriment. It is in any event difficult to conceive of this situation arising, because the breadwinner is not likely to consent to the risk that the negligent conduct of another person may cause his death; and the person who acted negligently will therefore almost invariably be unable to prove consent. If there was no negligence on the part of such other person there will in any event be no liability. Even if there was consent by the breadwinner to the risk that the negligent conduct of another person may cause his death, such consent is likely to be regarded as *contra bonos mores* and therefore invalid. An agreement by the breadwinner undertaking that no claim will be instituted in the event of injury or death (*pactum de non petendo*), even if it purports to bind his estate and his dependants, will also not affect the right of his dependants to claim compensation for loss of support in the event of his death.[1336] The dependants are not bound by such an agreement, because they are not parties to it, and the breadwinner cannot contract on behalf of his dependants to their detriment.

621. A prior agreement not to claim damages, should harm be caused by the conduct of another person (*pactum de non petendo in anticipando*), is contractual and therefore differs from consent, which involves unilateral conduct indicating that the person consenting is willing to suffer harm or run the risk of some harm. Theoretically, the effects of these two legal phenomena also differ, in that consent justifies the causing of harm, whereas a *pactum de non petendo in anticipando* merely excludes the recovery of damages for unlawfully caused harm. The practical effect of a *pactum de non petendo in anticipando* is the same as that of consent, however, in that it provides a complete defence against a claim for damages as a result of the anticipated and later realized harm. In certain circumstances, the conclusion of such an agreement could at the same time indicate a willingness to suffer the harm or to run the risk of harm and could therefore also constitute consent, for instance where the parties informally agree prior to undertaking a dangerous activity that their involvement would be at their own risk, and that liability for damages would be excluded. The requirements for a valid *pactum de non petendo in anticipando* are the same as for any other contract. One person cannot conclude a *pactum de non petendo in anticipando* on behalf of another without authorization. As noted in the

1335. *Ibid.*
1336. *Jameson's Minors v. CSAR* 1908 TS 575.

preceding paragraph, an agreement by a breadwinner undertaking that no claim will be instituted in the event of his injury or death, even if it purports to bind his estate and his dependants, will not affect the right of his dependants to claim compensation for loss of support in the event of his death.[1337] The courts appear to accept that a parent or guardian can validly conclude a *pactum de non petendo in anticipando* on behalf of a minor child, for instance where a school or sport club requires such an undertaking from the parent or guardian as a condition for the child's participation in an educational activity or sport.[1338] Arguably, such an undertaking is not to the benefit of the child, who should be entitled to *restitutio in integrum* to have the effects of the agreement set aside.[1339] The effect of a *pactum de non petendo in anticipando* will in any event depend on the precise ambit of the agreement, and the courts will tend to interpret such agreements restrictively.[1340] An agreement purporting to exclude liability for harm caused intentionally will not be valid, but an agreement excluding liability for harm caused by negligence or even gross negligence is regarded as valid.[1341]

§3. Necessity

622. A state of necessity justifies infringement of the interests of an innocent person (i.e., someone not causing or threatening to cause harm unlawfully) in a situation where such infringement is the only reasonable means of protecting one's own interest or that of another person against danger created by natural phenomena or human conduct.[1342] For example, it may be justified to break a window and enter another person's house to telephone for help in the event of injury, or to rescue someone trapped inside the house. In such a case, necessity justifies the causing of damage to the house.

623. An attack by an animal and danger created by forces of nature are natural phenomena that do not cause harm unlawfully; unlawfulness being an attribute of the outcome of a causal sequence set in motion by human conduct. Defensive conduct in the face of an attack by an animal or danger from forces of nature therefore does not constitute private defence, but can be justified on the ground of necessity.[1343]

1337. *Ibid*; and *see also Payne v. Minister of Transport* 1995 (4) SA 153 (C).
1338. *See Minister of Education and Culture (House of Delegates) v. Azal* 1995 (1) SA 30 (A), where the court decided that the undertaking by a parent, which limited the school's liability for damage to property or personal injury of the child, did not have effect where there was negligence on the part of the responsible teacher. *See also Durban's Water Wonderland (Pty) Ltd v. Botha* 1999 (1) SA 982 (A), where it was held that a parent had agreed on behalf of a child to conditions excluding the liability of an amusement park owner for injury to a person using the park's facilities.
1339. *See* P.Q.R. Boberg, *The Law of Delict, Vol. 1 Aquilian Liability*, 732.
1340. *See Minister of Education and Culture (House of Delegates) v. Azal* 1995 (1) SA 30 (A).
1341. *See Government of the Republic of South Africa v. Fibre Spinners & Weavers (Pty) Ltd* 1978 (2) SA 794 (A) 807; and *Afrox Healthcare Bpk v. Strydom* 2002 (6) SA 21 (SCA).
1342. Cf. *S v. Adams, S v. Werner* 1981 (1) SA 187 (A) 220; *S v. Bailey* 1982 (3) SA 772 (A) 796.
1343. The courts have nevertheless sometimes referred to private defence in this situation; cf. *Van der Bijl v. Richter* 1921 CPD 316; *Du Plessis v. Van Aswegen* 1931 TPD 332 (where the defendant

624. The essential difference between necessity and private defence is that necessity justifies the causing of harm to an innocent person (i.e., someone who is himself not causing or threatening to cause harm unlawfully), whereas private defence justifies the causing of harm to a person who is himself causing or threatening to cause harm unlawfully. The requirements to be satisfied for the recognition of private defence and necessity differ accordingly, in particular regarding the requirement of proportionality between the protected interest and the infringed interest for the purposes of necessity.

625. Necessity, as a ground of justification, simply involves an application of the general criterion of reasonableness or *boni mores*. To justify the conclusion that the infringement of the interest was lawful the person who relies on necessity must prove that the protection of a legally recognized interest against danger created by natural phenomena or human conduct was, in terms of the proportionality of the interests involved and the nature and extent of the danger and the means of protection, acceptable in terms of the *boni mores* or the legal convictions of the community.

626. The requirements for reliance on necessity are as follows.

627. There must have been actual danger to a legally recognized interest. In accordance with the general approach to the assessment of unlawfulness, the existence and extent of the danger must be determined objectively, on the basis of the circumstances actually prevailing, and not on the basis of the perception or reaction of the person who relies on the state of necessity. However, as in the case of private defence, the courts have in certain cases adopted what amounts to a qualified objective approach, by determining whether the person who purported to act in necessity reacted to the situation reasonably, instead of taking into account all the facts of the situation as known after the event.[1344] This approach involves an overlap between the inquiry into unlawfulness and the inquiry into negligence, both of which are then governed by the criterion of the reasonable person. The end result will be the same, however, whether one concludes, on the one hand, that the person relying on necessity had overreacted and therefore unlawfully exceeded the bounds of necessity, but lacked fault because he acted as a reasonable man would have done under the circumstances, and therefore cannot be held liable for causing harm in protection of his interests; or, on the other hand, that the person relying on necessity acted as a

---

was found to have been justified in killing the plaintiff's donkey, which had created havoc on defendant's property); and *S v. Moller* 1971 (4) SA 327 (T).

1344. *See R v. Mahomed* 1938 AD 30 36, where the court held that the fear created by the situation was reasonable and that the conduct of the persons who acted defensively must be judged in the light of that fear. *See also S v. Pretorius* 1975 (2) SA 85 (SWA), where necessity was raised as a defence against a charge of speeding. A parent rushed to hospital with his child after the child had taken a number of tablets. The parent believed that his child's life was in danger. It turned out that the child had taken pain tablets and could at most suffer from an upset stomach. Nevertheless, the court held that the parent had acted reasonably in a situation of necessity and therefore set the conviction for speeding aside.

reasonable person would have done under the circumstances, and therefore acted lawfully within the bounds of necessity and therefore cannot be held liable for causing harm in protection of his interests.

628. The *endangered interest can be that of the defendant himself or of another person.* For instance, where a child's life is in danger a parent may take protective measures that may infringe the interests of another person.[1345] The necessity induced conduct may be to both the benefit and the detriment of the same person, for instance where a physician needs to perform an emergency operation on an unconscious patient, who then suffers the pain and discomfort of an operation, but gains a greater health benefit.

629. Any legally recognized interest may be protected on the ground of necessity, for example life or physical integrity[1346] and property.[1347] Subject to the principle of proportionality, the necessity induced conduct may also infringe any kind of interest, for instance life or physical integrity,[1348] honour[1349] or freedom.[1350]

630. The danger can be created by any natural phenomenon, such as fire or flood; or by human conduct, such as duress.[1351] There are conflicting views on whether the defendant can rely on necessity where he himself had created a situation of danger and then, in the course of protecting his own interests or that of others from such danger, he caused harm to others. In criminal cases, it has been held on the one hand that an accused cannot rely on necessity to escape the consequences of a situation which he himself had created,[1352] while on the other hand the Appellate Division has accepted that defensive conduct may be justified where a situation of danger resulted from prior unlawful conduct on the part of the accused.[1353] If one sets in motion a sequence of events that creates danger and then, in the course of protecting one's own interests or that of others from such danger, causes harm to others, the focus of the inquiry into unlawfulness should not be restricted to that part of the sequence of events which involved a situation of necessity. The entire sequence of events must be taken into account for the purposes of

1345. Cf. *S v. Pretorius* 1975 (2) SA 85 (SWA).
1346. *S v. Goliath* 1972 (3) SA 1 (A).
1347. There are examples in Roman law where necessity justifies the protection of property in a manner that involves the causing of damage to the property of others; *see* D 19 5 14 pr (throwing cargo from a ship to prevent it from sinking), and D 47 9 3 7 (breaking down a neighbour's house to protect one's own from fire). *See also Van der Bijl v. Richter* 1921 CPD 316; and *Du Plessis v. Van Aswegen* 1931 TPD 332 (where the defendant was found to have been justified in killing the plaintiff's donkey, which had created havoc on defendant's property).
1348. *S v. Goliath* 1972 (3) SA 1 (A).
1349. *See Fayd'Herbe v. Zammit* 1977 (3) SA 711 (D) 719.
1350. Cf. *Robbertse v. Minister van Veiligheid en Sekuriteit* 1997 (4) SA 168 (T).
1351. *S v. Goliath* 1972 (3) SA 1 (A).
1352. *S v. Kibi* 1978 (4) SA 173 (E) 179; *S v. Bradbury* 1967 (1) SA 387 (A) 393 404 (in this case, the view was expressed that a person who voluntarily joins a violent gang cannot rely on a situation of necessity if he is later forced by the gang to commit murder).
1353. *R v. Mahomed* 1938 AD 30, where the accused had kidnapped a girl and were later attacked by a group of people who wanted to free the girl.

assessing unlawfulness. For example, where a parent has started a fire that endangers the life of his child and then, in the process of saving the life of the child, causes damage to a third party, he clearly had a duty to save the child, but nevertheless, when the entire sequence of events is taken into account, the conclusion should be that he unlawfully caused damage to the third party. The same applies in the case of a person who hides away in a shop after closing hours and then needs to break a window to get out.[1354]

631. The *danger must be present or imminent.* As in the case of private defence, anticipatory defensive conduct is not justified on the ground of necessity. Where one expects a dangerous situation to develop some time in the future, it is not justified to cause harm to others in the course of protecting one's interests in anticipation of the danger.[1355] A declaratory order or interdict may be the appropriate remedy where future danger is expected to emanate from human conduct, and also where danger is expected to be caused by a natural phenomenon such as a flood and reasonable measures to avert harm will affect the interests or require the cooperation of another person. Where the danger is imminent, although not yet present, one may reasonably protect one's interests without having to wait until the danger has actually commenced.[1356] Where the danger has already ceased, one cannot rely on necessity to justify retaliation, for instance where a neighbour's dog has bitten a child the parent of the child cannot follow the dog and shoot it.

632. The *person wishing to rely on necessity must not be legally obliged to endure the consequences of the dangerous situation.* For instance, the owner of a lower lying property must receive run-off water from an adjacent higher property, even if it causes damage on his property, and may not take preventative steps harmful to the other landowner on the ground of necessity.[1357]

633. There must be *proportionality between the protected interest and the interest infringed by the protective conduct.* Because necessity justifies the causing of harm to an innocent person (i.e., someone who is himself not causing or threatening to cause harm unlawfully) it will be unreasonable if the harm caused to the innocent person outweighs the harm prevented by the protective conduct. Furthermore, even if the protected interest outweighs the infringed interest, protective conduct will not necessarily be justified. A blood donation may not be enforced to save the life of a critically ill person with the same blood group; and the wearer of an expensive leather jacket may not in the event of sudden rain take an umbrella from the wearer of an inexpensive garment, because it will generally be unreasonable to force a person against his will to sacrifice his interests in order to protect the endangered interests of another.[1358] The general criterion of reasonableness applies; and all the surrounding circumstances must be taken into account to assess whether protective

1354. *See* Von Bar, *Gemeineuropäisches Deliksrecht*, Band II, 527.
1355. Cf. *S v. Mogohlwane* 1982 (2) SA 587 (T); *S v. Kibi* 1978 (4) SA 173 (E).
1356. Cf. *Hope v. R* 1917 NPD 145 146; *R v. Patel* 1959 (3) SA 121 (A).
1357. *See Dickens v. Lake* (1906) 23 SC 201 204; *Hugo v. Page* 1944 CPD 119.
1358. Cf. Von Bar, *Gemeineuropäisches Deliksrecht*, Band II, 530–531.

conduct in a situation of necessity is justified. In the examples referred to above, the proportionality of interests involved will be outweighed as a relevant factor by the absence of a special duty or relationship between the parties and by the unwillingness of the person whose interests are to be infringed to sacrifice those interests, albeit that the interests to be sacrificed are less valuable or generally regarded as less important than the interests to be protected.

634. The issue of proportionality of interests also gives rise to the question *whether the protection of life in a situation of necessity can justify the taking of another life*. Taking one life to save another is regarded as justifiable neither in the English law[1359] nor in other European jurisdictions,[1360] on the basis that one life may not be regarded as more valuable than another. This was also the view adopted in earlier South African cases,[1361] but in 1972 in *S v. Goliath*[1362] the Appellate Division held in a criminal case that necessity, in the form of compulsion or duress, can be a complete defence to a charge of murder. It was emphasized, however, that the success of this defence will depend on the particular circumstances of each case, and that such a defence will be considered with the utmost circumspection.[1363] In this instance, the accused, A, was forced by B to take part in the killing of an innocent person C. B threatened to kill A if he did not assist in the killing of C; and A, fearing for his life, complied. In a key passage of the majority judgment, Rumpff JA held that the ordinary person regards his own life as more important than the life of another and that only a person with qualities of heroism will sacrifice his own life for that of another. The law does not require that a person acting under duress should conform to a higher standard than that of the average person, and compulsion or duress can therefore be a complete defence to a charge of murder.[1364] In a minority judgment, Wessels JA agreed that held that necessity in the form of compulsion or duress can be a complete defence to a charge of murder, but differed on the reasons. His conclusion was that compulsion cannot justify the killing of an innocent person, but could lessen and even exclude fault.[1365]

1359. *See R v. Dudley & Stevens* (1884) 14 QBD 273. This case dealt with the situation where two of the people adrift in a small boat after the sinking of their ship, after twenty-one days at sea and eight days without food, had cut the throat and eaten the cabin boy, who was the weakest of the persons on the boat. They were later rescued and subsequently charged with murder and raised the plea of necessity. This plea was rejected as a defence against a charge of murder, on the basis that necessity can never justify the killing of an innocent person.

1360. *See* Von Bar, *Gemeineuropäisches Deliksrecht*, Band II, 531.

1361. *See R v. Mtetwa* 1921 TPD 227 231–232; *R v. Werner* 1947 (2) SA 828 (A) 837; *S v. Mneke* 1961 (2) SA 240 (N) 243.

1362. 1972 (3) SA 1 (A).

1363. *See also S v. Bailey* 1982 (3) SA 772 (A).

1364. At 25.

1365. Fault in the form of intention was in issue in the *Goliath* case, where the charge was murder; and intention requires that the person who acted had the will or knowledge that the death of another person would ensue and also knowledge of the unlawfulness of causing the death. Both these requirements appear to have been satisfied in the *Goliath* case and it is therefore not clear on what basis fault could have been excluded on account of compulsion or duress. Wessels JA did not expand on this aspect in his judgment. Two possible arguments in support of the view that fault was excluded are that: (i) that the accused lacked knowledge of unlawfulness, because he assumed that it was justified to sacrifice the life of another to save his own; or (ii) that the accused lacked

635. In terms of *the general criterion of reasonableness*, which is to be applied according to the *boni mores* or legal convictions of the community, as held by Rumpff JA three years after *Goliath* in the *Ewels* case,[1366] the effect of the majority judgment in the *Goliath* case is that the *boni mores* or legal convictions of the community require no more of the person acting under duress than to act as the average or reasonable person would under the circumstances. The courts will be very circumspect in recognizing necessity as a defence where the loss of life of an innocent person is concerned, but the standard will be that of the ordinary, average or reasonable person. There is no basis for suggesting that the courts will apply a different standard in a civil case; and consequently the dependants of the victim in the *Goliath* case would not have succeeded with a claim for loss of support against the accused.

636. In terms of the general criterion of reasonableness, the necessity induced conduct must have been *necessary or the only reasonable means of protecting the interests concerned.* If the defendant could have escaped from the dangerous situation by taking flight, he should have done so.[1367] In *Petersen v. Minister of Safety and Security*,[1368] the police attempted to seize a number of bags of illegally harvested perlemoen (abalone) in an area known for perlemoen poaching. A belligerent crowd gathered and began stoning the police, forcing their retreat. That allowed the crowd to carry away most of the perlemoen. The police attempted to stave off the attack by firing rubber bullets into the crowd and, when they ran out of rubber bullets, shooting into the ground near the crowd with sharp point ammunition. The plaintiff claimed damages for injuries sustained by her son in the shooting. The police alleged that the shooting was justified by necessity. The plea of necessity was upheld on appeal. The court decided that the defence of necessity does not require the harmful action to be directed at a person engaged in a wrongful attack. There was no need for the police to establish that the injured boy was himself part of the attacking crowd. They had to prove that danger existed, or was imminent; that there was no other reasonable means of averting the danger; and that the means used and measures taken to avert the danger of harm were not excessive, having regard to all the circumstances of the case, including that, at the stage when the police started to fire live ammunition, their attackers simply did not allow them to flee. The causing of the injuries by the police was therefore not wrongful but justified by necessity.

§4. Self-help and Self-defence (Private Defence)

637. Private defence justifies the protection of a legally recognized interest against actual or imminent unlawful attack.

---

capacity for fault, because he acted under compulsion and therefore could not choose freely between right and wrong, even though he may have known that he was doing wrong. The requirements for intention and the capacity for fault are discussed below in §3.

1366. 1975 (3) SA 590 (A).

1367. *See S v. Bradbury* 1967 (1) SA 387 (A) 390 392 393 404.

1368. [2010] 1 All SA 19 (SCA).

638. The policy considerations underlying private defence have been formulated as follows in *Ntsomi v. Minister of Law and Order*:[1369]

> The principle that right does not have to yield to wrong has been a touchstone of civilized legal systems through the ages. The victim of an unlawful attack has been entitled to defend his person or property by virtue of a rule of law which has existed in all familiar legal systems for many centuries. 'Non scripta sed nata lex' as Cicero put it (Pro Milone Cap. 4) and in the words of Geib, '*Notwehr hat keine Geschichte*' (Lehrbuch vol. I at 228).

639. The requirements for reliance on private defence are set out in the following paragraphs.[1370]

640. There must have been an *unlawful attack*. The conduct of the attacker must have unlawfully caused or threatened to cause the infringement of an interest. Private defence is not justified against a lawful infringement of an interest, for instance against a lawful arrest.[1371] The mere fact that a person who has committed a crime for which he may be arrested without a warrant is running away from the scene of his crime pursued by those who saw him do it does not change him into a threatened innocent with the right to use violence against those who are trying to effect his arrest.[1372] An attack by an animal and danger created by forces of nature are natural phenomena that do not cause harm unlawfully, unlawfulness being an attribute of a causal sequence set in motion by human conduct. Although danger created by animals or forces of nature therefore does not constitute an unlawful attack for the purposes of private defence, defensive conduct in the face of such danger can nevertheless be justified on the ground of necessity.[1373] However, where a person uses an animal as an instrument of attack, for instance inciting a dog to bite, there can be private defence against what is essentially human conduct causing or threatening infringement of a right. In most cases, private defence involves an attack in the form of positive conduct, but an omission can conceivably also give rise to private defence, for instance where a salesman refuses to leave another person's house, or where a fireman refuses to extinguish a fire on request of a house owner. Some measure of coercion may be reasonable in such cases, but South African courts have not decided on this question, and in European jurisdictions private defence is not recognized in such instances.[1374]

1369. 1990 (1) SA 512 (C) 526.
1370. *See Ntsomi v. Minister of Law and Order* 1990 (1) SA 512 (C) 526–527.
1371. Cf. *R v. Moloy* 1953 (3) SA 659 (T).
1372. *See R v. Ndara* 1955 (4) SA 182 (A).
1373. In respect of defensive conduct against attacks by animals, cf. *R v. Staalmeister* 1912 EDL 308; and *S v. Moller* 1971 (4) SA 327 (T). In the *Moller* case the court used the terminology of private defence in respect of defensive conduct a situation of necessity. In European jurisdictions the dominant view is that an attack for the purposes of private defence presupposes human conduct, but in English law, which sees self- or private defence as a form of necessity, private defence against dangers created by animals or natural phenomena is recognized; *see* Von Bar, *Gemeineuropäisches Deliksrecht*, Band II, 519.
1374. *See* Von Bar, *Gemeineuropäisches Deliksrecht*, Band II, 520.

641. The attack must be directed against *a legally recognized interest.* The courts have recognized that private defence may be justified against attacks on the following interests: life;[1375] bodily integrity;[1376] honour;[1377] property.[1378] There is no closed list and in principle an unlawful attack on any legally recognized interest can give rise to a plea of private defence.

642. The attack must have *commenced or be threatening.* Anticipatory defence is not justified. Where one expects another person to attack a legally recognized interest some time in the future, it is not justified to use force against the attacker in anticipation.[1379] In such a case, an interdict may be the appropriate remedy. Where an attack is threatening, the defender does not need to wait until the attack has actually commenced.[1380] Where a harmful attack has already ceased the person who suffered the harm cannot rely on private defence to justify retaliation.[1381]

643. Fault on the part of the attacker is not required. Essentially, private defence justifies warding off unlawfully caused harm, regardless of whether the causing of the harm is intentional, negligent or without fault. Private defence is therefore also justified against an attack by a person incapable of fault, such as an infans or an insane person.[1382]

644. The *attack need not be directed at the defender.* One person may defend the person or property of another against unlawful attack. For instance, one policeman may be justified in using force to ward off an attack on a fellow policeman,[1383] and a husband may prevent an infringement of his wife's honour.[1384] Because private defence is based on the policy consideration that right should not yield to wrong, one person may defend the interests of another against unlawful attack for purely altruistic reasons and no special relationship between the defender and the person whose interests are unlawfully infringed or threatened should be required.

1375. *Ntanjana v. Vorster and Minister of Justice* 1950 (4) SA 398 (C); *Ntsomi v. Minister of Law and Order* 1990 (1) SA 512 (C).
1376. *R v. Nomahleki* 1928 GWL 8.
1377. Cf. *R v. Van Vuuren* 1961 (3) SA 305 (E), where the appellant grabbed the complainant by the arm after the complainant had insulted the appellant's wife. The appellant was prosecuted for assault and successfully relied on private defence. The court held that he had acted reasonably to prevent further injury in the form of insult and that his conduct therefore did not amount to assault. Cf. also *S v. Ndlangisa* 1969 (4) SA 324 (E), where spitting in another's face in reaction to insult was held not to be justified by private defence. In European jurisdictions, private defence against the infringement of honour or other personality rights is not generally recognized, but in German law private defence against invasion of privacy, for instance by unlawful taking of photographs, has been recognized in a few cases; *see* Von Bar, *Gemeineuropäisches Deliksrecht,* Band II, 518.
1378. *Ntai v. Vereeniging Town Council* 1953 (4) SA 579 (A); *Ex Parte Minister van Justisie: In re S v. Van Wyk* 1967 (1) SA 488 (A); *S v. Mogohlwane* 1982 (2) SA 587 (T).
1379. *S v. Mogohlwane* 1982 (2) SA 587 (T); *S v. Kibi* 1978 (4) SA 173 (E).
1380. *Hope v. R* 1917 NPD 145 146; *R v. Patel* 1959 (3) SA 121 (A).
1381. Cf. *S v. Mogohlwane* 1982 (2) SA 587 (T).
1382. Cf. *R v. K* 1956 (3) SA 353 (A).
1383. *Ntanjana v. Vorster and Minister of Justice* 1950 (4) SA 398 (C).
1384. *R v. Van Vuuren* 1961 (3) SA 305 (E).

645. The *defence must be directed at the attacker.* Private defence justifies the causing of such harm as is reasonably necessary to ward off an unlawful attack and does not justify causing harm to a person other than the attacker.

646. The *means of defence must have been necessary and reasonable to prevent or ward off the threatened harm.* It is lawful for any person to use a reasonable degree of force for the protection of himself or any other person against any unlawful attack. However, a harmful means of defence is not justified when the threat could have been avoided in some non-harmful or less harmful way.[1385] Causing harm in the course of private defence is not justified if the harm is either unnecessary, that is, if the infringement of interest could have been prevented in some other way, or disproportionate to the protected interest.[1386] The issues of necessity and proportionality raise several further questions.

647. It is also relevant whether it was necessary to defend against the attack. Could the defender have protected his interests by taking flight? The courts have accepted that the victim of an attack is not expected to flee from his assailant if flight would be dangerous or if it would amount to a dereliction of duty.[1387]

648. The question of proportionality between defence and attack is often the most difficult facet of the inquiry into private defence. The means used and the harm caused by the defender must not be out of proportion to the threatened harm.[1388] In a number of cases, the courts have taken into account in this regard what the person who acted in private defence could reasonably have known or how he could reasonably be expected to react to the situation, instead of taking into account all the facts of the situation as known after the event. Van Winsen AJ formulated this approach as follows in *Ntanjana v. Vorster and Minister of Justice*:[1389]

> The very objectivity of the test, however, demands that when the Court comes to decide whether there was a necessity to act in self-defence it must place itself in the position of the person claiming to have acted in self-defence and consider all the surrounding factors operating at the time he acted. The Court must be careful to avoid the role of the armchair critic wise after the event, weighing the matter in the secluded security of the courtroom. ... Furthermore, in judging the matter it must be ever present to the mind of the Judge that, at any rate in the particular circumstances of this case, the person claiming to act in self-defence does so in an emergency, the creation of which is the work of the person unlawfully attacking. The self-defender is accordingly

1385. *See Chetty v. Minister of Police* 1976 (2) SA 450 (N) 455-6; *Thabethe v. Minister of Police* 1981 (3) SA 569 (D) 573.
1386. *Ntsomi v. Minister of Law and Order* 1990 (1) SA 512 (C) 527-8.
1387. *See R v. Zikalala* 1953 (2) SA 568 (A); *R v. Molife* 1940 AD 202; *R v. Patel* 1959 (3) SA 121 (A); *Ntsomi v. Minister of Law and Order* 1990 (1) SA 512 (C) 530.
1388. *Ex Parte Minister van Justisie: In re S v. Van Wyk* 1967 (1) SA 488 (A) 501; *Ntsomi v. Minister of Law and Order* 1990 (1) SA 512 (C) 526.
1389. 1950 (4) SA 398 (C) 406A-D. *See also S v. Ntuli* 1975 (1) SA 429 (A) 437E, and *Ntsomi v. Minister of Law and Order* 1990 (1) SA 512 (C) 527-8.

> entitled to have extended to him that degree of indulgence usually accorded by the law when judging the conduct of a person acting in a situation of imminent peril. 'Men faced in moments of crisis with a choice of alternatives are not to be judged as if they had had both time and opportunity to weigh the pros and cons', per Innes JA in *Union Government (Minister of Railways & Harbours) v. Buur* 1914 AD 273 at 286.

In terms of this approach, the defender may be judged to have acted reasonably even if it appears with hindsight that he was not really in danger, or that he caused more harm in defence than was required to ward off the attack.[1390] In effect, therefore, the *boni mores* or legal convictions of the community require no more of the defender than to act as a reasonable person would under the circumstances. For example, the use of force by an armed policeman faced with a threat of violence will be judged according to the norm of a reasonable policeman.[1391]

649. The foundations of this 'reasonableness of conduct' approach to unlawfulness were laid at a time when the concept of unlawfulness in the law of delict was poorly developed, if at all. There is a strong dissent from the reasonableness of conduct approach to putative defence in *Kgaleng v. Minister of Safety and Security.*[1392] The court said the following:

> The defendants may yet escape liability on the basis that the second defendant's bona fide (although erroneous) belief that his conduct was justified, excluded consciousness of wrongfulness – and thus fault in the form of dolus – on his part, and provided a reasonable man would not have reacted differently to the way in which the second defendant reacted under the circumstances – thereby excluding fault in the form of culpa.[1393]

650. However, in *Mugwena and Another v. Minister of Safety and Security*, the Supreme Court of Appeal also applied the test of a reasonable person to determine whether the causing of injury was justified by defence.[1394] The two approaches will almost invariably produce the same result, but the *Kgaleng* approach seems preferable, because it takes account of the reasonableness of the belief in the threat with reference to the well-defined concepts of intent and negligence.

651. The end result will invariably be the same, whether one concludes, on the one hand, that the defender used disproportionate force and therefore unlawfully exceeded the bounds of private defence, but lacked fault because he acted as a reasonable man would have done under the circumstances; or, on the other hand, that

---

1390. Cf. *Ntanjana v. Vorster and Minister of Justice* 1950 (4) SA 398 (C) 406A-D; *S v. Ntuli* 1975 (1) SA 429 (A) 437E; *Ntsomi v. Minister of Law and Order* 1990 (1) SA 512 (C) 526–527.
1391. *Ntanjana v. Vorster and Minister of Justice* 1950 (4) SA 398 (C); *Ntsomi v. Minister of Law and Order* 1990 (1) SA 512 (C) 527–528.
1392. 2001 (4) SA 854 (W).
1393. *Kgaleng v. Minister of Safety and Security* 2001 (4) SA 854 (W) 865–866, para. 16.
1394. 2006 (4) SA 150 (SCA) 158–159.

the defender caused harm lawfully in the course of private defence, according to the standard of a reasonable person in the particular circumstances.[1395]

652. The interest that the defender seeks to protect need not be commensurate with or similar in character to the interest of the attacker that is infringed by the defence.[1396] The interest threatened by the attack and the interest affected by the defence are often different in nature and of unequal value. On the basis that right should not yield to wrong, the attacker who causes or threatens harm unlawfully should not have a cause of action against the defender for causing more harm in defence than he would have suffered as a result of the attack.[1397] However, an extreme imbalance, for instance where the defender fatally wounds the attacker to prevent a petty theft, will indicate that the defence was unreasonable.[1398]

653. A prominent instance of private defence involving an imbalance of interests is *Ex Parte Minister van Justisie: In re S v. Van Wyk.*[1399] In this case, a shop-owner set up a gun in his shop to protect his property against thieves. His shop had been the target of repeated burglaries in the past, and other protective measures such as burglar proofing, night watchmen and watchdogs had proved ineffective. He set up the gun with a tripwire, so that an intruder setting off the wire would be hit in the legs. He also put up a notice on the door of the shop, warning of the presence of a gun inside. An intruder set off the gun and was wounded in the hip and later died as a result of the wound. The shop-owner was prosecuted for murder and eventually the Appellate Division had to decide whether one may in principle rely on private defence where defence of property had resulted in injury or death; and whether the bounds of defence were exceeded in this particular case. All the judges answered the first question affirmatively, holding in essence that killing in defence of property, where the defender was in no personal danger, can be justified *in particular circumstances.* In respect of the second question the judges differed, the majority holding in essence that, in view of the repeated burglaries and the failure of other methods of protection, the setting up of the gun was a reasonable method of defence.[1400]

1395. *See* in this regard Von Bar, *Gemeineuropäisches Deliksrecht*, Band II, 524, who states that the theoretical distinction between unlawfulness and fault in respect of private defence exceeding the bounds of necessity amounts to *l'art pour l'art.*

1396. *Ex Parte Minister van Justisie: In re S v. Van Wyk* 1967 (1) SA 488 (A) 496-7.

1397. *Ex Parte Minister van Justisie: In re S v. Van Wyk* 1967 (1) SA 488 (A) 497.

1398. *Ex Parte Minister van Justisie: In re S v. Van Wyk* 1967 (1) SA 488 (A) 498.

1399. 1967 (1) SA 488 (A) 498.

1400. In his dissenting judgment Rumpff JA held that the reasonableness of setting up a gun that killed the intruder must be determined as if the shop-owner himself had fired the gun, because what is unlawful in the form of direct conduct cannot be lawful in the form of indirect conduct (504-5). However, this argument does not take into consideration that the shop-owner could not reasonably have protected his shop by guarding it himself every night and therefore needed to employ indirect protection, the reasonableness of which was in issue.

It must be noted that the *S v. Van Wyk* judgment belongs to the era before the new Constitution, and that the approach of the courts to the taking of life in defence of property is likely to be different, in accordance with the sanctity of life as enshrined in the Constitution.[1401]

654. In cases where the proportionality of the defence is in issue, the courts will have regard to all the surrounding circumstances, including factors such as the means of defence at the disposal of the defender;[1402] the nature and the danger of the attack;[1403] and a possible imbalance of interests.[1404]

§5. Provocation

655. There is authority in South African law for the view that provocation, in the form of inciting words or conduct, can be a complete defence to a claim for compensation based on alleged infringement of personality rights. For instance, where the provocative words or conduct of A causes B to insult or assault A, a claim by A for compensation based on the infringement of his personality rights may be met by B with a plea of provocation.[1405] Should A also suffer pecuniary loss, however, B cannot rely on provocation to escape liability for such loss.[1406]

656. Provocation differs from private defence and necessity in that the person acting in response to provocation does not anticipate or prevent harm, but responds to it and retaliates. The courts are circumspect in recognizing a complete defence in respect of provocation, because no one should be encouraged to take the law into his own hands.[1407]

657. There are different views on the basis for recognition of provocation as a complete defence. One view is that provocation can exclude fault on the part of the person who responded to the provocation, because his mental capacity to decide

---

1401. Act 108 of 1996, s. 11.
1402. *Ntsomi v. Minister of Law and Order* 1990 (1) SA 512 (C) 529–530.
1403. *R v. Patel* 1959 (3) SA 121 (A) 124.
1404. *Ex Parte Minister van Justisie: In re S v. Van Wyk* 1967 (1) SA 488 (A) 498.
1405. According to D 48.5.22.3, a father, A, will not be liable for assaulting a man whom he catches having intercourse with his (A's) daughter. Voet, as translated by Gane, Commentary on the Pandects) XLVII.10.20 (vii), states as follows: 'It is not unlike this (self-defence) when on being provoked a person has retaliated with a wrong, since wrongs appear in that way to have been set off insofar as a civil action could have been brought. The retaliation of a wrong does not involve a wrong, since to suffer what you have done is no wrong, and he who has meant on being challenged to avenge himself is to be pardoned.' In the following cases, provocation was accepted as a defence: *Powell v. Jonker* 1959 (4) SA 443 (T) 445-6; *Dzvairo v. Mudoti* 1973 (3) SA 287 (RA); *Bennett v. Minister of Police* 1980 (3) SA 24 (C); *Bester v. Calitz* 1982 (3) SA 864 (O) 875 880-1; *Wapnick v. Durban City Garage* 1984 (2) SA 414 (D) 419–420.
1406. *See* D 9 2 45 4; but cf. *Mehnert v. Schlemmer* (1908) 18 CTR 783.
1407. *Bester v. Calitz* 1982 (3) SA 864 (O) 876-7.

between right and wrong and to act accordingly may be affected by the provocation, and he may therefore lack the capacity for fault.[1408] However, there is no example in reported cases where a court has found that provocation affected a person's mental abilities to such an extent. Another view is that provocation merely affects the amount of the compensation to which the person who acts provocatively is entitled for the consequent infringement of his personality rights: he may be entitled to less compensation or may forfeit the right to compensation entirely.[1409] The right to compensation may even be denied altogether in terms of this approach, without exposition of the theoretical basis for denial of the right. The third view is that provocation can be a ground of justification; in other words, the person who caused infringement of personality rights in response to provocation may be regarded as having acted reasonably and therefore lawfully.[1410]

658. The view that provocation can be a ground of justification was adopted in *Bester v. Calitz*,[1411] the case that has hitherto dealt most comprehensively with the theoretical basis for recognition of provocation as a defence. This case dealt with a claim for damages arising from insulting remarks made in anger and elicited by provocative prior conduct and an insult of a similar nature. The court held that in such circumstances the elicited response is not unlawful. The traditional justification grounds are merely crystallized manifestations of the application of the general criterion of unlawfulness, and should not be regarded as a numerus clausus of defences. Where the traditional justification grounds cannot appropriately be applied, but it nonetheless appears that the conduct of the person who responded to provocation was reasonable, liability should not be imposed. Unlawfulness is determined according to the general criterion of reasonableness, which is an objective standard based on the *boni mores* or legal convictions of the community. In applying this standard, the approach should not be an idealistic one. Account should be taken of human weaknesses and the inclination of the average person to respond angrily to insult or other forms of provocation. According to the legal convictions of the community, it must therefore be regarded as reasonable and not unlawful to react angrily and to swear at a person whose conduct was provocative.

659. The decision in the *Bester* case is another example of the 'reasonableness of conduct' approach to unlawfulness, as adopted in cases of private defence and necessity. The court enquired whether the person who was incited by provocation reacted as a normal reasonable person would, instead of adopting the idealistic approach that an aggressive response to provocation is unnecessary and pointless in

1408. *Powell v. Jonker* 1959 (4) SA 443 (T); *Wessels v. Pretorius* 1974 (3) SA 299 (NC) 301; *Winterbach v. Masters* 1989 (1) SA 922 (E) 925. Cf. also *Jeftha v. Williams* 1981 (3) SA 678 (C) 683, where it was held that provocation in the course of an argument can exclude intention for the purposes of defamation, i.e., be a defence excluding fault.

1409. *Powell v. Jonker* 1959 (4) SA 443 (T) 444-5; *Winterbach v. Masters* 1989 (1) SA 922 (E) 925.

1410. *Mordt v. Smith* 1968 (4) SA 750 (RA); *Dzvairo v. Mudoti* 1973 (3) SA 287 (RA); *Bester v. Calitz* 1982 (3) SA 864 (O) 875 878–881; *Wapnick v. Durban City Garage* 1984 (2) SA 414 (D) 419–420.

1411. 1982 (3) SA 864 (O) 880.

the light of all the facts of the situation as known after the event; and that self-control is required in the face of provocation.[1412] It is suggested that the approach in the *Bester* case provides a sound theoretical basis for the recognition of provocation as a complete defence, by application of the general criterion of reasonableness according to the *boni mores* or legal convictions of the community.

660. The requirements for reliance on provocation as a ground of justification are the following.

661. The provocation must be of such a nature that the conduct in reaction to it, whether by way of insult, defamation or even physical assault, can be regarded as reasonable.[1413] The general standard for determining unlawfulness in this case involves the question whether a reasonable person in the position of the defendant would have been similarly provoked.

662. The reaction to the provocation must have been 'an immediate and reasonable retaliation'.[1414] An immediate, spontaneous reaction in the heat of the moment may be regarded as reasonable, whereas a deliberate or premeditated later retaliation may not be reasonable.

663. The nature of the conduct in reaction to the provocation must have been reasonably in proportion to or commensurate with the provocation.[1415] The proportionality will be assessed objectively with regard to all the circumstances of the case, including the value and nature of the interests affected by the provocative and retaliatory conduct respectively. As a rule, verbal provocation will not justify physical assault, even if the verbal provocation was gravely insulting or defamatory.[1416] Provocation in the form of physical assault may justify a retaliatory assault, provided the retaliation is proportionate to the provocation.[1417] Both physical provocation and verbal provocation may justify insulting or defamatory remarks in retaliation.[1418] Where the retaliatory conduct was disproportionate to the provocative conduct the defence of provocation will not succeed as a complete defence, but the damages of the claimant who provoked the retaliation may nevertheless be reduced.[1419]

1412. P.Q.R. Boberg, *The Law of Delict Vol. 1 Aquilian Liability,* 829 argues, with reference to *Blou v. Rose Innes* 1914 TPD 102 104, that self-control should be displayed in the face of provocation and that an aggressive response is 'natural, but is against the law'.
1413. *Bester v. Calitz* 1982 (3) SA 864 (O) 875 878–881.
1414. *Powell v. Jonker* 1959 (4) SA 443 (T) 445; *Dzvairo v. Mudoti* 1973 (3) SA 287 (RA).
1415. *Powell v. Jonker* 1959 (4) SA 443 (T) 446; *Bennett v. Minister of Police* 1980 (3) SA 24 (C) 31-2.
1416. *Blou v. Rose Innes* 1914 TPD 102; *Bantjes v. Rosenberg* 1957 (2) SA 118 (T); *Bennett v. Minister of Police* 1980 (3) SA 24 (C) 31-2; but *see* D 48 5 22 3, stating that a father, A, will not be liable for assaulting a man whom he catches having intercourse with his (A's) daughter.
1417. *Powell v. Jonker* 1959 (4) SA 443 (T) 446; *Bennett v. Minister of Police* 1980 (3) SA 24 (C) 31-2.
1418. Cf. *Kernick v. Fitzpatrick* 1907 TS 389 394; *Kirkpatrick v. Bezuidenhout* 1934 TPD 155 158-9. Cf. also *Jeftha v. Williams* 1981 (3) SA 678 (C) 683, where Grosskopf J stated: 'My own sense

§6. STATUTORY AUTHORITY

664. A statutory provision can justify the causing of harm that would otherwise be unlawful.[1420] The effect of such a statutory provision is to authorize the infringement of certain rights and correspondingly to restrict the rights of the persons affected. The person who purports to act in terms of statutory authority must not exceed the bounds of that authority and bears the onus of proving that the causing of harm was within the bounds of the statutory authority.[1421]

665. The question whether the causing of harm was authorized by a statutory provision is one of interpretation, and the normal rules of statutory interpretation will apply. However, the courts have also adopted certain guidelines and presumptions to determine whether the causing of harm in a particular instance is authorized by statute. These guidelines and presumptions are used as aids in the process of interpretation and are not conclusive.[1422]

666. The general rule is that the intention of the legislature will determine whether the causing of harm in a particular instance is authorized. The intention of the legislature is determined according to the normal rules of statutory interpretation.[1423]

667. If the statute is *directory* in respect of an action involving the infringement of private interests, and it does not provide for compensation, this will indicate that the infringement of rights and consequent harm is justified.[1424]

668. If the statute is merely *permissive* and *general* in respect of an action involving the infringement of private interests, and does not provide for compensation, there is a presumption that the infringement of rights and consequent harm

---

of what is reasonable leads me to consider that it should not be lawful for a person to publish defamatory matter about another merely because he loses his temper, whatever the provocation may be.' In this case, it was held that provocation can exclude fault in the form of intention rather than unlawfulness.

1419. *Mulvallha v. Steenkamp* 1917 CPD 571 573; *Powell v. Jonker* 1959 (4) SA 443 (T) 446.

1420. *See* generally *Union Government (Minister of Railways) v. Sykes* 1913 AD 156; *Johannesburg Municipality v. African Realty Trust* 1927 AD 163; *East London Western Districts Farmers' Association v. Minister of Education and Development Aid* 1989 (2) SA 63 (A); *Simon's Town Municipality v. Dews* 1993 (1) SA 191 (A), *Government of the RSA v. Basdeo* 1996 (1) SA 355 (A).

1421. *Johannesburg Municipality v. African Realty Trust* 1927 AD 163 175; *Sambo v. Milns* 1973 (4) SA 312 (T) 320; *During v. Boesak* 1990 (3) SA 661 (A) 673.

1422. *Johannesburg Municipality v. African Realty Trust* 1927 AD 163 172–173; *East London Western Districts Farmers' Association v. Minister of Education and Development Aid* 1989 (2) SA 63 (A) 70.

1423. *Johannesburg Municipality v. African Realty Trust* 1927 AD 163 172; *Simon's Town Municipality v. Dews* 1993 (1) SA 191 (A) 195-6.

1424. *Johannesburg Municipality v. African Realty Trust* 1927 AD 163 171–172.

is not justified. However, there is no such presumption where a *public body* is permitted to act in the *public interest* or where the permission to act is *localized* or *specific.*[1425]

669. In the case of certain empowering statutes, the intrinsic physical nature of the works or acts authorized is such that their execution necessarily and inevitably involves the disturbance of private rights.[1426] In the case of *Johannesburg Municipality v. African Realty Trust,*[1427] it was held that it was impossible to exercise the power conferred (the construction of streets and drains) without increasing the flow of water onto the plaintiff's land. In *Breede River (Robertson) Irrigation Board v. Brink,*[1428] it was held that it is impossible to build an irrigation canal for miles across the countryside without interfering with the natural flow of surface drainage water. In *Bloemfontein Town Council v. Richter,*[1429] it was held to be proved on the evidence that the removal of silt from the dam would inevitably cause some damage to the plaintiff's adjacent property. In *Germiston City Council v. Chubb & Sons Lock and Safe Co. (SA) (Pty) Ltd,*[1430] the conclusion of fact was inescapable that the construction of roads on sloping ground must interfere with the rights of adjoining landowners by modifying the natural drainage of the locality concerned.

670. The general criterion of reasonableness will be applied to determine whether the bounds of statutory authority have been exceeded. Where alleged statutory authority for the infringement of property rights is concerned, for instance, the question is whether there has been unreasonable interference with the rights of the appellants to the enjoyment of their property.[1431] In earlier cases, the courts referred in this regard to the question whether the statutory powers have been *negligently* exceeded,[1432] but subsequently it has been recognized that the question is one of unlawfulness.[1433] The courts will take into account the extent to which it was reasonably possible to avoid the infringement of private interests or to minimize harm

1425. *See Johannesburg Municipality v. African Realty Trust* 1927 AD 163 172–173; *Breede River (Robertson) Irrigation Board v. Brink* 1936 AD 359 366.
1426. *East London Western Districts Farmers' Association v. Minister of Education and Development Aid* 1989 (2) SA 63 (A) 72.
1427. 1927 AD 163.
1428. 1936 AD 359.
1429. 1938 AD 195.
1430. 1957 (1) SA 312 (A).
1431. *See East London Western Districts Farmers' Association v. Minister of Education and Development Aid* 1989 (2) SA 63 (A) 68.
1432. *See Johannesburg Municipality v. African Realty Trust* 1927 AD 163 172–173; *Bloemfontein Town Council v. Richter* 1938 AD 195 231.
1433. *Simon's Town Municipality v. Dews* 1993 (1) SA 191 (A) 196.

resulting from the exercise of statutory powers; and in this regard the cost and effectiveness of measures to prevent harm will be relevant.[1434] In cases of alleged unlawful arrest or excessive use of force in the course of making an arrest, the courts will take into account the possibility of alternative or less harmful conduct.[1435]

§7. Official Capacity

671. Certain public officials such as judges, magistrates or members of statutory licensing boards are authorized to perform functions that may detrimentally affect the interests of other persons, for instance where a judgment by a judge or magistrate contains negative comments on the credibility of a witness. The infringement of personality or other interests as a result of the reasonable performance of official duties are justified in the public interest.[1436] In many cases, official authority is conferred by statute, for example the authority of the police to make arrests and to conduct searches, and the rules of statutory authority as set out in section 6 above will apply. Where official duties involve the exercise of discretion and are not defined in detail by statutory provisions, the question is whether the performance of such duties was reasonable and within the bounds of the official authority.[1437] An official who performs official duties with an ulterior motive, malice or dishonesty acts unreasonably and outside the bounds of his authority and the resultant infringement of private interests will be unlawful.[1438]

§8. Obedience to Orders

672. Obedience to orders as a ground of justification has so far been raised in criminal cases only, but could also arise as a defence in a civil action, for instance where a policeman is given an unlawful order by his superior officer to shoot at a person running away. The question is to what extent the causing of injury or death

1434. *Johannesburg Municipality v. African Realty Trust* 1927 AD 163 172–173; *Breede River (Robertson) Irrigation Board v. Brink* 1936 AD 359 366.

1435. *Matlou v. Makhubedu* 1978 (1) SA 946 (A) 958; *Minister of Justice v. Hofmeyr* 1993 (3) SA 131 (A); *Shoba v. Minister van Justisie* 1982 (2) SA 554 (A); *Minister van Polisie v. Goldschagg* 1981 (1) 37 (A); *Macu v. Du Toit en 'n Ander* 1982 (1) SA 272 (C); *Minister van Wet en Orde v. Van den Heever* 1982 (4) SA 16 (K); *Botha v. Lues* 1983 (4) SA 496 (A); *George v. Minister van Wet en Orde* 1987 (4) SA 222 (EC); *Prince v. Minister van Wet en Orde* 1987 (4) SA 231 (EC); *Govender v. Minister of Safety and Security* 2001 (4) SA 273 (SCA); *Ex Parte Minister of Safety & Security: In re S v. Walters* 2002 (4) SA 613 (CC).

1436. *See May v. Udwin* 1981 (1) SA 1 (A) 19, where it was held that public policy and sound administration of justice require that a magistrate, in discharging his judicial duties, 'should be able to speak his mind freely without fear of incurring liability for damages for defamation'.

1437. *See* generally *Basner v. Trigger* 1945 AD 22; *Ingram v. Minister of Justice* 1962 (3) SA 225 (W); *May v. Udwin* 1981 (1) SA 1 (A); *Moeketsi v. Minister van Justisie* 1988 (4) SA 707 (T).

1438. *See Moeketsi v. Minister van Justisie* 1988 (4) SA 707 (T) 713; and *May v. Udwin* 1981 (1) SA 1 (A) 19.

by the junior policeman is justified by his obedience to orders. In *S v. Banda*,[1439] it was held that obedience to an unlawful order can be a ground of justification in the following circumstances.

673. The order must issue from a person in a position of lawful authority over the accused. This requirement involves a question of fact.

There must be a duty on the accused to obey the order given. This second requirement involves the essential problem, that is, when is there a duty to obey an unlawful order; or when can obedience to an unlawful order be a ground of justification for causing harm? The courts have accepted that there is no absolute or blind duty to obey orders.[1440] According to some decisions, there can never be a duty to obey an unlawful order,[1441] whereas others hold that only the execution of a *manifestly* or *palpably* unlawful order is itself unlawful.[1442] Whether or not an order is manifestly or palpably unlawful must then be determined according to the judgment of a reasonable person.[1443] This approach accords with the approach of the Appellate Division in *S v. Goliath*,[1444] where it was held that the law does not require of a person acting under duress to conform to a higher standard than that of the average person; and compulsion or duress can therefore be a complete defence, even to a charge of murder. A person who is under pressure to obey an order from a superior and who needs to decide at the same time whether such an order is lawful or not, is acting under compulsion or duress. In terms of the general criterion of reasonableness, which accords with the *boni mores* or legal convictions of the community, as held by Rumpff JA three years after *Goliath* in the *Ewels* case,[1445] no more is required of the person acting under compulsion or duress than to act as the average or reasonable person would under the circumstances.

674. The accused must have done no more harm than was necessary to carry out the order. This requirement again involves the general criterion reasonableness. All the circumstances of the case must be taken into account to determine whether it was possible to avoid harm or to cause less harm.

1439. 1990 (3) SA 466 (B) 480.
1440. *R v. Smith* (1900) 17 SC 561 567; *S v. Banda* 1990 (3) SA 466 (B) 480.
1441. *R v. Arlow* 1960 (2) SA 499 (T) 452; *R v. Van Vuuren* 1944 OPD 35 38.
1442. *R v. Smith* (1900) 17 SC 561 567; *S v. Mule* 1990 (1) SACR 517 (SWA); *S v. Banda* 1990 (3) SA 466 (B) 480.
1443. *S v. Banda* 1990 (3) SA 466 (B) 496.
1444. 1972 (3) SA 1(A).
1445. 1975 (3) SA 590 (A).

§9. DISCIPLINARY POWERS

675. Persons who exercise lawful authority over children such as parents,[1446] and persons in loco parentis, for example guardians and teachers,[1447] may in terms of such authority lawfully administer punishment for purposes of education and correction.

676. The authority of persons in loco parentis to exercise disciplinary powers is an original authority and does not derive from delegation by parents,[1448] although a parent or guardian may delegate disciplinary powers to another person. Delegated authority to discipline cannot be wider or more comprehensive than the original authority,[1449]and involves a discretion,[1450] which must be exercised reasonably and not in a capricious manner.[1451]

677. Section 10 of the South African Schools Act[1452] prohibits corporal punishment in public as well as independent (private) schools, by school principals, teachers and persons in charge of school hostels. The implication of the section is also that parents may not delegate the power to administer corporal punishment to a person in a public or private school.

678. The authority to discipline must be exercised moderately and reasonably,[1453] in accordance with the general criterion of reasonableness. The purpose of punishment must be correctional and educational.[1454] The repetition of punishment that has not had the desired effect,[1455] and malice or improper motive[1456] will indicate unreasonableness. Punishment that may be regarded as cruel, inhuman or degrading will be unreasonable and unlawful.[1457]

679. The following factors will be taken into account to determine the reasonableness of the punishment:[1458] the nature and seriousness of the transgression; the means and degree of punishment or force used; the physical and mental condition

1446. *R v. Janke and Janke* 1913 TPD 382 385 392; *Tshabalala v. Jacobs* 1942 TPD 310 313; *Du Preez v. Conradie* 1990 (4) SA 46 (B) 51.
1447. *R v. Scheepers* 1915 AD 337 338; *R v. Schoombie* 1924 TPD 481; *R v. Le Maitre and Avenant* 1947 (4) SA 616 (C); *R v. Muller* 1948 (4) SA 848 (O); *Hiltonian Society v. Crofton* 1952 (3) SA 130 (A); *Du Preez v. Conradie* 1990 (4) SA 46 (B) 51.
1448. *R v. Muller* 1948 (4) SA 848 (O) 860.
1449. *Du Preez v. Conradie* 1990 (4) SA 46 (B) 53.
1450. *R v. Le Maitre and Avenant* 1947 (4) SA 616 (C) 621-2.
1451. *S v. Legathe* 1982 (3) SA 104 (B) 109.
1452. Act 84 of 1996.
1453. *R v. Scheepers* 1915 AD 337 338; *R v. Roux* 1932 OPD 59 61; *R v. Jacobs* 1941 OPD 7 9 10; *Du Preez v. Conradie* 1990 (4) SA 46 (B) 53.
1454. *R v. Janke and Janke* 1913 TPD 382 385; *Du Preez v. Conradie* 1990 (4) SA 46 (B) 51–52.
1455. *R v. Janke and Janke* 1913 TPD 382 388.
1456. *R v. Janke and Janke* 1913 TPD 382 385.
1457. Section 12(1) of the Constitution of the Republic of South Africa Act 108 of 1996.
1458. *See* generally *R v. Janke and Janke* 1913 TPD 382 385–386; *Du Preez v. Conradie* 1990 (4) SA 46 (B) 51–52.

of the child; the gender and age of the child; the physical disposition of the child; and the purpose and motive of the person inflicting the punishment.

680. Punishment by a person in a position of lawful authority is presumed to be imposed reasonably and without malice,[1459] and the person who alleges the opposite bears the onus of proving the punishment unreasonable.[1460]

§10. Impossibility

681. The law will not enforce impossibility. Where the circumstances indicate the existence of a duty to act positively to prevent harm to another person, but it was impossible for the defendant to act, the failure to prevent harm will not be unlawful. For example, a strong swimmer who would normally be able to save a person from drowning may be prevented by cramp from doing so. One could say that impossibility is a ground of justification in such a case, because the defendant's failure to prevent harm is reasonable in the circumstances. In terms of the *boni mores* or the legal convictions of the community[1461] the swimmer is not in breach of a legal duty to save the drowning person, because it was impossible to do so. One could also say that a duty to act positively does not arise at all in such circumstances, because it is not unreasonable for the defendant, according to the *boni mores* or the legal convictions of the community, to fail to rescue. Impossibility has so far not arisen as a defence in a delictual action and it is suggested that physical or economic impossibility[1462] is more likely to be considered in the process of applying the general criterion of reasonableness for determining unlawfulness than in the guise of a separate ground of justification.

1459. *R v. Janke and Janke* 1913 TPD 382–385.
1460. *Hiltonian Society v. Crofton* 1952 (3) SA 130 (A).
1461. *See Minister van Polisie v. Ewels* 1975 (3) SA 590 (A) 596-7; *Administrateur, Natal v. Trust Bank van Afrika Bpk* 1979 (3) SA 824 (A) 833-4; *Lillicrap, Wassenaar and Partners v. Pilkington Brothers (SA) (Pty) Ltd* 1985 (1) SA 448 (A) 498; *Nkumbi v. Minister of Law and Order* 1991 (3) SA 29 (E) 35; *Macadamia Finance Ltd v. De Wet* 1991 (4) SA 273 (T) 278; *Kadir v. Minister of Law and Order* 1992 (3) SA 737 (C) 740; *McCann v. Goodall Group Operations (Pty) Ltd* 1995 (2) SA 718 (C) 722-3; *Administrateur Transvaal v. Van der Merwe* 1994 ($) SA 347 (A) 358; *Mukheiber v. Raath* 1999 (SCA) para. 26.
1462. For instance, where it is physically possible to prevent harm, but so costly that it would be unreasonable in terms of the legal convictions of the community to expect preventative conduct; as in *Regal v. African Superslate (Pty) Ltd* 1963 (1) SA 102 (A).

Chapter 3. Contributory Fault and Joint Wrongdoers

§1. Background to the Apportionment of Damages Act

682. In Roman and Roman-Dutch law, contributory negligence on the part of a plaintiff was a complete defence to a claim for damages. To alleviate the inequitable results of this all-or-nothing approach the courts in England and South Africa accepted the 'last opportunity rule', in terms of which the party who had the last opportunity of avoiding the harmful result was held to be solely responsible.[1463] The rule was difficult to apply and also produced inequitable results. The Apportionment of Damages Act[1464] abolished the common law doctrine of contributory negligence and the last opportunity rule[1465] and introduced the principle of apportionment of liability in accordance with the respective degrees of fault of the parties.

683. Section 1(1)(a) of the Act provides:

> Where any person suffers damage which is caused partly by his own fault and partly by fault of any other person, a claim in respect of that damage shall not be defeated by reason of the fault of the claimant but the damages recoverable in respect thereof shall be reduced by the court to such extent as the court may deem just and equitable having regard to the degree in which the claimant was at fault in relation to the damage.

§2. Application of the Apportionment of Damages Act

684. Apportionment of damages, based on apportionment of fault, applies where the plaintiff has suffered harm partly as a consequence of own fault and partly as a consequence of the fault of another. The section involves a comparative evaluation of the respective degrees of fault and a proportionate reduction of the damages recoverable by the plaintiff.

685. The reference to 'own fault' in section 1(1)(a) refers to fault on the part of the plaintiff, and this means that where the plaintiff claims damages as a result of the injury or death of another, for instance the medical costs incurred as a result of the injuries of a child, or the loss of support as a result of the death of a parent, there is no own fault on the part of the plaintiff, and damages are not to be reduced proportionate to the contributory negligence of the injured or the deceased person. Instead, in such cases, the injured person who was negligent, or the estate of the deceased person who was negligent, is considered to be a joint wrongdoer in terms of section 2(1B) of the Act, and the defendant has a right to claim a contribution

1463. *See Moore v. Minister of Posts and Telegraphs* 1949 (1) SA 815 (A); *Coetzee v. Van Rensburg* 1954 (4) SA 616 (A).

1464. Act 34 of 1954.

1465. Sections 1(1)(b) and 2(14).

from the joint wrongdoer. In an action based on vicarious liability contributory fault on the part of a person who is not the plaintiff can be taken into account: the defendant-employer can rely on the contributory fault of an employee of the plaintiff, to effect a reduction of damages, or even to exclude liability.[1466]

686. The Act does not apply to actions based on breach of contract. This was established in *Thoroughbred Breeders' Association v. Price Waterhouse*,[1467] where the Supreme Court of Appeal held that contributory negligence in terms of the Apportionment of Damages Act[1468] does not apply in the contractual relationship between auditor and client.

687. The Act also does not apply to actions involving strict liability, for example the *actio de pauperie* for damage done by animals. However, where the owner of an animal is sued for damage done by the animal, the owner can raise the defence that the harm was caused by the plaintiff's own fault.[1469] Culpable conduct in the form of 'substantial negligence or imprudence' will defeat the claim.[1470] Although the South African courts have to date adopted an all-or-nothing approach in respect of the *actio de pauperie*, the possibility of apportionment has not been specifically excluded.[1471] Apportionment on the basis of causal contribution, as applied in *General Accident Versekeringsmaatskappy SA Bpk v. Uijs*[1472] could be applied.

§3. Concept of Fault

688. The concept of fault as used in the Act includes both negligence and intent. Intent is regarded as a more reprehensible form of fault, and the common law rule is that a defendant who intentionally caused harm to the plaintiff cannot claim a reduction of damages based on the plaintiff's contributory negligence.[1473] However, apportionment has been applied where there was negligence on the part of the plaintiff and intent on the part of the defendant,[1474] or negligence on the part of one joint

1466. Cf. *Becker v. Kellerman* 1971 (2) SA 172 (T); *Greater Johannesburg Transitional Metropolitan Council v. Absa Bank Ltd* 1997 (2) SA 591 (W) 605–606; *Randbond Investments (Pty) Ltd v. FPS (Northern Region) (Pty) Ltd* 1992 (2) SA 608 (W); *Absa Bank Ltd v. Bond Equipment (Pretoria) (Pty) Ltd* 2001 (1) SA 372 (SCA).

1467. 2001 (4) SA 551 (SCA). *See also Barclay Bank DCO v. Straw* 1965 (2) SA 93 (O); *OK Bazaars (1929) Ltd v. Stern & Ekermans* 1976 (2) SA 521 (C).

1468. Act 34 of 1956.

1469. *O'Callaghan v. Chaplin* 1927 AD 310 329.

1470. McQuoid-Mason, *LAWSA* vol. 1 §335; *O'Callaghan v. Chaplin* 1927 AD 310 329.

1471. *See Svamvur v. Portwood* 1970 (1) SA 144 (R) 145; *Swart v. Honeyborne* 1981 (1) SA 974 (C) 976B.

1472. 1993 (4) SA 228 (A) 235.

1473. *Mabaso v. Felix* 1981 (3) SA 865 (A) 877; *Wapnick v. Durban City Garage* 1984 (2) SA 414 (D) 418, *Minister van Wet en Orde v. Ntsane* 1993 (1) SA 560 (A) 570.

1474. *Minister van Wet en Orde v. Ntsane* 1993 (1) SA 560 (A) 570.

wrongdoer and intent on the part of the other,[1475] and also between employers where employees on both sides acted intentionally.[1476]

§4. Criterion of Apportionment

689. The criterion for apportioning damages is not set out in section 1(1)(a) of the Apportionment of Damages Act.[1477] This section merely requires an assessment of what is 'just and equitable having regard to the degree in which the claimant was at fault in relation to the damage'.

690. One approach to apportionment is to regard 'fault' in the form of negligence as referring to the proportionate degree of deviation from the standard of the reasonable person. This approach to section 1(1)(a) was accepted in *South British Insurance Co. Ltd v. Smit*,[1478] where Ogilvie Thompson JA said the following:

> What the Court is required to do is to determine, having regard to the circumstances of the particular case, the respective degrees of negligence of the parties. In assessing 'the degree in which the claimant was at fault in relation to the damage' the Court must determine in how far the claimant's acts or omissions, causally linked with the damage in issue, deviated from the norm of the bonus paterfamilias. In thus assessing the position, the Court will, as explained above, determine the respective degrees of negligence, as reflected by the acts and omissions of the parties, which have together combined to bring about the damage in issue.

691. In *Jones v. Santam Bpk*,[1479] the court accepted that a comparative assessment of negligence should be done. The court noted that the judgment in the *Smit* case referred to determination of 'the respective degrees of negligence' of the parties, not just the degree of negligence on the part of the claimant. Although section 1(1)(a) refers only to the 'the degree in which the claimant was at fault', consideration of the section as a whole indicates that the fault of both parties should be taken into account. Otherwise, 'the degree in which the claimant was at fault' will also automatically determine the degree in which the defendant was at fault in relation to the damage.[1480] The court in the *Jones* case therefore adopted the so-called mathematical approach. This involves determining the respective degrees of fault of the plaintiff and the defendant, by assessing the extent (percentage) by which the conduct of both the plaintiff and the defendant deviated from the norm of the reasonable person. The 'fault' of each in relation to the harm is then expressed as a

1475. *Lloyd-Gray Lithographers (Pty) Ltd v. Nedcor Bank Ltd t/a Nedbank* 1998 (2) SA 667 (W); *Nedcor Bank Ltd t/a Nedbank v. Lloyd-Gray Lithographers (Pty) Ltd* 2000 (4) 915 (SCA).
1476. *Randbond Investments (Pty) Ltd v. FPS (Northern Region) (Pty) Ltd* 1992 (2) SA 608 (W); *Greater Johannesburg Transitional Metropolitan Council v. Absa Bank Ltd* 1997 (2) SA 591 (W).
1477. Act 34 of 1956.
1478. 1962 (3) SA 826 (A) 836.
1479. 1965 (2) SA 542 (A) 554–555.
1480. An approach accepted in *AA Mutual Insurance Association Ltd v. Nomeka* 1976 (3) SA 45 (A).

ratio, for example, two equal percentages of deviation represent a 1:1 ratio and the plaintiff's claim will be reduced by 50%, whereas a 60% deviation by the plaintiff and a 20% deviation by the defendant represent a ratio of 3:1 and the plaintiff's claim will be reduced by 75%, or, the plaintiff will be entitled to only one-quarter of the damages claimed.

692. The courts thus initially eschewed the view that the term 'fault' indicates 'blameworthiness', a concept that would introduce moral considerations into the apportionment process. However, a purely objective standard of comparative negligence as criterion for apportionment may produce unjust results, particularly where children are involved, as noted by Jansen JA in *Weber v. Santam Versekeringsmpy Bpk.*[1481] In terms of the *Weber* judgment, the courts should not be averse to applying the concept of 'blameworthiness' in the apportionment process, on the basis of the reference in section 1(1)(a) to what is 'just and equitable, having regard to the degree in which the claimant was at fault in relation to the damage'. For example, in the case of contributory negligence on the part of a child, where the other party involved is an adult, who ought to have foreseen and guarded against the conduct of the child, justice and equity may require that the mathematical result be adjusted in favour of the child.

693. Another approach is to assess the relative causal significance or potency of the parties' culpable conduct. In *General Accident Versekeringsmaatskappy SA Bpk v. Uijs*,[1482] the court applied the notion of 'causal negligence' in a case where the plaintiff was a passenger in a vehicle driven by the defendant. The plaintiff had failed to comply with defendant's request to wear a seat belt and was seriously injured in an accident caused by the defendant's negligent conduct. In the court's assessment, the plaintiff and the defendant had deviated from the norm of the reasonable person in the same degree. However, justice and equity demanded that the plaintiff's fault be assessed differently, because the plaintiff did not contribute to the accident. A one-third reduction was found to be proper in the circumstances.

694. It is not necessary to claim or plead specifically an apportionment of damages, provided that the fault of the plaintiff has been placed in issue. The court must give judgment in accordance with the imperative of section 1(1)(a).[1483] The onus of proving fault on the part of the plaintiff rests on the defendant.[1484]

1481. 1983 (1) SA 381 (A) 401.
1482. 1993 (4) SA 228 (A) 235.
1483. *AA Mutual Insurance Association Ltd v. Nomeka* 1976 (3) SA 45 (A).
1484. *Mabaso v. Felix* 1981 (3) SA 865 (A) 877; *Damba v. AA Mutual Insurance Association Ltd* 1981 (3) SA 740 (E) 742; *Willmers v. Cape Provincial Administration* 1992 (1) SA 310 (E) 316.

§5. Joint Wrongdoers

695. Section 2 of the Apportionment of Damages Act[1485] abolishes the common law distinction between joint and concurrent wrongdoers and provides for a right of contribution between joint wrongdoers as defined in the section.

Section 2(1) provides:

> Where it is alleged that two or more persons are jointly or severally liable in delict to a third person (hereinafter referred to as the plaintiff) for the same damage, such persons (hereinafter referred to as joint wrongdoers) may be sued in the same action.

The subsection places joint and concurrent wrongdoers on the same footing and indicates that a joint wrongdoer refers to a person who is alleged in an action to be jointly and severally liable to the plaintiff, whether or not that is in fact the case, and also to persons who are in fact wrongdoers.

696. In terms of section 2(1A), a spouse married in or out of community of property may be regarded as a wrongdoer against the other spouse. Also, in terms of sections 18 and 19 of the Matrimonial Property Act[1486] spouses married in community of property may claim non-patrimonial damages arising from bodily injuries from one another and such damages, as well as non-patrimonial damages recovered from another person, do not become part of the joint estate. In *Van der Merwe v. Road Accident Fund and Another*,[1487] the Constitutional Court decided that the distinction between patrimonial and non-patrimonial damages in section 18(b) of the Matrimonial Property Act is unconstitutional. In this case, the distinction would have prevented the plaintiff spouse, who was married in community of property, from recovering damages for patrimonial loss from her former husband, who assaulted and injured her by running her over with a car, while they were still married. The court held that the distinction made by section 18(b) in respect of claims for patrimonial damages between spouses married in and out of community is a relic of the common law of marriage. The distinction drawn by section 18(b) displays a preoccupation with the conceptual cohesion of a joint estate and, by in effect depriving a physically brutalized spouse a claim for patrimonial loss against the other spouse, it fails the test of rationality.

697. As noted above, damages claimed as a result of the injury or death of another person, for instance the medical costs incurred as a result of the injuries of a child or the loss of support as a result of the death of a parent, cannot be reduced proportionate to the contributory negligence of the injured or deceased person – there is no 'own fault' on the part of the claimant. Instead, the negligent injured person or the estate of the deceased is considered to be a joint wrongdoer in terms of section 2(1B) of the Act, and the defendant liable to pay damages to a parent for the

1485. Act 34 of 1956.
1486. Act of 1984.
1487. [2006] ZACC 4; 2006 (4) SA 230 (CC).

injuries of a child or to a dependant for the death of a breadwinner has a right of contribution against the child or the estate of the deceased breadwinner.

698. Section 2(1) provides that joint wrongdoers may be sued in the same action and section 2(2) provides that notice of any action may be given by a plaintiff or any joint wrongdoer sued in the action, at any time before *litis contestatio*, to any other joint wrongdoer not sued in the action; and such a joint wrongdoer may then intervene as a defendant in the action. Section 2(4) provides that if no such notice was given timeously, the plaintiff can sue the non-notified joint wrongdoer only with the leave of the court on good cause shown; and a joint wrongdoer sued by the plaintiff can likewise claim a contribution from the non-notified joint wrongdoer only with the leave of the court. In terms of section 2(6)(c), a person from whom a contribution is claimed may raise against the claimant (the other joint wrongdoer) any defence which the claimant could have raised against the plaintiff.

699. In terms of section 2(7)(a), any joint wrongdoer who pays damages to the plaintiff in excess of the amount which the court deems just and equitable, having regard to the degree in which he was at fault in relation to the damage suffered by the plaintiff, may recover from any other joint wrongdoer a contribution in an amount which the court deems just and equitable having regard to the degree to which such other joint wrongdoer was at fault in relation to the damage suffered by the plaintiff.

700. In terms of section 2(8)(a) a court may, in its judgment in favour of the plaintiff against two or more joint wrongdoers, either order that such joint wrongdoers pay the amount of the damages awarded jointly and severally, the one paying the other to be absolved; or, if it is satisfied that all the joint wrongdoers have been joined in the action, apportion the damages awarded against the said joint wrongdoers in such proportions as it deems just and equitable having regard to the degree in which each joint wrongdoer was at fault in relation to the damage suffered by the plaintiff.[1488]

701. In terms of section 2(8)(b), any joint wrongdoer who pays more than the amount apportioned to him may recover a contribution from any joint wrongdoer who has paid less than or nothing of the amount apportioned to him.

702. In terms of section 2(9), a court may make an order as to costs between joint wrongdoers, as it considers just.

703. In terms of section 2(10), a plaintiff who exempts any joint wrongdoer from liability or limits such a joint wrongdoer's liability, cannot recover a portion based on the full amount of the damages from another joint wrongdoer.

1488. *See Wright v. Medi-Clinic Ltd* 2007 (4) SA 327 (C), a medical negligence case, where the court apportioned damages payable for brain injury sustained by the plaintiffs' child at time of birth on the basis that the obstetrician in attendance should pay 20% of recoverable damages, and the hospital 80%.

704. In terms of section 2(11)(a), a joint wrongdoer who is entitled to recover a contribution from another joint wrongdoer, but is unable to recover by reason of the other wrongdoer's insolvency or otherwise, may recover from any other joint wrongdoer such portion of that contribution as the court may deem just and equitable, having regard to the degree in which that other joint wrongdoer was at fault in relation to the damage suffered by the plaintiff.

Chapter 4. Exemption Clauses

§1. Validity and Effect

705. A prior agreement not to claim damages should harm be caused by the conduct of another person (*pactum de non petendo in anticipando*) can exclude the recovery of damages. Such an agreement or exemption clause in an agreement can provide a complete defence against a claim for damages as a result of the anticipated and later realized harm, excluding liability for negligence in breach of contract as well as delict.[1489] If the defendant had contractually excluded liability for negligent-caused harm, the plaintiff cannot evade this limitation by suing in delict, provided the defendant discharges the onus of proving that the terms of the exemption exclude liability in the particular circumstances.[1490] The Consumer Protection Act 68 of 2008 limits the scope of contractual exemption clauses in transactions where the Act applies.[1491]

706. The requirements for a valid agreement to exclude liability (*pactum de non petendo in anticipando*) are the same as for any other contract. The requirement of authorization to contract on behalf of another person applies. One person cannot conclude a *pactum de non petendo in anticipando* on behalf of another without authorization. This means that a prior agreement by a breadwinner undertaking that no claim will be instituted in the event of his negligently caused injury or death, even if such an agreement purports to bind his estate and his dependants, will not exclude the right of his dependants to claim compensation for loss of support in the event of his death.[1492] An exemption clause that would have been effective against a deceased person need not be effective against his or her dependants; and it is questionable whether an exemption from liability for causing death will be considered valid.[1493]

707. The courts appear to accept generally that a parent or guardian can validly conclude a *pactum de non petendo in anticipando* on behalf of a minor child, for instance where a school or sport club requires such an undertaking from the parent or guardian as a condition for the child's participation in an educational activity or

1489. *Government of the Republic of South Africa v. Fibre Spinners & Weavers (Pty) Ltd* 1978 (2) SA 794 (A) 807.
1490. *Durban's Water Wonderland (Pty) Ltd v. Botha* 1999 (1) SA 982 (A) 990B-C.
1491. Section 51.
1492. *Jameson's Minors v. CSAR* 1908 TS 575; and *see also Payne v. Minister of Transport* 1995 (4) SA 153 (C).
1493. *Johannesburg Country Club v. Stott* 2004 (5) SA 511 (SCA) paras 6, 9, 12 and 14–17.

sport,[1494] or where the terms for entry into an amusement park excludes liability.[1495] Although participation in an educational activity or sport is to the benefit of the child, an agreement excluding liability for negligently caused injury to the child is not, and arguably the child should be entitled to *restitutio in integrum*, to have the effects of the agreement set aside.[1496] The effect of such an agreement will in any event depend on the precise ambit of the agreement, and the courts will tend to interpret such agreements restrictively.[1497]

708. An agreement purporting to exclude liability for harm caused intentionally will not be valid, but under common law an agreement excluding liability for harm caused by negligence or even gross negligence is regarded as valid.[1498] In a transaction governed by the Consumer Protection Act,[1499] a purported exclusion of liability for gross negligence is void.[1500]

709. Under common law, exemption clauses have been enforced even where the effect appears to be to undermine a basic purpose of the contract, such as to be treated with due care in a hospital,[1501] or to store valuables safely in a bank vault.[1502]

§2. INTERPRETATION

710. Where a contractual term is raised as a defence to a claim founded in delict, the defendant bears the onus of establishing the terms of the contract.[1503] The extent

1494. *See Minister of Education and Culture (House of Delegates) v. Azal* 1995 (1) SA 30 (A), where the court decided that the undertaking by a parent, which limited the school's liability for damage to property or personal injury of the child, did not have effect where there was negligence on the part of the responsible teacher.
1495. *See Durban's Water Wonderland (Pty) Ltd v. Botha* 1999 (1) SA 982 (A), where it was held that a parent had agreed on behalf of a child to conditions excluding the liability of an amusement park owner for injury to a person using the park's facilities.
1496. *See* P.Q.R. Boberg, *The Law of Delict Vol. 1 Aquilian Liability*, 732.
1497. *Minister of Education and Culture (House of Delegates) v. Azal* 1995 (1) SA 30 (A).
1498. *Government of the Republic of South Africa v. Fibre Spinners & Weavers (Pty) Ltd* 1978 (2) SA 794 (A) 807; *Sasfin (Pty) Ltd v. Beukes* 1989 (1) SA 1 (A) 15; *First National Bank of SA Ltd v. Rosenblum* 2001 (4) SA 189 (SCA); and *Afrox Healthcare Bpk v. Strydom* 2002 (6) SA 21 (SCA).
1499. Act 68 of 2008.
1500. Section 51(1)*(c)*(i).
1501. *Afrox Healthcare Bpk v. Strydom* 2002 (6) SA 21 (SCA).
1502. *First National Bank of SA Ltd v. Rosenblum* 2001 (4) SA 189 (SCA); *ABSA Bank Ltd v. Fouche*[2002] 4 All SA 245; 2003 (1) SA 176 (SCA).
1503. *See Durban's Water Wonderland (Pty) Ltd v. Botha* 1999 (1) SA 982 (A) 990B-C: 'The respondents' claims were founded in delict. The appellant relied on a contract in terms of which liability for negligence was excluded. It accordingly bore the onus of establishing the terms of the contract.' (The position would have been otherwise had the respondents sued in contract. *See Stocks & Stocks (Pty) Ltd v. T.J. Daly & Sons (Pty) Ltd* 1979 (3) SA 754 (A) at 762E–767C.).

of the exclusion or limitation of liability depends on the interpretation of the exemption clause. General principles of interpretation apply, but the courts will scrutinize such clauses carefully. In *Van der Westhuizen v. Arnold*,[1504] Lewis AJA said the following in this regard:

> [40] There does not, therefore, appear to be any clear authority for a general principle that exemption clauses should be construed differently from other provisions in a contract. But that does not mean that courts are not, or should not be, wary of contractual exclusions, since they do deprive parties of rights that they would otherwise have had at common law. In the absence of legislation regulating unfair contract terms, and where a provision does not offend public policy or considerations of good faith, a careful construction of the contract itself should ensure the protection of the party whose rights have been limited, but also give effect to the principle that the other party should be able to protect himself or herself against liability insofar as it is legally permissible. The very fact, however, that an exclusion clause limits or ousts common law rights should make a court consider with great care the meaning of the clause, especially if it is very general in its application. This requires a consideration of the background circumstances ... and a resort to surrounding circumstances if there be any doubt as to the application of the exclusion.

711. If there is no express reference to negligence in the exemption clause – for example, in the case of a so-called owner's risk clause – the court must consider whether the words are extensive enough in their ordinary meaning to cover negligence on the part of the defendant. If negligence is the only basis of liability, either in the case of breach of contract or delict, an exclusionary clause (e.g., an 'owner's risk' clause) can be construed to exclude liability on the basis of negligence.[1505] In case of doubt, the issue will be decided against the party relying on the exemption, as the person considered responsible for drafting the contract (proferens).[1506] If the words are extensive enough in meaning to cover negligence, the court must consider the possibility of another ground of action which does not require proof of

1504. 2002 (6) 452 (SCA).

1505. *Essa v. Divaris* 1947 (1) SA 753 (A) 763–764 766–767; *Hughes v. SA Fumigation Co. (Pty) Ltd* 1961 (4) SA 799 (C) 805; *Bristow v. Lycett* 1971 (4) SA 223 (RA) 236. However, in *Drifters Adventure Tours CC v. Hircock*[2007] 1 All SA 133 (SCA), a case concerning the negligent driving of a tour bus, an exemption clause purported to absolve the tour operator 'of any liability whatsoever', was in the context of the contract as a whole interpreted not to exclude liability for negligent driving, a risk which the court regarded as being inherent in ordinary road transportation, so that contracting out would be so perverse that it could not be accepted that this was the intention of the clause.

1506. *Durban's Water Wonderland (Pty) Ltd v. Botha* 1999 (1) SA 982 (A) 989G-I: 'Against this background it is convenient to consider first the proper construction to be placed on the disclaimer. The correct approach is well established. If the language of a disclaimer or exemption clause is such that it exempts the proferens from liability in express and unambiguous terms, effect must be given to that meaning. If there is ambiguity, the language must be construed against the proferens. (*See Government of the Republic of South Africa v. Fibre Spinners & Weavers (Pty) Ltd* 1978 (2) SA 794 (A) at 804C.) But the alternative meaning upon which reliance is placed to demonstrate the ambiguity must be one to which the language is fairly susceptible; it must not be "fanciful" or "remote" (cf. *Canada Steamship Lines Ltd v. Regem* [1952] 1 All ER 305 (PC) at 310C-D)'.

negligence, for example strict liability of the owner of an animal or a common carrier.[1507] It must be clear that the parties intended the cause of action that is in issue to be covered by the exemption.[1508] As noted above, the Consumer Protection Act 68 of 2008 limits the scope of contractual exemption clauses in transactions where the Act applies.[1509]

§3. Exemption Clauses and the Constitution

712. Exemption clauses, like other contractual clauses, are subject to the broad principle of legality, and will be unenforceable if contrary to public policy. The values enshrined in the Constitution[1510] inform the content of public policy and are therefore relevant to the validity of exemption clauses.

713. The effect of the Constitution in this regard was considered in *Afrox Healthcare Bpk v. Strydom.*[1511] The plaintiff had been admitted to the hospital owned by the defendant, for an operation and post-operative medical treatment. Upon admission, the plaintiff signed an agreement containing an exemption clause, providing that the patient:

> absolved the hospital and/or its employees and/or agents from all liability and indemnified them from any claim instituted by any person (including a dependant of the patient) for damages or loss of whatever nature (including consequential damages or special damages of any nature) flowing directly or indirectly from any injury (including fatal injury) suffered by or damage caused to the patient or any illness (including terminal illness) contracted by the patient whatever the cause/causes are, except only with the exclusion of intentional omission by the hospital, its employees or agents.

The plaintiff alleged that it was also a tacit term of this agreement that the defendant's nursing staff would treat him in a professional manner and with reasonable care. After the operation, certain negligent conduct by a nurse led to complications setting in, which caused the plaintiff to suffer damages. The respondent argued that

1507. *Essa v. Divaris* 1947 (1) SA 753 (A) 763–764 766–767; *Government of the Republic of SA (Department of Industries) v. Fibre Spinners and Weavers (Pty) Ltd* 1978 (2) SA 794 (A) 807. In *Walker v. Redhouse* 2006 [JOL] 18175 (SCA), concerning an action based on the strict liability of the owner of an animal *action de pauperie*, an exemption 'for any loss or damage sustained … in the course of my horse riding' was held to exclude liability of the owner for an injury that occurred when a hired horse bolted and so acted contra naturam sui generic (there was no negligence on the part of the owner).

1508. *Cardboard Packing Utilities (Pty) Ltd v. Edblo Tvl Ltd* 1960 (3) SA 178 (W); *Hughes v. SA Fumigation Co. (Pty) Ltd* 1961 (4) SA 799 (C); *Bristow v. Lycett* 1971 (4) SA 223 (RA) 235–240; *Government of the Republic of SA v. Fibre Spinners & Weavers (Pty) Ltd* 1978 (2) SA 794 (A) 803–806; *Lawrence v. Kondotel Inns (Pty) Ltd* 1989 (1) SA 44 (D) 53–54.

1509. Section 51.

1510. Act 108 of 1996.

1511. 2002 (6) SA 21 (SCA). *See also*, on a non-variation clause in a lease, *Brisley v. Drotsky* 2002 (4) SA 1 (SCA).

the negligent conduct of the nurse had constituted a breach of contract by the defendant and instituted an action for damages suffered. The defendant relied on the exemption clause to avoid liability.

The plaintiff contended that the exemption clause was contrary to the public interest, that it was in conflict with the principles of good faith or bona fides, and that the admission clerk had had a legal duty to draw his attention to the relevant clause, which he had not done. The public policy grounds for the plaintiff's attack on the validity of the exemption clause were the alleged unequal bargaining positions of the parties; the fact that the defendant was the provider of medical services, which entailed the duty to provide medical treatment in a professional and caring manner; and the wide ambit of the exemption, which could encompass even gross negligence on the part of the nursing staff. Furthermore, section 39(2) of the Constitution[1512] obliged every court, when developing the common law, to promote the spirit, purport and object of the Bill of Rights, so that account had to be taken of the fundamental rights contained in the Constitution. It was argued that the exemption clause conflicted with the spirit, purport and object of section 27(1)(a)of the Constitution, which guaranteed each person's right to medical care, and as such it was in conflict with the public interest, or, alternatively, it was unreasonable, unfair and in conflict with the principle of bona fides or good faith.

The court noted that exclusionary and indemnity clauses should be interpreted restrictively. Specific exclusionary clause could be declared contrary to public policy and as such unenforceable. The relevant considerations of public policy were no different from those applicable to other contractual terms. There was no evidence indicating that the plaintiff had occupied a weaker bargaining position than the defendant during the conclusion of the contract. The plaintiff had not relied on gross negligence on the part of the nursing staff, and the question of whether the contractual exclusion of a hospital's liability for damages caused by the gross negligence of its nursing staff was in conflict with the public interest was accordingly not relevant. Even if that were the case, it would not mean the automatic invalidity of the relevant clause. The provisions would probably rather have been restricted to exclude gross negligence.

With regard to the constitutional argument, that it first had to be decided whether section 39(2) of the Constitution empowered, and obliged, the court to consider constitutional provisions not yet in operation when the contractual relationship between the parties had commenced. For the purposes of the judgment, it was accepted in favour of the respondent that the provisions of section 27(1)(a)of the Constitution had to be taken into account. However, the exemption clause was not in conflict with that right, and the elementary and basic general principle was that it was in the public interest that contracts entered into freely and seriously by parties having the necessary capacity should be enforced. The contention that the exemption clause was contrary to the public interest therefore failed.

714. In *Johannesburg Country Club v. Stott*,[1513] the court considered an exemption clause that sought to exclude any liability on the part of the club for personal

1512. Act 108 of 1996.
1513. 2004 (5) SA 511 (SCA).

injury or harm to its members or their children whilst on the club premises, however caused. One of the members of the club was killed by lightning whilst playing golf, and his wife instituted a dependant's action in which she sought damages for loss of support and funeral costs. The court issued a directive requesting that the legal representatives of the parties provide it with argument on whether or not the exemption clause ought to be unenforceable on the grounds that it violates public policy, because it is inconsistent with the constitutionally entrenched right to life. However, despite the directive that it issued, the court found that it was able to decide the matter without having to resort to a constitutional inquiry. It was held that the terms of the exemption clause in any event did not cover liability for loss of support as claimed by the plaintiff.

715. The application of an exemption clause in contract and delict was in issue in *Freddy Hirsch Group (Pty) Ltd v. Chickenland (Pty) Ltd.*[1514] The appellant, Freddy Hirsch, was a manufacturer and supplier of spices. The respondent, Chickenland, was the operative arm of Nando's, a chain of fast food chicken outlets. Chickenland bought spices from Freddy Hirsch to use in its sauces and other condiments. The supply agreement contained a liability exemption clause in favour of Freddy Hirsch. However, the employee of Chickenland who signed the agreement on behalf of Chickenland made a note that the standard conditions were not checked. At some stage, it was discovered by health inspectors in the United Kingdom that Chickenland's peri-peri hot sauce contained a banned substance. It was common cause that the banned substance was part of a spice that Freddy Hirsch supplied to Chickenland. Chickenland had to recall these sauces and suffered a loss of ZAR 12 million. Chickenland brought claims in contract and delict and alleged, *inter alia*, that the material, express and/or implied and/or tacit terms of the supply agreement of the spices were that:

- each of the spice packs would be fit for human consumption; and
- the spice packs would be free of any banned substance.

The Supreme Court of Appeal decided that a supplier of goods (here Freddy Hirsch) cannot rely on a clause excluding liability for defects in the goods supplied where the *res* delivered is an entirely different *res* from that bargained for. Where the supplier supplied a foodstuff that contained a banned contaminant rendering it unfit for human consumption, it failed to perform in terms of the contract because what was delivered was different in substance from what was purchased. Because the present case dealt with non-performance rather than defective performance, the exemption did not avail the supplier. As far as the exemption clause purported to exclude all terms, warranties or representations (whether statutory or common law) as to the quality or fitness of the foodstuff, it was contrary to public policy and unenforceable. The appeal by Freddy Hirsch was accordingly dismissed with costs.

1514. 2011 (4) SA 276 (SCA).

716. The constitutional validity of exemption and limitation clauses was considered by the Constitutional Court, in the case of *Barkhuizen v. Napier*,[1515] which involved a constitutional challenge to a time limitation clause in a short-term insurance contract. The clause in question required the claimant to institute court proceedings within ninety days after the insurance company had rejected the claim.

The majority of the court held that the proper approach to the constitutional challenge is to determine whether the time limitation clause is contrary to public policy as evidenced by constitutional values, in particular, those found in the Bill of Rights. The question was whether a time limitation clause is contrary to public policy and whether it allowed an adequate and fair opportunity to seek the assistance of a court. The period of ninety days allowed was not inadequate or unfair. When the ninety days period commenced to run, the plaintiff had all the information that was necessary for him to sue the insurance company as he had already lodged his claim with the insurance company and the insurance company had rejected his claim. In addition, there was no evidence that the contract was not freely concluded between persons with equal bargaining power or that the insured was not aware of the clause. The insured waited for two years after being told of the rejection of his claim, but did not furnish any reason for non-compliance with the clause. In the circumstances, the clause was not unfair or unreasonable.

In a minority judgment, Sachs J held that considerations of public policy, as animated by the Constitution, dictated that the time-bar clause, which limited access to courts, should not be enforced. This was not merely because it was in small print, or because it bore harshly on the insured, but because the clause was contained in a standard form document; and generally failed to comply with standards of notice and fairness which contemporary notions of consumer protection required in open and democratic societies. In another minority judgment Moseneke DCJ, with whom Mokgoro J concurred, agreed with Sachs J that the clause was against public policy and should be unenforceable. The proper approach, according to this judgment, was whether the clause clashes with public norms and whether the contractual term is so unreasonable as to offend against public policy. Moseneke DCJ held that the impugned time clause is, on the facts of this case, unreasonably short and inflexible with the result that it precludes a reasonable and adequate opportunity to seek legal redress.

717. In the cases referred to above, specific exemption clauses were examined in specific circumstances. Further constitutional challenges to such clauses may follow, in particular where such clauses are contained in standard contracts and where personal injury is involved. The focus is likely to be on the impact of such clauses on the right to access to the courts, as guaranteed in section 34 of the Constitution.[1516] As noted above, the Consumer Protection Act 68 of 2008 limits the scope of contractual exemption clauses in transactions where the Act applies.[1517]

1515. 2007 (5) SA 323 (CC).
1516. Act 108 of 1996.a.
1517. Section 51.

Part V. Causation

§1. Requirement of Causation in Delict

718. The existence of a causal nexus between the defendant's conduct and the harm suffered by the plaintiff is an essential element of a delict. This was recognized in Roman and Roman-Dutch law, but no comprehensive theory for determining legal causation was developed. It was recognized that an independent intervening act which neutralizes or substantially reduces the causative effect of another act interrupts the chain of causation; and also that the negligent intervening conduct of a third party normally interrupts the chain of causation.[1518] The intervention of natural phenomena, such as wind or lightning, interrupts the chain of causation, unless the chain of events was put in motion in circumstances where such intervention was reasonably foreseeable.[1519]

§2. Two Elements of Causation

719. Causation involves two different questions, namely whether the defendant's conduct factually caused the plaintiff's harm; and whether the defendant should be held legally responsible for such harm. In the leading case of *Minister of Police v. Skosana*,[1520] this is stated as follows:

> Causation in the law of delict gives rise to two rather distinct problems. The first is a factual one and relates to the question whether the negligent act or omission in question caused or materially contributed to … the harm giving rise to the claim. If it did not, then no legal liability can arise and *cadit quaestio*. If it did, then the second problem becomes relevant, viz whether the negligent act or omission is linked to the harm sufficiently closely or directly for legal liability to ensure or whether, as it is said, the harm is too remote. This is basically a juridical problem in which considerations of legal policy may play a part.

1518. D 9 2 11 3; D 9 2 15 1; D 9 2 51 pr.
1519. D9 2 30 4; D 9 2 52 pr; D9 2 7 5; D 9 2 30 3; D 19 2 57.
1520. 1977 (1) SA 31 (A) 34–35.

720. The factual consequences of an act may extend indefinitely, and the law does not impose liability for all the harmful consequences of an act. Causation-in-fact is necessary to found liability, but not in itself sufficient.

§3. Factual Causation

721. Factual causation concerns the factual link between the defendant's conduct and the harm suffered by the plaintiff. In *International Shipping Co. (Pty) Ltd v. Bentley*,[1521] the court accepted the 'but-for' or *conditio sine qua non* test for factual causation:

> The inquiry as to factual causation is generally conducted by applying the so-called 'but-for' test, which is designed to determine whether a postulated cause can be identified as a *causa sine qua non* of the loss in question. In order to apply this test one must make a hypothetical inquiry as to what probably would have happened but for the wrongful conduct of the defendant. This inquiry may involve the mental elimination of the wrongful conduct and the substitution of a hypothetical course of lawful conduct and the posing of the question as to whether upon such an hypothesis plaintiff's loss would have ensued or not. If it would in any event have ensued, then the wrongful conduct was not a cause of the plaintiff's loss; *aliter*, if it would not so have ensued. If the wrongful act is shown in this way not to be a *causa sine qua non* of the loss suffered, then no legal liability can arise.

722. The conduct complained of can only be a factual cause of the harmful consequence if it was a necessary condition for the existence of that consequence. In terms of the *conditio sine qua non* theory, the conduct of the defendant can only be considered a cause-in-fact of the harmful consequence if the elimination of that conduct would have meant the non-occurrence of the harmful consequence. The application of the 'but-for' test therefore requires a process of mental elimination – if the defendant's positive act is hypothetically eliminated from the complex set of conditions prevailing at the time, would the harmful consequence still have occurred?

723. In determining the causative effect of an omission in terms of the 'but-for' test, a mental substitution of the defendant's omission with reasonable positive conduct is usually done. If the hypothetical reasonable positive conduct would have prevented the harmful consequence, the omission was a necessary condition and therefore a cause of that consequence.[1522] In *S v. Van As*,[1523] the issue was whether

1521. 1990 (1) SA 680 (A).

1522. In *Moses v. Minister of Safety & Security* 2000 1 Al SA 89 (C); 2000 (3) SA 106 (C), the liability of the police for the death of a person detained in a police cell was in issue. The detainee had died after an assault by fellow-detainees. The assault occurred between cell inspections, which were twenty-five minutes apart. The police were unaware of the propensity of the fellow-detainees towards violence – they had not exhibited any signs of aggressiveness. In view of the relatively limited manpower available, number of matters to be attended to more regular inspections could not reasonably be expected. In any event, a cell inspection would have prevented the assault only

the failure by policemen to conduct an extensive search for children who had left the scene of an arrest could be regarded as the cause of the death of two of the children by exposure to cold and rain. The court took into account what reasonable policemen would have done in the situation and decided that such conduct would not have saved the children. The failure to conduct an extensive search was therefore not regarded as the cause of the death of the children.

724. The *conditio sine qua non* approach cannot be regarded as the exclusive test for factual causation. As a theory, it is logically flawed in that mental elimination of one factor creates a new causation problem and leads to circular reasoning; and it also deals inadequately with multiple contributory causes. The courts apply common sense standards and the *conditio sine qua non* approach is in effect a means of expressing an a priori conclusion on factual causation, based on knowledge (expert and general) and experience.

725. In *Minister of Finance v. Gore and Others*,[1524] the question of factual causation concerned the outcome of a tender process, if it had not been affected by fraud. Cameron JA noted that factual causation involves an inquiry where the answer depends on fact, but the question itself is formulated in law.[1525] The time-honoured way of formulating the question in South African law is in the form of the 'but-for' test. Can it be said that, but for the wrongful act complained of, the loss concerned would not have ensued? Applying this test requires a process of inferential reasoning as described by Corbett CJ in the *International Shipping Co.* case, cited above. What would have happened if the wrongful conduct is mentally eliminated and hypothetically replaced with lawful conduct? A plaintiff who can establish that, in such event, the loss would, on a preponderance of probabilities, not have occurred, recovers his damages in full, because causation is regarded as having been established as a fact. A plaintiff who cannot do so will get nothing. That there is no discount either way stems from the nature of the inferential process: the verdict must go one way or the other even if the scales are tipped only slightly in one direction.[1526]

726. The court in the *Gore* case noted, with reference to the onus resting on plaintiff, that the requirement of proof on the basis of a more-than-50% chance has an all-or-nothing effect that is arguably unsatisfactory and unfair. The plaintiff who can establish a 51% chance, so it is said, gets everything, while a 49% prospect results in total failure. This, however, said Cameron JA, is not how the process of

---

if it had coincided with the assault, which took place shortly after the deceased's assailants had been admitted to the cell. Accordingly, the plaintiff had not succeeded in showing that, if more regular inspections were held, that would have prevented the assault and its consequences. In the premises, the plaintiff had failed to discharge the onus of showing that the conduct attributed to the defendant's servants had been causally (in the sense of factual causation) linked to any loss suffered by the plaintiff.

1523. 1967 (4) SA 594 (A).
1524. 2007 (1) SA 111 (SCA).
1525. Paragraph 31.
1526. Paragraph 32.

legal reasoning works. The legal mind enquires: what is more likely? The issue is one of persuasion, which is ill-reflected in formulaic quantification. The question of percentages does not arise. Application of the 'but-for' test is not based on mathematics, pure science or philosophy. It is a matter of common sense, based on the practical way in which the ordinary person's mind works against the background of everyday life experiences.[1527] In this regard, Nugent JA said the following in *Minister of Safety and Security v. Van Duivenboden*:[1528]

> A plaintiff is not required to establish the causal link with certainty, but only to establish that the wrongful conduct was probably a cause of the loss, which calls for a sensible retrospective analysis of what would probably have occurred, based upon the evidence and what can be expected to occur in the ordinary course of human affairs rather than metaphysics.

727. In *mCubed International (Pty) Ltd and Another v. Singer and Others NNO*,[1529] the respondents were trustees of the Leon John Singer Family Trust who wanted to invest ZAR 40 million overseas through various investment companies. They wished to invest ZAR 10 million of the ZAR 40 million through the appellants (mCubed) by converting the ZAR 10 million into US dollars. Employees of mCubed proposed an investment structure and the funds were invested overseas. However, the investment structure proposed by mCubed later proved to be unlawful, and when the trustees learned about this, they terminated the investment through the early withdrawal of the investment funds. However, they could not recover the whole of the ZAR 10 million invested, because of an unfavourable change in the Rand-Dollar exchange rate. The trustees then instituted legal proceedings against mCubed to recover the balance of the invested funds. The trustees alleged that, but for the misrepresentations made by mCubed, they would not have invested the money through mCubed, and they would have retained the money in Rand. The also argued that, but for the misrepresentations made by mCubed, they would have terminated the investment immediately and would not have suffered the loss.

The court confirmed the 'but-for' test as being the appropriate test to determine factual causation, and in applying this test, it asked what mCubed should have done in the circumstances. The court was satisfied that, but for the misrepresentation by mCubed, the ZAR 10 million would not have been invested with mCubed at that stage.

The trustees contended that this was the end of the 'but-for' inquiry, and that factual causation had thus been established. The court disagreed, having taken the following two factors into consideration: (i) the unpredicted strengthening of the Rand against the US Dollar, and (ii) the likelihood that, had the trustees known about the proposed investment structure's illegality, the ZAR 10 million would likely have been converted to US Dollars and invested through some other investment company. The court reasoned that but for the unexpected strengthening of the Rand against the Dollar, the loss would not have been sustained. If the Rand-Dollar

1527. *Minister of Finance v. Gore and Others* 2007 (1) SA 111 (SCA) para. 33.
1528. 2002 (6) 431 (SCA) para. 25.
1529. 2009 (4) SA 471 (SCA).

exchange rate performed as was predicted, the trust would have made a profit despite the trustees' dissatisfaction with mCubed and despite the early withdrawal of investment funds. The court furthermore took into account the fact that even if mCubed had acted as it should have and the trustees accordingly did not invest the ZAR 10 million with it, there was enough evidence to indicate that the trustees would have invested the ZAR 10 million, converted to US Dollars, through other investment companies where they could have sustained a similar loss due to the stronger Rand. Thus, the misrepresentation was not the cause of the loss; it was merely the cause of the investment through mCubed. Factual causation was therefore not established because but for the misrepresentations made by employees of mCubed, the trust would probably still have suffered the loss.

728. In *The Minister of Correctional Services v. Lee*,[1530] the plaintiff, Lee, was detained in prison for some four years and contracted tuberculosis. After his release from prison Lee sued the State, nominally represented by the Minister of Correctional Services, for damages. Essentially, he alleged that the prison authorities had failed to take adequate precautions to protect him against contracting tuberculosis, that he had contracted the illness in consequence of their omission, and that the omission violated his right to protection of his physical integrity under the common law, the Correctional Services Act 8 of 1959, and the Constitution. The Supreme Court of Appeal held that the difficulty faced by Lee was lack of knowledge about the source of his infection. Had he been able to prove its source, it is possible that he might have established a causal link between his infection and specific negligent conduct on the part of the prison authorities. Instead, he had to rely on systemic omission to prevent infection. In the absence of proof that reasonable systemic adequacy would have altogether eliminated the risk of contagion, which would be difficult to prove, it cannot be found that but for the systemic omission he probably would not have contracted the disease. On that ground his claim failed. However, his appeal to the Constitutional Court succeeded. The court held that the law does not require evidentiary proof of the alternative, but merely substitution of a notional and hypothetical lawful, non-negligent alternative. The purpose of the exercise is to evaluate the evidence presented by a plaintiff, not to require more evidence. On this basis probable factual causation was found to have been established.

729. Where the plaintiff proves that a particular consequence was caused by more than one factor the courts do not require him or her to quantify the extent of the causal connection. This approach was confirmed in *Humphrys NO v. Barnes*.[1531] The appellant (plaintiff) bought immovable property from the respondent (defendant). The defendant had raised the height of a pre-existing retaining wall which was previously erected by the owner of the adjoining property. The defendant then sold the property to the appellant, subject to a voetstoots clause. After heavy rain, the wall collapsed, resulting in extensive damage to both properties. It was accepted in the magistrates' court that the defendant had been negligent in constructing the wall, and that such negligence was a contributory cause of the collapse. In the High

1530. [2012] ZASCA 23 (SCA judgment); and [2012] ZACC 30 (Constitutional Court Judgment).
1531. 2004 (2) SA 577 (C).

Court Griesel J held that the correct approach to be followed was set out in *Kakamas Bestuursraad v. Louw* where Schreiner JA held:

> [A] plaintiff can hold a defendant liable whose negligence has materially contributed to a totality of loss resulting partly also from the acts of other persons or from the forces of nature, even though no precise allocation of portions of the loss to the contributing factors can be made.[1532]

This dictum in the *Kakamas Bestuursraad* case, as explained by Boberg,[1533] places the onus of proof in its proper perspective. It is not for the *plaintiff* to prove *which part* of the loss the defendant caused, but the *defendant* can escape liability for the whole loss by proving *which part* he caused. In short, the harm is presumed to be indivisible, and the plaintiff need prove only that the defendant contributed materially to the totality of it. The onus is then on the defendant to rebut the presumption by proving that the harm is in fact divisible and that he did not cause all of it – which he does by proving which part he *did* cause.

730. Where the plaintiff's damage was caused partly by the negligent conduct of A and partly by the negligent conduct of B, the same presumption of indivisibility of the damage applies. Both A and B will be liable for the loss, as 'joint wrongdoers' in terms of section 2(1) of the Apportionment of Damages Act,[1534] which makes them jointly and severally liable for the whole damage with a right of recourse *inter se*. The application of the Act presupposes that A and B caused 'the same damage' (as section 2(1) expressly states) – that is, that the plaintiff's damage is one and indivisible. It is presumed that the damage is indivisible, but a defendant who can discharge the onus of proving that he caused only a distinct part of the plaintiff's harm is liable only for that part which he caused.

731. At the court in the *Humphrys* case, Griesel J confirmed the position as follows:

> [17] In the present instance it was therefore incumbent upon the plaintiff to prove only a material factual link between the defendant's negligent conduct and the collapse of the wall. He was not required to quantify the extent of its causal contribution. On the evidence as a whole, I am satisfied that the plaintiff had discharged that onus. It was then for the defendant to discharge the onus of proving that he caused only a distinct part of the plaintiff's harm, which he failed to do.[1535]

1532. 2004 (2) SA 577 (C) 581 citing from 1960 (2) SA 202 (A) 222A-C.
1533. *See* the citation in the *Humphrys* case 2004 (2) SA 577 (C) 581 of P.Q.R. Boberg, *Law of Delict*, 404–405 (1984) (emphasis added).
1534. Act 34 of 1956.
1535. 2004 (2) SA 577 (C) para. [17].

§4. MULTIPLE CAUSES

732. Where any one of concurrent events would have been sufficient to produce the harmful result, both will be regarded as contributory factual causes of the harm, although neither can be regarded as a *conditio sine qua non* of the harm. This accords with the common sense approach as accepted by the Supreme Court of Appeal in cases such as *Minister of Safety and Security v. Van Duivenboden*[1536] and *Minister of Finance v. Gore and Others.*[1537]

733. Section 2(1) of the Apportionment of Damages Act[1538] abolished the common law distinction between joint and concurrent wrongdoers. Joint wrongdoers are defined as persons who are jointly or severally liable in delict for the same damage. Either of the wrongdoers who concurrently caused the same damage could be held liable, with a right of recourse against the other; or both could be held liable jointly and severally.

734. Where any one of successive events would have been sufficient to produce the harmful result, but the result was in fact produced by the first event, the first event is likely to be regarded as the cause of the harm. For example, if two fires are started from different directions by two persons acting independently, both fires being sufficient to destroy a house, but the fire from the one direction reaches the house first and destroys it, the first fire will be regarded as the cause of the damage, while the hypothetical result (destruction of the house) of the second fire is likely to be disregarded.[1539]

735. The decision in *Minister of Communications and Public Works v. Renown Food Products*[1540] is in line with this approach. In that case, a claim was based on damage caused by collisions occurring in quick succession. The first defendant's vehicle collided with and caused damage to the plaintiff's vehicle, and within seconds the second defendant's vehicle collided with first defendant's vehicle, causing it to collide again with plaintiff's vehicle. It was not clear what damage, if any, was caused to plaintiff's car by the second collision. The court held that at common law the plaintiff must prove the damage caused by each defendant. Section 2(1) of the Apportionment of Damages Act[1541] provides that where it is alleged that two or more persons are jointly or severally liable in delict to a third person (the plaintiff) for the same damage, such persons (the joint wrongdoers) may be sued in the same action. However, for that provision to be applicable the two defendants must have caused the same damage. There was no evidence in this case that the two defendants in fact caused the same damage. Whether the time separation between occurrences of damage is ten minutes or a few seconds the principle remains the same,

---

1536. 2002 (6) 431 (SCA) para. 25.
1537. 2007 (1) SA 111 (SCA) para. 33.
1538. Act 34 of 1956.
1539. *See* B. Winiger, H. Koziol, B.A. Koch & R. Zimmermann eds., *Digest of European Tort Law Volume 1: Essential Cases on Natural Causation* 479–484 (Springer-Verlag/Wien 2007).
1540. 1988 (4) SA 151 (C).
1541. Act 34 of 1956.

namely that where two separate acts of negligence have caused different damage, each defendant will be liable at common law only for the damage personally caused. There is nothing in the Apportionment of Damages Act which detracts from that position. To interpret section 2(1) of the Act so as to widen the scope of the words 'the same damage' is not justified. There is nothing in the Act to indicate that 'the same damage' also refers to a situation where damage-causing events follow in quick succession and where the damage attributable to each separate event cannot be determined. However equitable it may be to place an onus on the defendants in such a case to prove allocation of damage, there is no such rule in South African law. The onus is on the plaintiff to prove the damage attributable to each defendant. If this cannot be proved with mathematical exactness, evidence must be presented to enable the court to assess as accurately as possible with the material before it the liability of each defendant.[1542] The plaintiff in this case called a loss adjuster as a witness, who testified that he was not qualified to determine which collision caused what damage. He also appears not to have been instructed even to attempt to do so, notwithstanding the fact that he was called upon to examine the plaintiff's vehicle within a few days of the accident. The plaintiff therefore failed to establish that the second defendant is liable for any damage at all.

736. Where successive damage-causing events produce different results, principles relating to both causation and damages may be in issue. For example, where one person has administered a fatal dose of poison to a horse, and, before the poison kills the horse, another person sets fire to the stable and the horse dies in the fire,[1543] the person who administered the poison will be liable for causing injury by poisoning, thereby reducing the value of the horse; whereas the person responsible for the fire will be liable for the death of the horse, but the reduced (or non-existent) value of the horse at that time will be taken into account.

737. Where an event creates circumstances conducive to the causing of harm by a second event of a particular kind, the person responsible for the first event will be liable if the second event was reasonably foreseeable. In *Vigario v. Afrox Ltd*,[1544] the plaintiff claimed damages for loss of support resulting from the death of her husband in a fire. It appeared that the defendant was responsible for the occurrence of oxygen enrichment in an area where it should not have occurred (a cold box), and the deceased was responsible for the ignition of a fire by the lighting of a cigarette lighter, which produced a naked flame and ignited either his beard or his clothing, causing it to burn intensely in the oxygen-enriched atmosphere. Had the same lighter been lit in a non-oxygen-enriched atmosphere, there would in all likelihood have been no fire of any consequence and the probability would have been that the deceased would merely have singed his beard and would have been able to put out any resultant fire to his beard or clothing. The court in this case held, by application of the *sine qua non* or 'but for test', that it was a combination of all the factors

1542. *See* in this regard *Prinsloo v. Luipaardsvlei Estates & GM Co. Ltd* 1933 WLD 6 at 23–24.
1543. *See* J. Spier ed., *Unification of Tort Law: Causation, Principles of European Tort Law: Volume 4*, 3–4, 97 (Kluwer L. Intl. 2000).
1544. 1996 (3) SA 450 (W) 459.

which was the factual cause of the resulting intense fire and the death. The defendant should reasonably have foreseen the death of the deceased. The lighting of the cigarette lighter was the probable cause of the fire starting, but this act was not a *novus actus interveniens*, but rather the very type of act which the defendant could and should have anticipated as being possible if oxygen enrichment was allowed to occur in the area in question. The defendant could and should have taken reasonable and simple steps to guard against such an event happening. In the result, the plaintiff succeeded in establishing upon a balance of probabilities that:

(1) the harm to the deceased, including the possibility that he might light a cigarette lighter in the cold box in the particular conditions was reasonably foreseeable;
(2) the necessary nexus was present;
(3) there was no legally recognizable *novus actus interveniens*; and
(4) with due consideration being given to matters of legal policy and reasonableness, there was adequate causation in law.

§5. Legal Causation

738. Proof of causation-in-fact is necessary to found liability, but not in itself sufficient. In addition, a legally relevant causal connection is required.

739. Historically, the South African courts have adhered to two main theories of legal causation. The first was the theory of *direct consequences* as applied in *In re Polemis v. Furness, Withy & Co. Ltd*[1545] in terms of which a defendant is liable in respect of harm which is a direct result of his or her wrongful conduct, irrespective of whether such results were foreseeable.[1546] If extraneous factors such as an act of God or of a third party – a *novus actus interveniens* – intervened, then the causal chain is broken. The test is derived largely from English law. However, in an Australian case some forty years later, *The Wagon Mound*,[1547] the Privy Council held that it was insufficient that the damage should be a direct result of the allegedly tortuous act if that damage could not reasonably have been foreseen. According to the direct consequences test, the defendant will be liable for the direct factual consequences of his actions. Although there is authority for the application of this test in the case law,[1548] most writers are in agreement that it does not form an independent test for causation in the modern law.[1549] In particular, it is difficult to sever this test from the foreseeability criterion, and the assessment of whether a supervening event

1545. 1921 3 KB 560.
1546. J.C. van der Walt & J.R. Midgley, *Principles of Delict*, paras 132 & 134 (3rd ed., Butterworths 2005).
1547. [1961] AC 388.
1548. *Alston v. Marine and Trade Insurance Co. Ltd* 1964 (4) SA 112 (W); *Smit v. Abrahams* 1992 (3) SA 158 (C) 164.
1549. P.Q.R. Boberg, *The Law of Delict Vol. 1*, 442 (1984); J.C. van der Walt & J.R. Midgley, *Principles of Delict*, para. 134 (3rd ed., Butterworths 2005).

constitutes a *novus actus*, breaking the direct chain of causation, often resolves into an inquiry whether the event was foreseeable.

740. The second theory is that of *foreseeability*, which limits liability to those consequences of the defendant's actions which he or she could reasonably have been expected to have foreseen.[1550] It differs from the reasonable foreseeability test for negligence in that the latter not only enquires as to foreseeability, but also preventability.[1551] The defendant need not reasonably foresee all the consequences of his or her actions, merely the general nature or the kind of harm which actually occurred.[1552] The exact extent[1553] or precise manner of occurrence[1554] need not have been reasonably foreseeable, but the risk of harm must have been a real risk, which a reasonable person would not have brushed aside as being far-fetched.[1555]

741. As the foreseeability criterion attaches to the general nature of the harm, rather than to its extent or the exact way it occurred, liability also arises in the case of any pre-existing weakness. In cases where the plaintiff suffers more extensive damage as a result of the defendant's conduct than would normally have been the case, because of some physical, psychological or financial weakness, the rule 'you must take your victim as you find him' (also referred to as the 'talem qualem rule' or the 'thin skull rule') applies, and the defendant is liable to compensate the plaintiff to the full extent of the damage.[1556]

742. The importance of the foreseeability test, as a suitable subsidiary factor in the application of the more flexible and comprehensive test adopted in later cases, is demonstrated in *Standard Chartered Bank of Canada v. Nedperm Bank,* where the Appellate Division referred to the flexible test[1557] and thereafter proceeded with the causation inquiry in terms of reasonable foreseeability.[1558]

1550. J.C. van der Walt & J.R. Midgley, *Principles of Delict*, paras 132 & 136 (3rd ed., Butterworths 2005).
1551. *Ibid.*, at para. 136.
1552. *Masiba v. Constantia Insurance Co. Ltd* 1982 (4) SA 333 (C) 342; *Standard Chartered Bank of Canada v. Nedperm Bank Ltd* 1994 (4) SA 747 (A) 768; *Smit v. Abrahams* 1992 (3) SA 158 (C) 163–164.
1553. *Masiba v. Constantia Insurance Co. Ltd* 1982 (4) SA 333 (C) 342; *Smit v. Abrahams* 1992 (3) SA 158 (C) 163; *Paget v. Santam Insurance Co. Ltd* 1981 (1) SA 814 (Z).
1554. *Da Silva v. Coutinho* 1971 (3) SA 123 (A) 148; *Minister van Polisie v. Van Aswegen* 1974 (2) SA 101 (A) 108; *Smit v. Abrahams* 1992 (3) SA 158 (C) 164.
1555. *Standard Chartered Bank of Canada v. Nedperm Bank Ltd* 1994 (4) SA 747 (A) 766–768.
1556. *Wilson v. Birt (Pty) Ltd* 1963 (2) SA 508 (D) 516; *Potgieter v. Rondalia Assurance Corporation of SA Ltd* 1970 (1) SA 705 (N); *Boswell v. Minister of Police* 1978 (3) SA 268 (E); *Masiba v. Constantia Insurance Co. Ltd* 1982 (4) SA 333 (C); *Silver v. Premier, Gauteng Provincial Government* 1998 (2) SA 643 (T); *Gibson v. Berkowitz* 1997 (1) All SA 99 (W); 1996 (4) SA 1029 (W) 1048–1050. In *Smit v. Abrahams* 1994 (4) SA 1 (A), the '*talem-qualem*' rule was applied to a case where the plaintiff, owing to financial inability, was unable to purchase a substitute vehicle but was compelled to hire one.
1557. 1994 (4) SA 747 (A) 764–765.
1558. 1994 (4) SA 747 (A) 766–769.

743. It is clear therefore that reasonable foreseeability features prominently in the inquiry into legal causation, and that it is not the precise nature of the harm that must be foreseeable, but the kind of harm that occurred, the general manner of occurrence and the possibility that a person in the position of the plaintiff would suffer harm. Boberg points out that it is not clear whether reasonable foreseeability is invoked as a test of legal causation, or as part of the inquiry into negligence. He argues that a relative approach to negligence, focusing on the kind of harm, the general manner of occurrence and the possibility of harm to a person in the position of the plaintiff, leaves little scope for legal causation or remoteness, liability being coextensive with, and limited by, fault.[1559] Boberg makes a cogent argument, and there is undeniably a measure of structural vagueness in many of the judgments in this regard. However, generally the content and focus of reasonable foreseeability is clear enough, and in most judgments the courts regard reasonable foreseeability as a subsidiary factor in the legal causation inquiry, even if that involves a certain degree of duplication with negligence.

744. A third theory that has been used to a lesser extent in determining legal causation is *adequate cause*. This theory combines factual and legal enquiries and considers whether the defendant's conduct is adequately or appropriately connected with the harm which allegedly resulted. The point of reference for this inquiry is the 'normal' expectation of the consequences following from the conduct in question.[1560] What is normal in this regard is expressly distinguished from what is foreseeable, yet the dividing line between adequate causation and foreseeability seems problematic. This criterion is not used as an independent test, but as one of the combination of factors relevant to legal causation.[1561]

745. In the leading case of *S v. Mokgethi*,[1562] the Appellate Division reassessed the approach of the courts to legal causation. The case was an appeal from the Provincial Division where the accused were convicted of murder which had been committed during a robbery. The deceased was a bank teller at First National Bank and was shot between the shoulder blades during the course of an armed robbery by the appellants. As a result of the shot, the deceased became a paraplegic and had to make use of a wheelchair. During his treatment, he was taught how to turn himself and to lift himself up from the wheelchair from time to time, in order to prevent the formation of pressure sores. The teller became very depressed. Although the teller returned to work at the bank, he was later readmitted into hospital with serious pressure sores and septicaemia which had developed because he failed to sufficiently shift his position in the wheelchair as he had been advised to do by medical practitioners who treated him. The teller subsequently died when the septicaemia spread

---

1559. P.Q.R. Boberg, *The Law of Delict Vol. 1*, 445–451 (Juta & Co. Ltd 1984).
1560. P.Q.R. Boberg, *The Law of Delict Vol. 1*, 443 (Juta & Co. Ltd 1984).
1561. *International Shipping Co. Ltd v. Bentley* 1990 (1) SA 680 (A).
1562. 1990 (1) SA 32 (A).

to all his organs. The question before the court was whether a causal link existed between the shot wound inflicted more than six months previously in the armed robbery, and the bank teller's death.[1563]

On the question of factual causation, there was no doubt that the shot wound was the *conditio sine qua non* of the teller's death.[1564] The real question was therefore whether the shot wound incurred by the deceased was the legal cause of his death. The court referred to a number of criteria as relevant to the determination of legal causation – (the absence of a *novus actus interveniens*, proximate cause, direct cause, foreseeability and adequate cause). Van Heerden JA then stated that no single test of legal causation could be applied to all types of cases.[1565] In all cases, public policy considerations would determine whether a sufficiently close causal nexus existed between the conduct in question and the harm sustained.[1566] The court favoured a more general approach using a flexible criterion that would allow for informed differences of opinion.[1567] Applying these dicta, the Appellate Court found that the teller's death was too remote a consequence of the shot wound to attach liability for murder to the accused. In general, the court found that the perpetrator's action which is the factual cause of death of the deceased is too remote to give rise to criminal liability if:

(a) a failure on the part of the deceased to obtain medical or similar advice or follow prescribed treatment is the immediate cause of death;
(b) the wounding is not in itself lethal or was no longer lethal at the relevant time; and
(c) the deceased's failure to obtain or follow treatment was unreasonable in the circumstances.

746. The flexible and comprehensive nature of the inquiry into legal causation was confirmed as follows in *International Shipping Co. (Pty) Ltd v. Bentley*:[1568]

> [D]emonstration that the wrongful act was a *causa sine qua non* of the loss does not necessarily result in legal liability. The second inquiry then arises, viz whether the wrongful act is linked sufficiently closely or directly to the loss for legal liability to ensue or whether, as it is said, the loss is too remote. This is basically a juridical problem in the solution of which considerations of policy may play a part. This is sometimes called 'legal causation'.

747. Where the defendant's conduct unlawfully causes a series of harmful consequences, as a matter of policy delictual liability is not imposed for all the harmful consequences. The concept of legal causation essentially serves to limit the boundaries of legal liability.

1563. 1990 (1) SA 32 (A) 37J–38A.
1564. 1990 (1) SA 32 (A) 39D.
1565. 1990 (1) SA 32 (A) 40–41.
1566. 1990 (1) SA 32 (A) 40I.
1567. 1990 (1) SA 32 (A) 45H.
1568. 1990 (1) SA 680 (A) 700E–701F.

748. The courts have stated that the issue is essentially a practical one and that expedience and good sense often dictate where the line is to be drawn. A proper and equitable balance must be struck between the interests of the defendant and that of the plaintiff. Essentially, therefore, the question of legal causation involves not only logical reasoning, but also a moral reaction, involving a value judgment and applying common sense, to assess whether harm can be fairly said to be imputable to the defendant.

749. In the *International Shipping Co. (Pty) Ltd v. Bentley*[1569] case, a financing company in 1977 made facilities available to a group of companies. Thereafter Bentley was appointed auditor to the group. From 1979, he issued unqualified financial statements that were to some extent false and misleading. The company alleged that it had relied on the statements in reviewing its facilities to the group and in deciding to increase the facilities. The group was liquidated in 1981 and the financing company suffered loss. The court found that Bentley's conduct was wrongful and blameworthy, and a *conditio sine qua non* of the company's loss.

However, a number of other factors intervened: the loss was sustained two years after the statements were reported; the financing company implemented a support programme in 1980, knowing that the group's position was bleak, when it could have terminated the facility; the group's indebtedness was allowed to escalate beyond formally authorized credit limits; the result of the support programme was that the relationship between the parties was no longer one in which the debtor and creditor dealt at arm's length, but a kind of unofficial judicial management; the company's executives must have been aware of deceptive conduct on the part of the group's chief executive officer that also contributed to the company's loss; the company must have relied on the 1978 financial statements as well; and, generally, the support programme was conducted in an uninhibited manner. Consequently, the ultimate loss was regarded as not linked sufficiently closely or directly to the loss for legal liability to ensue, or being too remote, for Bentley to be held liable.

750. Following the *Mokgethi* and *Bentley* cases, the South African courts now accept that legal causation involves the basic question whether there is a close enough relationship between the wrongdoer's conduct and its consequence for such consequence to be imputed to the wrongdoer, taking into account policy considerations based on reasonableness, fairness and justice.[1570] In order to determine the closeness of the connection, the courts apply a combination of criteria as subsidiary tests, including the 'direct consequences' test, the 'adequate causation' test and reasonable foreseeability.[1571]

751. In *Fourway Haulage SA (Pty) Ltd v. SA National Roads Agency Ltd*,[1572] the issue of causation arose in the context of economic loss. The South African National

1569. 1990 (1) SA 680 (A).
1570. *S v. Mokgethi* 1990 (1) SA 32 (A) per Van Heerden JA at 40–41.
1571. J.C. van der Walt & J.R. Midgley, *Principles of Delict*, para. 132 (3rd ed., Butterworths 2005).
1572. 2009 (2) SA 150 (SCA).

Roads Agency was authorized to collect toll fees at two toll plazas. Fourway Haulage was transporting asbestos and one of their drivers caused an accident, which resulted in this highly toxic substance spilling all over the road. The road was closed and traffic diverted to a non-toll road while the spillage was being cleaned up. Because of this, the South African National Roads Agency lost money and sued Fourway Haulage for damages. On the test for legal causation, Brand JA said the following:[1573]

> What Van Heerden JA said in that case (Mokgethi) is not that the 'flexible' or 'supple' test supersedes all other tests such as foreseeability, proximity or direct consequences, which were suggested and applied in the past, but merely that none of these tests can be used exclusively and dogmatically as a measure of limitation in all types of factual situations. Stated somewhat differently: the existing criteria of foreseeability, directness, and so on, should not be applied dogmatically, but in a flexible manner so as to avoid a result which is so unfair or unjust that it is regarded as untenable. If the foreseeability test, for example, leads to a result which will be acceptable to most right-minded people, that is the end of the matter … .
>
> In this case it can, in my view, be accepted with confidence that any of the various criteria will lead to the conclusion that the loss suffered by the Agency is not too remote. If, for example, the direct consequences criterion is applied, it is clear that the loss followed directly from the wrongful and negligent conduct of Fourway's driver; there was no so-called novus actus interveniens that broke the chain of events. If, on the other hand, one applies the foreseeability test, it was in my view reasonably foreseeable that a collision could cause spillage and that, because of the dangerous nature of the cargo, spillage could result in the closure of the toll road which could lead to a revenue loss by the Agency.

The court thus set out the relationship between the flexible approach and the subsidiary tests. However, it also cautioned as follows against using concepts such as reasonableness, fairness and justice to determine legal causation:[1574]

> Considerations of fairness and equity must inevitably depend on the view of the individual judge. In considering the appropriate approach to wrongfulness, I said that any yardstick which renders the outcome of a dispute dependent on the idiosyncratic view of individual judges is unacceptable. The same principle must, in my view, apply with reference to remoteness. That is why I believe we should resist the temptation of a response that remoteness depends on what the judge regards as fair, reasonable and just in all the circumstances of that particular case. Though it presents itself as a criterion of general validity, it is, in reality, no criterion at all.

1573. At paras 34–35.
1574. At para. 33.

752. The flexible criterion for determining legal causation is similar to the policy-based test used to determine unlawfulness.[1575] Both have an important function in limiting liability, but the legal causation test focuses on the extent to which liability should be imposed for damage or harm factually caused by the defendant's conduct, whereas the unlawfulness inquiry is essentially concerned with the scope of protection afforded to various rights and interests, the scope of responsibility to act and overall policy considerations relating to the question whether the law of delict should intervene at all.[1576] In this regard, the Supreme Court of Appeal said the following in *Fourway Haulage SA (Pty) Ltd v. SA National Roads Agency SA (Pty) Ltd*:[1577]

> In the final analysis, the issue of remoteness is again determined by considerations of policy. Broadly speaking, wrongfulness – in the case of omissions and pure economic loss – on the one hand, and remoteness on the other, perform the same function. They are both measures of control. They both serve as a 'longstop' where most right-minded people, including judges, will regard the imposition of liability in a particular case as untenable, despite the presence of all other elements of delictual liability.
>
> Since wrongfulness – in the context of omissions and pure economic loss – and remoteness are both determined by considerations of policy, a certain degree of overlapping is inevitable. However, wrongfulness and remoteness are not the same. They involve two different enquiries in respect of two different elements of delict, each with its own characteristics and content … . Even where negligent conduct resulting in pure economic loss is for reasons of policy found to be wrongful, the loss may therefore, for other reasons of policy, be found to be too remote and therefore not recoverable. An example of a case where this happened is to be found in a decision of this court in *International Shipping Co (Pty) Ltd v. Bentley* (*supra*).

§6. Intended Consequences

753. It is generally accepted that intended consequences can never be too remote.[1578] This approach ties in with the flexible criterion for determining legal causation, in that considerations of reasonableness, fairness and justice demand that a person should be held liable for harm deliberately caused. However, the approach to legal causation remains a flexible one and the possibility cannot be excluded that where consequences, although intended, came about in an unusual or an unexpected manner, or through the intervention of another causative factor, liability for intentional causing of harm will not be imposed.

1575. J.C. van der Walt & J.R. Midgley, *Principles of Delict*, para. 132 (3rd ed., Butterworths 2005).
1576. *Ibid.*
1577. 2009 (2) SA 150 (SCA).
1578. *Thandani v. Minister of Law & Order* 1991 (1) SA 702 (E) 705; J.C. van der Walt and J.R. Midgley, *Principles of Delict*, para. 133 (3d ed., Butterworths 2005).

754. In a deprivation of liberty case, for example, where a wrongful arrest is followed by detention through proper judicial process, the correct approach will be to enquire whether the subsequent lawful period of detention was an intended consequence of the wrongful arrest and sufficiently closely connected to it to be considered a consequence for which liability should be imposed.[1579]

§7. *Novus Actus Interveniens*

755. An intervening and independent causative factor or event may interrupt the chain of causation between the defendant's conduct and the harm suffered by the plaintiff. The concept of an intervening cause or *novus actus interveniens* is usually referred to in the context of legal causation, and historically this concept served primarily to limit liability when the direct consequences test was applied. An independent intervening act or event neutralizes the causative effect of the defendant's conduct and indicates that the connection between such conduct and the harm suffered is not sufficiently close to impose liability. However, the concept of an intervening cause or *novus actus interveniens* also has a place in the context of factual causation, in cases where a natural phenomenon or independently occurring human action causes harm in a way that interrupts and renders irrelevant the causative effect of the defendant's conduct.

756. In the cases, the concept of a *novus actus interveniens* features primarily in the process of reasoning to determine legal causation. The assessment of causative factors such as the presence of a *novus actus interveniens* forms part of the comprehensive flexible approach adhered to by the courts since *S v. Mokgethi.*[1580] A *novus actus interveniens* is an independent, unconnected event which interrupts the chain of causation by contributing to the occurrence of harm subsequent to the defendant's conduct.[1581] The intervening event negates the effect of the defendant's original conduct to such an extent that the link between the conduct and the harm is considered too weak. The event may present itself in the way of perfectly normal conduct,[1582] natural occurrences, conduct of a third party, or conduct of the plaintiff.[1583] However, if the intervening event or conduct was reasonably foreseeable,[1584] or can be considered to be a risk inherent in the situation created by the

1579. *Thandani v. Minister of Law & Order* 1991 (1) SA 702 (E) 705; *Ebrahim v. Minister of Law & Order* 1993 (2) SA 559 (T).

1580. 1990 (1) SA 32 (A).

1581. J.C. van der Walt & J.R. Midgley, *Principles of Delict* para. 135 (3rd ed., Butterworths 2005).

1582. *Alston v. Marine and Trade Insurance Co. Ltd* 1964 (4) SA 112 (W) where the plaintiff suffered a stroke after a reaction between a slice of cheese eaten, and the drug parstellin which was being used to treat injuries sustained in a motor collision caused by the negligence of the driver of the car insured by the defendant.

1583. *Alston v. Marine and Trade Insurance Co. Ltd* 1964 (4) SA 112 (W); *Mafesa v. Parity Versekeringsmaatskappy Bpk* 1968 (2) SA 603 (O); J.C. van der Walt & J.R. Midgley, *Principles of Delict*, para. 135 (3rd ed., Butterworths 2005).

1584. *Ebrahim v. Minister of Law and Order and Others* 1993 (2) SA 559 (T) at 566B–C; *Vigario v. Afrox Ltd* 1996 (3) SA 450 (W) 459.

defendant's conduct, as in the case of depression-induced suicide on the part of an accident victim,[1585] it will not qualify as a *novus actus interveniens*.

§8. Illustrative Cases on Legal Causation and *Novus Actus Interveniens*

757. The following examples illustrate the reasoning of the courts in determining legal causation, a process often involving consideration of a possible *novus actus interveniens*.

758. In *Mafesa v. Parity Versekeringsmpy Bpk*,[1586] the plaintiff sustained a leg fracture in an accident caused by another person's negligent driving. After the leg had set clinically, the plaintiff was discharged from hospital. Using crutches the plaintiff negligently walked on a smooth floor and fell and had to undergo a second operation. The court decided that the plaintiff's negligent conduct was an intervening cause which broke the causal effect of the original negligent driving.

759. In *Alston v. Marine and Trade Insurance Co. Ltd*,[1587] the plaintiff suffered a brain injury in an accident caused by another person's negligent driving. The injury led to manic depression that was treated with a drug called parstellin. The plaintiff ate cheese and suffered a stroke that was directly attributable to the interaction of parstellin and cheese. The possibility of this serious side effect was unknown and considered to be highly extraordinary and unpredictable at the time, and the court held that the stroke was attributable to an intervening cause, for which the negligent driver was not responsible.

760. In *Standard Chartered Bank of Canada v. Nedperm Bank Ltd*,[1588] the respondent was held to have acted wrongfully by furnishing a favourable bank report on the creditworthiness of a customer. The bank report was inaccurate and misleading and the respondent knew, and had in fact been greatly perturbed by the fact that the customer was in a parlous financial position. On the issue of loss and causation, Corbett CJ accepted that the untrue report was the *conditio sine qua non* of the loss.[1589] Whether the furnishing of such a report was linked sufficiently closely or directly to the loss for liability to ensue, or whether the loss was too remote depended on the following general test:

> [T]he test to be applied is a flexible one in which factors such as reasonable foreseeability, directness, the absence or presence of a novus actus interveniens, legal policy, reasonability, fairness and justice all play their part.[1590]

1585. *RAF v. Russell* 2001 (2) SA 1106 (SCA).
1586. 1968 (2) SA 603 (O).
1587. 1964 (4) SA 112 (W).
1588. 1994 (4) SA 747 (A).
1589. 1994 (4) SA 747 (A) 767H-I.
1590. 1994 (4) SA 747 (A) 765A.

The respondent's conduct was found to be the legal cause of the appellant's loss. It was reasonably foreseeable that the appellant might suffer pecuniary loss as a result of its reliance on a false bank report issued by the respondent.

761. In *Clinton-Parker v. Administrator Transvaal*,[1591] the plaintiffs' babies were swapped at birth by the staff at the hospital where the babies were born. The swap was discovered eighteen months after they gave birth. The plaintiffs decided to keep the children as handed to them in the hospital. They sued for damages, including the cost of treatment for the severe psychological harm they had suffered and travelling costs they would have to incur in visiting their natural children. It was common cause that the plaintiffs suffered from a 'mixed anxiety depressive disorder'.[1592] It was also accepted that the hospital staff had been negligent in swapping the babies and factual causation was established.[1593] The other questions were whether, in terms of the principles relating to emotional shock as accepted in *Bester v. Commercial Union Versekeringsmaatskappy van SA Bpk*,[1594] serious psychiatric injury was reasonably foreseeable in this case, and whether the negligent act was sufficiently closely or directly linked to the harm for legal liability to ensue.[1595] In this regard, the defendant argued that serious harm of the kind actually experienced by the plaintiffs had not been foreseeable (only some psychological disturbance was foreseeable); that the plaintiffs' decision to retain the children given to them at birth constituted a *novus actus interveniens*; and that the fortuitous discovery of the swap was an event which could not have been foreseen.

Navsa J held that:

> foreseeability may well be a factor to be considered in determining liability. The *Mokgethi* and *International Shipping* cases allow a flexible approach, enabling the totality of the situation including policy considerations to be assessed, to answer the question of whether the act complained of and the consequential harm is sufficiently closely connected for liability to ensue.[1596]

On the defendant's own expert evidence, 20%–30% of a sample of people with profiles similar to those of the plaintiffs, that is single, young, first-time mothers, were likely to develop a psychiatric illness in the present circumstances. A maternity ward 'could hardly be heard to say that it is less informed than [the defendant's expert] about the relationship between a mother and child and the devastating effects (a 20%–30% likelihood) a swop [sic] at birth could have on the mental health of parents like the plaintiffs'.[1597] Reasonable staff members in a maternity ward would have been alive to the risks attendant on the negligent swopping of babies at birth. Furthermore, the defendant's own expert evidence in relation to the reaction of the majority of mothers showed that the risk of some sort of psychiatric harm was not

---

1591. 1996 (2) 37 (W).
1592. 1996 (2) SA 37 (W) 51J.
1593. 1996 (2) SA 37 (W) 56A-B.
1594. 973 (1) SA 769 (A).
1595. 1996 (2) SA 37 (W) 55B-C, applying *Minister of Police v. Skosana* 1977 (1) SA 31 (A) 34F-G.
1596. 1996 (2) SA 37 (W) 57E-F.
1597. 1996 (2) SA 37 (W) 59A-C.

inconsequential. Therefore, the rule that the extent or precise nature of the harm need not be foreseen by the negligent actor operated against the defendant.[1598]

On the question of a *novus actus interveniens*, the court held that the defendant was not entitled to rely on the plaintiffs' decision to keep the children given to them at birth. Experts agreed that it was a complex situation with no right or wrong answer. The decision to retain the children handed to them at birth was made when the plaintiffs were devastated, and bonding had already occurred between the mothers and their babies.

On the fortuitous nature of the discovery of the swap, the court took into account that comprehensive records are kept, blood tests are commonly required and medical and genetic histories are vital to medical treatment.[1599] It must have been foreseen that at some stage the true state of affairs would be discovered.

On the possibility of indeterminate liability, Navsa J rejected the analogy of *Alcock v. Chief Constable of the South Yorkshire Police*,[1600] concerning the communication of the news of the death or injury of loved ones in an accident. In this case, the mothers were the proximate victims of the negligence of the defendant's employees and continued to be directly affected.[1601] The harm suffered by the plaintiffs was sufficiently close to the negligence of the defendant's employees, and the defendant was held liable.

762. In *Napier v. Collett*,[1602] the Appellate Division confirmed that the general approach to questions of causation as applied in the criminal law and the law of delict, is equally applicable to insurance law, although its application will be subject to the provisions of the policy in question. However, a particular policy will seldom affect the basic approach, which requires, in the first place, an inquiry into the presence of factual causation. If this initial inquiry leads to the conclusion that the prior event was a *causa sine qua non* of the subsequent one, the further question of whether the relationship between two events is sufficiently close for the former to constitute the legal cause of the latter arises. In answering this question in the context of insurance law, prime regard must be had to the provisions of the policy in question, which may extend or limit the consequences covered. In addition to specific provisions, matters such as the type of policy, the nature of the risk insured against and the conditions of the policy may be relevant. The insurance of a race horse was in issue, with the policy covering loss arising from death as a result of the accident. The policy further provided that '(t)his insurance does not cover intentional slaughter … except that underwriters will not invoke this particular exclusion as a defence … where the underwriters shall have expressly agreed to the destruction of the animal … .' The horse in question suffered an accident during a race, and experts disagreed as to whether injuries were serious enough to warrant putting the horse to death. The animal eventually died during surgical examination conducted under anaesthetic two months later, to ascertain the extent of injuries.

1598. 1996 (2) SA 37 (W) 59D-G.
1599. 1996 (2) SA 37 (W) 60A-C.
1600. 1991 (4) All ER 907 (HL).
1601. 1996 (2) SA 37 (W) 63J-64A.
1602. 1995 (3) SA 140 (A).

The court considered whether the relationship between the accident and the death was sufficiently close to constitute legal causation, and decided that the causal relationship between the accident and the death was indirect and fortuitous. The effective cause of the death was the administration of anaesthetic flowing from attempts to secure underwriters' consent to putting the horse to death. The death was therefore not the result of an accident within meaning of the policy.

763. In *Groenewald v. Groenewald*,[1603] the plaintiff was physically assaulted by her estranged husband, and locked up inside his office on the third floor of a building. In an attempt to escape, the wife climbed through a window and attempted to lower herself onto a ledge on the second floor. She fell from the ledge and sustained serious injuries, and claimed damages from her husband. The court found that the husband's assault on his wife, his threats and the fact that he locked her up, caused the plaintiff to attempt escape: '[h]ad it not been for those acts of the defendant there would have been no reason for the plaintiff to escape by climbing through the window and attempting to reach the ground from the ledge outside the building'.[1604] The court applied the flexible and comprehensive approach to legal causation as accepted in earlier cases, noting that reasonable foreseeability is merely 'one of many criteria which might flexibly be applied as a matter of policy to determine whether or not the damages actually suffered by the plaintiff are or are not too remote to hold the defendant liable'.[1605] The court held that the injuries sustained were reasonably foreseeable:

> The defendant threatened to kill the plaintiff and must have intended the plaintiff to take his threats seriously. She in fact took him seriously. This was not unreasonable in the circumstances. A reasonable person in the appellant's position would have foreseen that, if there were a way for the respondent to escape and possibly avoid being killed, she would try to escape. Unless there had been a way of avoiding being killed other than by escaping through the window and jumping from the third storey that was so obvious and so certain to be successful as to make an escape through the window unreasonable even for a person in the respondent's frame of mind, a reasonable person might have foreseen that she might do so.[1606]

As to the defendant's argument that the plaintiff's attempt to lower herself from the ledge constituted a *novus actus interveniens*, the court took into account that the plaintiff feared for her life, had no idea when help would arrive, and knew that she was not out of the appellant's reach, and therefore a reasonable person might do exactly as she had done, and her conduct did not constitute a *novus actus interveniens*.[1607] Furthermore, Streicher JA held that '[t]here [were] no considerations of

1603. 1998 (2) SA 1106 (SCA).
1604. 1998 (2) SA 1106 (SCA) 1113G-H.
1605. 1998 (2) SA 1106 (SCA) 1113A-B.
1606. 1998 (2) SA 1106 (SCA) 1113J–1114B.
1607. 1998 (2) SA 1106 (SCA) 1114E-H.

legal policy which militate against holding the defendant liable for the plaintiff's damages ... [and] it would ... be eminently reasonable, fair and just to hold the defendant liable'.[1608]

764. In *Meevis v. Sheriff, Pretoria East,*[1609] the plaintiff claimed patrimonial loss flowing from the wrongful attachment of jewellery by the sheriff of the court. While the jewellery was in the possession of the sheriff, a robbery took place at the sheriff's premises and the jewellery was stolen. It was clear that, had the property not been attached, it would not have been in the sheriff's possession to be stolen. The wrongful attachment therefore factually caused or materially contributed to the plaintiff's loss. On the question of legal causation, the court confirmed that the test to be applied is a flexible one in which factors such as reasonable foreseeability, directness, the absence or presence of a *novus actus interveniens*, legal policy, reasonability, fairness and justice all play their part. In this case, it could not reasonably have been foreseen that the jewellery would be stolen from the sheriff's premises, but the general nature of the harm and the general manner of the harm occurring was reasonably foreseeable. The robbery could therefore not be regarded as a *novus actus interveniens*. The loss suffered by the plaintiff was accordingly not too remote and the defendant was held liable.

765. In *RAF v. Russell,*[1610] the plaintiff claimed damages for loss of support as a result of the death by suicide of her husband. He had suffered severe multiple injuries, including brain damage, in a motor vehicle accident, caused by the negligent driving of a motor vehicle, for which the defendant was liable. The question was whether the negligent causing of the accident could be regarded as the legal cause of the death by suicide. After the accident, the deceased had at first been hospitalized, in a comatose state, and then lived with his wife and their children for a while. He was not only physically disabled, but also suffered from severe depression. After two failed attempts at suicide he was admitted to a nursing home, where he committed suicide. The question was whether the suicide constituted a *novus actus interveniens*, interrupting the causative effect of the negligence of the driver that caused the accident. The evidence clearly established that the brain injury sustained in the accident was the cause of or the major factor inducing the depression.[1611] In delivering the judgment of the court, Chetty AJA said that the deceased 'cannot be said to have acted with unimpaired volition in forming the decision to commit suicide' and it follows that the act of suicide, although deliberate, did not constitute a *novus actus interveniens.*[1612] The brain injuries sustained in the accident left the deceased mentally impaired and in a state of depression. He had lost the ability to make a balanced decision and therefore his act of suicide, although deliberate, did

1608. 1998 (2) SA 1106 (SCA) 1114I.
1609. 1998 (2) All SA 602 (T); 1999 (2) SA 389 (T).
1610. 2001 (2) SA 34 (SCA).
1611. 2001 (2) SA 34 (SCA) 38I.
1612. 2001 (2) SA 34 (SCA) 40H–41F.

not interrupt the causative effect of the negligence of the driver that caused the accident.[1613] With regard to foreseeability, the court held that it was unnecessary for the negligent driver to have foreseen in detail that the injuries of the deceased could lead to suicide.

766. In the case of *Van der Spuy v. Minister of Correctional Services*,[1614] an innocent bystander was shot by a prisoner who had managed to escape as a result of the negligence of the prison authorities. It was accepted that the negligence constituted the factual cause of the plaintiff being shot – had it not been for the escape, the plaintiff would not have been injured.[1615] The question was whether the loss suffered by the plaintiff was too remote for the defendant to be held liable. The case therefore turned on the issue of legal causation. The court referred to the criteria of reasonable foreseeability, directness, the absence or presence of a *novus actus interveniens*, legal policy, fairness and justice.[1616] The court held that:

> [W]hile foreseeability may only be one of the criteria to which one must have regard in the assessment of remoteness, it is an important factor to be taken into account. In this regard, it is important to remember that, while the general manner of its occurrence must be reasonably foreseeable, the precise or exact manner in which the harm occurs need not be foreseeable.[1617]

In this regard the court took into account several factors: at least one of the escapees was considered a dangerous person; and the defendant and its employees owed a duty to the public at large to prevent potentially dangerous persons escaping into the community if they were likely to commit acts of violence once they escaped. The general manner in which harm was caused to the plaintiff was reasonably foreseeable.[1618] Prison escapes inevitably implied the use of violence to overcome resistance and the possibility of harm being done to persons not necessarily resisting was also foreseeable.[1619] In short: a reasonable man would generally have foreseen violence being done to persons in the vicinity of a prison should prisoners (particularly potentially dangerous prisoners) attempt to escape, the shooting of the plaintiff should be regarded as being part and parcel of the general type of harm which was reasonably foreseeable.

The damages suffered by the plaintiff were not so remote that the chain of causation could be regarded as having been interrupted.

1613. 2001 (2) SA 34 (SCA) 41F–H.
1614. 2004 (2) SA 463(SE).
1615. 2004 (2) SA 463 (SE) 472D.
1616. 2004 (2) SA 463 (SE) 474J–475A.
1617. 2004 (2) SA 463 (SE) 476C. The court cited with approval *Sea Harvest Corporation (Pty) Ltd v. Duncan Dock Cold Storage (Pty) Ltd* 2000 (1) SA 827 (SCA).
1618. 2004 (2) SA 463 (SE) 476D.
1619. 2004 (2) SA 463 (SE) 476D–F.

Part VI. Remedies

Chapter 1. General Principles

§1. Damages the Main Aim of the Law of Delict

767. The main aim of the law of delict is to provide compensation (damages) for unlawfully caused damage, loss or harm. Damage, loss or harm occurs when a legally recognized patrimonial or personality right or interest is lost or reduced in value, quality or utility. The term 'damages' is used to refer to either or both of two different kinds of compensation, namely the monetary equivalent of patrimonial loss, and the monetary compensation awarded as reparation or satisfaction for injury to personality rights.

768. The duality of the origins of the South African law of damages is reflected in its terminology. Terms deriving from Roman and Roman-Dutch law, such as 'id quod interest', 'interesse', 'positive and negative interest', '*damnum emergens*' and '*lucrum cessans*' are used together with terms deriving from English law, such as 'special', 'general', 'nominal', 'punitive' and 'exemplary' damages. Certain of the terms derived from English law, such as 'nominal', 'punitive' and 'exemplary' damages, play a relatively minor part in the modern South African law of damages, which is dominated by the three actions deriving from Roman and Roman-Dutch law, the Aquilian action, the action for pain and suffering and the *actio iniuriarum*.

769. The Aquilian action is aimed at recovery of damages for patrimonial loss or damnum, flowing from damage to property, bodily injury or pure economic loss. Aquilian liability is aimed at restoring the difference between the plaintiff's patrimonial position after the damage or loss occurred and the patrimonial position as it would have been had the damage or loss not occurred.[1620]

770. The *actio iniuriarum* is aimed at recovery of damages for non-patrimonial harm to personality interests, providing reparation or satisfaction for the plaintiff insofar as it is possible for an award of money to do so. The purpose of an award for pain and suffering in cases of personal injury is similar to that of an award under the *actio iniuriarum*, providing solace for psychological harm in the form of pain,

---

1620. In *Transnet Ltd v. Sechaba Photoscan (Pty) Ltd* 2005 (1) SA 299 (SCA) para. 11, the court referred to 'the perennially true statement that the aim in awarding delictual damages is to put the injured party in the same position as he would have been in but for the delict'.

disfigurement, loss of amenities and the like.[1621] Damages recoverable by these two actions serve a compensatory function only in a broad sense, because the harm in question does not have an economic or pecuniary value.[1622]

771. The Constitutional Court has confirmed in *Fose v. Minister of Safety and Security*,[1623] that the aim of the law of delict is not to award punitive damages:

> Serious judicial doubts have been expressed concerning, and considerable academic criticism levelled against, the award of punitive damages in delictual claims. Prof Van der Walt, whose views are broadly representative of academic criticism generally, expresses his misgivings succinctly as follows:
>
> The historical approach of awarding additional sentimental damages as a penalty for outrageous conduct on the part of the defendant is not justifiable in a modern system of law. The basic purpose of a civil action in delict is to compensate the victim for the actual harm done. In the case of impairment of personality by wrongful conduct it may be difficult to determine the amount of *solatium* which will confer personal satisfaction or compensation for the injury, but in principle all factors and circumstances tending to introduce penal features should be rigorously excluded from such an assessment. The aim of discouraging evil and high-handed conduct is foreign to the basic purposes of the law of delict. It is for criminal law to punish and thereby discourage such conduct. The policy of awarding punitive damages unduly enriches the plaintiff who is entitled only to compensation for loss suffered. This policy has the added disadvantage of putting a wrongdoer in jeopardy of being punished twice – in the civil proceedings and in the criminal proceedings which could conceivably follow or which have preceded the civil action.

772. The Constitutional Court in *Dikoko v. Mokhatla*[1624] took a similar view of the purpose of a damages award in a defamation case:

> [68]The primary purpose of a compensatory measure, after all, is to restore the dignity of a plaintiff who has suffered the damage and not to punish a defendant.
>
> [76]In our law a damages award therefore does not serve to punish for the act of defamation. It principally aims to serve as compensation for damage caused by the defamation, vindicating the victim's dignity, reputation and integrity. Alternatively, it serves to console. (Footnotes omitted.)

1621. *Hoffa v. SA Mutual Fire & General Insurance Co. Ltd* 1965 (2) SA 944 (C) 954–955: 'The damages awarded to him are in a certain sense analogous to the solatium which is awarded under the actio injuriarum to someone as a salve to his wounded feelings.'
1622. *Mutual & Federal Insurance Co. Ltd v. Swanepoel* 1988 (2) SA 1 (A) 10–11; *Sandler v. Wholesale Coal Suppliers Ltd* 1941 AD 194 199.
1623. 1997 (3) SA 786 (CC) para. 63.
1624. 2006 (6) SA 235 (CC).

773. The general aim of the law of delict is therefore compensatory, not punitive. The modern delictual actions have not retained their erstwhile punitive characteristics.[1625] This is also true of the *actio iniuriarum*, which in the more recent past appears to have retained a punitive element.[1626] If there is malice or other aggravating circumstances,[1627] a larger award (solatium) or 'aggravated damages' is appropriate under the *actio iniuriarum*, to provide appropriate solace to the plaintiff.[1628] The focus should be on the plaintiff's feelings, not on meting out retribution to the defendant.

§2. The Constitution and Damages

774. Damages may also be awarded under the Constitution,[1629] which provides in section 38 for the right to approach a competent court, where it is alleged that a right in the Bill of Rights has been infringed or threatened; in which case the court may then grant appropriate relief, including a declaration of rights and, although it is not expressly stated, an award of damages. The effect of this provision is not to replace a common law award of damages. In *Fose v. Minister for Safety and Security*,[1630] for example, the Constitutional Court refused to award constitutional damages to a plaintiff who was seriously assaulted and tortured by the police. The court held that ordinary delictual damages would be a sufficiently powerful vindication of the plaintiff's rights.[1631] The Supreme Court of Appeal has awarded constitutional damages in a matter involving the infringement of the right to property (land), as protected by section 25(1) of the Constitution, viewing such an award in the circumstances of the case as appropriate relief.[1632] Section 38 of the Constitution also allows collective action for damages, as detailed in Chapter 2 section 1 below.

1625. *Collins v. Administrator, Cape* 1995 (4) SA 73 (C) 93–94, where the court confirmed that neither the Aquilian action nor the action for pain and suffering is punitive. The purpose is compensatory, and there is no basis in South African law for a nominal award to an unconscious victim, to reflect society's demand that some retribution be made for the injustice done to the plaintiff, or to express society's sympathy with the victim and its sense of outrage at his grievous loss, or to serve as a symbolic reparation of the damage and to soothe the community. Such an award would mean an import into the modern delictual action of a penal element for which there can be no justification.

1626. *Salzmann v. Holmes* 1914 AD 471 483; *Manamela v. Minister of Justice* 1960 (2) SA 395 (A) 401; *Gelb v. Hawkins* 1960 (3) SA 687 (A) 693; *SA Associated Newspapers Ltd v. Yutar* 1969 (2) SA 442 (A) 458.

1627. *See*, for example, *Kahn v. Kahn* 1971 (2) SA 499 (RA) 501–502.

1628. *Whittaker v. Roos & Bateman*; *Morant v. Roos & Bateman* 1912 AD 92 118 125; *Manamela v. Minister of Justice* 1960 (2) SA 395 (A) 401; *Fose v. Minister of Safety & Security* 1997 (3) SA 786 (CC) para. 62.

1629. Act 108 of 1996.

1630. 1997 (3) SA 786 (CC) para. 63.

1631. *See also Tobani v. Minister of Correctional Services* 2000 (2) All SA 318 (SE); *Minister of Correctional Services v. Tobani* 2001 (1) All SA 370 (E); 2003 (5) SA 126 (E).

1632. *Modderfontein Squatters, Greater Benoni City Council v. Modderklip Boerdery (Pty) Ltd* and *President of the RSA v. Modderklip Boerdery (Pty) Ltd* 2004 (6) SA 40 (SCA) 61.

§3. Other General Principles of Delict and Damages

775. Liability for damages can arise only if there is a causal link between the defendant's conduct and harm suffered by the plaintiff. The existence of compensable damage therefore depends in the first instance on determination of factual causation of harm. If a factual causal links exists, liability for damages can arise if the requirements of unlawfulness, fault and legal causation are also met.

776. The principles for determining damages, with reference to different kinds of damages, the methods for assessment of damages, the 'once-and-for-all' rule, equitable limitation of damages (remoteness) and accounting for inflation, tax and interest, are detailed in Chapters 2 and 3 below.

§4. Other Remedies Afforded by the Law of Delict

777. The law of delict also has a preventative function, affording the possibility of obtaining an interdict to restrain a person who presents a threat from unlawfully causing harm, or from continuing with the unlawful causing of harm, where this has already occurred. The principles of the law of delict can also form the basis for a declaratory order, for example to correct inaccurate information, or to resolve a conflict of rights. Retraction and apology can also be remedies in defamation cases.[1633] Restitution can be ordered in the case of unlawful dispossession of property. These alternative remedies are dealt with in Chapter 7 below.

1633. *See Mineworkers Investment C (Pty) Ltd v. Modibane* 2002 (6) SA 512 (W) paras [17]ff.

Chapter 2. Kinds of Damages

§1. Individual and Collective Damage

778. Under South African law prior to 1994, there was no equivalent to a class action as it exists in the United States, enabling one or more claimants who litigate against a defendant to recover damages not only on their own behalf, but also on behalf of similar claimants.[1634] The most important feature of a class action is that other members of the class, although not formally and individually joined, benefit from, and are bound by, the outcome of the litigation, unless they invoke prescribed procedures to opt out of it. Prior to the constitutional changes in South Africa in 1994, a claimant could participate in court proceedings only by becoming formally associated with the proceedings by compliance with the formalities of joinder.[1635]

779. There are inherent difficulties with joining all interested parties to an action for damages, because the various parties who have the common interest are isolated, scattered and strangers to each other. While the need for group action through joinder may clearly exist, the conditions for it may not. What is needed is something over and above the possibility of joinder – some affirmative technique for bringing everyone into the case and for making recovery available to all. It is not so much a matter of permitting joinder as of ensuring it.[1636]

780. Section 38 of the Constitution confers on specified persons the right to approach a competent court in the event of a constitutional right being infringed; and this provision has been used by the courts to recognize class actions. In *Ngxuza v. Secretary, Department of Welfare, Eastern Cape Provincial Government,*[1637] the applicants, who were the recipients of social grants, had their grants cancelled or suspended unilaterally by the government department of welfare concerned. The applicants contended that the suspension or cancellation of the grants was unlawful and sought a declaration to that effect, and for the retrospective reinstatement of the grants. They claimed the same relief on behalf of many others in the same position as themselves. To this end, the applicants required the government department to provide them with a list of all the people who had been similarly deprived of their grants. The department disputed that the applicants had the standing to act on behalf of the other persons referred to, or that they were entitled to an order for the disclosure of the information sought.

The court in the *Ngxuza* case found that the applicants did have standing to sue in terms of section 38(b), (c) and (d) of the Constitution,[1638] by means of a class action. The court also found that there was no reason not to grant the relief sought by the applicants. The court pointed out that in a constitutional state, the exercise of

1634. *See Permanent Secretary, Department of Welfare, Eastern Cape Provincial Government v. Ngxuza* 2001 (10) BCLR 1039 (SCA) para. 4 1043; 2001 (4) SA 1184 (SCA).
1635. *See* G.E. Devenish, LAWSA vol. 5(3) *Constitutional Law* para. 177.
1636. *Ibid.*
1637. 2000 (12) BCLR 1322 (E); 2001 (2) SA 609 (E).
1638. Act 108 of 1996.

public power is dependent on the principle of legality. The role of the courts in this regard is to control the exercise of public power so that it conforms to the principle of legality. Section 38 of the Constitution confers on specified persons the right to approach a competent court in the event of a constitutional right being infringed, and there is no justification for interpreting this section restrictively. As no formally binding precedent on the interpretation of section 38 existed, the court had to look at the Constitution as a whole to see what changes it has wrought to the social context in which it must be applied. The Constitution explicitly provides that public administration must be governed by the democratic values and principles set out therein. It also grants the right to lawful, reasonable and fair administrative action to all its citizens. The courts must ensure accountability in the exercise of public power. This together with the hardships faced by persons reliant on social grants formed the background against which the issue of standing was determined in favour of the applicants.[1639]

A class action of this kind involves one or more claimants litigating against a defendant not only on their own behalf, but on behalf of similar claimants. Consequently, other members of a class, although not formally joined before the court, benefit from and are bound by the outcome of the litigation, unless they opt out.

781. In *Highveldridge Residents Concerned Party v. Highveldridge TLC*,[1640] the High Court adopted an expansive interpretation of section 38 in dealing with a class action. The requirements for an unincorporated voluntary association to have locus standi in court under the common law include that the association had to be a corporate body. The key issue in this case was whether the 'association' referred to in section 38(e) had to meet the requirements of the common law pertaining to a voluntary association to have locus standi. The court held that the restrictions placed by the common law on the standing in law of voluntary associations could not apply without qualification to voluntary associations, seeking redress under section 38 for the violation or threatened violation of rights contained in the Bill of Rights.[1641]

782. The judgments referred to above liberalized the law in relation to locus standi, thereby making possible collective action, also for the recovery of damages, in cases where the violation or threatened violation of constitutional rights is in issue. However, the details of awarding damages to interested persons by means of such a class action are yet to be established in case law.

783. In *Children's Resource Centre Trust v. Pioneer Food (Pty) Ltd*,[1642] the Supreme Court of Appeal set out the factors that should be weighed in deciding

1639. *See also Koelman & Others v. MEC for Social Services & Population Development, Northern Cape* [2006] JOL 17964 (NC).
1640. 2003 (1) BCLR 72 (T); 2002 (6) SA 66 (T).
1641. *See also Rail Commuter Action Group v. Transnet Ltd t/a Metrorail* 2003 (3) BCLR 288 (C); 2003 (5) SA 518 (C), in which the court held that s. 38 of the Constitution had extended the common law rules of locus standi. This case involved an application brought by an action group in the interests of rail commuters as a class. They sought relief to ensure safety against violence against passengers on trains.
1642. 2013 (2) SA 213 (SCA) at para. 26.

whether to certify a class action. These factors are as follows: the existence of a class identifiable by reference to objective criteria; the proposed class representative is suitable to conduct the action and represent the class; a cause of action raising a triable issue; the right to relief requires the determination of issues of fact or law, or both, common to all members of the class; the relief sought or damages claimed flow from the cause of action and are ascertainable and capable of determination; where damages are claimed, there is a procedure by which to allocate the damages to members of the class given the composition of the class and the nature of the proposed action; and that a class action is the most appropriate means by which the claims of the class may be determined. The court recognized that these factors may not be exhaustive, but required that a court should be satisfied that the factors are present before granting certification. In *Mukaddam v. Pioneer Foods (Pty) Ltd*,[1643] the Constitutional Court clarified the position. The factors referenced by the Supreme Court of Appeal are not prerequisites for the grant of certification. Rather, they are considerations to be weighed under the overarching principle of what is required by the interests of justice.

§2. Direct and Indirect Damage

784. The distinction between direct and indirect or consequential damage is relevant to the limitation of liability or remoteness of damage. Indirect or consequential damage may not be recoverable for being 'too remote'. In the context of property damage, the diminution in the value of the property constitutes direct loss, whereas the damage resulting from the loss of use of the property, for example in the case of a vehicle used for business purposes, constitutes indirect loss. In the context of damages for personal injury medical costs constitutes a direct loss, whereas loss of income resulting from the injury may be regarded as indirect or consequential loss. The principles in question relate to the assessment of damages, as detailed in respect of personal injury and death in Part VI, Chapter 4 below; and in respect of property damage in Part VI, Chapter 5 below.

§3. Pecuniary and Non-pecuniary Losses

785. In *Van der Merwe v. Road Accident Fund and Another (Amicus Curiae Women's Legal Centre)*,[1644] the Constitutional Court explained the concept of damages and the difference between pecuniary and non-pecuniary damage or loss, as follows:

> [37] The notion of damages is best understood not by its nature but by its purpose. Damages are 'a monetary equivalent' of loss 'awarded to a person with the object of eliminating as fully as possible [her or] his past as well as future damage.' The primary purpose of awarding damages is to place,

---

1643. 2013 (5) SA 89 (CC) at paras 34–40.
1644. 2006 (4) SA 230 (CC); [2006] JOL17069 (CC) paras 37–39.

to the fullest possible extent, the injured party in the same position she or he would have been in, but for the wrongful conduct. Damages also represent 'the process through which an impaired interest may be restored through money.' To realize this purpose our law recognizes patrimonial and non-patrimonial damages. Both seek to redress the diminution in the quality and usefulness of a legally protected interest. It seems clear that the notion of damages is sufficiently wide to include pecuniary and non-pecuniary loss and it is understood to do so ordinarily in practice.

[38] Thus patrimonial damages, which in practice are also called special damages, aim to redress, to the extent that money can, the actual or probable reduction of a person's patrimony as a result of the delict or breach of contract. In this sense patrimonial damages are said to be a 'true equivalent' of the loss. Ordinarily they are calculable in money. Well-settled examples in bodily injury claims are past and future medical expenses, past and future loss of income, loss of earning capacity, and loss of support.

[39] On the other hand non-patrimonial damages, which also bear the name of general damages, are utilized to redress the deterioration of a highly personal legal interests that attach to the body and personality of the claimant. However, ordinarily the breach of a personal legal interest does not reduce the individual's estate and does not have a readily determinable or direct monetary value. Therefore, general damages are, so to speak, illiquid and are not instantly sounding in money. They are not susceptible to exact or immediate calculation in monetary terms. In other words, there is no real relationship between the money and the loss. In bodily injury claims, well-established variants of general damages include 'pain and suffering', 'disfigurement', and 'loss of amenities of life'. (Footnotes omitted.)

786. Damages under the *lex Aquilia* serve to restore the plaintiff's patrimonial state to the position it would have been in had the damage or loss not occurred, and not to compensate for mental suffering, distress, inconvenience, discomfort or annoyance.[1645] Patrimonial or pecuniary loss occurs when a legally recognized interest with a monetary value, such as ownership of an asset or some other right to property is reduced in value, quality or utility (as when property is damaged or lost); or when the plaintiff incurs a cost or debt (as when physical injury entails medical costs); or suffers a prospective loss (as when the damage-causing event entails loss of future income or loss of business or professional profits).

787. Damages for non-patrimonial harm, including damages for pain and suffering in personal injury cases, do not serve a compensatory function, for such harm does not have an economic or pecuniary value. Instead the emphasis is on providing satisfaction for the plaintiff insofar as it is possible for an award of money to do

1645. *Monumental Art Co. v. Kenston Pharmacy (Pty) Ltd* 1976 (2) SA 111 (C) 124.

so.[1646] The *actio iniuriarum* is aimed at recovery of damages as reparation or satisfaction for injury to personality rights. Damages of this kind constitute compensation for the non-patrimonial loss in the form of, for example, insult, indignity and impairment of reputation.

788. In respect of both pecuniary and non-pecuniary damages, the terminology of 'general' and 'special' damages is sometimes used, a derivation from English law. There appears to be no logical foundation for the classification of damages in this manner, and the terminology appears to find application mainly for purposes of pleading.[1647] The term 'general damages' refers to the kind of harm which the law presumes to flow from the wrong complained of, as a natural and probable consequence. A plaintiff need only allege generally that such harm was suffered and the extent of the harm; the nature of the harm need not be detailed in the pleadings. Patrimonial loss which falls into this category includes loss of support resulting from the death of a breadwinner, as well as prospective loss which has not yet crystallized at the date of trial, such as future medical expenses and future loss of earnings. All forms of non-patrimonial loss, such as pain and suffering, disfigurement and loss of amenities are also classified as 'general damages'.[1648] The term 'special damages' refers to harm that must be detailed in pleadings, and in respect of which further particulars may be required, and this includes, in cases of bodily injury, all patrimonial loss actually incurred by the plaintiff, such as medical and hospital expenses, and past loss of earnings.[1649] The categories overlap and the logic of the classification itself is questionable.

The general principles for the assessment of both pecuniary and non-pecuniary damages are detailed in Part VI, Chapter 3.

§4. Pure Economic Loss

789. Pure economic loss can best be described negatively, as patrimonial loss that does not result from the claimant's own bodily injury or damage to the claimant's property. Such loss can occur in a wide variety of circumstances and includes losses arising from misrepresentation, harmful advice, unlawful competition and from the injury, death or damage to property of another person. The measure of such loss is the same as for other forms of patrimonial loss, namely the difference

1646. *Mutual & Federal Insurance Co. Ltd v. Swanepoel* 1988 (2) SA 1 (A) 10–11.
1647. *See* M.M. Corbett, *The Quantum of Damages in Bodily and Fatal Injury Cases,* 2–3 (4th ed., J.J. Gauntlett ed. 1995).
1648. *See*, for example, *Venter v. Nel* 1997 (4) SA 1014 (D) 1016–1017, where general damages were awarded in respect of 'the possibility of a reduction in life expectancy, psychological stress, contumelia and pain and suffering'.
1649. *See* generally M.M. Corbett, *The Quantum of Damages in Bodily and Fatal Injury Cases,* 3 (4th ed., J.J. Gauntlett ed. 1995); and *see*, for example *Guardian National Insurance Co. Ltd v. Van Gool* 1992 (4) SA 61 (A) 68.

between the plaintiff's financial position at the time of assessment and the financial position the claimant would have been in were it not for the harmful conduct.[1650]

790. Generally, therefore, the principles applied by the courts in cases of pure economic loss are no different from the principles applied in other cases, as appears from the following statement in *Jowell v. Bramwell-Jones*:[1651]

> The element of damage or loss is fundamental to the Aquilian action and the right of action is incomplete until damage is caused to the plaintiff by reason of the defendant's wrongful conduct (see *Oslo Land Co. Ltd v. The Union Government* 1938 AD 584 at 590; *Evins v. Shield Insurance Co. Ltd* 1980 (2) SA 814 (A) at 838H-839C). This applies no less to claims arising from pure economic loss than it does to claims arising from bodily injury or damage to property (see *Siman & Co. (Pty) Ltd v. Barclays National Bank Ltd* 1984 (2) SA 888 (A) at 911B-D). Whether a plaintiff has suffered damage or not is a fact which, like any other element of his cause of action and subject to what is said below, must be established on a balance of probabilities. Once the damage or loss is established a court will do its best to quantify that loss even if this involves a degree of guesswork. (See *Turkstra Ltd v. Richards* 1926 TPD 276 at 282-3.)

791. The question of limitation of damages is particularly important in the context of pure economic loss, because the economic effects of harmful conduct can reach much further than the physical effects, and the courts are wary of imposing liability in an indeterminate amount towards an indeterminate class of claimants. This appears from the judgment in *Shell and BPSA Petroleum Refineries (Pty) Ltd v. Osborne Panama SA*,[1652] where the defendant's employee caused damage to a mooring buoy in Durban harbour, and that in turn caused economic loss to the charterer of an oil tanker waiting outside the harbour, because of the consequent delay in discharging the cargo and additional liability for charter fees. The court held that this kind of loss was foreseeable only in relation to an unascertained class of potential victims, namely the owners or charterers of all vessels intending the discharge oil at that particular mooring buoy. Only insofar as the plaintiff-charterer was a member of that unascertained class was its loss reasonably foreseeable. The court was therefore unwilling to recognize a legal duty on the part of the defendant towards one of an unknown number of potential claimants.

1650. In *Transnet Ltd v. Sechaba Photoscan (Pty) Ltd* 2005 (1) SA 299 (SCA) para. 11, the court referred to 'the perennially true statement that the aim in awarding delictual damages is to put the injured party in the same position as he would have been in but for the delict'.
1651. 2000 (3) SA 274 (SCA) at 286G–I.
1652. 1980 (3) SA 653 (D).

792. Exact quantification can be a problem in cases where loss of profit or of some other future financial gain is in issue. This is evident in cases of unlawful competition, where loss normally occurs in the form of a loss of custom to competitors.[1653] In most cases, it is possible to show that some loss has been suffered,[1654] but the extent of the loss is often difficult to prove with precision.[1655] In such cases, the courts will not require mathematically precise proof of loss and will, on the probabilities indicated by the evidence, make an assessment of the loss on an equitable basis.[1656] However, before a court will make an assessment of the quantum it must be satisfied on a balance of probabilities that *some* damages have actually been suffered by the plaintiff. In cases of pure economic loss, the two questions can be closely related, as explained in *Hendricks v. President Insurance Co. Ltd*:[1657]

> In this case, and indeed in other cases of its type, the inquiry to ascertain whether damages have, in fact, been suffered is almost identical to that which has to be undertaken to quantify those damages. In order to answer both questions similar, if not identical, facts will have to be considered and evaluated. This is so because the loss which is claimable does not result from physical damage which is obvious and observable but results from a comparison of two financial situations which, although real and ascertainable, are unseen. Where property is damaged ... the existence of damage and the fact of a loss are prima facie easily established. ... *Per contra*, in claims involving financial loss such as claims for loss of profits, which are less obvious and which require arithmetic demonstration, often both the question as to whether damages have been suffered and the question of the *quantum* thereof are placed in issue.

The general principles for the assessment and limitation of damages are further detailed in Chapter 3.

1653. *See* generally *Dun & Bradstreet (Pty) Ltd v. SA Merchants Combined Credit Bureau (Cape)Pty Ltd* 1968 (1) SA 209 (C) 221; and *Harchris Heat Treatment (Pty) Ltd v. Iscor* 1983 (1) SA 548 (T).

1654. *Van Heerden v. Paetzold* 1917 CPD 221 224 (concerning damages for the effect of malicious statements); *Atlas Organic Fertilizers (Pty) Ltd v. Pikkewyn Ghwano (Pty) Ltd* 1981 (2) SA 173 (T) 204–206 (concerning the assessment of loss of profit); *Link Estates (Pty) Ltd v. Rink Estates (Pty) Ltd* 1979 (2) SA 276 (E) 286–287.

1655. *See Lorimar Productions Inc v. Sterling Clothing Manufacturers (Pty) Ltd* 1981 (3) SA 1129 (T) 1138; *Hushon SA (Pty) Ltd v. Pictech (Pty) Ltd* 1997 (2) All SA 672 (SCA); 1997 (4) SA 399 (SCA).

1656. *International Tobacco Co. (SA) Ltd v. United Tobacco Co. (South) Ltd (1)* 1955 (2) SA 1 (W) 17; *Caxton Ltd v. Reeva Forman (Pty) Ltd* 1990 (3) SA 547 (A) 573; *Hushon SA (Pty) Ltd v. Pictech (Pty) Ltd* 1997 (4) SA 399 (SCA) 412–413.

1657. 1993 (3) SA 158 (C) 164. In this case, the plaintiff failed to establish that he had suffered loss as a result of the death of his wife. He claimed the expenses of having to employ a housekeeper, but did not prove that the expenses in regard to the housekeeper exceeded the costs saved as a result of no longer having to maintain his wife. The evidence failed to establish what amount plaintiff's late wife contributed to the household income; for what period she worked; what share of the household income she used or can reasonably be apportioned to her maintenance.

§5. Actual and Future Loss

I. Actual Loss

793. Actual loss that has been incurred up to the date of assessment (sometimes referred to as '*damnum emergens*') is determined according to the normal measure for loss and damages, namely the difference between the plaintiff's patrimonial position at the time of assessment and the patrimonial position the claimant would have been in were it not for the harmful conduct.[1658] Actual loss can take a wide variety of forms, including expenses incurred, earnings lost and property diminished in value.

794. Although it is said that the time for the assessment of damages is the date of the delict, it is clear that actual loss is assessed by also taking into consideration facts that occurred after the delict.[1659] In the case of bodily injury, for example, medical expenses and loss of income occur after the injury; and in the case of damage to property repair costs indicating the diminution in value of property are incurred after the date when the damage occurred. Furthermore, in respect of prospective loss the courts are both entitled and bound to take account of subsequently occurring facts.[1660] Generally, therefore, the courts take into account all facts that occur between the date of the delict and the date of assessment which may affect the extent of the damages,[1661] and in respect of prospective loss the course of future events is gauged on a balance of probabilities.

795. Actual loss typically manifests itself in the form of expenses, and the plaintiff can recover damages for all necessary medical and other expenses which were reasonably incurred as a result of the delict.[1662] Where the plaintiff suffers personal injuries, such expenses include medical expenses,[1663] hospitalization costs,[1664] cost

1658. In *Transnet Ltd v. Sechaba Photoscan (Pty) Ltd* 2005 (1) SA 299 (SCA) para. 11, the court referred to 'the perennially true statement that the aim in awarding delictual damages is to put the injured party in the same position as he would have been in but for the delict'.

1659. *See* M.M. Corbett, *The Quantum of Damages in Bodily and Fatal Injury Cases*, 8 (4th ed., J.J. Gauntlett ed. 1995); J.C. van der Walt & J.R. Midgley, *Principles of Delict*, para. 163 (3rd ed., Butterworths 2005).

1660. *See* generally M.M. Corbett, *The Quantum of Damages in Bodily and Fatal Injury Cases*, 8 (4th ed., J.J. Gauntlett ed. 1995)

1661. *General Accident Insurance Co. SA Ltd v. Summers*; *Southern Versekeringsassosiasie Bpk v. Carstens*; *General Accident Insurance Co. SA Ltd v. Nhlumayo* 1987 (3) SA 577 (A) 611–613, where the court viewed loss of earning capacity caused by bodily injuries as damage which continues into the future well after the time of the commission of a delict. The court discounted damages for loss of earning capacity and loss of support only to the date of trial and not the date of delict. *See also Sigournay v. Gillbanks* 1960 (2) SA 552 (A) 557. *See also Wigham v. British Traders Insurance Co. Ltd* 1963 (3) SA 151 (W) (life expectancy of dependant taken at date of trial).

1662. *Ngubane v. SA Transport Services* 1991 (1) SA 756 (A) 784–785.

1663. *Botha v. Minister of Transport* 1956 (4) SA 375 (W) 376; *Muller v. Mutual & Federal Insurance Co. Ltd* 1994 (2) SA 425 (C) 432.

1664. *Watt v. Van der Walt* 1947 (2) SA 1216 (W) 1228; *Botha v. Minister of Transport* 1956 (4) SA 375 (W) 376.

of post-operative care,[1665] travel expenses,[1666] cost of artificial limbs and paramedical aids,[1667] additional accommodation costs[1668] and the cost of procuring the services of an attendant.[1669] In the case of death, funeral expenses, including the cost of a tombstone, may be claimed.[1670]

II. Prospective or Future Loss

796. Damages can be recovered for prospective or future loss likely to arise after the date upon which the damages are assessed, and this includes prospective loss of income and prospective loss of profit.[1671] The assessment of prospective or future loss necessarily involves speculation, and courts must gauge the probable course of future events as best they can on the basis of available evidence.[1672] Future expenses need only be proved as a reasonable possibility, and a contingency adjustment is made to account for the possibility that such future expenses may not be necessary.[1673] A distinction needs to be drawn between causation and quantification of damages, because the standards of proof are different. The plaintiff must prove a likelihood of some prospective loss occurring (causation of damages) on a balance of probabilities. Once it is proven that some loss is likely to occur, the court has to assess the likelihood of loss for purposes of quantification. Allowance is then made for the contingency that the loss might not occur, or that any unforeseen event, such as an earlier than expected death, might intervene. The award will then be reduced by a percentage to allow for such possibility.[1674] Contingencies may have a positive or negative impact on the award.[1675]

797. Although courts have warned against following too mathematical an approach, actuarial calculations of the present values of future income and expenses

1665. *Muller v. Mutual & Federal Insurance Co. Ltd* 1994 (2) SA 425 (C) 437.
1666. *Broom v. The Administrator, Natal* 1966 (3) SA 505 (D) 526.
1667. *Watt v. Van der Walt* 1947 (2) SA 1216 (W) 1228; *Botha v. Minister of Transport* 1956 (4) SA 375 (W) 376; *Ngubane v. SA Transport Services* 1991 (1) SA 756 (A) 783–785; *Blyth v. Van den Heever* 1980 (1) SA 191 (A) 224–227.
1668. *General Accident Versekeringsmpy SA Bpk v. Uijs* 1993 (4) SA 228 (A) 235–238.
1669. *Esterhuizen v. Administrator, Tvl* 1957 (3) SA 710 (T) 726; *Ngubane v. SA Transport Services* 1991 (1) SA 756 (A) 785; *Troos Transport t/a Ekonoliner Luxury Coach Lines v. Abrahams* 1999 (2) SA 142 (C) 145–146.
1670. *Commercial Union Assurance Co. of SA Ltd v. Mirkin* 1989 (2) SA 584 (C).
1671. *Transnet Ltd v. Sechaba Photoscan (Pty) Ltd* 2005 (1) SA 299 (SCA).
1672. *Sigournay v. Gillbanks* 1960 (2) SA 552 (A) 557; *General Accident Insurance Co. SA Ltd v. Summers; Southern Versekeringsassosiasie Bpk v. Carstens; General Accident Insurance Co. SA Ltd v. Nhlumayo* 1987 (3) SA 577 (A) 615.
1673. *Blyth v. Van den Heever* 1980 (1) SA 191 (A) 225; *Van der Plaats v. SA Mutual Fire & General Insurance Co. Ltd* 1980 (3) SA 105 (A) 113–115; *Erdmann v. Santam Insurance Co. Ltd* 1985 (3) SA 402 (C) 404–405.
1674. *Burger v. Union National South British Insurance Co.* 1975 (4) SA 72 (W) 75; *De Klerk v. ABSA Bank Ltd* 2003 (1) All SA 651 (SCA); 2003 (4) SA 315 (SCA) paras 27–28; *Minister van Veiligheid & Sekuriteit v. Geldenhuys* 2003 (4) All SA 330 (SCA), 2004 (1) SA 515 (SCA) para. 41.
1675. *Southern Insurance Association Ltd v. Bailey* 1984 (1) SA 98 (A) 117; *Minister of Defence v. Jackson* 1991 (4) SA 23 (ZS) 34–35; *Ngubane v. SA Transport Services* 1991 (1) SA 756 (A) 781–782; *Van der Plaats v. SA Mutual Fire & General Insurance Co. Ltd* 1980 (3) SA 105 (A) 114–115.

serve as useful guides.[1676] However, sometimes the imponderables are such that actuarial calculation would be inaccurate and serve little purpose.[1677] Before a court will make an assessment of the quantum, it must be satisfied on a balance of probabilities that *some* damages have actually been suffered by the plaintiff.[1678]

798. While it is clear that a plaintiff may, and must, claim both actual and prospective damages in one action, it has been held that a plaintiff cannot sue solely for prospective damages, on the basis that such a plaintiff has not yet suffered damage. Prospective damages may be awarded as ancillary to accrued damages, but, according to this approach, prospective damage cannot separately constitute a cause of action.[1679] Arguably, however, damage as an element of a delictual cause of action includes such prospective damage as can be proved on a balance of probabilities, and where only prospective damage can be proved, this should be regarded as sufficient for the purposes of a delictual cause of action.[1680]

III. The Once-and-for-All Rule

799. In delict, the plaintiff must claim damages in a single action for all harm arising from a particular cause of action. This is known as the once-and-for-all rule. A plaintiff who fails to claim for some of damages arising from a cause of action will be precluded from claiming such damages by means of a subsequent action.[1681] The one claim must therefore include all loss that has already occurred at the date of assessment, as well as such prospective loss as can be proved on a balance of probabilities. The rule is based on the policy consideration that a single cause of action should not give rise to a multiplicity of actions or splitting of claims, to ensure that there is an end to litigation.[1682] The rule also has important implications for prescription, in that the prescription period begins to run in respect of the debt arising from a particular cause of action as soon as some damage is caused.

1676. *Goldie v. City Council of Johannesburg* 1948 (2) SA 913 (W) 920; *Gillbanks v. Sigournay* 1959 (2) SA 11 (N) 14–15; *Southern Insurance Association Ltd v. Bailey* 1984 (1) SA 98 (A) 113–114; *Gallie v. National Employers General Insurance Co. Ltd* 1992 (2) SA 731 (C) 736.

1677. *Griffiths v. Mutual & Federal Insurance Co. Ltd* 1994 (1) SA 535 (A) 546.

1678. *Hendricks v. President Insurance Co. Ltd* 1993 (3) SA 158 (C) 164. In this case, the plaintiff failed to establish that he had suffered loss as a result of the death of his wife. He claimed the expenses of having to employ a housekeeper, but did not prove that the expenses in regard to the housekeeper exceeded the costs saved as a result of no longer having to maintain his wife. The evidence failed to establish what amount the plaintiff's late wife contributed to the household income; for what period she worked; what share of the household income she used or can reasonably be apportioned to her maintenance.

1679. *Coetzee v. SAR&H* 19333 CPD 565 576.

1680. *See* M.M. Corbett, *The Quantum of Damages in Bodily and Fatal Injury Cases*, 8–9 (4th ed., J.J. Gauntlett ed. 1995).

1681. *See* M.M. Corbett, *The Quantum of Damages in Bodily and Fatal Injury Cases*, 7 (4th ed., J.J. Gauntlett ed. 1995); J.C. van der Walt and J.R. Midgley, *Principles of Delict*, para. 152 (3rd ed., Butterworths 2005).

1682. *Evins v. Shield Insurance Co. Ltd* 1980 (2) SA 814 (A) 835.

800. The application of the once-and-for-all rule for purposes of damages and prescription depends essentially on what is regarded as constituting a separate cause of action. The question is whether different kinds of damage or loss arising from a particular event constitute a single cause of action or multiple causes of action. A 'cause of action' is the factual basis or set of material facts that 'begets' the plaintiff's right of action and its correlative, the defendant's debt.[1683] The prevailing view is that different kinds of damage or loss that arise from a particular event constitute a single cause of action if the same set of material facts (*facta probanda*) need to be proved to claim compensation for such damage or loss.

801. In *Evins v. Shield Insurance Co. Ltd*,[1684] the court applied this test to determine whether the plaintiff's claim for damages arising from an accident in which she was injured and her husband died was based on one or two causes of action:

> From this analysis it is evident that, although there is a measure of overlapping, the *facta probanda* in a bodily injury claim differ substantially from the *facta probanda* in a claim for loss of support. Proof of bodily injury to the plaintiff is basic to the one; proof of death of the breadwinner is basic to the other. Proof of a right to support and the real expectation that, but for the breadwinner's death, such support would have been forthcoming is basic to the one, irrelevant to the other. ... even where both claims flow from the same accident, the cause of action in each case may arise at a different time. ... the cause of action in respect of bodily injury will normally arise at the time of the accident, i.e., when the bodily injury and the consequent damnum are inflicted; in the case of the cause of action for loss of support, this will arise only upon the death of the deceased, which may occur some considerable time after the accident. Until such death there is, of course, no wrongful act qua the plaintiff; only a wrongful act qua the person who is later to become the deceased.

The application of this test depends of course on what facts are regarded as material to claim a particular kind of damages. The distinction between a single and multiple causes of action in the cases is sometimes challenging to logical analysis.

802. In a case where damage to a motorcycle and personal injury occurred in the same accident, the court held that both kinds of damages arose from the same cause of action.[1685] However, where an accident involves both bodily injury giving rise to a claim under the Road Accident Fund Act[1686] and property damage, two causes of action are involved, because there is no compensation for property damage under the Road Accident Fund Act:[1687] a common law claim is required to recover the property damage. Where different kinds of damage or loss arise from injuries sustained in a motor vehicle accident, the claim is based on the same set of

1683. *CGU Insurance v. Rumdel Construction (Pty) Ltd* 2004 (2) SA 622 (SCA) para. 6.
1684. 1980 (2) SA 814 (A) 839.
1685. *Green v. Coetzer* 1958 (2) SA 697 (W).
1686. Act 56 of 1996.
1687. *Ibid.*

material facts (*facta probanda*), and all damages flowing from the injuries, for losses already incurred and prospective, must be claimed in one action.

803. Where harmful conduct causes a particular kind of damage to occur repetitively over a period of time, all damages must normally be claimed in one action. In *Oslo Land Corporation v. Union Government*,[1688] for example, the spraying of excessively strong locust poison by a government agency caused death of cattle over a period of three years, and it was held that all the damage arose from a single cause of action, and, consequently, that prescription began to run when the first damage occurred, and all damages, for losses already incurred and prospective, had to be claimed in one action. However, where the damage-causing event is in the nature of a continuing wrong causing continuing harm, the courts recognize multiple causes of action, or a cause of action which in effect subsists continually over the period of time during which the harm occurs, so that the claimant can recover damages for all the harm that occurred within the applicable prescription or limitation period.[1689] In *Lombo v. African National Congress*,[1690] where the plaintiff contended that he had been assaulted on various occasions, the court found that every actionable form of maltreatment constituted a separate cause of action, and each was independently subject to extinctive prescription from the time of its infliction. The Supreme Court of Appeal noted that continuing unlawful detention 'would notionally have given rise to a separate cause of action for each day he was so detained'.[1691]

804. The once-and-for-all rule thus applies even if the full extent of the damage has not manifested itself at the date of the trial, or even if the plaintiff did not know of such further damage at the date of the trial. Generally, in deciding whether a single or multiple causes of action exist, the courts will have regard to differences in the nature of the various items of damage that occurred; the evidence required to prove these items of damage; the duration of the conduct that gave rise to the damage; and whether the damage arose from a single act or event.

1688. 1938 AD 584.
1689. On the concept of a continuing act causing continuing harm, *see* generally Max Loubser, *Extinctive Prescription* (2nd ed, 2019) 77-81. In *Slomowitz v. Vereeniging Town Council* 1966 (3) SA 317 (A), the plaintiff claimed damages for business losses suffered as a result of the unlawful closing of a road, from Feb. 1960 until 17 Dec. 1963. Summons had been served on 24 Mar. 1964. A limitation period applicable in this case required the action to be brought within six months of the time when the cause of action arose. The Appellate Division held that, on account of damage caused by the continuance of the unlawful closing of the road, the claimant had a cause of action against the defendant throughout the period that the road remained closed. However, in view of the six-month limitation period, the plaintiff was only entitled to such damages as he could prove he sustained during the period of six months prior to the serving of the summons on the defendant – for the period from 25 Sep. to 17 Dec. 1963.
1690. 2002 (3) All SA 517 (SCA); 2002 (5) SA 668 (SCA).
1691. At para. 26. *See also Ngcobo v. Minister of Police* 1978 (4) SA 930 (D).

§6. Costs

805. The award of costs is in the discretion of the court. The general rule is that a litigant who is substantially successful in an action for damages is entitled to the legal and other costs involved in bringing the action, including the costs of preparing the claim. Costs follow a successful claim, despite the fact that the damages awarded are less than the claim. In cases where the claim was so much greater than the amount awarded that the claim can be regarded as grossly extravagant, courts can decline to award costs. The fundamental rule is that costs should be borne by the party responsible for such costs having been incurred. Accordingly, costs should be paid by the defendant who caused damage or loss to the plaintiff by harmful conduct, and who, by failure to pay compensation voluntarily, in effect compelled the plaintiff to go to court to recover damages. If the plaintiff secures an award of the substantial balance of damages claimed, this is normally accompanied by a costs order in favour of the plaintiff.[1692]

§7. Mitigation of Damages

806. A plaintiff should take reasonable steps to minimize the loss caused by the defendant's harmful conduct.[1693] A plaintiff cannot recover damages for loss that could have been prevented had the plaintiff taken reasonable steps to limit initial loss or further accumulation of loss. The duty to mitigate loss arises as soon as the plaintiff in fact suffers loss. Arguably, the issue is essentially one of legal causation or remoteness – the plaintiff cannot recover damages that can be attributed to his or her own conduct or lack of it, instead of to the defendant's conduct.[1694] A plaintiff who has incurred costs by taking reasonable steps to mitigate loss may also recover such costs. Where there is a choice the plaintiff should choose the less expensive method.[1695] A plaintiff may be expected to seek alternative employment in the event of disability, but it is not reasonable to expect the plaintiff to qualify academically for a different career.[1696] The onus of proving that the plaintiff did not properly mitigate loss rests on the defendant.[1697]

1692. *See* generally M.M. Corbett, *The Quantum of Damages in Bodily and Fatal Injury Cases*, 79–80 (4th ed., J.J. Gauntlett ed. 1995).
1693. *Swart v. Provincial Insurance Co. Ltd* 1963 (2) SA 630 (A) 633; *Da Silva v. Coutinho* 1971 (3) SA 123 (A) 145; *De Pinto v. Rensea Investments (Pty) Ltd* 1977 (4) SA 529 (A).
1694. *Da Silva v. Coutinho* 1971 (3) SA 123 (A) 145; *Burger v. Union National South British Insurance Co.* 1975 (4) SA 72 (W) 74–75.
1695. The use of private medical services and hospital facilities instead of State facilities may, in some instances, be reasonable: *Ngubane v. SA Transport Services* 1991 (1) SA 756 (A) 784.
1696. *Swart v. Provincial Insurance Co. Ltd* 1963 (2) SA 630 (A) 634.
1697. *Shrog v. Valentine* 1949 (3) SA 1228 (T) 1237.

Chapter 3. Assessment and Compensation of Damages

§1. Objective Versus Subjective

807. Damages are assessed on an objective basis, without regard to the subjective value of money to the person who suffered the injury.[1698] In *Radebe v. Hough*,[1699] the Appellate Division said the following in this regard:

> It is true that compensation must sound in money and that 'there are no scales by which pain and suffering can be measured and there is no relationship between pain and money which makes it possible to express the one in terms of the other with any approach to certainty' (*per* Watermeyer J.A. in *Sandler v. Wholesale Coal Suppliers, Ltd* 1941 AD 194 at p. 199). But that does not mean that further uncertainty must be introduced by taking into consideration the value of money to the person injured. A millionaire is not entitled to a higher award of damages for pain and suffering because money means very little to him, and conversely a pauper is not to be prejudiced by the fact that money means a great deal to him. What would be the position if the financial status of the millionaire or of the pauper changed in the interval between the suffering of the pain and the award of damages?

These remarks appear to be directed specifically to the assessment of damages for pain and suffering, but the same approach is followed in the assessment of all non-pecuniary damages, although considerations of social or financial status may be relevant in determining the extent of non-pecuniary damages for loss of amenities.[1700]

§2. Concrete Versus Abstract

808. It is now well settled that the aim with an award of delictual damages is to put the plaintiff in the same position he or she would have been in but for the harm-causing event.

809. In *Dippenaar v. Shield Insurance Co. Ltd*,[1701] the Appellate Division, per Rumpff JA, formulated the position as follows:

> In our law, under the lex Aquilia, the defendant must make good the difference between the value of the plaintiff's estate after the commission of the delict and the value it would have had if the delict had not been committed.

1698. Pain and suffering, for example, do not vary according to the financial status of the plaintiff; *see Radebe v. Hough* 1949 (1) SA 380 (A) 386; *Minister of Defence v. Jackson* 1991 (4) SA 23 (ZS) 27.

1699. 1949 (1) SA 380 (A) 386.

1700. *See* generally M.M. Corbett, *The Quantum of Damages in Bodily and Fatal Injury Cases*, 6–7 (4th ed., J.J. Gauntlett ed. 1995).

1701. 1979 (2) SA 904 (A) 917A-B.

810. In *Transnet Ltd v. Sechaba Photoscan (Pty) Ltd,*[1702] the Supreme Court of Appeal, per Howie P, referred to the 'perennially true statement that the aim in awarding delictual damages is to put the injured party in the same position as he would have been in but for the delict'; and added:[1703]

> It is now beyond question that damages in delict (and contract) are assessed according to the comparative method. Essentially, that method, in my view, determines the difference, or, literally, the interesse. The award of delictual damages seeks to compensate for the difference between the actual position that obtains as a result of the delict and the hypothetical position that would have obtained had there been no delict. That surely says enough to define the measure. There appears to be no practical value in observing the distinction between positive and negative interesse in determining delictual damages. It is a distinction that tends to obscure rather than clarify. If to award the difference means necessarily awarding loss of profits then it does not assist first to ask what positive interesse and negative interesse comprise. (Footnotes omitted.)

This comparative or differential approach, also termed the 'sum-formula' approach, as developed in German jurisprudence, notably by Mommsen,[1704] has become part of the South African law on damages.[1705] The approach involves the comparison of two patrimonial positions, expressed as sum totals. The plaintiff's present patrimonial position (after the occurrence of the damage-causing event) is compared to (subtracted from) the hypothetical patrimonial position in which the plaintiff would have been had the damage-causing event not occurred.

811. The comparative method is usually formulated in the abstract, purporting to involve the comparison of the plaintiff's total patrimonial position at two points in time. However, it is clear that the method is in practice applied in a concrete way, with reference to the particular asset or interest affected. In the case of property damage, for example, the loss is calculated with reference to the diminution in value of the property and the effect of the loss of use of the property, given its particular integration in the plaintiff's patrimonial structure. The property damage of course also affects the plaintiff's total patrimonial position, but the inquiry into the extent

---

1702. 2005 (1) SA 299 (SCA) para. 11, at 304E–F.
1703. Paragraph 15.
1704. *See* Reinhard Zimmermann, *The Law of Obligations: Roman Foundations of the Civilian Tradition*, 824 (Juta & Co. Ltd 1990).
1705. *See Union Government (Minister of Railways & Harbours) v. Warneke* 1911 AD 657 665; *Oslo Land Co. Ltd v. Union Government* 1938 AD 584 590; *Erdmann v. Santam Insurance Co. Ltd* 1985 (3) SA 402 (C) 406; *Dippenaar v. Shield Insurance Co. Ltd* 1979 (2) SA 904 (A) 917; *President Insurance Co. Ltd v. Mathews* 1992 (1) SA 1 (A) 5; *Rudman v. Road Accident Fund* 2002 (4) All SA 422 (SCA); 2003 (2) SA 234 (SCA) 240–241; *Transnet Ltd v. Sechaba Photoscan (Pty) Ltd* 2005 (1) SA 299 (SCA) 302.

of the loss focuses concretely on the asset or interest affected and often does not proceed to the abstract comparison of the plaintiff's total patrimonial position at different points in time.[1706]

812. Theoretically non-pecuniary harm can also be determined by means of a comparison. The state of the plaintiff's personality interests as it is after the harmful event can be compared to the State had the harmful event not occurred, to estimate the existence and extent of the harm involved. However, as in the case of pecuniary loss, the inquiry in practice mostly focuses concretely on the extent to which a particular interest has been negatively affected, and it often does not involve the abstract comparison of the state of the plaintiff's personality interests at different points in time.

§3. Methods of Assessing Damages

I. General Principles

813. The assessment of damages in delict is fundamentally determined by the comparative, differential or sum-formula method, as set out in the preceding section. The application of this method for the assessment of damages in cases of personal injury and death is detailed in Chapter 4 and in respect of property damage in Chapter 5. Ancillary principles on assessment as detailed in other sections concern equitable limitation of damages (Chapter 3 section 4), and collateral benefits (Chapter 6).

814. The principles on assessment of damages that are dealt with in this section concern the role of interest, inflation and tax, the currency in which the award is made and non-pecuniary damages.

II. Interest

815. Interest on damages in a liquidated amount runs from the date when payment is due, that is when the defendant is in mora. The rule is that mora begins to run from the date of receipt of a letter of demand, and where there has been no letter of demand, there is no mora until summons has been served on defendant.[1707] In the past a plaintiff was not entitled to recover interest on damages awarded where the claim is unliquidated.[1708] The Prescribed Rate of Interest Act[1709] as amended in

1706. P.Q.R. Boberg, *The Law of Delict Vol. 1*, 481–482 (1984); J.C. van der Walt & J.R. Midgley, *Principles of Delict*, paras 145–146 (3rd ed., Butterworths 2005).

1707. *West Rand Estates Ltd v. New Zealand Insurance Co. Ltd* 1926 AD 173 at 182; *Standard Chartered Bank of Canada v. Nedperm Bank Ltd* 1994 (4) SA 747 (A) 778A-B; *Thoroughbred Breeders Association of South Africa v. Price Waterhouse* 2001 (4) SA 551 (SCA) para. 86.

1708. *Muller v. Mutual & Federal Insurance Co. Ltd* 1994 (2) SA 425 (C) 446–448; *Standard Chartered Bank of Canada v. Nedperm Bank Ltd* 1994 (4) SA 747 (A) 777–779.

1709. Act 55 of 1975.

1997[1710] provides that interest at the legal rate is payable on unliquidated debts from the date of demand or service of summons, whichever date is the earlier.[1711] The distinction between interest on damages (mora interest) and interest constituting a part of damages, for example where the plaintiff was forced to borrow money as a result of the delict, should be noted.[1712]

III. Inflation

816. Inflation, involving a change in the purchasing power of money, is a relevant factor in assessing damages, not only in comparing past awards made in analogous situations,[1713] but also in assessing the extent of any future harm and the future purchasing power of the award.[1714]

817. No adjustment is made for inflation in respect of loss suffered prior to the date of assessment.[1715] In this regard, the Appellate Division held in *SA Eagle Insurance Co. Ltd v. Hartley*[1716] that the principle of currency nominalism applies. The respondent had suffered a loss of income, expressed in Rands, prior to the trial. That loss had to be made good by the appellant (the authorized insurer of the motor vehicle) by paying to the respondent the number of Rands which he had lost, irrespective of whether the purchasing power of the Rand had varied in the interim. This did not mean that the effects of inflation were never relevant in the computation of damages. Where, for example, damages for future loss of earnings or loss of

1710. By Act 7 of 1997, introducing s. 2A.
1711. *See David Trust v. Aegis Insurance Co. Ltd* 2000 (2) All SA 297 (SCA); 2000 (3) SA 289 (SCA) 303–304; *Van der Berg v. Coopers & Lybrand Trust (Pty) Ltd* 2001 (1) All SA 425 (SCA); 2001 (2) SA 242 (SCA) para. 48; *Adel Builders (Pty) Ltd v. Thompson* 1998 (2) All SA 534 (SE); 1999 (1) SA 680 (SE) 688–692; *Skilya Property Investments (Pty) Ltd v. Lloyds of London Underwriting* 2002 (3) SA 765 (T) 815–816.
1712. *See Davidson v. Bonafede* 1981 (2) SA 501 (C) 507–508; and *Thoroughbred Breeders Association of South Africa v. Price Waterhouse* 2001 (4) SA 551 (SCA) paras 77–78, where the main claim for interest was calculated at the rate of interest levied by the plaintiff's banker on every individual amount stolen from the plaintiff, from the date upon which that particular amount was stolen. Because of the thefts, the plaintiff's overdraft, so it was contended, was inflated and the excess attracted interest at the higher rates charged by a banker to its customer on overdraft. Thus formulated, the plaintiff's claim was one not for ordinary mora interest, but for additional damages in the form of interest.
1713. *Norton v. Ginsberg* 1953 (4) SA 537 (A) 541 551; *Ramakulukusha v. Commander, Venda National Force* 1989 (2) SA 813 (V) 847–848; *Burger v. Union National South British Insurance Co.* 1975 (4) SA 72 (W) 77; *Blyth v. Van den Heever* 1980 (1) SA 191 (A) 227.
1714. *Spencer v. Barclays Bank* 1947 (3) SA 230 (T) 245; *Legal Insurance Co. Ltd v. Botes* 1963 (1) SA 608 (A) 619; *Van der Plaats v. SA Mutual Fire & General Insurance Co. Ltd* 1980 (3) SA 105 (A) 113–114; *Southern Insurance Association Ltd v. Bailey* 1984 (1) SA 98 (A) 116; *Stephenson v. General Accident Fire & Life Assurance Corporation Ltd* 1974 (4) SA 503 (RA) 506; *Beverley v. Mutual & Federal Insurance Co. Ltd* 1988 (2) SA 267 (D) 271 272; *Moekoena v. President Insurance Co. Ltd* 1990 (2) SA 112 (W) 114–115; but *see SA Eagle Insurance Co. Ltd v. Hartley* 1990 (4) SA 833 (A) 840–841.
1715. *SA Eagle Insurance Co. Ltd v. Hartley* 1990 (4) SA 833 (A) 840; *Adel Builders (Pty) Ltd v. Thompson* 1998 (2) All SA 534 (SE); 1999 (1) SA 680 (SE) 687.
1716. 1990 (4) SA 833 (A).

support had to be computed, regard should be had to what the plaintiff or the bread-winner would have earned in the future and the court ultimately had to calculate what such loss was likely to be in Rand terms, so that the loss of purchasing power of the currency was relevant to the inquiry, but only indirectly. General damages concerned the valuation of a non-monetary debt, and such a valuation must be made in terms of currency values as they are at the time of valuation and not in terms of the values of an earlier time, an approach which did not offend against the principle of currency nominalism. The court remarked that a mechanism was needed by which a court could compensate a plaintiff for the ravages of inflation in respect of monetary losses incurred prior to the trial, in the form of a statutory power to award interest. Such a power was subsequently conferred on the courts by means of the amendment to the Prescribed Rate of Interest Act referred to above.

818. Although it is customary to base an assessment of the effects of inflation on evidence, the courts have, in the absence of such evidence, taken judicial notice of inflation.[1717] Since any allowance for the change in the value of money cannot be exact, courts are inclined to adopt a cautious and conservative approach,[1718] and do not adhere slavishly to the consumer price index, especially in cases involving non-patrimonial harm.[1719]

IV. Tax

819. An award of damages is regarded for tax purposes as being of a capital nature, and is not subject to tax,[1720] unless the award is in the nature of compensation for lost income or profit.[1721] Tax is considered in assessing the extent of past and future earning capacity,[1722] provided that there is sufficient certainty as to the extent of the tax, and the onus in this regard is on the plaintiff.[1723]

V. Currency

820. It is competent for a plaintiff to seek and for a South African court to award damages in a foreign currency.[1724] A debt sounding in money is paid in terms of its

1717. *Burger v. Union National South British Insurance Co.* 1975 (4) SA 72 (W) 77.
1718. *Norton v. Ginsberg* 1953 (4) SA 537 (A) 541; *Legal Insurance Co. Ltd v. Botes* 1963 (1) SA 608 (A) 619.
1719. *AA Onderlinge Assuransie Assosiasie Bpk v. Sodoms* 1980 (3) SA 134 (A) 141.
1720. *Minister of Defence v. Jackson* 1991 (4) SA 23 (ZS) 32 36.
1721. *Minister of Defence v. Jackson* 1991 (4) SA 23 (ZS) 38; *Omega Africa Plastics (Pty) Ltd v. Swisstool Manufacturing Co. (Pty) Ltd* 1978 (3) SA 465 (A) 475–476.
1722. *Oberholzer v. Santam Insurance Co. Ltd* 1970 (1) SA 337 (N) 342; *Krugell v. Shield Versekeringsmpy Bpk* 1982 (4) SA 95 (T) 104; *Minister of Defence v. Jackson* 1991 (4) SA 23 (ZS).
1723. *Sigournay v. Gillbanks* 1960 (2) SA 552 (A) 568; *Muller v. Mutual & Federal Insurance Co. Ltd* 1994 (2) SA 425 (C) 454–455; *Snyders v. Groenewald* 1966 (3) SA 785 (C) 789C.
1724. *Standard Chartered Bank of Canada v. Nedperm Bank Ltd* 1994 (4) SA 747 (A) 774–777; *Radell v. Multilateral Motor Vehicle Accidents Fund* 1995 (4) SA 24 (A) 29; *Elgin Brown & Hamer (Pty)*

nominal value irrespective of currency fluctuations.[1725] This means that the amount to be paid is the monetary value of the loss at the time of the delict, but there may be an award of appropriate interest. Payment can be made in South Africa either in the foreign currency or its South African Rand equivalent on the date of payment.[1726]

VI. Assessment of Non-pecuniary Damages (Solatium)

821. Damages for non-patrimonial harm, including damages for pain and suffering in personal injury cases, do not serve a compensatory function, for such harm does not have an economic or pecuniary value. Instead the emphasis is on providing satisfaction for the plaintiff insofar as it is possible for an award of money to do so.[1727] The purpose of awards for the infringement of personality rights under the *actio iniuriarum* and for pain and suffering in cases of personal injury is to provide solace and to assuage wounded feelings.[1728] There is no formula for the assessment of non-pecuniary damages, the award being in the discretion of the court. Common to all awards under the *actio iniuriarum* is the fact that harm is presumed once it is proved that the plaintiff's personality interest has been infringed.[1729] The court determines the monetary amount awarded for damages *ex aequo de bono* according to the particular facts of the case.[1730]

822. Although courts are prepared to award substantial damages,[1731] the courts are generally conservative, as stated in *Argus Printing and Publishing Co. Ltd v. Inkatha Freedom Party*:[1732]

> Our courts have not been generous in their awards of *solatia*– an action for defamation has been seen as the method whereby a plaintiff vindicates his reputation, and not as a road to riches.

Ltd v. Dampskibsselskabet Torm Ltd 1988 (4) SA 671 (N); *Skilya Property Investments (Pty) Ltd v. Lloyds of London Underwriting* 2002 (3) SA 765 (T) 815.

1725. *SA Eagle Insurance Co. Ltd v. Hartley* 1990 (4) SA 833 (A) 840; *Radell v. Multilateral Motor Vehicle Accidents Fund* 1995 (4) SA 24 (A) 28–29; *Skilya Property Investments (Pty) Ltd v. Lloyds of London Underwriting* 2002 (3) SA 765 (T) 815.

1726. *Standard Chartered Bank of Canada v. Nedperm Bank Ltd* 1994 (4) SA 747 (A) 777; *Radell v. Multilateral Motor Vehicle Accidents Fund* 1995 (4) SA 24 (A) 29; *Skilya Property Investments (Pty) Ltd v. Lloyds of London Underwriting* 2002 (3) SA 765 (T) 816.

1727. *Mutual & Federal Insurance Co. Ltd v. Swanepoel* 1988 (2) SA 1 (A) 10–11.

1728. *Hoffa v. SA Mutual Fire & General Insurance Co. Ltd* 1965 (2) SA 944 (C) 954–955: 'The damages awarded to him are in a certain sense analogous to the solatium which is awarded under the actio injuriarum to someone as a salve to his wounded feelings.'

1729. On impairment of dignity *see Matthews v. Young* 1922 AD 492 503; *Bull v. Taylor* 1965 (4) SA 29 (A) 38; and on defamation *see Walton v. Cohn* 1947 (2) SA 225 (N) 229; *Smith v. Die Republikein (Edms) Bpk* 1989 (3) SA 872 (SWA) 875.

1730. *Smith v. Die Republikein (Edms) Bpk* 1989 (3) SA 872 (SWA) 875. In *Van der Berg v. Coopers & Lybrand Trust (Pty) Ltd* 2001 (1) All SA 425 (SCA) para. 48; 2001 (2) SA 242 (SCA), the court referred to the result in a defamation case as 'little more than an enlightened guess'.

1731. *Caxton Ltd v. Reeva Forman (Pty) Ltd* 1990 (3) SA 547 (A).

1732. 1992 (3) SA 579 (A) 590.

823. Earlier cases of a similar nature may serve as an approximate guide, but are applied with circumspection.[1733] Factors relevant to the assessment of damages generally include the nature and seriousness of the *iniuria*,[1734] the circumstances in which the infringement took place,[1735] the behaviour and motive of the defendant,[1736] the extent of the plaintiff's humiliation or distress,[1737] the abuse of a relationship between the parties[1738] and the attitude of the defendant after the *iniuria* had taken place.[1739]

824. In assessing the monetary amount awarded for damages on account of defamation, a court will have regard to the nature and content of the words used and the effect they were intended to have upon the plaintiff, the nature and extent of the publication, the conduct of the defendant, both at the time of the defamation and subsequently (if relevant), any attempts to rectify the harm, such as an apology, the character and status of the plaintiff and the actual consequences of the defamation. In *Muller v. SA Associated Newspapers Ltd*,[1740] the court summarized the general approach to the assessment of damages as follows:

> In estimating the monetary amount of damages to be awarded the Court must have regard to all the circumstances of the case. It must, *inter alia*, have regard to the character and status of the plaintiff, the nature of the words used, the effect that they are calculated to have upon him, the extent of the publication, the subsequent conduct of the defendant and, in particular, his attempts, and the effectiveness thereof, to rectify the harm done.[1741]

825. In *Dikoko v. Mokhatla*,[1742] Mokgoro J made further comments on the assessment of damages in defamation cases:

> [71] When assessing damages for defamation, courts have in the past considered a range of factors arising from the circumstances and facts of the case: The nature and gravity of the defamatory words; falseness of the statement; malice on the part of the defendant; A rank or social status of the parties; the absence or nature of an apology; the nature and extent of the publication and

1733. *Norton v. Ginsberg* 1953 (4) SA 537 (A) 551; *Pont v. Geyser* 1968 (2) SA 545 (A) 557–558.
1734. *Norton v. Ginsberg* 1953 (4) SA 537 (A) 550; *SA Associated Newspapers Ltd v. Yutar* 1969 (2) SA 442 (A) 458.
1735. *Brenner v. Botha* 1956 (3) SA 257 (T) 262; *Ramakulukusha v. Commander, Venda National Force* 1989 (2) SA 813 (V) 849.
1736. *Guggenheim v. Rosenbaum (2)* 1961 (4) SA 21 (W) 36; *SA Associated Newspapers Ltd v. Yutar* 1969 (2) SA 442 (A) 458; *Ramakulukusha v. Commander, Venda National Force* 1989 (2) SA 813 (V) 845 849; *Hofmeyr v. Minister of Justice* 1992 (3) SA 108 (C) 132 135; *Bentley v. McPherson* 1999 (2) All SA 89 (E); 1999 (3) SA 854 (E) 866.
1737. *Fuller v. Viljoen* 1949 (3) SA 853 (G) 855.
1738. *Jansen van Vuuren v. Kruger* 1993 (4) SA 842 (A) 857–858.
1739. *Bruwer v. Joubert* 1966 (3) SA 334 (A) 338.
1740. 1972 (2) SA 589 (C) 595.
1741. *See also Buthelezi v. Poorter and Others Marais v. Groenewald* 2000 (2) All SA 578 (T) 592; 2001 (1) SA 634 (T) 649; *Van der Berg v. Coopers & Lybrand Trust (Pty) Ltd* 2001 (1) All SA 425 (SCA) para. 48; 2001 (2) SA 242 (SCA).
1742. 2006 (6) SA 235 (CC).

the general conduct of the defendant. The court must therefore have regard to all the circumstances of a case where the assessment is always context specific. The list is non-exhaustive. Although earlier cases of a similar nature give guidance, they must always be applied with the necessary circumspection.

826. In assessing damages for malicious prosecution, a court will take into account the seriousness of the charge and the potential penalty, any period of incarceration, the period during which the charge was pending, and the personal insult, indignity, humiliation and defamation which the plaintiff suffers.[1743] Similar factors will be taken into account for the assessment of damages for infringement of bodily integrity and deprivation of liberty by unlawful arrest,[1744] and invasion of privacy.[1745]

§4. Equitable Limitation of Damages

827. Liability for damages will only be imposed if there is a factual link between the defendant's conduct and the damage, loss or harm suffered by the plaintiff. The plaintiff must prove on a balance of probabilities the actual loss that has occurred and that prospective loss will occur. The first question is therefore one of factual causation of damage, loss or harm. The standard of proof is the balance of probabilities – the factual causal link must be more probable than not.

828. Once the probability of prospective loss has been proved, the court has to assess the likelihood of such loss for purposes of quantification. As noted in Chapter 2 section 5 above, a distinction needs to be drawn between causation and quantification of damages in cases of prospective loss, because the standards of proof are different. Allowance is made for the contingency that the loss might not occur, or that any unforeseen event, such as an earlier than expected death, might intervene. The award will then be reduced by a percentage to allow for such possibility.[1746] Contingencies may have a positive or negative impact on the award.[1747]

1743. *Law v. Kin* 1966 (3) SA 480 (W) 482; *Ramakulukusha v. Commander, Venda National Force* 1989 (2) SA 813 (V) 851; *Ochse v. King William's Town Municipality* 1990 (2) SA 855 (E) 860; *Mthimkhulu v. Minister of Law & Order* 1993 (3) SA 432 (E) 441.

1744. *Makomberedze v. Minister of State (Security)* 1986 (4) SA 367 (ZH) 270; *Ochse v. King William's Town Municipality* 1990 (2) SA 855 (E) 860; *Thandani v. Minister of Law & Order* 1991 (1) SA 702 (E) 707; *Mthimkhulu v. Minister of Law & Order* 1993 (3) SA 432 (E) 440.

1745. *O'Keeffe v. Argus Printing & Publishing Co. Ltd* 1954 (3) SA 244 (C) 249; *Kidson v. SA Associated Newspapers Ltd* 1957 (3) SA 461 (W) 468–469; *Mhlongo v. Bailey* 1958 (1) SA 370 (W) 371–373; *Jansen van Vuuren v. Kruger* 1993 (4) SA 842 (A) 857–858; *Jooste v. National Media Ltd* 1994 (2) SA 634 (C) 647.

1746. *Burger v. Union National South British Insurance Co.* 1975 (4) SA 72 (W) 75; *De Klerk v. ABSA Bank Ltd* 2003 (1) All SA 651 (SCA); 2003 (4) SA 315 (SCA) paras 27–28; *Minister van Veiligheid & Sekuriteit v. Geldenhuys* 2003 (4) All SA 330 (SCA), 2004 (1) SA 515 (SCA) para. 41.

1747. *Southern Insurance Association Ltd v. Bailey* 1984 (1) SA 98 (A) 117; *Minister of Defence v. Jackson* 1991 (4) SA 23 (ZS) 34–35; *Ngubane v. SA Transport Services* 1991 (1) SA 756 (A) 781–782; *Van der Plaats v. SA Mutual Fire & General Insurance Co. Ltd* 1980 (3) SA 105 (A) 114–115.

Furthermore, no legal system holds a defendant liable for all the consequences suffered by the plaintiff as a result of the defendant's harmful conduct, even if the causal link between such consequences and the harmful conduct is proved on a balance of probabilities. Some line must be drawn, and this involves the question of legal causation or remoteness of damage, as detailed in Part V above.

829. Following the leading cases of *Mokgethi,*[1748] *Bentley,*[1749] and *Fourway Haulage SA (Pty) Ltd v. SA National Roads Agency Ltd,*[1750] the South African courts now accept that legal causation involves the basic question whether there is a close enough relationship between the wrongdoer's conduct and its consequence for such consequence to be imputed to the wrongdoer, taking into account policy considerations based on reasonableness, fairness and justice.[1751] In order to determine the closeness of the connection, the courts apply a combination of criteria as subsidiary tests, including the 'direct consequences' test, the 'adequate causation' test and reasonable foreseeability.[1752] The flexible criterion is similar to the policy-based test used to determine unlawfulness.[1753] Both have an important function in limiting liability, but the legal causation test focuses on the extent to which liability should be imposed for damage or harm factually caused by the defendant's conduct, whereas the unlawfulness inquiry is essentially concerned with the scope of protection afforded to various rights and interests, the scope of responsibility to act and overall policy considerations relating to the question whether the law of delict should intervene at all.[1754]

830. In cases where the plaintiff suffers more extensive damage as a result of the defendant's conduct than would normally have been the case, because of some physical, psychological or financial weakness, the rule 'you must take your victim as you find him' (also referred to as the 'talem qualem rule' or the 'thin skull rule') applies, and the defendant is liable to compensate the plaintiff to the full extent of the damage.[1755]

831. Where damages are difficult to prove with precision and the plaintiff has produced evidence that enables the court to make an estimate of the damage, the fact that damages cannot be assessed with certainty will not relieve the defendant of

1748. 1990 (1) SA 32 (A).
1749. 1990 (1) SA 680 (A) 700E–701F.
1750. 2009 (2) SA 150 (SCA).
1751. *S v. Mokgethi* 1990 (1) SA 32 (A) per Van Heerden JA at 40–41.
1752. J.C. van der Walt & J.R. Midgley, *Principles of Delict,* para. 132. (3rd ed., Butterworths 2005).
1753. *Ibid.*
1754. *Ibid.*
1755. *Wilson v. Birt (Pty) Ltd* 1963 (2) SA 508 (D) 516; *Potgieter v. Rondalia Assurance Corporation of SA Ltd* 1970 (1) SA 705 (N); *Boswell v. Minister of Police* 1978 (3) SA 268 (E); *Masiba v. Constantia Insurance Co. Ltd* 1982 (4) SA 333 (C); *Silver v. Premier, Gauteng Provincial Government* 1998 (2) SA 643 (T); *Gibson v. Berkowitz* 1997 (1) All SA 99 (W); 1996 (4) SA 1029 (W) 1048–1050. In *Smit v. Abrahams* 1994 (4) SA 1 (A), the 'talem-qualem' rule was applied to a case where the plaintiff, owing to financial inability, was unable to purchase a substitute vehicle but was compelled to hire one.

liability. The first question in such cases is whether the plaintiff has proved on a balance of probabilities that damage was caused by the defendant, and the second question is whether the plaintiff has produced all the evidence reasonably available to him or her at the trial, to enable the court to make an assessment of damages. In *Hersman v. Shapiro & Co*,[1756] Stratford J said in this regard:

> Monetary damage having been suffered, it is necessary for the Court to assess the amount and make the best use it can of the evidence before it. There are cases where the assessment by the Court is very little more than an estimate; but even so, if it is certain that pecuniary damage has been suffered, the Court is bound to award damages. It is not so bound in the case where evidence is available to the plaintiff which he has not produced; in those circumstances the Court is justified in giving, and does give, absolution from the instance. But where the best evidence available has been produced, though it is not entirely of a conclusive character and does not permit of a mathematical calculation of the damages suffered, still, if it is the best evidence available, the Court must use it and arrive at a conclusion based upon it.

832. Provided the plaintiff has adduced the evidence that is reasonably available, the court will in these circumstances assess the damages on an equitable basis.[1757]

§5. Methods of Payment

833. An award of damages is expressed as a sum of money and will usually, although not invariably, be converted into South African currency where the damages are calculable in a foreign currency.[1758] The award of damages takes the form of lump sum; a court will not of its own accord make an order for periodic payments by way of an annuity. However, the parties can agree to payment of damages by way of an annuity, and such an agreed form of payment can be made an order of court. Although the quantification of the award is often done on an annuity basis, particularly for loss of future income and loss of support, the award is for a lump sum.[1759] The annuity method of calculation requires of the court to arrive at a lump

1756. 1926 TPD 367 at 379.

1757. *See Esso Standard SA (Pty) Ltd v. Katz* 1981 (1) SA 964 (A) 969–970; *Turkstra Ltd v. Richards* 1926 TPD 276; *Hersman v. Shapiro & Co.* 1926 TPD 367 379; *Lazarus v. Rand Steam Laundries 1946 (Pty) Ltd* 1952 (3) SA (T) 50H-C 51G; *Mkwanazi v. Van der Merwe and Another* 1970 (1) SA 631B–632H; *Monumental Art Co. v. Kenston Pharmacy (Pty) Ltd* 1976 (2) SA 111 (C) 118A–F.

1758. *Standard Chartered Bank of Canada v. Nedperm Bank Ltd* 1994 (4) SA 747 (A) 774–777; *Radell v. Multilateral Motor Vehicle Accidents Fund* 1995 (4) SA 24 (A) 29; *Elgin Brown & Hamer (Pty) Ltd v. Dampskibsselskabet Torm Ltd* 1988 (4) SA 671 (N); *Skilya Property Investments (Pty) Ltd v. Lloyds of London Underwriting* 2002 (3) SA 765 (T) 815.

1759. *See* M.M. Corbett, *The Quantum of Damages in Bodily and Fatal Injury Cases*, 46–48, 64–66 (4th ed., J.J. Gauntlett ed. 1995).

sum that will, by investment, render to the plaintiff a periodic payment, and the sum arrived at should be such that at the end of the period there would be no capital sum left.[1760]

834. There is provision for periodic payment of compensation under statutory compensation schemes. The Road Accident Fund Act[1761] allows the fund to pay a claim for future expenses arising from injuries in a motor vehicle accident, for example hospital and other medical expenses, after they have been incurred; and also to pay compensation for future loss of income by instalments. Section 17(4) of the Act provides as follows in this regard:

> Where a claim for compensation under subsection (1) –
>
> a. includes a claim for the costs of the future accommodation of any person in a hospital or nursing home or treatment of or rendering of a service or supplying of goods to him or her, the Fund or an agent shall be entitled, after furnishing the third party concerned with an undertaking to that effect or a competent court has directed the Fund or the agent to furnish such undertaking, to compensate the third party in respect of the said costs after the costs have been incurred and on proof thereof;
> b. includes a claim for future loss of income or support, the Fund or an agent shall be entitled, after furnishing the third party in question with an undertaking to that effect or a competent court has directed the Fund or the agent to furnish such undertaking, to pay the amount payable by it or the agent in respect of the said loss, by instalments in arrear as agreed upon.

835. The COIDA[1762] provides for compensation in the form of periodic payments or pension, for example in the case of temporary total or partial disablement;[1763] permanent disablement[1764] and death,[1765] but also for a lump sum in lieu of a pension in certain circumstances.[1766]

1760. *Esso Standard SA (Pty) Ltd v. Katz* 1981 (1) SA 964 (A) 970; *Constantia Versekeringsmpy Bpk v. Victor* 1986 (1) SA 601 (A) 623.
1761. Act 56 of 1996.
1762. Act 130 of 1993.
1763. Section 47(4).
1764. Section 49(4).
1765. Section 54.
1766. *Ibid.*

Chapter 4. Personal Injury and Death

§1. Pecuniary Losses

I. Personal Injury: Medical and Other Expenses

836. Damages for personal injury can include medical and other expenses reasonably incurred as a result of the injury.[1767] Such expenses are special damages and must be specifically alleged and proved, while future expenses need only be proved as a reasonable possibility.[1768] A contingency adjustment is made to account for the possibility that future expenses may not be necessary.[1769] A distinction needs to be drawn between causation and quantification of damages, because the standards of proof are different. The plaintiff must prove a likelihood of some future expenses occurring (causation of damages) on a balance of probabilities. Once it is proven that some expenses are likely to be necessary, the court has to assess the likelihood of specific expenses for purposes of quantification. Allowance is then made for the contingency that the loss might not occur, or that any unforeseen event, such as an earlier than expected death, might intervene. The award will then be reduced by a percentage to allow for such possibility.[1770]

837. Medical expenses reasonably incurred and causally linked to the injury can include hospitalization costs,[1771] costs of post-operative care,[1772] travel expenses,[1773] cost of artificial limbs and paramedical aids,[1774] additional accommodation costs,[1775] the purchase of a motor vehicle,[1776] costs of procuring the services of an attendant or caregiver.[1777]

1767. *Ngubane v. SA Transport Services* 1991 (1) SA 756 (A) 784.
1768. *Ngubane v. SA Transport Services* 1991 (1) SA 756 (A) 785.
1769. *Blyth v. Van den Heever* 1980 (1) SA 191 (A) 225; *Van der Plaats v. SA Mutual Fire & General Insurance Co. Ltd* 1980 (3) SA 105 (A) 113–115; *Erdmann v. Santam Insurance Co. Ltd* 1985 (3) SA 402 (C) 404–405.
1770. *Burger v. Union National South British Insurance Co.* 1975 (4) SA 72 (W) 75; *De Klerk v. Absa Bank Ltd* 2003 (1) All SA 651 (SCA); 2003 (4) SA 315 (SCA) paras 27–28; *Minister van Veiligheid & Sekuriteit v. Geldenhuys* 2003 (4) All SA 330 (SCA), 2004 (1) SA 515 (SCA) para. 41.
1771. *Watt v. Van der Walt* 1947 (2) SA 1216 (W) 1228; *Botha v. Minister of Transport* 1956 (4) SA 375 (W) 376.
1772. *Muller v. Mutual and Federal Insurance Co. Ltd* 1994 (2) SA 425 (C) 437.
1773. *Broom v. The Administrator, Natal* 1966 (3) SA 505 (D) 526.
1774. *Watt v. Van der Walt* 1947 (2) SA 1216 (W) 1228; *Botha v. Minister of Transport* 1956 (4) SA 375 (W) 376; *Ngubane v. SA Transport Services* 1991 (1) SA 756 (A) 783–785; *Blyth v. Van den Heever* 1980 (1) SA 191 (A) 224–227.
1775. *General Accident Versekeringsmaatskappy SA Bpk v. Uijs* 1993 (4) SA 228 (A) 235–238.
1776. *Ngubane v. SA Transport Services* 1991 (1) SA 756 (A) 782–783.
1777. *President Insurance Co. Ltd v. Mathews* 1992 (1) SA 1 (A) 5; *Hendricks v. President Insurance Co. Ltd* 1993 (3) SA 158 (C) 163; *Erdmann v. Santam Insurance Co. Ltd* 1985 (3) SA 402 (C) 404–405.

II. Personal Injury: Loss of Earnings and Earning Capacity

838. Loss of earnings must be causally linked to the plaintiff's injuries, and it must be determined what past and future earnings would have been were it not for the injuries.[1778] The onus is on the plaintiff to produce sufficiently detailed and reliable evidence to prove the lost earnings.[1779]

839. The courts have characterized damages awarded for loss of future earnings as compensation for loss of earning capacity. In *Dippenaar v. Shield Insurance Co. Ltd* the court explained this as follows:[1780]

> In our law, under the *lex Aquilia*, the defendant must make good the difference between the value of the plaintiff's estate after the commission of the delict and the value it would have had if the delict had not been committed. The capacity to earn money is considered to be part of a person's estate and the loss or impairment of that capacity constitutes a loss, if such loss diminishes the estate.

840. The monetary value of loss of earning capacity may be proved in a variety of ways, depending on the facts of each case. Actual income, in terms of a contract of employment effective at the time of the injury, is often used as the measure of the loss of earning capacity.[1781]

841. The loss of income can occur in the form of loss of a salary, commission not earned,[1782] or lost profits.[1783] In the case of a self-employed person with a fluctuating income, it will be more difficult for the plaintiff and the court to determine with precision the extent of the loss.[1784] Compensation for loss of potential earnings not received is subject to an adjustment in respect of tax[1785] and contingencies.[1786] However, because of the principle of currency nominalism, no adjustment is made for inflation in respect of past loss of earnings,[1787] but interest can now be awarded

1778. *SA Eagle Insurance Co. Ltd v. Hartley* 1990 (4) SA 833 (A) 836; *Ngubane v. SA Transport Services* 1991 (1) SA 756 (A) 781; *Minister of Defence v. Jackson* 1991 (4) SA 23 (ZS) 35–36.
1779. *Sigournay v. Gillbanks* 1960 (2) SA 552 (A) 558.
1780. 1979 (2) SA 904 (A) 917: and *see also Santam Versekeringsmaatskappy Bpk v. Byleveldt* 1973 (2) SA 146 (A) 150; *Southern Insurance Association Ltd v. Bailey* 1984 (1) SA 98 (A) 111.
1781. *Dippenaar v. Shield Insurance Co. Ltd* 1979 (2) SA 904 (A) 920.
1782. *Sigournay v. Gillbanks* 1960 (2) SA 552 (A) 559; *Griffiths v. Mutual & Federal Insurance Co. Ltd* 1994 (1) SA 535 (A) 546–547.
1783. *Sandler v. Wholesale Coal Suppliers Ltd* 1941 AD 194; *Transnet Ltd v. Sechaba Photoscan (Pty) Ltd* 2005 (1) SA 299 (SCA) para. 17.
1784. *See* M.M. Corbett, *The Quantum of Damages in Bodily and Fatal Injury Cases*, 39 (4th ed., J.J. Gauntlett ed. 1995).
1785. *Minister of Defence v. Jackson* 1991 (4) SA 23 (ZS) 35–36; *Snyders v. Groenewald* 1966 (3) SA 785 (C) 789C.
1786. *Ngubane v. SA Transport Services* 1991 (1) SA 756 (A) 781–782.
1787. *SA Eagle Insurance Co. Ltd v. Hartley* 1990 (4) SA 833 (A) 841–842.

on past loss of income, in terms of the Prescribed Rate of Interest Act,[1788] as amended in 1997.[1789] Interest will run from the date of demand or service of summons, whichever date is the earlier.[1790]

842. Quantification of the loss of earnings or earning capacity mostly cannot be done with mathematical precision, but an actuarial calculation on an annuity basis is an appropriate guide.[1791] The annuity method of calculation requires of the court to arrive at the present value of the prospective loss.[1792] Damages are awarded as a lump sum that will, by investment, render to the plaintiff a periodic payment, and the sum arrived at should be such that at the end of the period there would be no capital sum left.[1793] The period is computed on the basis of life expectancy. If life expectancy is shorter than the period over which the injured person would have worked, had it not been for the injury, damages are recoverable only for the shortened life expectancy, an approach described by the saying 'there are no wages in heaven'.[1794]

843. The courts have a wide discretion and are not bound to a standard method of calculation. Allowance is made for the contingency that the income might not have been earned, on account of, for example, an earlier than expected death. The award will then be reduced by a percentage to allow for such possibility.[1795] However, contingencies may have a positive or negative impact on the award.[1796]

844. Where the plaintiff has suffered a permanent impairment of earning capacity, the method for assessing loss of future earnings can be summarized as follows: the present value of the future income which the plaintiff would have earned but for the injury and consequent disability is determined, and from it is subtracted the

---

1788. Act 55 of 1975.
1789. By Act 7 of 1997, introducing s. 2A.
1790. *See David Trust v. Aegis Insurance Co. Ltd* 2000 (2) All SA 297 (SCA); 2000 (3) SA 289 (SCA) 303–304; *Van der Berg v. Coopers & Lybrand Trust (Pty) Ltd* 2001 (1) All SA 425 (SCA); 2001 (2) SA 242 (SCA) para. 48; *Adel Builders (Pty) Ltd v. Thompson* 1998 (2) All SA 534 (SE); 1999 (1) SA 680 (SE) 688–692; *Skilya Property Investments (Pty) Ltd v. Lloyds of London Underwriting* 2002 (3) SA 765 (T) 815–816.
1791. *Minister of Defence v. Jackson* 1991 (4) SA 23 (ZS) 30.
1792. *Southern Insurance Association Ltd v. Bailey* 1984 (1) SA 98 (A) 113.
1793. *Esso Standard SA (Pty) Ltd v. Katz* 1981 (1) SA 964 (A) 970; *Constantia Versekeringsmpy Bpk v. Victor* 1986 (1) SA 601 (A) 623; *Goldie v. City Council of Johannesburg* 1948 (2) SA 913 (W) 920; *Gillbanks v. Sigournay* 1959 (2) SA 11 (N) 14–15; *Sigournay v. Gillbanks* 1960 (2) SA 552 (A) 565–571.
1794. *Lockat's Estate v. North British & Mercantile Insurance Co. Ltd* 1959 (3) SA 295 (A).
1795. *Burger v. Union National South British Insurance Co.* 1975 (4) SA 72 (W) 75; *De Klerk v. ABSA Bank Ltd* 2003 (1) All SA 651 (SCA); 2003 (4) SA 315 (SCA) paras 27–28; *Minister van Veiligheid & Sekuriteit v. Geldenhuys* 2003 (4) All SA 330 (SCA), 2004 (1) SA 515 (SCA) para. 41.
1796. *Southern Insurance Association Ltd v. Bailey* 1984 (1) SA 98 (A) 117; *Minister of Defence v. Jackson* 1991 (4) SA 23 (ZS) 34–35; *Ngubane v. SA Transport Services* 1991 (1) SA 756 (A) 781–782; *Van der Plaats v. SA Mutual Fire & General Insurance Co. Ltd* 1980 (3) SA 105 (A) 114–115.

present value of the plaintiff's estimated future income, if any, having regard to the disability. The figure arrived at is then adjusted in the light of all relevant factors and contingencies.[1797]

III. Personal Injury: Illegal Earnings

845. Loss of income from unlawful activity is not recoverable. This rule applies where the income is derived from transactions which are void and unenforceable,[1798] and included in this category are criminal activities, whether morally colourless or not, and any other activity which is contrary to good morals or public policy.[1799] The rule has also been extended to the action of dependants, so that dependants may not claim damages from the defendant if the breadwinner supported them with income from unlawful activities. However, where claims for future losses are concerned, the criterion is loss of earning capacity, which, unlike actual past earnings, cannot be characterized as 'illegal'. Evidence indicating a reasonable possibility that the earning capacity could in the future have been exploited lawfully, is a sufficient basis for an award of damages, even if past earnings were illegal.[1800] Illegal earnings can therefore be relied upon as some indication of earning capacity.[1801] However, in the absence of such evidence the courts have refused to award damages for losses arising from earning income in an illegal manner.[1802] Where the evidence indicates a mere possibility that earning capacity might in future have been put to use lawfully, it could be argued that an appropriate contingency adjustment should be made.[1803]

846. A more flexible approach would also be appropriate for dependants' claims for loss of support, where the support had been provided out of a breadwinner's illegal earnings. The courts have on occasion refused to award any damages to such dependants.[1804] Arguably, an award should in such cases depend on what the deceased could legally have earned, even if it is probable that the deceased would in fact have continued to earn income illegally, because the focus should be on the

1797. M.M. Corbett, *The Quantum of Damages in Bodily and Fatal Injury Cases*, 48–56 (4th ed., J.J. Gauntlett ed. 1995).

1798. *Dhlamini v. Protea Assurance Co. Ltd* 1974 (4) SA 906 (A) 915.

1799. *Ibid*; *Mba v. Southern Insurance Association Ltd* 1981 (1) SA 122 (Tk) 124.

1800. *See Lebona v. President Versekeringsmpy Bpk* 1991 (3) SA 395 (W) 405; *Dhlamini v. Multilaterale Motorvoertuigongelukkefonds* 1992 (1) SA 802 (T) 806, where the evidence indicated what the deceased would have earned in lawful employment.

1801. *Shield Insurance Co. Ltd v. Booysen* 1979 (3) SA 953 (A) 964 965; *Dhlamini v. Multilaterale Motorvoertuigongelukkefonds* 1992 (1) SA 802 (T) 806.

1802. In *Santam Insurance Co. Ltd v. Ferguson* 1985 (4) SA 843 (A) 852, the court noted that there was no factual basis upon which it could determine what income the deceased could have earned lawfully. In *Nkwenteni v. Allianz Insurance Co. Ltd* 1992 (2) SA 713 (Ck) 716, the court said: 'The basis of these decisions is that if the only measure of income earned by a plaintiff is derived from illegal activity, then there is nothing to go on to establish his loss of future earning capacity.'

1803. *See Dhlamini v. Multilaterale Motorvoertuigongelukkefonds* 1992 (1) SA 802 (T) 806–807; *Fortuin v. Commercial Union Assurance Co. of SA Ltd* 1983 (2) SA 444 (C) 446.

1804. *Booysen v. Shield Insurance Co. Ltd* 1980 (3) SA 1211 (SE); *Santam Insurance Ltd v. Ferguson* 1985 (4) SA 843 (A); *Mankebe v. AA Mutual Insurance Association Ltd* 1986 (2) SA 196 (D).

dependants' loss of a right to support. Alternatively, the courts should at least take into account the contingency of lawful future income; a source which was illegal in the past may become legal in future.[1805]

IV. Death: Loss of Support

847. The claim for loss of support arising from the unlawful and negligent or intentional causing of the death of a breadwinner is founded in family law, and the claim was historically restricted to cases where a duty of support derives from a valid marriage, mainly concerning spouses and children. However, the group of claimants has been extended in modern law, to include those whose right to support derives from a relationship akin to marriage, but not constituting a legally valid marriage, for instance 'a solemn marriage in accordance with recognized and accepted faith',[1806] or a same-sex permanent life relationship similar in other respects to marriage,[1807] or a permanent heterosexual life partnership involving a reciprocal duty of support established by tacit agreement[1808] and also the right to support of a divorced person under a court order dealing with maintenance after dissolution of the marriage.[1809]

848. Claims by dependants are limited to patrimonial loss in the form of loss of support and certain expenses, such as for a funeral or tombstone,[1810] and no solatium for loss of companionship or grief can be recovered. The dependants are entitled to be placed in the position they would have been in had the breadwinner not died.[1811]

849. The dependants have to establish that they have suffered patrimonial loss, when both losses and benefits (such as inheritances) are taken into account.[1812] For example, where the deceased's estate generates sufficient income to support the dependents in full, no loss is suffered.[1813] The general principles were formulated as follows in *Victor v. Constantia Insurance Co. Ltd*:[1814]

1805. *Xatula v. Minister of Police, Transkei* 1993 (4) SA 344 (Tk) 348.
1806. *Amod v. MVA Fund* 1999 (4) SA 1319 (SCA).
1807. *Du Plessis v. RAF Fund* 19 Sep. 2003 (SCA).
1808. *Paixão v. Road Accident Fund* [2012] ZASCA 130.
1809. *Santam v. Henery* 1999 (3) SA 421 (SCA).
1810. *Commercial Union Assurance Co. of SA Ltd v. Mirkin* 1989 (2) SA 584 (C). *Hendricks v. President Insurance Co. Ltd* 1993 (3) SA 158 (C).
1811. *Legal Insurance Co. Ltd v. Botes* 1963 (1) SA 608 (A) 614; *Groenewald v. Snyders* 1966 (3) SA 237 (A) 246; *Constantia Versekeringsmpy Bpk v. Victor* 1986 (1) SA 601 (A) 611; *Lambrakis v. Santam Ltd* 2002 (3) SA 710 (SCA) para. 12.
1812. *See Santam Insurance Co. Ltd v. Fourie* 1997 (1) SA 611 (A), where a claim by a husband based on the death of his wife failed, because the deceased in fact earned less than the benefits which she derived from the pooling of her and her husband's income.
1813. *Lambrakis v. Santam Ltd* 2002 (3) SA 710 (SCA) para. 19; and *see Mqolomba v. RAF* 2002 (4) All SA 214 (Tk), where the benefits of a trust fund were taken into account in assessing whether or not harm had been suffered.
1814. 1985 (1) SA 118 (C) 120.

> A dependant's claim is limited to the actual pecuniary loss he has suffered as a result of the death of the person upon whom he was dependent and the measure of his damages is the difference between the dependant's position as a result of the loss of support he has suffered and the position he could reasonably have been expected to be in had the deceased not died. … From such difference there falls to be deducted any financial benefit accruing to the dependant in consequence of the breadwinner's death.

850. The precise mathematical computation of an award for the loss of future support is not possible, as in the case of loss of prospective income, but it is recognized that a calculation upon an annuity basis is an appropriate guide, based on assumptions indicated as reasonable by the available evidence. The accuracy of the calculation of course depends on the soundness of the assumptions, and these may vary from the strongly probable to the speculative.[1815] The purpose of the award is to provide the dependant with a lump sum that will render a periodic income for the period of expected dependency, at the end of which there will be no capital left.

851. The general approach of the courts is to use the annuity basis of calculation as a starting-point and to adjust the figure so obtained in accordance with the general equities of the case. The general approach of the courts to annuity calculations is as follows.[1816] The first issue relevant to the annuity calculation is the period during which the dependant would have received support from the deceased. This period of dependency is computed on the basis of the life expectancy of the deceased breadwinner as at the time of death, taking into account the circumstances relevant to the expected period of dependency, including the life expectancy and a period of dependence of the dependant. The second issue is the net annual income of the deceased over that period. In this regard, the courts make allowance for hazards and uncertainties pertaining to work and employment, including the nature of the work, the possibilities of increases and decreases of income, taxation, inflation, living expenses and expenses involved in producing income. The third issue is how much of the deceased's net income would have been devoted to the support of the dependant. Where the dependants are a surviving spouse and children, a common method of division is to allocate equal shares of the income to each parent and half of such a share to each child. However the division may vary according to the circumstances of the case. Other relevant facts that will be taken into account include benefits accruing to the dependants by reason of the deceased's death; the capacity of the dependant to earn an income; and the possibility and financial implications of marriage or remarriage by the dependant.[1817]

1815. *Lambrakis v. Santam Ltd* 2002 (3) SA 710 (SCA) para. 14.
1816. *See* generally M.M. Corbett, *The Quantum of Damages in Bodily and Fatal Injury Cases*, 64–74 (4th ed., J.J. Gauntlett ed. 1995).
1817. *See* generally *Lambrakis v. Santam Ltd* 2002 (3) SA 710 (SCA); *Legal Insurance Co. Ltd v. Botes* 1963 (1) SA 608 (A); *Groenewald v. Snyders* 1966 (3) SA 237 (A); *Constantia Versekeringsmpy Bpk v. Victor* 1986 (1) SA 601 (A); *Ongevallekommissaris v. Santam Bpk* 1998 (4) All SA 507 (SCA); 1999 (1) SA 251 (SCA).

852. In *Ongevallekommissaris v. Santam Bpk*,[1818] the Supreme Court of Appeal confirmed that in calculating the loss of support of a surviving spouse allowance must be made for the benefits that might accrue from a possible future marriage, but noted that such a marriage will not necessarily restore a person's previous financial position. The real issue is therefore the extent of any financial benefit that might result from a remarriage.[1819]

853. A child's subsequent adoption is not analogous to a woman's remarriage, and has been treated as irrelevant to the child's loss of support as a result of the death of a parent.[1820]

854. In assessing the dependant's loss of support, some benefits which the dependant receives as a result of the death of a breadwinner will be taken into account, but others are considered irrelevant as collateral benefits. Benefits that will be taken into account (deducted) include the following: the proceeds of an insurance policy received as nominated beneficiary under the policy;[1821] and the benefit of receiving an inheritance earlier than would otherwise have been the case (accelerated benefit).[1822] Benefits that will not be taken into account (disregarded) include the division of the joint estate upon the death of the deceased (although, in certain instances, the accelerated benefit of full ownership of assets might be considered a benefit);[1823] the benefit of adoption, in the case of a child;[1824] and a benefit received by a surviving spouse, which does not affect the position of the dependent children;[1825] and insurance money, pension or a benefit which has been or will or may be paid as a result of the death, as provided in the Assessment of Damages Act.[1826]

855. Loss of support which derived from income unlawfully earned by the deceased is not recoverable. This rule applies where the income was derived from transactions which are void and unenforceable,[1827] and included in this category are criminal activities, whether morally colourless or not, and any other activity which is contrary to good morals or public policy.[1828] However, evidence indicating a reasonable possibility that the earning capacity could in the future have been exploited lawfully, is a sufficient basis for an award of damages to dependants, even if past earnings were illegal.[1829] Arguably, a more flexible approach would be appropriate

1818. 1998 (4) All SA 507 (SCA); 1999 (1) SA 251 (SCA).
1819. At 511 (All SA); 258–259 (SA).
1820. *Constantia Versekeringsmpy Bpk v. Victor* 1986 (1) SA 601 (A).
1821. *Groenewald v. Snyders* 1966 (3) SA 237 (A) 246.
1822. *Groenewald v. Snyders* 1966 (3) SA 237 (A) 248; *Lambrakis v. Santam Ltd* 2002 (3) SA 710 (SCA) para. 13.
1823. *Santam Insurance Ltd v. Meredith* 1990 (4) SA 265 (Tk AD) 267.
1824. *Constantia Versekeringsmpy Bpk v. Victor* 1986 (1) SA 601 (A).
1825. *Groenewald v. Snyders* 1966 (3) SA 237 (A).
1826. Act 9 of 1969, ss 1(1) and 1(2).
1827. *Dhlamini v. Protea Assurance Co. Ltd* 1974 (4) SA 906 (A) 915.
1828. *Ibid*; *Mba v. Southern Insurance Association Ltd* 1981 (1) SA 122 (Tk) 124.
1829. *See Lebona v. President Versekeringsmpy Bpk* 1991 (3) SA 395 (W) 405; *Dhlamini v. Multilaterale Motorvoertuigongelukkefonds* 1992 (1) SA 802 (T) 806, where the evidence indicated what the deceased would have earned in lawful employment.

for dependants' claims for loss of support, and an award should in such cases depend on what the deceased could legally have earned, even if it is probable that the deceased would in fact have continued to earn income illegally, because the focus should be on the dependants' loss of a right to support. However, the courts have on occasion refused to award any damages to dependants in such cases.[1830] Alternatively, the courts should at least take into account the contingency of lawful future income; a source which was illegal in the past may become legal in future.[1831]

§2. Non-pecuniary Losses

856. A claim for pain, suffering, shock, disfigurement or loss of amenities as a result of bodily injury is regarded as an extension of the Aquilian action for patrimonial loss. The general approach to such claims was formulated as follows in *Sandler v. Wholesale Coal Suppliers Ltd*:[1832]

> The question now arises whether this Court should increase the amount awarded to the appellant for pain and suffering and permanent disability. In considering that question it must be recognized that though the law attempts to repair the wrong done to a sufferer who has received personal injuries in an accident by compensating him in money, yet there are no scales by which pain and suffering can be measured, and there is no relationship between pain and money which makes it possible to express the one in terms of the other with any approach to certainty. The amount to be awarded as compensation can only be determined by the broadest general considerations and the figure arrived at must necessarily be uncertain, depending upon the judge's view of what is fair in all the circumstances of the case.

857. Pain and suffering include both that experienced at time of injury and subsequent and prospective discomfort, either physical or mental. Facts relevant to the assessment of damages for pain and suffering include the severity and duration of the pain or loss of amenities, even if unremembered; the extent of any disability or disfigurement; the plaintiff's awareness of and response to the injuries, both physically and mentally; whether any pain and suffering will occur in future; the plaintiff's life expectancy; and the plaintiff's erstwhile lifestyle.[1833]

1830. *Booysen v. Shield Insurance Co. Ltd* 1980 (3) SA 1211 (SE); *Santam Insurance Ltd v. Ferguson* 1985 (4) SA 843 (A); *Mankebe v. AA Mutual Insurance Association Ltd* 1986 (2) SA 196 (D).
1831. *Xatula v. Minister of Police, Transkei* 1993 (4) SA 344 (Tk) 348.
1832. 1941 AD 194 199. *See also AA Mutual Insurance Association Ltd v. Maqula* 1978 (1) SA 805 (A) 809.
1833. *Radebe v. Hough* 1949 (1) SA 380 (A) 387; *Botha v. Minister of Transport* 1956 (4) SA 375 (W) 379–380; *Mair v. General Accident Fire & Life Assurance Corporation Ltd* 1970 (3) SA 25 (RA) 26–27; *Van der Plaats v. SA Mutual Fire & General Insurance Co. Ltd* 1980 (3) SA 105 (A) 115–116; *Solomon NNO v. De Waal* 1972 (1) SA 575 (A) 585; *Reyneke v. Mutual & Federal Insurance Co. Ltd* 1991 (3) SA 412 (W) 426; *Gibson v. Berkowitz* 1997 (1) All SA 99 (W) 122–123; 1996 (4) SA 1029 (W) 1055.

858. There are conflicting views on whether or not damages for pain and suffering should be awarded to a person who is unconscious or in a vegetative state. In *Gerke v. Parity Insurance Co. Ltd*,[1834] the court awarded damages, taking into account a certain objective element of harm. In *Reyneke v. Mutual and Federal Insurance Co. Ltd*,[1835] the court took the view that where a victim is fully or partially unconscious, one should distinguish two categories: pain, suffering, mental anguish, fear and anxiety on the one hand; and loss of amenities of life, reduced expectation of life, disfigurement and disability on the other. In the former, category subjective awareness is required, whereas in the latter an objective or functional assessment can be made. In *Collins v. Administrator, Cape*[1836] the court declined to make an award for non-pecuniary loss to a baby who had been in a permanently vegetative state almost from birth, on the grounds that the award would serve no purpose at all, given that she had no awareness of her existence, or of any pain.

859. Emotional distress or nervous shock can be regarded as a form of physical or bodily injury, but special considerations apply, because existence and extent of this type of harm can be difficult to determine, and some limitation must be placed on liability towards victims of accidents who suffer shock as a result of the injury or death of others (often referred to as secondary victims). There is no similar concern for limitation of liability in cases of emotional distress or nervous shock suffered by primary victims of bodily injury.[1837] Liability is imposed only in cases of serious nervous shock, psychiatric injury or post-traumatic stress, and the criterion employed by the courts for limiting liability in such instances is that of the reasonable foreseeability.[1838] The compensation scheme under the Road Accident Fund Act 56 of 1996 does not allow for the recovery of damages for emotional distress or nervous shock. The Act provides that the Road Accident Fund is not liable for 'compensation in respect of loss or damage resulting from emotional shock sustained by a person, other than a third party, when that person witnessed or observed or was informed of the bodily injury or the death of another person as a result of the driving of a motor vehicle'. The claimant must therefore institute a common law action against the negligent driver or owner for loss or harm that results from emotional shock.[1839]

1834. 1966 (3) SA 484 (W).
1835. 1991 (3) SA 412 (W) 426.
1836. 1995 (4) SA 73 (C).
1837. *Gibson v. Berkowitz* 1997 (1) All SA 99 (W) 124–125; 1996 (4) SA 1029 (W).
1838. *See* generally *Bester v. Commercial Union Versekeringsmpy van SA Bpk* 1973 (1) SA 769 (A); *Barnard v. Santam Bpk* 1999 (1) SA 202 (SCA).
1839. Section 21 provides as follows: ' …

1. No claim for compensation in respect of loss or damage resulting from bodily injury to or the death of any person caused by or arising from the driving of a motor vehicle shall lie:
   a. against the owner or driver of a motor vehicle; or
   b. against the employer of the driver.
2. Subsection (1) does not apply:
   a. if the Fund or an agent is unable to pay any compensation; or
   b. to an action for compensation in respect of loss or damage resulting from emotional shock sustained by a person, other than a third party, when that person witnessed or

860. The following factors are relevant to the reasonable foreseeability of emotional distress or nervous shock: The occurrence of ordinary physical injury or the apprehension of such injury;[1840] the threat of damage to property;[1841] a close relationship between the secondary and the primary victim of an accident;[1842] and whether the nervous shock resulted from personal experience and simultaneous sensory perception of the event, or from subsequently being informed about the event.[1843] These factors are not essential requirements, however, and a person may claim damages for nervous shock without having suffered other physical injury, or as a result of being told afterwards of the death of a close relation,[1844] or as a result of witnessing damage to property and the accompanying threat of injury to a child.[1845] Where the nervous shock is caused intentionally, intention will be an overriding factor indicating liability. The principle that 'you take your victim as you find him' applies, and if nervous shock was foreseeable, there will be liability for all the harm, even though such harm was aggravated by a pre-existing condition, such as high blood pressure or hypertension.[1846]

observed or was informed of the bodily injury or the death of another person as a result of the driving of a motor vehicle.'

1840. *Bester v. Commercial Union Versekeringsmpy van SA Bpk* 1973 (1) SA 769 (A).
1841. *Masiba v. Constantia Insurance Co. Ltd* 1982 (4) SA 333 (C).
1842. *Bester v. Commercial Union Versekeringsmpy van SA Bpk* 1973 (1) SA 769 (A); *Road Accident Fund v. Sauls* 2002 (2) SA 55 (SCA).
1843. *Barnard v. Santam Bpk* 1999 (1) SA 202 (SCA).
1844. *Ibid.*
1845. *Masiba v. Constantia Insurance Co. Ltd* 1982 (4) SA 333 (C).
1846. *Ibid*; *Gibson v. Berkowitz* 1997 (1) All SA 99 (W) 124–125; 1996 (4) SA 1029 (W).

Chapter 5. Damage to Property

861. Generally compensation for property damage is assessed according to the reduction in the market value of the property as a result of the damage.[1847] The difference between the pre-damage market value and the post-damage market value of the property usually indicates the extent of the loss.[1848] The cost of repairs will often be an appropriate indicator of such reduction in value, where the repairs were necessary, fair and reasonable, and where the repairs can in fact restore the thing to its prior condition.[1849] Cost of repairs cannot serve as the measure where these exceed the replacement cost or where repairs do not restore the pre-damage value.[1850] The loss of the owner of damaged property may include the cost of hiring a substitute. This cost will be compensated even if the damaged property was not used in the generation of income, but nevertheless reasonably required in the normal course of the owner's personal or family affairs.[1851] Consequential loss reasonably connected to the property damage will also be recoverable.[1852] Losses as a result of damage to a vehicle may include the cost of towing a vehicle to a garage.[1853] Where the property was used for business purposes, damages include compensation for actual lost profits owing to the deprivation of its use, but not for potential profits.[1854]

1847. *Philip Robinson Motors (Pty) Ltd v. NM Dada (Pty) Ltd* 1975 (2) SA 420 (A) 428–429; *Mpisi v. Trebble* 1994 (2) SA 136 (A) 146.
1848. *Erasmus v. Davis* 1969 (2) SA 1 (A) 5 7–8 9 17; *Lazarus v. Rand Steam Laundries (1946) (Pty) Ltd* 1952 (3) SA 49 (T) 51; *Heath v. Le Grange* 1974 (2) SA 262 (C) 263; *Monumental Art Co. v. Kenston Pharmacy (Pty) Ltd* 1976 (2) SA 111 (C) 118; *Botha v. Rondalia Versekeringskorporasie van SA Bpk* 1978 (1) SA 996 (T) 1005.
1849. *Erasmus v. Davis* 1969 (2) SA 1 (A); *Shrog v. Valentine* 1949 (3) SA 1228 (T) 1234–1238; *Botha v. Van Zyl* 1955 (3) SA 310 (SWA) 312; *Heath v. Le Grange* 1974 (2) SA 262 (C) 263–267; *Romansrivier Koöperatiewe Wynkelder Bpk v. Chemserve Manufacturing (Pty) Ltd* 1993 (2) SA 358 (C) 367–368.
1850. *Erasmus v. Davis* 1969 (2) SA 1 (A); *Botha v. Van Zyl* 1955 (3) SA 310 (SWA).
1851. *Shrog v. Valentine* 1949 (3) SA 1228 (T) 1237; *Kellerman v. SA Transport Services* 1993 (4) SA 872 (C); *Zweni v. Modimogale* 1993 (2) SA 192 (B) 195–196; *Smit v. Abrahams* 1994 (4) SA 1 (A) 11–12, 19–20.
1852. *Zweni v. Modimogale* 1993 (2) SA 192 (B) 195.
1853. *Shrog v. Valentine* 1949 (3) SA 1228 (T) 1234, 1237.
1854. *Shrog v. Valentine* 1949 (3) SA 1228 (T) 1237; *Smit v. Abrahams* 1994 (4) SA 1 (A) 11–12.

Chapter 6. Collateral Benefits

862. A damage-causing event may not only cause loss, but may also produce some benefit for plaintiff, for example where the plaintiff's vehicle is damaged, but the loss is made good by an insurance payment. In assessing damages, it must be determined whether a benefit following the damage or loss should be taken into account to reduce the defendant's liability for damages, or should be ignored as a collateral benefit (*res inter alios acta*). No generally satisfactory theory has been developed to determine whether to deduct or disregard benefits flowing from a damage-causing event.[1855] The courts take into account considerations of fairness and justice, and that compensation should not exceed actual loss, but in fact the problem is dealt with from case to case. However, the cases have established precedents in the cases referred to below, and these cases provide practical guidelines.

863. Charitable or ex gratia benefits will be disregarded.[1856] Examples are discretionary medical or sick leave,[1857] and the ex gratia disability benefit under a group life insurance scheme funded by an employer.[1858]

864. Benefits contracted for will generally be regarded as collateral or *res inter alios acta*, and will be disregarded. This includes life insurance and indemnity insurance benefits.[1859] If damage or loss is covered by indemnity insurance, both a delictual action against the wrongdoer and a contractual claim against the insurer will be available. The insured (plaintiff) is then entitled to both the damages recovered from the wrongdoer and the proceeds of the insurance claim. However, in the case of indemnity insurance the insured who has recovered damages equal to or in excess of the insurance payment from the wrongdoer will be obliged in terms of the insurance contract to repay the insurance benefit, to prevent double compensation. Alternatively, where the insured has not claimed damages from the wrongdoer the insurer will be entitled to institute such a claim against the wrongdoer in the name of the insured, without cession of action, in terms of the principle of subrogation. In respect of liability insurance, this principle also entitles the insurer to defend a delictual claim in the name of its insured, so as to limit or exclude liability. The

1855. *See* generally J.C. van der Walt & J.R. Midgley, *Principles of Delict,* paras 156, 232–234 (3rd ed., Butterworths 2005).

1856. *Santam Versekeringsmpy Bpk v. Byleveldt* 1973 (2) SA 146 (A). The following statement in often-cited dictumin *Parry v. Cleaver* 1970 AC 1 at 14 has often been cited:

> It would be revolting to the ordinary man's sense of justice, and therefore contrary to public policy, that the sufferer should have his damages reduced so that he would gain nothing from the benevolence of his friends or relatives or of the public at large, and that the only gainer would be the wrongdoer.

1857. *Gehring v. Unie Nasionaal Suid-Britse Versekeringsmpy Bpk* 1983 (2) SA 266 (C).

1858. *Standard General Insurance Co. Ltd v. Dugmore NO* 1997 (1) SA 33 (A).

1859. *Standard General Insurance Co. Ltd v. Dugmore* 1996 (4) All SA 415 (A) 418–418; 1997 (1) SA 33 (A) 41.

operation of the principle of subrogation is described as follows in *Commercial Union Insurance Company of South Africa Ltd v. Lotter*:[1860]

> It is trite law that an insurer under a contract of indemnity insurance who has satisfied the claim of the insured is entitled to be placed in the insured's position in respect of all rights and remedies against other parties which are vested in the insured in relation to the subject-matter of the insurance. This is by virtue of the doctrine of subrogation, which is part of our common law.

865. The contractual right of an owner-seller of property to claim reinstatement from the purchaser in the event of damage to the property will not be taken into account where the owner claims damages from the wrongdoer.[1861]

866. In the leading case of *Dippenaar v. Shield Insurance Co. Ltd*,[1862] the Appellate Division decided that the benefits flowing from an existing employment contract, such as accelerated pension benefits, should be taken into account in the assessment of loss of earning capacity, where the plaintiff relies on the contract to prove the loss. In such a case, the entire contract should be looked at, and the benefits derived from the contract should be deducted to assess the extent of the loss of earning capacity. Likewise, medical or sick leave or other benefits to which an employee is entitled in terms of an employment contract will be deducted from damages recoverable.[1863] Thus the benefit of receiving medical treatment free of charge in a provincial hospital will not be disregarded when assessing damages for medical costs.[1864]

867. In assessing claims by dependants for loss of support, some benefits resulting from the death of a breadwinner will be taken into account, but others are considered irrelevant as collateral benefits. Benefits that will be taken into account (deducted) include the following: the proceeds of an insurance policy received as nominated beneficiary under the policy;[1865] and the benefit of receiving an inheritance earlier than would otherwise have been the case (accelerated benefit).[1866] Benefits that will not be taken into account (disregarded) include the division of the joint estate upon the death of the deceased (although, in certain instances, the accelerated

1860. 1999 (2) SA 147 (SCA) 154. *See also Ackerman v. Loubser* 1918 OPD 31; *Teper v. McGees Motors (Pty) Ltd* 1956 (1) SA 738 (C); and *Avex Air (Pty) Ltd v. Borough of Vryheid* 1973 (1) SA 617 (A) at 625H.

1861. *Botha v. Rondalia Versekeringskorporasie van SA Bpk* 1978 (1) SA 996 (T) 1001; and *see also Joubert v. Santam Versekeringsmpy Bpk* 1978 (3) SA 328 (T) 332.

1862. 1979 (2) SA 904 (A) 917: and *see also Santam Versekeringsmaatskappy Bpk v. Byleveldt* 1973 (2) SA 146 (A) 150; *Southern Insurance Association Ltd v. Bailey* 1984 (1) SA 98 (A) 111.

1863. *Serumela v. SA Eagle Insurance Co. Ltd* 1981 (1) SA 391 (T); *Krugell v. Shield Versekeringsmpy Bpk* 1982 (4) SA 95 (T); *Mutual & Federal Insurance Co. Ltd v. Swanepoel* 1988 (2) SA 1 (A) 8–9.

1864. *Free State Consolidated Gold Mines Ltd v. Multilateral Motor Vehicle Fund* 1997(4) SA 930 (O).

1865. *Groenewald v. Snyders* 1966 (3) SA 237 (A) 246.

1866. *Groenewald v. Snyders* 1966 (3) SA 237 (A) 248; *Lambrakis v. Santam Ltd* 2002 (3) SA 710 (SCA) para. 13.

benefit of full ownership of assets might be considered a benefit);[1867] the benefit of adoption, in the case of a child;[1868] and a benefit received by a surviving spouse, which does not affect the position of the dependent children;[1869] and insurance money, pension or a benefit which has been or will or may be paid as a result of the death, as provided in the Assessment of Damages Act.[1870]

868. Whether benefits are deducted or disregarded may depend on specific statutory provisions. The COIDA[1871] provides that if an occupational injury or disease in respect of which compensation is payable was caused in circumstances resulting in some person other than the employer of the employee concerned (the 'third party') being liable for damages, the employee who is entitled to compensation in terms of this Act may also claim damages from the third party; and the Director-General or the employer by whom compensation is payable may also claim from the third party for recovery of compensation payable in terms of the Act. In awarding damages in an action against the third party, the court shall have regard to the compensation paid in terms of this Act.[1872] The effect of this provision is that the 'third party' (the wrongdoer) is liable for the total monetary amount recoverable as damages under common law, this total being made up by the compensation payable under the Act (which must be repaid to the Director-General) and the balance of damages recoverable under common law (which must be paid to the employee).

1867. *Santam Insurance Ltd v. Meredith* 1990 (4) SA 265 (Tk AD) 267.
1868. *Constantia Versekeringsmpy Bpk v. Victor* 1986 (1) SA 601 (A).
1869. *Groenewald v. Snyders* 1966 (3) SA 237 (A).
1870. Act 9 of 1969, ss 1(1) and 1(2).
1871. Act 130 of 1993.
1872. Section 36(1) and (2) of the Act; and *see RAF v. Maphiri* 2004 (2) SA 258 (SCA).

Chapter 7. Other Remedies

§1. Restitution

869. There is no general restitutional remedy in the South African law of delict – damage or loss is generally compensated for by an order to pay damages. However, in the case of unlawful dispossession of property a spoliation order, or mandament van spolie, can be obtained.[1873] The mandament van spolie is a remedy that derives from Roman-Dutch law, with roots in canon law.[1874]

870. The spoliation order or mandament van spolie is available where a person has been deprived unlawfully of the whole or part of his possession of movable or immovable property.[1875] The underlying principle is that a person who has been deprived of his possession must first be restored to his former position before the merits of the case can be considered, as indicated by the maxim spoliatus ante omnia restituendus est. The main purpose of the remedy is to preserve public order by restraining persons from taking the law into their own hands and by inducing them to submit the matter to the jurisdiction of the courts.[1876]

871. It has been accepted in South African law that any person who exercises physical control over a thing with the intention of deriving some benefit from it (*animus ex re commodum acquirendi*) is in principle entitled to the mandament van spolie, even against the owner of the thing.[1877]

872. The application or motion procedure can be used, instead of the more cumbersome action procedure, and the person who has been deprived of possession will apply to court for a spoliation order directing the respondent to return the thing to him immediately. The respondent will then be served with a rule nisi ordering him to give reasons why he should not be ordered to restore possession at a particular date. Such an order can also contain an interim interdict restraining the respondent from alienating the thing. If the applicant can prove on the return date that he was in peaceful possession of the thing, and that he has been deprived of his possession the order will be made final; if not, the rule nisi lapses.[1878]

873. To obtain a *mandament van spolie*, the applicant must show that he or she was in peaceful and undisturbed possession of the thing; and he or she was unlawfully deprived of such possession.[1879] The respondent can resist the application by raising any of the following defences:[1880]

1873. *See* generally C.G. van der Merwe, THINGS, in LAWSA vol. 27, paras 263–277.
1874. *Ibid.*, at para. 263.
1875. C.G. van der Merwe, THINGS, in LAWSA vol. 27, para. 264.
1876. *Ibid.*, at para. 265.
1877. *Ibid.*, para. 266.
1878. *Ibid.*, para. 267.
1879. *Ibid.*, para. 269.
1880. *Ibid.*, at para. 270.

(a) that the applicant was not in peaceful and undisturbed possession of the thing in question at the time of dispossession;
(b) that the dispossession was not unlawful and therefore did not constitute spoliation;
(c) that restoration of possession is impossible; or
(d) that the respondent acted within the limits of counter-spoliation in regaining possession of the article.

The defence that restoration of possession is impossible is only valid where it is objectively impossible to restore possession of the spoliated thing, and in such a case the applicant will have to look to other remedies. Although the courts differ as to when restoration is actually impossible, the weight of authority supports the view that the *mandament van spolie* will not succeed where the spoliated thing has been destroyed, materially damaged, or alienated to a bona fide third party.[1881]

The respondent cannot raise the defence of a better title to the possession of the thing than the applicant (the so-called defence on the merits of the case) – the *status quo ante* must first be restored before the merits will be adjudicated.[1882]

874. If the applicant succeeds, the respondent must restore the *status quo ante* by restoring the property to the state it was at the time of the spoliation. This does not merely entail the return of the spoliated property to the applicant, but also the restoration of the property to its previous state. The respondent will be ordered, for example, to rebuild a fence, to reconnect a spoliated electrical panel to the electricity supply, to restore the ceiling of a house, or to rebuild the wall of a storeroom that has been knocked down.[1883] In *Fredericks v. Stellenbosch Divisional Council*,[1884] where the applicants' huts were unlawfully demolished and the building materials removed by the respondent council, the court not only ordered the return of the materials, but also the re-erection of the huts.

875. The *mandament van spolie* must be instituted within a reasonable time, and in practice this has been interpreted to mean that a *mandament van spolie* should be allowed within a year after spoliation has taken place. If an application is brought later than a year after spoliation has taken place, the applicant will have to show special circumstances to allow him to proceed with the application.[1885]

876. As in any other claim, an order as to costs is normally given against the unsuccessful party, but the order as to costs is in the discretion of the court.[1886]

1881. *Ibid.*, at para. 271.
1882. *Ibid.*, at para. 277.
1883. *Ibid.*, para. 273.
1884. 1977 (3) SA 113 (C).
1885. C.G. van der Merwe, THINGS, in LAWSA vol. 27, para. 276.
1886. *Ibid*, para. 277.

§2. RETRACTION, APOLOGY

877. Traces of a remedy involving retraction or apology remain, where the infringement of personality rights is concerned. In Roman-Dutch law, the *actio iniuriarum* appears to have split into two remedies, the *amende honorable* and the *amende profitable*.[1887] The *amende profitable* provided a claim for damages, as in the modern law.[1888] The *amende honorable*, which enabled the plaintiff to claim that the defendant should withdraw hurtful words and deny their truth, or admit guilt and request forgiveness, has fallen into disuse.[1889] In practice, this means that the plaintiff can no longer claim an apology, as in Roman-Dutch law, and courts are unable to order that an apology be published, even where this appears to be the most appropriate remedy.[1890] It follows that a contrite defendant also cannot raise an apology and retraction as a defence to a claim for damages. However, such an apology is likely to be regarded as a mitigating factor, resulting in a lesser award of damages.[1891]

878. In *Mineworkers Investment Co. (Pty) Ltd v. Modibane*,[1892] the court held that the remedy of retraction or apology, although no longer current, has not been abrogated by disuse, and found that the *amende honorable* remains part of the South African law.[1893] The court held that even if this was an incorrect conclusion, it was desirable to formulate innovative remedies, tailored to the needs of a particular case, provided that they are fair and balanced:[1894]

> Even if the *amende honorable* had never existed, the imperatives of our times would have required its invention. … [I]t is entirely consonant with 'the spirit, purport and objects' of the Bill of Rights in our Constitution that a person who has committed a wrongful act by defaming another should, in suitable circumstances, be given an opportunity to make an appropriate public apology in *lieu* of paying damages; and, no less importantly, that the victim of a defamation should similarly have the opportunity of having a damaged reputation restored by the remedy of a public apology.

879. The lack of a recognized procedure for retraction and apology is a shortcoming in the law, even though such a remedy is clearly not suitable and adequate

1887. *See Mineworkers Investment Co. (Pty) Ltd v. Modibane* 2002 (6) SA 512 (W) paras 17ff.
1888. *Van Zyl v. African Theatres Ltd* 1931 CPD 61 65; *Maisel v. Van Naeren* 1960 (4) SA 836 (C) 840.
1889. *Hare v. White* (1865) 1 Roscoe 246 247 250; *Lumley v. Owen* (1882) 3 NLR 185 186; *Ward-Jackson v. Cape Times Ltd* 1910 WLD 257 263.
1890. *Kritzinger v. Perskorporasie van SA (Edms) Bpk* 1981 (2) SA 373 (O) 389; *Mineworkers Investment Co. (Pty) Ltd v. Modibane* 2002 (6) SA 512 (W) para. 25.
1891. *Norton v. Ginsberg* 1953 (4) SA 537 (A) 540 550; *Kidson v. SA Associated Newspapers Ltd* 1957 (3) SA 461 (W); *SA Associated Newspapers Ltd v. Samuels* 1980 (1) SA 24 (A) 41; *Smith v. Die Republikein (Edms) Bpk* 1989 (3) SA 872 (SWA) 878–879.
1892. 2002 (6) SA 512 (W) para. 25.
1893. Paragraph 24.
1894. Paragraph 28.

in all cases of infringement of personality rights. To be adequate, an apology should involve both a retraction and an expression of regret. In *Ward-Jackson v. Cape Times Ltd*,[1895] the court said:

> [T]he essence of an apology is that it should not only contain an unreserved withdrawal of all imputations made, but that it should also contain an expression of regret that they were ever made. Where there is no unreserved withdrawal of imputations and no expression of regret, a mere retraction cannot be called a full and free apology.

880. For an apology to be effective, the following elements are likely to be required: An admission of liability is not necessary and the apology may be stated in hypothetical terms, but it should be a comprehensive apology; it should be given prominence and publicity that is equal to that of the offending words or conduct; and it should be made within a reasonable time.

§3. Interdicts (Injunctive Relief)

881. The most common remedies available under the modern law of delict are damages and an interdict to prevent or to stop the unlawful causing of harm.

882. An interdict is an order of court restraining a person from the threatened unlawful causing of harm or from the continued unlawful causing of harm. The order can take the form of a prohibition or a mandate. A prohibitory order instructs a person to abstain from the threatened unlawful causing of harm, or from the continued unlawful causing of harm, whereas a mandatory order instructs a person to act positively to redress a state of affairs created by the unlawful causing of harm, as in the case of a spoliation order instructing the respondent, for example, to re-erect dwellings which have been unlawfully demolished.[1896]

883. The interdict has a preventative function, so that a person who is about to suffer injury is not compelled to wait for the harm to occur and claim damages afterwards, but may take steps to prevent the harm from occurring. However, such preventative action is not always appropriate, for instance where it involves prior restraint of the constitutional right of free speech, in particular where it concerns free and fair political activity,[1897] or restraint of the constitutional right of freedom of assembly.[1898]

1895. 1910 WLD 257 263.
1896. *Fredericks v. Stellenbosch Divisional Council* 1977 (3) SA 113 (C); and *see* the preceding section on spoliation.
1897. *Diepsloot Residents & Landowners Association v. Administrator, Tvl* 1993 (1) SA 577 (T) 578; *Mandela v. Falati* 1994 (4) BCLR 1 (W); 1995 (1) SA 251 (W) 259–260.
1898. *Minister of Law & Order, Bophuthatswana v. Committee of the Church Summit of Bophuthatswana* 1994 (3) SA 89 (B) 100–101.

884. An interdict can be either final or temporary. A temporary (or interim) interdict operates pendente lite, pending an action between the respective parties. An interim interdict protects a right until it is established in the main action whether final relief should be granted.[1899] A final or permanent interdict unconditionally and permanently prohibits the unlawful causing of harm by the respondent. A final interdict may be granted in motion proceedings if the facts in issue are not in dispute; otherwise, an action must be instituted.[1900]

885. The basic requirements for the granting of a final interdict are the following: some conduct on the part of the respondent; a clear right on the part of the applicant; the actual or threatened infringement of the applicant's right; and the absence of another appropriate remedy, so that irreparable harm for the applicant may ensue.[1901] These are also the requirements for an interim interdict, but for an interim interdict there is the additional requirement that the balance of convenience must favour the granting of the interdict.[1902] As a delictual remedy, the interdict requires the actual or threatened unlawful causing of harm to the plaintiff. Fault on the part of the respondent, in the form of either intent or negligence, is not a requirement.[1903]

886. The conduct by the respondent can be either positive action or an omission, which is either actually taking place or reasonably apprehended to occur in future.[1904] The following explanation of the meaning of 'reasonable apprehension' has been approved by the Appellate Division:[1905]

> A reasonable apprehension of injury has been held to be one which a reasonable man might entertain on being faced with certain facts. The applicant for an interdict is not required to establish that, on a balance of probabilities flowing from the undisputed facts, injury will follow: he has only to show that it is reasonable to apprehend that injury will result. However, the test for apprehension is an objective one. This means that, on the basis of the facts presented to

1899. *Fourie v. Uys* 1957(2) SA 125 (C) 127F.
1900. *Prinsloo v. Shaw* 1938 AD 570; *Hilleke v. Levy* 1946 AD 214.
1901. *Setlogelo v. Setlogelo* 1914 AD 221; *Minister of Law & Order, Bophuthatswana v. Committee of the Church Summit of Bophuthatswana* 1994 (3) SA 89 (B) 89 98; *Sanachem (Pty) Ltd v. Farmers Agri-Care (Pty) Ltd* 1995 (2) SA 781 (A) 789.
1902. *Transkei v. JALC Holdings (SA) (Pty) Ltd* 1991 (4) SA 646 (Tk) 648; *Knox D'Arcy Ltd v. Jamieson* 1995 (2) SA 579 (W) 592–593.
1903. *Setlogelo v. Setlogelo* 1914 AD 221 227; *Free State Gold Areas Ltd v. Merriespruit (OFS)Gold Mining Co. Ltd* 1961 (2) SA 505 (W); *Regal v. African Superslate (Pty) Ltd* 1963 (1) SA 102 (A); *Hawker v. Life Offices Association of SA* 1987 (3) SA 777 (C) 780; *Elida Gibbs (Pty) Ltd v. Colgate-Palmolive (Pty) Ltd (1)* 1988 (2) SA 350 (W) 353; *R & I Laboratories (Pty) Ltd v. Beauty Without Cruelty International (SA Branch)* 1990 (3) SA 746 (C) 753–755.
1904. *Regal v. African Superslate (Pty) Ltd* 1963 (1) SA 102 (A); *Liss Shoe Co. (Pty) Ltd v. Moffett Building & Contracting (Pty) Ltd* 1952 (3) SA 484 (O); *Condé Nast Publications Ltd v. Jaffe* 1951 (1) SA 81 (C); *Performing Right Society Ltd v. Berman* 1966 (2) SA 355 (R); *Stern & Ruskin v. Appelson* 1951 (3) SA 800 (W); *Elida Gibbs (Pty) Ltd v. Colgate-Palmolive (Pty) Ltd (1)* 1988 (2) SA 350 (W) 353.
1905. *Minister of Law & Order v. Nordien* 1987 (2) SA 894 (A) 896G–H.

him, the Judge must decide whether there is any basis for the entertainment of a reasonable apprehension by the applicant.

887. The conduct must be harmful to the applicant by infringement or threatened infringement of a right.[1906] The applicant must have a clear right, so that the infringement is clearly unlawful, in accordance with the principles for determining unlawfulness in the law of delict.[1907] There must be no other appropriate remedy available, or, as often said, the infringement must involve irreparable harm to the applicant.[1908]

888. The requirements for an interdict are not considered in isolation, but in the context of the case as a whole. The stronger the right established by the applicant, the less strict the court will be in the assessment of the other requirements.[1909]

889. As far as the proof required is concerned, a final interdict will be granted only if the applicant can prove a clear right on a balance of probabilities.[1910] For temporary interdicts, providing only temporary relief, the courts accept a lesser degree of proof. The requirement for an interim interdict is that the applicant must have established a prima facie right, even if there is still some doubt.[1911] The test for establishing a prima facie right for the purposes of an interim interdict has been formulated as follows:[1912]

> The accepted test for a prima facie right in the context of an interim interdict is to take the facts averred by the applicant, together with such facts set out by the respondent that are not or cannot be disputed and to consider whether, having regard to the inherent probabilities, the applicant should on those facts obtain final relief at the trial. The facts set up in contradiction by the respondent should then be considered and, if serious doubt is thrown upon the case of the applicant, he cannot succeed.

1906. *Setlogelo v. Setlogelo* 1914 AD 221 227; *Prinsloo v. Shaw* 1938 AD 570.
1907. *Ibid*; *Hilleke v. Levy* 1946 AD 214 218; *Swanepoel v. Botha* 1951 (3) SA 853 (T) 861; *Welkom Bottling Co. (Pty) Ltd v. Belfast Mineral Waters (OFS) (Pty) Ltd* 1967 (3) SA 45 (O) 56–57; *Erasmus v. Afrikander Pty Mines Ltd* 1976 (1) SA 950 (W); *Simonlanga v. Masinga* 1976 (2) SA 732 (W); *Harchris Heat Treatment (Pty) Ltd v. Iscor* 1983 (1) SA 548 (T) 554; *Aetiology Today CC t/a Somerset Schools v. Van Aswegen* 1992 (1) SA 807 (W) 816–821.
1908. *Celliers v. Lehfeldt* 1921 AD 509; *Ebrahim v. Twala* 1951 (2) SA 490 (W); *Free State Gold Areas Ltd v. Merriespruit (OFS) Gold Mining Co. Ltd* 1961 (2) SA 505 (W); *Lubbe v. Die Administrateur, OVS* 1968 (1) SA 111 (O); *Erasmus v. Afrikander Pty Mines Ltd* 1976 (1) SA 950 (W); *Bristow v. Coleman* 1976 (2) SA 252 (R).
1909. *Eriksen Motors (Welkom) Ltd v. Protea Motors, Warrenton and Another* 1973 (3) SA 685 (A) 691F.
1910. *Nienaber v. Stuckey* 1946 AD 1049 1053–1054.
1911. *Webster v. Mitchell* 1948 (1) SA 1186 (W) 1189; *Gool v. Minister of Justice and Another* 1955 (2) SA 682 (C) 688A-E; *LF Boshoff Investments (Pty) Ltd v. Cape Town Municipality, Cape Town Municipality v. LF Boshoff Investments (Pty) Ltd* 1969 (2) SA 256 (C) 267 E-F; *Simon NO v. Air Operations of Europe AB and Others* 1999 (1) SA 217 (SCA) 228G-I.
1912. *Simon NO v. Air Operations of Europe AB and Others* 1999 (1) SA 217 (SCA) 228G-I; and *see also Webster v. Mitchell* 1948 (1) SA 1186 (W) 1189.

890. For the purposes of an interim interdict, the court will assess the possible prejudice to the parties and exercise its discretion to grant or refuse an interdict on the balance of convenience.[1913] If the refusal of an interim interdict would have the effect of depriving the applicant of the rights that are sought to be protected, the court should exercise its discretion to grant the interdict.[1914]

§4. Punitive Damages

891. In *Fose v. Minister of Safety and Security*,[1915] the Constitutional Court has noted serious doubt as to the awarding of punitive damages in the law of delict:

> Serious judicial doubts have been expressed concerning, and considerable academic criticism levelled against, the award of punitive damages in delictual claims. Prof Van der Walt, whose views are broadly representative of academic criticism generally, expresses his misgivings succinctly as follows:
>
> The historically anomaly of awarding additional sentimental damages as a penalty for outrageous conduct on the part of the defendant is not justifiable in a modern system of law. The basic purpose of a civil action in delict is to compensate the victim for the actual harm done. In the case of impairment of personality by wrongful conduct it may be difficult to determine the amount of *solatium* which will confer personal satisfaction or compensation for the injury, but in principle all factors and circumstances tending to introduce penal features should be rigorously excluded from such an assessment. The aim of discouraging evil and high-handed conduct is foreign to the basic purposes of the law of delict. It is for criminal law to punish and thereby discourage such conduct. The policy of awarding punitive damages unduly enriches the plaintiff who is entitled only to compensation for loss suffered. This policy has the added disadvantage of putting a wrongdoer in jeopardy of being punished twice – in the civil proceedings and in the criminal proceedings which could conceivably follow or which have preceded the civil action.

892. Similar statements are made in the judgment in *Dikoko v. Mokhatla*:[1916]

> Even if a compensatory award may have a deterrent effect, its purpose is not to punish. Clearly, punishment and deterrence are functions of the criminal law. Not the law of delict. In our law a damages award therefore does not serve to punish for the act of defamation. It principally aims to serve as compensation

---

1913. *Webster v. Mitchell* 1948 (1) SA 1186 (W) 1192–1193.
1914. *Candid Electronics (Pty) Ltd v. Merchandise Buying Syndicate (Pty) Ltd* 1992 (2) SA 459 (C) 463E–465D; *v.& A Waterfront Properties (Pty) Ltd and Another v. Helicopter & Marine Services (Pty) Ltd and Others* 2006 (1) SA 252 (SCA) 258C.
1915. 1997 (3) SA 786 (CC) para. 63.
1916. [2006] JOL 18035 (CC) paras 75–76.

for damage caused by the defamation, vindicating the victim's dignity, reputation and integrity. Alternatively, it serves to console.

893. The modern delictual actions have not retained their erstwhile punitive characteristics.[1917] This is also true of the *actio iniuriarum*, which in the more recent past appears to have retained a punitive element.[1918] If there is malice or other aggravating circumstances,[1919] a larger award (solatium) or 'aggravated damages' is appropriate under the *actio iniuriarum*, to provide appropriate solace to the plaintiff.[1920] The focus should be on the plaintiff's feelings, not on meting out retribution to the defendant.

894. The modern South African law of delict therefore does not provide for the award of punitive damages.

1917. *Collins v. Administrator, Cape* 1995 (4) SA 73 (C) 93–94, where the court confirmed that the neither the Aquilian action nor the action for pain and suffering is punitive. The purpose is compensatory, and there is no basis in South African law for a nominal award to an unconscious victim, to reflect society's demand that some retribution be made for the injustice done to the plaintiff, or to express society's sympathy with the victim and its sense of outrage at his grievous loss, or to serve as a symbolic reparation of the damage and to soothe the community. Such an award would mean an import into the modern delictual action of a penal element for which there can be no justification.

1918. *Salzmann v. Holmes* 1914 AD 471 483; *Manamela v. Minister of Justice* 1960 (2) SA 395 (A) 401; *Gelb v. Hawkins* 1960 (3) SA 687 (A) 693; *SA Associated Newspapers Ltd v. Yutar* 1969 (2) SA 442 (A) 458.

1919. *See*, for example, *Kahn v. Kahn* 1971 (2) SA 499 (RA) 501–502.

1920. *Whittaker v. Roos & Bateman*; *Morant v. Roos & Bateman* 1912 AD 92 118 125; *Manamela v. Minister of Justice* 1960 (2) SA 395 (A) 401; *Fose v. Minister of Safety & Security* 1997 (3) SA 786 (CC) para. 62.

Selected Bibliography

Boberg, P.Q.R. *The Law of Delict Vol. 1: Aquilian Liability*. Cape Town: Juta, 1984.

Boberg, P.Q.R. 'Oak Tree or Acorn? Conflicting Approaches to Our Law of Delict'. *SALJ* 83 (1966): 150.

Boberg, P.Q.R. 'The Role of Fault in Determining the Lawfulness of Competition'. *THRHR* 54 (1991): 43.

Bruggemeier, G. 'Common Principles of Tort Law A Pre-Statement of Law'. *British Institute of International and Comparative Law* (2004).

Burchell, J.M. *The Law of Defamation in South Africa.* Cape Town: Juta, 1985.

Burchell, J. 'Media Freedom of Expression Scores as Strict Liability Receives the Red Card: National Media v Bogoshi'. *SALJ* 116 (1999): 1.

Burchell, J. *Personality Rights and Freedom of Expression: The Modern Actio Injuriarum.* Kenwyn: Juta, 1998.

Cameron, E. 'Legal Chauvinism, Executive-Mindedness and Justice – LC Steyn's Impact on South African Law'. *SALJ* 99 (1982): 38.

Corbett, M.M. 'Aspects of the Role of Policy in the Evolution of Our Common Law'. *SALJ* 104 (1987): 52.

Corbett, M.M. 'The Quantum of Damages in Bodily and Fatal Injury Cases'. 4th edn, edited by J.J. Gauntlett. Cape Town: Juta, 1995.

Currie, I. & De Waal, J. *The Bill of Rights Handbook*, 5th ed. Cape Town: Juta, 2005.

Dean, O.H. 'Intellectual Property and Comparative Advertising'. *Stell LR* 1 (1996): 25.

De Villiers, M. *The Roman and Roman-Dutch Law of Injuries: A Translation of Book 47, Title 10 of Voet's Commentary on the Pandects.* Cape Town: Juta, 1899.

European Group on Tort Law: Principles of European Tort Law Text and Commentary. Springer Verlag Wien, 2005.

Fairgrieve D, Andenas, M. & Bell, J. (eds). *Tort Liability of Public Authorities in Comparative Perspective.* London: The British Institute of International and Comparative Law, 2002.

Fagan, A. 'Rethinking Wrongfulness in the Law of Delict', *SALJ* 122 (2005): 90, *Africa* Oxford: Clarendon Press (1996) 399.

Galligan, T.C. Jr. 'Contortions along the Boundary Between Contracts and Torts', *Tulane Law Review* 69 (1994): 457.

Grobbelaar, C-G. *'n Regsvergelykende studie na die regmatigheid van paralelle invoere, getoets aan die beginsels van handelsmerkereg, outeursreg en mededingingsreg.* unpublished LLM thesis, University of Stellenbosch (1998).

Hart, H.L.A. & Honore, T. *Causation in the Law.* 2nd edn. Oxford: Clarendon Press, 1985.
Heuston, R.F.V. & Buckley, R.A. (eds). *Salmond and Heuston on the Law of Torts.* 21st edn. London: Sweet and Maxwell, 1966.
Horton Rogers, W.V. 'Wrongfulness under English Tort Law'. In *Unification of Tort Law: Wrongfulness,* edited by Helmut Koziol. Kluwer Law International, 1998.
Hosten, W.J. 'Kodifikasie in Suid-Afrika –'n Heroorweging'. *Huldigingsbundel vir WA Joubert* (1968): 59.
Hutchison, D. 'Relational Economic Loss (or Interference with Contractual Relations): The Last Hurdle'. In *Developing Delict: Essays in Honour of Robert Feenstra,* edited by Scott, T.J. & Visser, D. Lansdowne: Juta, 2000, 133 (First published as *Acta Juridica* 2000, Cape Town: Juta).
Hutchison, D. 'Aquilian Liability II'. In *Southern Cross: Civil Law and Common Law in South Africa,* edited by Zimmermann, R. & Visser, D. Cape Town: Juta, 1996, 627.
Joubert, W.A. *Grondslae van die Persoonlikheidsreg.* unpublished LLD thesis, University of Stellenbosch (1950).
Keeton, W.P. (ed.). *Prosser and Keeton on the Law of Torts.* 5th edn. St Paul, Minn.: West, 1984.
Kötz, H. & Wagner, G. *Deliktsrecht,* 10th edn., 2006.
LAWSA Joubert, W.A. (founding ed) *The Law of South Africa* (and reissues).
Lawson, F.H. & Markesinis, B.S. *Tortious Liability for Unintentional Harm in the Common Law and Civil Law,* vol 1. Cambridge University Press, 1982.
Loubser, M. & Midgley, R. (eds), with Phumelele Jabavu; James Linscott; André Mukheibir; Liezel Niesing; Devina Perumal; Priya P. Singh; Bernard Wessels. *The Law of Delict in South Africa.* 3rd ed., Cape Town: Oxford University Press, 2017.
Loubser, M.M. 'Principles and Policy in Unlawful Competition: An Aquilian Mask?'. In *Developing Delict: Essays in Honour of Robert Feenstra,* edited by Scott, T.J. & Visser, D. Lansdowne: Juta, 2000, 168 (First published as *Acta Juridica* 2000, Cape Town: Juta).
Loubser, M.M. *Extinctive Prescription.* Kenwyn: Juta, 1996.
Loubser, M.M. 'Concurrence of Contract and Delict'. *Stell LR* 2 (1997): 146.
Loubser, M. & Reid, E. 'Strict Liability'. In *Mixed Legal Systems in Comparative Perspective: Property and Obligations in Scotland and South Africa,* edited by Zimmermann, R., Visser, D. & Reid, K. Oxford: Oxford University Press, 2004, 605.
Lunney, M. & Oliphant, K. *Tort Law Text and Materials.* 2nd ed. Oxford University Press, 2003.
Markesinis, B.S. & Deakin, S.F. *Tort Law.* 3rd edn. Oxford: Clarendon Press, 1994.
McKerron, R.G. *The Law of Delict: A Treatise on the Principles of Liability for Civil Wrongs in the Law of South Africa.* 7th edn. Cape Town: Juta, 1971.
McQuoid-Mason, D.J. 'Invasion of Privacy: Common Law v. Constitutional Delict – Does it Make a Difference?'. *Acta Juridica* (2000): 227.
McQuoid-Mason, D.J. *The Law of Privacy in South Africa.* Kenwyn: Juta, 1978.
McQuoid-Mason, D.J. 'Privacy'. In *Constitutional Law of South Africa,* edited by Chaskalson, M., et al. Cape Town: Juta, 1996, 18–11.

Midgley, J.R. 'The Role of Foreseeability in Psychiatric Injury Cases'. *THRHR* 55 (1992): 441.
Midgley, J.R. 'Fault under the *actio iniuriarum*: Custer's Last Stand?'. In *Vita Perit, Labor non Moritur: Liber Memorialis PJ Visser, edited by* Boezaart, T. & De Kock, P. Durban: LexisNexis Butterworths, 2009, 187.
Midgley, J.R. 'Intention Remains the Fault Criterion under the *actio injuriarum*'. *SALJ* 118 (2001): 433.
Midgley, J.R. *Lawyers' Professional Liability.* Cape Town: Juta (1992).
Midgley, J.R. 'Media Liability for Defamation'. *SALJ* 116 (1999): 211.
Midgley, J.R. 'The Nature of the Inquiry into Concurrence of Actions'. *SALJ* 107 (1990): 621.
Midgley, J.R. 'Revisiting Factual Causation'. In *Essays in Honour of AJ Kerr, edited by* Glover, G.B. Durban: LexisNexis, 2006, 277.
Mostert, F. 'Aanleuning: skending van 'n handelsmerk en die reg op werfkrag buite mededingingsverband'. *THRHR* 49 (1986): 173.
Mostert, F. 'The Right to the Advertising Image'. *SALJ* 99 (1982): 413.
Mukheiber, A. 'Comparing the Casuistry of Compensating Advantages and Collateral Sources'. *Obiter* 23 (2002): 328.
Neethling, J. 'The Conflation of Wrongfulness and Negligence: Is It Always Such a Bad Thing for the Law of Delict?'. *SALJ* 123 (2006): 204.
Neethling, J. 'Misappropriation or Copying of a Rival's Performance as a Form of Unlawful Competition (Prestasieaanklamping)'. *SALJ* 110 (1993): 711.
Neethling, J. 'Persoonlike immaterieelgoedereregte: 'n nuwe kategorie subjektiewe regte?'. *THRHR* 50 (1987): 316.
Neethling, J. 'Die Reg op die Verdienvermoë en die Reg op Korrekte Inligting as Selfstandige Subjektiewe Regte'. *THRHR* (1990): 101.
Neethling, J. & Potgieter, J.M. 'Wrongfulness and Negligence in the Law of Delict: A Babylonian Confusion?'. *THRHR* 70 (2007): 120.
Neethling, J., Potgieter, J.M. & Visser, P.J. *Law of Delict* 5th edn. Durban: LexisNexis Butterworths, 2006.
Neethling, J., Potgieter, J.M. & Visser, P.J. *Neethling's Law of Personality.* 2nd edn. Durban: LexisNexis Butterworths, 2005.
Nugent, R.W. 'Yes, It Is always a Bad Thing for the Law: A Reply to Professor Neethling'. *SALJ* 123 (2006): 557.
Pauw, P.C. *Persoonlikheidskrenking en Skuld in die Suid-Afrikaanse Privaatreg: 'n Regshistoriese en Regsvergelykende Ondersoek.* Pijnacker: Dutch Efficiency Bureau, 1976.
Rutherford, B.R. 'Misappropriation of the Advertising Value of Trade Marks, Trade Names and Service Marks'. In *Onregmatige Mededinging / Unlawful Competition*, edited by Neethling, J. Pretoria: University of South Africa, 1990, 55.
South African Law Reform Commission Project 96 *The Apportionment of Damages Act 34 of 1956 Report* (2003).
Spier, J. (ed.). *Unification of Tort Law: Causation, Principles of European Tort Law Volume* 4. The Hague: Kluwer Law International (2000).
Stapleton, J. 'Restatement (Third) of Torts: Products Liability, an Anglo-Australian Perspective'. *Washburn Law Journal* 39 (2000): 363.

Van Aswegen, A. *Die Sameloop van Eise om Skadevergoeding uit Kontrakbreuk en Delik.* unpublished LLD thesis, University of South Africa (1991).
Van Aswegen, A. 'Die toets vir die bestaan van 'n "onafhanklike delik" in die geval van kontrakbreuk'. *THRHR* 55 (1992): 271.
Van Aswegen, A. 'Policy Considerations in the Law of Delict'. *THRHR* 56 (1993): 171.
Van Dam, C. *European Tort Law*. Oxford: Oxford University Press, 2006.
Van der Merwe, C.G. *Skuldlose Aanspreeklikheid vir Skade Veroorsaak deur Diere.* unpublished LL.D thesis, University of South Africa (1970).
Van der Merwe, C.G. 'The Defence of Conduct of a Third Party in View of the Rationale for Strict Liability in Terms of the Pauperian Action Revisited'. *SALJ* 47 (1994): 47.
Van der Merwe, D. 'Die impak van toenemende eentaligheid in die regstelsel op Afrikaans'. *Tydskrif vir Geesteswetenskappe* 40, no. 3 (2000): 255.
Van der Merwe, N.J. & Olivier, P.J.J. *Die Onregmatige Daad in die Suid-Afrikaanse Reg.* 6th edn. Pretoria: Van der Walt, 1989.
Van der Merwe, S. & De Jager, F. 'Products Liability: A Recent Unreported Case'. *SALJ* 97 (1980): 83.
Van der Walt, J.C. & Midgley, J.R. *Principles of Delict.* 3rd edn. Durban: LexisNexis Butterworths, 2005.
Visser, D.P. 'Die rol van opset en die *boni mores* by onregmatige mededinging'. *THRHR* 52 (1989): 115.
Visser, P.J. & Potgieter, J.M. *Visser and Potgieter's Law of Damages.* 2nd edn. Lansdowne: Juta, 2003.
Von Bar, C. *Gemeineuropäisches Deliktsrecht Band II.* Verlag CH Beck, 1999.
Walker, D.M. *The Law of Delict in Scotland.* 2nd edn. Edinburgh: Green, 1981.
Weir, T. 'Complex Liabilities'. *International Encyclopaedia of Comparative Law* Vol XI Ch. 12. The Hague: Brill & Nijhoff,, 1983.
Weir, T. *Tort Law.* Oxford: Clarendon Press, 2002.
Winiger, B., et al. (eds). *Digest of European Tort Law Volume I: Essential Cases on Natural Causation.* Wien: Springer-Verlag, 2007.
Zimmermann, R. *The Law of Obligations: Roman Foundations of the Civilian Tradition.* Cape Town: Juta, 1990.
Zimmermann, R. & Visser, D. (eds). *Southern Cross: Civil Law and Common Law in South Africa.* Cape Town: Juta, 1996.
Zimmermann, R. 'Comparative Law and the Europeanization of Private Law'. In *The Oxford Handbook of Comparative Law*, edited by Reimann, M. & Zimmermann, R. (2006).

Index

The numbers here refer to paragraph numbers.

Index

www.ingramcontent.com/pod-product-compliance
Ingram Content Group UK Ltd.
Pitfield, Milton Keynes, MK11 3LW, UK
UKHW020131290926
15471UKWH00003B/421

9 789403 526232